Becoming a Teacher

ACCEPTING THE CHALLENGE
OF A PROFESSION   SECOND EDITION

FORREST W. PARKAY
Washington State University

BEVERLY HARDCASTLE STANFORD
Azusa Pacific University

ALLYN AND BACON
Boston / London / Toronto / Sydney / Tokyo / Singapore

This book is dedicated to our students—
their spirit continually renews us
and inspires confidence in
the future of teaching in America.

Series Editor: Sean W. Wakely
Developmental Editor: Mary Ellen Lepionka
Series Editorial Assistant: Carol L. Cherniak
Production Administrator: Annette Joseph
Editorial-Production Service: Karen Mason
Text Designer: Karen Mason
Composition Buyer: Linda Cox
Photo Researcher: Laurel Anderson/Photosynthesis
Cover Administrator: Linda K. Dickinson
Cover Designer: SRZS Designs
Manufacturing Buyer: Megan Cochran

Copyright © 1992, 1990 by Allyn and Bacon
A Division of Simon & Schuster, Inc.
160 Gould Street
Needham Heights, Massachusetts 02194-2310

Library of Congress Cataloging-in-Publication Data

Parkay, Forrest W.
    Becoming a teacher : accepting the challenge of a profession /
Forrest W. Parkay, Beverly Hardcastle Stanford. —2nd ed.
        p.   cm.
    Includes bibliographical references and index.
    ISBN 0-205-13327-4
    1. Teaching—Vocational guidance.   2. Education—Study and
teaching—United States.   3. Teachers—United States—Attitudes.
I. Stanford, Beverly Hardcastle   II. Title.
LB1775.P28   1991
371.1'0023'73—dc20   91-22404
                                                                CIP
                                                                r91

Printed in the United States of America.

10 9 8 7 6 5 4 3 2   97 96 95 94 93

Photo and Cartoon Credits
Listed on last page, which constitutes a continuation of the copyright page.

Contents

PART TWO   FOUNDATIONS OF AMERICAN EDUCATION

Chapter 5   Schools and Society   127

Chapter 6   Historical Foundations of American Education   163

Chapter 9   Legal Concerns in
         American Education   265

PART THREE   STUDENTS AND CLASSROOMS

Chapter 10   Students: The Focus of
          Our Teaching   297

Chapter 11   Dynamics of Classroom Life   333

Chapter 12   The School Curriculum   371

Preface

The second edition of *Becoming a Teacher: Accepting the Challenge of a Profession* is designed to introduce you to the exciting and complex world of teaching. Included are many new features designed to help you prepare for an exciting future as a successful teacher.

- A "Consider This" feature in each chapter gives you an opportunity to assess your own opinions, knowledge, and preparation for teaching.
- So that you may learn from outstanding teachers, we have added a "Keepers of the Dream" feature that profiles teachers who are committed to touching lives through teaching, to helping others realize their dreams.
- In addition, a "Teachers on Teaching" section in each chapter gives you an opportunity to learn what teachers around the country think about important educational issues.
- Each chapter also has a feature titled "Fact Finding" that presents current, eye-opening data on important educational trends.
- "Education in the News" reports highlight recent developments and controversies in education that have attracted media attention.
- The new "Glossary" at the end of the book helps you quickly locate the definitions of key terms and concepts and the text pages on which the terms and concepts appear.
- Finally, the new "Teacher's Resource Guide" at the end of the book provides a rich array of materials, strategies, and contacts to help you as you enter the teaching profession.

The second edition of *Becoming a Teacher* also retains features from the first edition that proved useful and popular with readers. Each chapter begins with a realistic scenario and a set of focusing questions to orient you to that chapter's topics. We have retained the "Five-Minute Focus" writing exercises—short, optional, writing activities based on the writing-to-learn and writing-across-the-curriculum concepts. To encourage you to actively reflect as you learn about teaching, your instructor may ask you to keep a journal for your Five-Minute Focus writing assignments.

After reading Part One of this book, "Teachers and Teaching," you will be better able to determine whether teaching is a good career for you. Among the topics we address here are why people choose to teach, the "realities" of teaching, the paths you may follow to become a teacher, and the process of finding your first teaching position. Part Two, "Foundations of American Education," focuses on what professional teachers need to know about the social, historical, philosophical, political, and legal dimensions of education. In Part Three, "Students and Classrooms," we meet the students and enter the real world of the school. We examine the characteristics of students at various stages of development, the dynamics of classroom life, and the curricula that are taught in schools. In Part Four, "The Future of Education," we consider four major issues and trends that will impact your quest to become an effective teacher: the professionalization of teaching, the equalizing of educational opportunity, promising educational innovations, and the challenge of acquiring the knowledge and skills you and your students will need to meet the future.

We congratulate you on accepting the challenge of becoming a professional teacher. We hope this text will serve you well as you begin your quest. Best wishes!

Many individuals in the editorial and production departments of Allyn and Bacon provided us with invaluable help during the preparation of the second edition of *Becoming a Teacher.* Clearly, our greatest debt is owed to Mary Ellen Lepionka, our developmental editor. Always cheerful and encouraging, she worked tirelessly on all phases of the project and provided us with expert guidance and feedback throughout. The long hours she spent on the book—from developing a comprehensive, detailed outline to providing extensive, thoughtful critiques of chapters—are deeply appreciated. A significant amount of credit for the final text, then, belongs to Mary Ellen.

Sean Wakely, Senior Education Editor at Allyn and Bacon, gave critical support for the second edition. His creative, insightful suggestions for improving the manuscript and consistent encouragement were much appreciated. We would also like to thank Annette Joseph, Production Administrator, who ably and smoothly directed the production of the second edition, and Karen Mason, the designer and packager, who gave us a beautiful book.

Our special thanks to colleagues who contributed to the first edition and to those who helped us gather material for the second edition. For the "Teachers on Teaching" feature, we are indebted to Jane Applegate, Kent State University; William Bechtol, Southwest Texas State University; Deborah Byrnes, Utah State University; Rona Flippo, Fitchburg State College; Nathale Gehrke, University of Washington; Ed Greene, Chattanooga Public Schools; Mark Mahlios, University of Florida; Sharon O'Bryan, William Woods College; Mary Olson, University of North Carolina at Greensboro; Anne Patterson, University of Central Arkansas; John Rhodes, University of Florida; and Jo Roberts, University of Georgia. We are also indebted to the many teachers who contributed material for the "Teachers on Teaching" feature. Their comments bring to life the concepts and issues addressed in the text.

For their willingness to help others in the quest to become professional teachers and for their time and cooperation in the publishing process, we would also like to thank the eleven teachers we interviewed for our "Keepers of the Dream" feature: Jessamon Dawe, Jaime Escalante, Thelma Holmes, Shirley Hopkinson, Bruce Johnson, Eric McKamey, Karin Marchant, Gloria Marino, Joyce Roberta Miller, Shirley Rau, and Yvonne Wilson.

We are grateful to the many people throughout the United States who have used the previous edition and who provided suggestions and materials for this edition, including our students. We also received invaluable help in the form of ideas, resources, and suggestions from the following colleagues: Roy Bolduc, Phillip Clark, Tom Fillmer, Sevastian Foti, David Honeyman, Peggy Johnson, Dorene Ross, Mary Budd Rowe, Paul Sindelar, and Rod Webb, all of the University of Florida; Laura Faseler and Amy Tayler of Southwest Texas State University; and Cindy Clausen of Washington State University at Spokane; and a special thanks to Patricia Bonner, Dean of the School of Education and Behavioral Studies at Azusa Pacific University. Additionally, we owe a profound debt of gratitude to Herbert A. Thelen and Kaoru Yamamoto, two great teachers who have touched our professional lives and shaped our views of teaching. In many ways their rich ideas have found their way into this book.

We thank the following reviewers who provided concise, helpful suggestions during the developmental stages of this and the previous edition of the book: John J. Bruno, Buffalo State College; Jerrold Burnell, Cleveland State University; David David, Texas A&M University; Robert Isaf, State University of New York at Cortland; Robert Kinderman, Kutztown University; Dwane Kingery, University of North Texas; William Matthias, Southern Illinois University; Alfonso E. Ortiz, Jr., New Mexico Highlands University; Morgan G. Otis, California State University, Sacramento; Joseph J. Pizzillo, Glassboro State College; Alan F. Quick, Central Michigan University; Janice Streitmatter, University of Arizona; John P. Strouse, Ball State University; and Walter Yoder, University of Akron.

Finally, the personal support of our families and friends as we worked on this project was invaluable. Forrest W. Parkay would like to thank Arlene, Anna, Catherine, and Rebecca; their understanding and constant encouragement made the second edition possible. Beverly Hardcastle Stanford expresses her appreciation of her late mother, Jessamine Hardcastle, and sister, Valerie Schamel, for their steadfast encouragement of this effort; her children, Jennifer Hopkins Lewis and Daniel Clayton Lewis, for their belief and understanding; new members of her family, Virginia Westergard and Vaughan and Statia Stanford, for their assistance both spiritual and mechanical; and most of all her husband, Dick Stanford, for his patient, cheerleading support throughout.

F.W.P.
B.H.S.

Choosing to Teach

*T*he experience of becoming a teacher needs to be acknowledged for what it is: complex and demanding.

Frances F. Fuller and Oliver H. Bown
"Becoming a Teacher"

*I*magine that you have completed a course of study to become a teacher and are about to have your first job interview. It is 7:45 in the morning and you have just parked your car in the faculty parking lot at a school in a medium-sized city. The school is located on a quiet, tree-lined street in a middle-class neighborhood. It is late summer, and the early morning air is still sweet and cool; by midafternoon it will be hot and humid. Several small children are racing across a wide expanse of grass toward a swingset, while three adults stroll after them. On a playing field to your left, two older boys are trying, unsuccessfully, to get a kite up in the air.

After entering the school through a set of heavy wooden doors, you see the main office straight ahead. You hold the office door open a moment as a courtesy to the pleasant-looking man who is just leaving with an enormous pile of books in his outstretched arms.

"Thanks much," he gasps as he struggles to keep the books from falling. "I knew I should have gotten a cart," he says as he moves quickly down the hallway.

You approach the counter and introduce yourself to the school's head secretary. She remains seated behind a desk that is covered with loose papers, file folders, and assorted three-ringed notebooks.

"Mr. Henderson said he would interview me at 7:45," you inform her. "He told me today was about the only day he could squeeze me in."

"Well, he's going to be late. He's got a student in there right now," the secretary responds, glancing at the closed door to Mr. Henderson's office. She looks at the note-filled calendar on her desk. "You're right, I've got you down for 7:45. Why don't you have a seat over there." She motions for you to sit in one of the hard, armless chairs that line the wall across from the principal's office.

While waiting for the principal, you prepare mentally for the interview. You review the questions you expect to be asked. Why did you decide to become a teacher? How would you meet the needs of the students at this school? How would you manage classroom activities? What is your philosophy of education? What new approaches would you use in your teaching? Why should the district hire you?

As you reflect on these questions, you realize that they are actually quite difficult. You also realize that your answers may determine whether or not you get the job.

FOCUS QUESTIONS

1. Why do people choose to teach?
2. What are some of the rewarding aspects of teaching? What are some of the challenging aspects?
3. What are some contemporary images of teachers and teaching?
4. How do your personality characteristics relate to a career in teaching?

Though predictable, the interview questions just posed are surprisingly challenging. Why *did* you decide to become a teacher? How *will* you meet the needs of all students? What *do* you have to offer students? The answers to these and similar questions are, of course, not easy, and they are dependent upon the personality and experiences of the person responding. However, they are questions that professional teachers recognize as important and worthy of careful consideration.

The primary purpose of this book is to orient you to the world of education and to help you begin to formulate answers to such questions. In addition, this book will help you answer *your own* questions about the career you have chosen. What is teaching really like? What are the trends and issues in the profession? What problems can you expect to encounter in the classroom? What kind of rewards do teachers experience?

We begin this book by examining why people choose to teach because we believe that "good teachers select themselves."[1] They know why they want to teach and what subjects and ages they want to teach. They are active in the choosing process, aware of the options, informed about the attractions and obstacles in the field, and anxious to make their contributions to the profession.

ATTRACTIONS TO TEACHING

People are drawn to teaching for many reasons. For some, the desire to teach emerges early and is nurtured by positive experiences with teachers during the formative years of childhood. For others, teaching is seen as a way of making a significant contribution to the world and experiencing the joy of helping others grow and develop. And for others, life as a teacher is attractive because it is exciting, varied, and stimulating. In the "Five-Minute Focus" that follows, discuss your reasons for choosing to teach.

Motivation for teaching is often based on a combination of attractions to the profession, such as love of both the student and the subject and a love of the teaching-learning process.

FIVE-MINUTE FOCUS Now that you have begun to move in earnest from the *dream* of becoming a teacher to the *reality* of becoming one, reflect on what has drawn you to teaching. Describe or list your reasons for deciding to become a teacher. Date your journal entry and write for five minutes.

Five-Minute Focus   2-28

In high school I was a C student with D motivation. I had some fun teachers, but only one that showed me I had a good head on my shoulders, and that I was pretty smart when I used it.

After two and a half years of being out of high school, I decided to go back to college. I had just counseled at a junior high camp and found out that I had a deep love for kids. I began to go to school full-time and also teach Sunday School at my church. I found that learning was great, and teaching kids was fantastic. Watching kids discover and learn is an extremely exciting thing, especially when you are a part of it. The joy that fills your heart when you see that kid with the D motivation giving 100% because you invested your time into his life, cannot be found on any pay scale. Parents are too busy now trying to make ends meet. It's up to teachers to show these kids that they do have a place in this world. I can't think of a more worthwhile job.

In this example of a journal entry, an education student reflects and writes on a "Five-Minute Focus" question.

A Love of Teaching

A 1989 Metropolitan Life survey of a nationally representative sample of 2,000 teachers (kindergarten through grade 12) revealed that 81 percent of teachers "strongly agree" that they love to teach, while 16 percent "agree somewhat." What does it mean to *love* teaching?

Love of Students   The teachers in the survey might have meant a love of students. Though the conditions under which they work may be poor, their salaries modest, and segments of their communities unsupportive, many teachers teach simply because they care about students. As one elementary school teacher put it: "I love kids; I love kids; I love kids. . . . I get lots from the kids. I get a reason to get up in the morning. I get—definite reasons to be able to go to sleep at night!"[2]

The day-to-day interactions between teachers and students build strong bonds between them. Daily contact also enables teachers to become familiar with the personal as well as the academic needs of their students, and this concern for students' welfare and growth outweighs the difficulties and frustrations of teaching. Teachers who know they are needed find it hard to leave the profession.

Others, no doubt, love students because they appreciate the unique qualities of youth. Like the following teacher, they enjoy the liveliness, curiosity, freshness, openness, and trust of young children or the abilities, wit, spirit, independence, and idealism of adolescents:

> I have always enjoyed teaching, and I like the children. I've taught first, third, and fifth grades, and I think each grade level was the best age to teach. I stay in teaching because it keeps me connected to the spirit and vitality of childhood, a connection I don't want to lose.[3]

The opportunity to work with young people, whatever their stage of development, is a key reason people are drawn to teaching and remain in the profession.

Love of Subject   Some teachers who expressed a love of teaching may have meant that they love teaching in their discipline. The opportunity to continually learn more in one's profession and to share that knowledge with students is a definite attraction. Most of us can recall teachers who were so excited about their subjects that they were surprised when students were not equally enthusiastic. The affinity of such teachers toward their subjects was so great that we tended to see the two as inseparable—for instance, "Miss Gilbert the French teacher" or "Mr. Montgomery the math teacher." Though other factors may draw teachers to their work, a love of subject is clearly one of them.

Love of the Teaching Life   For those teachers who always enjoyed school, it is often the life of a teacher that has appeal—to be in an environment that encourages a high regard for education and the life of the mind. John Barth, novelist and English professor, wrote eloquently of his love of the teaching life: "There is chalkdust on the sleeve of my soul. In the half-century since my kindergarten days, I have never been away from classrooms for longer than a few months. I am as at home among blackboards, half-desks, lecterns, and seminar tables as among the furniture of my writing-room; both are the furniture of my head."[4] These are the teachers who are ready to return to the classroom when fall begins or when merchants display their back-to-school signs. The rhythm of their lives is synchronized with that of the school.

Others enjoy the drama and unpredictability of teaching. A new class or school year offers them an excitement similar to opening night in the theater. They view themselves—at least in part—as actors who enjoy performing for their audience of students.

Love of the Teaching-Learning Process   To love teaching can also mean to love the act of teaching and the learning that can follow. Many teachers, like the following high school special education teacher, focus on the *process* rather than on the subject or even the students: "I enjoy what I do. . . . I've been teaching long enough that when the fun stops . . . I'll get out. But it hasn't stopped yet, after thirty-four years. Every day is different. Every day is interesting."[5] Persons with this orientation are attracted by the live, spontaneous aspects of teaching and are invigorated by the need to think on their feet and to capitalize on teachable moments when they occur. They relish the "simultaneity" of teaching,[6] the times when several learning opportunities occur at once, and they constantly work to identify the full array of chesslike moves they can make in leading students to new insights. For them, the teaching-learning process is fascinating.

The Influence of Teachers

It seems reasonable to assume that the process of becoming a teacher begins early in life. Although it is not true that some people are born teachers, their early life experiences often encourage them to move in that direction.[7] A teacher's influence during his or her formative years may have been the catalyst. In most cases, the adults who have the greatest influence on children—beyond their parents or guardians—are their teachers. As one student teacher put it: "As a child, I used to think a teacher was next to God."

Evidence also suggests that those in teacher training programs recall their teachers more positively than others. For example, educational researchers Benjamin Wright and Shirley Tuska, in a study of nearly 4,500 teacher trainees, found a much higher incidence of teachers being remembered as "admired" and "influential" than in a group of almost one thousand nonteachers. The nonteachers recalled their teachers with negative associations more often than the teacher trainees.[8] Similarly, it has been suggested that teachers behave according to "internalized" models of their own teachers.[9] These internalized models are not always based on good teachers; when they are, however, students and the teaching profession benefit.

FIVE-MINUTE FOCUS   Describe a former teacher who has had a positive influence on your decision to teach. In what ways would you like to become like that teacher? Date your journal entry and write for five minutes.

The Practical Benefits of Teaching

Not to be overlooked as attractions to teaching are its practical benefits. These include working hours and vacations, rising salaries, and the accessibility of a teaching career.

TABLE 1.1   Estimated Starting Salaries for New
College Graduates, 1990–91

Bachelor's Degree Graduates	Estimated Percent Change	Estimated Starting Salary, 1990–91
Academic Majors		
Chemical Engineering	8.1%	$38,114
Mechanical Engineering	7.9%	$34,715
Electrical Engineering	7.5%	$34,658
Computer Science	8.3%	$33,238
Industrial Engineering	7.4%	$32,784
Physics	6.0%	$30,504
Civil Engineering	7.9%	$29,508
Nursing	8.3%	$29,449
Chemistry	6.8%	$29,364
Accounting	2.8%	$27,866
Financial Administration	2.2%	$25,869
General Business Administration	2.8%	$24,992
Geology	5.0%	$24,636
Marketing/Sales	3.1%	$24,273
Mathematics	6.5%	$24,168
Personnel Administration	3.3%	$23,863
Agriculture	3.0%	$23,486
Communications	4.7%	$22,882
Social Science	6.1%	$22,610
Education	4.9%	$21,662
Liberal Arts/Arts and Letters	5.8%	$21,655
Hotel, Restaurant Institutional Management	3.9%	$21,555
Advertising	2.3%	$21,483
Telecommunications	3.0%	$20,499
Retailing	5.0%	$20,360
Human Ecology/Home Economics	2.5%	$20,202
Journalism	2.1%	$19,516
Natural Resources	2.3%	$19,496
Averages for Graduate Degree Levels		
MBA	6.6%	$38,563
Masters	6.5%	$35,634
Ph.D.	4.0%	$39,591

Source: Scheetz, L. Patrick, *Recruiting Trends 1990–91* (East Lansing, Mich.: Collegiate Employment Research Institute, Michigan State University, 1990).

Hours and Vacations Teachers' hours and vacations are widely recognized as benefits. Though the number of hours most teachers devote to their work goes far beyond the number of hours they actually spend at school, their schedules do afford them a measure of flexibility not found in other professions. For example, teachers with school-age children can often be at home when their children are not in school.

For most of those who make the transition from college to a nonteaching career, the reduced vacation time is an adjustment. The lengthy holiday breaks of college are replaced by a scant week or two in their new workplaces. Only after an employee has worked for several years will vacation time be increased significantly, if ever. In contrast, all teachers, regardless of their years of experience, receive the same generous vacation time: Thanksgiving and Christmas breaks, a spring or Easter break, and a long summer vacation. During these vacations, teachers may earn extra money working part-time or consulting for their school districts. They may also pursue graduate work, participate in career development programs, travel, or simply rest and enjoy themselves.

Rising Salaries Though the general consensus is that teachers are still underpaid (in 1990–91 their average salary was $33,015, and $20,652 was the average starting salary for 1990 graduates with a bachelor's degree in education), the situation is improving, as Table 1.1 shows. An analysis of salary trends during the 1980s conducted by the American Federation of Teachers revealed that average teacher salaries jumped 69 percent. For the 1989–90 school year, the average salary of teachers in eight states (Alaska, Connecticut, California, New York, Maryland, Rhode Island, New Jersey, and Michigan) and the District of Columbia was more than $35,000.

Increasingly, teachers' salaries are becoming more competitive and more geared to the significance of their work. School district officials in Rochester, New York, for example, implemented a 1988–89 salary schedule that enabled some teachers to earn as much as $70,000 per year, and the Dade County, Florida, school board approved a teachers' contract that enabled some teachers in the Miami area to earn up to $64,000 during 1990–91. Clearly, then, salaries are becoming one of the attractions of the profession.

Career Accessibility Entry into teaching is relatively accessible because teaching has a "wide decision range," according to Dan Lortie, the author of *Schoolteacher: A Sociological Study.*[10] In other words, it is rarely too late or too early to decide to become a teacher. People may decide to teach when they are very young or they may decide to teach after they have completed a full career in another field.

Teaching is also perceived as easy to enter. Lortie refers to this as the "subjective warrant" and notes that "occupations with stringent warrants will lose more would-be members through self-discouragement than will those with permissive warrants."[11] While teaching may in some respects be an easier field to enter than others, it is our thesis throughout this book that teaching is a complex, demanding profession. In short, it is not easy to become a professional teacher.

While the practical benefits of teaching are legitimate factors to consider, the needs of students require that those who commit themselves to teaching do so primarily because of the attractions we discussed previously. Students lose out, sadly and some-times irreparably, when taught by teachers who view their work as just another job with decent pay, short hours, and good vacations.

Nonteaching duties may be challenges for managing time and stress, but they also provide opportunities for getting to know students better and for participating fully in the life of the school.

CHALLENGES OF TEACHING

Why should an introductory text on teaching confront undesirable or difficult aspects of the profession? Shouldn't such discussions be reserved for those who have already entered the field? Won't students learn soon enough the hazards of being a teacher?

We do not think so. We believe that prospective teachers need to consider the problems as well as the pleasures they are likely to encounter. Students need to be informed of what to expect if they are to make the most of their professional preparation programs. With greater awareness of the realities of teaching, they can more purposefully and meaningfully go about the business of (1) reflecting on and refining their personal philosophies of education, (2) acquiring teaching strategies and management techniques, and (3) developing a knowledge base of research and theory to guide their actions. In this manner, they can become true professionals—free to savor the joys and satisfactions of teaching while confident of their ability to deal with its frustrations and challenges.

By dealing openly with the problems of teaching, you can acquire strategies for dealing with them. Such awareness should make your study relevant, focus your preparation for teaching, and ease your entry into the profession.

Stressful Working Conditions

While we have noted that the work schedule and vacations for teachers are quite good, other working conditions need improvement. Though working conditions vary from school to school and from district to district, some problems are common to many schools. We briefly discuss five of them here: (1) lack of discipline, (2) drug abuse, (3) high teacher-student ratios, (4) long working hours, and (5) frustrations with the system.

Lack of Discipline   For 15 of the 21 years between 1969 and 1990, the public ranked lack of discipline as the most important problem facing the schools in the annual Gallup Polls of the Public's Attitudes Toward the Public Schools. Not surprisingly, discipline is a major concern among students in introductory education classes. Before teachers can teach they must have control in their classrooms. Even when parents and the school community are supportive and problems are relatively minor, dealing with discipline can be a disturbing, emotionally draining aspect of teaching.

Drug Abuse   In the 1986–1990 Gallup Polls of the Public's Attitudes Toward the Public Schools, drug abuse became the top-ranking problem facing the public schools. Students' drug problems are not always easy to detect. Their low productivity rates, inability to learn, and attitude problems demand teacher attention; yet teachers may be unaware of the source of those difficulties. Even when teachers do recognize a drug problem, they may lack the resources or expertise to offer help. Obviously, teachers feel frustrated when faced by the wasted potential they observe in their students. In addition, when the public calls for schools to curb the drug problem, that expectation can increase the stress teachers experience.

High Teacher-Student Ratios   Many schools have high teacher-student ratios, which are a source of stress for some teachers. Feeling the press of numbers and valiantly resisting the realization that they cannot meet the needs of all their students, teachers may try to work faster and longer to give their students the best possible education. All too often, however, they learn to put off, overlook, or otherwise attend inadequately to many students each day. The problem of high teacher-student ratios becomes even more acute when complicated by the high student-mobility rates in many schools. In such situations, teachers have trouble not only in meeting their students' needs but also in recognizing them and remembering their names!

Long Working Hours   The official working hours for teachers are attractive, but the *real* working hours are another matter. Not built into contracts are the after-hours or extra assignments found at all levels of teaching—from recess duty and parent conferences to high school club sponsorships and coaching. Also not obvious are the hours of preparation that occur before and after school—frequently late into the night and over the weekend.

The need to complete copious amounts of paperwork, most related to various forms of record keeping, may be the most burdensome of the teacher's nonteaching tasks. Other nonteaching tasks include supervising student behavior on the playground, at extracurricular events, and in the halls, study halls, and lunchrooms; attending faculty meetings, parent conferences, and open houses; and taking tickets or selling concessions at athletic events. Individually, such assignments and responsibilities may be enjoyable; too many of them at once, however, become a burden and consume the teacher's valuable time.

Frustrations with the System   Though teachers are in the best position to recognize the needs of their students and to select teaching methods, management strategies, and materials to address those needs, they are commonly excluded from participating in the decision-making processes concerning these issues. Administrators, legislators, and even architects—all of whom are removed from the realities of classroom life and the concerns of teachers and students—make decisions that profoundly affect teachers. In addition to the frustration caused by their lack of efficacy in matters of immediate concern to them, teachers may be demoralized when they realize how little respect decision makers often have for them as professionals. Albert Shanker, the articulate president of the American Federation of Teachers, contends, "Although [teachers'] personal lives now may be much freer of monitoring by school boards and administrators, . . . teachers in most of the United States still are treated with a great deal of paternalism. The difference is that today the paternalism mostly affects their *professional* lives."[12]

Other Sources of Stress

Other challenges of teaching, though not as obvious as the conditions described above, can be quite stressful. The following, for example, are significant sources of stress that teachers must learn to cope with:

- Isolation
- Conflicts with administrators and other teachers
- Lack of support in dealing with problems
- Little time to reflect and share with other teachers
- Continuous interruptions
- Stress of continually being "on stage"
- Budget constraints
- Deteriorating physical plants

Fortunately, it is unlikely that all of these stresses will characterize your life as a teacher. Furthermore, you can develop specific strategies for managing these stresses and other challenges of teaching. In the following excerpts, for example, several teachers tell how they manage stress.

I keep talking and try to smile. I look for positive signs. I listen to loud music and dig the garden over-zealously. I try to organize my teaching day very carefully.

In coping with stress, different things may help at different times. Obviously if it's pressure of work then a "blitz" may in itself reduce tension. At other times deciding to do nothing connected with work over a weekend can distance school and put things back in perspective.

I reduce stress by talking things through with my husband, who isn't in the profession.

CONSIDER THIS . . .

Managing Stress

After graduating from the state university, you accept a job at a local school. For the most part, you're pleased with the position—the kids are great, your colleagues helpful, and the parents concerned. After a few months, however, things have begun to "pile up." You feel overloaded with assignments to grade each evening; you still haven't received the books you ordered last month; and you're worried about how your students will perform on the state-mandated test of basic skills in February. There just doesn't seem to be enough time in the day to do everything! You wonder how other teachers manage and whether you're becoming burned out before the first year is even over. What can you do? Write five actions you could take to prevent burnout and to better manage stress.

1. _____
   _____
2. _____
   _____
3. _____
   _____
4. _____
   _____
5. _____

Now compare your ideas to the ones listed below.

"A Teacher's Ten Commandments for Avoiding Burnout"

I.   Keep alert to changing methods and philosophies.
II. Attend conferences, workshops, and inservice programs with an open mind.
III. Listen to other teachers in your school.
IV. Avoid like the plague the stereotype of talking only about school after hours.
V.   Keep alert physically and mentally.
VI. Keep in step with students and find out about their hobbies, movies, and music.
VII. Discard . . . discard . . . discard old ideas, old prejudices, old materials.
VIII. Read more than "Dick and Jane" books and subscribe to professional magazines.
IX. Be flexible and avoid doing something just because it's always been done that way.
X.   Keep your senses sharpened, your mind keen, and your heart open to remain an enthusiastic teacher!

Source: Peggie Case Paulus, "Teacher Burnout," *Instructor* (January 1979):59.

I reduce pressure within myself by getting involved in outside activities which have nothing to do with teaching.

I consciously relax body muscles when I notice them becoming tense.

Jogging is a great relief in all sorts of ways . . .

I reduce stress by ensuring that my life is not on a single track. I do this by pursuing other interests—mainly music and sports—so that on Monday mornings my body and spirit are refreshed.[13]

PAST IMAGES OF TEACHERS AND TEACHING

Rarely have teachers and their profession received praise or even neutral recognition in the media or by the public at large. From the community scrutiny in colonial times to the frequently negative press reports of recent times, the public in general has done little to boost the morale of those to whom it entrusts the minds of its young.

As you will learn in Chapter 6, the status of teachers in colonial America was low. And while the need for teachers had increased dramatically by the early 1900s, their status had improved only slightly. It was not until the late 1950s and early 1960s that the public began to acknowledge that the status of the United States as a world leader was directly related to the quality of its educational system.

The image of teachers became worse again during the 1970s. The decade was a mixed one for American education, marked by drops in enrollment, test scores, and public confidence, as well as progressive policy changes that promoted a more equal education for all Americans. Calls for "back to basics" and teacher accountability drives initiated by parents, citizens groups, and politicians who were unhappy with the low academic performance level of many students were also prominent during this troubled decade.

During the 1980s, the image of teachers was badly battered by ominous sounding commission reports, a dramatically negative press, and the resultant public outcry for better schools. Several national reports declared that American education was shockingly inadequate, if not a failure.

CONTEMPORARY IMAGES OF TEACHERS AND TEACHING

A mismatch or delay between the perceptions and expectations of reality, held by people in a culture and a change in reality itself : CULTURAL LAG

In contrast with earlier times, teachers today participate much more widely in their communities, and their status is much higher. But, as educational researcher and author Sara Lawrence Lightfoot observes, "One recognizes a severe **cultural lag** between our stereotypic images of 'teacher' and real teachers who are demanding the prerogatives and power that other professionals have been accustomed to"[14] (boldface ours).

FIVE-MINUTE FOCUS   What is your view of the current image of teachers? What factors in today's world might be contributing to the attention, or lack of attention, that is paid to teachers? Date your journal entry and write for five minutes.

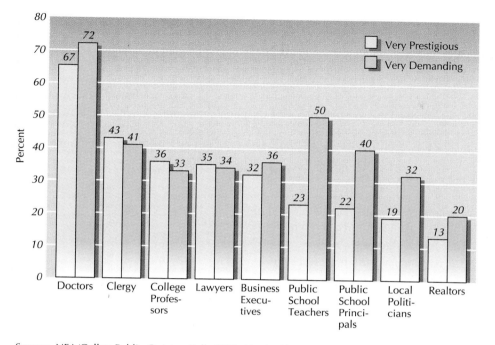

FIGURE 1.1
How the Public Regards Professions

Source: NEA/Gallup Public Opinion Poll, 1985. Used with permission.

Public Opinion Polls

The annual Gallup Poll of the Public's Attitudes Toward the Public Schools, the Metropolitan Life Surveys of American Teachers conducted by Louis Harris and Associates, and the polls conducted for the National Education Association (NEA) are useful barometers of the public's image of teachers. While some questions vary from year to year, depending upon the concerns of educators at the time, other questions remain the same and thus indicate changing attitudes.

These opinion polls reveal interesting patterns and trends. In 1969, for example, 75 percent of parents said that they would like to see one of their children pursue a teaching career, but in 1990 only 51 percent said so.[15] Another poll, taken in 1985, revealed the public perception of teaching as a lower-status but highly demanding profession, as shown in Figure 1.1.

Teachers' Views   Between 1985 and 1986, the percentage of American teachers who at some time seriously considered leaving teaching to go into another occupation rose by 4 percent to 55 percent, while the percentage of teachers reporting that they were very satisfied with teaching fell by 7 percent to only 33 percent.[16] However, teachers' perceptions of whether or not they are respected showed definite improvement during the mid- to late 1980s. In 1984, 47 percent of teachers who responded to the Metropolitan Life Survey of the American Teacher agreed with the statement, "As a teacher I feel respected in today's society." By 1989, this figure had increased to 53 percent.

By 1990, people's attitudes toward the public schools had become more positive. In 1980, for example, 35 percent of the respondents to the annual Gallup survey

FACT FINDING

Are Teachers Optimistic or Pessimistic About the Future?

A Louis Harris and Associates survey of 2,000 teachers examined school reforms, accountability, teaching as a career, the societal problems teachers face in classrooms, and teachers' views of the future. Teachers expressed optimism about their future when asked, "On the whole, are you optimistic or pessimistic that the following will be better five years from now?"

	Optimistic	Pessimistic
The quality of teaching in your school	80%	19%
The principal-teacher relationship	76%	22%
Educational changes	69%	30%
The educational performance of students	64%	35%
The professional status of teachers	61%	38%
Working conditions for teachers	61%	38%
The job satisfaction of teachers	57%	41%

Source: The American Teacher 1989: Preparing Schools for the 1990s (New York: Louis Harris and Associates, 1990) p. 108. To obtain a copy of the report, write: Metropolitan Life Insurance Company, The American Teacher Survey 1989, P.O. Box 807, Madison Square Station, New York, NY 10159–0807.

rated their local public schools with a grade of A or B. In 1990, however, 41 percent gave their schools high grades. The public's image of elementary teachers had also improved. In 1987, 53 percent gave elementary teachers in their communities an A or a B; in 1990, 58 percent did so. Perceptions of local high school teachers, however, remained the same, with 43 percent of respondents giving them an A or a B.

The results of one question on the 1990 Gallup survey suggested that the public may place less blame on teachers than in the past for problems in the schools. When asked, "Which is more at fault for the problems currently facing public education in this community—the performance of the local public schools or the effect of societal problems?" 73 percent of the respondents assigned the blame to society.

The Improving Image of Teachers   The image of teachers received a boost in 1984 when President Reagan announced plans for a teacher to be the first civilian in space. The tragedy that followed and the personality and spirit of Christa McAuliffe gave the United States a new kind of hero—a teacher. The less publicized continuation of the program keeps outstanding teachers affiliated with the Challenger Center, working together in programs that promote education and interest in space exploration.

During the early 1990s, deliberate efforts were made to restore dignity to the profession of teaching. To highlight the important work of teachers, public and commercial television stations aired programs with titles such as "Learning in America: Schools that Work," "America's Toughest Assignment: Solving the Education Crisis," "The Truth About Teachers," and "Why Do These Kids Love School?" First Lady Barbara Bush hosted a series of television programs highlighting exceptional teachers, and many national corporations initiated award programs to recognize excellence among teachers.

What Students Think

What do students who are preparing to enter the profession think about the public's view of teachers? One of the authors of this book informally surveyed seventy undergraduate and graduate students to explore their perceptions of the public's regard for teachers. The students were asked to write responses to three basic questions: *What do Americans think of elementary teachers? What do they think of secondary teachers?* and *What is the current stereotype of teachers?* In addition, those who were parents and teachers as well were asked to share their perceptions of teachers from those points of view. No one found the questions difficult to answer.

> Unfortunately for those who do not understand and believe in the importance of an education, they seem to view teachers as babysitters or caretakers. However . . . I believe that the majority see teachers as role models and educators. Parents depend on teachers to teach their children the skills and knowledge that will enable them to become self-sufficient members of society.
> —Chrisee Huffman

> Most Americans see teachers as only adequate. They seem to think that anyone is capable of organizing a classroom and maintaining a learning environment. Although much thought and training go into teaching, and teachers sacrifice much energy and personal time for their classrooms, the majority of the American public has little respect for today's educators. I think one way to fix this is to ask Dr. Smith, heart surgeon, to take a second grade class for a week.
> —Susan Pope

Many graduate students qualified their generalizations about the public image of teachers by noting the influences of socioeconomic status, cultural background, school district philosophies, the positive or negative nature of an individual's own school experiences, and parents' attitudes toward their children.

> A lot depends upon how the parents feel about their own kids. Some parents wouldn't wish their kids on anyone and are amazed that anyone could get them to do anything. Others want to take part in their [children's] education and some feel that teachers are hiding behind their education.
> —Annette Malinak

> In higher socioeconomic areas, I have seen that some parents think we must produce perfect people, and we are looked down upon if the children are not perfect. Others regard us very highly, and appreciate the fact that we are trying to provide their children with the best possible education. In lower socioeconomic areas, I noticed that most parents regarded me as a babysitter, and didn't really seem to care whether or not their children learned anything. Those who did regard me highly felt as if they did not know how to help their children, so they were happy that I took an interest at all.
> —Peggy Arp

A number of students had contrasting images for elementary and secondary teachers.

> In my opinion, most people feel that elementary teachers are too absorbed in their jobs, that they lose touch with the world outside of the classroom. They do, however, keep a good tie between the school and the parents. Secondary teachers, on the other hand, are definitely more reality-based, but they are the least likely to communicate with parents. I think that most parents feel left out of the secondary portion of their child's education, except when Johnny is in detention.
> —Wayne Ellison

Keepers of the Dream

Joyce Roberta Miller
1989 Texas Teacher of the Year
Memorial High School, Spring Branch Independent
School District, Houston

Joyce Roberta Miller, who received her master's and specialist's degrees from the College of Education at the University of Florida, wanted to become a teacher since she was a small child. "I always had a desire to educate others, to work with people," she says. "When I entered the University of Florida, I was a pre-law major, but during my second year I decided that's not what I wanted to do. I really wanted to teach and combine my interests in history and politics with working in a classroom."

Joyce taught in Gainesville for nine years at Buchholz High School and in 1977 went to India as a Fulbright scholar. Since 1980, Joyce has taught economics and government at Memorial High School in Houston. In 1989, she was named Texas Teacher of the Year. In 1991, Ann Richards, governor of Texas, appointed Joyce to the Texas School Assembly, a group set up to advise the governor on educational issues.

Known as a task master in the classroom, Joyce has been lovingly nicknamed "Killer Miller" by her students. She typically puts in a 60-hour work week and sponsors the school's Model United Nations team, teaches summer school at Rice University, is active in the National Association of Teachers of the Year and the Texas State Teacher's Association (TSTA-NEA), and has just been elected to the district's site-based leadership committee. "Teaching is not a job you can walk away from at 3:00," she says. "I would tell new teachers that they have to be willing to become involved."

The key to her successful teaching can be found in her belief that education should extend beyond the classroom walls. "If learning is limited to the confines of the classroom, then the purpose of education is defeated," she says. She describes how she is able to bring the world into the classroom:

During my government class each year, more than two dozen politicians visit the classroom and give the students the opportunity for input, questioning, and interaction. This has stimulated students to attend district political conventions, work in campaigns, write letters to their representatives, and conduct individual research on critical local, state, and national issues. As a result of these experiences, some of my students have expanded their education beyond the classroom and have been selected as Congressional interns, have attended Washington Close-Up, and have become leaders in their colleges.

Joyce has high expectations of her students. "I set out my goals and requirements at the beginning of the year, and I expect students to meet those challenges," she says. "High expectations," she adds, "should apply to *all* students, not just high-ability students."

Joyce believes that beginning teachers need to be supported as they learn to adjust to the challenges of teaching.

The first thing I would say to a new teacher is, "Find a mentor—somebody you can trust as a friend, someone you can work with and respect as a colleague. This person should help you along the way and yet allow you to make decisions to fit your personality."

Joyce has developed an unwavering commitment to teaching as a profession. She is truly a "keeper of the dream"—dedicated to touching the lives of her students, to helping them realize their dreams.

With the exception of one year that was difficult, I've never regretted becoming a teacher. If I had the opportunity to do it again, I'd become a teacher. I recently made an educational videotape for Texas A&M University, and I ended it by saying "Come back and see me in 20 years—I'll still be teaching; I'll still be in the classroom."

"Lovingly Nicknamed 'Killer Miller'"

The students in the informal survey included undergraduates in an introductory education course, undergraduates in their last course before student teaching, and graduate students seeking certification or career development. At all levels, the students were well aware of the negative stereotypes and the public's criticism of teachers. Nearly all gave either a mixture of the public's positive and negative views or only negative ones. The few who gave only positive images explained that while in the past teachers had been viewed poorly, teachers had become better prepared and thus were more respected. What impresses us is the students' undaunted spirit and determination to overcome negative images. They did not waver in their commitment to the teaching profession. Clearly, they were guided by matters other than the public's perceptions of teaching.

Keepers of the Dream

Fortunately, in spite of persisting stereotypes and a frequent lack of public appreciation, many of our country's most talented youth and dedicated veterans in the teaching field retain the desire to teach. In part, the desire endures because teachers have been positively influenced by one or more teachers of their own, who enriched, redirected, or significantly changed their lives. The desire also endures because teachers recognize the many joys and rewards the profession offers.

Reflecting on dedicated teachers and their contributions to us, we are guided to teaching for the benefit of others. In doing so, we become keepers of the American dream—the belief that education can improve the quality of children's lives. That dream, more powerful than all our images of teachers, is alive throughout the country in classrooms where outstanding teachers work.

FOUR VIEWS OF ESSENTIAL KNOWLEDGE AND ABILITIES

Contemporary images of the teaching profession aside, we must ask what knowledge and abilities teachers need to teach well. Unfortunately, the complexities of teaching make it very difficult to answer this question without a good deal of elaboration and qualification. For one thing, there is no single, universally accepted definition of what good teaching is. For another, the **knowledge base** upon which teaching as a profession rests is uncertain. Educational researchers are still learning *what* good teachers know and *how* they use that knowledge. As a result, statements about what teachers need to know and what they need to be able to do are varied, ranging in language from the concrete, specific, and scientific to the abstract, indefinite, and artistic. An examination of different views of teachers' knowledge and abilities follows.

A Personal-Development View

One view of what teachers need to know and be able to do places primary emphasis on who the teacher is as a person. According to this view, teachers should be concerned with developing themselves as persons so that they may learn to use themselves more effectively. Arthur Combs, a well-known advocate of this view, has suggested that "teacher effectiveness . . . is a function of how teachers use themselves. . . . The skillful use of self and the creation of conditions for significant learning is a truly professional achievement."[17]

What this approach requires, then, is that teachers continually develop their powers of observation and reflection so that they can most effectively respond to the needs of students. Thus, teaching is seen as more than a mechanical, craftlike implementation of specific procedures; it becomes an authentic, growth-oriented encounter between teacher and students.

Another important dimension of the **personal-development view** is the teacher's need for self-knowledge, particularly in regard to oneself as a learner. As Arthur Jersild wrote in *When Teachers Face Themselves,* a 1955 book still timely today, "A teacher's understanding of others can be only as deep as the wisdom he possesses when he looks inward upon himself."[18] If teachers do not know themselves well, if they have not taken time to reflect on what they think and feel, on how they have grown and developed as human beings, they present and model a hollow self for others. In turn, they are unable to see beyond the surface of their students' behavior.

Some teachers may be so caught up in their presentation of themselves as teachers, acting as they imagine teachers should act, that they fail to behave in accordance with their true thoughts and feelings.[19] If their students also act inauthentically and put on performances as students, then classroom activities amount to little more than a lifeless imitation of true education. Regarding yourself as separate from a role and taking time to reflect on your beliefs and values about education will help you become a more unique and authentic teacher.

Research-Based Views

Within the last half decade, several states and a few large cities have developed their own lists of research-based competencies that beginning teachers must demonstrate. These competencies are derived from educational research that has identified what effective teachers do. Typically, the states have developed *behavioral indicators* for each competency, which trained observers from universities and school districts use to determine to what extent teachers actually exhibit the target behaviors in the classroom.

The Florida Performance Measurement System (FPMS) was the first evaluation system of this sort to be implemented on a statewide basis. Beginning teachers in Florida must now demonstrate behaviors in nine domains: planning, management of student conduct, instructional organization and development, presentation of subject matter, verbal and non-verbal communication, testing, counseling, consultation, and library/media services. (The Appendix to this chapter presents the Summative Observation Instrument for the FPMS and the "effective" and "ineffective" behavioral indicators for four of these domains.)

Similarly, Virginia has developed a Beginning Teacher Assistance Program that requires teachers to demonstrate competency behaviors in fourteen areas: academic learning time, accountability, clarity of structure, individual differences, evaluation, consistent rules, affective climate, learner self-concept, meaningfulness, planning, questioning skill, reinforcement, close supervision, and awareness.

An example of the approach taken by some large-city school districts is that of the Dade County school system (Miami, Florida). It employs a Teacher Assessment and Development System (TADS) that, like the previous examples, requires teachers to demonstrate certain behavior in the classroom. Dade County teachers must achieve an acceptable rating in six categories: preparation and planning, knowledge of subject matter, classroom management, techniques of instruction, teacher-student relationships, and assessment techniques.

A Job-Analysis View

A third view of what teachers need to know and be able to do is based on the job analyses that some school districts conduct. Typically, a **job analysis** begins with a review of existing job descriptions and then proceeds to interviews with those currently assigned to the job and their supervisors regarding the activities and responsibilities associated with the job. These data are then analyzed to identify the dimensions of the job. Finally, interview questions based on the dimensions are developed and used by district personnel responsible for hiring.

To illustrate the job-analysis view of the knowledge, skills, and attitudes needed by teachers, we present the twelve dimensions identified by the Washington County, Florida, School District as essential for the position of elementary teacher.

Oral Communication/Presentation: Effective expression in individual or group situations (includes gestures and nonverbal communication).

Written Communication: Effective expression of ideas in writing and in good grammatical form.

Initiative: Active attempts to influence events to achieve goals; self-starting rather than passive acceptance. Taking action to achieve goals beyond what is necessarily called for; originating action.

Tolerance for Stress: Stability of performance under pressure and/or opposition.

Job Motivation: The extent to which activities available in the job overlap with activities and responsibilities that result in personal satisfaction.

Sensitivity: Actions that indicate a consideration for the feelings and needs of others.

Individual/Group Leadership: Utilization of appropriate interpersonal styles and methods in guiding individuals and groups toward task accomplishment.

Technical/Professional Knowledge: Level of understanding and ability to use technical/professional information.

Planning and Organizing: Establishing a course of action for self and/or others to accomplish a specific goal; planning proper assignments of personnel and appropriate allocation of resources.

Control/Monitoring: Establishing and/or using procedures to monitor and/or regulate processes, tasks, or activities of students and personal job activities and responsibilities.

Judgment/Decisiveness: Developing alternative courses of action and decisions that are based on logical assumptions and that reflect factual information. Decisiveness is the readiness to make decisions, render judgments, take action, or commit oneself.

Work Standards: Setting high goals or standards of performance for self, subordinates, others, and the organization.[20]

A Professional View

In 1983, the American Association of Colleges for Teacher Education (AACTE) issued a paper entitled "Educating a Profession: Profile of a Beginning Teacher," which outlined what a beginning teacher should know and be able to do. In addition to a solid foundation in the liberal arts and sciences, the social and behavioral sciences, and an academic specialty area, the paper stated that beginning teachers should possess the following knowledge and skills—regardless of subject field, grade level, school size, or student population.

Generic Teaching Knowledge and Skills

Teacher candidates should be able to:

1. Analyze and interpret student abilities, cultural backgrounds, achievements, and needs:
   - Use school records, including standardized test scores, and anecdotal data, to identify the learner's needs;
   - Recognize and interpret various exceptional conditions of children (e.g., limited sight or hearing, cognitive ability or outstanding gifted abilities);
   - Identify cultural backgrounds of students and interpret impact on learning.
2. Design instruction that will meet learner needs through appropriate instructional materials, content, activities, format, and goals:
   - Plan a course of action for instruction over a school year, a semester, a grading period, a day, and a lesson;
   - Develop lesson plans with objectives or expected outcomes, instructional sequences and activities, and an evaluation design;
   - Decide the subject matter to be taught, including sequencing, pacing, emphases, activities, and evaluation;
   - Select appropriate print, audiovisual, and computer materials according to established criteria and the needs of students.
3. Conduct instruction to best facilitate learning:
   - Present subject matter and manage activities to maximize learning;
   - Use a variety of instructional strategies including individual and small or large group instruction, peer teaching, independent study, field projects, computer-assisted instruction, lecture, etc.;
   - Use instructional technology, including computers, as appropriate.
4. Manage the classroom to promote productive learning:
   - Regulate classroom time to focus on learning activities;
   - Manage student interaction with each other and the teacher;
   - Organize the classroom physical setting to be an effective environment for learning activities.
5. Manage student conduct to create a positive climate for student learning:
   - Develop, explain, and monitor rules for student conduct;
   - Deal with distractions and competing tasks to maintain a smooth flow of attractive and challenging tasks for students;
   - Maintain a focus on productive learning by correcting deviant behavior, varying teaching strategies, and praising desirable conduct.
6. Promote classroom communication to evoke and express academic information as well as personal feelings and relationships:
   - Use and elicit Standard English in writing and speaking;
   - Use correct mathematical symbols and processes;
   - Use body language and other forms of nonverbal communication to express emotions as well as approval, disapproval, permission, etc.

7. Evaluate learning to determine the extent to which instructional objectives are achieved by students:
   - Relate evaluation to instructional objectives and be able to select and develop appropriate questions and types of tests;
   - Elicit students' best efforts in preparation for and in taking examinations;
   - Create an appropriate environment for test-taking that encourages conscientious and ethical behavior;
   - Help students develop an acceptance of tests as an opportunity to demonstrate the accomplishment of goals and to identify areas that need strengthening;
   - Summarize students' performance on units of instruction and report that performance honestly and accurately to both students and parents;
   - Analyze test results and interpret achievement information meaningfully to students.
8. Arrange for conferral and referral opportunities:
   - Refer parents/pupils to appropriate professional expertise as necessary following detection of apparent student problems;
   - Conduct conferences as necessary with parents and special school personnel, such as the school nurse, psychologist, social worker, librarian/media specialist, and guidance counselor.[21]

In light of the four differing views of what teachers ought to know and be able to do, it seems clear that becoming a teacher *is* complex and demanding. We believe that effective teachers use five kinds of knowledge and skills to meet the challenges of the profession. As Figure 1.2 shows, such teachers are guided by **reflection** and a **problem-solving orientation.** On the basis of this reflection and problem solving, they use knowledge of self and students (including cultural differences), subject matter, and educational theory and research to create optimum conditions for learning.

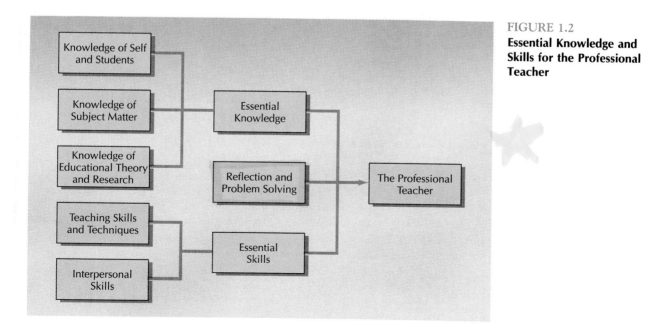

FIGURE 1.2

Essential Knowledge and Skills for the Professional Teacher

CONSIDER THIS . . .

The Characteristics of Effective Teachers: A Self-Assessment

One of the most comprehensive studies of the attributes of effective teachers was the Teacher Characteristics Study directed by David G. Ryans and reported in his 1960 book, *Characteristics of Teachers*. The study spanned six years and involved 100 separate research projects in which 6,000 teachers in 1,700 schools participated.

Data from this study indicated that several characteristics tend to be associated with "outstanding" teachers. For each of the following 13 characteristics identified by Ryans, indicate on a 1–5 scale the extent to which it applies to you.

	Very applicable			Not at all applicable
1. Superior intellectual abilities	1	2	3	4	5
2. Above-average school achievement	1	2	3	4	5
3. Good emotional adjustment	1	2	3	4	5
4. Favorable attitudes toward pupils	1	2	3	4	5
5. Enjoyment of pupil relationships	1	2	3	4	5
6. Generosity in the appraisal of the behavior and motives of other persons	1	2	3	4	5
7. Strong interests in reading and literary matters	1	2	3	4	5
8. Interest in music and painting	1	2	3	4	5
9. Participation in social and community affairs	1	2	3	4	5
10. Early experiences in caring for children and teaching (such as reading to children and taking a class for the teacher)	1	2	3	4	5
11. History of teaching in the family	1	2	3	4	5
12. Family support of teaching as a vocation	1	2	3	4	5
13. Strong social service interest	1	2	3	4	5
				Total score _____

Now that you have completed the self-assessment, calculate your total score; the highest score = 65, the lowest = 13. Interpret the results of your self-assessment with caution. A low score does not necessarily mean that you will be an effective teacher, nor does a high score mean that you would be ineffective.

Source: David G. Ryans, *Characteristics of Teachers: Their Description, Comparison, and Appraisal* (Washington, D.C.: American Council on Education, 1960) p. 366.

THE IMPORTANCE OF SELF-ASSESSMENT

Self-assessment is a necessary process in the professional development of teachers. Now that you have begun your journey toward becoming a teacher, you should acquire the habit of assessing your growth in knowledge, skills, and attitudes. As you do so, however, remember that professional development is a lifelong process; any teacher, at any stage of development, has room for improvement.

At this point, you should have a general idea of the extent to which you currently possess the knowledge, skills, and attitudes reviewed in the previous section. In which areas are you already strong? Which areas will require hard work on your part? How will you acquire the knowledge you need? How will you develop the skills you need? How can you come to know yourself more fully and deeply?

FIVE-MINUTE FOCUS   Reflect on yourself as a teacher. What knowledge, skills, and attitudes do you already have that suit you well for teaching? What ones that you currently lack are your chief concerns? Date your journal entry and write for five minutes.

SUMMARY

We began this chapter by reviewing why people are drawn to teaching, pointing out that most teachers love certain aspects of their work. We considered the influence that early life experiences can have on the decision to become a teacher, as well as the rewards and practical benefits of teaching that make the profession attractive. Next, we turned to the conditions under which teachers work and briefly considered the sources of stress with which some teachers must cope: lack of discipline, drug abuse, high teacher-student ratios, long working hours, and frustrations with the system.

Next, we examined the changing image of teachers and teaching in the United States. We also explored the vision of teachers as keepers of the dream and found hope in the determined spirits of those who choose to teach. Four different views were then presented of the knowledge and abilities that teachers need: a personal-development view, a research-based view, a job-analysis view, and a professional view. We also presented a model of how the professional teacher, guided by reflection and problem solving, uses three kinds of knowledge (knowledge of self and students, subject matter, and educational theory and research) and two kinds of skills (teaching skills and techniques and interpersonal skills).

KEY TERMS AND CONCEPTS

cultural lag, 12
knowledge base, 17
personal-development view, 18
job analysis, 19

reflection, 21
problem-solving orientation, 21
self-assessment, 23

DISCUSSION QUESTIONS

1. What attractions to teaching have not been discussed in this chapter? What challenging aspects?
2. What significant experiences in your life have contributed to your decision to become a teacher?
3. What do you think is the public's image of teachers in your community today?
4. Are elementary school teachers regarded more positively than teachers in secondary schools? Why do you think as you do?
5. Which view of essential knowledge and skills for teachers seems most useful: the professional view, the personal-development view, the research-based view, or the job-analysis view? Least useful?
6. How can the image of teachers be improved? What strategy for changing it can you recommend?

APPLICATION ACTIVITIES

1. Consider your reasons for deciding to become a teacher. How do they compare with those described in this chapter?
2. Make a list of recent portrayals of teachers in the movies, television, and other media. Analyze the portrayals in terms of the type of teacher image they present—positive, neutral, or negative.
3. Survey the students taking education courses in your college to see what they think Americans think of teachers. Try to include in your survey students in introductory courses, exit courses, and graduate courses. Compare the responses you obtain to those discussed in this chapter.
4. Clip all education-related articles in a major newspaper for a two-week period. Analyze the clippings in terms of the type of teacher image they present—positive, neutral, or negative.

FIELD EXPERIENCES

1. Design a questionnaire and conduct a survey of students who are planning to become teachers. Why did they decide on teaching as a career, and what do they think they need to know and be able to do in order to teach?
2. Visit a local school and interview several teachers for their perceptions on the rewarding and challenging aspects of teaching. Present your findings to the rest of your class in the form of a brief oral report.
3. Interview a school administrator to find out what kind of knowledge, skills, and attitudes he or she looks for in a new teacher. Exchange your findings with others in your class. Do you note any differences according to level (i.e., elementary, middle, or secondary)?
4. Interview the dean or assistant dean of your college of education. Ask him or her to discuss the public's current image of teachers. Share the results of your interview in a report to the class.

SUGGESTED READINGS

Bullough, Robert V., Jr. *First-Year Teacher: A Case Study.* New York: Teachers College Press, 1989. *Bullough describes the skills and coping strategies a seventh-grade teacher develops during her first year-and-a-half of teaching.*

Godar, John. *Teachers Talk.* Macomb, Ill. Glenbridge Publishing, 1990. *Godar spent a year interviewing 282 teachers in 10 states and, through verbatim transcriptions, gives them an opportunity to have "their say in the debate over what's wrong with public education."*

Kohl, Herbert. *Growing Minds: On Becoming a Teacher.* New York: Harper and Row, 1984. *Kohl shares his perspectives on teaching in a series of insightful, well-written essays.*

Kysilka, Marcella L. (Ed.). *Honor in Teaching: Reflections.* West Lafayette, Ind.: Kappa Delta Pi Publications, 1990. *Fourteen eminent educators address what must be done to restore honor to the teaching profession.*

Lortie, Dan. *Schoolteacher: A Sociological Study.* Chicago: University of Chicago Press, 1975. *The first chapter entitled "The Hand of History" provides an excellent overview of the changing images of teachers.*

Rubin, Louis D. (Ed.). *An Apple for My Teacher: Twelve Authors Tell About Teachers Who Made the Difference.* Chapel Hill, N.C.: Algonquin Books of Chapel Hill, 1987. *In a set of lively, graceful sketches, twelve distinguished authors reflect on the teachers who helped them discover their vocation.*

APPENDIX: Florida Performance Measurement System

Summative Observation Instrument

Domain	Effective Indicators		Frequency	Frequency	Ineffective Indicators
3.0 Instructional Organization and Development	1. Begins instruction promptly				Delays
	2. Handles materials in an orderly manner				Does not organize or handle materials systematically
	3. Orients students to classwork/maintains academic focus				Allows talk/activity unrelated to subject
	4. Conducts beginning/ending review				
	5. Questions: academic comprehension/ lesson development	asks single factual question			Poses multiple questions asked as one, unison response
		requires analysis/ reasons			Poses nonacademic questions/nonacademic procedural questions
	6. Recognizes response/amplifies/gives corrective feedback				Ignores student or response/expresses sarcasm, disgust, harshness
	7. Gives specific academic praise				Uses general, nonspecific praise
	8. Provides for practice				Extends discourse, changes topic with no practice
	9. Gives directions/assigns/checks comprehension of homework, seatwork assignment/gives feedback				Gives inadequate directions/no homework/ no feedback
	10. Circulates and assists students				Remains at desk/circulates inadequately

APPENDIX: Florida Performance Measurement System (continued)

Summative Observation Instrument

Domain	Effective Indicators	Frequency	Frequency	Ineffective Indicators
4.0 Presentation of Subject Matter	11. Treats concept–definition/attributes/examples/nonexamples			Gives definition or examples only
	12. Discusses cause-effect/uses linking words—applies law or principle			Discusses either cause or effect only/uses no linking word(s)
	13. States and applies academic rule			Does not state or does not apply academic rule
	14. Develops criteria and evidence for value judgment			States value judgment with no criteria or evidence
5.0 Communication: Verbal and Nonverbal	15. Emphasizes important points			
	16. Expresses enthusiasm verbally/challenges students			
	17.			Uses vague, scrambled discourse
	18.			Uses loud, grating, high-pitched, monotone, inaudible talk
	19. Uses body behavior that shows interest—smiles, gestures			Frowns, deadpan, or lethargic
2.0 Mgmt. of Student Conduct	20. Stops misconduct			Delays desist/doesn't stop misconduct/desists punitively
	21. Maintains instructional momentum			Loses momentum, fragments nonacademic directions, overdwells

Source: Florida Department of Education, Tallahassee, Fla.

TEACHERS . . .

What attracted you to teaching?
Would you choose the same career again?

I have always enjoyed the school environment. I had several very good teachers when I was in school and their methods of presenting the material, as well as the excitement they created in the classroom, made me want to do the same. Yes, I would choose teaching as a career again, because it is a gratifying profession for helping others. Also, when working with children as opposed to machinery, each day is unpredictable in terms of rewards and accomplishments. Teaching is not, by any means, a monotonous job.

—Rose Ann Blaschke
Vivian Elementary School, Lakewood, Colorado

As a child I had the good fortune to attend a small country school. The best year of my school career was spent in sixth grade with Mr. Deutscher. "Mr. D." was from Holland and so spoke with a curious (to us) accent. He was a rather imposing man (large, bald, small spectacles); all the kids were afraid of him. This fear was not unfounded, for he administered discipline with a firm hand.

In spite of his menacing image, I liked Mr. D. His class was always a place of learning and adventure. We studied French, read about pirates, collected stamps, sculpted models of African wildlife in clay, drew maps, and much more. Mr. D. also fostered our interest in reading. I read many books that year in sixth grade. Among my favorites were *The Adventures of Tom Sawyer, Robinson Crusoe,* and the entire collection of *Tarzan* books by Edgar Rice Burroughs!

Today I am very thankful that Mr. D. was my teacher. He inspired in me a love of learning and a thirst for knowledge that has never left me. In part, he is why I became a teacher.

—William Jody Dyer
Menifee Valley Middle School, Menifee, California

For eight years I was president/owner of a commercial development company, managing over 500,000 square feet of retail space. I was successful—my dream of becoming a business person had come true. Over time, however, the stress of the "dog eat dog" world of business became overwhelming. I was a mother and had a need to "give" instead of to "get." I enrolled in a graduate school of education and

ON TEACHING

found teaching the most satisfying work I have ever experienced. Becoming a teacher was a major career change for me, and yes, I would do it again.
—Jennifer Cronk
Rocky Mountain Hebrew Academy, Denver, Colorado

I want to become a teacher because I love children and value education. I have been drawn to the field of education since I was a small child "playing school" in a makeshift basement classroom. I feel that the future of our nation depends on our children receiving the best education we can provide for them. All children have a right to this education and I want to be a part of the process. I'm a creative person and teaching offers me unlimited ways of expressing that creativity in an area where I can make a positive and lasting contribution. I find the challenge of making learning relevant and fun for each child exciting! Teaching is a career where I can continue to learn and grow; a career that can never be described as dull or routine. Teaching is a way I can remember and repay teachers who contributed to my own education. I'm looking forward to all teaching has to offer!
—Joy Brandveld
Azusa Pacific University, Azusa, California

Teaching offers me a creative climate, a place to express and receive love, a chance to develop talents, be a leader, and be home during the summer with my children.
—Charlotte McDonald
Canyon Rim Elementary School, Salt Lake City, Utah

My third grade teacher was Mrs. Walters. I was a student in her class as our friendship began; then in fifth grade I was a student helper and worked with some of her first graders on reading. In sixth grade I moved away, but from then until I was a senior in high school, each September just before school began I would go to her school and put up all of her bulletin boards. During those three days each year we spent many hours talking, not realizing that many of those talks would become an inspiration to me now as I begin my teaching career. I find myself doing things in my classroom just as Mrs. Walters had done them. As I look at my future in educating young children, I have one hope: that I can impact and nurture just one life and become a mentor to that one as Mrs. Walters became to me.
—Karen S. Kusayanagi
Jean Hayman Elementary School, Lake Elsinore, California

CHAPTER

2

What Is Teaching Really Like?

We need to become more aware than we presently are of the fleeting and ephemeral quality of the teacher's work.

Philip Jackson
"The Way Teaching Is"

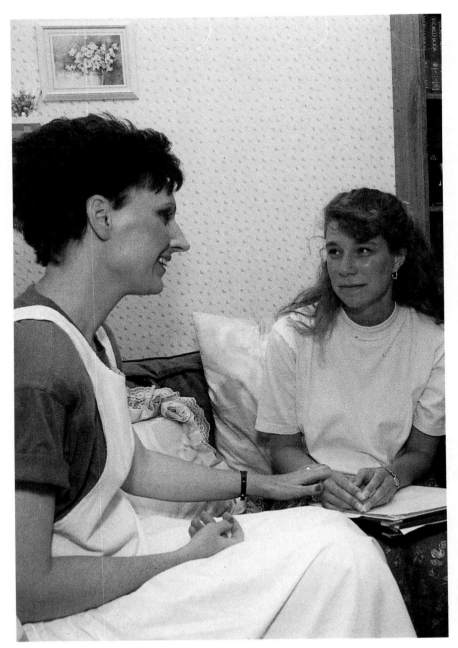

*L*incoln School is near a busy expressway in an urban area in the South. The school has just under 1,200 pupils, of whom about 45 percent are African American, 35 percent Hispanic, 15 percent white, and 5 percent Asian. As recently as the early 1970s, the neighborhood surrounding Lincoln was predominantly middle-income. Since then, however, the more upwardly mobile families began to move out of the area and into the suburbs. Today, most of the families that remain are low-income.

Often, students at urban schools such as Lincoln have below-average achievement; however, the performance of Lincoln students on the annual state-mandated test of reading, writing, and mathematics skills has been just below the mean score for all schools in the state. And, compared to the other schools in the city, the achievement of Lincoln students is above average. As a result, Lincoln has a reputation throughout the city for providing students with an above-average education.

Built in the mid 1960s, Lincoln is a well-maintained two-story building. The principal, Karen Long, takes special pride in the appearance of the school and believes that it contributes to the overall morale of students and teachers.

After looking for a job for a month, you were thrilled when Karen called in early August and asked if you wanted to teach at Lincoln. Other teachers had told you how supportive Karen was of first-year teachers, and you couldn't imagine a better place to begin your teaching career.

Near the end of your first three months at Lincoln, Nancy, who is also a beginning teacher and a good friend, comes into your room after the students have left for the day.

"I'm so tired," she begins. "I don't know if I can make it until Christmas." She drops into a student's desk at the front of the room and, with a vacant look on her face, begins to watch you organize materials for tomorrow's classes.

"What's the matter?" you ask, continuing to staple worksheets together. "Maybe it'll help to talk about it."

"I'm just not sure I'm cut out for teaching," Nancy says. "I like my students, and I think they like me—but I'm not sure if I'm doing a good job. It's just that . . . teaching is much more difficult than I thought it would be. I didn't think being on the other side of the teacher's desk would be so hard."

"I know what you mean," you respond.

"It seems as though I'll have days where everything goes great. The kids are motivated and really seem to learn a lot. On those days I absolutely love teaching."

"That makes it all worthwhile, doesn't it?"

"Then, other days things are really hard," Nancy continues. "The kids don't respond like I think they should, and I start putting myself down because I think I ought to be able to be that terrific teacher all the time. What do you think . . . is this what teaching is really like?"

How would you respond to your friend? What are the realities of teaching that she is beginning to discover?

FOCUS QUESTIONS

1. What are the realities of teaching?
2. How do good teachers describe teaching?
3. In what ways is teaching different from other professions?
4. How do teachers and students influence each other?
5. How can educational research help teachers understand their work more fully?

Each of us is able to recall, at least dimly, the years during which we were taught the basics—reading, writing, mathematics, and oral communication. We also remember, no doubt, reading and writing about other subjects—geography, science, and history, for example. In addition, we acquired other knowledge and skills that school boards, teachers, curriculum committees, and an array of interest groups felt we ought to learn. Courses such as woodworking, health, music, art, physical education, typing, home economics, and a foreign language rounded out the curriculum we experienced at the elementary, middle, junior, and senior high schools we attended.

Although the teachers who taught us had different personalities, methods, and expectations, we would probably find that our lives as students were more alike than different. The recollections we share with one another about teachers who were good or bad, easy or hard, interesting or dull are drawn from a commonly shared set of experiences. The universality and apparent sameness of these experiences, then, lead us to conclude that we *know* what teaching is really like and what teachers do.

Teachers control the behavior of students. Teachers assign work and give directions. They ask questions and judge the rightness or wrongness of students' responses. They lecture and occasionally demonstrate what students are to do. They assign chapters to read in the text and then conduct recitations or give quizzes on that material. They praise some students for right answers or good work, and they prod, chastise, and, at times, humiliate others in the hope that their work will improve. And, near the end of the term or semester, of course, they decide who has passed and who has failed.

But, is teaching the sum total of the overt behaviors that students have observed in their teachers? Clearly not. Teaching is much more complex. As you move ahead in your journey toward becoming a teacher, you will discover that teaching involves much more than simply performing certain behaviors in front of a group of students. Throughout this book, we contend that a significant portion of the teacher's work is mental and involves a continuous inner dialogue about purposes and appropriate actions. The hallmark of a truly professional teacher, then, is the skill and sensitivity with which he or she maintains this dialogue and draws upon it to become more effective. To help you begin such a dialogue, this chapter addresses four questions: How do "effective" teachers view their work? What other views of teaching can help you understand what teaching is really like? What are the "realities" of teaching? And, how can educational research help to increase your understanding of teaching?

THE COMPLEXITIES OF TEACHING

It may seem odd for a chapter titled "What Is Teaching Really Like?" to point out that we do not fully understand what teaching is and what teachers do. To admit what we don't know about teaching, however, is where we must begin.

One of the most important steps you can take toward becoming a professional teacher is to try to appreciate the complexity of the career you have chosen. As you progress through your teacher education program, you will come to realize that it is impossible to know all of the factors that determine how much any student learns, and, as a teacher, you can influence only a scant few of those factors that you can identify. Our hope, though, is that you will become an expert at determining just where to target your energies and resources in the classroom. If you can develop that skill, you may be confident in your ability to be maximally successful in any teaching situation.

The Challenge of the Profession

To meet the challenge of the profession of teaching, however, will not be easy. At best, the task is very difficult; at worst, it may be close to impossible. As Haim Ginott suggests: "Teachers are expected to reach unattainable goals with inadequate tools. The miracle is that at times they accomplish this impossible task."[1]

In spite of the difficulties that confront all teachers, we want you to keep this important distinction in mind: Though the outcomes of teaching may be unsatisfying if students do not learn all that you would like them to learn, the *experience* of teaching others is very satisfying. Compared to all other professions, the work of the teacher matters the most. After all, the drive to become educated, to inquire into the nature of the world, is what distinguishes human beings from other life forms on this planet. And the teacher, more than any other professional, is centrally concerned with facilitating this highest human need.

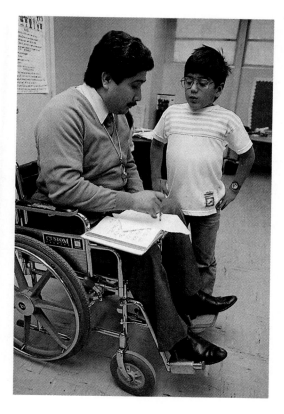

With vision and commitment, teachers can meet personal challenges in addition to mastering the professional challenges of becoming an effective teacher.

CONSIDER THIS . . .

The Teaching Commitment Scale

How committed are you to achieving excellence in your teaching? For an indication of your level of job commitment, respond to the Teaching Commitment Scale that follows. The scale contains 16 items that ask how you will feel once you have become a teacher. Indicate the extent to which you agree or disagree with each item by circling the appropriate number. When you total your score, reverse-score items 6, 8, and 16. Your total score will range from a low of 16 to a high of 64, with 64 representing the highest level of commitment to teaching.

Responses: 1-Strongly Disagree, 2-Disagree, 3-Agree, 4-Strongly Agree

After I have become a teacher:	1	2	3	4
1. Most of the important things that will happen to me will involve my work.	—	—	—	—
2. I will spend a great deal of time on matters related to my job, both during and after school.	—	—	—	—
3. I will feel badly if I don't perform well as a teacher.	—	—	—	—
4. I will think about teaching even when I'm not working.	—	—	—	—
5. I would probably continue teaching even if I didn't have to work.	—	—	—	—
6. I will have a perspective on my job that will not let it interfere with other aspects of my life.	—	—	—	—
7. Performing well as a teacher will be extremely important to me.	—	—	—	—
8. Most things in my life will be more important to me than teaching.	—	—	—	—
9. I will avoid taking on extra duties and responsibilities in my work.	—	—	—	—
10. I will enjoy teaching more than anything else I do.	—	—	—	—
11. I will stay overtime to finish a job even if I don't have to.	—	—	—	—
12. Sometimes I will lie awake thinking about the next day at school.	—	—	—	—
13. I will be able to use abilities I value.	—	—	—	—
14. I will feel depressed when my teaching does not go well.	—	—	—	—
15. I will feel good when I teach well.	—	—	—	—
16. I would not teach if I didn't have to.	—	—	—	—

Total _____

Source: Adapted from the Occupational Commitment Scale developed by Ladewig and White (1984, *Journal of Family Issues, 5,* 343–362).

The Importance of Vision and Commitment

Anyone who aspires to become an effective teacher should have a personal vision—a sense of what he or she values and is committed to. As Roland Barth observes in *Improving Schools from Within,* vision and a sense of purpose can help one respond to the complex realities of school life:

> [The] lives of teachers, principals, and students are characterized by brevity, fragmentation, and variety. During an average day, for instance, a teacher or principal engages in several hundred interactions. A personal vision provides a framework with which to respond and to make use of the many presciptions and conceptions of others. Without a vision, I think our behavior becomes reflexive, inconsistent, and short-sighted as we seek the action that will most quickly put out the fire so we can get on with putting out the next one. . . . As one teacher put it in a powerful piece of writing, "Without a clear sense of purpose we get lost, and our activities in school become but empty vessels of our discontent."[2]

Commitment is also a vital component of professional effectiveness. However, as Tom Peters and Nancy Austin point out in their best-selling book, *A Passion for Excellence,* it is not easy to make a commitment to excellence:

> Whether we're looking at a billion dollar corporation or a three-person accounting department, we see that excellence is achieved by people who muster up the nerve (and the passion) to step out—in spite of doubt, or fear, or job description. . . . They won't retreat behind office doors, committees, memos or layers of staff, knowing this is the fair bargain they make for extraordinary results. They may step out for love, because of a burning desire to be the best, to make a difference, or perhaps, as a colleague recently explained, "because the thought of being average scares the hell out of me."[3]

HOW GOOD TEACHERS VIEW THEIR WORK

Let's begin by examining how four junior and senior high school teachers, identified as highly successful by their principals, view their work. We asked these teachers to describe those moments when they knew they were teaching effectively. As you "listen" to their individual voices, notice how they try to describe "something" that is beyond easy observation and measurement. And note, too, how they convey the idea that teaching is not entirely a logical, sequential process.

> *Teacher 1:* Sometimes you see this little light . . . especially in math. You're explaining something, and you see all these puzzled looks on their faces. And you think, "Oh, gosh, they don't understand any of this." And then all of a sudden it hits them and I think, "Aha, I got it!" And they really do! . . .
>
> *Teacher 2:* I don't really know how to determine when I'm definitely reaching kids. That's what makes this job so difficult. But it's when they respond. . . . I don't know how to measure it exactly. It's just a feeling. I just feel like I have the kids with me.
>
> *Teacher 3:* Well, sometimes it's lightbulb clear. Boom . . . it's there, and you can see it. The kids really responding, actually learning. I don't know how you see it, but you know it.

Teacher 4: I have to grab the kids that don't want to do math at all and somehow make them want to do this work. I'm not sure how I do it, but kids just want to do well in my class. For some mysterious reason, and I don't care why, they really want to do well.

In some respects, the essence of teaching is difficult to describe. Certainly, we can describe in elaborate detail the interactions of effective teachers and their students—and these data are rightly included in quality teacher education programs—but our descriptions cannot capture, with richness and completeness, *all* that a teacher does (or doesn't do) in order to teach. Just as the attraction between two persons may be the result of a mysterious chemistry, the relationships between teachers and their students are charged with a difficult-to-measure emotional energy. The more effective teachers are somehow able to direct this energy toward learning the subject at hand.

The comments of these teachers confirm the difficulty of arriving at a comprehensive definition of teaching. Our quest to answer the question "What is teaching really like?" leads us to the inescapable conclusion that we can't fully define what *it* is. It may be in the way we describe the good teachers we have had that we find the closest approximation of what teaching really is. David Denton describes that special quality this way: "We come close to the 'It' of teaching with such terms as 'magic,' or 'the vibrations are great,' or 'he's altogether.' Student language, not scientific language, but student language emerges from that shared existential space where teaching is—whatever It is."[4]

MODES OF TEACHING

When we recall our favorite teachers, we likely think of particular people, not idealizations of the teacher's many roles. Though each was a teacher, each was unique, distinct from the others; indeed, their ability to be themselves fully is, most likely, an essential part of why we value them so. The many roles of the teacher, then, should not be regarded as a limitation on behavior, a straitjacket that binds and reduces people to mediocre sameness, but as a responsibility to be accepted and fulfilled in an individual manner—a full academic robe drawing respect while allowing for freedom of movement and individual expression.

By teaching dynamically without overdoing the performance and power-wielding modes of teaching, you can capture students' attention and invite active rather than passive learning.

Five **modes of teaching,** more general and significant than a discussion of the teacher's roles, can help you understand what teaching is really like. You may recognize these modes in the writings of gifted teachers when they reflect on their work, and may even acknowledge them as deeper reasons for your decision to teach. We discuss these modes of teaching here because they subtly but powerfully influence the way people think and act when they become teachers.

A Way of Being

As noted earlier, teaching is ideally more like wearing an academic robe than a stiff and binding straitjacket, and once you put it on, you rarely take it off. When you travel, when you read, and when you learn something, the robe is there, its weight prompting you to think, "How can I use this in class?"

The robe is also with you as you move about in your interpersonal life outside of school, reminding you when you encounter students, parents, and others in the community that you are no longer just yourself. For good or ill, you are also "Mr. Burke, the varsity basketball coach," "Mr. Montgomery, the new math teacher," or "Miss Rodriguez, our son's sixth-grade teacher."

In much the same way that becoming a husband or wife or parent changes you, so does becoming a teacher, for you must take on the role and let it become a part of you. You think like Eliot Wigginton did when he introduced himself to an audience by saying simply and directly: "I am a teacher. That is not what I do, but who I am. When I am not teaching, I am thinking about teaching."[5] Indeed, being a teacher is a way of being, much more than it is a set of roles, and the experience is a comprehensive one.

A Creative Endeavor *lose most*

Perhaps one of the most creative teachers in our society today is Eliot Wigginton, an English teacher who has taught in Rabun Gap, Georgia, for over 20 years. His guidance in the creation and development of what has become known as the Foxfire experience has brought him national attention, accolades, and awards. The project, which began when Wigginton was frustrated by not being able to motivate his students, has blossomed from a student-produced literary magazine, *Foxfire,* into a full-blown student-run corporate enterprise devoted to the furtherance of Rabun Gap's oral history and the development and expression of the students' skills and talents.

In his intriguing book *Sometimes a Shining Moment,* an account of the Foxfire experience and the author's personal reflections on teaching, Wigginton refers to the creative dimension of teaching. "I teach because it is something I do well; it is a craft I enjoy and am intrigued by; there is room within its certain boundaries for infinite variety and flexibility of approach, and so if I become bored or my work becomes routine, I have no one to blame but myself."[6]

Teaching is a creative endeavor in which teachers are continually shaping and reshaping the lessons, events, and experiences of their students. Ann Lieberman and Lynne Miller discuss this dimension of teaching in their book *Teachers, Their World, and Their Work* when they share their perceptions of teaching as a craft and teachers as craftspeople:

Teachers struggle to adjust and readjust, to make routines, and establish patterns, only to recast what has been done in a new form to meet a new need or a new vision.

[Thus] the reality of teaching is of a craft learned on the job, [and] when viewed as a craft, teaching makes sense as a messy and highly personal enterprise, for it concerns itself with the making and remaking of an object until it satisfies the standards of its creator.[7]

The creative dimension of teaching may indeed be the life source for those who remain in the profession for many years. It replenishes the spirit.

A Live Performance

Teaching is a live performance with each class period, each day, containing the unpredictable. Further, teachers are engaged in live dialogues with their classes and individual students. The experience of teaching is thus an intense, attention-demanding endeavor—an interactive one that provides minute-to-minute challenges.

Some teachers embrace the live performance aspect of teaching more than others, believing that within it lies true learning. Sybil Marshall, who is such a teacher, writes about the process and effect of teaching dynamically in her book *An Experiment in Education,* an account of her experiences as a teacher in a one-room school in England: "To control a class in freedom, to learn with each child instead of instructing a passive class, to be a well of clear water into which the children can dip all the time, instead of a hosepipe dousing them with facts, is the most exhausting way of doing a teacher's job."[8] This mode of teaching can be best understood through actual experience. The more practice you have in actual teaching situations—as Saturday morning coach, camp counselor, Sunday school teacher, and guest teacher in schools—the more comfortable you become with teaching as a live performance.

A Wielding of Power

Power is the dimension of teaching most immediately evident to the new teacher. It is recognized in the first-grader's awed "Teacher, is this good?" on through the high school senior's "How much will this paper count?" Customarily, teachers get respect, at least initially, the deference deriving from their power to enhance or damage their students' academic status and welfare.

Even in the most democratic classrooms, teachers have more influence than their students because they are responsible for what happens when students are with them, establishing the goals, selecting the methods, setting the pace, evaluating the progress, and deciding whether students should pass or fail. Accordingly, teachers' authority can be regarded as the heaviness of the academic robe we mentioned earlier, the part of teaching that is particularly serious.

How you use this power is crucial. The late teacher and writer John Holt wrote about the psychological wars that insecure and frightened teachers conduct with their students. In his book *How Children Fail,* Holt gave a vivid example of one battle in such a war:

A mother told me not long ago that on one of her five-year-old son's first days in kindergarten he began to talk to a friend. Having never in his short life been told that he couldn't talk to people, he didn't know this was a crime. Instead of just telling him her rule, the teacher scolded him loudly in front of the class. Then she made a long red paper "tongue," which she pinned to his shirt, after which she began to make fun of him, calling him Long Tongue and inviting the other children to do the same—an invitation they could hardly refuse. In such ways is the war waged. Not much will be learned while it goes on.[9]

The war is not confined to kindergarten, as we all know, for students at any level can be humiliated by teachers who misuse their power. Wigginton writes, "Most of us have forgotten what it's like to be young. The image is burned into my mind of an eighth-grade boy, handsome, active, popular, aggressive, healthy, whole, standing beside our assistant principal, Alvin Smith, crying great, choking, gasping sobs because he had just been scolded by a teacher for forgetting his textbook."[10]

You can support as well as defeat with your power, turning students around and swaying them to appreciate your subjects, or school, or most importantly themselves through your belief in them. Sometimes your influence will surprise you when a passing comment or words of genuine praise come back to you as reasons for a student's success.

The mixed potential inherent in the power wielded by teachers should not lie outside of your awareness. Like doctors, teachers should vow first to do no harm with their power and then to use it to promote health and growth.

FIVE-MINUTE FOCUS Think back to your experiences in school—at the elementary, middle school, or high school level. Were you ever made uncomfortable because of a teacher's power over you? Have you ever been ridiculed or diminished by a teacher? Or have you experienced the opposite—being elevated by a teacher's regard for you? Write about a specific incident illustrating either experience. Date your journal entry and write for five minutes.

An Opportunity to Serve

To become a teacher is to serve others professionally—students, the school, the community, and the country, depending upon how broad the perspective is. Most who come to teaching do so for altruistic reasons. As Herbert Kohl, the inner-city schoolteacher who first drew the nation's attention 20 years ago with his book *36 Children*,[11] notes in a recent work,

> I believe the impulse to teach is fundamentally altruistic and represents a desire to share what you value and to empower others. Of course, all teachers are not altruistic. Some people teach in order to dominate others or to support work they'd rather do or simply to earn a living. But I am not talking about the job of teaching so much as the calling to teach. Most teachers I know, even the most demoralized ones who drag themselves to oppressive and mean schools where their work is not respected and their presence not welcome, have felt that calling at some time in their lives.[12]

The altruistic dimension of teaching is at the heart of the motivation to teach. The paycheck, the public regard, and the vacations have little holding power compared to the opportunity to serve. When teachers speak of this, their reason for remaining in the profession becomes obvious. Torey Hayden, a special education resource room teacher and popular author, enlivens her accounts of her teaching experiences with frequent illustrations of just such satisfaction.

What was important was a scrawny seven-year-old kid waving a twenty-five-year-old pre-primer at me from across the room, squealing delightedly, reading out the text to Boo and Benny and the finches. Come what might in her future, I knew I had given her the best I had. Never again could anyone say she could not read. She now could prove that false. Lori Sjokheim was not anybody to be messed with. Lori Sjokheim could read.[13]

Sara Lawrence Lightfoot describes a similar phenomenon at the secondary-school level when she writes about certain special relationships between teachers and students in her book *The Good High School:*

In every school I visited, several students spoke of developing these bonds that were highly individualized and mutual, and very different from the generalized affection of a kind and popular teacher. A lanky, awkward senior at Carver told me how it felt when, in his sophomore year, an English teacher described his writing as "poetic." "I couldn't believe what she was saying . . . so I asked her to say it again." Every day he finds a way of stopping by her room, even if it is just for a brief greeting. She traces him through the day, knows most of the details of his life, and gets "a rare pleasure" from their relationship.[14]

Whatever form the altruistic rewards of teaching take, they ennoble the profession and remind teachers of the human significance of their work.

A word of caution. Altruism alone cannot teach students; indeed, without the necessary knowledge and skills, the well-intentioned efforts of teachers are likely to be counterproductive, if not dangerous. However, the opportunity to serve others is the fuel that drives teachers to learn continually so that they can better guide their students.

Of the five perspectives on teaching discussed here, the opportunity to serve is most likely to be familiar to you, and for most of you, we hope, it is the reason you want to teach. Perhaps to your surprise, it is, in our minds, your greatest asset. We know that new teachers with their high ideals, determined optimism, and belief that the impossible is possible, often do work miracles. Their fresh hope makes up for their lack of experience and is a gift to the veterans they join.

SIX REALITIES OF TEACHING

In this section of the chapter we will examine six basic **realities of teaching,** which illustrate why teaching is so demanding *and* why it can be so exciting, rewarding, and uplifting. And when we say that teaching is demanding we mean more than the fact that Mr. Smith's third-period plane geometry students just can't seem to learn how to compute the area of a triangle; or that Miss Ellis' sixth-grade composition class can't remember whether to use *there* or *their;* or even that one out of four Chicago teachers has said that teaching makes him or her physically ill.[15] While there are many frustrating, stressful events with which teachers must cope, the difficulty of teaching goes much further, or deeper, than these examples suggest.

Before we look at the six realities of teaching, we want to clarify our perspective. Though these six realities highlight the demanding (perhaps even impossible) dimensions of teaching, we *do not* mean to suggest that the efforts of teachers are wasted or that teachers do not make a difference. Clearly, what teachers do in the classroom matters a great deal. Every school year, thousands upon thousands of young people learn much from their teachers. The very fact that you are beginning your study of the teaching profession is a testament to the effectiveness of *your* teachers. However, as we contend throughout this book, you will be more effective as a teacher if you deepen your appreciation of the complexities and difficulties of teaching and then use this understanding to guide your actions as a teacher.

Reality 1: The Unpredictability of Outcomes

The outcomes of teaching, even in the best of circumstances, are neither predictable nor consistent. Any teacher, beginner or veteran, can give countless examples of how the outcomes of teaching are often unpredictable and inconsistent. Life in most classrooms usually proceeds on a fairly even keel—with teachers able to predict, fairly accurately, how their students will respond to lessons. Adherence to the best laid lesson plans, however, may be accompanied by students' blank stares, yawns of boredom, hostile acting out, or expressions of befuddlement. On the other hand, lack of preparation on the teacher's part does not necessarily rule out the possibility of a thoroughly exciting discussion in class, a real breakthrough in understanding for an individual student or the entire class, or simply a good, fast-paced review of previously learned material. In short, teachers are often surprised at students' reactions to a lesson.

In an article titled "The Way Teaching Is," Philip Jackson quotes Sir William Osler, the famous Canadian physician and professor of medicine, who had an apt metaphor for the unpredictable quality of teaching. As Osler put it: "No bubble is so iridescent or floats longer than that blown by the successful teacher." Jackson then goes on to say, "Osler's metaphor intrigues me because it calls attention to the fragile quality of the psychological condition that is created and maintained by the teacher.

In facing the reality of uncertainty about students' responses, teachers must be able to present themselves and their instructional content in a manner that inspires students to respond.

Class sessions, like bubbles, tend to be shortlived, and after a teaching session is finished, its residue, like that of a burst bubble, is almost invisible."[16]

We believe it may be helpful, in the spirit of Osler and Jackson, to think of teaching as akin to blowing bubbles. If our aim while blowing bubbles is to blow the largest, most beautiful, longest lasting bubble we can, we must be able to maintain a perfectly balanced set of conditions while blowing our bubble—not an easy task, as anyone who has ever tried it will attest! In a similar way, the teacher's ability to conduct a perfect (or even a good) class depends upon his or her ability to orchestrate a wide variety of classroom events. And when the dismissal bell rings, the perfect class, like the burst bubble, is gone forever.

Students' Responses   The point to remember is that whether or not students are turned on to learning during a particular lesson may, at times, depend upon factors that are beyond the teacher's awareness and, therefore, control. Contrary to the popular notion that teaching consists entirely of a specific number of competencies or observable behaviors, the reactions of students to any given lesson cannot be guaranteed. Furthermore, it is incorrect to assume that teachers, like other professionals, can control all the results of their efforts.

For example, one of us spent eight years as an English teacher at a ghetto high school on Chicago's South Side and can vividly recall both the good and bad classes during those years. As often as not, those classes—whether good or bad—just seemed to happen. One experience in particular stands out.

> To motivate a freshman remedial English class during a review for a grammar test, I planned to give each student several pieces of Halloween candy if the review went well. Since the review was well planned and the form of reinforcement (candy) was known to be important to students, I was prepared to have a "good" class.
>
> During the review session, however, students were almost totally preoccupied with the candy they were to receive. Surprisingly, students did not put forth much effort at mastering the material. Many students gave wild, crazy answers to my review questions. Some interrupted me repeatedly to ask how many pieces of candy they would get, when they would get it, what kind it was, and would they get candy in all their classes that day.
>
> Contrary to basic theories of reinforcement, my students were unable, or unwilling, to see that behavior during the review and the reward of candy were connected—one led to the other. When I finally gave students their (unearned) reward—after weighing the pros and cons of not "rewarding" them at all—several became angry because they did not get more! Still others tried to steal the candy of their less aggressive classmates. The unexpected reactions of students forced me to spend the final few minutes of class, originally set aside to present new material, restoring order.

Another example of how the outcomes of teaching are unpredictable is given in a teacher's account of his first year on the job. Here we see how creativity and planning do not necessarily ensure a successful lesson and how the inability to obtain positive outcomes can lower a teacher's professional self-esteem.

> I brought in movies, had exercises with the newspaper, had the class write their own newspaper, did map exercises, and had them work on problems I brought in, but I felt that I was only occupying them—a sort of military holding action. I sensed no growth. I felt like Mr. Jonas, the teacher I had observed the year before on the West side. What a disappointing self-image! I began watching the clock, hoping the minutes would race by. They never did. It seemed like an eternity before the bell would ring.

It would finally come, and I would drag myself to the first floor and prepare to get away from it all. Thank God it was my last class. I would be completely drained of emotional and psychic energy. Some days I would come home and fall asleep from four o'clock to ten o'clock. I am sure it was a symbolic return to the womb.

The next morning I would be reborn again and I would trudge off to school to face another day of trying to be a teacher.[17]

As the two preceding examples show, students' unexpected reactions may cause teachers either to scrap their carefully executed plans or to press ahead and make the best of things. However, surprises in the classroom are not always bad. One teacher we interviewed, for example, describes how her sixth-graders let her know that they enjoyed, not disliked, a particular lesson.

Yesterday, the kids seemed real lethargic when I questioned them about the paragraphs they had read. They hardly had anything to say and I thought to myself, "I am really boring these kids with this stuff. So why don't we get off this tomorrow?"

So, for today I had the greatest lesson plan in the world ready—a lesson on speed reading. Well, I couldn't even get into it. Two or three kids said "Let's read some more paragraphs. Let's do what we did yesterday." Then the whole class started in. They wanted more paragraphs!

When you have a positive response like that from the kids, they must be getting something out of it. So I shelved the speed reading lesson and we read more paragraphs. It was absolutely the best class I've ever had with this group. Everyone was just about frantic to read aloud and answer questions. It was beautiful! It was like I could see them begin to understand what reading for comprehension is all about.

Philip Jackson describes this dynamic dimension of teaching in his well-known book *Life in Classrooms* when he notes that "as typically conducted, teaching is an opportunistic process. . . . Neither the teacher nor his students can predict with any certainty exactly what will happen next. Plans are forever going awry and unexpected opportunities for the attainment of educational goals are constantly emerging."[18]

One reality of teaching, then, is that teachers must cope with the erratic ebb and flow of their students' responses—sometimes they react as hoped to lessons; at other times, they don't. Furthermore, the outcome of any lesson is not wholly determined by either the teacher's intentions or behavior. As a result, teachers are never certain that they have once and for all triumphed over the demands of their profession. To what extent was that good class on Monday the result of planning and skill in delivery? To what extent a matter of chance? There is always room for doubt and, we would add, professional growth.

The Future Orientation of Teaching   Teachers strive to effect behavioral changes in their students for the future as well as for the here and now. In *Life in Classrooms*, Jackson labels this the preparatory aspect of teaching. Few teachers have the sole purpose of having students perform better on next Monday's unit exam or on a criterion-referenced test mandated by the state. Instead, students are expected to apply their newly acquired skills and knowledge at some indeterminant, usually distant, point in the future. In fact, some students are slower than others at displaying what they have learned from teachers—only later do these students provide evidence that their teachers were effective. Perhaps you have noticed changes in your behavior that you would attribute to the efforts of a teacher whom you had long ago.

Our inability to determine the actual effects that teachers *might* have on students in the future leads to some interesting problems regarding how teachers are evaluated.

Who is to say, for example, that Catherine's phenomenal reading gains in the fourth grade are not the result of her second-grade teacher's determination to make the resistant child complete her phonics drills? Or consider Sam, a college freshman, who one day appreciates Miss Schmid for "forcing" him to write all those compositions back in sophomore English. Should Sam's current composition instructor, or Miss Schmid, take credit for the excellent papers he now writes? Is Miss Schmid necessarily any less effective because the fruits of her labors with Sam were not immediately apparent?

Reality 2: The Difficulty of Measurement

It is difficult to measure what students learn as a result of being taught. The ultimate purpose of teaching is to lead the student to a greater understanding of the things of this world. But, as even the most casual appraisal of human nature will confirm, it is very difficult, perhaps impossible, to determine precisely what another human being does or does not understand. Although the aims or intentions of teaching may be specified with exacting detail, one of the realities of teaching is that some of what students learn may be indeterminate and beyond direct measurement.

In spite of state-by-state efforts to institute standardized tests of basic skills and thereby hold teachers accountable, the conventional wisdom among teachers is that they are often uncertain about just what their students learn. We have miles of computer printouts with test data, but very little knowledge of what lies behind a child's written response, little understanding of how the child experiences the curriculum. As one educational researcher concludes: "The inaccessibility of data is similar both in science and in learning. We cannot directly 'see' subatomic particles, nor can we 'see' the inner-workings of the mind and emotions of the child. Both are inferential: both are subject to human interpretation."[19]

Years ago, John Dewey called for teachers who would be sensitive to the inner lives of children and therefore aware of what students were learning (or failing to learn) as a result of their exposure to the curriculum. That he refers to this high degree of sensitivity as "insight into soul-action" suggests how difficult it is for teachers to develop the capacity to know what their students learn:

> As every teacher knows, children have an inner and an outer attention. The inner attention is the giving of the mind without reserve or qualification to the subject at hand. It is the first-hand and personal play of mental powers. As such, it is a fundamental condition of mental growth. To be able to keep track of this mental play, to recognize the signs of its presence or absence, to know how it is initiated and maintained, how to test it by results attained, and to test *apparent* results by it, is the supreme mark and criterion of a teacher. It means insight into soul-action, ability to discriminate the genuine from the sham and capacity to further one and discourage the other.[20]

On the one hand, then, teachers must recognize their limited ability to determine what students actually learn; on the other, they must continuously work to become more sensitive to what students learn. To reduce "uncertainties" about students' learning, Philip Jackson suggests four basic approaches available to teachers (see Figure 2.1). The first two are indirect: carefully observing students for signs of involvement and creating a classroom climate in which they feel comfortable enough to admit learning problems. The second two are more direct: questioning students to determine their level of understanding and testing them on material that has been taught. None of these approaches, however, will tell teachers all they might wish to know about students' learning.

FIVE-MINUTE FOCUS Reflect upon your experiences as a student. Describe a time when you learned something other than what the teacher thought he or she was teaching. Date your journal entry and write for five minutes.

Reality 3: The Need for Teacher-Student Partnership

The teacher's ability to influence student behavior is actually quite limited. To the extent that we believe that learning *always* results in observable, measurable changes in student behavior (a currently popular, though limited, view), teaching becomes even more of a challenge. Arthur Combs rejects the notion of a direct correlation in a book aptly titled *Myths in Education: Beliefs That Hinder Progress and Their Alternatives:*

> A teacher's influence on all but the simplest, most primitive forms of student behavior, even in that teacher's own classroom, cannot be clearly established. The older children get, the less teachers can influence even those few, primitive forms of behavior. The attempt to hold teachers responsible for what students do is, for all practical purposes, well nigh impossible.[21]

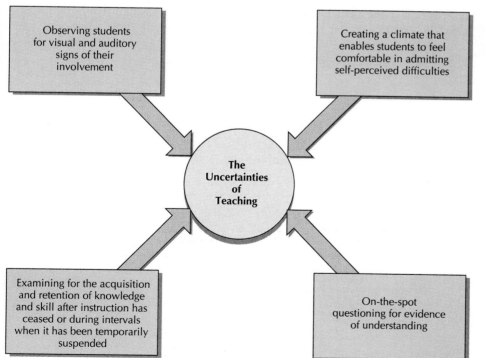

FIGURE 2.1
Reducing the Uncertainties of Teaching: Four Strategies

Source: Reprinted by permission of the publisher from Jackson, Philip W., *The Practice of Teaching.* (New York: Teachers College Press, © 1986 by Teachers College, Columbia, University. All rights reserved.), list that appears on page 61.

It should be obvious that a teacher cannot change a student's behavior with the ease with which a surgeon removes a patient's tonsils or a factory worker tightens a nut and bolt. At best, a teacher tries to influence a student so that he or she makes an internal decision to behave in the desired manner—whether it be reading the first chapter of *The Pearl* by Friday or solving ten addition problems during a mathematics lesson. In contrast, the patient under anesthesia is passive, and the surgeon is no more dependent upon the vagaries of an interactive doctor-patient relationship than an auto assembly-line worker is dependent upon a worker-chasis relationship.

The very fact that we refer to the *teaching-learning process* indicates the extent to which classroom events are "jointly produced"[22] and depend upon a teacher-student partnership. In regard to this partnership, Dewey suggests that the teacher sells and the student must buy:

> Teaching may be compared to selling commodities. No one can sell unless someone buys. We should ridicule a merchant who said that he had sold a great many goods although no one had bought any. But perhaps there are teachers who think that they have done a good day's teaching irrespective of what pupils have learned. There is the same exact equation between teaching and learning that there is between selling and buying.[23]

Teaching, therefore, is a uniquely demanding profession because the work of teachers is evaluated not in terms of what teachers do but in terms of what their "clients" (students) do. "It is the student who does the learning, and he or she is the most powerful person in the teaching/learning situation. His or her intelligence, adaptability, creativity, motivation, and general configurations of personality are much more important determiners of how much he or she will learn than anything the teacher or curricular system can do."[24] To be an effective teacher, then, requires more than the ability to cover the text, deliver a lecture, or divide third-grade students into appropriate reading groups; the teacher must also be able to present him- or herself in a manner that inspires students to behave in certain ways.

FIVE-MINUTE FOCUS   What are the characteristics of teachers with whom students willingly establish teacher-student "partnerships"? The characteristics of teachers with whom students do not develop such partnerships? Date your journal entry and write for five minutes.

Reality 4: The Impact of Teachers' Attitudes

With the role of teacher also comes the power to influence others by example. Albert Bandura writes that "virtually all learning phenomena resulting from direct experience occur on a vicarious basis by observing other people's behavior and its consequences for them."[25] Clearly, students learn much by imitation, and teachers are the ones they often choose to imitate. In the primary grades, teachers are idolized by their young students. At the high school level, teachers have the potential to inspire their students' emulation, and at the very least, to establish the classroom tone by modeling expected attitudes and behaviors.

Teachers' attitudes toward individual students, groups of students, the subjects taught, and learning itself can have powerful effects on their students' thinking and behavior. The specific attitudes teachers provide for imitation can significantly influence the quality of life in classrooms and, in some cases, the future lives of students.[26]

Teachers model attitudes toward the subjects they teach as well as the way they treat their students. This helps to explain why many principals report first looking for enthusiasm in teacher candidates, no doubt thinking that if they feel positive about the subject matter, students also are more likely to.

While the love of what one teaches is a crucial ingredient for good teaching, it is something that cannot be feigned, because students of all ages are too perceptive to believe the counterfeit. If teachers become bored with the subjects they teach, they need to find new ways to be interested in them again—new approaches for teaching them, new dimensions of the subjects to study. If they feel inadequate in a subject area, they must master the skills and change their attitudes or they will pass on their insecurities and dislikes, twenty- or thirtyfold.

Finally, teachers' attitudes toward learning are important models for their students. The teachers who are learning to ski, sketch, play the piano, speak French, or who continually seek more information about nutrition, investments, politics, literature, or archeology are teachers who show students through their example that learning is an ongoing, life-enriching process that does not end with diplomas and graduations. With their love of learning, they confirm the timeless message of Sir Rabindranath Tagore that is inscribed above the doorway of a public building in India: "A teacher can never truly teach unless he is still learning himself. A lamp can never light another lamp unless it continues to burn its own flame."[27]

Reality 5: The Drama and Immediacy of Teaching

Interactive teaching is characterized by events that are rapid-changing, multidimensional, and irregular. We have already discussed how the outcomes of teaching are unpredictable and inconsistent. Yet the challenges of teaching go beyond this. The face-to-face interactions teachers have with students—what Jackson has termed "**interactive teaching**"[28]—are themselves rapid-changing, multidimensional, and irregular. One of us realized during his first year of teaching that "from the moment I and my students encountered one another in the classroom, the flux of counter-educative events I had to contend with was often confusing, if not overwhelmingly chaotic, in its complexity.

"Of course I believe that a teacher should offer a positive role model; however . . ."

What any [teacher] found in a given classroom was not a cohesive, task-oriented group but several small, very strong, often opposing subgroups that somehow the teacher had to rally around the common goal of learning."[29]

When teachers are in the **preactive teaching** stages of their work—preparing to teach or reflecting on previous teaching—they can afford to be consistently deliberate and rational. Planning for lessons, grading papers, reflecting on the deviant behavior of a student—such activities are usually done alone and lack the immediacy and sense of urgency that characterize interactive teaching. While actually working with students, teachers must be able to think on their feet and respond appropriately to complex, ever-changing situations. They must be flexible and ready to deal with the unexpected. During a discussion, for example, the teacher must operate on at least two levels. On one level, he or she must respond appropriately to students' comments, monitor other students for signs of confusion or comprehension, formulate the next comment or question, and be alert for signs of misbehavior. On another level, the teacher must ensure that participation is evenly distributed among students, evaluate the content and quality of students' contributions, keep the discussion focused and moving ahead, and emphasize major content areas.

Interactive teaching also has a dramatic, spontaneous quality to it. The teacher is on stage and must perform so that all students, including those who are resistant and marginally motivated, will want to learn.

During interactive teaching, the awareness that one is solely responsible for the forward movement of the group never lets up. Teachers are the only professionals who practice their craft almost exclusively under the direct, continuous gaze of up to 30 or 40 clients. Jackson sums up the experience: "The *immediacy* of classroom events is something that anyone who has ever been in charge of a roomful of students can never forget."[30]

 **FIVE-MINUTE FOCUS**   Describe an activity that has required you to think on your feet and make spontaneous decisions about what to do. What is the best way for you to prepare for that activity? Date your journal entry and write for five minutes.

Reality 6: The Uniqueness of the Teaching Experience

Teaching involves a unique mode of being between teacher and student—a mode of being that can be experienced but not fully defined or described. On your journey to become a teacher, you will gradually develop your capacity to listen to students and to convey an authentic sense of concern for their learning. Unfortunately, we can offer no precise, easy-to-follow formula for demonstrating this to students. You will have to take into account your personality and special gifts to discover your own best way for showing this concern.

One reason it is difficult to describe teaching is because an important domain of teaching, teachers' thought processes, cannot be observed directly. Figure 2.2 shows how this domain interacts with and is influenced by the observable domain of teachers' actions and their effects. The model also illustrates a further complexity of teaching—namely, that the relationships between teacher behavior, student behavior, and student achievement are reciprocal. What teachers do is influenced not only by their

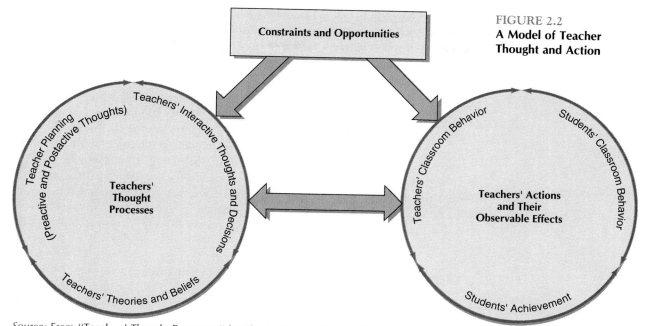

FIGURE 2.2
A Model of Teacher Thought and Action

Source: From "Teachers' Thought Processes," by Christopher M. Clark and Penelope L. Peterson. Reprinted by permission of Macmillan Publishing Company from *Handbook of Research on Teaching,* Third Edn. Edited by Merlin C. Wittrock. Copyright © 1986 by the American Educational Research Association.

thought processes before, during, and after teaching but also by student behavior and student achievement. This complexity contributes to the uniqueness of the teaching experience.

As you continue your study of teaching, you will steadily increase your appreciation of the seen and unseen factors that influence every moment of classroom life. You will come to an intuitive understanding of how to realize the possibilities for student learning and growth inherent in any situation. And, lastly, you will know how to determine and bring into being the potentialities of most of your students.

HOW EDUCATIONAL RESEARCH HELPS TEACHERS TEACH

Since the 1970s, educational researchers have developed increasingly sophisticated methods for observing and analyzing the behavior of teachers and their students. This line of research, often referred to as **teacher effectiveness research,** has shown us that, while we may not fully understand the artistic dimensions of teaching, there are particular teacher behaviors that tend to result in greater student learning. Much of what goes on in classrooms can have significant, measurable effects on student attitudes and achievement. For example, researchers have identified the following as strongly associated with how much students actually learn:

- Teacher praise and reinforcement
- Students' time-on-task
- Teachers' thought processes
- Teachers' expectations that students will (or will not) learn
- The amount of time students spend practicing what they have learned

- The amount of time teachers spend actively (or directly) teaching students
- How teachers organize and manage their classrooms
- How teachers respond to low and high achievers
- The instructional strategies teachers use

Although research can provide teachers with useful tools for analyzing their teaching, it should not be viewed as a recipe or a set of easy-to-follow steps for solving particular problems. Instead, it is most accurate to think of educational research as providing general rules of thumb for teachers to follow. After all, part of being a professional is the ability to decide *how* and *when* to use research to guide one's actions. Teaching is a very complex activity, and research findings should not be applied without considering the setting within which they are to be implemented. It is important to remember that the results of a single research study conducted in, say, a culturally homogeneous third-grade classroom in an inner-city school in the Midwest may not be applicable to a culturally diverse group of fourth-graders in a rural area of the Southwest.

Research on Students and Teachers   We believe that teachers for the 1990s need to be aware of theories and research that can be applied to teaching students from different backgrounds. Increasingly, teachers will find in their classrooms students whose race, first language, religion, values, and social class differ from their own. Moreover, these teachers will be expected to carry out programs designed to provide equal educational opportunities to the more than 4 million people aged 3–21 who are handicapped.

In a chapter in the 1990 *Handbook of Research on Teacher Education*, Carl Grant and Walter Secada point out another reason why teachers must be prepared for diversity: "The current demographic makeup of our student and teaching populations, as well as of the projections for the future, shows a striking discontinuity between teacher and student diversity."[31] Currently, the school population in the United States is about 29 percent nonwhite, while only 12 to 14 percent of teachers are nonwhite. Furthermore, the teaching population is becoming older (the median age increased from 33 in 1976 to 39 in 1983), and these teachers will be replaced by an increasingly female and white cohort. Thus, a teaching force that is becoming more homogeneous is being called upon to prepare for a student population that is becoming increasingly diverse.

Sources of Research Reports   Utilizing methods that range from carefully designed experiments with intricate statistical analyses of data—often termed *quantitative* research—to studies that make use of methods borrowed from the field of anthropology—often termed *qualitative* research—educational researchers are continuing their quest to understand teaching more fully. Their findings are reported in scores of educational research journals (see "Resources in Educational Research: Publications" in the Teacher's Resource Guide). In addition, there are several excellent reviews of research with which you should become familiar during your professional preparation. The most impressive of these is the third edition of the *Handbook of Research on Teaching* (Macmillan, 1986), a project sponsored by the American Educational Research Association. Its more than one thousand pages are devoted to synthesizing research in the following five areas: (1) theories and methods of research on teaching, (2) research on teaching and teachers, (3) the social and intellectual context of teaching, (4) adapting teaching to differences among learners, and (5) research on teaching at

FACT FINDING

How Do Teachers Use Instructional Time?

Research suggests that the attitudes of elementary school teachers toward a subject influence the amount of time they spend teaching that subject.

Teachers' Time Allocations (in Minutes) to Different Subject Matter Areas

Teacher	Reading	Mathematics	Language Arts	Science	Social Studies
A	67.4	43.7	53.7	2.0	2.4
B	50.6	29.1	48.1	6.7	13.3
C	80.3	32.0	25.3	43.2	43.2
D	95.5	49.9	41.1	10.6	6.0
E	32.0	30.6	46.5	25.7	30.5
F	26.5	34.6	72.0	3.7	26.5

The data clearly suggest that teachers need to maintain an awareness of how they use time in their classrooms and should not allow their attitudes toward content to determine whether they instruct students in that content.

Source: William H. Schmidt and Margaret Buchmann, "Six Teachers' Beliefs and Attitudes and Their Curricular Time Allocations," *The Elementary School Journal* (November 1983): 162–172.

various grade levels and in various subject areas. Another fine review of research on teaching is the very readable fourth edition of *Looking in Classrooms* (Harper and Row, 1987) by noted educational researchers Thomas L. Good and Jere E. Brophy. Their book contains excellent chapters on teacher expectations, preventing management problems in the classroom, coping with management problems effectively, and motivating students to learn. A third extensive review of research on teaching is Richard Kindsvatter, William Wilen, and Margaret Ishler's *Dynamics of Effective Teaching* (Longman, 1988). Their book summarizes several areas of teacher effectiveness research, including teacher decision making, instructional techniques, classroom discipline, and evaluation of pupil performance.

Government Sources for Research Application   The federal government supports several efforts designed to help teachers improve their practice through the application of research findings. In 1966, three new agencies were created to support and disseminate research: **Educational Resources Information Center (ERIC), Research and Development Centers,** and **Regional Educational Laboratories.**

ERIC is a national information system made up of 16 **ERIC Clearinghouses** and four "adjunct" Clearinghouses—all coordinated by the central ERIC agency in Washington, D.C. (see "Educational Resources Information Clearinghouses (ERIC)" in the Teacher's Resource Guide). The ERIC system, available in most college and university libraries, contains descriptions of exemplary programs, the results of research and development efforts, and related information that can be used by teachers, administrators, researchers, and the public to improve education. Each Clearinghouse

Keepers of the Dream

Jessamon Dawe
Retired After 41 Years of Teaching
Gonzales, Texas

Jessamon Dawe, Ph.D., was 82 when she wrote the following paper. In addition to 21 years as a college professor, she was a school teacher for 20 years.

LIFE OF TEACHING

In my forty-one years as a teacher (beginning in 1928 and ending in 1969), I touched the lives of several thousand students. But did I make a difference? Frankly, not much, I suppose. In times of frustration, it seemed to me that good students would learn in spite of me and that I really could not help the poor ones a great deal. That first year as a duenna of a one-teacher school in the middle of a south Texas prairie was not actually good for my 22-year-old health. The residences nearest to the school were at least a mile away; so there I was on my own with nobody to help me. . . .

My next venture was in a small town 23 miles from San Antonio the year the stock market crashed—1929. I taught second grade for half a year before they decided I was not much good at it and put me in the high school. . . .

A fine boy at that high school (a good athlete, average student) gave me some discipline problems that caused me to retain him after class. At the end of an hour we would close up our books and he would walk home with me as happily as if I had arranged a special occasion for him—not a punishment. After the second such instance, I recognized his misconduct as a plea for attention. . . . Did I help him? Personal success is hard to measure. He won some sort of Golden Gloves title in the military during World War II and ended up owning an acreage back home for raising livestock. . . .

"Did I Make a Difference?"

In 1948 when the military services were coming back from World War II, I was blissfully settled as an instructor in the College of Business Administration at The University of Texas at Austin. A wide variety of challenging students rolled in: colonels, majors, captains, G.I.'s, and the usual run of the younger generation, many with the capabilities to become corporation presidents, judges, and what have you. . . .

The war brought back some paraplegics in wheel chairs, but this boy at the front below the rostrum from me was too young. Almost child size, he had no legs below the knees and no arms below the elbows. He was industriously taking notes with a pencil stuck in a groove where his right elbow should be. After several trips he made to my office (where I tried to reflect a "what a regular guy you are" attitude, being careful where I looked), I learned that he typed his assignment with that pencil in his elbow groove. As his graduation approached, I said, "What will you do next, John?"

"I'm going to law school. A guy in the shape I'm in has to make it from the neck up." Well! The die was cast. "Whatever happened to you?" "I was born this way. A thalidomide baby. . . ." As he picked up his burdens and left, all I could do for him was to cry big tears. . . .

As I reflect on the values of my teaching career, my concentration centers on those students with whom I most needed to make a difference. I won some and lost some. . . . I did manage to impart to the majority—competent, good citizens—the psychology and techniques of communication with which to work magic in their business and personal lives. . . .

Source: Excerpted from Jessamon Dawe, "Life of Teaching," *The Educational Forum,* Winter 1990, pp. 147–149. Used by permission of the author and publisher.

specializes in one area of education and searches out relevant documents or journal articles, which are screened according to ERIC selection criteria, abstracted, and indexed.

Within the **Office of Educational Research and Improvement (OERI)** in Washington, D.C., the Office of Research (formerly the National Institute of Education) maintains 14 research centers at universities around the country (see the "Office of Educational Research and Improvement (OERI) Centers" in the Teacher's Resource Guide). The centers are devoted to high-quality, fundamental research at every level of education, with most of the research done by scholars at the host university. Among the areas these centers focus on are the processes of teaching and learning, school organization and improvement, the content of education, and factors that contribute to (or detract from) excellence in education.

OERI also houses Programs for the Improvement of Practice (PIP), which support exemplary projects at the state and local levels. PIP also maintains nine regional educational laboratories (see the "Regional Education Laboratories" in the Teacher's Resource Guide) that emphasize the application of research findings. Each laboratory serves a geographic region and is a nonprofit corporation not affiliated with a university. Laboratory staff work directly with school systems, state educational agencies, and other organizations to improve education.

As you progress through the professional component of your teacher education program, you will become increasingly aware of how educational research can contribute to your understanding of teaching. And, equally important, you will learn how it can provide you with guidelines for increasing your effectiveness in the classroom.

SUMMARY

We began this chapter with the observation that we have all spent hundreds of hours being taught, and we therefore tend to believe that the skills of teaching may be easily described and readily acquired. We suggested, however, that this is not the case.

Teaching is more than the sum total of observable teacher behaviors. Teaching also involves the teacher's inner dialogue about how to respond appropriately to the complex and constantly changing conditions of the classroom. Diligently pursued, such reflections lead the teacher toward greater understanding of the factors that promote and hinder learning.

We also looked at how several teachers view their work. The comments of each demonstrated how difficult it is to put into words just what teachers do in the classroom that makes them effective. We concluded that students' descriptions of their teachers may give us the most complete picture of what teaching is.

To explore further what teaching is really like, we then considered five modes of teaching—teaching as a way of being, a creative endeavor, a live performance, a wielding of power, and an opportunity to serve.

We then examined the following six realities of teaching, each of which illustrates a different aspect of the challenging nature of teaching: (1) The outcomes of teaching, even in the best of circumstances, are neither predictable nor consistent; (2) It is difficult to measure what students learn as a result of being taught; (3) The teacher's ability to influence student behavior is actually quite limited; (4) With the role of teacher also comes the power to influence others by example; (5) Interactive teaching is characterized by events that are rapid-changing, multidimensional, and irregular;

and (6) Teaching involves a unique mode of being between teacher and student—a mode of being that can be experienced but not fully defined or described.

Finally, we took a brief look at some of the dimensions of teaching that are being studied by educational researchers. While teachers can use research findings to increase their understanding of teaching, we cautioned that research should not be viewed as providing specific solutions to particular problems. We concluded the chapter with a brief review of three major federal programs designed to put research into practice.

KEY TERMS AND CONCEPTS

modes of teaching, 37
realities of teaching, 40
interactive teaching, 47
preactive teaching, 48
teachers' thought processes, 48
teacher effectiveness research, 49
Educational Resources Information
    Center (ERIC), 51

Research and Development Centers,
    51
ERIC Clearinghouses, 51
Regional Educational Laboratories, 51
Office of Educational Research and
    Improvement (OERI), 53

DISCUSSION QUESTIONS

1. Which of the five modes of teaching discussed in this chapter is most neglected by experienced teachers? Defend your choice. *Creative endeavor*
2. Think about a time when a teacher truly motivated you to learn. What are some of the things that teacher did to motivate you? Do you believe other students in the class had the same reaction to this teacher? Why or why not? Does the analysis of your experience suggest any basic principles about how people learn? How might you incorporate these principles into your own teaching?
3. Meet with three to four of your classmates and share recollections of the "good" and "bad" teachers each of you has had, from elementary school through college. Are there any characteristics that each set of teachers seems to share? What are your group's conclusions about "good" and "bad" teachers?
4. This chapter discussed several of the characteristics of teaching that make it a challenging profession. Can you think of other challenging aspects of teaching? How will you cope with these challenges when you become a teacher? What steps could teachers, individually and in groups, take in order to meet these challenges?
5. Review carefully the quote from Dewey on page 44. What does Dewey mean by children's inner and outer attention? How do they differ? Why is the inner attention a "fundamental condition" of mental growth? How does a teacher differentiate between outer and inner attention? To what extent is Dewey correct in suggesting that the teacher "sells" and the student must "buy"? Are there any limitations to this comparison?

APPLICATION ACTIVITIES

1. In small groups, analyze the following episode from a sophomore English class at a high school in a low-income urban neighborhood. What unseen factors might have caused the teacher's students to act as they did? Which of the five realities discussed in this chapter are evident in this description? Be prepared to share your group's conclusions with the rest of the class.

Miss Martinez's Third-Period Class

At 9:42 A.M., a loud bell signals the start of Miss Martinez's third-period class; however, only six students are present. During the next few minutes, though, eight more students arrive one by one. As these stragglers enter the room, they talk loudly, and without restraint, to their friends. . . .

"Gimmie that pen," one boy snaps as he snatches a Bic pen from a girl's desk. As the girl rises out of her desk to pursue her stolen property, the boy tosses it back. Satisfied, the girl lets the matter drop.

Three students leave their desks to get their journal folders from a cardboard box on Miss Martinez's desk. Miss Martinez helps them locate their journals and then directs them to retake their seats. She also moves about the room passing out folders to other students, some of whom sit at their desks as though waiting to be served.

During these opening minutes of class, three boys wander aimlessly about the room. One, a tall, thin boy, presses his nose against the window, surveying the sidewalk two stories below. Just then a fat boy skips past and jabs him playfully in the ribs, rudely interrupting his dreamy state. . . .

"Dave. Julio. Sit down right now!" Miss Martinez matter-of-factly corrects her students who, with admirable obedience, take their seats.

The third boy lopes around the entire circumference of the room. As he moves down the wall opposite the windows, he flicks the chains and padlocks that secure the room's two built-in cabinets. He catches Miss Martinez's disapproving glance and then heads back to his seat.

"Good morning, people," Miss Martinez officially begins at 9:45. She points to the chalkboard and explains the two topics for the day's journal entry (each class period is begun with a five-minute journal entry): "What was the most frightening thing that ever happened to you?" and "What did you do yesterday after school?"

As Miss Martinez repeats the assignment and gives necessary directions, all but four or five students continue to talk in small groups about matters clearly unrelated to the journal writing assignment.

Several social interaction groups are quite evident at this time. In the back of the room, Bao and Ry chat and exchange an occasional comment with Joan who sits in front of them. . . .

Maria, Lara, and Julio form another talkative trio. Maria turns around in her seat and rests her elbow on Lara's desk. At this moment, all three appear oblivious to their teacher and unmindful of the task they have been assigned.

For those students in the front row, however, the journal entry is the main concern. Leon, Raelene, and Karen write and occasionally look up at the board to recheck the day's topics. They do not talk to any of their classmates. Meghan and Sue are also at work, though they exchange a comment every now and then.

Suddenly, Matthew prods Meghan in the back and makes an insult which [the observer] can't hear. Meghan turns around, her tightly pursed lips indicating that she is ready for battle. . . .

Miss Martinez talks softly with Leon and Raelene at the front of the room. A moment later, she begins to move down the window side of the room, toward those students who still have not yet begun to write. The combined conversations of the three main social cliques are now quite loud. Their talk includes a great deal of clownlike nonsense.

At 9:48, the noise level has increased even more. "Let's please have it silent while we work on our journals," Miss Martinez announces. Her tone is one of mild irritation. The talking continues, though perhaps not as loudly. Carlo, Jamie, and Dave continue to be the loudest.

Miss Martinez continues, at 9:49, to move about the room to see how individual students are progressing with their work. Her plan seems to include interaction with each small group. Those students in the front row work silently while the rest of the class continues to talk in their subgroups, stopping occasionally for a perfunctory spurt of writing or a nonchalant glance at Miss Martinez. . . . Obviously, she gets along well with all of them. With uncanny precision, the boys seem to calculate their foolish behavior both to escape work and to remain in Miss Martinez's good graces. Their teacher's smiles indicate that they are very successful indeed.[32]

2. You are not having major discipline problems, but your students seem to have lost all enthusiasm for your class. Work with others to develop a questionnaire you could use to get feedback from your students as a first step toward remedying the situation. Design your questions to help you learn what students really think.

3. Invite a group of first-year teachers to your class, possibly graduates from your institution, and ask them about their first impressions of becoming a teacher. What aspects of teaching were difficult for them? Which easy? What surprises did they find? How would they have prepared themselves differently? Prepare a list of questions and present them to your guests before their visit. Also, you may need to schedule the visit during the evening or on a weekend because of their teaching schedules.

4. Review the comments made by the four teachers on pages 35–36. Do you agree with the language they use to describe those moments when they knew they were teaching effectively? Are there more concrete measures that teachers might use to gauge their effectiveness? Describe them.

5. This chapter focuses on the complex, spontaneous qualities of teaching. What aspects of teaching are predictable? What aspects are *within* the teacher's ability to control?

6. Identify an area of teaching about which you are concerned (e.g., discipline, salaries, curriculum, instructional strategies, school choice, teacher unions, etc.) and use the ERIC system to obtain current information on that topic. Ask a reference librarian for assistance in using ERIC. Report your findings to the class in the form of a brief presentation.

FIELD EXPERIENCES

1. Ask your instructor to arrange a group interview session between students in your class and several school teachers. Ask the teachers to comment on the extent to which they agree or disagree with each of the five realities of teaching discussed in this chapter.

2. Arrange to observe a teacher's class. During your observation, note evidence of the five modes of teaching discussed in this chapter. Following your observation, arrange to check your perceptions with the teacher during an informal, post-observation interview.

3. Have your instructor arrange group interviews between students in your class and students at the local elementary, middle, junior, and senior high schools. At each interview session, ask the students what characterizes good and bad teachers. Also, ask the students what advice they would give a university student in the process of becoming a teacher. Following the interviews, compare the characterizations and advice given by students at the different levels.

4. Interview members of your college's faculty to learn from them what they regard as the most important realities of teaching that teachers must address. Share their thoughts with the class.

5. Make arrangements to sit in on several of the meetings student teachers have with their supervisors. These are often held weekly as student teaching seminars. Take note of the topics discussed and the areas of concern and of pleasure expressed by the student teachers. Share these with your class, being careful to maintain the anonymity of the students you observed.

SUGGESTED READINGS

Arends, Richard I. *Learning to Teach.* New York: Random House, 1988. *A comprehensive, research-based introduction to teaching organized around the executive, interactive, and organizational functions of teaching.*

Gehrke, Nathalie J. *On Being a Teacher.* West Lafayette, Ind.: Kappa Delta Pi, 1987. *The author mixes step-by-step guidance with thoughtful reflection to help students anticipate their upcoming teaching experiences and challenges. Unique features of the book are the projections into the second year of teaching, when one's sense of humor returns (!), and the reasons teachers leave the profession.*

Greenwood, Gordon E. and Forrest W. Parkay. *Case Studies for Teacher Decision Making.* New York: Random House, 1989. *Presents 30 case studies based on actual problem situations encountered by beginning and experienced teachers.*

Hayden, Torey. *Somebody Else's Kids.* New York: Avon Books, 1981. *A teacher's account of her problems and pleasures teaching six children in a resource room. Enjoyable and moving reading.*

Marquis, David. *I Am a Teacher.* New York: Simon & Schuster, 1991. *This collection of dramatic photographs and quotations is a vivid portrait of America's teachers. Marquis designed the book to be a "fitting tribute to teachers, one that would let America's teachers speak for themselves."*

Parkay, Forrest W. *White Teacher, Black School: The Professional Growth of a Ghetto Teacher.* New York: Praeger 1983. *Parkay shares his personal struggle and growth in this honest and involving tale of teaching in a challenging setting.*

Rubin, Louis J. *Artistry in Teaching.* New York: Random House, 1985. *An interesting discussion of teaching as art and teaching as theater.*

TEACHERS . . .

**What did you think teaching would be like?
How did you feel on your first teaching assignment?**

I was scared. I asked myself, "Do I have what it would take to teach? Can I earn the respect/control of my students? I have the knowledge; but is it enough?" Yes, there were serious doubts about my preparation and ability to perform this job. I signed a contract and told myself that I can and will do the best job possible. My first experience was the beginning of 19 wonderful years in teaching. You gain confidence and experience every year. Now, I cannot see myself doing anything else other than my chosen profession. And just like any job, you have to start somewhere—so dive in, believe in yourself, and ENJOY.

—Suzanne Neal
William Woods College, Fulton, Missouri

I thought teaching would be a quiet, worthy career. The job was actually much more exciting than I supposed. I adored teaching from the first and still do. I think it's very important not to take student reactions personally. I try to "lighten up"—by discussion, by going off somewhere and relaxing, by reading something detached. Generally, you have to work on the process of being a calm person and mature emotionally in a volatile profession like teaching.

—Paula Tyler
Austin Independent School District, Austin, Texas

Before I became a teacher, I thought that all students would be eager to learn. They would come to school and try to do their best at everything. I also thought that I would spend at least 95 percent of my time actually teaching children. The most surprising thing I have found is that the job encompasses much more than teaching students. Sometimes the "other" responsibilities are overwhelming, making me less effective as a teacher.

My first teaching assignment was in a very low socioeconomic area of Denver in the 1960s. Most of my students were black or Hispanic and I felt apprehensive about the way I would relate to them as a white, middle-class teacher. I was not confident about my ability or knowledge of the subject matter. Now, however, I am a much more confident person in the classroom. I don't give a second thought

ON TEACHING

to the racial background of my students. I am very familiar with the curriculum and I like seeing students grow in their knowledge and understanding of my subject area.

—Rose Ann Blaschke
Vivian Elementary School, Lakewood, Colorado

I thought that all kids would like school and would be willing to sit quietly and cooperate with the teacher. My eyes were opened! I realized that a big part of teaching was motivating students so that they wanted to learn. I also learned that the teacher continues learning just as the students do.

—Amy Orcutt
Green Gables Elementary School, Jefferson County, Colorado

Before I became a teacher, I thought that I would teach the students, they would take a test on what I taught, and I would assess my teaching on that. I am surprised constantly by how little that type of learning matters. It is a part of teaching, but relating to the students, being able to encourage growth within them, being able to laugh and cry with them matters more with each year as my confidence as a teacher develops. Encouragement, respect, trust—these are found in the interpersonal relationships between teachers and students. For me these things have come to matter more and more. I am genuinely interested in my subject matter (English), but I have found what matters most to the students and to me is that I am sharing my "treasures" with young people who are in need of genuine interests themselves.

—Jeanne Brostrom
Baldwin Park High School, Baldwin Park, California

The most surprising thing I discovered in teaching is the work load. Planning, preparing materials, teaching, grading, and conferring with parents are only a small portion of the teacher's day. Faculty meetings, college courses, conferences, special events, holidays, bus duty, lunch duty, playground duty, etc., make up the unseen and sometimes thankless portion of a teacher's busy day.

On my first teaching assignment, I was elated. I will never forget my first class and the immense sense of responsibility I felt. I was full of optimism and ideas. I felt there was not a child there I could not "reach." I still feel this way, though my definition of "reach" has changed. I feel I can make a positive difference in each student's life.

—Jennifer Cronk
Rocky Mountain Hebrew Academy, Denver, Colorado

CHAPTER 3

Your Education as a Teacher

We maintain that teachers should have a liberal education equivalent to that of the best-educated members of their community. . . . that [they] should know and understand the intellectual and practical content from which school curricula are drawn . . . that [they] should have both the skills to teach and the knowledge of the research and experiential bases for those skills.

American Association of Colleges for Teacher Education
A Call for Change in Teacher Education

Sara taught in a heterogeneously grouped kindergarten in a rural community. The problem she discussed concerned five children with special needs: three were emotionally handicapped, two developmentally delayed. Each child was experiencing academic problems as well as disrupting the class. According to Sara, the children (all boys) "took time away from the whole class. . . . They really drained me, disrupted my class."

Sara described factors contributing to the academic and behavioral problems of the children. One had been sexually abused. The father of one child had died the previous year. Another child was living with his grandparents during his parents' divorce proceedings and was consequently experiencing considerable emotional distress. Two children, who exhibited signs of developmental delay, were from economically disadvantaged homes. Sara believed that the children's impoverished environments contributed to their delay.

In describing these children, Sara was sensitive to the psychological, social, and developmental factors contributing to their problems in school. She was concerned with each individual's problems as well as the effect of the problems on the class. Despite the complexity and the severity of the problems that she faced in attempting to teach these children, Sara consistently sought a variety of solutions to reach them.

In seeking solutions, Sara used methods learned during her college education, sought the advice of college classmates, and discussed the problems with school colleagues, administrators, the guidance counselor, and the children's parents. She tried several approaches: time out in the classroom (in a chair), time out in another classroom, referrals to the principal, conferences with the child, notes to parents, calls to parents, punishment, and rewards for good behavior.

According to Sara, "The most effective strategy was time out from the activities in the classroom," but she was not satisfied with this solution.

> I was satisfied with the short-term effect of time out but not with the long-term. I kept thinking that I needed to dig deeper, that there was a way to reach these children, something special for each child. . . . I had so many other concerns, being a beginning teacher. If this were to happen again [having five children with serious problems] I would ask that they be split up, ask for some of them to be put in another class.

Despite these difficulties, Sara "took a deep breath and tried not to be insecure." Sara said that she hoped, in the future, for "more confidence to do what I know is best for the children." Although Sara faced a difficult situation, she maintained a reflective attitude. . . .

At the end of the year, Sara believed that she was doing very well for a beginning teacher. However, she expressed reservations concerning the effectiveness of the solutions she developed. Sara persevered in her attempts to resolve the situation. She saw herself as capable of meeting the challenges in her situation and free to implement a variety of solutions. She was supported, both professionally and emotionally, by the faculty and administrative staff. Sara's belief in her capabilities as a teacher as well as the support she received from those around her helped Sara maintain a reflective attitude during a stressful year.[1]

FOCUS QUESTIONS

1. What do reform proposals say teachers should know and be able to do?
2. Why should teachers be "transformative intellectuals"?
3. What is a reflective teaching log and why should you bother to keep one?
4. How can induction and internship programs help you during your first year of teaching?

What accounted for Sara's success in handling the problem she encountered during her first year? No doubt, two factors contributed to her success: (1) she drew from what she had learned in her teacher education program, a program that emphasized the development of reflective teachers and (2) she received support and encouragement during the critical first year of teaching. As the case of Sara illustrates, the professional development of teachers begins in teacher education programs and *continues* in a supportive environment during the first years of teaching. During the last decade, widespread efforts have been made to ensure that all beginning teachers are as successful as Sara.

CALLS FOR CHANGE IN TEACHER EDUCATION

During the 1980s and into the 1990s, the nation experienced an unprecedented push for reform in education. Numerous commissions were established and more than fifty major reports were made outlining what should be done to improve America's schools. Most of these reports called for changes in the education of teachers. In fact, the preparation program you are now involved in has been influenced, most likely, by this **educational reform movement.** Further evidence of the movement is revealed in the fact that 75 percent of America's teachers in 1989 reported that educational reforms such as merit pay plans, mentor teacher programs, and career ladders had been enacted in their states (an increase of 12 percent over 1985), and 59 percent reported that reform had occurred at their schools (see Figure 3.1).

Increasingly, teachers are being prepared according to the suggestions made in these reports. As you read about three of these major efforts to transform teacher education and then explore the kinds of knowledge we regard as essential for teachers, think about how the advice given and the issues raised fit your needs and expectations as you prepare to teach.

FIGURE 3.1
Educational Reform: How Widespread Is It?

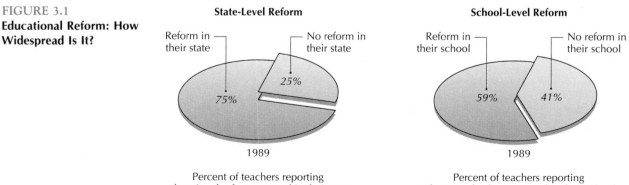

Source: Based on data from *The Metropolitan Life Survey of the American Teacher, 1989* (New York: Louis Harris and Associates, 1990), p. 52.

The Commission for Excellence

In its report, *A Call for Change in Teacher Education,* the **National Commission for Excellence in Teacher Education** urged the adoption of new, higher, and fairly specific standards for the preparation of teachers. The report recommended that the new generation of teachers needs to be:

- Competent in their subjects
- Skilled in teaching
- Informed about children and their development
- Knowledgeable about cognitive psychology
- Schooled in technology
- Informed about the latest, most relevant research
- Able to work with peers and others in diverse environments
- Confident of their roles and contributions.[2]

The Commission also specified three areas for teacher education: liberal education, subject specialization, and the study and application of pedagogy.

First, teachers should have a liberal education equal to "that of the best-educated members of their community." To gain this, according to the report, future teachers need a cohesive, liberal education, which includes the general education or academic foundations requirements established for all graduates of their institution, as well as courses in sociology, psychology, anthropology, history, language, literature, and the arts. A strong background in general or liberal education that prepares teachers to understand the context of their world empowers teachers to be comfortable with their own education and that of others. As Alfred North Whitehead said, "Education is the process of catching up with one's generation."[3] If teachers fall behind in their knowledge of subject matter, they fall behind their generation—a strange, contra-dictory place for teachers to be. Coupled with these requirements is the need for a regard for learning and growth. "All teachers . . . must profoundly value learning, ideas, and artistic expression," the report stressed.[4]

The commission's second recommendation, for a thorough knowledge in subject specializations, varied according to school level. Secondary teachers should have a subject specialization in the field they plan to teach as well as two related areas. For elementary teachers, the commission reported a need for "an extended liberal arts program in the content areas of the elementary school, as well as specialization in child development with particular emphases on language development and thinking."[5]

For the third recommendation, the study and application of pedagogy, the authors of the report called for a strong professional education program and outlined five objectives for such a program. We share them here so that you can consider them as a checklist for your own education as a teacher. According to the Commission, teachers need the following understandings:

1. How to instruct well, selecting appropriate material for students' learning levels, using effective strategies to reteach difficult concepts, and leading discussions and seminars
2. How to observe and diagnose students' academic needs and how to indivi-dualize instruction accordingly
3. How to apply findings from research on teacher and school effectiveness
4. How to integrate technology and how to promote higher-order thinking
5. How to appropriately relate concepts learned in advanced academic courses to those that are taught in elementary, middle, and high schools[6]

The report also included recommendations for field experiences and student teaching as part of a professional education program and recognized the value to students of studying and analyzing their own and others' videotaped and live teaching.

The Holmes Group

Another group that called for the reform of teacher education was the **Holmes Group,** named after Henry W. Holmes, dean of the Harvard Graduate School of Education during the 1920s. The Holmes Group was initially made up of 96 major universities. In *Tomorrow's Teachers,* a 1986 report written by 13 deans of education and one college president, the Holmes Group recommended that all teachers have a bachelor's degree in an academic field and a master's degree in education. While the Holmes Group viewed additional academic preparation as a means of enhancing the professional status of teachers, critics maintained that students' education would be delayed and be more expensive, with no assurance that students who spent five years obtaining a teaching certificate would be paid more.

The members of the Holmes Group endorsed a five-part platform for improving teaching in America:

- To make the education of teachers more intellectually sound; to make prospective teachers thoughtful students of teaching and its improvement.
- To recognize differences in teachers' knowledge, skills, and commitment, and in their education, certification, work, and career opportunities by distinguishing among novices, competent professional teachers, and high-level professional leaders. The Holmes Group labels these distinctive practitioners Instructors, Professional Teachers, and Career Professionals.
- To create standards of entry into the profession—examinations and educational requirements—that are professionally relevant and intellectually defensible.
- To connect institutions of higher and professional education with schools in order to make better use of expert teachers in the professional education and induction of other teachers and in research on teaching, and to build demonstration sites where new career opportunities, working conditions, and administrative arrangements can be developed and refined.
- To make schools better places for teachers to work and for students to learn by altering the professional roles and responsibilities of teachers.[7]

Like the National Commission for Excellence in Teacher Education, the Holmes Group recommended that teachers should have a broad, liberal education. Similarly, the five components of professional education advocated by the Holmes Group echoed many of those recommended by the Commission:

- The study of teaching and schooling as an academic field
- Knowledge of the pedagogy of subject matter
- Skills and understanding implicit in classroom teaching
- Values, dispositions, and a sense of ethical responsibility
- Clinical experiences.

The Carnegie Forum

In 1985, the prestigious Carnegie Foundation established the **Carnegie Forum on Education and the Economy** to examine the relationship between economic growth

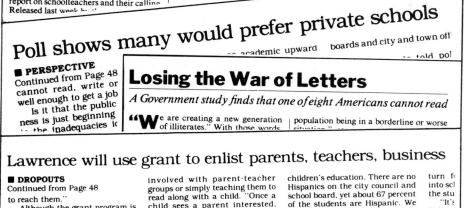

In the 1980s, the image of teachers was badly battered by ominous-sounding commission reports, a dramatically negative press, and the resultant public outcry for better schools.

and education. To prepare its first report, *A Nation Prepared: Teachers for the 21st Century*, the Forum established the **Task Force on Teaching as a Profession.** The Task Force report, released in May 1986, outlined six sweeping recommendations for transforming American education:

- Increased professional autonomy for teachers, including opportunity for collegial decision making involving "lead teachers"
- The creation of a National Board for Professional Teaching Standards
- The elimination of the undergraduate degree in education and the establishment of a Master in Teaching degree
- A concerted effort to increase the number of minorities who become teachers
- Incentives based on teacher performance and productivity
- Increased salaries to attract and retain the best teachers—salaries to be determined according to level of responsibility, competence as determined by level of Board certification, experience, and productivity as measured by student performance.

HOW EDUCATIONAL REFORMS AFFECT TEACHING

Currently, teachers' views of reform are somewhat mixed, though they have improved recently. The 1989 Metropolitan Life Survey of 1175 teachers who reported that their state had implemented reforms such as merit pay, career ladders, and mentor teacher programs, for example, revealed that 53 percent believed the effect of reform had been positive *on students* (an increase of 11 percent from 1985), while 40 percent perceived not much effect, and 6 percent a negative effect. Their view of the impact of reform *on teachers* was less positive, however: 43 percent believed it was positive (an increase of 7 percent from 1985), while 27 percent saw not much effect, and 29 percent a negative effect (see Figure 3.2).

Many teachers, such as the following elementary teacher, believe teachers have not been sufficiently involved in the reform movement:

> One of the problems is legislative people deciding what the education reforms should be and how they should be handled. I think it entails a lack of trust in the teachers by these authorities, and I think it's passed on to the public by the authorities. . . . Every time they start reforming education, they start reforming the teachers. For example, there's all the talk about competency testing and we're going to get rid of all the bad teachers. Teachers have the feeling that they're talking about all of us. We sometimes are used as public relations by authorities. And then often they take credit for what we do.[8]

Others, like the following high school teacher, are critical of what they see as change for the sake of change:

> In education I think the goals or the objectives change with every passing fad. Administrators say we should go to competency testing, we should be master teachers, we should have ability groupings . . . we should not have ability grouping[s] . . . we should get back to basics, we should have more electives. Education has changed so much, even just from district to district or year to year—they have [such] different goals and different approaches that I think there's no steady course of where you're heading. I think this district has just been incredible as far as their planning on how many buildings, how many high schools, etc. I think what they've been doing is just running around in circles.[9]

FIGURE 3.2

The Overall Impact of Reforms on Teachers and Students: 1985 and 1989

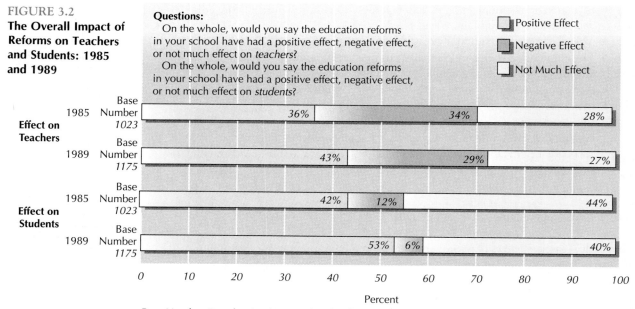

Questions:
On the whole, would you say the education reforms in your school have had a positive effect, negative effect, or not much effect on *teachers*?
On the whole, would you say the education reforms in your school have had a positive effect, negative effect, or not much effect on *students*?

☐ Positive Effect
☐ Negative Effect
☐ Not Much Effect

Effect on Teachers
1985 Base Number 1023: 36% | 34% | 28%
1989 Base Number 1175: 43% | 29% | 27%

Effect on Students
1985 Base Number 1023: 42% | 12% | 44%
1989 Base Number 1175: 53% | 6% | 40%

Percent

Base Number: State has implemented such reforms.

Source: The Metropolitan Life Survey of the American Teacher, 1989 (New York: Louis Harris and Associates, 1990), pp. 54–55.

Though it will be some time before the impact of reform on teacher education can be fully determined, it is clear that recent proposals for reform are united in calling for an intellectually challenging and thorough education for students preparing to teach. Many of the nearly 1,400 colleges and universities that prepare teachers have begun to follow through on their recommendations. While reform proposals provide the setting for change, the real difference will come from the students themselves. Their desire and commitment to become well educated can bring about true change.

THREE KINDS OF ESSENTIAL KNOWLEDGE

In Chapter 1, we identified three kinds of knowledge that students preparing to become teachers must have before they can enter the classroom legitimately and confidently: knowledge of self and students, knowledge of subject, and knowledge of educational theory and research. It is to this essential knowledge that we now turn.

Knowledge of Self and Students

Effective teachers are aware of themselves and sensitive to the needs of their students. While it is evident that teachers should understand their students as fully and deeply as possible, it is less evident that this understanding depends upon their level of self-knowledge.

The Importance of Self-Knowledge If teachers are knowledgeable about their needs (and, most importantly, able to take care of those needs), they are better able to help their students. As Arthur Jersild wrote in 1955, "The teacher's understanding and acceptance of himself is the most important requirement in any effort he makes to help students to know themselves and to gain healthy attitudes of self-acceptance."[10]

Two somewhat surprising emotions that teachers experience when they teach are anxiety and loneliness. Promoting the anxiety are three conditions clouding teachers' efforts: (1) the interminable nature of teaching (i.e., their work is never completed), (2) the intangible and often unpredictable characteristics of teaching results, and (3) the inability to attribute learning results to specific teachers' instruction. Unlike architects, lawyers, and doctors, teachers can never stand back and admire *their* work. If a student does well, that success rightfully belongs to the student. Furthermore, the work teachers do with certain students one year may not take effect until the next, while, on the other hand, the sudden blooming of students this year may be due to the fine work of last year's teachers. Teachers thus need to develop the ability to tolerate ambiguities and to reduce their anxieties about being observably effective.

The second emotion, loneliness, is hardly to be expected in a profession devoted to the service of others; yet both elementary and secondary school teachers commonly experience it, albeit for different reasons. Elementary teachers tend to feel isolated from adult companionship because of their need to remain in their classrooms, supervising their students at all times for safety, legal, and pedagogical reasons. Even to leave the classroom to go to the restroom, they must make arrangements with other teachers to cover their classes while they are away. In addition, elementary teachers are separated from other adults by the ways in which schools structure time and space.

Secondary teachers usually find more free time in common, but they too experience loneliness and isolation because of their subject matter separations. "So strong is subject matter compartmentalization that it is common for the shop teacher and the English teacher to never interact in the course of a school day, or in fact, in the course of a school year," write Ann Lieberman and Lynne Miller.[11] The physical space of high schools, they note, is also designed to separate subject areas, with the math department sectioned off in one corridor, the foreign language in another.

In their book, *Beyond Bias: Perspectives on Classrooms*, Jean Carew and Sara Lawrence Lightfoot describe the sense of isolation that exists for teachers psychologically, as well as physically: "Behind closed doors, they are asked to perform a complex and demanding job alone, without companionship and supportive criticism, often without reinforcement and reward; and their lack of adult contact and interaction gives them a distorted view of their own power and maturity."[12]

What can teachers do about the loneliness? As with anxiety, self-awareness and a willingness to confront the issue seem to be important. In addition, elementary teachers can encourage the administration to schedule common planning periods and relieve them of lunch duties, or they can design team teaching arrangements that go beyond the mere exchanging of students, calling instead for cooperative planning and instructing. Secondary teachers can encourage more interdisciplinary meetings that address common teaching concerns, such as improving writing skills across the curriculum, handling homework better, or dealing with discipline needs. Simply providing a forum for sharing solutions to common problems would reduce the sense of isolation.

FIVE-MINUTE FOCUS   One of our primary responsibilities in life is to learn more about ourselves. What would you like to learn about yourself? What steps could you take to increase your level of self-knowledge in this area? Date your journal entry and write for five minutes.

Characteristics of Students   The case study of Sara presented at the beginning of this chapter illustrates how important it is for teachers to be knowledgeable about student characteristics such as their developmental levels. Without an understanding of these characteristics, teachers' efforts to help students learn and grow are likely to be inappropriate and, in some cases, counterproductive. Chapter 10 examines the intellectual development of students at various stages of growth, considers their cultural differences and special needs and talents, and identifies several areas of special concern to students as individuals and as members of society.

In addition, teachers need to understand their students in the context of their lives outside of the classroom. What are the attributes of the communities in which they live? Are they members of particular subcultures or ethnic groups that influence their values, attitudes, and beliefs? These and other questions about students and their communities provide the focus for Chapter 5.

In the case of Sara, we saw how family backgrounds can contribute to students' academic and behavioral problems. As our society becomes more culturally diverse, more teachers will encounter challenges similar to those Sara faced. And, like Sara, they will need to be skilled at reflective problem solving and willing to try alternative strategies to best meet students' needs. To understand more fully students with cultural backgrounds different from your own, you may wish to take courses in multicultural education, English as a second language (ESL), or a foreign language.

FACT FINDING

Are You an Introvert or an Extravert?

Research shows that extraverts (persons attracted to the outer world of action, people, and things) and introverts (those attracted more to the inner world of ideas and feelings) are about equally represented at all levels of teaching.

Source: Gordon Lawrence, *People Types and Tiger Stripes: A Practical Guide to Learning Styles,* 2nd ed. (Gainesville, Fla.: Center for Application of Psychological Type, Inc., 1982).

Knowledge of Subject

Our review of educational reform stressed how important it is for teachers to have a deep, comprehensive knowledge of subject matter. Competence in subject areas relates to the following three important roles of teachers.

Teachers as Scholars   James Conant's 1963 work, *The Education of American Teachers,* contained recommendations that resemble those found in the reform literature. Significantly, he believed that teachers needed to become knowledgeable in areas outside of their specializations and to become well educated themselves. The following comments should sound familiar: "If teachers are to be considered learned persons in their communities, and if they are to command the respect of the professional men and women they meet, they must be prepared to discuss *difficult topics*" (our emphases).[13]

With the title of teacher comes an assumption of knowledge. Those outside the field of education expect a teacher to be a ready reference for all sorts of information: How do you spell *esophagus?* When should *mother* be capitalized? What is the plot of *King Lear?* Which countries border the Mediterranean? Who is the prime minister of Israel? What is the significance of the Monroe Doctrine? Teachers are expected to be informed and to hold defensible positions on a full range of issues, from local politics to English literature to American history to world geography. Obviously, training in methods of classroom instruction alone will not provide the knowledge, perspective, and intellectual habits that facilitate the development of an educated person, which in turn is what the public expects a teacher to be.

Teachers as Agents of Change   According to an increasingly vocal group of educators, teachers also need to be "transformative intellectuals" and agents of change. Maxine Greene, perhaps the most eloquent of these educators, writes that teaching "is an undertaking oriented to empowering persons to become different, . . . to pursue meanings, to make increasing sense of their actually lived worlds."[14] In other words, teaching, rather than simply showing students the way, must guide students from a position where they can be easily swayed by others to one in which they are agents in their own behalf.

Henry Giroux and Peter McLaren, two educators who express views similar to Greene's, state that teachers should be "transformative intellectuals" who teach their students to be critical thinkers and active, informed citizens.[15] They complain that the idea of democracy has been forgotten in an educational program that seems to be designed more toward preparing efficient and productive workers than responsible, critical citizens. A democratic form of government is not possible if voters are ignorant and unable to think critically. Kenneth Zeichner's advice to his fellow educators was that "educational, moral and political commitments ought to guide our work . . . rather than merely dwelling on which procedures and organizational arrangements most effectively help us realize tacit and often unexamined ends."[16]

It is in this respect that teachers play more the role of philosopher than skilled worker, making sense of their worlds rather than merely following orders and meeting expectations. In turn, teachers should model critical thinking skills and actively teach and exhort their students to do the same.

Teachers as Models of Inspiration   The recent focus on the knowledge of the mechanics of effective teaching overlooks the complex and significant human dimension that exists when students and teachers come together. Although scholars may prescribe behaviors, it is the unique personalities of teachers and their students and how they regard each other that will make the difference in the long run.

For a hopeful alternative to the mechanistic view of teaching, we recommend that you draw on literature and read John Barth's essay "Teacher: The Making of a Good One," a brief memoir that combines a deft analysis of good teaching with a gently enthusiastic tribute to his wife, a high school English teacher. He reminds us of how important the individuality of the teacher is: "One does not speak of taking 'Mrs. Barth's course' in myth and fantasy, or in the short story, or in the nineteenth-century Russian novel, or in the literature of alienation; one speaks of 'taking Barth.' "[17]

When selecting a course, experienced college students know that gaining information about the professor teaching the course is much more useful than reading the course description. Furthermore, sections of the same course vary widely because of the personalities, teaching styles, and academic interests of the individual professors teaching them.

Unquestionably, teachers have unique opportunities to be inspiring models for their students. Their enthusiasm for learning, high regard for the subjects they teach, personal integrity and character, and styles of encountering life and overcoming obstacles are qualities that can deeply influence their students. We recognize this when we consider our own Mrs. Barths. The perspectives, attitudes, and example of such teachers last far longer than any subject matter they teach.

In order to be scholars, agents of change, and models of inspiration, teachers must be well educated themselves. To bring this about, colleges must include in their teacher programs a place for knowledge of subject matter. While much has been gained from the recent teacher education reform work, the emphasis seems to be more focused on the *how* questions rather than the *what* and the *what for* ones. Unfortunately, teaching technology per se, though helpful, is not substantive. Teachers can indeed learn management skills and techniques for promoting on-task behavior, but if they know little and have little ability to evaluate and critique what they are asked to teach, they can be detriments to their students, albeit skilled and efficient detriments! A knowledge of subject matter is essential.

FIVE-MINUTE FOCUS   Should you have a solid background in general studies? Why or why not? Are you comfortable with your background in history, literature, the sciences, and philosophy? Should teachers be scholars, agents of change, and models of inspiration? Why or why not? Date your journal entry and write for five minutes.

SIPRESS

Knowledge of Educational Theory and Research

When Eliot Wigginton became discouraged by his students' disruptiveness and lack of interest, he took a hard look at what was happening in his classroom and remembered that the same thing happened when he was in high school, which led to his having to repeat ninth grade.

> I realized that all those kids in my classroom had the same question that I had, which went something like . . . why are you making us sit here and do this . . . what is this for? And I realized that Richard Brautigan was right and that a lot of what was happening . . . in my school and what had happened to me was about boredom and about restlessness and about a feeling that we have abilities that aren't being tapped . . . a feeling that something is profoundly wrong. You get to the point in high school where you see life passing in front of your eyes, you know. Brautigan, in the last stanza of a poem from a book he wrote called *Rommel Drives On Into Egypt,* perhaps said it best when he says as a conclusion, "My teachers could have ridden with Jesse James for all the hours they stole from me."[18]

A teacher can steal hours from students or enrich them. The vital difference, as we suggested in the previous chapter, may be the teacher's ability to use educational theory and research to understand teaching more fully.

When Educational Theory Is Ignored In a provocative article entitled "How Not to Fix the Schools," several leaders and writers in the field of education critiqued the 1980s wave of educational reform. A key point in their discussion was that the reformers had apparently ignored what had been learned about learners and the learning process. According to these writers, educational theories regarding motivation, learning styles, critical thinking skills, and individualized learning were apparently being overlooked and, instead, changes were advocated that adapted easily to measurement and assessment. These proposals were reductive in terms of the type of knowledge students gained (in most cases simple recall) and destructive to the spirit and excitement of real inquiry.

One of the discussion participants, Walter Karp, a contributing editor to *Harpers Magazine,* stated: "America's high schools characteristically breed conformity and mental passivity. This they do through large, impersonal classes, a focus on order as the first priority, and an emphasis on standardized short answer tests among other things."[19] Theodore Sizer concurred: "The recent reforms reinforce the tendency toward fact-stuffing, short answers, and mental passivity by emphasizing tighter requirements and standardized testing. . . . The degree to which the reform movement ignores the current concepts about learning is astonishing."[20] These supposed reforms leave the individual student submerged by numbers, rules, and test scores and squeezed into categories, with lists of supposedly mastered competencies, rather than empowered to pursue meaning, as Greene urged, to think creatively and critically and to grow optimally.

One member argued that the reformers showed a disturbing lack of concern for the attitudes of learners. Ernest L. Boyer, president of the Carnegie Foundation for the Advancement of Teaching and the former U.S. Commissioner of Education, observed that "business leaders are discovering that if they don't find a way to engage their employees, their companies won't be competitive. Is it too much to expect people in education to accept the same message?"[21]

What We Know about Learners and Learning   In spite of the difficulties of teaching students with diverse needs and backgrounds, much is known about learners and learning that can be of great value to teachers. Study of the contributions of Jean Piaget, Maria Montessori, John Dewey, Jerome Bruner, Erik Erikson, B.F. Skinner, Albert Bandura, and other cognitive and learning theorists, for example, can provide future teachers with several perspectives on the learner and the learning process. You may also wish to take courses in child or adolescent development and educational psychology to increase your understanding of how learning takes place.

Theories about learners and learning, while they are helpful, are not intended to set forth, in cookbook fashion, exactly what teachers should do in particular situations. Instead, such theories are "tools" that professional teachers use to understand the behavioral options open to them and the probable consequences of implementing those options. In other words, theories about learners and learning guide the decision making of professional teachers. Not only do such teachers know that a certain strategy "works," they know *why* it works. Because they recognize the importance of theories, they have at their disposal a greater range of options for problem solving than teachers who have not developed their repertoire of theories.

As you progress through your teacher education program, keep in mind that your ultimate goal as a professional will be to apply theoretical knowledge to the practical problems of teaching. To the extent that you realize this goal you will have confirmed what noted social psychologist Kurt Lewin said about theories: "There is nothing so practical as a good theory."[22]

To illustrate the usefulness of theories about learners and learning, we present the following findings from the report *What Works: Research About Teaching and Learning,* published by the United States Department of Education in 1986.[23] Each finding not only demonstrates a connection between specific student behaviors and learning, it also confirms an underlying theoretical perspective on learners and learning. It is no exaggeration to say, then, that without the theory, there would be no recommendation for practice.

- "Children who are encouraged to draw and scribble 'stories' at an early age will later learn to compose more easily, more effectively, and with greater confidence than children who do not have this encouragement."
- "Children in early grades learn mathematics more effectively when they use physical objects in their lessons."
- "Students tutoring other students can lead to improved academic achievement for both student and tutor, and to positive attitudes toward coursework."

EDUCATION
in the
N   E   W   S

The "Comer Process"

America's schools share the problem of ensuring educational quality and equity for all students, including students at risk of failing or dropping out. One creative approach to this problem is to forge special interrelationships among members of a community for meeting all students' needs. Such school-based community collaborations take on a variety of forms. In New Haven, Connecticut, for example, parents, mental-health specialists, and school staff collaborate in a successful School Development Program. Created by Yale child psychiatrist James Comer, this program has become a national model for school reform, publicized in education news.

Comer's ideas flow from his basic assumption that "all kids can learn regardless of their income and their background . . . at the level needed to be successful in society." Applying principles of child development and behavior, Comer developed a process for giving children the stable support and role models they need.

The "Comer process" is built around three elements: a school-governance team, a mental-health team, and parents. The governance team includes teachers, administrators, and parents, and may also include a curriculum specialist, a union representative, a counselor, and a custodian. Focusing on the needs of the students, they make decisions by consensus. In the New Haven school system, the mental-health team includes psychologists, social workers, and special-education teachers. They focus on preventing problems, intervening on students' behalf, and giving all students the support they need to succeed.

In addition to serving on the school-governance team, parents participate in the PTO, volunteer in the classrooms, and attend community social events—such as Black History Month dinners, Halloween parades, book fairs, and student concerts—that are held in the school. The school also offers parents workshops on how to help their children with homework and on nutrition, finance, substance abuse, and parenting skills.

By emphasizing the students' needs and the social contexts of teaching and learning, schools in low-income communities that are using the Comer process have been remarkably successful. In New Haven, for example, the schools were ranked at the bottom statewide in both achievement and attendance, but today they are at or near the top. More than 70 schools in other states have adopted the Comer process, and the experiment has even attracted major funding. The Rockefeller Foundation recently awarded a multimillion-dollar grant for the dissemination of Comer's ideas nationally. Through such innovative school-community collaborations, it is hoped, "schools of failure" will become a thing of the past.

Source: Daniel Gursky, "A Plan that Works," *Teacher Magazine* (June/July 1990): 46–54.

- "Memorizing can help students absorb and retain the factual information on which understanding and critical thought are based."
- "The best way to learn a foreign language in school is to start early and to study it intensively over many years."

In order to keep current on educational theory and research, preservice and inservice teachers need to review reports like these and survey new findings that appear in education journals and references like the *Handbook of Research on Teaching.* We also encourage teachers to attend professional conferences, enroll in university courses, and initiate arrangements to bring to their schools experts in the field to act as speakers or consultants.

PRESERVICE TRAINING

Although programs in teacher education vary throughout the country, they provide preservice teachers with an enduring set of resources and experiences they can draw from as teachers. Recall how Sara, profiled at the beginning of this chapter, turned to what she learned in her preservice program to solve the problems she faced.

In a similar manner, a beginning junior high school teacher quoted in Robert Bullough's book, *First-Year Teacher: A Case Study*, describes how a course provided her with specific techniques that she could apply to meet the challenges of her first teaching assignment:

> [The professor] always said, "Take the students from where they are to where you want them to go." She was always very questioning about what your [purposes] were [but she didn't just ask,] "What's your objective?" It was more than that: "What is the student thinking? Where is he or she? What do you want [them] to be doing?" Whenever I have to prepare a lesson, I'm thinking about how to be creative [with it]; she always [emphasized] creative things. I go back to those [things she taught]. Sometimes I even go back and thumb through lessons that [the students in her classes] did [and shared] with each other. That helps a lot.[24]

In the following sections, we take a brief look at how teacher education programs differ with regard to admission procedures and program structure and focus. As you read, keep in mind that there is *no one best way* to prepare teachers. What does make a difference, however, is the quality of experiences offered in the program and the teacher education student's commitment to becoming what educator and philosopher John Dewey termed a "thoughtful and alert student of education."[25]

Admission Procedures

For some teacher education programs, admission into the university is all that is needed for acceptance into their programs; for others, students must pass tests in basic skills and general studies content; while still others require students to obtain certain Scholastic Aptitude Test scores. Most universities consider college grade point averages (GPA's) rather than high school GPA's as admission criteria. When students are admitted varies from university to university; most are admitted in their sophomore or junior years, though some programs begin during their freshman year and others are limited to graduate students. Until recently, students wishing to enter teacher education programs were rarely rejected; however, efforts to reform teacher education have resulted in higher standards of admission at most universities.[26]

Program Structure and Focus

Should teacher education students be thoroughly prepared with a liberal arts degree and then receive professional training or should the mixture of general and professional courses be more equal and occur simultaneously during the undergraduate years? The balance between the two types of knowledge—liberal and professional—has been a fundamental concern in teacher education over the years.

Citing M. L. Borrowman's review of teacher education programs, Judith Lanier and Judith Little outline three stances commonly taken regarding the mixture of professional and liberal education studies: (1) future teachers need to receive a thorough four-year liberal education and then study an additional year for professional training; (2) the two types of courses should be mixed and organized "around a set of professional functions of teaching or a general social problems core"; and (3) "the eclectic or ad hoc approach," which mixes the professional and liberal education courses early in students' academic study, should be used.[27]

There is still no consensus on the value of making graduate work necessary for certification, though a number of universities are experimenting with the five-year program. Expressing the opinion of those who prefer a year of graduate work is David Imig, executive director of the American Association of Colleges for Teacher Education: "Eliminating the undergraduate degree is part of a series of interventions necessary to educate a workforce that can maintain our standard of living 20 years from now. . . . Requiring graduate study for teachers may not be as radical a change as it appears. Sixty percent of all teachers now hold master's degrees, and many school systems already require them."[28]

Replacing undergraduate teacher education programs with a year of intense professional preparation at the graduate level is a dramatic and, to many, an extreme alternative. Its proponents argue that it would raise standards and make teaching more accessible to graduates in other disciplines and people who wish to change their fields of work.

Using a fifth year for internships or the extension of professional coursework while continuing undergraduate programs in teacher education may be a less disruptive alternative.

FOUR APPROACHES TO TEACHER EDUCATION

Teacher education programs also differ in that many present students with experiences that are oriented toward a particular focus or view of effective teaching. Among those that have been widely documented are the extended preparation approach, the reflective teaching approach, the theory-into-practice approach, and the collaborative approach.

The Extended Preparation Approach

Several teacher education programs around the country now require students to complete an extended course of study before becoming eligible to receive a teaching certificate. Normally, **extended preparation programs** require that students acquire a broad, liberal education and extensive preparation in an academic area before taking professional education courses.

An extended (five-year) program that has received national recognition is the PROTEACH (short for *professional teacher*) program at the University of Florida at Gainesville. Initiated in 1983 as a result of the expanding knowledge base in teaching, PROTEACH is designed to prepare professional teachers who will make decisions based on teacher effectiveness research and the ability to reflect on classroom experiences. PROTEACH students earn both bachelor's and master's degrees before they are certified. Compared to other programs, PROTEACH requires more study in the academic teaching fields, more clinical/field work, more coursework in professional education, and a more comprehensive final evaluation of students. In addition, program components stress the role of teachers as producers, as well as consumers, of research on teaching.

The Reflective Teaching Approach

Teacher education programs oriented around the concept of **reflective teaching** are designed to prepare teachers who are reflective decision makers. As Donald Cruickshank, one of the primary architects of reflective teaching, observed: "Rather than behaving according to technique, impulse, tradition, and authority [reflective teachers] deliberate on their teaching."[29] The teacher education program at The Ohio State University was among the first to emphasize reflective teaching. In that program, students learn to become more reflective about their teaching through the structured use of classroom diaries or journals, observational systems such as interaction analysis, problem-solving simulations, and video protocols.

The Theory-into-Practice Approach

Several teacher education programs are designed to enable students to master the **Instructional Theory into Practice (ITIP)** model developed by Madeline Hunter at the University of California at Los Angeles. According to Hunter, teaching consists of a series of professional decisions that influence student learning. These decisions are in three areas: those involving content to be learned, those that focus on how students will learn, and those that involve specific teacher behaviors. In terms of this three-part framework, then, teacher education students learn how to develop lessons that contain the seven essential elements shown in Figure 3.3: anticipatory set, objective and purpose, input, modeling, check for understanding, guided practice, and independent practice.

FIGURE 3.3
Seven Elements of Instructional Theory into Practice

1. *Anticipatory Set:* The teacher develops in students a "mental set" that focuses them on the content to be learned. For example, "How many of you know how to find out the area of a circle?"

2. *Objective and Purpose:* The teacher tells students what they are going to learn and why it will be useful to them. For example, "Today we are going to learn how to write a business letter so that you will be able to write for information about careers that interest you."

3. *Input:* The teacher presents new information related to the knowledge, processes, or skills students are to learn. This may be accomplished through lecture, demonstration, simulation, or other appropriate activity.

4. *Modeling:* In this step, the teacher provides examples of the knowledge, processes, or skills being taught. In other words, the teacher "models" what students are expected to do.

5. *Check for Understanding:* As the lesson unfolds, the teacher conducts periodic checks to see what students have learned. The teacher may check for understanding concurrently with the next step.

6. *Guided Practice:* Students are given an opportunity to practice the new knowledge, processes, or skills under the teacher's guidance.

7. *Independent Practice:* In the final step, the teacher assigns activities that require students to practice on their own what they have learned.

The Collaborative Approach

Several innovative teacher education programs are exploring ways to collaborate with school-based teachers and administrators in the preparation of teachers. The University of Oregon, for example, has a Resident Teacher Program that combines graduate study with a year of full-time teaching in a public school. The resident teacher is supervised by school district faculty and university faculty.

In 1987, the University of Houston and the Houston Independent School District collaborated to create the Houston Teaching Academy. The Academy is a multiethnic K–8 school that serves as a site for the preparation of teachers for inner-city schools— a model of the **collaborative approach** to teacher training. As another example, the University of Wisconsin at Whitewater has developed a Teacher Induction Team approach to teacher education. A "team" consisting of a school administrator, a mentor teacher, and a university consultant works with students who have been admitted to the university's graduate program. The team and the student prepare a personal development plan, and students attend monthly seminars.

FIELD EXPERIENCES

Field experiences are designed to give students opportunities to experience firsthand the world of the teacher. Through field activities, students are given limited (and usually, carefully structured) exposure to various aspects of teaching. Observing, tutoring, instructing small groups, operating instructional media, and completing various noninstructional tasks are among the most common field experience activities.

Observation

A vital element in all field experiences is classroom observation. Students report that these experiences aid them greatly in making a final decision about entering the teaching field. Most become more enthusiastic about teaching and more motivated to learn the needed skills; a few decide that teaching is not for them. Recognizing the value of observations, a number of universities are attempting to incorporate such fieldwork earlier in their teacher education programs.

Observations of classrooms in session and of child behavior play an important part in your preparation for becoming a teacher. Many education students report that of all their field experiences, observation proved most valuable.

Currently, some universities and communities are cooperating on cable television projects designed to enable college students on campus to tune in to live coverage of teaching and learning activities in school classrooms off campus. Such an approach recognizes the power of models for learning how to teach. Further, the approach is relatively inexpensive, less intrusive, and more time-efficient.

Focused Observations   Observations are more meaningful when they are focused and conducted with clear purposes. Observers may focus on the students, the teacher, the interactions between the two, the structure of the lesson, or the setting. More specifically, for example, observers may wish to note students' interests and ability levels, to study student responses to a particular teaching strategy, or to analyze the question and response patterns in a class discussion. Much of what observers notice will be determined by the questions that have been raised before they enter the classroom.

When conducting observations, students need to guard against three types of observation "errors"—errors of omission, commission, and transmission—according to Martin O. Juel, retired professor, Southwest Texas State University. Errors of omission result from not having the necessary information or not seeing or understanding the whole story; errors of commission are caused by including more information than is actually there (i.e., projecting one's opinions into the situation); and errors of transmission occur when careless mistakes are made while keeping a written record of the observation. Because our expectations strongly influence what we see, observer bias is difficult to overcome. It can be reduced by using such tactics as writing comments in two columns—one for objective reporting of what is seen and a second for subjective reactions—or viewing a lesson from two perspectives, a student's and the teacher's, and comparing the two.

Instruments of Observation   With recent reform efforts to improve education in the United States has come the development of instruments to facilitate the evaluation of teacher performance, a task now widely required of school administrators. Students preparing to teach can benefit by using these evaluative instruments in their observations, such as the one from the Toledo, Ohio, school system shown in the Appendix at the end of this chapter.

Observations may also be guided by sets of questions related to specific areas. For instance, since beginning teachers are frequently frustrated by their lack of success in interesting their students in learning, asking questions specifically related to motivation can make an observation more meaningful and instructive. Figure 3.4 presents a helpful set of focused questions on motivation. Similar questions can be generated for other focus areas such as classroom management, student involvement, questioning skills, evaluation, and teacher-student rapport. Select one of these focus areas for the following Five-Minute Focus.

FIVE-MINUTE FOCUS   Think about the focus area that you have selected and brainstorm a set of questions to ask about it. After three minutes, order your questions in a logical sequence and use the results to guide you in your next observation. Date your journal entry and write for five minutes.

Directions: As you observe, note the ways that students are motivated intrinsically (from within) and extrinsically (from factors outside themselves).

FIGURE 3.4
Guiding Questions for Observing Motivation

Intrinsic Motivation

What things seem to interest students at this age?

Which activities and assignments seem to give them a sense of pride?

When do they seem to be confused? bored? frustrated?

What topics do they talk about with enthusiasm?

In class discussions, when are they most alert and participating most actively?

What seems to please, amuse, entertain, or excite them?

What do they joke about? What do they find humorous?

What do they report as being their favorite subjects? favorite assignments?

What do they report as being their least favorite subjects and assignments?

How do they respond to personalized lessons (e.g., using their names in exercises)?

How do they respond to activity-oriented lessons (e.g., fieldwork, project periods)?

How do they respond to assignments calling for presentations to groups outside the classroom (e.g., parents, another class, the chamber of commerce)?

How do they respond to being given a choice in assignments?

Extrinsic Motivation

How do teachers show their approval to students?

What phrases do teachers use in their praise?

What types of rewards do teachers give (e.g., grades, points, tangible rewards)?

What reward programs do you notice (e.g., points accumulated toward free time)?

What warnings do teachers give?

What punishments are given to students?

How do teachers arouse concern in their students?

How do students motivate other students?

What forms of peer pressure do you observe?

How do teachers promote enthusiasm for an assignment?

How do teachers promote class spirit?

How do teachers catch their students' interest in the first few minutes of a lesson?

Which type of question draws more answers—recall or open-ended?

How do teachers involve quiet students in class discussions?

How do teachers involve inactive students in their work?

In what ways do teachers give recognition to students' accomplishments?

Participation

Because of the need to provide practice with theory before the student teaching period, many teacher education programs include elements of facsimile teaching, usually in the form of microteaching and/or simulations.

Microteaching Introduced in the 1960s, **microteaching** was received enthusiastically and remains a popular practice. The process calls for students to teach brief, single-concept lessons to a small group of students (5–10) while concurrently practicing a specific teaching skill, such as positive reinforcement. Often the microteaching is videotaped for later study.

As originally developed, microteaching includes six steps. The student:

1. Is assigned, or may select, a specific teaching skill to learn about and practice
2. Reads about the skill in one of several pamphlets
3. Observes a master teacher demonstrate the skill in a short movie or on videotape
4. Prepares a 3- to 5-minute lesson to demonstrate the skill
5. Teaches the lesson, which is videotaped, to a small group of peers
6. Critiques, along with the instructor and the students' peers, the videotaped lesson

Based on the level of skill performance shown, the student may either reteach the skill or prepare a new lesson from nearly 20 skills that have been categorized into five clusters: response repertoire, creating student involvement, questioning skills, increasing student participation, and presenting skills.

Simulations   As an element of teacher training, **teaching simulations** provide opportunities for vicarious practice of a wide range of teaching skills. In simulations, students analyze teaching situations that are presented in writing, on audiotape, in short films, or on videotape. Typically, they are given background information about a hypothetical school or classroom and the pupils they must prepare to "teach." After this orientation, students role-play the student teacher or the teacher who is confronted with the problem situation. Following the simulation, participants discuss the appropriateness of solutions and work to increase their problem-solving skills and their understanding of the teacher's multifaceted role.

Classroom Aides   Serving as a teacher aide is another popular means of providing field experience before student teaching. Assisting teachers in classrooms familiarizes college students with class schedules, record-keeping procedures, and students' performance levels, and provides ample opportunity for observations. In exchange, the classroom teacher receives much needed assistance.

Student Teaching

The most extensive and memorable field experience in teacher preparation programs is the period of student teaching. States require students to have a five-week to semester-long student teaching experience in the schools before certifying them as teachers. The nature of student teaching varies considerably among teacher education programs. Typically, a student is assigned to a cooperating (or master) teacher in the school, and a university supervisor makes periodic visits to observe the student teacher. Some programs even pay student teachers during the student teaching experience.

The most frequent criticism of student teaching is that student teachers pay more attention to classroom management and the mechanics of scheduling and record keeping than they do to the promotion of learning. The sink-or-swim phenomenon of working with 30 or more students at once results in a desire to quickly master survival skills. The concern among teacher educators is that students will not continue to grow and move beyond the coping strategies they gain in student teaching when they enter their own classrooms as teachers. Students are encouraged to regard the student teaching experience as an opportunity to experiment as well as to cope, to question as well as to imitate, and to discover avenues for continuing their professional development after certification.

Student teaching is a time of responsibility. As one student teacher put it, "I don't want to mess up [my students'] education!" It is also, as two other student teachers suggest, an opportunity for growth, a chance to master critical skills.

I went in with some confidence and left with lots of confidence. I felt good about what was going on. I established a comfortable rapport with the kids and was more relaxed. Each week I grew more confident. When you first go in you are not sure how you'll do. When you know you are doing O.K. your confidence improves.

I had some bad days, but overall I felt like I improved. I felt like, wow, I can deal with these kids. They're not so intimidating. They're not so smart. But the first few days it was kind of scary.

According to data gathered from 902 teacher education institutions in the United States, about 60 percent of the student teacher's time is actually spent teaching (see Figure 3.5). The remaining time is devoted to observing and participating in classroom activities. The amount of time one actually spends teaching, however, is not as important as one's willingness to reflect carefully on the student teaching experience. Two excellent ways to promote reflection during student teaching are journal writing and maintaining a reflective teaching log.

Journal Writing Many supervisors require student teachers to keep a journal of their classroom experiences so that they can engage in reflective teaching and begin the process of criticizing and guiding themselves. We share here two entries that give brief glimpses of the student teaching experience and illustrate the instructive benefit of journal writing. The first was written by a student teaching in a third-grade classroom.

February 3

If there is one thing that *really* drives me crazy about these kids, it's how they don't listen to directions. Today in my language lesson all they had to do was rewrite a paragraph—not make corrections, just rewrite. We are working on paragraph form. I explained the directions once and had one of the students read it out loud again. Then I asked for any questions—none. Then as soon as I said "begin" the questions started flying. But what really got me was that they were all questions I had already explained or that were in the directions right there on their papers. I finally said they would have to ask their neighbors for the answer. It was *so* frustrating. Mrs. B. said for me to tell them next time that I would explain the directions once and ask for questions, then that was it. They would have to ask someone else! What a day!

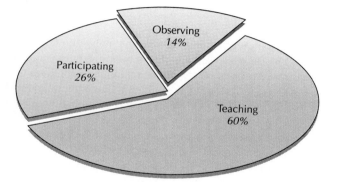

FIGURE 3.5
Student Teaching Activities by Percent of Time

Source: Based on data in Johnson, J. and Yates, J., "A National Survey of Student Teaching Programs" (DeKalb, Ill.: Northern Illinois University, 1982). (ERIC Document Reproduction Service No. ED 232 963.)

Gaining skill in giving directions effectively resulted from this student's exasperation. The next entry is from a student teacher in a fifth-grade classroom who discusses a problem less easily remedied—the recurrence of misbehavior.

> He turned right around 30 minutes later and took another person's pencil. Needless to say I was very disappointed in the little boy who stole and in myself for my ineffective discipline. My cooperating teacher saw the disappointment in my face. She sat down next to me, patted me on the back and said, "You know the song 'We've only just begun . . .'? Well, you have just started in this business and even someone like me with 15 years of experience still thinks about that song every time I discipline a new child each year. Sometimes you're effective and sometimes you're not." That made me feel so much at ease with myself and with my career choice.

Relatively unstructured, open-ended journals, such as the ones from which these entries were selected, provide student teachers with a medium for subjectively exploring the practicum experience.

Reflective Teaching Logs   To promote the practice of reflecting more analytically, some supervisors ask their student teachers to use a more directed and structured form of journal keeping, the **reflective teaching log.** In this a student lists and briefly describes the daily sequence of activities, selects a single episode to expand on, analyzes the reason for selecting it and what was learned from it, and considers the possible future application of that knowledge.

To illustrate the reflective teaching approach to keeping a log, we share here a complete entry for one episode that was recounted and critiqued by a college student tutoring a high school student in life sciences. The entry is of particular interest because it provides us with a glimpse of a college student's first experience teaching an academic subject and it addresses two common problems: failure to pay attention and apparent lack of motivation.

Log for February 17, 2:30–4:15

Events

We went over her old notes, homework, quizzes and tests, looking for the relationship between them. We also talked about her lab work and how she liked that aspect of the course. We then shifted our attention to the textbook and worked about halfway through chapter one.

Episode

When I talked to Anne's teacher and his assistant, they both felt her main problem was attention and motivation. Perhaps that is why I so easily noticed the former problem today. I realize it was a Friday afternoon and few people are into schoolwork at that point, but it was still amazing how quick[ly] her attention would wander.

We were working in the school library, trying to pull the central meaning out of the text sections. For instance, we would read the section on bacteria characteristics and then try to make an outline, but she wasn't really there. I don't wish to exaggerate this because she was paying some attention though I felt it wasn't much. I felt annoyed, but I also felt anxious because I might be just boring and not teaching "right." This is really the first teaching I've done dealing with an academic subject and consequently I am in need of improvement.

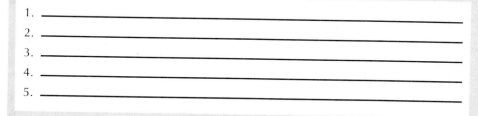

CONSIDER THIS . . .

How Can You Get the Most Out of Student Teaching?

Teacher education students consistently rank student teaching as the most valuable component of their teacher education program. In most cases, students establish constructive, growth-promoting relationships with their cooperating teachers. For some student teachers, however, the relationship is less positive. You can reduce the likelihood of experiencing difficulties if you learn as much as possible about your cooperating teacher. Write five questions you would ask your cooperating teacher.

1. _____
2. _____
3. _____
4. _____
5. _____

Now compare your questions to the following suggestions.

1. I've noticed some special areas in your room. (Specify one of them.) What do you and the kids do in this area? Who gets to use it? How are they selected? (Repeat for each area.)
2. Did you arrange the room this way? (If no): Who did? (If yes): What were you trying to do with this arrangement? How long has it been this way?
3. I've been looking through the textbook. How was it selected and by whom? How do you like it? What are its strengths? Weaknesses? Is it successful with some kids but not with others? (Repeat this set of questions for each text.)
4. I also looked over the worksheets, labs, and/or quizzes you've been using. Did you write them? (If no): Where did you get them? (If yes): When did you make them up? Did you base them on anything in particular? Are you happy with them?
5. I enjoyed the lesson(s) (or classes) that I had the opportunity to observe. When I compared your lesson plan with the actual lesson, I noticed that you did not follow your plan precisely. (This question is used only if you noticed some discrepancies.) What caused you to modify your plan?
6. What rules do you expect the kids in your class to follow? (*Probe:* rules for waiting their turn to speak and to receive help, rules for moving around the classroom, leaving the classroom, being on time, what to do when finished with work, working together, resolving conflicts among kids, homework, forms to follow, procedures for work, language, noises, who may speak, etc.) Does the school have rules or regulations with which you disagree? (If yes): Why do you disagree? Do you follow them anyway? Which rules are the most important to you? How do you handle infractions? Are there some kids [who] break rules more than other kids? Tell me about those kids.
7. Suppose you accidentally happened to overhear a group of your former students discussing you as a teacher. What kinds of things would you like to hear them saying?
8. Why did you ask to have a student teacher (or aide, depending upon your role)?
9. What do you expect from me?*

*Source: List from George J. Posner, *Field Experience: Methods of Reflective Teaching*, 2d ed. (New York: Longman, 1989), pp. 54–55. Copyright © 1989 by Longman Publishing Group. Reprinted with permission from Longman Publishing Group.

Analysis

I can't truthfully say I gave any solution to this problem or that I had previously thought about it. I just assumed we would work on the material and on "understanding-type problems." Understanding is not the main problem; bringing attention to the subject is. At first glance through her biology book I thought, at the risk of sounding arrogant, that it was so basic that even people who are not considered smart could work through it. But I'm beginning to see that I was really off the mark as to the problem. One reason this is so interesting to me is because it sounds somewhat like myself in high school. Attention is something both Anne and I have a problem with, but in my case I rely on my relatively good learning ability. Anne can't. I don't see how to change her attitude or even if it is my responsibility or right, but I do think her attention can be worked on.[30]

Field experiences, including observations, microteaching, simulations, working as a teacher aide, and student teaching, are valuable elements in teacher education programs. That they be regarded as *initial* rather than *terminal* learning opportunities is essential. Though personal enthusiasm, energy, and optimism, combined with the knowledge and skills gained from teacher preparation programs should help new teachers complete their first year with relative success, it is the development of the habits of self-evaluation, reflective teaching, and a desire for continuing professional growth that will lead them to become the master teachers children and young people need and deserve.

You may begin your student teaching experience by observing your cooperating teacher in action conducting a class. Inviting first-year teachers to observe mentor or master teachers at work is a common strategy for helping new teachers learn their job.

Keepers of the Dream

Bruce D. Johnson
PROTEACH Student Teacher
University of Florida at Gainesville

Bruce D. Johnson, a student in the five-year teacher education program at the University of Florida at Gainesville, has specific advice for those preparing to student teach:

First, if you're not organized, get organized real quickly. Also, make time for yourself. If you're not happy, the kids won't be happy. Finally, develop a positive relationship with your cooperating teacher and volunteer for everything. Everyone likes a person who is industrious and has initiative.

Johnson just completed a ten-week internship (student teaching) at a local elementary school. Now halfway through a second internship at a middle school, Johnson reports:

The more I teach, the more excited I get. Before I began my first internship, I was concerned about taking on all of that responsibility. It just came all at once. That was the first time I felt the responsibility of actually teaching the kids. If I didn't do my job, they wouldn't learn. That weighed on my shoulders pretty heavily.

That Johnson met the challenges of his first student teaching assignment was confirmed by his cooperating teacher, the university supervisor, his students, and, he's proud to report, his students' parents. "When the parents came up at a PTA meeting and said, 'Thank you, you're doing a wonderful job,' that made it all worthwhile."

Johnson has had a long-term commitment to teaching, a commitment that becomes deeper as next fall nears, when he hopes to begin teaching at a middle school.

I wanted to be a teacher since high school. When I came to the University of Florida I had various majors—electrical engineering, architecture, journalism—but I wasn't really happy until I went into teaching. Now it's really becoming a passion.

"It's Really Becoming a Passion"

Johnson chose Florida's extended teacher education program because of the "added experience in the classroom." In addition to a sixteen-week one-half day and a ten-week, full-day internship, Johnson had four "placements" (field experiences), each about eleven hours a week over an eight-week period.

Those placements in the first, fifth, seventh, and eighth grades made me realize that I really don't have the patience for extremely young children. I'd consider fourth or fifth grade, but middle school is where I want to be. There's something about that age group—there are so many changes going on. That's really an exciting age.

Prior to student teaching, Johnson was not overly concerned about classroom management. "Mainly, I was anxious about my ability to teach the information," he says. Now halfway through his second internship, however, Johnson has had some management problems.

I have a few students who are playing angry young men and women. It has a lot to do with their home lives—problems outside of school. They're testing me, resisting. So, I've been honest with them. I've let them know that I'm not the omnipotent teacher. Teachers make mistakes. I'm just a human being.

They're starting to come around. It's really nice. Things started to improve last week, and I'm still excited about it.

A lot of people say, "Never smile until Christmas—never become a friend to a student." I don't believe that. I'm friends with all my students. I've seen them in plays, at football games. We may joke around, but they still respect me. I'm their teacher.

INDUCTION AND INTERNSHIP PROGRAMS

In response to widespread efforts to improve education, many states and local school districts, often in collaboration with colleges and universities, have begun teacher induction and/or internship programs. Among the programs that have received national attention are the Florida Beginning Teacher Program, the California Mentor Teacher Program, the Virginia Beginning Teacher Assistance Program, and the Kentucky Beginning Teacher Internship Program.

Induction programs provide beginning teachers with continued assistance at least during the first year. **Internship programs** also provide participants with support, but they are usually designed primarily to provide training for those who have not gone through a teacher education program. In some instances, however, the terms *induction* and *internship* are used interchangeably.

Most induction and internship programs serve a variety of purposes:

1. To improve teaching performance
2. To increase the retention of promising beginning teachers during the induction years
3. To promote the personal and professional well-being of beginning teachers by improving teachers' attitudes toward themselves and the profession
4. To satisfy mandated requirements related to induction and certification
5. To transmit the culture of the system of beginning teachers.[31]

To accomplish these purposes, induction programs offer such resources as workshops based on teacher-identified needs, observations by and follow-up conferences with individuals not in a supervisory role, support from mentor (or "buddy") teachers, and support group meetings for beginning teachers.

SUMMARY

We began this chapter with a look at how a beginning teacher, Sara, used a reflective problem-solving approach to meet the challenges she encountered during her first year of teaching. We pointed out how recent calls for change in teacher education are aimed at ensuring that all beginning teachers are as successful during the first year as Sara was.

Then we looked at the recommendations made by three influential reform groups: the National Commission for Excellence in Teacher Education, the Holmes Group, and the Carnegie Forum's Task Force on Teaching as a Profession. To determine how educational reforms have affected teaching, we turned to teachers' views of the reform movement.

Next, we examined three kinds of knowledge that must be part of your education as a teacher: knowledge of self and students, knowledge of subject, and knowledge of educational theory and research. Here, we looked at teachers as scholars, agents of change, and models of inspiration.

We then considered the differences among teacher education programs, and, to illustrate the range of these differences, we briefly described four widely documented programs. Next, our review of field experiences focused on observations, microteaching, simulations, and student teaching. Finally, we discussed the critical role that induction and internship programs can play in the professional growth of teachers.

KEY TERMS AND CONCEPTS

educational reform movement, 62
National Commission for Excellence
  in Teacher Education, 63
Holmes Group, 64
Carnegie Forum on Education and the
  Economy, 64
Task Force on Teaching as a
  Profession, 65
extended preparation, 75
reflective teaching, 76

Instructional Theory into Practice, 76
collaborative approach, 77
field experiences, 77
focused observations, 78
microteaching, 79
teaching simulations, 80
reflective teaching log, 82
induction programs, 86
internship programs, 86

DISCUSSION QUESTIONS

1. What elements do the reform reports on teacher education have in common?
2. Who were the Mrs. Barths in your educational experience and what did they do that made them different?
3. Do you believe that teachers should be able to discuss most topics or do you think that they need to be specialists in their area of expertise only? Explain your answer.
4. Do you believe that America's high schools "breed conformity and mental passivity," as Walter Karp has complained? Justify your answer.
5. What is the chief merit of each of the four approaches to teacher education?
6. Which of the field experiences mentioned in this chapter, other than student teaching, is the most important?

APPLICATION ACTIVITIES

1. Divide your class in half and have one group design an ideal four-year teacher preparation program and the other an ideal five-year program. Share the results and debate the merits and weaknesses of each.
2. Invite several teachers or graduate students to your class to discuss their student teaching experiences.
3. Locate and read the article "How Not to Fix the Schools" (*Harpers*, February 1986). Formulate your position for or against the way educators have responded to the challenge to reform.
4. Read a recent article in a professional journal that calls for educational reform. Share the article with the rest of your class in the form of a brief oral report.

FIELD EXPERIENCES

1. Make several classroom observations using a set of focused questions of your own. Discuss the results.
2. Interview two teachers to obtain their views on school reform. In particular, ask them if reform has had a positive effect *on students* and *on teachers*. Pool your findings with those obtained by other students in your class. Finally, compare your group results with data from the Metropolitan Life Survey of 1990 in Figure 3.2.

3. Visit a school and interview a first-year teacher to find out what kinds of support he or she is receiving. What support is most helpful? Least helpful? What kind of support would the teacher like to be receiving but is not?

4. Interview a student who has completed student teaching at your college or university. What tips does he or she have for developing a positive relationship with a cooperating teacher?

SUGGESTED READINGS

Cruickshank, Donald R. *Research that Informs Teachers and Teacher Educators.* Bloomington, Ind.: Phi Delta Kappa, 1990. *A short, readable book that presents summaries of research on effective schools, effective instruction, effective teachers, and teacher education.*

Grossman, Pamela L. *The Making of a Teacher: Teacher Knowledge and Teacher Education.* New York: Teachers College Press, 1990. *A fascinating book that compares the effectiveness of graduates of a teacher education program with those who were not. Teacher education graduates were more flexible, innovative, and better able to comprehend students' perspectives.*

Hayden, Torey. *Somebody Else's Kids.* New York: Avon Books, 1981. *A teacher's account of her problems and pleasures teaching six children in a resource room. Enjoyable and moving reading.*

Posner, George J. *Field Experience: Methods of Reflective Teaching,* 2d ed. New York: Longman, 1989. *This clearly written handbook teaches readers how to observe effectively by providing numerous logical and perceptive questions, interesting exercises, and realistic sample log entries. Enjoyable style, relevant information.*

Wigginton, Eliot. *Sometimes a Shining Moment: The Foxfire Experience.* Garden City, N.Y.: Doubleday, 1985. *In this award-winning book a gifted teacher reflects on his own teacher preparation and the 20 years of teaching high school English that followed, describing along the way the development and success of the Foxfire experience, a daring, effective, and inspiring adventure in teaching and learning.*

APPENDIX   Teacher Summary Evaluation Report

Name _____ Date _____

College _____ School _____

Grade or Subject _____ Period of Sept.–Dec. ☐   Period of Jan.–March ☐   Period of Apr.–Dec. ☐

Observation Time _____ Conference Time _____

Check on March and Dec. Report	*Check on March Report Only*	*Contract Status*

Check on March and Dec. Report

☐ Outstanding
☐ Satisfactory
☐ Unsatisfactory

Check on March Report Only

☐ Recommended for first one-year contract
☐ Recommended for second one-year contract
☐ Recommended for initial four-year contract
☐ Recommended for third one-year contract
☐ Not recommended for reappointment

Contract Status

☐ First year contract
☐ Second year contract
☐ Four-year contract
☐ One-year contract
☐ Continuing contract
☐ Long-term substitute (60 or more days)

- **Outstanding (O):** Performance shows exceptional professional qualities and growth.
- **Satisfactory (S):** Performance shows expected and desired professional qualities and growth.
- **Unsatisfactory (U):** Performance shows serious weaknesses or deficiencies.
- For more complete definition refer to page 12 in The Toledo Plan.
- Unsatisfactories and/or outstandings must have a written supportive statement.

	O	S	U		O	S	U
I. Teaching Procedures				c. Efficient classroom routine			
a. Skill in planning				d. Appropriate interaction with pupils			
b. Skill in assessment and evaluation				e. Is reasonable, fair, and impartial in dealing with students			
c. Skill in making assignments				**III. Knowledge of Subject— Academic Preparation**			
d. Skill in developing good work-study habits				**IV. Personal Characteristics and Professional Responsibility**			
e. Resourceful use of instructional materials				a. Shows a genuine interest in teaching			
f. Skill in using motivating techniques				b. Personal appearance			
g. Skill in questioning techniques				c. Skill in adapting to change			
h. Ability to recognize and provide for individual differences				d. Adheres to accepted policies and procedures of Toledo Public Schools			
i. Oral and written communication skills				e. Accepts responsibility both inside and outside the classroom			
j. Speech, articulation, and voice quality				f. Has a cooperative approach toward parents and school personnel			
II. Classroom Management				g. Is punctual and regular in attendance			
a. Effective classroom facilitation and control							
b. Effective interaction with pupils							

Evaluator's Signature
(when required)

Teacher's Signature

Principal's Signature
(when required)

Evaluator's Position

Date of Conference

Directions

1. Rate all categories, bold face and subcategories; 2. Attach all signed or initiated supporting documents.

Source: The Toledo Plan: Intern, Intervention, Evaluation. Toledo Public Schools, 1986, p. 13. Reprinted by permission.

TEACHERS . . .

What did you find most helpful in your teacher education? In your opinion how can teacher education be improved?

My classes that have been most beneficial have been those in which fellow teachers shared strategies, lesson plans, and ideas for discipline and motivation that have been most successful for them. I have also attended several Sensory Motor Workshops that utilize body movement to further develop cognitive thinking, introduce specific activities to better develop and maintain children's attention span, and demonstrate exercises that keep the children calm and quiet.

—Sherry Reeve
Acacia Academy, West Covina, California

Most helpful to me were student teaching experiences and observations in real classrooms in the public schools. I also benefitted from peer teachings and evaluations. Nothing has helped me more than actually teaching by trial and error and exchanging ideas with other public school educators.

Increasing the number of courses teachers take in their subject areas would help improve teacher education. I only had to take a few classes in my minor (Biology) and this is what I am teaching now. I also think classes on how to teach Biology would have been more beneficial to me than more technical courses within the field of Biology per se.

—Janiece Nelson
Hutto High School, Hutto, Texas

The most helpful input in my education as a teacher was the field experience of student teaching. I found that many of the ideas presented in the university classes simply were not applicable or not feasible in the real world of teaching.

As an elementary teacher, I teach all subjects. I'm not convinced that more courses on the subjects [are] the answer for improved teaching; rather, more teaching experiences in the subject areas may improve teaching. Teachers who specialize in one subject area would probably benefit from extension courses in their particular subject.

—Angela Swann
Palm Elementary School, Austin, Texas

ON TEACHING

The most helpful and least helpful aspects of my education were my professors. The attitude and personality of a professor either inspired me or turned me off. The subject matter was not the issue. The best way to improve teacher education is to give teachers more time in the classroom, not more courses.

—Julie A. Addison
Rock Ridge Elementary School,
Castle Rock, Colorado

The classes that involved extensive hands-on classroom experience were the most helpful to me as an educator. The guidance I received from my cooperating teachers was priceless. It is true that the only way to learn to teach is to teach. I am happy to say that no course I took seemed unnecessary.

I think teachers should take more courses in their subject areas. To maintain credibility we must be good in our field[s]. As educators we must also keep current in our area[s] of expertise, even if this requires taking courses on a regular basis after certification. CPAs must keep current with tax laws and medical personnel must keep abreast of medical procedures and breakthroughs, so why should educators be any exception?

—Jennifer Cronk
Rocky Mountain Hebrew Academy, Denver, Colorado

I found the classes where actual "hands-on" experiences took place helped me the most. The times I had to actually teach lessons, games, and activities to the class gave me the valuable practical learning that I believe helped me to become a better teacher. The least helpful classes were the lecture courses, in which only "textbook" learning was expected. A novice needs some reassurance as to how to go about this wonderful thing called "teaching." The way to improve teaching, in my opinion, is to improve how and what future teachers are taught. Teachers need to grow in their profession and adapt to changes but also need a good foundation on which to build.

—Suzanne Neal
William Woods College, Fulton, Missouri

I feel that every class is worth something—some more than others. The classes that got me out into the teaching field were the most useful, allowing me to sample the real thing and then bring it back into the classroom for discussion. I feel that teachers should receive more training in the schools and should spend as much time as possible with mentor teachers. Curriculum classes were also very helpful.

—Amy Orcutt
Green Gables Elementary School, Jefferson County, Colorado

CHAPTER 4

Your First Teaching Position

*B*efore I began teaching, I was unsure about whether I could do everything that teachers have to do. But now that the first year's about over, I know I can do it. I feel really great.

A First-Year Teacher

Near the end of your teacher education program, you receive a letter from a friend who graduated two years earlier. She informs you that she is now teaching in a rural school in a southern state, a job she thoroughly enjoys. She says she feels very fortunate to have the job she does, given her initial difficulty finding the "right" teaching position.

"I know we're in the middle of a teacher shortage, and it's not that hard to find a job," she says in her letter. "But I didn't want to take just any job. It had to be the right one."

She goes on to describe the frustration of sending off "nearly twenty" letters of inquiry, to be granted only two interviews.

"One interview I went on was really different. Three people kept asking me these questions like, 'When did you first decide you wanted to become a teacher?' and, 'What do you think students want out of school?' They took notes [on] what I said, and they even tape recorded it. It was almost like they were looking for 'right' answers. I'm not sure how I did on that one."

"The other interview was just as different. I spent half an hour in the principal's office, and it was just like we were having a conversation. She was really a nice person."

After those two interviews, she heard about an opening at her present school from a friend. "I was so excited when she told me about this job. I was just a nervous wreck before the interview. But it went great—I got the job!"

Her account of how difficult it was to find a job that matched her expectations and her description of the group interview worry you. Now you're wondering what steps you can follow to increase your chances of finding the best possible teaching position.

FOCUS QUESTIONS

1. How can one find out about the current job market for teachers in different specialty areas and in different regions of the country?
2. How can one find out about current average salaries for teachers and which regions of the country have the highest pay scales?
3. In addition to their base salaries, what fringe benefits do teachers typically receive?
4. What is the sequence of job search strategies that nearly every applicant for a teaching position should follow?
5. What other career opportunities are available in education and noneducation fields?

Upon completion of your teacher education program, you will still have several important steps to take before securing your first teaching position. Preparing well for these steps will go a long way toward helping you begin teaching with confidence.

It is natural that you feel both excited and a bit fearful when thinking about your first job. While taking the courses required in your teacher education program you will probably feel secure in your role as a student; you will know what is expected of you. As a teacher, however, you will assume an entirely new role—a role that will require some time before it becomes comfortable. The aim of this chapter, then, is to help make the transition from student to professional teacher a positive, pleasant one. We will first look at the steps you can take to identify current trends related to teacher supply and demand and teachers' salaries. Then, we will discuss three major concerns shared by all beginning teachers: obtaining the first teaching position; creating a pleasant, work-oriented climate on the first day of school; and developing cooperative, productive relationships with other school personnel, parents, and the community. Finally, we will take a look at other career opportunities in education and noneducation fields.

FIVE-MINUTE FOCUS   Describe your view of the ideal teaching position. What kind of climate would the school have? How would you describe the faculty and students? Date your journal entry and write for five minutes.

TEACHER SUPPLY AND DEMAND

When you think ahead to a career in teaching, one question you are likely to ask yourself is, How hard will it be to find a job? From time to time, **teacher supply and demand** figures have painted a rather bleak picture for those entering the teaching profession. At other times, finding a position has been relatively easy.

In response to a shortage of teachers during the 1960s, many college students decided to earn their teacher certification. As we moved into the 1970s, however, the demand for teachers was suddenly replaced by a teacher surplus. Declining enrollments and cutbacks in educational spending cost many teachers their jobs, and finding a teaching position became highly competitive. At nearly all levels of schooling and in most sections of the country, there was a definite surplus of teachers.

Even during times of teacher surplus, however, talented, qualified teachers have been able to find jobs. Teaching is one of the largest professions in the United States; during 1989–90, for example, the total instructional staff in our nation's public schools was estimated at 2,645,327.[1] Within such a large profession, annual openings resulting from retirements and career changes alone are sizable.

Source: Based on data from the National Center for Education Statistics and the U.S. Bureau of the Census. Graph and illustration in *Introduction to the Foundations of American Education,* 8th ed. James A. Johnson et al. Boston: Allyn and Bacon, 1991, p. 33. Used by permission of the publisher.

FIGURE 4.1
Number of School-Age Children, 1970–2020

Improvement in the Job Market

While the need for new teachers is difficult to determine, most analysts predict a much more favorable job market for teachers in all regions of the country during the 1990s. The school-age population began to increase in 1985, and that trend is expected to continue until the year 2000 (see Figure 4.1). These increased enrollments contrast sharply with the declining numbers of students who are entering teacher education programs, indicating that we may be headed for an acute teacher shortage. The

FIGURE 4.2
Projected Annual Demand for Hiring of Teachers, by Level, 1989–1997

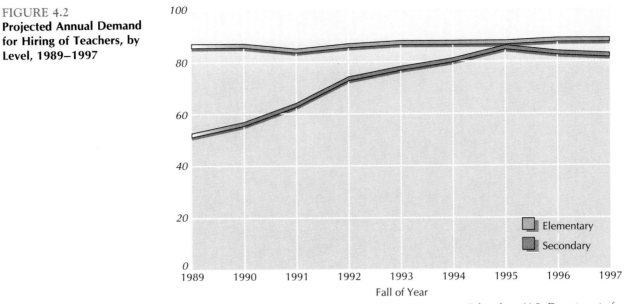

Source: "Projections of Education Statistics to 1997–98," 1988. Taken from U.S. Department of Education, National Center for Education Statistics, *1989 Educators Indicators,* p. 47.

National Center for Education Statistics reported, for example, that the 1985–86 school year began with a shortage of 12,000 teachers.

Though we cannot be certain that supply and demand projections are accurate (some analysts suggest that such data are incomplete and often inaccurate), it appears that there will be considerable need for new teachers during the 1990s. Figure 4.2 shows that the demand for the hiring of new elementary teachers will stabilize through 1997, while the demand for secondary teachers is expected to increase rapidly until 1995, and then decline slightly. These projections mean that qualified teachers— those with a real commitment to children—should have little difficulty securing desirable positions.

Need According to Specialty Area and Geographic Region

The ease with which you will find your first teaching position is also related to your area of specialization and to the part of the country where you wish to locate. In 1991, for example, job seekers able to teach bilingual education or special education were in an especially favorable position. Also, Alaska had the greatest demand for teachers, followed by the Southeast, the South Central region, and the West. For current employment opportunities according to specialty area and geographic region, check the teacher supply and demand report published annually by the Association for School, College, and University Staffing, Inc. (ASCUS, 1600 Dodge Avenue, S-330, Evanston, IL 60201-3451, tel. (708) 864-1999). When considering supply and demand estimates, remember that jobs *are* to be had in oversupplied areas. Job hunting will be more competitive, though, and you may have to relocate to another region of the country.

TEACHERS' SALARIES AND BENEFITS

It is widely recognized that teachers teach, in large part, because of the satisfaction of helping young people learn and grow. While such intangible rewards represent a significant attraction to teaching, teachers are demanding that the public acknowledge the value and professional standing of teaching by supporting higher salaries. Ninety-four percent of teachers surveyed in the "Metropolitan Life Survey of the American Teacher 1985," for example, said that "providing a decent salary" would "help a lot" in encouraging good teachers to remain in teaching.

There is considerable evidence that, after losing ground to the ravages of inflation in the 1970s, teacher salaries are on the upswing. Governors and educational leaders have come to the realization that in education, as in other walks of life, you get what you pay for. As the 1983 *Nation at Risk* report reminded the American public in its plea for fiscal support of quality education: "Excellence costs. But in the long run mediocrity costs far more."

In an effort to boost paychecks, states such as Florida, California, Texas, and Tennessee have devised merit pay plans, master teacher programs, and career ladders. Some local districts have even developed their own salary incentive plans. Dade County, Florida, for example, initiated a 5 million dollar meritorious school program in 1985, which provided cash bonuses to all faculty and staff at 58 schools. Teachers at these meritorious schools received a special bonus paycheck of over $2,400.

The National Education Association reported that, during the 1990–91 school year, public school teachers earned an average salary of $33,013. Table 4.1 shows a state-by-state comparison of teachers' salaries for 1988–89, 1989–90, and 1990–91 and the percent of change between 1988–89 to 1989–90 and 1989–90 to 1990–91 salaries.

It is important to remember that higher salaries are frequently linked to higher costs of living. During an interview for a teaching position in northern Alaska several years ago, one of us was shocked to learn that a primitive, tar-paper dwelling in Nome rented for over $900 a month! Be aware, too, that salary differences within a state can be considerable. Generally, salaries are significantly higher in metropolitan areas and lower in rural areas. Average salaries for teachers in the Chicago area, for instance, can be as much as $10,000 higher than the average for teachers in other parts of Illinois.

Teachers' salaries are typically determined by years of experience and advanced training as evidenced by graduate credit hours or advanced degrees. Additional duties, such as coaching an athletic team, producing the yearbook and school newspaper, sponsoring clubs, or directing the band, bring extra pay for many teachers. Most districts offer at least limited summer employment for teachers who wish to teach summer school or develop curriculum materials.

Teachers also receive various **fringe benefits,** such as medical insurance and retirement plans, which are usually given in addition to base salary. These benefits vary from district to district and are determined during collective bargaining sessions. Table 4.2, based on a survey of 1,808 school districts, shows the percentage that offered different fringe benefits during the 1987–88 school year. When considering a school district for your first position, carefully examine the fringe benefits package as well as the salary schedule and opportunities for extra pay.

TABLE 4.1   Trends in Teachers' Average Salary, 1988–89, 1989–90 and 1990–1991

State	Average Salary 1988–89	Rank	Average Salary 1989–90	Rank	Average Salary 1990–91	Rank	Percent Change 1988–89 to 1989–90	Percent Change 1989–90 to 1990–91
Alaska	$41,752	1	$43,097	1	$43,661	1	3.2%	1.6%
Connecticut	37,659	2	40,768	2	43,647	2	8.3%	8.3%
D.C.	37,232	3	39,850	3	42,256	3	7.0%	11.4%
New York	36,654	4	38,925	4	41,600	4	6.2%	6.6%
California	35,495	5	37,625	5	39,598	5	6.0%	4.2%
Maryland	34,159	7	36,481	6	38,806	6	6.8%	6.0%
Michigan	34,128	8	36,427	7	37,682	8	6.7%	4.6%
Rhode Island	34,233	6	36,057	8	37,674	9	5.3%	4.4%
New Jersey	33,037	9	35,676	9	38,790	7	8.0%	8.7%
Massachusetts	32,221	10	34,175	10	36,090	10	6.1%	3.9%
Pennsylvania	31,248	12	33,435	11	35,471	11	7.0%	6.4%
Delaware	31,585	11	33,377	12	35,200	12	5.7%	5.4%
Illinois	31,148	13	32,917	13	34,729	13	5.7%	5.9%
Wisconsin	31,046	14	32,600	14	33,100	16	5.0%	3.6%
Hawaii	29,835	16	32,252	15	32,541	14	8.1%	1.5%
Minnesota	30,661	15	32,190	16	33,264	15	5.0%	3.4%
Indiana	29,330	19	30,978	17	32,178	22	5.6%	5.9%
Virginia	28,976	22	30,926	18	32,382	19	6.7%	4.6%
Oregon	29,387	18	30,842	19	32,200	21	5.0%	4.4%
Colorado	29,557	17	30,758	20	32,020	23	4.1%	4.1%
Nevada	28,836	23	30,587	21	32,209	20	6.1%	5.2%
Ohio	29,171	21	30,567	22	32,615	18	4.8%	4.4%
Washington	29,200	20	30,475	23	32,975	17	4.4%	8.2%
Arizona	28,499	24	29,402	24	30,760	26	3.2%	4.6%
Wyoming	28,400	25	28,991	25	28,966	31	2.1%	2.8%
New Hampshire	26,703	29	28,986	26	31,329	24	8.5%	8.0%
Vermont	27,106	26	28,849	27	30,986	25	6.4%	7.6%
Florida	26,974	27	28,787	28	30,387	27	6.7%	5.5%
Georgia	26,920	28	28,013	29	28,855	32	4.1%	3.0%
North Carolina	25,646	34	27,814	30	29,082	29	8.5%	4.3%
Texas	26,513	30	27,400	31	26,321	38	3.3%	3.0%
Missouri	26,006	31	27,229	32	26,607	36	4.7%	5.0%
Kansas	25,926	32	27,220	33	29,923	28	5.0%	4.1%
Tennessee	25,619	35	27,052	34	26,246	39	5.6%	4.4%
Maine	24,938	38	26,881	35	26,700	35	7.8%	6.7%
Iowa	25,778	33	26,747	36	27,949	33	3.8%	4.4%
South Carolina	25,185	37	26,638	37	26,174	43	5.8%	3.5%

TABLE 4.1 *(continued)*

State	Average Salary 1988–89	Rank	Average Salary 1989–90	Rank	Average Salary 1990–91	Rank	Percent Change 1988–89 to 1989–90	Percent Change 1989–90 to 1990–91
Kentucky	24,933	39	26,275	38	29,069	30	5.4%	10.6%
Nebraska	23,841	42	25,522	39	26,592	37	7.1%	4.1%
Alabama	25,190	36	25,500	40	27,300	34	1.2%	7.9%
New Mexico	24,092	41	26,302	41	26,194	42	5.0%	4.2%
Montana	24,421	40	25,081	42	26,210	41	2.7%	4.5%
Mississippi	22,579	46	24,365	43	24,443	48	7.9%	0.3%
Louisiana	22,469	47	24,300	44	26,240	40	8.1%	7.9%
Oklahoma	23,521	43	23,944	45	24,649	47	1.8%	6.8%
Idaho	22,732	45	23,861	46	25,485	45	5.0%	6.8%
Utah	22,852	44	23,652	47	25,415	46	3.5%	7.3%
North Dakota	22,249	48	23,016	48	23,576	49	3.4%	2.4%
West Virginia	21,904	50	22,842	49	25,956	44	4.3%	13.6%
Arkansas	21,955	49	22,471	50	23,040	50	2.4%	3.0%
South Dakota	20,925	51	21,300	51	22,363	51	3.8%	4.9%
U.S. AVERAGE	$29,636	—	$31,325	—	$33,013	—	5.7%	5.3%
Guam	25,842	—	25,842	—	—	—	0.0%	—
Virgin Islands	26,572	—	28,000	—	—	—	5.4%	—

Source: Survey & Analysis of Salary Trends 1990 (Washington, D.C.: The American Federation of Teachers), 11 and National Education Association, 1991, "Estimates of School Statistics, 1990–91" (Washington, DC: N.E.A.). Reprinted with permission.

TABLE 4.2 Percentage of School Districts Offering Selected Fringe Benefits, 1987–88

Benefit Offered	Percent of School Districts	Benefit Offered	Percent of School Districts
Sick Leave	99	Professional Liability Insurance	71.3
Retirement Plan	98	Sabbatical Leave	70.2
Medical Insurance	97.1	Severance Pay	39.9
Dental Insurance	78	Vision Care	35.1
Life Insurance	73.8	Tuition Reimbursement	34.7
Prescription Drugs	72.7		

Note: Based on a survey of 1,808 districts.
Source: Based on data from *Fringe Benefits for Teachers in Public Schools, 1987–88* (Arlington, VA: Education Research Service, Inc., 1988): 52–54.

FIVE-MINUTE FOCUS   Why is it that society generally regards teaching as very important but continues to pay teachers at a level that is often below that received by workers in business and industry? Date your journal entry and write for five minutes.

BECOMING CERTIFIED

Successful completion of a college or university teacher training program will not automatically enable you to teach. State certification is required for teaching in the public schools, and in many private schools as well. In some cases, large cities (e.g., Chicago, New York, Buffalo) have their own certification requirements that must be met. And certain local school districts have installed additional requirements, such as a written examination, before one can teach in those districts.

A **teaching certificate** is actually a license to teach. The department of education for each of the fifty states and the District of Columbia sets the requirements for certification. A certificate usually indicates at what level and in what content areas one may teach. One might, for example, be certified for all-level (K–12) physical education or art, or secondary English, or elementary education. In addition, a certificate may list other areas of specialization, such as driver's training, coaching, or journalism. If one plans to go into nonteaching areas such as counseling, librarianship, or administration, special certificates are usually required.

State Certification Requirements

In order for a person to receive a teaching certificate, all states require successful completion of an approved teacher education program that culminates with at least a bachelor's degree. Approved programs include a particular sequence of education courses and a student teaching or internship experience. The professional education component for elementary teachers in 1984, for example, ranged from a minimum requirement of 20 semester hours in Michigan to a maximum of 33 hours in Mississippi. For secondary certification, New York required a minimum of 12 hours and Tennessee required 24.[2] Many states also require teachers to complete a fifth year of study or a master's degree after becoming certified. Additional requirements may also include U.S. citizenship, an oath of loyalty, or a health examination.

One consequence of the national dialogue on education during the early 1980s has been that all but seven states now require testing of teachers for initial certification (see the Teacher's Resource Guide for "States Requiring Testing for Initial Certification of Teachers"). States use either a standardized test (usually the NTE, formerly called the National Teacher Examination) or a test developed by outside consultants. Areas covered by the states' tests usually include basic skills, professional knowledge, and general knowledge. Also, many states require an on-the-job performance evaluation for certification.

There is a trend away from granting teaching certificates for life. Some states, for example, issue three- to five-year certificates, which may be renewed only with proof of coursework completed beyond the bachelor's degree. And, amid considerable controversy, Arkansas, Georgia, and Texas have enacted testing for recertification of experienced teachers.

While there is definitely a national movement to make certification requirements more stringent, the teacher shortage that began in the mid-1980s has resulted in increasing use of "alternative" certification. More than 20 states have developed some system of **alternative certification.** Since the fall of 1985, for example, New Jersey's Provisional Teaching Program has allowed people who have completed college but not a teacher education program to become teachers. Trainees must take 80 hours of instruction before the school year begins and complete about 200 hours of education classes after school and on weekends. During the 1989–90 school year, about one-third of New Jersey's new teachers went through the alternative-certification program.

The Los Angeles District Intern Program is another approach to alternative certification. After passing the National Teachers' Examination, participants receive only three weeks of training before the start of school. Once school begins, interns receive advice from mentor teachers and attend classes one afternoon a week throughout a two- or three-year period.

All but two states may grant certification to those who don't meet current requirements. Half of the states may even give a substandard credential to those who hold less than a bachelor's degree. Though strongly resisted by professional teacher organizations, alternative certification is likely to become even more widespread if the teacher shortage escalates during the 1990s.

Unfortunately, certification requirements differ from state to state, and they are frequently modified. To remain up-to-date on the requirements for the state in which you plan to teach, it is important that you keep in touch with your teacher placement office or certification officer at your college or university. You may also wish to refer to *Requirements for Certification for Elementary and Secondary Schools* (The University of Chicago Press), an annual publication that lists state-by-state certification requirements for teachers, counselors, librarians, and administrators. Or, you may contact the teacher certification office in the state where you plan to teach (see the Teacher's Resource Guide for a "Directory of State Teacher Certification Offices in the United States").

Well over half of the states are members of the **Interstate Certification Compact,** a reciprocity agreement whereby a certificate obtained in one state will be honored in another (see the Teacher's Resource Guide). If you plan to teach in a state other than the one in which you are currently studying, you should find out if both states have a reciprocity agreement.

Some time during your last term of study, you will need to file for certification. The certification officer at your college or university will verify to the state that you have met all the requirements for the certificate you are seeking; an application fee may also be required. You will receive the teaching certificate four to eight weeks after your application is submitted.

The National Teacher Examination

Currently, the **National Teacher Examination (NTE),** required in most states for initial certification, consists of tests of communication skills, general knowledge, and professional knowledge (see Figure 4.3). Each test is a separate two-hour examination. Specialty tests in 28 subject areas are also available.

In late 1988, Educational Testing Service (ETS), the developers of the NTE, announced plans to replace the examination with a more sophisticated battery of tests by 1992. The new testing system, currently being developed with input from the

National Education Association and the American Federation of Teachers, will consist of examinations administered at specific intervals over two or more years in a student's teacher education program and early teaching career.

In a 1990 report, *Working Papers Toward A New Generation of Teacher Assessments*, ETS announced that the successor to the NTE will consist of three "stages."

Stage I Tests   Stage I tests will assess the "enabling skills" or "basic skills" needed by beginning teachers in reading, writing, and mathematics. These tests will most likely be given early in a student's teacher education program. To help students pass the Stage I tests, ETS plans to provide computer-delivered instructional components that would consist of practice tests, a diagnostic skills assessment, and 20 to 30 hours of instructional modules.

FIGURE 4.3
The National Teacher Examination

The NTE consists of three tests organized according to the chart below.

Area Tested	Section (30 min. each)	Number of Questions
Communications Skills	Listening	40
	Reading	30
	Writing (multiple choice)	45
	Writing (essay)	essay
General Knowledge	Literature and Fine Arts	35
	Mathematics	25
	Science	30
	Social Studies	30
Professional Knowledge	Part I	35
	Part II	35
	Part III	35
	Part IV	35

Typical Questions from the Test of Professional Knowledge

1. ____   Which of the following is *not* part of the mastery learning approach to instruction? (A) Clearly specified objectives. (B) Preset mastery standards. (C) Additional time and help for those who don't achieve mastery. (D) Ability grouping.

2. ____   Which of the following is the best example of an extrinsic motivation? (A) Material reward such as a prize or money. (B) Opportunity to interact with friends. (C) Chance to participate in favorite activity. (D) Learning something that will help with a personal problem.

3. ____   John Dewey believed that (A) the teacher should try to structure the classroom like a democracy, (B) children should be allowed to do whatever they please, (C) students cannot learn much outside of the classroom, (D) students should not learn basic skills, (E) the school curriculum should be based on the entrance requirements of the best colleges and universities.

4. ____   You believe that one of your students is being physically abused at home. Legally, you should (A) do nothing, (B) tell your principal or a social worker what you believe is happening, (C) talk with the student and try to find out the truth, (D) visit the student's home and talk to a parent or guardian.

Note: The questions presented above are not from the NTE but are samples of the kind of questions found on the examinations.

Stage II Tests   Stage II tests will measure subject matter knowledge, pedagogy, and, to some extent, subject matter pedagogy. In most cases, Stage II tests will be taken upon completion of an undergraduate program. ETS plans to "modularize" the Stage II tests, allowing a state to select the modules that best match its regulations. The tests will have a core content module required by every state, with the remaining modules selected on an individual basis by the states. The format of these tests will include multiple-choice, short-answer, essay, and other types of performance responses. In addition, interactive video, computer simulations, and other new assessment techniques may be used in Stage II.

Stage III Assessment   According to ETS, Stage III will be a "performance-based assessment system," not a "test." Stage III will involve the assessment of actual teaching skills of the beginning teacher. The test will focus on planning for instruction, implementing instruction, classroom management, and evaluating student progress and instructional effectiveness. Moreover, the test will assess the teacher's sensitivity to developmental levels and cultural differences among students. Classroom observations conducted by state and local personnel will be the main component of Stage III. The observations will be supplemented by work samples in the form of lesson plans, for example, and structured interviews. Following the Stage III assessments (which normally will be completed by the end of the first year of teaching), the state will make a decision about whether to grant a license to teach.

FINDING YOUR FIRST TEACHING JOB

During the last year of your teacher education program, you will probably become increasingly concerned about finding a teaching position. The "Job Search—A Timetable Checklist" presented in the Teacher's Resource Guide may help you plan your job search. Through systematic preparation a few months before graduation, you can maximize your chances of landing a position that suits you. In addition, such preparation will give you greater control of your professional future and ensure that your first year of teaching is rewarding.

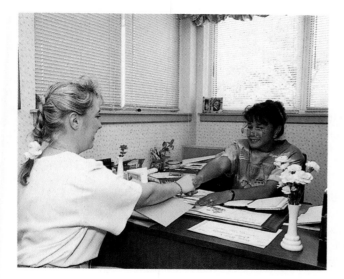

Signing a contract to teach in a school district of your choice is a welcome, and often well-earned, reward for your job-search efforts. With information, planning, and perseverance, those efforts can be both efficient and fruitful.

The Teacher's Resource Guide contains a chart showing a sequence of job search strategies that nearly every applicant for a teaching position should follow (see "Job Search: A Sequence of Planned Strategies"). In the remainder of this section we will discuss five critical steps in that sequence: finding out about teaching vacancies, preparing a résumé, writing letters of inquiry and letters of application, being interviewed, and selecting a position.

Finding Out about Teaching Vacancies

There are many ways to find out about teaching vacancies, some worth pursuing more than others.

College Placement Services   Your college or university probably has a **placement service** designed to help graduates find jobs. If your school is large enough, it may have a placement service devoted exclusively to locating positions for teachers. Each year, placement services receive hundreds of job vacancy notifications, most from school districts within the state. On a regular basis, placement offices usually publish lists of vacancies, which are posted and, in many cases, mailed to students who have registered with the office and set up a credentials file.

A **credentials file** (known as placement papers at some institutions) usually includes the following: background information on the applicant, the type of position sought, a list of courses taken, performance evaluations by the applicant's cooperative teacher, and three or more letters of recommendation. With each job application, the candidate requests that his or her credentials be sent to the appropriate person at the school district, or the school district itself may request the applicant's papers. Placement offices usually charge a small fee for each time a candidate's papers are sent out.

When selecting individuals to write letters of recommendation, select those who have recently had the opportunity to evaluate your abilities and character. Your education professors, subject area professors, and employers would be appropriate persons to ask to write a recommendation. When you make your request, tell the person the kind of position you are looking for and offer any information he or she might need to write the letter. Also, supply the letter writer with a stamped, addressed envelope and the placement form on which the letter is to be written.

A job announcement describes the position and its requirements and provides the name and address of the individual to contact at the school district. For each position you are interested in, send a letter of application to the appropriate person along with your résumé. In addition, you may have your placement office send your credentials file.

Placement offices also frequently set up on-campus interviews between candidates and representatives of school district personnel departments. The office will announce the date and time when a particular school district representative will be interviewing. Interested candidates then schedule an appointment with the placement office.

State Department of Education Employment Offices   Many state departments of education will help teachers locate positions. Like college and university placement offices, states publish lists of job openings, which are then distributed to registered candidates. Since most of these states will assist out-of-state candidates, you can register in more than one state.

Personal Networking   There is considerable truth to the well-known maxim that *it's who you know* that is important in landing the right job. Personal contacts can be a very effective source of information about openings, and a contact might even be able to help you get an interview. It makes sense, then, to let people know you're looking for a job—friends, teachers at schools you've attended, faculty at the school where you student teach, and people you meet at workshops and conferences.

Newspapers   For the most part, teaching vacancies are listed in the help-wanted ads of newspapers only during times of acute teacher shortages. However, a few large-city newspapers, especially the Sunday edition of the *New York Times,* regularly carry such notices. In addition, *Education Week,* a weekly newspaper devoted to educational news, occasionally carries notices of teaching vacancies.

Commercial Placement Services   These agencies will, for a fee ranging from 6 to 10 percent of your first year's salary, help you locate a teaching position. You need to pay the fee only if you accept a position that you learned about through the agency. Actually, most of the information provided by commercial placement services can be obtained on one's own. As a job-hunting strategy, commercial agencies are seldom worth the money.

Letters to School Districts   Though a mass mailing of your résumé to all school superintendents in your state might seem like a good idea, it usually isn't. As one director of a placement office put it: "The unsolicited shotgun approach to job hunting—mass mailing to any and all school systems—is the most popular and least effective strategy."[3] It is possible, however, that if the shortage of teachers becomes more acute during the 1990s, mass mailings might become more effective, particularly if your specialty is in an area currently experiencing a critical shortage or if you are willing to relocate to sections of the country that typically have more difficulty attracting teachers.

Preparing Your Résumé

A résumé presents a concise summary of an individual's professional experiences and education. Résumés must be typed and preferably no longer than one page, two pages at most. Though there is no right way to prepare a résumé, it should present—in a neat, systematic way—key information that will help an employer determine your suitability for a particular position. Since your résumé will most likely be your first contact with an employer, it must make a good impression. If your résumé contains errors, is poorly organized, or looks messy, an employer will likely conclude that your performance on the job would have the same qualities.

Ordinarily, a résumé contains the following information:

- Personal data
- Education
- Certificates held
- Experience
- Activities and interests
- Honors and offices held
- Professional memberships
- References

Figure 4.4 is a résumé prepared by Kevin A. Walker. When preparing your résumé, use Walker's as a model. His is clear, well organized, and presents an overall attractive appearance. Depending upon your background, you may wish to use categories other than those Walker has used. If you have no honors or professional memberships to list, it would be best to omit those categories. To prepare an effective résumé, read "15 Rules for Effectively Updating Your Résumé" in the Teacher's Resource Guide.

FIGURE 4.4
Résumé

KEVIN A. WALKER

Personal Data

Born: August 20, 1971.
Address and Phone: 811 West Indiana
Urbana, Illinois 61801
(217) 344-1234

Education

B.A., Secondary English Education, University of Illinois at Urbana,
June 1992.

Certificates Held

English/Language Arts, 9–12; Journalism.

Experience

Student Teaching, Willow Senior High School, 123 Rand Road,
Urbana, Illinois 61801, Spring 1992. Cooperating teacher: Mrs.
Hilda Walker.
Volunteer Telephone Counselor, Urbana Crisis Hotline, June 1989–
June 1990.
Summer Recreation Director, Urbana Park District, Summer 1990
and 1991. Directed summer recreation program comprised of 10
counselors and 140 elementary-aged boys and girls.

Activities and Interests

Urbana Heritage Association, Treasurer, 1991.
Center for Performing Arts, Student Representative.
Hobbies: Jogging, Physical Fitness, Piano, Fishing, Water Skiing.

Honors

B.A. with Honors, University of Illinois, June 1992.
Illinois State Scholarship, 1988–1992.

Professional Memberships

National Council of Teachers of English.

References

References and credentials file available upon request.

Writing Letters of Inquiry and Letters of Application

As a job seeker, you will most likely have occasion to write two kinds of letters: letters of inquiry and letters of application. A **letter of inquiry** is used to determine if a school district has, or anticipates, any teaching vacancies. This type of letter states your general qualifications and requests procedures to be followed in making a formal application (see Figure 4.5). A letter of inquiry should also include your résumé as well as a self-addressed, stamped envelope for the school district's convenience.

Be prepared not to receive a reply for each letter of inquiry you send out. Because of the volume of mail they receive requesting information on vacancies, many school districts are unable to respond to all inquiries.

FIGURE 4.5
Letter of Inquiry

811 West Indiana
Urbana, Illinois 61801
May 5, 1992

Dr. Mary Bond
Office of Personnel Services
Metropolitan School District
Wacker Office Building
773 Ranier Avenue
Seattle, Washington 98504

Dear Dr. Bond:

    This letter is to express my interest in a teaching position in the Seattle Metropolitan School District. In particular, I would like to know if you anticipate any vacancies in secondary English for fall of 1992. This June I will receive my B.A. in secondary English education from the University of Illinois at Urbana.

    As a student teacher this spring semester, I taught American literature to gifted junior students and remedial writing to freshmen. I also assisted my cooperating teacher in the design, layout, and production of a school literary magazine.

    My education at Illinois, I feel, has prepared me well to teach today's high school students. In addition to several courses in English and American literature, I have had a course in teaching secondary-level writing and two courses in secondary reading. If possible, I would like a position that would enable me to become involved in developing a school-wide reading program.

    Enclosed you will find my résumé, which provides additional information about my experiences and activities. If there are any positions for which you think I might be suited, please send application materials in the enclosed stamped, self-addressed envelope. I appreciate your consideration, and I look forward to hearing from you.

Sincerely,

Kevin A. Walker

Kevin A. Walker

FIGURE 4.6
Letter of Application

811 West Indiana
Urbana, Illinois 61801
May 20, 1992

Dr. John Smith
Associate Superintendent for Personnel
Urban School District
720 Cedar Street
Springfield, Illinois 62777

Dear Dr. Smith:

This letter is in support of my application for the position in the English department at Urban High School. This June I will receive my B.A. in secondary English education from the University of Illinois at Urbana.

As my enclosed résumé indicates, I just completed my student teaching at Willow Senior High School in Urbana. During that eight-week period, I taught American literature to gifted junior students and remedial composition to freshmen. I also worked with my cooperating teacher, Mrs. Hilda Walker, on Willow High's literary magazine.

As a result of my rewarding experiences at Willow High and in light of my academic record, I believe I could make a significant contribution to Urban High's educational program.

I have arranged for my credentials to be forwarded from my placement office. If you require additional information of any sort, please feel free to contact me. At your convenience, I am available for an interview in Springfield. In advance, I thank you for your consideration.

Sincerely,

Kevin A. Walker

Kevin A. Walker

A **letter of application** indicates your interest in a particular position and outlines your qualifications for that job. As most districts have several vacancies at any given time, it is important that the first sentence of your letter refer to the specific position for which you are applying. The body of the letter should then highlight why you would be an excellent choice to fill that position. Also, inform the reader that your credentials file will be sent upon request or is being sent by your placement office. Close the letter by expressing your availability for an interview. (See Figure 4.6.)

Being Interviewed

The interview is one of the most important steps in your search for an appropriate position. You will find that districts handle interviews differently. Some ask a set of structured questions of all candidates; others hold interviews that are more informal

CONSIDER THIS . . .

How Can You Prepare for Your Interview?

The following questions were gathered from school hiring officials and are representative of those that you are likely to encounter in your job interviews.

Circle the *one* question in each section that you feel *least* prepared to answer and develop answers on a separate sheet.

Motivation/Experience/Training

1. Tell us about yourself.
2. Why did you enter the field of teaching?
3. What experiences have you had related to teaching?
4. What qualities do you have that make you an effective teacher?
5. What grade levels or subjects do you prefer to teach?
6. Have you taught or are you interested in teaching combination classes?
7. Do you have experience with special education students?
8. Why do you want to teach in our school district?
9. Do you have (multicultural, urban, learning problems) teaching experience?
10. What do you remember most about your own education?

Teaching Effectiveness

11. How do you meet the range of skills and needs commonly present in a classroom?
12. When do you use an individual, group and/or whole class teaching approach? Why?
13. Let's imagine we are going to observe a teacher teaching a lesson. I tell you in advance to expect a superb lesson. What would you expect to see in that lesson?
14. If a teacher wants to be sure pupils will learn a skill to be taught, what should he/she be sure to do when teaching?
15. How do you diagnose your students' needs?
16. How do you make sure your lessons are taught at the correct level?
17. How do you stimulate active participation in the classroom?
18. How would you use parents in the classroom?

Teacher Planning/Preparation

19. What kinds of planning do you see a teacher doing?
20. How do you plan for a year? a week? a day?
21. How do you know what you will cover?

Classroom Management/Discipline

22. What are some characteristics of a well-managed classroom?
23. Talk to us about classroom control.
24. What discipline methods work for you?
25. What is your primary goal with student discipline?
26. What are some examples of rules you would have in your classroom?
27. How would you be sure your rules are carried out?
28. How much responsibility for their learning do you feel students should have to take?
29. Are you a "let 'em go to the pencil sharpener whenever they want" type of person or a "raise your hand and ask permission" type of person?
30. What types of rewards and consequences would you use?
31. Describe your most difficult student discipline situation and how you handled it.

Staff Development/Professional Growth

32. What do you see yourself doing over the course of the next several years to improve your abilities as a professional?
33. What professional development topics most interest you?

Staff Rapport/Relationships

34. As a teacher new to a school, what would you see yourself doing to contribute to healthy staff relationships and to become part of the staff?
35. What should a principal expect from teachers?
36. What should teachers expect from the principal?

Grading Systems

37. What grading system works for you?
38. Under what conditions, if any, would most of your pupils receive D's and F's? How and why could this happen?

Closing Comments/Questions

39. What additional talents and skills do you have?
40. What extracurricular activities can you supervise?
41. Do you have questions or additional comments for us?

Source: C. Bruce Johnston, "Practice Makes Perfect: Sample Interview Questions," *1991 ASCUS Annual: A Job Search Handbook for Educators* (Evanston, Ill.: Association for School, College and University Staffing, Inc.), 18. Used with permission.

And now, Miss Miller, would you just briefly tell me your methods for teaching reading, your philosophy of education, your views on testing, your ideas on discipline in the classroom, your opinions about homework, where you think education is heading in this country and how you would upgrade math skills in our school should you be hired?.....

sipress

and open-ended. In some districts, you might be interviewed by the principal only; in others, the superintendent, the principal, and the department chairperson might interview you; and in still others, classroom teachers might interview you. Regardless of format, the interview enables the district to obtain more specific information regarding your probable success as an employee, and it gives you an opportunity to ask questions about what it is like to teach in the district.

When you are interviewed you may expect the session to begin with a short period of light conversation in order to put you at ease and to begin to develop rapport between you and the interviewer(s). The interviewer will then typically present a brief overview of the community, the school district, and the position to be filled. Following this, you will be asked a series of questions. Figure 4.7 indicates the topics which a group of newly hired teachers were asked to discuss during their interviews.

In addition to responding to questions in these areas, you will certainly have the opportunity to ask questions about the position. It is important that you have some questions prepared in advance; these will demonstrate your interest in working in the district. (For suggestions about appropriate questions, see "Critical Information to Know About School Districts" in the Teacher's Resource Guide.)

At the conclusion of the interview, you may wish to indicate your availability for additional interviews with district personnel. Inform the interviewer how you may be contacted, and then thank him or her for considering your application.

Accepting an Offer

One day—after preparing an attractive résumé, setting up a credentials file, sending off numerous letters of application, and carefully preparing for interviews—you are notified that a school district would like to hire you. Your job search efforts have paid off!

At first you will certainly feel justifiably proud and excited. In the competition for positions, you have been successful. Beneath these feelings, however, may be some

FIGURE 4.7 **Frequent Interview Topics**

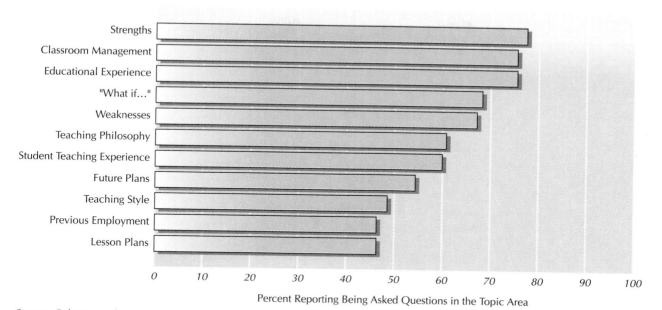

Source: Rebecca Anthony and Steve Head, "National Survey of Recruitment Practices," *ASCUS Staffer: Newsletter of the Association for School, College and University Staffing, Inc.,* Winter 1990, p. 10.

doubt and anxiety about whether this position is the best for you. Accepting your first teaching position is a major personal and professional step. Before signing a contract with a district, then, you should carefully consider some job-related questions, such as the following:

- In regard to my abilities and education, am I suited to this position?
- Would I like to work with this school's students, administrative staff, and teachers?
- Is the salary I am being offered sufficient?
- Will this position likely be permanent?

In addition, think about the lifestyle you would have if you accepted the position. In this regard, ask yourself these questions:

- Would I like to live in this community? Is its quality of life appealing?
- Would the cost of living in this community enable me to live comfortably?
- Are opportunities for continuing education readily available?
- What cultural and recreational activities are available in the community?

You must decide to accept or reject the offer after carefully considering the preceding questions and the possibility that you will receive another, more attractive, offer. If you accept, you will need to return a signed contract to the district along with a short letter confirming your acceptance. As a professional courtesy, you should notify other districts to which you have applied that you have accepted a position elsewhere.

FIVE-MINUTE FOCUS   It is the first day of school and you are about to begin your career as a teacher. Describe what that first day would be like if it turned out perfectly. Date your journal entry and write for five minutes.

BEGINNING TO TEACH

Once you accept the professional challenge of teaching, it is important to prepare well in advance of the first day of school. During these weeks, you will want to review the texts your students will use and develop general strategies for presenting that material. This interlude before school begins is a critical time. When school is underway, you will find that your days are full and frequently hectic—with very little time available for study.

In addition to reviewing the material you will teach, you should use this time to find out all you can about the school's students and the surrounding community. Perhaps you can find another teacher or counselor who might be willing to spend some time orienting you to the culture of the school. If your class rosters have been finalized, you could use this time to examine students' cumulative record folders. Additional, specific information about the students you will teach will enable you to plan more effectively.

The First Day

Nearly every beginning teacher has found the first day of school both exciting and frightening. Such feelings are a natural part of beginning one's professional career. We believe that a beginning teacher who is not anxious about performing well probably lacks the sensitivity and commitment to become an effective teacher. Though you may not realize it while you are waiting for the bell to ring, signaling the start of school, the nervous energy you feel will probably enhance your performance on that first day.

The need for a good beginning is true in all human endeavors, but especially so with teaching. If you can create a pleasant, work-oriented climate on the first day, this will contribute greatly to your success during the remainder of the year.

On the first day, students are eager to learn and are hopeful that the year will be a productive one. In addition, nearly all students will be naturally receptive to what you have to say. To them, you are a new, unknown quantity, and one of their initial concerns is to find out what kind of a teacher you will be. It is therefore critical that you be well organized and ready to take charge. Use this initial period to your advantage, and it will be you, not your students, who determines what classroom life will be like that year.

As we have suggested in earlier chapters, there is no recipe or set of easy-to-follow steps that ensures success in the classroom. In short, there is no right way to act when you meet your students for the first time. However, the guidelines in Table 4.3 and the advice given in the "Teachers on Teaching" feature at the end of this chapter should prove helpful in planning for that moment. Be assured, too, that you will learn how to implement classroom skills as you pursue additional coursework in your teacher education program.

TABLE 4.3   Guidelines for the First Days of School

General Guidelines for First-Day Activities

Maintain a whole-group focus.

Stay in charge of all of the students all of the time.

Keep students involved; avoid dead time.

Plan adequate time for teaching classroom procedures and rules.

Plan activities that will allow students to experience success.

Establish a content focus, some positive expectations.

Provide variety, changes of pace.

Presenting Procedures and Rules

1. Teach rules and procedures systematically using:
   - Explanation: definition in concrete terms, discussion of rationale, demonstration, examples of specific behaviors.
   - Rehearsal or practice, using cues or signals (e.g., bell, hand raised, certain word) when appropriate.
   - Feedback: specific and accurate information about compliance.
   - Review and reteach, if necessary.

2. Sequence your teaching of rules and procedures so that they are presented to students as they are needed. Don't overload students the first day with discussion of procedures that will not be used the first week.

3. Discuss school rules and policies regarding other school areas (playground, lunchroom, hallways) prior to their use. Give feedback on students' behavior when they return.

4. Remember that a necessary and important part of the teaching of rules and procedures is consistent enforcement and use of consequences (positive as well as negative).

5. After the first day, review and reinforce procedures and rules, and teach additional procedures as they are needed.

Suggested Activities for the First Day of School

1. Teach classroom rules and procedures.
2. Introduce students to important features of the room.
3. Teach class routines, such as warm-up or end-of-day routines.
4. Show materials and supplies needed.
5. Conduct a get-acquainted activity.
6. Do *simple* academic activities, such as review.
7. Introduce an exciting new topic of study.
8. Play a game students already know or can easily learn.
9. Do a *simple* art or craft activity.

Source: "Guidelines for the First Day of School" (Austin, Tex.: Research on Classroom Learning and Teaching Project, The Research and Development Center for Teacher Education, University of Texas, September 1982, mimeographed). Used with permission.

Advice from Experienced Teachers

In our work with schools and teachers, we have gathered recommendations on preparing for the first day from experienced elementary through secondary teachers in urban, suburban, and rural schools. Their recommendations fall into three categories: planning, managing, and following up.

Planning   Without exception, experienced teachers stress the importance of planning. As the following teachers put it:

> An important part of preparation is having the room and all your materials ready. Ask yourself, "Where do I want students to sit?" "Do I have all the supplies I need?" You should be one-hundred percent prepared on the first day.
> —High-school mathematics teacher

> From the start, plan to get students involved. On the first day there are a lot of clerical, paperwork-type things that need to be done—distributing books, lockers, fee receipts, etc. *Before* taking care of those things, give students a short assignment or some task. With their attention focused, they're less likely to fool around. They'll know that in your class they're expected to work.
> —Middle-school science teacher

> It really helps on the first day to have plenty of material to cover and things to do. I'd recommend taking the material you plan to cover that day and doubling it. It's better to have too much than to run out. What you don't use the first day, you use the next. It takes a while to get a feeling for how fast the kids are going to go.
> —Third-grade teacher

Managing   Experienced teachers are unanimous in pointing out the importance of establishing effective management practices on the first day. Two of their recommendations follow.

> From the beginning, it's important to do what you're there to do—that's teach. Teach the class something, maybe review material they learned last year. That lets them know that you're in charge, you expect them to learn. They'll look to you for direction—as long as you give it to them, you're fine.
> —Junior-high language arts teacher

> The first day is a good time to go over rules and procedures for the year. But don't overdo it. Be very clear and specific about your expectations for classroom behavior.
> —Sixth-grade teacher

Following Up   Several experienced teachers stressed the importance of following up on procedures established during the first day.

> What you want to establish on the first day is a businesslike atmosphere. But you have to keep that going beyond the first day. Don't let up. Don't get lazy. Remember, there are 179 days left.
> —High-school mathematics teacher

> What I've found very helpful is to get in touch with all my kids' parents right after the first day. I tell them a bit about how I run my class, what we're going to do that year, and how pleased I am to have their child in my room. I keep it upbeat, very positive. We're going to have a great year! It takes time to do that—everyone's so busy at the start of the year—but it's worth it. It pays off during the rest of the year.
> —First-grade teacher

Keepers of the Dream

Shirley A. Rau
1991 Idaho Teacher of the Year
Nampa High School, Nampa

hirley A. Rau, the 1991 Idaho Teacher of the Year, offers straightforward advice to those interviewing for their first teaching position: "Be honest. Talk about specific things you've done and your ideas about students. Above all else, be as honest as you can."

Her advice for that all-important first day of teaching is also concise and to-the-point.

It's important on the first day to start building a community of learners. Rather than simply going over class rules, engage students immediately in a typical activity—talking, reading, writing about ideas. It's a great day for teachers to listen to students' ideas. Provide them with a forum so you can learn about their needs, the directions they would like the class to take during the year.

Rau teaches senior English at Nampa High School in Nampa, Idaho, serves as head of the English Department, and coaches the school's two-time national champion cheerleading squad. In 1989, she was named Cheerleading Coach of the Year by the International Cheerleading Foundation.

Rau received a Bachelor of Arts in Education from Idaho State University in 1978 and a Master of Liberal Arts from the Middlebury College Bread Loaf School of English in 1985. She has presented workshops on learning styles, cooperative learning, and women and writing at state and national conferences.

"Actually, I wasn't going to become a teacher when I entered college," she says. "I was going to be a pharmacy major. In fact, I was doing my practicum—counting pills, washing bottles—and I just couldn't imagine myself doing that for the rest of my life. I knew teaching was for me."

Rau credits her fellow teachers for making her first year of teaching a success.

That was an exciting year. I was on a staff with a group of teachers who really supported me. They

made it a part of their day to come into my room and see how I was doing and to share things. They made it easy to ask questions and work with them. They started me on the track of cooperating with other teachers and sharing my successes and failures with them.

They did such a good job of taking care of each other that my needs were always met. I had plenty of supplies, counseling help, administrative help. The school was a community. Anything I needed to be successful was provided.

Not every year of teaching was as successful as that first year, Rau admits.

About six years into my teaching career, I had a difficult year—a tough class, a difficult cheerleading squad, a difficult administrator. I thought about leaving the profession. I had to think through what I was doing. I had to look for ways to love teaching. Instead of just *being* in love with teaching, I had to look for ways to *build* some love so I could continue. I had to reassess what I had loved for so many years and ask myself whether I could begin to love it again.

I kept a log that year. I kept notes about the things that bothered me and the things I could celebrate, the small victories. During the summer I went back and looked over that log and reflected on it. That's how I made my decision to continue. I was able to look back and see a pattern of successes that outweighed everything else.

Rau is a reflective teacher who also encourages her students to be reflective. "I share the power of language with my students," she says. "I try to help my students find a voice in silence. My classroom is a community of readers, writers, and learners—my students are the creators, questioners, and thinkers."

> *" Above All Else, Be as Honest as You Can. "*

ON-THE-JOB RELATIONSHIPS

How successful your first year of teaching is will be determined not only by the relationships you develop with your pupils but also by the contacts you have with other staff, parents, and the community. All four of these groups can contribute significantly to your effectiveness as a teacher.

Relationships with Colleagues and Other Staff

Each working day, you will be in close contact with other teachers and staff members. It will definitely be to your advantage to establish friendly, professional relationships with all of them. During your first few months at the school, it would be wise to communicate to colleagues that you are willing to learn all you can about your new job. You can do this by listening carefully to what other staff say about their work and paying attention to how they carry out their responsibilities.

In addition to being an astute observer on the job, it is important to indicate your willingness to cooperate and to be a "team player." In most schools it is common practice to give junior faculty members less desirable assignments, reserving the more desirable ones for senior faculty. By demonstrating your willingness to take on these responsibilities with good humor and to give them your best effort, you will do much to establish yourself as a valuable faculty member. Taking into account your assigned duties, you might consider volunteering for a few of the numerous tasks that must be done to make any school's program a success: sponsoring a club, helping with a Parent-Teacher Association program, organizing a fund-raising drive, or helping with the library inventory.

It is important that you get along with your fellow staff members. Some you will enjoy being around; others you may wish to avoid. Some will express obvious enthusiasm for teaching; others may be bitter and pessimistic about their work. Be pleasant and friendly with both types. Accept their advice with a smile, and then act on that which is worthwhile.

Though you may find some staff members who are openly critical of certain school policies and practices, avoid expressing any criticisms of the school until you are more established as a group member. By withholding negative comments, you might acquire additional information that would cause you to change your opinions. Act in a manner that will cause others to view you as a task-oriented professional.

Relationships with Administrators

Pay particular attention to the relationships you develop with administrators, department heads, and supervisors. Though your contacts with them will not be as frequent as with other teachers, they can do much to ensure your initial success. They are well aware of the difficulties you might encounter as a first-year teacher, and they are there to help you succeed.

The principal of your new school will, most likely, be the one to introduce you to other teachers, members of the administrative team, and staff. He or she should inform you if there are assistant principals or (on the high school level) department heads who can help you enforce school rules, keep accurate records, and obtain supplies, for example. The principal may also assign an experienced teacher to serve as a mentor during your first year. In addition, your principal will indicate his or her availability to discuss issues of concern, and you should not hesitate to do so if the need arises.

Your relationships with parents are a key factor in your quest to become an effective teacher. Parents and other concerned members of the community can become valuable allies in the teaching-learning process, in problem-solving, and in multicultural awareness programs.

Relationships with Parents

Establishing friendly relationships with your pupils' parents can be an important component of your success as a teacher. A Metropolitan Life Survey of 1,002 new teachers who began teaching in 1990–91, for example, revealed that 91 percent "strongly agreed" and 9 percent "somewhat agreed" that teachers need to work well with their students' parents. In reality, teachers and parents are partners—both concerned with the learning and growth of their children. It is important that you become acquainted with parents at school functions, at meetings of the Parent-Teacher Association (PTA or PTO), at various community events and in other social situations. To develop good communication with parents, you will need to be sensitive to their needs, such as their work schedules and the language spoken in their home.

You will find that parents differ greatly in terms of how much they wish to be (or *can* be) involved with their children's school. Some parents, such as the author of the following letter, monitor quite closely their children's education:

> The time my son spends in fifth grade seems important as a period of transition. Ninth grade seems so far away, but middle school seems right upon us. And I am concerned that he will be able to move from elementary school into middle school successfully.
>
> I like the idea of the longer school day and more requirements for graduation. Right now, as a fifth-grader, my child is a little weak in math. When he starts the ninth grade, he already will know that he has to take math all through high school, so it is very important to me that in the next four years his math skills are improved.
>
> We want him to be involved in as many things as possible when he starts high school. As a fifth-grader, he is interested in band and hears a lot about student government from his older sister, who is a junior.
>
> We expect that by the time our fifth-grader reaches the ninth grade the schools will give a lot of attention to technology and computer training. Right now, he is very enthusiastic about school; we certainly hope that will last.
>
> We were a little surprised by how much our involvement in what he is doing could make a difference. We plan to keep in touch with the teacher and to attend all the programs the school sets up.[4]

FACT FINDING

How Does Parental Involvement Affect Student Achievement?

A survey by the National Center for Education Statistics revealed a direct relationship between grades and parental involvement in students' lives at home and school. High parental involvement included knowing the child's whereabouts, communicating on a daily basis, and tracking the child's school progress.

Parental Involvement in Relation to Self-Reported Student Achievement

Survey Questions Asked of Students	Percentage of Affirmative Responses to Survey Question, by Students' Self-Reported Grade			
	Received Mostly A Grade	Received Mostly B Grade	Received Mostly C Grade	Received Mostly D Grade
Parents almost always know child's whereabouts	88%	81%	72%	61%
Child talks with mother or father almost every day	75	67	59	45
Parents attend PTA meetings at least once in a while	25	22	20	15
Mother keeps close track of how well child does in school	92	89	84	80
Father keeps close track of how well child does in school	85	79	69	64
Child lives in household with both parents	80	71	64	60

Source: National Center for Education Statistics *Bulletin,* "The Relationship of Parental Involvement to High-School Grades." Education Department (March 1985).

Other parents will be known to you only by the fact that they sign their children's report cards and other routine school forms. For this reason, it is important that you consider taking the initiative and keeping parents informed of events in your classroom via a monthly newsletter. Parents greatly appreciate hearing about the good things their children are doing; unfortunately, though, parents are usually contacted only when their children are in trouble. For this reason, perhaps, 14 percent of the beginning teachers in the Metropolitan Life Survey sample referred to above "strongly agreed" and 56 percent "somewhat agreed" that too many parents treat schools and teachers as adversaries. To improve the perceptions parents have of schools and teachers, you might consider making it a point to telephone at least one parent each day to report something positive.

By maintaining contact with parents, you can significantly enhance the achievement of your students. A study of 60,000 high school students, for example, revealed that 32 percent of the students with an A average said their parents helped them decide what courses to take; only 13 percent of the C students reported the same. In the same way, 66 percent of the A students said their parents met with or telephoned a teacher when an academic problem arose; less than 50 percent of the C students reported the same parental involvement.[5] Research has also shown, for example, that parental involvement is a key factor in children's reading achievement and reading group placement.[6]

While teachers know that students learn more when parents participate, and most parents do wish to be more involved, there is a gap between the rhetoric of parental involvement and its practice. The rise in single-parent families and families in which both parents work has left parents with very little time to supervise their children's studies. For this reason, it is important that you be willing to take the extra time and energy to ask for parental help; most parents will gratefully respond.

Strategies for Involving Parents

- Ask parents to read aloud to the child, to listen to the child read, and to sign homework papers.
- Encourage parents to drill students on math and spelling and to help with homework lessons.
- Encourage parents to discuss school activities with their children and suggest ways parents can help teach their children at home. For example, a simple home activity might be alphabetizing books; a more complex one would be using kitchen supplies in an elementary science experiment.
- Send home suggestions for games or group activities related to the child's schoolwork that parent and child can play together.[7]
- Encourage parents to participate in school activities such as a sports booster club, career day, and music and drama events.
- Involve parents in their children's learning by having them co-sign learning contracts and serve as guest speakers.

Relationships with Students

Needless to say, the relationships you establish with students will be among the most important (and complex) you will have as a teacher. As the range of topics addressed by this book suggests, these relationships will have many dimensions. You must see that each student learns as much as possible; this is your primary responsibility as a professional teacher. You will need to establish relationships with a great diversity of students based on mutual respect, caring, and concern. Without attention to this personal realm, your effectiveness as a teacher will be significantly limited. You will also have numerous legal responsibilities to your students, which are explained in Chapter 9. In addition, you will act in the role of disciplinarian in your classroom and you will be a role model to your students, who will be influenced by your attitudes.

Relationships with the Community

You should remember that the community provides significant support for the education of its young people. In fact, up until 1980, most of the money to support schools came from the local communities. Though federal and state regulations set general guidelines for schools, it is the local community that actually determines what a school is like.

Most communities hold high expectations of teachers. Don't view these expectations as an imposition, however; see them as a sign that community members view teachers as leaders—not unlike physicians, members of the clergy, or lawyers. As a professional, it is important that you take an active part in community affairs and, if the occasion arises, take a stand in regard to political and moral issues. By participating fully in the life of the community in which you live, you will also make many important contacts. Some of these individuals, for example, may have expertise related to your specialty and may be willing to visit with your students.

OTHER CAREER OPPORTUNITIES IN EDUCATION

Our primary focus throughout this book is on becoming a professional teacher at the elementary through secondary levels. However, we wish to point out that there are a great many nonteaching jobs in education and education-related fields. Several of these were alluded to earlier: principal, assistant principal, librarian, and counselor. In addition, there are many jobs that, while removed from the world of the classroom, would nevertheless enable you to use your teaching skills. In fact, a sourcebook of career information, *New Roles for Educators*, suggests that "the usual concepts of careers in education should . . . be expanded to include the roles of federal and state government, community agencies, private industry, professional and education-related associations, foundations, study councils, and research organizations."[8]

In the following outline, we list several places other than schools where individuals with teaching backgrounds are often employed. We believe that the number of education-related careers will increase dramatically during the next two decades.

Alternative Careers in Education

Industry
- Publishers
- Educational materials and equipment suppliers
- Specialized educational service firms
- Communications industries
- Research and development firms
- Management consulting firms
- Education and training consultants
- Educational divisions of large corporations—Xerox, IBM, CBS, General Electric, Westinghouse, etc.

Government
- Federal agencies—U.S. Office of Education, Bureau of Prisons, Department of Labor, Office of Economic Opportunity, Department of Justice, Department of Health, Education and Welfare, etc.
- Federal programs—Bureau of Indian Affairs Schools, Bureau of Prisons Schools, Job Corps, Overseas Dependent Schools, Peace Corps, Teacher Corps, Upward Bound, VISTA, etc.
- Regional educational networks—Research and development centers, Regional educational laboratories, 16 clearinghouses of the Educational Resources Information Center (ERIC), etc.
- Jobs in state departments of education

Education-Related Associations
- Research centers and foundations
- Professional associations—National Council of Teachers of English, National Association of Mathematics Teachers, National Education Association, American Federation of Teachers, Phi Delta Kappa, Kappa Delta Pi, Educational Testing Service, etc.

Community Organizations

- Community action programs—Upward Bound, neighborhood health centers, legal services, aid to migrant workers, etc.
- Social service agencies—United Fund agencies, Boy Scouts, Girl Scouts, YMCA's and YWCA's, settlement houses, boys' and girls' clubs, etc.
- Adult education centers
- Museums
- Hospitals

FIVE-MINUTE FOCUS Select one of the areas from the list above and describe why your knowledge, skills, and attitudes might suit you for a career in that area. Date your journal entry and write for five minutes.

CAREER OPPORTUNITIES IN NONEDUCATION FIELDS

As a former teacher who went on to become vice president of a firm that trains clients in communication skills put it, "Those who can teach also can . . . sell, compute, write, design, organize, market, advertise, run day-care centers, start meals-on-wheels programs, set up business task forces, lead community projects, and so on, ad infinitum."[9] In short, teaching requires a wide variety of aptitudes and skills that are valuable assets in many careers. Effective teachers have organizational and administrative abilities, communication skills, leadership abilities, the ability to influence and motivate, and high levels of creativity.

If you are unable to find a desirable teaching position, or if, after a few years of teaching, you realize that teaching is not for you, you may join those educators who eventually pursue careers outside of teaching. The following four steps should help you make an effective career transition:

1. Identify the special skills and aptitudes you possess
2. Do research to find out which careers require those skills and aptitudes (The *Dictionary of Occupational Titles* [to be found at most libraries] lists over 30,000 careers and may give you some ideas)
3. Prepare a résumé and cover letter
4. Initiate an aggressive, creative job search campaign

If you need more guidance than these brief steps provide, several publications on career opportunities in noneducation fields are available.[10]

SUMMARY

This chapter has given you information and strategies to enable you to make a smooth transition from being a student to being a teacher. We first considered how to find out about current trends relating to teacher supply and demand and pointed out that there will be a steady increase in the need for new teachers throughout the 1990s.

Our look at teachers' salaries indicated that the financial rewards teachers receive are increasing. Base salaries are being pushed up, fringe benefits are increasing, and various programs to provide bonuses to teachers are being tried out.

Next, we discussed several steps to be followed in obtaining a teaching position: becoming certified, finding out about teaching vacancies, preparing a résumé, writing letters of inquiry and letters of application, being interviewed, and selecting a position.

We then presented several suggested guidelines for actually beginning to teach. We also discussed the importance of establishing positive relationships with other staff, parents, and the community. Finally, we took a brief look at other career opportunities in education and noneducation fields.

KEY TERMS AND CONCEPTS

teacher supply and demand, 94
fringe benefits, 97
teaching certificate, 100
alternative certification, 101
Interstate Certification Compact, 101

National Teacher Examination, 101
placement service, 104
credentials file, 104
letter of inquiry, 107
letter of application, 108

DISCUSSION QUESTIONS

1. Do you feel there are any limitations regarding the extent to which a teacher should become involved in community affairs? As a teacher, what community activities might you become involved in?
2. Based on current data for teacher supply and demand, what is the estimated need for teachers in the field that interests you? in the geographic region where you would like to settle? What is the average salary in that region?
3. Other than teaching on the elementary through secondary levels, what other careers do you think you might be suited for after receiving your teaching certificate?
4. Looking ahead to your first teaching assignment, do you anticipate any conflict in on-the-job relationships? Explain. How do you plan to handle these conflicts?
5. Next to the medical profession, the public sees teaching as the most demanding profession, yet the public has been reluctant to grant teachers higher salaries. Why do you think this is so?

APPLICATION ACTIVITIES

1. Help your instructor set up a series of role-play interview sessions during which some members of your class take the part of applicants for a teaching position and others act as personnel directors. If possible, exchange résumés. The remaining class members should observe the role-plays, noting strengths and weaknesses. Review the role-plays during postinterview discussions.
2. Arrange for a member of your school's placement office to visit your class and discuss procedures to be followed in obtaining a teaching position.
3. Invite a personnel director from a local school district to your class. Plan to have him or her address a set of predetermined concerns identified by your class.
4. Ask your instructor if he or she can arrange to have two or three persons who have pursued nonteaching careers in education visit with your class. What strategies did these individuals follow in order to obtain their positions? How satisfied are they with their career choices?

FIELD EXPERIENCES

1. Review the list of education-related careers on pages 120–121 and then visit one of the organizations mentioned. Talk to a person who can tell you what specific jobs might be appropriate for someone with a teaching certificate. Report your findings to the class.
2. If one of your education instructors can arrange it, observe the first day of classes at a local elementary, middle/junior, or high school. What strategies did the teachers use to begin the year on a positive, task-oriented note? What things would you have done differently? Why?
3. Visit a school and interview several teachers in regard to their relationships with parents and the community. To what extent and in what ways are teachers involved with parents? with the community? What recommendations do the teachers have for improving relationships between themselves and both groups?
4. Attend a meeting of the Parent-Teachers Organization at a school in your local community. After the meeting, interview a few parents for their perceptions of the school. In regard to the school's program, what are they most satisfied with? least satisfied with? Report your findings to the class.

SUGGESTED READINGS

The ASCUS Annual: A Job Search Handbook for Educators. Evanston, Ill.: Association for School, College, and University Staffing, Inc. *This excellent annual publication is available from the ASCUS office (1600 Dodge Avenue, S-330, Evanston, IL 60201-3451, (708) 864-1999).*

Emmer, Edmund and Carolyn Evertson, *How to Start the Year,* vols. I & II. New York: Prentice-Hall, 1990. *Presents a comprehensive, research-based set of strategies for beginning the new year. Volume I focuses on the elementary level; Volume II on the secondary.*

Howard, Edrice Margurite and Carol Weeg (eds.), *Teaching Abroad.* New York: Institute of International Education, 1988. *Part 1 describes teaching and administrative opportunities abroad. Part 2 lists nearly 200 study opportunities abroad for teachers and administrators.*

Kreider, Paul T. *The Interviewing Handbook for College Graduates.* San Anselmo, Calif.: KCE Publishing, 1981. *An excellent handbook designed to help the job applicant make the most of the interview opportunity.*

Pettus, Theodore, *One on One: Win the Interview, Win the Job.* New York: Random House, 1981. *Outlines a strategy for demonstrating to the interviewer that one is a top job candidate.*

Trimble, Richard M. *In the Classroom: Suggestions & Ideas for Beginning Teachers.* Lanham, Md: University Press of America, 1990. *An excellent set of strategies for meeting the challenges of beginning teaching.*

Tryneski, John (Ed.). *Requirements for Certification for Elementary and Secondary Schools.* Chicago: University of Chicago Press, 1991. *Since 1935, this annual publication has reported the certification requirements of the states.*

Webster, Steve. *Teach Overseas: The Educator's World-Wide Handbook and Directory to International Teaching in Overseas Schools, Colleges, and Universities.* New York: Maple Tree Publishing Company, 1984. *An excellent resource for those who desire the unique experience of teaching overseas.*

TEACHERS . . .

What advice would you give about being interviewed for a first-time teaching position?

My advice for those who are interviewing for their first teaching position is to be confident in yourself. I believe that while the interviewer has an agenda to discuss, he or she is looking to see how confident you are.

—Julie A. Addison
Rock Ridge Elementary School, Castle Rock, Colorado

Be confident and believe in yourself and what you can accomplish. You have to be yourself. Do not try to be someone or something that you think the interviewer wants for their school system. Honesty has to be observed so you each will be able to uphold your end of the contract.

—Suzanne Neal
William Woods College, Fulton, Missouri

Don't be negative. Negative people are a turnoff, especially in the teaching profession where adults are to work with young souls. Keep an open mind and be willing to accept a different grade level than the one you had your heart set on. Grade levels change yearly, a move easily made as you get used to your school. Questions you want to ask include these: What is the average class size? What is the discipline procedure at the school? Are students who fail every subject held back? Ask the principal what he [she] considers to be a good teacher. What extra duties are you expected to undertake?

I don't know anyone who likes to go on interviews. They are, at best, a learning experience. However, they are a necessary step toward teaching. If you want to teach, and it is really in your heart, whatever it takes to get there is worth it. I can't imagine any other job more rewarding!

One last thing: dress professionally! There is a time and place for everything.

—Jeanne Brostrom
Baldwin Park High School, Baldwin Park, California

Listen for the philosophy of the interviewer. Knowing his or her perspective on education will provide clues on the discipline, decision-making, and curriculum practices of the school—all of which affect a teacher's life on a daily basis.

—Olive Ann Slotta
Fred N. Thomas Career Education Center, Denver, Colorado

ON TEACHING

What sources of support helped you make the transition from student to teacher?

I was fortunate in that I did my student teaching at the same school where I was first assigned. This gave me the advantage of knowing some of the staff and many of the kids. I felt comfortable and welcomed, so the transition was quite easy. I also made sure I was as organized and prepared as possible for the opening day, which helped in my transition from student teacher to teacher.

This first teaching position was a half-time position, a wonderful way to break in to the teaching profession. It gave me time to stay organized and avoid the overwhelmed feeling many first-time teachers experience. It also gave me time to put extra effort into different programs, which was good for both the students and myself.

—Amy Orcutt
Green Gables Elementary School, Jefferson County, Colorado

The staff in my department assisted my teaching transition through their leadership and supportive attitude. Resources that assisted my success were training seminars and in-service workshops on classroom policy and techniques. Videos of other successful teachers were also a key resource.

—Gail Grau
Southwest State Texas University, San Marcos, Texas

During my first teaching assignment, I had a coordinator who met with me every Friday to go over the week's lesson plans. She also observed me quite regularly in the classroom and reported to the principal. My fellow teachers were also very supportive in letting me know the "routines" in that school, such as lunch procedure and checking out of materials.

—Rose Ann Blaschke
Vivian Elementary School, Lakewood, Colorado

In my teacher education program I received support from college instructors, cooperating teachers, the school principal, the school's staff and fellow teachers, my students, and the school secretary!

—Jennifer Cronk
Rocky Mountain Hebrew Academy, Denver, Colorado

CHAPTER

5

Schools and Society

*S*ociety can survive only if there exists among its members a significant degree of homogeneity; education perpetuates and reinforces this homogeneity by fixing in the child, from the beginning, the essential similarities collective life demands.

Emile Durkheim
Education and Sociology

Rick Warren has taught social studies at Hilltop High School for three years. Hilltop is located in an affluent suburb in a metropolitan area of the Northeast. The school has an enrollment of just under 2,000 students, most of whom are from families that are upper middle-class and above. Typical occupations of Hilltop parents are corporate lawyer, plastic surgeon, advertising executive, stock broker, and television producer. Some students are from families that are not as affluent—the son of the school superintendent and the daughter of a building contractor, for example.

Rick is married and has a nine-year-old son. He and his family live in a nearby suburb. His approach to the social studies is to teach students the important role they can play in addressing societal problems. He believes teachers must raise their students' level of awareness regarding societal inequities and motivate them to reduce those inequities. On one occasion, he even had two homeless persons visit his classes.

Rick's teaching strategies are varied and innovative. Students often participate in small-group projects, simulations, role-plays, and classroom debates on societal issues. Rick is a Vietnam veteran and frequently draws from his Vietnam experiences to illustrate some of the "errors" the United States has made in its foreign policy.

The reactions of Rick's colleagues to his methods have been mixed. Those who support him point to high levels of student involvement and learning that goes beyond the textbook. Last year, in fact, students voted Rick "Teacher of the Year." Other teachers, however, believe Rick uses the classroom as a "soapbox" to express his political views. Without apology, they maintain that Hilltop High parents (and students) want an education that will enable the students to get into the better colleges and universities—not to become social activists.

Since the Persian Gulf War, discussion among Hilltop teachers about Rick's teaching methods has increased. Rick and his students followed the war very closely, and a few of his students participated in an antiwar rally at a nearby college. "That was history in the making, and I wanted my kids to be in on it," Rick told a fellow teacher. "My kids are beginning to understand why we became involved in the Middle East. They're really beginning to think things through."

The other teacher at the end of the long table, silent until now, says, "I don't agree with what you're teaching. Where is it all going to lead? Our responsibility as teachers is to give them the knowledge they need to get a good score on the SAT or ACT. That's what the parents want—get 'em into a good college. After that, they can change the world if they want to."

What is the role of the teacher in American society in the 1990s? Do you agree or disagree with Rick's approach to teaching? If you were Rick, what would you say to this teacher?

FOCUS QUESTIONS

1. What roles do schools play in American society?
2. How does cultural diversity influence schools and teachers?
3. How are schools alike? How are they different?
4. What social issues currently challenge the schools?
5. What are the characteristics of "successful" schools?

The conflict between Rick and his fellow teachers highlights the different perspectives people have on the role schools (and teachers) should play in modern American society. Those who disagree with Rick's approach to teaching the social studies tend to believe that he should teach only content to students. Rick and his supporters, however, believe that students should acquire knowledge and skills to improve society. Underlying both positions are conflicting views on the aims of education.

AIMS OF EDUCATION

Americans agree that the purpose of schools is to educate. Unlike other institutions in society, schools have been developed exclusively to carry out that very important purpose. That we are not always in agreement about what the aims of education should be, however, is illustrated by the fact that we disagree about what it means to *be educated*. Is a person with a college degree educated? Is the person who has overcome, with dignity and grace, extreme hardships in life educated? Might a hermit who lives a serene life at the base of a remote mountain be more educated than the corporate attorney who received a degree from a prestigious university?

Debate about the **aims of education** is not new. Aristotle, for example, expressed the dilemma this way: "The existing practice [of education] is perplexing; no one knows on what principle we should proceed—should the useful in life, or should virtue, or should the higher knowledge, be the aim of our training; all three opinions have been entertained."[1] Definitive answers to Aristotle's questions have not been achieved; instead, each generation has developed its own response to what the aims of education should be.

Table 5.1 shows some of the results of two Gallup polls that surveyed the importance teachers attached to 25 goals of education in 1984 and in 1989, and the public's views of those goals in 1984. The results indicate that teachers in 1989 believed the primary aim of education was to teach students to think—creatively, objectively, and analytically. Also, a comparison of the 1984 and 1989 data shows a significant increase among teachers who believe that an important aim of schooling is "to develop respect for an understanding of other races, religions, nations, and cultures." Similarly, the 1989 sample of teachers gave a higher rating to developing the ability to deal with adult responsibilities and problems in areas such as sex, marriage, parenting, personal finances, and alcohol and drug abuse.

Data for the teachers and the public in 1984 reveal two important differences between the two groups. First, the public rated as much more important two vocational goals—"to help students get good/high-paying jobs" and "to develop an understanding about different kinds of jobs and careers, including their requirements and rewards." Second, nearly two-thirds of the public (64 percent) said that developing "standards of right and wrong" was most important, while only about half as many teachers (33 percent) gave this goal the highest rating.

TABLE 5.1   The Goals of Education

Please rate the importance of each of the following possible goals of education on a
scale of zero to 10. A zero means a goal is not at all important and should not be part
of the public school program. A 10 means a goal is the most important goal—before all
others.

	All Teachers		Elementary Teachers		High School Teachers		U.S. Public
	1984	1989	1984	1989	1984	1989	1984
To help develop good work habits, the ability to organize one's thoughts, the ability to concentrate	56	63	58	64	54	62	48
To develop the ability to think—creatively, objectively, analytically	56	80	54	83	58	77	51
To develop the ability to speak and write correctly	55	62	54	65	57	60	68
To develop the ability to use mathematics for everyday problems	53	55	55	59	52	37	54
To encourage the desire to continue learning throughout one's life	51	73	53	78	48	68	41
To encourage respect for law and order, for obeying the rules of society	46	55	48	57	42	51	52
To develop the ability to live in a complex and changing world	41	49	41	52	42	48	51
To prepare those who plan to attend college for college	36	46	37	49	36	43	46
To develop skills needed to get jobs for those not planning to attend college	34	50	37	52	31	48	54
To develop standards of what is "right and wrong"	33	48	36	51	30	43	64
To develop an understanding of democracy and to promote participation in the political process	31	49	31	50	31	49	33
To develop the ability to get along with different kinds of people	31	45	35	46	26	45	42
To develop respect for and understanding of other races, religions, nations, and cultures	30	51	31	54	27	47	39
To develop the ability to deal with adult responsibilities and problems, e.g., sex, marriage, parenting, personal finances, alcohol and drug abuse	28	43	28	45	28	41	46
To help students make realistic plans for what they will do after high school graduation	27	37	30	39	24	36	52
To develop an understanding about different kinds of jobs and careers, including their requirements and rewards	20	21	22	22	17	18	56
To help students get good/high-paying jobs	6	13	7	12	6	14	46

Percentage Giving Highest ("10") Rating

Source: "The 21st Annual Gallup Poll of the Public's Attitudes Toward the Public Schools," *Phi
Delta Kappan* (June 1989): 794.

FIGURE 5.1
What New Teachers Think Is Most Important for Helping Students to Learn

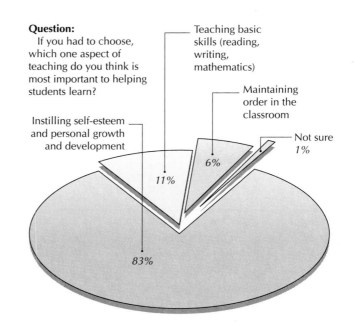

Question:
If you had to choose, which one aspect of teaching do you think is most important to helping students learn?

Teaching basic skills (reading, writing, mathematics)

Maintaining order in the classroom

Not sure
1%

Instilling self-esteem and personal growth and development

6%

11%

83%

Source: Louis Harris and Associates, *The Metropolitan Life Survey of the American Teacher 1990: New Teachers: Expectations and Ideals, Part I: Entering the Classroom* (New York: Louis Harris and Associates, 1990), p. 6. Used with permission.

New teachers believe that instilling self-esteem and personal growth and development is more important for helping students learn than either teaching basic skills or maintaining order in the classroom, according to a Metropolitan Life survey of 1,002 teachers who began teaching in the fall of 1990 (see Figure 5.1).

While different groups in our society—educators, parents, students, and politicians, for example—have conflicting views on the specific aims of education, there is greater agreement on a broader, more general level. Currently, our nation's schools are focused on four outcomes: socialization, achievement, personal growth, and social improvement.

Socialization

Schools are places where the young become socialized—where they learn to participate intelligently and constructively in American society. This purpose was contained in one of President Bush's national performance goals for education that he unveiled before a joint session of the Congress in 1990: "By the year 2000, . . . every school in America will ensure that all students learn to use their minds well, so they may be prepared for responsible citizenship, further learning, and productive employment in our modern economy."[2]

Education is the primary means of producing enlightened citizens. Without such a citizenry to hold it together, a society, especially a democratic society, is at risk. Therefore, schools reflect or "mirror" society. They reproduce the knowledge, values, and skills that society has identified as essential.

Additionally, schools, more than any other institution in our society, assimilate persons from different ethnic, racial, religious, and cultural backgrounds and pass on the values and customs of the majority. The Los Angeles Unified School District, for example, recently reported that its students represented 9 major language groups and 171 languages. It is through the schools that persons from such diverse backgrounds learn English and learn about the importance Americans attach to the Fourth of July or Veterans Day; about the contributions of George Washington, Abraham Lincoln, or Martin Luther King; and about the basic workings of capitalism.

Achievement

Schools are places where students acquire academic knowledge and skills that will prepare them either for additional schooling or for the world of work. Of the various aims that the schools have, achievement is the most universally agreed upon. Regardless of political ideology, religious beliefs, and cultural values, Americans want their schools to teach academic content. One of President Bush's national performance goals emphasized achievement: "By the year 2000, American students will leave grades four, eight, and twelve having demonstrated competency in challenging subject matter, including English, mathematics, science, history, and geography."[3]

Personal Growth

Our society places great value on the dignity and worth of the individual. Accordingly, one aim of our schools is to enable the young to become all that they are capable of becoming. Unlike socialization or achievement, the emphasis on personal growth puts the individual first, society second. According to this view, the desired outcomes of education go beyond achievement to include the development of a positive self-concept and interpersonal skills. Thus equipped, students are able to live independently and to seek out the "good" life according to their own values, needs, and wants.

Such a view, of course, places the child, not the subject matter, at the center of the curriculum. The knowledge and skills students acquire at schools are seen as enabling them to achieve personal growth and self-actualization.

Social Improvement

Schools also provide students with the knowledge and skills to improve society and the quality of life and to adapt to rapid social change. As we point out later in this chapter, many Americans expect schools to address such social issues as racial discrimination, poverty, child abuse, substance abuse, AIDS, and families in distress.

Naturally, there exists a wide range of opinions about how society might be improved. Some teachers, like Rick, believe that the purpose of schooling is to raise the awareness of students about global issues and social problems, such as class struggle and economic exploitation, to make the world a better place. Less controversial have been efforts to prepare students to serve others through volunteerism and to participate actively in the political life of the nation. The Carnegie Foundation for the Advancement of Teaching, for example, recommended that every high school student should complete a service requirement:

> to help students see that they are not only autonomous individuals but also members of a larger community to which they are accountable. [The program] would bring young people into contact with the elderly, the sick, the poor, and the homeless, as well as acquaint them with neighborhood and governmental issues.[4]

FIVE-MINUTE FOCUS   Examine Table 5.1 and then select the four or five goals that you consider most important. What do these goals say about your view of the central purpose of education? What additional goals (if any) should schools emphasize? Date your journal entry and write for five minutes.

EDUCATION IN A MULTICULTURAL SOCIETY

During your career as a teacher, you will teach students from many different cultural groups in our society—African Americans, Latin Americans, Asians, Native Americans, and whites from diverse ethnic groups. Many of these students will come from cultural backgrounds different from yours in religion, beliefs and values, and socioeconomic class.

The goal of providing equal educational opportunity for all has long distinguished American education from that found in most other countries. Since the 1850s, American schools have been particularly concerned with providing children from diverse backgrounds the education they need to succeed in our society. As Charles Silberman has suggested, America's schools were to be " 'the great equalizer of the conditions of men,' facilitating the movement of the poor and disadvantaged into the mainstream of American economic and social life."[5] Though many schools in the United States still have fairly uniform student populations—be they all-white suburban schools, schools on Indian reservations or in barrios, or inner-city schools—it is difficult today to ignore the fact that America is a **multicultural** society.

The number of students form diverse cultural backgrounds is increasing in most of America's schools. The percentage of ethnic minorities has been growing steadily since the end of World War II. Immigration, both legal and illegal, is at an all-time high, and the birth rate among the dominant white population is at an all-time low. For example, the birthrate among white females is 1.7, while that of Mexican-American females is 2.9. (A birth rate of 2.1 is needed to achieve a balance between births and deaths).[6]

Soon after the year 2000, one-third of Americans will be nonwhite, according to estimates contained in *One-Third of a Nation,* a report released in 1988 by the American Council on Education and the Education Commission of the States.[7] Table 5.2 shows the population of several ethnic groups in the United States for 1970 and 1980, with projected populations for 1990.

Many nonwhite students will come from homes where English is not spoken. Figure 5.2 shows that the number of people from non-English-speaking backgrounds in the United States has risen steadily since 1976 and is expected to increase from about 33 million in 1987 to almost 40 million by the year 2000.

This increase in minority populations is having a profound effect on our nation's schools. The District of Columbia now has a minority school enrollment of over 95 percent; Mississippi, 52 percent; Texas, 48 percent; New Mexico, 57 percent; and California, 45 percent. It is estimated that by the year 2000 the majority of students in most urban school districts will be members of those groups traditionally thought of as minorities. Among the urban school districts where white students already number less than 20 percent are Atlanta, Chicago, Detroit, New Orleans, Oakland, Richmond, and San Antonio.[8]

In the past, diversity was often seen as a "problem" in the classroom, with some teachers approaching the education of minority-group students from a perspective that was "remedial and deficit-oriented, rather than developmental and growth-oriented."[9] Today, however, multiculturalism is seen as a source of enrichment and as a challenge. In response to the changing nature of America's student population, then, it is imperative that teachers for the 1990s strive to "transform the challenges of ethnic, cultural, and racial diversity into educational and societal opportunities."[10]

TABLE 5.2   Population of Ethnic Groups in the United States, 1970, 1980, and Projected Population, 1990

Ethnic Group	1970 Population	1980 Population	1990 Projected Population
Total	203,211,926	226,504,825	252,293,000
White Americans*	177,748,975	188,340,790	191,594,000
African Americans	22,580,289	26,448,218	30,915,000
Hispanics	9,072,602	14,608,673	21,854,000
Mexican Americans	4,532,435	8,740,439	13,768,020
Puerto Ricans	1,429,396	2,013,945	2,666,188
Cubans	544,600	803,226	1,180,116
Central and South Americans			2,491,356
Other Spanish Origin			1,748,320
Jewish Americans			5,814,000**
American Indians	792,730	1,361,869	1,500,000**
Eskimos		42,149	64,000**
Aleuts		14,177	
Chinese Americans	431,583	812,178	1,260,000
Filipino Americans	336,731	781,894	1,410,000
Japanese Americans	588,324	716,331	800,000
Korean Americans	69,510	357,393	810,000
Asian Indians		387,223	680,000
Vietnamese Americans			860,000
Native Hawaiians	100,179	172,346	

*This figure includes the roughly 53% of Hispanics who classified themselves as White.

**1989 figure

Note: Not all of the racial and ethnic categories are mutually exclusive; for example, many Hispanic Americans are also White.

Sources: Based on several reports from the U.S. Census Bureau, including *National Origin and Language,* PC(2)–1A, 1973; *Race of the Population of States,* 1980. PC80–S1–3, 1981; *Projections of the Population of the U.S. by Age, Sex, and Race 1983–2080* (1989); and on projections reported in John W. Wright, Ed., *The Universal Almanac 1990.* (Kansas City: Andrews and McNeel, 1990.) Reprinted from James A. Banks, *Teaching Strategies for Ethnic Studies,* 5th ed. p. 16. Copyright © 1991 by Allyn and Bacon. Reprinted by permission.

FIGURE 5.2
Non-English Language Background Projections by Language Group, 1976–2000 (All Ages)

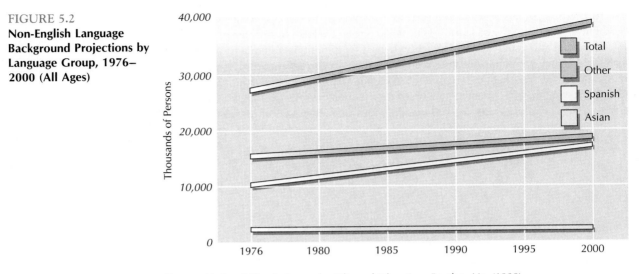

Source: National Clearinghouse for Bilingual Education, Rosslyn, Va. (1980).

American Cultural Diversity

In the preceding discussion of the aims of education, we pointed out that one mission of the schools is to maintain our culture. But what is the American culture? Is there a single culture to which all Americans belong? Before we answer that question we must define the term *culture*.

Definitions of Culture   This concept has been defined in many ways. Among the definitions suggested by sociologists and anthropologists are the following:

- The acquired knowledge that people use to interpret evidence and to generate social behavior[11]
- Whatever it is one has to know or believe in order to operate in a manner acceptable to its members[12]
- A shared organization of ideas that includes the intellectual, moral, and aesthetic standards prevalent in a community and the meanings of communicative actions[13]
- The world view or the way a cultural group perceives its environment, including stereotypes, role perceptions, norms, attitudes, values, ideals, and perceived relationships between events and behaviors[14]

Simply put, **culture** is *the way of life* common to a group of people. It consists of the values, attitudes, and beliefs that influence their behavior. It is also a way of looking at the world.

These definitions of culture remind us that there is no single American culture. While we may speak of "the American culture" in contrast to the cultures of India, Haiti, Saudi Arabia, China, or Sweden, we must remember that the primary distinguishing characteristic of American culture is its cultural diversity. Though at one time it was believed that America was a "melting pot" in which ethnic cultures would melt into one, ethnic and cultural differences have remained very much a part of American life.

"Of course it's misspelled. I'm preserving my indigenous cultural dialect."

Language and Culture   Culture is embedded in language, a fact that has resulted in conflict among different groups in our society. Some groups, while they support the preservation of ethnic cultures, believe that members of non-English-speaking groups must learn English if they are to function in the dominant culture. There is also conflict between those who wish to preserve linguistic diversity and those who wish to establish English as a national language. A few states have even passed, not without considerable controversy, English-only laws.

Much of the debate has focused on **bilingual education,** that is, using two languages as the medium of instruction. Bilingual education is designed to help students maintain their ethnic identity, encourage acculturation to the dominant culture, and integrate the home language and culture with a new one. Some people are staunchly opposed to any form of bilingual education, while others support it as a short-term way to teach English to students. At the very least, multicultural education must be bilingual to some extent in that it aims to teach *all* students to appreciate language diversity as an important dimension of cultural diversity.

Dimensions of Culture   Within our nation's boundaries, we find cultural groups that differ according to other distinguishing factors, such as religion, politics, economics, and region of the country. The regional culture of New England, for example, is quite different from that of the Southeast. Similarly, Californians are culturally different from Iowans.

Socioeconomic factors, such as income and occupation, also contribute to the culture of communities. Recall, for instance, the example at the beginning of this chapter. The culture of the surrounding community in which Rick taught included a distinct set of expectations for teachers and students at Hilltop High School that related to standards of living and occupational roles. If Rick had been teaching in an inner-city school, in a rural regional school, or in a factory town, different sets of expectations would undoubtedly have applied.

FIGURE 5.3
Ethnic Group Cultures and Their Relationship to the Shared National American Culture

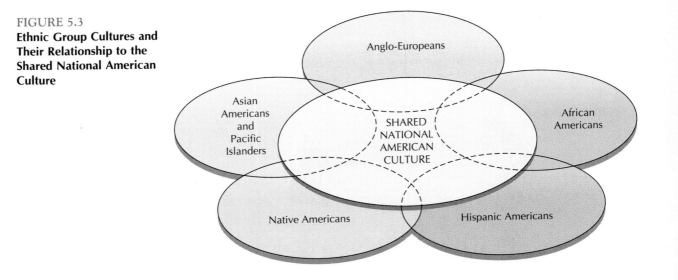

As Figure 5.3 illustrates, Americans do share some common dimensions of culture (represented by the large colored circle). James Banks, an authority on multicultural education, has termed this the "national American culture."[15] In addition, Americans are members of ethnic groups, represented by the five overlapping rings. An **ethnic group** is made up of individuals within a larger culture who share a racial identity and a set of beliefs, attitudes, and values. Members of an ethnic group are distinguishable from others in the society by either physical or cultural attributes, or both. Figure 5.3 shows that only a portion of any ethnic group's way of life is unique to that group.

Ethnic Groups in America

There are many ethnic groups in American society, and everyone belongs to one. However, as James Banks points out:

> an individual American is ethnic to the extent that he or she functions within ethnic subsocieties and shares their values, behavioral styles, and cultures. An individual, however, may have a low level of ethnicity or psychological identification with his or her ethnic group or groups.[16]

Table 5.3 shows the population of major social groups other than whites in the United States according to the 1990 census. In the following sections, we examine briefly some of these groups. First, however, we wish to present an important point that James Banks has made about the study of ethnic groups. Educators, he maintains, should guard against

> the assumption that . . . ethnic studies deals exclusively with groups of color, such as Asian Americans, American Indians, and African Americans. Conceptualizing ethnic studies exclusively as the study of ethnic groups of color also promotes a kind of *we-they* attitude among many White students and teachers. Many students think that ethnic studies is the study of *them*. . . .[17]

TABLE 5.3   Population by Selected Racial Group,* 1990

Race	Total Number	Increase Since 1980
African American	30.0 million	13.2%
Asian	7.3 million	107.8%
Native American	2.0 million	37.9%
Hispanic	22.4 million	53.0%
Other	9.8 million	

*Does not include whites of European or Middle-Eastern background.
Source: 1990 Census.

Anglo-Europeans   The Anglo-European subculture evolved from Western and Eastern Europe and is viewed by many as the dominant ethnic group in America. To a great extent, it has determined the "formal institutions, official language, social values, and other aspects of life in [our] society."[18]

While some may assume that this ethnic group currently shares a high degree of common identity, it is actually made up of people whose ancestors belonged to many different religious, cultural, and political groups in Western Europe. Americans whose ethnic heritage is Polish, German, Italian, Irish, Czechoslovakian, or Swedish, for example, often differ greatly in religious and political traditions, beliefs and values, and attitudes. Their individual ethnic identity is often strengthened by recent immigrants from the country of origin. European ethnics have, however, assimilated into the mainstream American society more completely than other ethnic groups.

African Americans   Of the more than 248 million persons living in America, approximately 13 percent are African Americans. The African-American population is expected to rise from 30 million in 1990 to 44 million by the year 2020. Among African Americans, the incidence of social problems such as unemployment, crime, drug abuse, poverty, inadequate housing, and school dropouts is significantly greater than it is for whites. The struggle of African Americans to improve their quality of life has been hampered for decades by various forms of racial discrimination, perhaps the most crippling of which has been school segregation and unequal educational opportunity.

The civil rights movement of the 1950s and 1960s made it clear that African Americans had been denied full access to many aspects of American life, including the right to a good education. One report, for example, revealed that a southern school district in the 1930s spent nearly 18 times as much for the education of white pupils as it did for the education of African Americans.[19]

Hispanic Americans   "Hispanic," or Spanish-speaking, Americans are the second-fastest growing minority in the United States. According to the 1990 census, 6.5 percent of Americans are Spanish-speaking, and it has been estimated that an additional five million migrants and illegal aliens who speak Spanish may be in the country. America's Hispanic population is expected to increase from 22.4 million in 1990 to around 47 million by 2020. Included in this category are people who report their ancestry as Mexican, Puerto Rican, Cuban, Central American, or South Amer-

Schools reflect the population, culture, and socioeconomic character of the surrounding community. This small, semirural, adobe school in the American Southwest has a high proportion of Native-American and Spanish-speaking students from families who rely on jobs in agriculture.

ican. Five states have populations that are more than 10 percent Latin American: New Mexico, Texas, California, Arizona, and Colorado.

Many Spanish-speaking immigrants come to the United States hoping to escape a life of poverty in their home country. Most of these immigrants lack job skills and have very little education—two characteristics that make it difficult for them to cope well with the complexities and demands of American life.

Native Americans   This group represents less than one percent of the total U.S. population and consists of 789 different tribal groups, each with its own language, religious beliefs, and way of life. Perhaps more than any other ethnic group, Native Americans have endured numerous attempts by the dominant white culture to eradicate their language and culture. Like many other ethnic groups in America, Native Americans reflect such school-related problems as low academic achievement, alcoholism, high dropout rate, and irregular attendance.

Those who teach Native Americans face the additional problem of dealing with a diversity of Indian languages. It has been estimated that there are from 12 to 21 language families that are used by Native Americans.[20] Moreover, these languages are frequently in transition, with older tribal members fluent in the original tribal language and younger members speaking a form of so-called "reservation English." The challenge of educating Native Americans from diverse language backgrounds is further compounded by the size of various native American populations. These range from the more than 100,000 Navajo to the 200 or so Supai of Arizona. According to the deputy commissioner for Indian education in the U.S. Office of Education, Native Americans are a culturally diverse group:

There is no such thing as an "Indian" heritage, culture, or value system. Some 250 tribes are recognized by the federal government, most of them differing from the others in culture, religion, and beliefs. Navajo, Cherokee, Sioux, and Aleut children are as different from each other in geographic and cultural background as they are from children growing up in New York City or Los Angeles.[21]

Asian Americans and Pacific Islanders Asian Americans and Pacific Islanders represent almost two percent of America's total population. This group includes, for example, Chinese, Japanese, Filipinos, Koreans, Vietnamese, Cambodians, Indians, Indonesians, Thais, Malaysians, Samoans, Guamanians, and native Hawaiians. With the exception of Hawaiians, persons from these groups usually arrive in the United States with little knowledge of English. About 60 percent of the total Asian American and Pacific Islander population live on the West coast of the United States.

Though Asian Americans and Pacific Islanders are usually grouped as "Orientals" and "Islanders," each subgroup is unique and has special educational needs. While some ethnic groups have been negatively stereotyped as lazy, undependable, or trouble-makers, Asian Americans are frequently viewed as hard-working, conscientious, and respectful of authority. The unreliability of such **stereotypes** notwithstanding, Asian-American parents do tend to require their children to respect authority and value education. In fact, one-third of the Asian-American adults immigrating to this country have a college degree.[22] As a result, stories of the outstanding academic accomplishments of Asian-American children who arrived in this country a few years earlier with no knowledge of English are common.

FIVE-MINUTE FOCUS   An important part of self-knowledge is being aware of one's cultural identity. Describe yourself in regard to the attitudes, values, beliefs, and ethnic group membership that make up your cultural identity. Date your journal entry and write for five minutes.

THE SCHOOL AS A SOCIAL INSTITUTION

During your career as a teacher, not only will you teach students with different cultural backgrounds, but you may also teach in different kinds of schools. An **institution** has been defined as "an established organization; especially, one dedicated to public service."[23] Clearly, then, schools are the institutions our society has established for the purpose of educating the young. For the last 200 years, American schools have developed complex structures, policies, and curricula to accomplish this mission. The Teacher's Resource Guide contains a chart showing "The Institutional Structure of Education in the United States."

Schools do not exist in a vacuum. They must continually respond to changing expectations on the part of students, parents, teachers, communities, and the public at large. As we pointed out earlier, schools "mirror" society, and this mirroring occurs at different levels. Schools mirror the national American culture while they also mirror the surrounding local culture and other special interests. Private, parochial, and religious schools, for example, are often maintained by groups that see the school as a means of perpetuating their preferred way of life.

The Culture of Schools

Schools are very much alike; in a sense, it is correct to say that a school is a school is a school. Students attend schools where they are grouped in various ways; taught

FACT FINDING

What Are Students' Attitudes About School Climate?

Research has shown that students' attitudes toward school can influence learning and other school-related behavior. In a 1990 report, the National Center for Education Statistics released data on the attitudes of eighth graders toward school according to their race/ethnicity.

Percent of Students Who Agree or Strongly Agree with the Statement, by Race/Ethnicity

Statement about School Climate	Percent		
	White	Black	Hispanic
Teaching is good	80	80	83
Teachers are interested in students	73	75	76
Teachers praise my effort when I work hard	60	72	71
Other students often disrupt class	78	80	79
Misbehaving students often get away with it	52	54	55
Disruptions by other students interfere with my learning	35	55	45
I don't feel safe at this school	10	18	15

Source: Adapted from graph in *The Condition of Education 1990: Volume 1, Elementary and Secondary Education* (Washington, D.C.: National Center for Education Statistics), p. 71.

by teachers who use textbooks, lecture, recitation, and drill and practice; and periodically examined on what they have learned. However, each school also differs significantly. Each has a culture of its own—a network of beliefs, values and traditions, and ways of thinking and behaving that distinguishes it from other schools.

Much like a community, a school has a distinctive culture—a collective way of life. Terms that have been used to describe this way of life include *climate, ethos, atmosphere,* and *character.* The culture of a school is reflected in such things as the quality of interpersonal relations within the school, the core beliefs and values to which students and teachers adhere, the mission of the school, and the degree of caring and support for those who spend their time at the school.

Some schools may be characterized as community-like places where there is a shared sense of purpose and commitment to providing the best education possible for students. Other schools lack a unified sense of purpose or direction and "drift," rudderless, from year to year. Still others are characterized by internal conflict and divisiveness; students, teachers, administrators, and parents may feel that the school is not sufficiently meeting their needs. Gerald Grant defines a school with a "strong positive ethos" (or culture) as follows:

> A school with a strong positive ethos is one that affirms the ideals and imparts the intellectual and moral virtues proper to the functioning of an educational community in a democracy. It attempts to commit its members to those ideals and virtues in at least a provisional way through the espousal of goals, exemplary actions and practices, ritual, celebrations and observance of norms.[24]

Formal Practices   The formal practices of schools are well known to anyone who has been educated in American schools. With few exceptions, students attend school from six years of age through sixteen, Monday through Friday, September through May, for twelve years. For the most part, students are assigned to grade level on the basis of age rather than ability or interest. Assignment to individual classes or teachers at a given grade level, however, may be made on the basis of ability or interest.

Teachers and students are grouped in several ways in the elementary school and in one dominant pattern in junior and senior high school. At the elementary school level, the **self-contained classroom** is the most traditional and prevalent arrangement. In this type of classroom, one teacher teaches all or nearly all subjects to a group of about 25 children, with the teacher and students remaining in the same classroom for the entire day. Often art, music, and physical education are taught in other parts of the school, so students may leave the classroom for scheduled periods. Individual students may also attend special classes for remedial or advanced instruction, speech therapy, or instrumental music and band lessons.

Another elementary school arrangement is **team teaching,** in which teachers share the responsibility for two or more classes, dividing up the subject areas between them, with one preparing lessons in mathematics, science, and health, for instance, while the other plans instruction in reading and language arts. The division of responsibility may also be made in terms of the performance levels of the children, so that, for example, one teacher may teach the lowest and highest reading groups and the middle math group, while the other teaches the middle reading groups and the lowest and highest mathematics group. In many schools, team teaching arrangements are so extensive that children move from classroom to classroom for 40- to 50-minute periods just as students do at the high school level.

In **open-space schools,** where **open-concept education** is practiced, students are free to move among various activities and learning centers. Instead of self-contained classrooms, open-space schools have large instructional areas with movable walls and furniture that can be rearranged easily. Grouping for instruction is much more fluid and varied. Students do much of their work independently, with a number of teachers providing individual guidance as needed.

In middle schools and junior and senior high schools, students typically study four or five academic subjects taught by teachers who specialize in them. In this organizational arrangement, called **departmentalization,** students move from classroom to classroom for their lessons. High school teachers often share their classrooms with other teachers and use their rooms only during scheduled class periods.

Though not prevalent, open-space schools and open-education practices can also be found at the high school level. Likewise, it is becoming more common to find departmentalization in elementary schools.

School Traditions   School traditions are those elements of a school's culture that are handed down from year to year. The traditions of a school reflect what students, teachers, administrators, parents, and the surrounding community believe is important and valuable about the school. One school, for example, may have developed a tradition of excellence in academic programs; another school's traditions may emphasize the performing arts; and yet another may focus on athletic programs. Whatever a school's traditions, they are usually a source of pride for members of the school community.

Ideally, traditions are the "glue" that holds together the diverse elements of a school's culture. They combine to create a sense of community, identity, and trust among people affiliated with a school. Traditions are maintained through stories that are handed down, rituals and ceremonial activities, and trophies and artifacts that have been collected over the years.

FIVE-MINUTE FOCUS   Select an elementary, junior, or high school that you attended. What were the traditions of that school? What school activities helped to maintain those traditions? Date your journal entry and write for five minutes.

The Hidden Curriculum   The cultures of schools also reflect the hidden, or implicit, curriculum. This refers to the behaviors, attitudes, and knowledge that schools teach students unintentionally. The **hidden curriculum** strongly influences the image students formulate of themselves and their beliefs about how they should relate to others and to society in general.

What students learn through the hidden curriculum may be either positive or negative. Some students learn positive behaviors, such as how to cooperate with others, how to postpone gratification for more significant rewards, or how to stay on task in spite of temporary setbacks. Others learn negative behaviors, such as how to manipulate adults, how to get by on the effort of others, or how to cheat. Important attitudes are also acquired through the hidden curriculum: one can trust/mistrust those in authority; hard work does/does not pay off; school is/is not worthwhile; or teachers do/do not care about their students. Finally, the hidden curriculum presents students with knowledge about the ways of the world: those in authority have more freedom than those who are not; the appropriateness of one's behavior depends upon the situation and the context; or misbehavior invites certain consequences.

The School Environment   The physical environment of the school both reflects and helps to create the school's overall culture. Some schools are dreary places or, at best, aesthetically bland. The tile floors, concrete block walls, long, straight corridors, and rows of fluorescent lights often found in these schools contribute little to their inhabitants' sense of beauty, concern for others, or personal comfort. As John Goodlad observed in his landmark study of 129 elementary, 362 junior-high, and 525 senior-high classrooms in schools around the country, "I can only conclude from our data that the schools we visited—like most of the schools I have visited over the past three decades—generally provided physical environments ranging from neutral to negative in their probable impact on the humans inhabiting them."[25]

Other schools are much more attractive. In their study of 100 "good" schools, for example, Jack Frymier and his associates found that they were "pleasant and clean places in which to be, and teachers and students [were] allowed to put things on the walls and rearrange furniture as desired."[26] Ninety-eight percent of the elementary teachers and 91 percent of the middle-level and secondary teachers reported that their school buildings were "always" or "often" pleasant.

The School Location   An additional dimension of a school's physical environment is its location. Schools in rural, urban, and suburban settings often have significantly different cultures. Rural schools are often the focal point for community life and reflect values and beliefs that tend to be more conservative than those associated with urban and suburban schools. Suburban schools are often much larger than rural schools and may lack their cohesiveness.

The cultures of urban schools vary considerably. Some are very academically oriented and serve parents who are just as involved in the education of their children as parents in the more affluent surrounding suburbs. Other urban schools, unfortunately, have the unpleasant distinction of being in the lowest percentiles of academic achievement—hardly a desirable tradition for a school to maintain.

Urban schools found in or near decaying centers of large cities often reflect the social problems of the surrounding area, such as drug abuse, crime, poverty, and broken families. One of the most serious problems confronting American education is the quality of such schools. Across the country—in Chicago, New York, Los Angeles, St. Louis, Detroit, and Cleveland—many middle-class white families, often in response to desegregation efforts, are moving away from urban centers or placing their children in private schools. As a result, students in urban school districts are increasingly from lower socioeconomic backgrounds.

Whether rural, suburban, or urban, each type of school presents the teacher with special challenges and opportunities. A teacher at a rural school, for example, may emphasize to students the importance of learning by enlisting the support of parents and others in the community. On the other hand, a teacher at an urban school has available a wider array of resources for enriching the curriculum—museums, theater, cultural events, businesses, and industry, for example. Also, as the following teacher suggests, the cultural diversity often found in the urban school can be an asset: "I work here in an inner-city high school. The advantages are that you meet very interesting students who come from a variety of backgrounds and make it very stimulating."[27]

Models of Schools

Given the wide variation in schools and their cultures, many "models" have been proposed for describing the distinguishing characteristics of schools. Schools can be categorized according to the focus of their curricula; for example, high schools may be college prep, vocational, or general. Another way to view schools is according to their organizational structure; for example, schools organized around open-concept education or the "magnet" concept (a model that allows students from an entire district to attend a school's specialized program).

Metaphors for Schools   Other models view schools metaphorically; that is, what is a school like? Some schools, for example, have been compared to factories; students enter the school as "input," move through the curriculum in a systematic way, and exit the school as educated "output." Arthur Powell has suggested that high schools are like shopping malls; there is something for everyone, and students are consumers looking for the best value.[28] Others have suggested that schools are like banks, gardens, prisons, mental hospitals, homes, churches, families, and teams.

Four Categories of Schools   In her study of several elementary schools in urban and suburban New Jersey, Jean Anyon identified four categories of schools that provide a useful way for talking about the cultural dimensions of schools in America.[29] Anyon maintains that schools "reproduce" the existing society by presenting different curricula and educational experiences to students from different socioeconomic classes. As a result of their experiences at school, students are prepared for particular roles in the dominant society.

The first kind of school she calls the *working-class school*. In this school, the primary emphasis is on having students follow directions as they work at rote, mechanical activities such as completing dittoed worksheets. Students are given little opportunity to exercise their initiative or to make choices. Teachers may make negative, disparaging comments about students' abilities and, through subtle and not-so-subtle means, convey low expectations to students. Additionally, teachers at working-class schools may spend much of their time focusing on classroom management, dealing with absenteeism, and keeping extensive records.

The *middle-class school* is the second type identified by Anyon. Here, teachers emphasize to students the importance of getting right answers, usually in the form of words, sentences, numbers, or facts and dates. Students have slightly more opportunity to make decisions, but not much. Most lessons are textbook based. Anyon points out that "while the teachers spend a lot of time explaining and expanding on what the textbooks say, there is little attempt to analyze how or why things happen. . . . On the occasions when creativity or self-expression is requested, it is peripheral to the main activity or it is 'enrichment' or 'for fun.' "[30]

The *affluent professional school*, unlike the previous two types of schools, gives students the opportunity to express their individuality and to make a variety of choices.

> Work [in affluent professional schools] involves individual thought and expressiveness, expansion and illustration of ideas, and choice of appropriate method and material. . . . The products of work are often written stories, editorials and essays, or representations of ideas in mural, graph, or craft form.[31]

Fewer rules govern the behavior of students in affluent professional schools, and teacher and student are likely to "negotiate" about the work the student will do.

Anyon provides the following definition of the *executive elite school*, the kind of school described in the opening scenario of this chapter:

> In the executive elite school, work is developing one's analytical intellectual powers. Children are continually asked to reason through a problem, to produce intellectual products that are both logically sound and of top academic quality. A primary goal of thought is to conceptualize rules by which elements may fit together in systems and then to apply these rules in solving a problem. Schoolwork helps one to achieve, to excel, to prepare for life.[32]

Teacher-student relationships are more positive than those in the working-class and middle-class schools. Teachers are polite to their students, seldom give few direct orders, and almost never make sarcastic or nasty remarks.

In applying Anyon's categories to schools in America, we should keep in mind that few schools are one type exclusively. Instead, most schools probably contain individual classrooms that represent the four types. Also, it is possible for one type of school to exist "within" a school of another type—for example, an advanced placement program (essentially, an affluent professional school) within an urban working-class school.

Also, we must remember that Anyon studied a small group of schools in one metropolitan area and that her criteria are linked almost exclusively to socioeconomic status. There are many schools in poor urban areas, for example, whose culture is more like the affluent professional school Anyon describes than the working-class school, and vice versa.

Strategic Planning

Experiments in school restructuring increasingly make headlines in education news. While these experiments vary in their levels of success, they share the same basic requirement: a great deal of "strategic planning." Because school reform involves an entire community and often has a long-term impact on a school system, planners have found that communication with all segments of a community is crucial, possibly even the most important element in the success of any program.

One method of strategic planning, proposed by Bill Cook of Cambridge Management Group in Montgomery, Alabama, includes selecting a Planning Team to represent the different groups, interests, and perspectives of the school district. The Planning Team's role is to develop statements of belief, a mission statement, a list of objectives, and a set of strategies for reform. After the Planning Team's work has been shared, everyone participates in the formation of Action Teams, which focus on developing more detailed plans for accomplishing each strategy. When the Action Teams' plans have been accepted by the Planning Team, a final Strategic Plan is presented to the school board.

During the 1988–1989 school year, the Tacoma, Washington, Public School District undertook this method of strategic planning in response to low student achievement, a high dropout rate, problems with integrating educational technology, and other concerns. Today most elements of the plan have been implemented or scheduled, but not without difficulty.

The problem came when the Planning Team failed to maintain the frequent, open communication with which the project began. At first the unions and members of the business community were not kept well enough informed. Later the school board, the community, and the local news media opposed a part of the Strategic Plan that called for "School Choice" enrollment caps ensuring that Tacoma schools would remain desegregated. The planners felt opposition was based on misunderstandings that could have been corrected if timely communication, more sensitive to the community's fears, had taken place. Even after three public hearings, however, the "School Choice" part of the plan was rejected.

School restructuring in any community is a difficult process at best. In addition to strategic planning, it requires a high level of power sharing and cooperation among diverse groups. Reporting on Tacoma's experience, former Deputy Superintendent of Tacoma Public Schools, Mary Nebgen, says:

> [It] is evident that communication has been the key to our success and that lack of communication has been the root of our failures. Since strategic planning can have a powerful affect on a district's future and its use of resources, district leaders must anticipate the need for extensive communication with all segments of the community at every stage of strategic planning.

Source: Mary Nebgen, "The Key to Success in Strategic Planning Is Communication," *Educational Leadership* 48, 7 (April 1991): 26–28.

SOCIAL ISSUES AND THE SCHOOLS

A complex and varied array of social issues impact the schools. These problems often detract from the schools' ability to educate students according to the four aims discussed at the beginning of this chapter: socialization, achievement, personal growth, and social improvement. Furthermore, the schools are often charged with the difficult (if not impossible) task of providing a front-line defense against such problems.

One of the most vocal advocates of the schools' role in solving social problems was George S. Counts, who said in his 1932 book *Dare the School Build a New Social Order?* that "If schools are to be really effective, they must become centers for the building, and not merely the contemplation, of our civilization."[33] Many people, however, believe that schools should not try to build a new social order. They should be concerned only with the academic and social development of students—not with solving society's problems. Nevertheless, the debate over the role of schools in regard to social problems will continue to be vigorous. In the following sections we examine several social problems that directly influence schools, teachers, and students.

Educational Equity

Ample evidence exists that certain groups in American society are denied equality of opportunity economically, socially, and educationally. For example, females have been, and still are, discriminated against in the marketplace. It is a well-established fact that women in our society are employed at lower levels than men, and, when they are employed at the same levels, they earn less.

Extensive programs at the federal, state, and local levels have been developed to ensure that all Americans—regardless of race, ethnicity, language, gender, or religion—have equality of opportunity. Our country has always derived strength from the diversity of its people, and *all* students should receive a quality education so that they may make their unique contributions to our society.

Poverty

Though the United States is one of the richest countries in the world, it has by no means achieved an enviable record in regard to poverty among children. It has been estimated, for example, that almost one million children in the United States are homeless. Consider the following data gathered by the Children's Defense Fund in 1986:

- Thirteen million children in America are poor.
- More than one in every five children is poor.
- Nearly one out of every four children under six is poor.
- Almost two out of every three poor children are white.
- Nearly two out of every five Hispanic children are poor.
- More than half of the children in families headed by females are poor.[34]

Poverty often encompasses a host of social problems that have proven especially difficult for schools to deal with. Typically, education has been viewed as an appropriate antidote to such poverty-related problems as unemployment, crime and delinquency, and drug addiction. In the 1960s, Presidents Kennedy and Johnson were instrumental in funneling massive amounts of money into a War on Poverty. Education was seen as the key to breaking the transmission of poverty from generation to generation. The strategy was to develop methods, materials, and programs such as Head Start, Upward Bound, and the Job Corps that would be appropriate to children who had been disadvantaged due to poverty.

The War on Poverty has proven much more difficult to win than imagined, and the results of programs initiated then have been mixed. The three- to six-year-olds who participated in Head Start did much better when they entered the public schools; however, academic gains appeared to dissolve over time. While the Job Corps enabled scores of youth to avoid a lifetime of unemployment, many graduates returned to the streets where they eventually became statistics in unemployment and crime records.

Moreover, the gains realized by educational programs targeted to low-income groups were diminished due to changes in funding. From time to time, support and services provided to participants were cut back or eliminated entirely.

Now, almost 30 years since the initiation of several major anti-poverty programs, it is clear that the problems associated with poverty cannot be solved by education alone. It will take time, patience, extensive financial resources, and the combined effort of all institutions in our society to reduce poverty in America.

Family Distress

The stress placed on families in our complex society is extensive and not easily handled. For some families, such stress can be overwhelming. The structure of families who are experiencing the effects of poverty, substance abuse, or violence, for example, can easily begin to crumble.

With the high rise in divorce and women's entry into the workforce, family constellations have changed dramatically. No longer is a working father, a mother who stays at home, and two or three children the only kind of family in America. The number of single-parent families, stepparent families, blended families, and extended families has increased dramatically during the last decade. Figure 5.4 shows the projected number of children not living with both parents between 1982 and 2020. This number is expected to increase from 16.2 million in 1984 to 21.1 million in 2020, an increase of 30 percent.

Stress within the family can have a significant negative effect on students and their ability to focus on learning while at school. Such stress is often associated with health and emotional problems, failure to achieve, and behavioral problems at school.

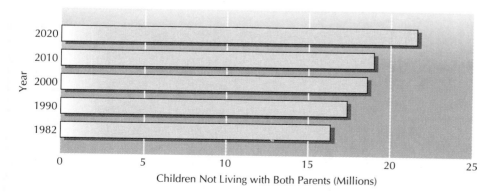

FIGURE 5.4
Projected Number of Children Not Living with Both Parents: U.S. Total, 1982–2020

Source: Aaron M. Pallas, Gary Natriello, and Edward L. McDill, "The Changing Nature of the Disadvantaged Population: Current Dimensions and Future Trends," *Educational Researcher* (June-July 1989): 20. Copyright 1989 by the American Educational Research Association. Reprinted by permission of the publisher.

Child Abuse

Fortunately, recent extensive publicity has made most children and adults aware of the problem of child abuse. It has been estimated that almost two million school-age children experience physical or psychological abuse each year. The burden of having to cope with abuse in the home environment clearly does not prepare a child to come to school to learn.

Teachers are now required by law to report suspected child abuse. Therefore, they must become well informed about physical, emotional, and sexual abuse and about the neglect and exploitation of children. These topics are discussed frequently in teachers' professional journals, but extensive, up-to-date information can also be obtained from local, state, and federal child welfare agencies. Usually such sources encourage teachers to be more observant of children's appearance and behavior in order to detect symptoms of child abuse.

Substance Abuse

One of the most pressing social problems confronting today's schools is the abuse of illegal drugs, tobacco, and alcohol. The 1990 Gallup Poll of the Public's Attitudes Toward the Public Schools, for example, revealed that 38 percent of the public identified the use of drugs as the number one problem faced by schools in their communities. Figure 5.5 shows the percentages of high school seniors who reported using alcohol, any illegal drug, or cocaine between 1975 and 1989.

The use of drugs among young people varies from community to community and from year to year, but overall it is disturbingly high. Mind-altering substances used by young people include the easily acquired glue, white correction fluid, and felt marker, as well as marijuana, amphetamines, and cocaine. The abuse of drugs not

FIGURE 5.5
Student Drug and Alcohol Use: Selected Years, 1975–1989 (Percent of high school seniors who reported using illegal drugs, cocaine, or alcohol)

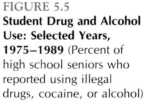

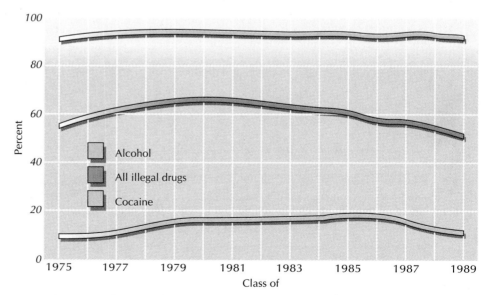

Source: U.S. Department of Health and Human Services: Alcohol, Drug Abuse, and Mental Health Administration; National Institute on Drug Abuse, Drug Use Among American High School Graduates, College Students, and Other Young Adults, 1989. Reprinted from National Center for Education Statistics, *The Condition of Education 1990: Volume 1, Elementary and Secondary Education* (Washington, D.C.: National Center for Education Statistics, 1990), p. 73.

only poses the risks of addiction and overdosing, but is also related to problems such as AIDS, teenage pregnancy, depression, suicide, automobile accidents, criminal activity, and dropping out of school.

For an alarming number of young people, drugs are an everyday part of life. As the following student, dangerously close to dropping out of high school, suggests, drugs are seen as a way of coping with life's problems:

> I've got too many problems, too many. It's too many problems to cope with and the problem is, you know, I like to take drugs. . . . See, it's that life is crazy, you know. And everybody, you know, comes down on me, and bothers me and the only way to get away from all that is by taking my drugs cuz that's, you know, they're my friends, they talk to me. . . . It'll set me straight for the whole day. And I go outside and play some handball, go to school first period, second period, third, fourth, I'm outta there, play handball right here in the handball court. I don't like to come to school, period, so I just come and sign in and go back out. And there's nothin' that's gonna stop me from doin' what I'm doin' now unless other things in life change me.[35]

Violence and Crime

As acts of terrorism, street crime, gang violence, and organized crime attest, ours is a violent, crime-ridden world. A widespread erosion of concern for the rights and property of others has steadily increased as a result of child abuse, television and movie violence, drug abuse, welfare and tax fraud, and corruption in business and government. Not surprisingly, violence and vandalism are also becoming more commonplace in our schools.

More than $600 million are spent each year on school vandalism, according to a report by the U.S. Senate Committee on Delinquency—a figure that the National Parent-Teacher Association pointed out exceeds the amount spent on textbooks for our nation's schools! The National Association of School Security Directors gives the following estimates of crimes committed each year in schools:

- 12,000 armed robberies
- 270,000 burglaries
- 204,000 aggravated assaults
- 9,000 rapes

While many schools have beefed up security measures, hired police officers, expelled students who commit violent acts, and taken steps to restore order, the problems, especially in large urban schools, can be hard to remedy. Clearly, students cannot learn in an atmosphere of fear and mistrust. School violence and vandalism is a reality that teachers in most settings must learn to deal with.

Children at Risk

An increasing number of young people live under conditions characterized by extreme stress, chronic poverty, crime, and lack of adult guidance. Frustrated and feeling powerless, many youths escape into rock music, video games, cults, movies, television, or cruising shopping malls. Others turn also to crime, gang violence, sex, or substance abuse. Not surprisingly, these activities place many young people "at risk" of dropping out of school.

Keepers of the Dream

Jaime Escalante
Mathematics Teacher in California
Subject of the Movie *Stand and Deliver*

Jaime Escalante, whose achievements were depicted in the 1988 movie *Stand and Deliver,* believes that students from all ethnic groups and socioeconomic backgrounds can achieve. "I don't think kids cannot learn," he says. "Anybody, any kid, can learn if he or she has the desire to do it."

Escalante, who taught mathematics for 17 years at Garfield High School in one of the roughest neighborhoods in East Los Angeles, has received numerous awards for his teaching, including the Presidential Medal for Excellence in Education and the National Outstanding Teacher of the Year award.

Escalante contends that all students can learn if they have *ganas,* Spanish for *desire.* When a student seems discouraged and ready to drop out of his AP calculus course, Escalante whispers to the student, "C'mon, Johnny, you can do it. You don't have to be gifted. The only thing you need is *ganas.*"

Escalante believes many students fail to succeed not because they lack ability, but because they lack confidence. A teacher's job, according to Escalante, is to motivate students and to set high standards. "Through teaching," he says, "I make small contributions to the dreams of my students. I teach from my heart and soul and not my mouth, and I am proud to be a teacher."

When Escalante began teaching at Garfield in 1973–74, he found it difficult to motivate students whose lives were so often impacted by poverty, family distress, and violence and crime.

The students were not interested in education. The parents were not interested in education. My first day was not really enjoyable. I noticed the language these kids used, and I noticed the kids without any supplies. I was disappointed. I decided to go back to my job—I had a good job, I was working with computers.

Going back home, I changed my mind. I said, "First, I'm going to teach them responsibility, and I'm going to teach them respect, and *then* I'm going to quit."[1]

Escalante continues to teach and to have high expectations of his students—and himself:

The teacher has to have the energy of the hottest volcano, the memory of an elephant, and the diplomacy of an ambassador. A teacher has to possess love and knowledge and then has to use this combined passion to be able to accomplish something.

When we talk about education, we're talking about the future of our country—the teacher plays an important role in that.[2]

"The Only Thing You Need Is GANAS."

1. Anne Meek, "On Creating *Ganas:* A Conversation with Jaime Escalante," *Educational Leadership* (February 1989): 46–47.
2. Shelagh Turner, "Jaime Escalante on Motivation: Be the Best You Can Be!" *Network Newsnotes: The National Network of Principals' Centers,* Vol. 5, No. 1 (November 1990): 1, 7.

Crowded older schools in decaying urban centers may reflect the poverty, indifference, or aggressiveness of community life. Despite appearances, however, with extra vigilance and the involvement of concerned adults such schools can become models of successful educational reform.

Among ethnic groups, dropout rates vary considerably. The National Center for Educational Statistics reported the following dropout rates for ethnic/racial groups in 1989: American Indians and Alaska Natives, 42.0 percent; Hispanic Americans, 39.9 percent; African Americans, 24.7 percent; whites, 14.3 percent; and Asians and Pacific Islanders, 9.6 percent.

Washington, D.C., has the highest dropout rate (45 percent), according to data released by the U.S. Department of Education in 1989, followed by Florida (38 percent); Arizona, Louisiana, Mississippi, and Georgia (37 percent); New York, South Carolina, and Texas (36 percent); Utah (35 percent); and Alabama and California (33 percent).

It has been estimated that one out of every four children will become a dropout statistic, at a cost to our society of about $145 billion annually.[36] **Students at risk** of dropping out tend to get low grades, perform below grade level academically, are older than the average student at their grade level because of previous retention, and have behavior problems in school.

Teenage Pregnancy Since 1970, there has been an epidemic in teenage pregnancies. Data from the National Center for Health Statistics indicate that the pregnancy rate among teenagers rose from less than 70 per 1,000 females aged 15–19 in 1970 to about 110 in 1982. The Alan Guttmacher Institute, a nonprofit research foundation affiliated with Planned Parenthood, estimated that more than a million teenagers would become pregnant in 1986, with half a million bearing and keeping their babies, 450,000 choosing abortions, and less than 100,000 giving their babies up for adoption.[37] Indeed, most teachers of adolescents today may expect to have at least some students who are, or have been, pregnant. At one inner-city Chicago high school, for example, the Chicago Board of Health estimates that one-third of the school's female students become pregnant each year.[38]

Because the physical development of girls in adolescence may not be complete, complications can occur during pregnancy and in the birthing process. Also, adolescents are less likely to receive prenatal care in the crucial first trimester, and they tend not to eat well-balanced diets free of harmful substances such as alcohol, tobacco, and drugs, which are known to be detrimental to a baby's development. These young mothers "are far more likely than mature women to have premature or low-birthweight babies, who . . . account for a substantial proportion of infant deaths and suffer a host of childhood illnesses, birth injuries, and neurological defects, including mental retardation."[39]

Teen pregnancy affects the lives of young mothers and children in other lasting ways. Because most teen mothers drop out of school, forfeiting their high school diplomas and limiting their access to decent, higher-paying job opportunities, they and their children stay at the bottom of the economic ladder. According to the National Urban League, "the poorest people in America today are children living in the homes of teenage mothers."[40]

AIDS   One of the most challenging social problems confronting the schools is providing for the education of young people who have AIDS (acquired immune deficiency syndrome), a condition, nearly always fatal, wherein the body is no longer able to defend itself against disease.

According to data gathered by the Centers for Disease Control (CDC), the number of AIDS cases is increasing at an alarming rate. As of June 1987, there were 36,058 cases reported; by the end of September of that same year, the number had risen to 45,000. The CDC has also reported that the number of active AIDS cases in this country has been doubling every 14 months. Researchers at Los Alamos National Laboratory predict that by 1994 AIDS will have spread to 10 percent of the U.S. population.

Increasingly, states are beginning to require that schools provide information on AIDS and how to avoid the disease. During the 1987–88 school year, 17 states had mandated AIDS education and another 18 states had gone on record as recommending that districts begin teaching about the disease.

Suicide   The increase in individual and multiple suicides among young people is alarming. The suicide rate for late adolescents, between the ages of 15 and 19, has tripled over the last two decades.[41] Suicide is now considered the leading cause of death among 15- to 24-year-olds, according to the Institute of Mental Health. Figure 5.6 shows how the number of suicides among young people aged 15–19 has skyrocketed since 1960.

The causes of the deep depression that drives some teenagers to suicide are many. Contributing factors may be conflict with parents, the end of a relationship with a boyfriend or girlfriend, rejection by peers, breakup of the family, or perceived poor performance in school. Often, as the following comments from a teenage girl who contemplated suicide indicate, no one event triggers thoughts of suicide:

> Well, lots of times I wanted to leave and sometimes just end this, end my life. . . . I mean actually yesterday. I was so upset. I was so depressed that I felt like my life was useless; I was worthless. I was so sad I didn't know what to do really.[42]

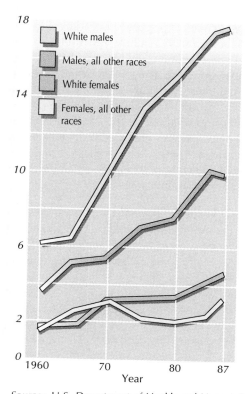

FIGURE 5.6
Suicides, Ages 15–19

Source: U.S. Department of Health and Human Services. As reported in *Newsweek Special Issue, Education: The New Teens: What Makes Them Different* (Summer/Fall 1990): 15.

When a young person commits suicide the effect on his or her peers can be very powerful. Therefore, school personnel should be understanding and supportive, ready to provide counseling to help students handle their feelings of loss and fear. Also, as the following comments from a ninth-grade science and computer teacher indicate, adolescent suicide is also deeply troubling to teachers:

> Of the kids I've had in class, I've had eight kill themselves in 16 years. One played football for me as a ninth grader. I joked with him when I had him; he was a good friend of mine. I knew him better than a lot of teachers; I'm sure I did, yet it didn't help him.[43]

Students with Special Challenges

Like many ethnic and racial groups in our society, **exceptional learners** have often not received the kind of education that most effectively meets their needs. More than 8 percent of the population aged 3–21 is classified as exceptional. Persons who have one or more of the following ten exceptionalities are included in this group: learning disabled, speech impaired, mentally retarded, emotionally disturbed, hard of hearing and deaf, orthopedically handicapped, visually handicapped, multi-handicapped, deaf and blind, and those with other health impairments.

Prior to the twentieth century, handicapped youngsters were usually totally segregated from regular classrooms. In state-run and private schools, mentally retarded, "crippled," and blind and deaf youngsters were taught by special education teachers. Around the turn of the century, however, some mildly handicapped students were placed in special education classes in regular schools. This trend toward self-contained special education classes within regular schools continued until 1975, when Congress passed the Education for all Handicapped Children Act (Public Law 94–142). This act guarantees to all handicapped children a free and appropriate public education. The law, which applies to every teacher and every school in the country, outlines extensive procedures to ensure that handicapped students are granted due process in regard to identification, placement, and educational services received. As a result of PL 94–142, the participation of handicapped students in "regular" school programs is routine; and to be "handicapped" no longer carries with it the stigma it once did.

Gifted and Talented Children   Another group of exceptional students who require special teaching methods and materials are the **gifted and talented.** Such children are quick, eager learners, often capable of mastering a subject or skill with an ease that other students (and some teachers) may resent. Gifted and talented students are often critical of teachers who fail to stimulate and challenge them.

There are many forms that giftedness may take; the trend during the last few decades has been to broaden our view of what characterizes giftedness. In 1961, Louis Fliegler proposed that gifted persons demonstrate at least two of the following qualities: high intelligence, high creativity, high achievement, or a talent.[44] An even more comprehensive definition, proposed by former U.S. Commissioner of Education Sidney Marland in his 1972 report to Congress, has since been widely used:

Gifted and talented children are those identified by professionally qualified persons who, by virtue of outstanding abilities, are capable of high performance. These are children who require differentiated educational programs and/or services beyond those normally provided by the regular school program in order to realize their contributions to self and society.

Children capable of high performance include those with demonstrated achievement and/or potential ability in one or more of the following areas:

1. General intellectual ability
2. Specific academic aptitude
3. Creative or productive thinking
4. Leadership ability
5. Visual and performing arts
6. Psychomotor ability

It can be assumed that utilization of these criteria for identification of the gifted and talented will encompass a minimum of 3 to 5 percent of the school population.[45]

Stereotypes of Gifted and Talented Children   Unfortunately, people commonly have a negative view of gifted and talented youngsters. Like ethnic groups, gifted students are different and thus have been the target of many myths and stereotypes, as Laurence Coleman points out:

The presence of negative images about gifted persons is obvious. . . . Popular sayings or proverbs, such as "the cream always rises to the top" and "a flash in the pan," are prime examples. The frail, bespectacled, loud-mouthed child and the idealistic, misguided professor are frequently seen on our TV screens. Perhaps the simplistic notion of compensation, that bright persons are physically weak, is a form of hostility toward high ability.[46]

In addition, the gifted are often stereotyped as emotionally or mentally unstable, socially unskilled, overspecialized, strange or odd, or conceited. Gifted students can also experience negative attitudes from their peers, as the following high-achieving student's comments indicate:

> Today, one of the students said I was frantic, you know, cause I got through with all my work. I felt funny about it, 'cause here I am trying to do all my work to try and get an "A" because we're supposed to finish eleven units for this marking period. I'm really trying and they're putting me down because I'm ahead.[47]

FIVE-MINUTE FOCUS Reflect on your experiences with social problems at the elementary, middle, or high school levels. Select one of the issues discussed in the preceding sections and describe its influence on you and/or your peers. Date your journal entry and write for five minutes.

THE SCHOOLS AND SOCIAL REFORM

Clearly, the social problems and issues we have examined in this chapter will continue to have a significant impact on America's schools. Although most social ills are beyond permanent solutions, the public looks to the schools to provide leadership for a host of social, political, and economic reforms. For example, the 1990 Gallup Poll of the Public's Attitudes Toward the Public Schools pointed out that more people would require drug abuse education in high schools than would require education in any subjects other than mathematics and English.

For some time, schools have served in the battle against social problems by offering an array of health, education, and social service programs. Schools provide breakfasts, nutritional counseling, diagnostic services related to health and family planning, after-school child care, job placement, and sex and drug education, to name a few.

Though the challenges posed by social problems are great and progress has been slow, schools will continue to play a key role in social reform. According to a Metropolitan Life Survey of 2,000 teachers in 1989, 78 percent of teachers favored integrated, collaborative health education and social services in the schools to respond to the mounting problems of at-risk students. However, 90 percent of the teachers believed that "Schools should mobilize these resources so that they can refer their students to them, but should not be expected to provide for all social/human needs."[48]

CHARACTERISTICS OF SUCCESSFUL SCHOOLS

The many social problems that impact the schools may seem daunting at this point in your professional education. However, a great many schools in all settings and with all kinds of students are highly successful, including inner-city and isolated rural schools and schools that serve pupils of all socioeconomic, racial, and ethnic backgrounds. What are the characteristics of these schools? Do they have commonalities that account for their success?

First, we must define what we mean by a *successful school*. One measure of success, naturally, is that students at these schools achieve at a high level and complete

CONSIDER THIS . . .

Should Social Problem Education Be Required in the Schools?

Examine the following set of twelve items from the 1990 Gallup Poll of the Public's Attitudes Toward the Public Schools. Estimate the percentage of respondents who believed that each item should be a *required* area or topic of study for high school students. Then indicate with an X whether *you* believe the item *should* or *should not* be required, and briefly write the reason for your answer. After completing the items, compare your responses with the research results on page 158. How do your responses differ from the public's?

	% Public View	My View	
	Should Require	Should Require	Should Not Require
1. Drug abuse education	_____	_____	_____
Main Reason: _____			
2. Alcohol abuse education	_____	_____	_____
Main Reason: _____			
3. AIDS education	_____	_____	_____
Main Reason: _____			
4. Sex education	_____	_____	_____
Main Reason: _____			
5. Environmental issues and problems	_____	_____	_____
Main Reason: _____			
6. Teen pregnancy	_____	_____	_____
Main Reason: _____			
7. Driver education	_____	_____	_____
Main Reason: _____			
8. Character education	_____	_____	_____
Main Reason: _____			
9. Parenting/parent training	_____	_____	_____
Main Reason: _____			
10. Dangers of nuclear waste	_____	_____	_____
Main Reason: _____			
11. Dangers of nuclear war	_____	_____	_____
Main Reason: _____			
12. Communism/socialism	_____	_____	_____
Main Reason: _____			

Source: Stanley M. Elam, "The 22nd Annual Gallup Poll of the Public's Attitudes Toward the Public Schools," *Phi Delta Kappan* (September 1990): 49–50. Reprinted by permission of Kappa Delta Pi, An International Honor Society in Education.

requirements for graduation. Whether reflected in scores on standardized tests or other documentation of academic learning gains, students at these schools are learning. They are achieving literacy in reading, writing, computation, and computer skills. They are learning to solve problems, think creatively and analytically, and, most importantly, they are learning to learn.

Another valid measure of success for a school is that it achieves results that surpass those expected from comparable schools in comparable settings. The achievement of students goes beyond what one would expect. In spite of surrounding social, economic, and political forces that impede the educative process at other schools, these schools are achieving results.

Finally, successful schools are those that are improving, rather than getting worse. School improvement is a slow process, and schools that are improving—"moving in the right direction" rather than "declining"—are also successful.

Much research has been conducted to identify the characteristics of successful (or "effective") schools.[49] The characteristics of successful schools have been described in different ways. In several research projects the following qualities have been identified.

- *Strong Leadership*—Successful schools have strong leaders—individuals who value education and see themselves as educational leaders, not just as managers or bureaucrats. They monitor the performance of everyone at the school— teachers, staff, students, and themselves. These leaders have a vision of the school as a more effective learning environment and they take decisive steps to bring that about.
- *High Expectations*—Teachers at successful schools have high expectations of students. These teachers believe that all students, rich or poor, can learn, and they communicate this to students through realistic, yet high, expectations.
- *Emphasis on Basic Skills*—Teachers at successful schools emphasize student achievement in the basic skills of reading, writing, and mathematical computation.
- *Orderly School Environment*—The environments of successful schools are or- derly, safe, and conducive to learning. Discipline problems are at a minimum, and teachers are able to devote greater amounts of time to teaching.
- *Frequent, Systematic Evaluation of Student Learning*—The learning of students in successful schools is monitored closely. When difficulties are noticed, ap- propriate remediation is provided quickly.
- *Sense of Purpose*—Those who teach and those who learn at successful schools have a strong sense of purpose. From the principal to the students, everyone at the school is guided by a vision of excellence.
- *Collegiality and a Sense of Community*—Teachers, administrators, and staff at successful schools work well together. They are dedicated to creating an en- vironment that promotes not only student learning but their own professional growth and development as well.

SUMMARY

This chapter reviewed the complex, multifaceted role that schools and teachers play in American society. First, we examined the various, sometimes conflicting, aims that the public expects the schools to attain. Our nation's schools are expected to contribute to the growth and development of students in four broad areas: socialization, achieve- ment, personal growth, and social improvement.

One of the primary challenges confronting the schools is to provide educational experiences that are appropriate for students from diverse cultural backgrounds. American society is made up of many different ethnic groups, five of which were briefly described in this chapter. Education in our multicultural society requires teachers who openly value diversity and recognize the unique contributions that each student makes to classroom life. Today's schools also require teachers who understand how students' values, beliefs, and lifestyles affect their performance in school.

We pointed out that, while schools are more alike than different, each has a unique culture. Various models of schools and metaphors, we learned, can help us understand the culture of schools. The more we know about a school's traditions, its identity, and the direction in which it is moving, the more successful we will be at meeting students' needs.

A wide array of social problems and issues impact the schools and, rightly or wrongly, many people look to the schools to provide leadership for addressing those problems. Among the problems and issues that will challenge teachers in the 1990s are educational equity, poverty, family distress, child abuse, substance abuse, violence and crime, children at risk, and children with special challenges.

The chapter concluded with a look at the characteristics of schools that successfully educate students, in spite of social problems that impact the educational process. In addition to possessing a set of common characteristics, successful schools are based upon the assumption that *all* students—regardless of ethnic background, socioeconomic status, special needs, culture of the surrounding community, or conditions of the home—can learn.

KEY TERMS AND CONCEPTS

aims of education, **128**	open-space schools, **141**
multicultural, **132**	open-concept education, **141**
culture, **134**	departmentalization, **141**
bilingual education, **135**	school tradition, **141**
ethnic group, **136**	hidden curriculum, **142**
stereotypes, **139**	equity, **146**
institution, **139**	students at risk, **151**
self-contained classroom, **141**	exceptional learners, **153**
team teaching, **141**	gifted and talented, **154**

ANSWER KEY FOR CONSIDER THIS . . .

"Should Social Problem Education Be Required in the Schools?"
Public's Responses: 1—90%, 2—84%, 3—77%, 4—72%, 5—66%, 6—64%, 7—59%, 8—57%, 9—46%, 10—30%, 11—28%, 12—24%.

DISCUSSION QUESTIONS

1. Select one of the social problems addressed in this chapter and discuss the steps that should be taken to solve that problem. Which of those steps should be undertaken by the schools?
2. Do you believe that schools "reproduce" the existing class and social structure— that students from the lower socioeconomic classes are not really being prepared for upward social mobility? Explain.
3. To what extent do you believe schools can improve society? Are those who believe

schools can provide leadership for social improvement unrealistic about the schools' ability to influence society? Why do you feel as you do?

4. Examine the list of characteristics of successful (effective) schools presented in this chapter. What steps can teachers take to develop each quality in their schools?

APPLICATION ACTIVITIES

1. Make a list of recent portrayals of ethnic groups in the movies, television, and other media. Analyze the portrayals in terms of the image they present of each group—positive, neutral, negative, or mixed.

2. Obtain a statement of philosophy from a school with which you are familiar. Analyze that statement in regard to the four major aims of education discussed in this chapter (socialization, achievement, personal growth, and social improvement). Are all four aims reflected in the document?

3. Collect and summarize several newspaper and magazine articles about public expectations of education and the schools. Discuss your findings.

4. Interview members of your local community about one of the social problems discussed in this chapter. How do your data compare with the information presented in this chapter?

5. Consider the extent to which schools have contributed to your upward mobility. In small groups, share your experiences with others in your class.

FIELD EXPERIENCES

1. Visit a school in your community recognized as being successful or effective. What evidence do you find of the characteristics of successful schools discussed in this chapter (pp. 155, 157)?

2. Use the Gallup Poll items presented in "Consider This: Should Social Problem Education Be Required in the Schools?" (p. 156) and interview several parents in your local school district. Which items do they believe should be taught in the schools?

3. Interview two or three teachers at the level for which you are preparing to teach. What do they believe are the major aims of education? How do their views compare with the aims discussed in this chapter?

4. Interview a social worker in your community. According to him or her, what kind of relationship should exist between the schools and social service agencies?

SUGGESTED READINGS

Banks, James A. *Teaching Strategies for Ethnic Studies,* 5th ed. Boston: Allyn and Bacon, 1991. *A comprehensive, authoritative guide for teaching in multi-ethnic settings. Includes an excellent list of videotapes and films on ethnic groups in the United States.*

Bennett, Christine I. *Comprehensive Multicultural Education: Theory and Practice,* 2d ed. Boston: Allyn and Bacon, 1990. *An excellent overview of key concepts in multicultural education, including several sample lesson plans and case study materials. Very useful chapters on the relationships between culture and learning styles.*

Davis, Gary and Margaret Thomas. *Effective Schools and Effective Teachers.* Boston: Allyn and Bacon, 1989. *A clear, concise summary of research on effective schools.*

Farrell, Edwin. *Hanging In and Dropping Out: Voices of At-Risk High School Students.* New York: Teachers College Press, 1990. *A fascinating, intimate glimpse into the lives of young people at risk of dropping out.*

TEACHERS . . .

How would you help a student at risk because of social problems to become more successful in school?

What do you think of the public's expectations that the schools help solve social problems?

I have dealt with many students who are affected by social problems. . . . I try to help them any way I can, but as a teacher you have to realize that you did not create the problem and you probably can't solve it. This is a difficult concept for most educators to confront.

Currently, the public is turning to the educational system to solve every social problem, but I believe the school system can only help individuals deal with these problems, not solve them.

—Julie A. Addison
Rock Ridge Elementary School, Castle Rock, Colorado

When I have a problem with an at-risk student, I contact the families and put in for a referral and a full staff evaluation. You have to find out what the problems are and what school and community support systems are available to assist.

—Anita Dollar
Mitchell Elementary School, Denver, Colorado

If I had a student with an overwhelming social problem that was interfering with his performance in class, I would try to give the child outside help. If that wasn't possible, I would assign a peer tutor to him.

I strongly disagree that the schools should help solve social problems. Teachers are not trained to be social workers and therefore cannot logically substitute for one. Also, with school budgets as tight as they are, we don't have the money to fund programs to deal with social problems at the rate they are increasing.

—Rose Ann Blaschke
Vivian Elementary School, Lakewood, Colorado

The schools do have certain responsibilities and should be accountable in those areas. However, I think the schools cannot solve the social problems. We can help educate the students about options and offer help and possible solutions. We also have to be careful about crossing the "fine line" into intruding on the roles and responsibilities of the family. Parents want you to take care of their child; then when you do, they may think you have gone too far! So where do we really stand and what are the expectations that we should deal with in the schools?

—Suzanne Neal
William Woods College, Fulton, Missouri

ON TEACHING

In the 90s educators must face problems that were nearly nonexistent in the past: drugs, AIDS, divorce, abuse, neglect, homelessness, child suicide, violence, and war. The role of education has expanded beyond reading, writing, and arithmetic. Educators must now teach or reinforce societal values, must report signs of abuse or neglect, must face a roomful of students who lack respect for authority, and must work under budgetary constraints—often with little job security.

I believe that we as educators should help with social problems, because we spend a significant [amount of] time with children. However, we cannot be the sole solution. Parents, grandparents, childcare facilities, and the whole community also need to become involved.

—Jennifer Cronk
Rocky Mountain Hebrew Academy, Denver, Colorado

I feel it is important to get the child to talk out his problem as much as possible in an unforced situation. Once communication is established, a more individual plan can be made for the classroom to meet the child's needs. Often, the parents should be involved so they can be supportive at home.

I feel that many social problems can be solved at school. There is a good support system and a generally shared standard of moral values. The environment promotes communication and problem solving. However, if problem solving is not supported at home it makes it very difficult for any solution to be permanent or effective.

—Amy Orcutt
Green Gables Elementary School, Jefferson County, Colorado

We enable at-risk students to feel successful in a number of ways. The curriculum is performance-based, encouraging regular experiences of success. Each semester we organize a learning project which solves a local social issue and provides a learning theme. Students are assigned to product-oriented teams and experience a great deal of success when their team's solutions receive praise from the larger community. Teachers often work behind the scenes to ensure that each team accomplishes at least one planned goal.

The semester learning projects have changed a state welfare program, publicized the issues of air pollution and water conservation, and researched the need for building a dam. I believe that today's graduates must feel empowered as well as responsible to help their community solve its problems. I believe that the schools should be a learning lab for social issues as well as for academic and vocational skills. Therefore, I also believe it is necessary to teach problem-solving strategies and consensus methods as "exit outcomes" for high school students.

—Olive Ann Slotta
Fred N. Thomas Career Education Center, Denver, Colorado

Historical Foundations of American Education

. . . the true business of the schoolroom connects itself, and becomes identical, with the great interests of society. The former is the infant, immature state of those interests; the latter, their developed, adult state. As "the child is father to the man," so may the training of the schoolroom expand into the institutions and fortunes of the state.

Horace Mann
Twelfth Annual Report on Education, 1848

*D*uring your first year of teaching you are talking with five colleagues in the teachers' lounge about some of the problems U.S. schools currently face. The discussion was sparked by a television special last night that most of the teachers watched about schools in America and how to improve them.

"Well, I think the program presented a realistic view of the challenges that confront today's teachers," one teacher says.

"Right, I was really glad to see a positive, honest portrayal of teachers," another offers. "The message to viewers seemed to be 'Let's get behind our teachers and support them more fully. The work they do is important to our nation's well-being.' " Two of the teachers nod their heads in agreement.

A third teacher looks up from the papers he is grading at a table near the window. "Exactly," he says, "I think the program helped people begin to understand that the problems in the schools are not the fault of the schools themselves. They just reflect what's happening in society." A few of the teachers murmur their approval of what they've just heard.

Then a teacher who recently announced that she will retire at the end of the year begins to speak. She is seated on the other end of the couch on which you're sitting. Everyone listens carefully, perhaps the group's way of communicating to her that her opinion is especially valued.

"When I began teaching in 1958," she says, "we didn't have the problems we have today. We had a job to do, and that was to teach kids. We were there to teach, and the kids, believe it or not, were there to learn."

Before she continues, her attention turns to you. "Then in the 60s and 70s the federal government got involved, and we started having problems. I can't think of any real good that has come out of the federal government's involvement in education. Can you?"

What do you say?

FOCUS QUESTIONS

1. How does teaching today differ from teaching in colonial America?
2. What working conditions did teachers experience in early American schools?
3. What are the major social forces that have shaped American education?
4. In what ways have U.S. schools become more democratic?
5. How has the federal government been involved in the development of our present system of education?

One of the authors once had the privilege of taking a Japanese educator on a tour of local public schools. Our first stop was an elementary school with an excellent reputation. After a short chat with the principal in her office, she took us on a tour of the building. As we strolled down the hallways, we looked in on several classrooms of which the principal was obviously proud. With each stop, the Japanese visitor's reaction was the same—a polite smile and a few carefully chosen words of English to say that he thought the teacher was doing an excellent job.

It was not until our next visit—to a middle school—that this educator revealed an animated, pressing interest in a particular aspect of American education. At this school, the principal just happened to be finishing up a meeting with a school board member. The Japanese educator was obviously pleased at the unexpected opportunity to speak with a school board member and immediately seized the opportunity, asking questions about her activities related to that district's schools. Had she been a teacher before? How frequently do American school board members make decisions about what is taught in the district's schools? How does the board determine organizational and administrative policies? How are board members selected?

Clearly, this Japanese educator was intrigued by the American practice of placing the control of schools in the hands of a local school board—a board made up of leading citizens rather than educators. He was struck by the fact that, in the United States, public schools are run not just *for* the public but *by* the public.

THE IMPORTANCE OF EDUCATIONAL HISTORY

What some might take for granted as the natural way that U.S. schools are organized and controlled by lay persons elected or appointed to boards of education is the result of several social, economic, political, and religious forces that have impacted our educational system. It is therefore impossible to understand schools today without a look at what they were yesterday. Our current system of public and private education is an ongoing reflection of the aspirations and the values brought to this country by our founders. It is an important part of your education as a professional to develop an appreciation for this tradition.

Still, you may wonder, what is the value of knowing about the history of American education? Will that knowledge help you to be a better teacher? First, a knowledge of this history will help you evaluate more effectively current proposals for change. It is very evident that education will continue to receive an unprecedented amount of public scrutiny between now and the turn of the century. Among those groups with a keen interest in schools—parents, politicians, teacher educators, teachers, students, and others—each has an agenda for changing the schools. You will be in a better position to evaluate these changes if you understand how schools have developed and how current proposals might relate to previous change efforts.

Second, a historical awareness of the development of schools and teaching is, by itself, an important part of professional knowledge. The more understanding you have about various aspects of the profession the more likely it is that you will make appropriate professional decisions. Just as an effective democracy demands enlightened, aware citizens, so, too, does a profession require knowledgeable professionals. An important step toward becoming that kind of professional, then, involves acquiring an appreciation of the historical roots of American education. In this chapter we present brief overviews of six periods in American education. At some point in your studies, you may wish to study these events in a course that deals exclusively with educational history.

EDUCATION IN COLONIAL AMERICA (1620–1750)

It is important to remember that education in colonial America had its roots in English culture. The settlers of our country tried initially to develop a system of schooling that paralleled the British two-track system. If students from the lower classes attended school at all it was at the elementary level for the purpose of learning the basics of reading, writing, and computation and receiving religious instruction. On the other hand, students from the upper classes had the opportunity to attend Latin grammar schools in preparation for college. At those schools they were given a higher education, which focused on Latin and Greek classics.

Above all, the early colonial elementary curriculum stressed religious objectives. Generally, no distinction was made between secular and religious life in the colonies. It was quite natural that the religious motives that compelled the Puritans to endure the hardships of settling in a new land should be reflected in the schools' curricula. The primary objective of elementary schooling, then, was to learn to read so that one might read the Bible and religious catechisms and thereby receive salvation.

The Status of Teachers

Since those who taught in colonial schools could do so with minimal qualifications—and for little pay—their status was relatively low. Respect increased with grade level and the amount of education required for the position. Elementary school teachers, the majority of whom had no more than an elementary education themselves, were given the least respect, while teachers in the few Latin grammar schools were accorded the highest status. The comments of one teacher who began to teach at age 19 reveal the low status accorded to teachers:

> . . . that I might appear more than common in a strange place, and be counted somebody, I got me an old wig, which, perhaps cast off by the master, had become the property of his slave, and from the slave it was conveyed to me.[1]

"Special but shadowed" is the way noted educator Dan Lortie describes the image of colonial teachers.[2] They were special because they, along with the clergy, were the only members of the community to have some education, and they were expected to have superior moral character. Teachers were shadowed because they were subordinate to the clergy, the main power of the community. Teachers' extra duties reflected their special but shadowed image: "Teachers rang the church bells, . . . swept up, . . . taught Bible lessons, and occasionally substituted for the ailing pastor. Those who wished to teach had to accept stern inspection of their moral behavior."[3]

Teaching was also shadowed by what was regarded as the real work of the community. According to one source, "Farming was the vital preoccupation. And though males were preferred as teachers, in the summer months, when men were needed to work the land, women were recruited to take their places."[4]

CONSIDER THIS . . .

Have Attitudes Toward Teaching Changed?

Examine the following excerpt from a survey of attitudes toward teachers and the teaching profession. The survey was given in 1934 to a representative sample of 500 last-semester high school seniors (269 males and 231 females) in Pittsburgh. Ten items from the original 52 are presented here. Estimate the percentage of respondents in 1934 who *agreed* with each item and then indicate with an X whether you *agree* or *disagree* with each statement.

After completing the survey, compare your responses to those made more than half a century ago, presented in the Answer Key at the end of this chapter. What differences do you note? Which survey items address issues that are still important today?

Attitudes Toward Teaching and the Teaching Profession

	1934	My View	
	% Agree	Agree	Disagree
1. It requires as much ability to be a worthwhile teacher as it does to be a worthwhile lawyer or physician.	——	——	——
2. Generally speaking, I like teachers and I am grateful for what they have done for me.	——	——	——
3. I think the teaching profession is the most undesirable of all professions.	——	——	——
4. After all, teachers are only human and they deserve much credit for the work they are doing.	——	——	——
5. I think the teaching profession is a very good one to enter even though I am not particularly interested in it.	——	——	——
6. The personnel of the teaching profession is gradually improving.	——	——	——
7. I believe school teachers are a hundred years behind the times and they cannot make the schools what they should be today.	——	——	——
8. Teaching is as good a profession as any other.	——	——	——
9. I would not choose teaching as my life's work because I think the salaries are not commensurate with the education required.	——	——	——
10. There is little chance of advancement in the teaching profession.	——	——	——

Source: Tressa C. Yeager, *An Analysis of Certain Traits of Selected High-School Seniors Interested in Teaching* (New York: Teachers College, Columbia University, 1935), pp. 52–54.

Not surprisingly, the image of teachers in colonial times was a masculine one. Schoolmasters were primarily men, who taught students who were usually boys. Girls were expected to stay at home to learn to read the Bible and to develop their skills as homemakers.

FIVE-MINUTE FOCUS What is your view of the current image of teachers? How does today's image compare with those of the past? What factors in today's world might be contributing to the attention, or lack of attention, that is paid to teachers? Date your journal entry and write for five minutes.

Colonial Schools

No one type of schooling was common to all the colonies. The most common types, however, were the dame schools, the reading and writing schools, and the Latin grammar schools.

The Dame School Dame schools provided initial instruction for boys and, often, the only schooling for girls. These schools were run by widows or housewives in their homes and supported by modest fees from parents. Classes were usually held in the kitchen, thus enabling the teacher to attend, simultaneously, to domestic chores. At **dame schools,** children learned only the barest essentials of reading, writing, and arithmetic. Females might also be taught sewing and basic homemaking skills. Students usually attended dame schools for no longer than a few weeks and only rarely for longer than a year.

Reading and Writing Schools Reading and writing schools offered boys an education that went beyond what their parents could teach them at home or what they could learn at a dame school. In spite of their name, **reading and writing schools** actually devoted little emphasis to writing—learning to read the Bible being the central business of colonial education. Reading lessons were based on the Bible, various religious catechisms, and the *New England Primer.* Students at these schools were also required to memorize the basic fundamentals of arithmetic.

Support for reading and writing schools came from public monies and from fees paid by parents. Due to limited financial support for schools, teachers at these schools frequently had other work to supplement their incomes.

Latin Grammar Schools The Boston Latin school was founded in 1635 to provide a precollege education for the new country's future leaders. At a mass meeting that April, the residents of Boston decided that "our brother Philemon Pormont, shall be entreated to become schoolmaster, for the teaching and nurturing of children with us."[5] The **Latin grammar school,** comparable to today's secondary school, was patterned after the classical schools of Europe. Boys enrolled in the Latin grammar schools at the age of seven or eight, whereupon they began to prepare to enter Harvard College (established in 1636). Following graduation from Harvard, they would assume leadership roles in the church.

At first, grammar schools were seven-year schools; later, they were made into four-year schools. The quality of teaching in the Latin grammar schools was higher

College prep

than that found in the dame schools or reading and writing schools. In addition, grammar school teachers assumed that students had learned to read and write, either at home or in dame schools.

Latin and Greek were the principal studies in these schools, though arithmetic was introduced in 1745. Students were required to read Latin authors and to speak Latin in poetry and prose as well as conjugate Greek verbs. As the following description indicates, both the curriculum and the mode of instruction were rigorous:

> In most of the Latin schools, the course of study lasted for seven years. Apparently school was in session six days a week and continued throughout the winter and summer. The school day was usually from six to eleven o'clock in the morning and from one to four or five o'clock in the afternoon. The boys sat on benches for long hours. Great faith was placed in the *memoriter* method of drill and rote learning. Through repeated recitations the students were conditioned to respond with a definite answer to a particular question. Class discussions were not permitted. The Latin schools inherited the English tradition of severe discipline. It was not unusual for a quick-tempered schoolmaster to hit a pupil for an unsatisfactory recitation. School regulations designated the punishments which should be meted out for fighting, lying, cursing, and playing cards or dice.[6]

The Puritan View of the Child

In addition to learning the rudiments of reading, writing, and arithmetic, colonial schoolchildren also learned their place in the world; they were continually reminded that they were born corrupt and sinful. Adults viewed natural childhood play as devil-inspired idleness, and the path to redemption lay in learning to behave like an adult as quickly as possible. A verse written by Massachusetts poet Anne Bradstreet in the middle 1600s sums up vividly the Puritan belief regarding how we all begin life:

> Stained by birth from Adam's sinful fact,
> Thence I began to sin as soon as act:
> A perverse will, a love of what's forbid,
> A serpent's sting in pleasing face lay hid.[7]

One of the goals of schooling, therefore, was to civilize the child, to compel him or her to set aside childish ways and to become an adult. If the child gave evidence of becoming more adult, this was assumed to be the result of divine intervention. To bring about this admittedly premature growth, the teacher had to correct the child constantly and try to curb his or her natural instincts. As historian S. Alexander Rippa puts it, the colonial schoolteacher was a harsh disciplinarian: "In colonial New England the whole idea of education presumed that children were miniature adults possessed of human degeneracy. The daily school routine was characterized by harshness and dogmatism. Discipline was strict, and disobedience and infractions of rules were often met with severe penalties meted out by quick-tempered, poorly qualified instructors."[8]

The dour, repressive atmosphere of the classroom was further supported by the most widely used reading primer of the time, *The New England Primer*. First printed in 1690, the **Primer** introduced children to the letters of the alphabet through the use of illustrative woodcuts and rhymed couplets. The first couplet began with the pronouncement that

> In Adam's fall
> We sinned all.

FIGURE 6.1   **Two Pages from a 1727 Edition of *The New England Primer***

Source: Facsimile of *The New England Primer, 1727* (New York: Teachers College Press, 1962). Used with permission.

And the final one noted that

> Zaccheus he
> Did climb the Tree
> His Lord to see.

The *Primer* also presented children with large doses of stern religious warnings about the proper conduct of life (see Figure 6.1).

With few exceptions, the learning materials encountered by children drove home the Puritans' religious beliefs. One of the most widely read pieces of the time, for example, was Michael Wigglesworth's poem about the Last Judgment. Written in 1662, *The Day of Doom* was memorized by countless children. An especially terrifying passage describes how innocent infants who died at birth were cast into Hell by a merciless Judge:

> You sinners are, and such as share
>   as sinner may expect
> Such you shall have, for I do save
>   none but mine own elect.
> Yet to compare your sin with their
>   who liv'd a longer time,

> I do confess yours is much less,
>   though ev'ry sin's a crime:
> A crime it is; therefore in bliss
>   you may not hope to dwell;
> But unto you I shall allow
>   the easiest room in hell.[9]

FIVE-MINUTE FOCUS Teachers' views of children have changed greatly from those held by colonial teachers. Write a paragraph or two that presents your view of the child and begins with the following phrase: *"I believe that children are. . . . "* Date your journal entry and write for five minutes.

The Origins of Mandated Education

In the United States today compulsory education laws require that parents, or those who have custody of children between certain ages, send their children to school. How did universal compulsory education develop?

[handwritten margin note: Act of 1642 — a law requiring each town to determine whether its young people could read and write.]

The Massachusetts Act of 1642   The compulsory nature of today's schools had its origins in the **Massachusetts Act of 1642.** Prior to this date, parents could decide whether they wished their children to be educated at home or at a school. Church and civil leaders in the colonies, however, decided that education could no longer remain voluntary. They saw that many children were receiving inadequate training. Moreover, they realized that organized schools would serve to strengthen and preserve Puritan religious beliefs.

[handwritten margin note: NOT mandated establishment]

Twenty-two years after their arrival in the New World, then, the Puritans decided to make education a civil responsibility of the state. The Massachusetts General Court passed a law in 1642 that required each town to determine whether young people could read and write. Parents and apprentices' masters whose children were unable "to read and understand the principles of religion and the capital laws of the country"[10] could be fined and, possibly, lose custody of their children.

While the Act of 1642 did not mandate the establishment of schools, it did make it clear that the education of children was a direct concern of the local citizenry. In 1648, the Court revised the 1642 law reminding town leaders that "the good education of children is of singular behoof and benefit to any commonwealth" and that some parents and masters were still "too indulgent and negligent of their duty."[11] As the first educational law in this country, the Massachusetts Act of 1642 was a landmark, and its impact continues to be felt today.

The Massachusetts Act of 1647   Often referred to as the Old Deluder Satan Act (because education was seen as the best protection against the wiles of the devil) the **Massachusetts Act of 1647** mandated the establishment and support of schools. In particular, towns of 50 households or more were to appoint a person to instruct "all such children as shall resort to him to write and read." Teachers were to "be paid either by the parents or masters of such children, or by the inhabitants in general."[12] This act furthermore required towns of 100 households or more to establish a Latin grammar school to prepare students for Harvard College. A town that failed to satisfy this law could be assessed a fine of five pounds.

As a result of the acts of 1642 and 1647, the colonies schooled all children by 1750. The extent of this schooling, however, was limited to just a few years of instruction in basic skills. The curriculum focused on the knowledge and skills needed to live a life of religious virtue—not on subjects that today we might call practical. Though the laws led to the creation of schools with very limited and narrow curricula, they did establish precedents for the compulsory support of schools and standards for judging their operation.

EDUCATION DURING THE REVOLUTIONARY PERIOD (1750–1820)

Education in America during the revolutionary period was characterized by a general waning of European influences on schools. Though religious traditions that had their origins in Europe continued to impact the curriculum, the young country's need to develop agriculture, shipping, and commerce also exerted its influence on the curriculum. By this time, the original settlers who had emigrated from Europe had been replaced by a new generation whose most immediate roots were in the new soil of America. This new, exclusively American, identity was also enhanced by the rise of civil town governments, the great increase in books and newspapers that addressed life in the new country, and a turning away from Europe toward the unsettled west.

America's break with Europe was most potently demonstrated in the American Revolution of 1776, which freed the 13 colonies of British rule. Following the Revolution, however, many leaders were concerned that new disturbances from within could threaten the well-being of the young country. In an analysis of the Revolution written in 1789, David Ramsay expressed his fear that the ability of Americans to overthrow a government could be used in the future by "factious demagogues" to undermine the American government.[13]

To preserve the freedoms that had been fought for, a system of education became essential. Through education, citizens would learn how to become intelligent, participating members in the new democracy. Prompted by their belief that human beings could be shaped through education, many leaders proposed plans to transform young people into good American citizens. Chief among these were Benjamin Franklin, Thomas Jefferson, and Noah Webster.

Benjamin Franklin's Academy

Benjamin Franklin (1706–1790) designed and promoted the Philadelphia Academy, a private secondary school, which opened in 1751. This school, which replaced the old Latin grammar school, had a curriculum that was broader and more practical. The academy was also a more democratically run institution than previous schools had been. Though **academies** were largely privately controlled and privately financed, they were often supported by public funds. Most academies were public in that anyone who could pay tuition could attend, regardless of church affiliation.[14]

academies *early secondary schools with broader and more practical curricula than those found in grammar schools of the previous era.*

In his *Proposals Relating to the Education of Youth in Pennsylvania,* written in 1749, Franklin noted that "the good Education of youth has been esteemed by wise men in all ages, as the surest foundation of the happiness both of private families and of commonwealths."[15] Toward this end, Franklin wanted the academy to be a vital part of the city and to involve citizens in school affairs. Franklin even urged the trustees of the academy to visit students frequently and to view them as their own children.

Unlike the curricula of earlier schools, the academy made history, not classical languages, the central focus of study. Franklin felt that the study of history would naturally lead students to pursue other subjects offered at the academy: Geography, Chronology, Ancient Customs, and Morality (what we would now call citizenship). Above all else, Franklin emphasized the utilitarian value of the curriculum: "As to their studies, it would be well if they could be taught everything that is useful, and everything that is ornamental: but art is long, and their time is short. It is therefore proposed that they learn those things that are likely to be *most useful* and *most ornamental.* Regard being had to the several professions for which they are intended."[16]

Franklin's proposals for educating youth called for a wide range of subjects: English grammar, composition, and literature; classical and modern foreign languages; science; writing and drawing; rhetoric and oratory; geography; various kinds of history; agriculture and gardening; arithmetic and accounting; and mechanics. The courses of study Franklin recommended undoubtedly reflected his experiences as statesman, diplomat, scientist, and inventor.

Franklin was also influenced greatly by the Enlightenment—a philosophical movement of the seventeenth and eighteenth centuries that stressed the power of human reason and resulted in numerous innovations in politics, religion, and education. He made frequent references to European writers associated with the Enlightenment, especially John Locke. And, not surprisingly, his proposals for the academy completely omitted religious instruction, with the exception of a course on the history of religion. To further promote such ideas, Franklin formed a *junto,* or discussion club, in 1727, and in 1743 he founded the American Philosophical Society. In 1769 these two joined to form the American Philosophical Society for Promoting Useful Knowledge. From 1769 to his death in 1790, Franklin was president of the society.

Academies multiplied across the country, reaching a peak of about six thousand in 1850.[17] They remained the most important kind of secondary school until the high school emerged near the end of the 1800s. High schools as we know them today have many characteristics that may be traced back to Franklin's academy:

1. A curriculum that is nonreligious.
2. A curriculum that offers students at least some choice among courses.
3. A curriculum that is concerned with preparing students to assume their responsibilities as citizens in a democracy.
4. A curriculum that places at least moderate emphasis on the practical value of schooling.

Thomas Jefferson's Philosophy

Thomas Jefferson (1743–1826) was born at Shadwell, Virginia, to a father who was a member of Virginia's landed gentry. Educated at the College of William and Mary, the second college to open in America, Jefferson went on to become one of this country's most influential leaders. Author of the Declaration of Independence at age 33, he also served the public as a member of the Virginia legislature, governor of Virginia, minister to France, secretary of state, vice-president, and a two-term President of the United States. His life demonstrated his wholehearted dedication to education. He was fluent in Latin, Greek, and many modern languages. He was strongly influenced by the work of the English philosopher John Locke, various British ideas on constitutional law, and the writings of French educators.

Above all, Jefferson viewed the education of common people as the most effective means of preserving liberty. As historian S. Alexander Rippa put it, "Few statesmen in American history have so vigorously striven for an ideal; perhaps none has so consistently viewed public education as the indispensable cornerstone of freedom."[18]

Jefferson was dedicated to human freedom and repulsed by any form of tyranny or absolutism. "I have sworn," he once said, "upon the altar of God, eternal hostility against every form of tyranny over the mind of man."[19] Toward this end, Jefferson was decidedly influential in the intellectual and educational circles of his day. He was a member of the American Academy of Arts and Sciences and president of the American Philosophical Society.

For a society to remain free, Jefferson felt, it must support a continuous system of public education. He proposed to the Virginia legislature in 1779 his Bill for the More General Diffusion of Knowledge. This plan called for state-controlled elementary schools that would teach, with no cost to parents, three years of reading, writing, and arithmetic to all white children. In addition, 20 state grammar schools would be created in which selected poor students would be taught free for a maximum period of six years. Jefferson's plan departed somewhat from the practical orientation of Franklin in that the grammar schools would teach boys a more academic curriculum: English grammar, Greek, Latin, geography, and advanced arithmetic.

Jefferson was unsuccessful in his attempt to convince the Virginia House of Burgesses of the need for a uniform system of public schools as outlined in his bill. The cost of supporting the bill and the special interests of various classes most likely led to its defeat. Jefferson was, however, able to implement many of his educational ideas through his efforts to found the University of Virginia. The last years of his life he devoted to developing the university, and he lived to see the university open with 40 students in March, 1824, one month before his eighty-first birthday.

While many leaders of Jefferson's time recognized the importance of an educated public, it was not until the 1830s that a tax-supported system of schools would become a reality. Though various religious groups were still wary of a state-supported system of schools that might not represent their interests, the influence of religion on education was beginning to decline. In addition, prosperous Virginians and conservative legislators who had been generally suspicious of any form of strong central government were beginning to recognize that good citizenship and a strong, free nation required an educational system that was available to all.

Noah Webster's Speller

In the years following the Revolution, several textbooks were printed in the United States. Writers and publishers saw the textbook as an appropriate vehicle for promoting democratic ideals and cultural independence from England. Toward this end, U.S. textbooks were filled with patriotic and moralistic maxims. One of the most widely circulated books of this type was Noah Webster's *Elementary Spelling Book.*

Born in Connecticut, Noah Webster (1758–1843) had successful careers as a lawyer, writer, politician, and schoolmaster. He also gained distinction as the author of *The American Dictionary,* a tremendously influential work based on 25 years of painstaking research.

Webster first introduced his speller in 1783 under the cumbersome title, *A Grammatical Institute of the English Language.* Later versions were titled the *American Spelling Book* and the *Elementary Spelling Book.* Webster's speller earned the nickname "the old blue-back" because early copies of the book were covered in light blue paper and later editions covered with bright blue paper.

In the introduction to his speller, Webster declared that its purpose was to help teachers instill in students "the first rudiments of the language, some just ideas of religion, morals and domestic economy."[20] Throughout, the little book emphasized patriotic and moralistic virtues (see Figure 6.2). Short, easy-to-remember maxims, taught pupils to be content with their lot in life, to work hard, and to respect the property of others. Readers were cautioned to "prefer solid sense to vain wit" and to "let no jest intrude to violate good manners." Webster also gave readers extensive instruction on how to behave in school:

FIGURE 6.2
A Page from Noah Webster's *American Spelling Book*

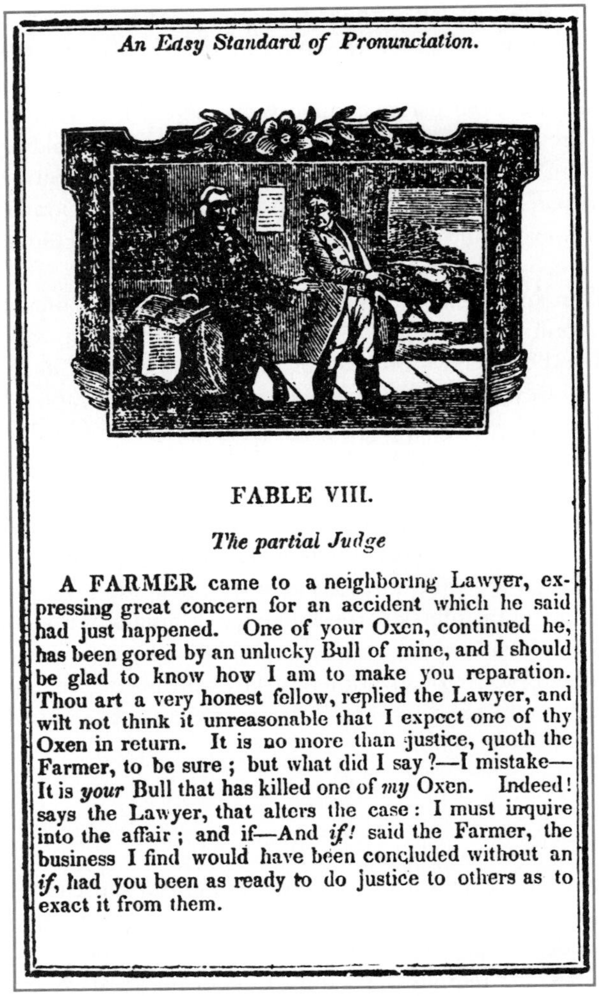

An Easy Standard of Pronunciation.

FABLE VIII.

The partial Judge

A FARMER came to a neighboring Lawyer, expressing great concern for an accident which he said had just happened. One of your Oxen, continued he, has been gored by an unlucky Bull of mine, and I should be glad to know how I am to make you reparation. Thou art a very honest fellow, replied the Lawyer, and wilt not think it unreasonable that I expect one of thy Oxen in return. It is no more than justice, quoth the Farmer, to be sure ; but what did I say ?—I mistake— It is *your* Bull that has killed one of *my* Oxen. Indeed! says the Lawyer, that alters the case : I must inquire into the affair ; and if—And *if!* said the Farmer, the business I find would have been concluded without an *if*, had you been as ready to do justice to others as to exact it from them.

Source: Noah Webster's *American Spelling Book* (New York: Teachers College Press, 1962). Used with permission.

He that speaks loud in school will not learn his own book well, nor let the rest learn theirs; but those that make no noise will soon be wise, and gain much love and good will.

Shun the boy that tells lies, or speaks bad words; for he would soon bring thee to shame.[21]

Webster's speller was so popular that it eventually sold over 24 million copies. Historian Henry Steele Commager said of the book, "The demand was insatiable. . . . No other secular book had ever spread so wide, penetrated so deep, lasted so long."[22] It has been estimated that more than one billion people have read Webster's book.

Webster's speller addressed so many topics that it has been called one of the first curriculum guides for the elementary grades.[23] Viewed by many as the "schoolmaster of the republic," Webster was a post-Revolutionary educational leader who had a profound impact on the American language and sense of national identity.

FIVE-MINUTE FOCUS   Think back to your days in elementary school. Do you recall learning any moral lessons similar to those that Webster included in his *Speller*? How did you learn these lessons? From the books you read? From your teachers? Date your journal entry and write for five minutes.

THE STRUGGLE FOR STATE-SUPPORTED SCHOOLS (1820–1865)

The first state-supported high school in the United States was the Boston English Classical School, established in 1821. The opening of this school, renamed English High School in 1824, marked the beginning of a long, slow struggle for state-supported **common schools** in this country. Those in favor of free common schools tended to be city residents and nontaxpayers, democratic leaders, philanthropists and humanitarians, members of various school societies, and working persons. Those opposed were rural residents and taxpayers, members of old aristocratic and conservative groups, owners of private schools, members of conservative religious sects, and Southerners and non-English-speaking residents. By far the most eloquent and effective spokesperson for the common school was Horace Mann.

free state-supported schools that provide education for all students

Horace Mann's Contributions

Horace Mann (1796–1859) was a lawyer, Massachusetts senator, and the first secretary of a state board of education. He is best known as the champion of the common school movement, which has led to the free, public, locally controlled elementary schools we know today.

The Free School   Mann worked tirelessly to convince people that their interests would be well served by a system of universal free schools for all. His eloquent appeals for a tax-supported school system stir the conscience even today.

reform school

> It [a free school system] knows no distinction of rich and poor, of bond and free, or between those, who, in the imperfect light of this world, are seeking, through different avenues, to reach the gate of heaven. Without money and without price, it throws open its doors, and spreads the table of its bounty, for all the children of the State. Like the sun, it shines, not only upon the good, but upon the evil, that they may become good; and, like the rain, its blessings descend, not only upon the just, but upon the unjust, that their injustice may depart from them and be known no more.[24]

Mann's humanitarian interests went far beyond the need to extend educational opportunity to all, and he became involved in several reform movements. He personally welcomed oppressed immigrants arriving in the United States; he was greatly concerned with the education of the blind; his concern over inhumane treatment of the mentally ill led him to secure a law establishing the first mental hospital in the United States; he promoted the separation of church and state and defended freedom of the press; and he worked for the abolition of slavery. Of all the humanitarian concerns of the day, however, the need for public education appealed most strongly to him.

Born on May 4, 1796, on a farm near Franklin, Massachusetts, Mann's boyhood was marked by poverty and hard work—experiences that no doubt contributed to his later involvement in humanitarian causes. Until he was 15, Mann's only formal schooling had been for brief periods of 8 to 10 weeks a year. However, he acquired from his parents a lifelong respect for learning. "If my parents had not the means to give me knowledge, they intensified the love of it," he wrote.[25] When he was twenty, Mann spent six months doggedly preparing for entrance to Brown University. He went on to graduate with honors in 1819 and even spoke at the commencement on "The Gradual Advancement of the Human Species in Dignity and Happiness."

The Reformed School   In 1837, Mann accepted the position of Secretary of the Massachusetts State Board of Education, a position he would hold for the next 12 years. At the time, conditions in Massachusetts schools were deplorable, and Mann immediately began to use his new post to improve the quality of schools. Through the 12 annual reports he submitted while secretary and through *The Common School Journal,* which he founded and edited, Mann's educational ideas became widely known in this country and abroad.

Mann's *First Report* in 1837 addressed the need for better schoolhouses and criticized the local community for its lack of interest in "the education of *all* its children."[26] In an address to the county common school convention that same year, Mann described the conditions of some of the one-room schoolhouses he had recently visited. One, heated by a central stove that winter, was about 90 degrees in the center of the room and below 30 degrees at the edge. Mann wryly observed that some students "suffered the Arctic cold of Captains Ross and Perry" while others endured "the torrid heat of the Landers," but none was awarded "the honors of a discoverer."[27]

In his widely publicized *Fifth Report* (1841), Mann told the moneyed conservative classes that support of common public schools would provide them "the cheapest means of self-protection and insurance." Where could they find, Mann asked, "any police so vigilant and effective, for the protection of all the rights of person, property and character, as such a sound and comprehensive education and training, as our system of Common Schools could be made to impart?"[28]

Several of Mann's annual reports stirred up controversy. His *Seventh Report* (1843), for example, roused the ire of Boston schoolmasters. In the report, Mann extolled the virtues of schools he had visited in Prussia (now Germany) that implemented the humane approaches of the great Swiss educational reformer Johann Heinrich Pestalozzi (1746–1827). "I heard no child ridiculed, sneered at, or scolded, for making a mistake," Mann wrote. He went on to wonder "whether a visitor could spend six weeks in our own schools without ever hearing an angry word spoken, or seeing a blow struck, or witnessing the flow of tears."[29]

Though initially well received, this report was attacked in writing by 31 Boston principals. One of their rejoinders was titled "Penitential Tears: or a Cry from the Dust, by 'the Thirty-one,' Prostrated and Pulverized by the Hand of Horace Mann." The principals felt that corporal punishment was necessary and that schools should be based on the "stern virtue, and inflexible justice, and scorn-despising firmness of the Puritan founders of our free schools."[30] Mann penned several responses to his critics that were so effective that public support for his ideas actually increased.

The Normal School   During the late 1830s, Mann put forth a proposal that today we take for granted. Teachers, he felt, needed more than a high school education to teach; they should be trained in professional programs. The French had established the *école normale* for preparing teachers, and Mann felt a similar two-year program was needed in the United States. Dedicated to the professionalization of teaching, Mann went on to be the prime mover behind the opening of the first public **normal school** in the United States at Lexington, Massachusetts, on July 3, 1839. The curriculum consisted of general knowledge courses plus courses in pedagogy (or teaching) and practice teaching in a model school affiliated with the normal school.

When Mann resigned as secretary in 1848, his imprint on American education was broad and deep. As a result of his unflagging belief that education was the "great equalizer of the conditions of men—the balance wheel of the social machinery,"[31] Massachusetts had a firmly established system of common schools and led the way for other states to establish free public schools. Financial support for common schools in the state was doubled; three normal schools were opened; salaries of male teachers were increased by 62 percent and female teachers by 51 percent; the school year was increased by one month; teaching methods reflected new and more humane educational theories; school physical plants and instructional materials were vastly improved; and, most importantly, children attended school in unprecedented numbers. The fact that this nation's first compulsory school attendance law was passed in Massachusetts in 1852 is certainly the direct result of Mann's tireless efforts.

Facsimile of 1883 teaching certificate.

Teacher's *2nd* Grade Certificate.

I, County Superintendent of Public Instruction of ...... *Guilford* ...... County, North Carolina, *certify that I have thoroughly and fully examined* .... *Julia C. Ross* .... *an applicant for a Teacher's Certificate,* on the several branches of study named below, and that .... *her* ...... *true grade of* Scholarship *in each is indicated by the number annexed to it, 100 indicating the* highest. (See section 38, School Law of 1881.)

Spelling, (including sounds of letters,)	90
Defining,	85
Reading,	90
Writing,	85
Arithmetic, (Mental and Written,)	80
English Grammar,	90
Geography,	85
History of North Carolina,	75
History of the United States,	75

The said applicant has also furnished satisfactory evidence of good moral char— acter. *This certificate will therefore authorize the said* .... *Julia C. Ross* .... *to teach in the Public Schools in* ...... *Guilford* ...... County *during one year only from date hereof.*

This ...*3rd*... *day of* ...... *Aug.* 188 *3*

J. R. Wharton
County Superintendent of Public Instruction

FIGURE 6.3   The Story of "The Wolf" Taken from McGuffey's *Third Reader*

42   ECLECTIC SERIES.

LESSON XIII.

| wolf | grieved | sleeve | neigh'bors | ear'nest |
| ax'es | clubs | or'der | sin'gle | de stroy' |

THE WOLF.

1. A boy was once taking care of some sheep, not far from a forest. Near by was a village, and he was told to call for help if there was any danger.

2. One day, in order to have some fun, he cried out, with all his might, "The wolf is coming! the wolf is coming!"

3. The men came running with clubs and axes to destroy the wolf. As they saw nothing they went home again, and left John laughing in his sleeve.

4. As he had had so much fun this time, John cried out again, the next day, "The wolf! the wolf!"

5. The men came again, but not so many as the first time. Again they saw no trace of the wolf; so they shook their heads, and went back.

6. On the third day, the wolf came in earnest. John cried in dismay, "Help! help!

THIRD READER.   43

the wolf! the wolf!" But not a single man came to help him.

7. The wolf broke into the flock, and killed

a great many sheep. Among them was a beautiful lamb, which belonged to John.

8. Then he felt very sorry that he had deceived his friends and neighbors, and grieved over the loss of his pet lamb.

> The truth itself is not believed,
> From one who often has deceived.

Source: Old Favorites from the McGuffey Readers, 1836–1936 (New York: American Book Company, 1936; reissued, Detroit: Singing Tree Press, 1969).

Reverend McGuffey's Reader

Though Mann was without question the educator who most influenced the organizational structure of schools from 1820 to 1860, Reverend William Holmes McGuffey had perhaps the greatest impact on what children learned while at school. Far exceeding Noah Webster's speller in sales were the famous **McGuffey readers.** It has been estimated that 122 million copies of the six-volume series were sold after 1836. The six readers ranged in difficulty from the first-grade level to the sixth grade. Through such stories as "The Wolf" (see Figure 6.3), "Meddlesome Matty," and "A Kind Brother," the readers emphasized such virtues as hard work, honesty, truth, charity, and obedience.

Refreshingly absent from these readers were the dour, pessimistic views of childhood so characteristic of earlier Puritan reading primers. Nevertheless, the McGuffey readers had a religious, moral, and ethical influence over millions of American readers. Through their reading of the "Dignity of Labor," "The Village Blacksmith," and "The Rich Man's Son," for example, readers learned that contentment outweighs riches in this world. In addition to providing explicit instructions on right living, the McGuffey readers also taught countless children and adults how to read and study.

Justin Morrill's Land-Grant Schools

In 1862, the **Morrill Land-Grant Act,** sponsored by Congressman Justin S. Morrill of Vermont, provided federal land for states either to sell or to rent in order to raise funds for the establishment of colleges of agriculture and mechanical arts. Each state was given a land subsidy of 30,000 acres for each representative and senator in its congressional delegation. Eventually, seven-and-a-half million dollars from the sale of over 17 million acres was given to land-grant colleges and state universities. A second Morrill Act in 1890 provided even more funds for land-grant colleges that did not benefit substantially from the earlier Morrill Act. The Morrill Act of 1862 set a precedent for the federal government to take an active role in shaping higher education in America.

THE EXPANSION OF COMMON SCHOOLS (1865–1920)

From the end of the Civil War to the end of World War I, publicly supported common schools steadily spread westward and southward from New England and New York. Beginning with Massachusetts in 1852, compulsory education laws were passed around the country. By the turn of the century, 32 states had enacted such laws, and all states had followed suit by 1930.

Because of compulsory attendance laws, an ever-increasing proportion of children attended school. In 1870, only 57 percent of school-age children were enrolled in school. By 1918, this proportion had risen to 75 percent.[32] The growth in enrollment on the high school level was exceptional. Between 1880 and 1920, the general population in the United States increased 110.8 percent, while high school enrollment increased 1,894.4 percent![33]

As common schools spread, school systems began to take on organizational features associated with today's schools: centralized control; increasing authority for state, county, and city superintendencies; and a division of labor among teachers and administrators at the individual school site.

The Kindergarten

Yet another form of schooling began to take hold following the Civil War—the **kindergarten.** Patterned after the theories of the German educator Friedrich Froebel (1782–1852), the kindergarten, or "garden where children grow," stressed the motor development and self-activity of children before they began formal schooling at the elementary level. Through play, games, stories, music, and language activities, a foundation beneficial to the child's later educational and social development would be laid.

Mrs. Carl Schurz, a student of Froebel, opened the first U.S. kindergarten in her home at Watertown, Wisconsin in 1855. Her small neighborhood class was conducted in German. In 1860, Elizabeth Palmer Peabody, sister-in-law of Horace Mann and the great American writer Nathaniel Hawthorne, opened the first private English-speaking kindergarten in this country in Boston. Initially, kindergartens were privately supported, but in St. Louis in 1873, Superintendent William T. Harris established the first publicly supported kindergarten.

Though advocates of kindergartens were divided as to whether the new form of schooling should stress preparation for the academic work of the first grade or foster

Compulsory attendance laws, the first of which was passed in Massachusetts in 1852, have significantly shaped the character of American education.

the moral, emotional, physical, and social development of children (a debate that, incidentally, continues today), kindergartens had become a major force in American education by 1900. The United States Bureau of Education recorded a total of 12 kindergartens in the country in 1873, with 72 teachers and 1,252 students. By 1898, kindergartens had mushroomed to 4,363, with 8,937 teachers and 189,604 students.[34]

The Rise of Professional Organizations

During this period, professional teacher organizations began to have a great influence on the development of schools in America. Two of these organizations, the National Education Association, founded in 1857, and the American Federation of Teachers, founded in 1916, labored diligently to professionalize teaching (see Chapter 13 for a detailed discussion of the NEA and the AFT). The NEA also appointed its Committee of Ten in 1892 and its Committee of Fifteen in 1893 to make recommendations for secondary and elementary curricula, respectively. In 1913, the NEA appointed the Commission on the Reorganization of Secondary Education to reexamine the secondary curriculum in regard to students' individual differences.

The Changing Status of Teachers

By the early 1900s, the demand for teachers had grown dramatically. Teachers came to be regarded as less special than they had been during the colonial era, simply

I promise to take a vital interest in all phases of Sunday-school work, donating of my time, service, and money without stint for the uplift and benefit of the community.

I promise to abstain from all dancing, immodest dressing, and any other conduct unbecoming a teacher and a lady.

I promise not to go out with any young men except in so far as it may be necessary to stimulate Sunday-school work.

I promise not to fall in love, to become engaged or secretly married.

I promise not to encourage or tolerate the least familiarity on the part of any of my boy pupils.

I promise to sleep at least eight hours a night, to eat carefully, and to take every precaution to keep in the best of health and spirits, in order that I may be better able to render efficient service to my pupils.

I promise to remember that I owe a duty to the townspeople who are paying me my wages, that I owe respect to the school board and the superintendent that hired me, and that I shall consider myself at all times the willing servant of the school board and the townspeople.

FIGURE 6.4
Teacher Contract

Source: Willard Waller, *The Sociology of Teaching* (New York: J. Wiley, 1932), p. 43. Copyright © 1932 by John Wiley. Reprinted with permission of John Wiley & Sons, Inc.

because their larger numbers made them more common. An increasing number of women entered the teaching field at this time but were given less respect from the community than their male predecessors, though they were still more highly regarded than women who worked in factories or as domestics.

As in the past, teachers during the early 1900s were expected to be of high moral character. They were subjected to a level of public scrutiny hard to imagine today, as illustrated by a public school contract that teachers were required to sign in 1927 (see Figure 6.4). Needless to say, the request to forego love, marriage, and even male companionship is one that would cause a severe teacher shortage today!

Though they had more years of education than their students' parents, teachers were still regarded suspiciously. Many teachers were outsiders brought into the community due to teacher shortages, and through a peculiar mix of respect and suspicion, they were kept separate from the life of the community. In his classic book *The Sociology of Teaching*, Willard Waller refers to this distancing as an "impenetrable veil" between the teacher and the rest of the community: "The teacher can never know what others are really like because they are not like that when the teacher is watching them. The community can never know what the teacher is really like because the community does not offer the teacher opportunities for normal social intercourse.[35]

Not only were teachers isolated, they continued to be clearly subordinate. In regard to community life in the 1930s, for example, "teachers were kept humble and socially isolated from the seats of power. This was more easily done because teaching, since the turn of the century, had been dominated by women, a group that had its own stigma of second-class citizenship."[36]

THE PROGRESSIVE ERA (1920–1945)

From the end of World War I to the end of World War II, the character of American education was profoundly influenced by the **progressive movement** in American society. During the late nineteenth and early twentieth centuries, supporters of progressive ideals were intent on improving the quality of American life in several areas. Educational progressives believed that the child's interests and needs should determine the focus of schooling. In 1919, the Progressive Education Association was founded and went on to devote the next two decades to implementing progressive theories in the classroom.

Progressives were not united by a single, overarching educational philosophy. For the most part, they were opposed to autocratic teaching methods; teaching styles that relied almost exclusively on textbooks, recitations, and rote memorization; the relative isolation of the classroom from the real world; and classroom discipline based on fear or physical punishment.

Teachers in progressive schools functioned as guides rather than taskmasters. They first engaged students through providing activities related to their natural interests, and then they moved students to higher levels of understanding. To teach in this manner was demanding: "Teachers in a progressive school had to be extraordinarily talented and well educated; they needed both a perceptive understanding of children and a wide knowledge of the disciplines in order to recognize when the child was ready to move through an experience to a new understanding, be it in history or science or mathematics or the arts."[37]

John Dewey's Laboratory School

Progressive educational theories were synthesized most effectively and eloquently by John Dewey (1859–1952). Born in the year that Darwin's *Origin of Species* was published, Dewey graduated when he was 20 from the University of Vermont. He later earned a doctorate at Johns Hopkins University, where his thinking was strongly influenced by the great psychologist William James.

From 1894 to 1904, Dewey served as head of the departments of philosophy, psychology, and pedagogy at the University of Chicago. From 1904 until he retired in 1930, Dewey was a professor of philosophy at Columbia University. Dewey's numerous writings have had a definite impact on U.S. schools, and, as the *New York Times* stated upon his death, he was the "foremost philosopher of his time."

While at the University of Chicago, Dewey established a Laboratory School with his wife. The school opened in January 1896 with two instructors and sixteen students. By 1902, Dewey's lab school had grown to its capacity of 140 students, with 23 teachers and 10 university graduate students as assistants. The children ranged in ages from four to fourteen and were placed in small groups of eight to ten. With Dewey as director and his wife as principal, the school became a virtual laboratory for testing Dewey's ideas. The school was so unique that historian Lawrence Cremin referred to it as "the most interesting experimental venture in American education."[38]

What made Dewey's Laboratory School so unique was that it was thoroughly child-centered. The curriculum was a natural outgrowth of the children's interests. The faculty was committed to following the lead set by students. In addition to giving students a meaningful, relevant education, Dewey's school had two purposes: "(1) to exhibit, test, verify, and criticize [Dewey's] theoretical statements and principles; and (2) to add to the sum of facts and principles in its special line with question marks, rather than fixed rules."[39]

Keepers of the Dream

John Dewey
(1859–1952)
Leader of the Progressive
Movement in Education

John Dewey, philosopher and educator, is perhaps most remembered as the leading advocate of progressive education. A strong believer in developing the school curriculum around the needs and interests of students, Dewey has had a profound and lasting impact on education in the United States, as this newspaper article attests.

Dr. John Dewey Dead at 92; Philosopher a Noted Liberal

The Father of Progressive Education Succumbs in Home to Pneumonia

Dr. Dewey's principal achievement was perhaps his educational reform. He was the chief prophet of progressive education. After twenty years that movement—"learning by doing"—had become a major factor in American education in the late Thirties, and in 1941 the New York State Department of Education approved a six-year experiment in schools embodying the Dewey philosophy.

But progressive education was long the center of controversy among educators, and in the early Forties criticism was becoming more outspoken. The revolt against Dewey and pragmatism in education was strongest in Chicago, the scene of his first and greatest triumphs. At the University of Chicago, where Dr. Dewey was head of the Department of Philosophy and for two years director of the School of Education, President Robert Hutchins has sponsored a system of "education for freedom" which seeks to separate the teaching of the "intellectual" from the "practical" arts. . . .

. . . Dr. Dewey dismissed as "a childish point of view" the criticism that progressive education, "a most reactionary philosophy," has led to undisciplined youth. . . .

President Hutchins calls for liberal education for a small, elite group and vocational education for the masses. I cannot think of any idea more completely reactionary and more fatal to the whole democratic outlook.

While Professor of Philosophy at the University of Michigan in 1893 Dewey wrote:

If I were asked to name the most needed of all reforms in the spirit of education I should say: 'Cease conceiving of education as mere preparation for later life, and make of it the full meaning of the present life.' And to add that only in this case does it become truly a preparation for later life is not the paradox it seems. An activity which does not have worth enough to be carried on for its own sake cannot be very effective as a preparation for something else . . . if the new spirit in education forms the habit of requiring that every act be an outlet of the whole self, and it provides the instruments of such complete functioning.

> "*Make of It the Full Meaning.*"

In a timeless way, the educational reform that Dewey advocated almost 100 years ago is still a valid focus for today's educational reform efforts. His dream for education is no less appropriate today than it was in 1893—that teachers understand the importance of professional reflection and commit themselves to making education truly meaningful for students.

Changing Expectations of the Schools

By the start of World War II, the progressive education movement, faced with rising public criticism, began a rapid decline. Many of the schools' deficiencies were blamed on progressive approaches that were seen as soft and lacking the structure and discipline children needed. In 1955, the Progressive Education Association ceased operation. Patricia A. Graham has observed that when the Association began in 1919, "progressive education meant all that was good in education; 35 years later nearly all the ills in American education were blamed on it."[40]

In spite of its short life, the progressive education movement had an unmistakable impact on American education. Many current practices in schools have their origins in the experimentation of the progressive era: inquiry or discovery learning, self-paced instructional approaches, field trips, flexible scheduling, open-concept classrooms, nongraded schools, small-group activities, and school-based counseling programs, to name a few.

The Impact of World War II

World War II created conditions in this country that led to increased federal involvement in education. The federal government funded several new educational programs. One of these, the Lanham Act (1941), provided funding for (1) the training of workers in war plants by U.S. Office of Education personnel, (2) the construction of schools in areas where military personnel and workers on federal projects resided, and (3) the provision of childcare for the children of working parents.

Another influential and extensive federal program in support of education was the Servicemen's Readjustment Act, popularly known as the **G.I. Bill of Rights.** Signed into law by President Franklin D. Roosevelt in 1944, the G.I. Bill has provided millions of veterans with payments for tuition and room and board at colleges and universities and at special schools. Similar legislation was later passed to grant educational benefits to veterans of the Korean and Vietnam conflicts. Not only did the G.I. Bill stimulate the growth of American colleges and universities, it also changed the character of the higher education student population. Generally, the returning veterans were older and more serious than students who had not served in the military.

THE MODERN POST-WAR ERA (1945–PRESENT)

The decades since the end of World War II have seen a series of profound changes in American education. These changes have addressed three as yet unanswered questions: (1) How can full and equal educational opportunity be extended to all groups in our culturally pluralistic society? (2) What knowledge and skills should be taught in our nation's schools? and (3) How should knowledge and skills be taught?

The 1950s

Teachers and education were put in the spotlight in 1957 when Russia launched the first satellite, named Sputnik, into space. Stunned American leaders immediately pointed an accusing finger at the schools and blamed the space lag on inadequacies in the education system. Interestingly, a concern about the quality of education had already existed but been ignored. In language disturbingly familiar, Diane Ravitch, author of *The Troubled Crusade: American Education, 1945–1980,* describes the time this way:

> Government officials repeatedly expressed concern about the shortage of graduates in scientific and technological fields. Additionally, the critics of progressivism complained about the neglect of the basic academic disciplines—English, history, science, mathematics, and foreign languages. . . . Sputnik came to be a symbol of the consequences of indifference to high standards. . . . Sputnik had happened not because of what the Russians had done but because of what American schools had failed to do.[41]

Sputnik and Defense Education   Russia was first into space, vocal critics told the public, because of the poor quality of U.S. public schools. Progressive approaches to schooling had so undermined academic rigor that students were taught less science, mathematics, and foreign language than their European counterparts. Americans, asserted Vice Admiral H.G. Rickover in his 1959 book *Education and Freedom,* needed to recognize that "education is our first line of defense."[42]

Prompted largely by charges that the public school curricula were not rigorous, the federal government appropriated millions of dollars over the next decade for educational reform. Through provisions of the National Defense Education Act of 1958, the United States Office of Education sponsored research and innovation in science, mathematics, modern foreign languages, and guidance. Out of their work came the new math, new science programs, an integration of anthropology, economics, political science, and sociology into new social studies programs, and renewed

Educational excellence became linked with national stature during the cold war period, when the United States embarked on a program of curriculum reform to "catch up" to Soviet achievements in the exploration of space.

interest and innovations in foreign language instruction. Teachers were trained in the use of new methods and materials at summer workshops, schools were given funds for new equipment, and research centers were established. In 1964, Congress extended the act for three years and expanded Title III of the act to include money for improving instruction in reading, English, geography, history, and civics.

School Desegregation   Since the end of World War II, significant gains have also been made in granting equal educational opportunity to all groups in our society. On May 17, 1954, the United States Supreme Court rejected the "separate but equal" doctrine that had been used as a justification for excluding blacks from attending school with whites. Declared Chief Justice Earl Warren, speaking for the Court in *Brown* v. *Board of Education of Topeka, Kansas:* to segregate schoolchildren "from others of similar age and qualifications solely because of their race generates a feeling of inferiority as to their status in the community that may affect their hearts and minds in a way unlikely ever to be undone."[43]

Brown v. *Board of Education of Topeka* made it clear that our country's well-being depended on our ability to provide equal educational opportunity—an opportunity essential for success in life. As Justice Warren stated in the text of the Supreme Court opinion:

> Today, education is perhaps the most important function of state and local governments. Compulsory school attendance laws and the great expenditures for education both demonstrate our recognition of the importance of education to our democratic society. It is required in the performance of our most basic public responsibilities, even service in the armed forces. It is the very foundation of good citizenship. Today it is a principal instrument in awakening the child to cultural values, in preparing him for later professional training, and in helping him to adjust normally to his environment. In these days, it is doubtful that any child may reasonably be expected to succeed in life if he is denied the opportunity of an education. Such an opportunity, where the state has undertaken to provide it, is a right which must be made available to all on equal terms.
>
> We come then to the question presented: Does segregation of children in public schools solely on the basis of race, even though the physical facilities and other "tangible" factors may be equal, deprive the children of the minority group of equal education opportunities? We believe that it does.[44]

The Supreme Court's ruling did not bring an immediate end to segregated schools. Though the Court one year later ordered that **desegregation** proceed with "all deliberate speed," opposition to school integration arose in school districts across the country. Some districts, whose leaders modeled restraint and a spirit of cooperation, desegregated peacefully. Other districts became battlegrounds, characterized by boycotts, rallies, and occasionally violence.

Process of eliminating Schooling practices based on the separation of racial groups

The 1960s

The 1960s, hallmarked by the Kennedy administration's spirit of action and high hopes, provided a climate supportive of change. Classrooms were often places of pedagogical experimentation and creativity. The open-education movement, team teaching, individualized instruction, the integrated-day concept, flexible scheduling, and nongraded schools were some of the innovations that teachers were asked to implement. Implied in these structural, methodological, and curricular changes was the belief that teachers were capable professionals.

The image of teachers and the significance of education was further enhanced by the publication and warm reception of a number of books written by educators in the 1960s. A.S. Neill's *Summerhill* (1960), Sylvia Ashton-Warner's *Teacher* (1963), John Holt's *How Children Fail* (1964), Herbert Kohl's *36 Children* (1967), James Herndon's *The Way It Spozed to Be* (1969), and Jonathan Kozol's *Death at an Early Age* (1967), a few of the classics that appeared at the time, gave readers inside views of teachers at work and teachers' perceptions of how students learn. These books made it clear that the teacher must be a theorist as well as a practitioner, one who can simultaneously analyze the educative process and teach students.

The Great Society   The education of poor youngsters received a boost in April 1965 when Congress passed the **Elementary and Secondary Education Act.** As part of President Lyndon B. Johnson's Great Society program, the act allocated funds on the basis of the number of poor children in school districts. Thus, schools in poverty areas that frequently had to cope with such problems as low achievement, poor discipline, truancy, and high teacher turnover rates, received much needed assistance in addressing their problems.

In 1968, the Elementary and Secondary Education Act was amended with Title VII, the Bilingual Education Act. This act provided federal aid to low-income children "of limited English-speaking ability." The act did not spell out clearly what bilingual education might mean other than to say that it provided money for local school districts to "develop and carry out new and imaginative elementary and secondary school programs" to meet the needs of non-English-speaking children. Since the passing of Title VII, debate over the ultimate goal of bilingual education has been intense: should it help students to make the *transition* to regular English-speaking classrooms, or should it help such students *maintain* their non-English language and culture?

The Lost Promise of Curriculum Reform   During the reform activity of the 1960s, public school enrollments rose dramatically. In 1950, about 25 million children were enrolled; in 1960, about 36 million; and in 1970, about 50 million. As a result of a decline in births, however, this trend stopped abruptly in the late 1970s. In the fall of 1979, for example, 41.5 million students were enrolled in K–12 classes, a decrease of 1,069,000 or 2.5 percent, from the year before.[45]

The curriculum reform movement of the 1960s did not bear the positive results that its supporters hoped for. The benefits of the new federally funded programs reached only a small percentage of teachers. In regard to some of the new materials—those related to the new math, for example—teachers complained that the recommended approaches failed to take into account the realities of classroom life. Many of the materials, it turned out, were developed by persons who had little or no classroom experience. Thus, many teachers of the 1960s ignored the innovations and continued teaching as they had always done. In fact, this tendency for teachers to resist many educational reforms has continued into the present. As Diane Ravitch points out,

> A teacher whose career began in 1960 has lived through an era of failed revolutions. One movement after another arrived, peaked, and dispersed. Having observed the curriculum reform movement, the free school movement, the minimum competency

movement, and, more frequently, the back-to-basics movement, a veteran teacher may be excused for secretly thinking, when confronted by the next campaign to "save" the schools, "This too shall pass."[46]

The 1970s

The image of teachers became worse again during the 1970s. The decade was a mixed one for American education, marked by drops in enrollment, test scores, and public confidence, as well as progressive policy changes that promoted a more equal education for all Americans. Calls for "back to basics" and teacher accountability drives initiated by parents, citizens groups, and politicians who were unhappy with the low academic performance level of many students were also prominent during this troubled decade.

The steadily downward trend in the Scholastic Aptitude Test (SAT) scores was taken as a sign that education was in serious trouble. And for the first time in polling history, more than half of the American adults polled in 1979 reported that they regarded themselves as better educated than the younger generation.[47]

Financial difficulties also confronted the schools, contributing to the gloom. Instead of increasing as it had since 1940, the enrollment of children in grades 1–8 in public and private schools declined by nearly five-and-one-half million during the seventies.[48] Schools found themselves in financial trouble with a reduction in state aid, which was determined on the basis of pupil attendance figures. Financial problems were exacerbated by reduced support from local taxpayers, who resisted tax increases for the schools because they were stressed by their own economic problems, or had lost confidence in the schools, or because fewer of them had children in school. Consequently, the ability to meet the needs of students was further reduced.

Many parents responded to the crisis by becoming education activists, seeking or establishing alternative schools, or joining the home education movement led by John Holt, who by then had given up on reforming the schools. For these parents, the image of teachers and schools was quite poor; they believed that they could provide a better education for their children than public school teachers could.

FACT FINDING

How Have SAT Scores Changed?

Between 1963 and 1980, combined SAT scores fell by nearly 100 points, but between 1980 and 1985 scores rose by 16 points. Between 1988 and 1990, however, scores again fell.

Scholastic Aptitude Test (SAT) Scores

Year*	Total	Verbal	Math
	Average Test Scores		
1963	980	478	502
1964	973	475	498
1965	969	473	496
1966	967	471	496
1967	958	466	492
1968	958	466	492
1969	956	463	493
1970	948	460	488
1971	943	455	488
1972	937	453	484
1973	926	445	481
1974	924	444	480
1975	906	434	472
1976	903	431	472
1977	899	429	470
1978	897	429	468
1979	894	427	467
1980	890	424	466
1981	890	424	466
1982	893	426	467
1983	893	425	468
1984	897	426	471
1985	906	431	475
1986	906	431	475
1987	906	430	476
1988	904	428	476
1989	903	427	476
Average 1963–1989	900	424	476

*Averages for 1972 through 1988 are based on college-bound seniors. Averages for 1963 through 1971 are estimates provided by the College Board; background information needed for specific identification of college-bound seniors was not collected before 1972.

Sources: Condition of Education 1990, Vol. 1, Elementary and Secondary Education, National Center for Education Statistics, p. 117, and *The Chronicle of Higher Education,* 5 September 1990, p. A33.

School Accountability   Those who kept their children in the public schools demanded teacher accountability, with the consequence that teachers' instructional flexibility was limited and their evaluation paperwork extended. Teacher-proof curricular packages descended on teachers, spelling out with their cookbook directions the deeper message that they were not to be trusted to teach on their own. Confidence in teachers reached a low point.

In addition, during the late 1960s and early 1970s increasing numbers of young people questioned what the schools were teaching and how they were teaching it. Thousands of young people mobilized in protest against an establishment they viewed as in support of an immoral, undeclared war in Vietnam and unconcerned with the oppression of minorities at home. In their search for reasons why these and other social injustices were allowed to exist, many militant youth groups singled out the schools' curricula. From their perspective, the schools were teaching subjects that were not relevant to finding solutions to pressing problems.

Responding in good faith to their critics' accusations, schools greatly expanded their curricular offerings and instituted a wide variety of instructional strategies. In making these changes, however, school personnel gradually realized that they were alienating other groups; taxpayers who accused schools of extravagant spending; religious sects who questioned the values that children were being taught; back-to-basics advocates who charged that students were not learning how to read, write, and compute; citizens who were alarmed at steadily rising school crime, drugs, and violence; and, finally, sharp-tongued critics who wondered why so many teachers couldn't teach. In short, the schools found themselves under siege from many quarters.

In spite of several well-documented failures, however, the reforms of the 1960s and 1970s resulted in a number of improvements that have lasted into the present. More young people graduate from high school now than in previous decades, more teachers have advanced training, school buildings are more adequate, and instructional methods and materials are more diverse.

Equal Opportunity   The 1970s were also the years, when some long overdue policy changes were made. For those people who had been marginalized by the educational system, the federal acts that were passed in this decade brought success and encouragement: the Title IX Education Amendment prohibiting sex discrimination (1972), the Indian Education Act (1972), the Education of All Handicapped Children Act (1975), and the Indochina Migration and Refugee Assistance Act (1975). Since teachers were the ones who had to put the laws into action, they could be viewed as America's reformers or as implementers of equal education practices.

Sex discrimination in federally supported school programs was addressed by Title IX of the Education Amendments Act, which Congress passed in 1972. The act, which was actually placed in effect in 1975, stated that "no person in the United States shall, on the basis of sex, be excluded from participation in, be denied the benefits of, or be subjected to discrimination under any education program or activity receiving Federal financial assistance." Following the act's implementation, charges of sex discrimination against females arose throughout the nation. Examples of the stereotypic portrayal of females in textbooks, the smaller proportion of female school administrators, and blatant discrepancies in salary schedules were easily found. An examination of other areas, such as athletic programs, special facilities for sports, and fraternities and sororities, revealed that both males and females had been discriminated against on the basis of sex.

The **Education for All Handicapped Children Act** (Public Law 94–142), passed by Congress in 1975 and signed into law by President Gerald Ford on November 28 of that year, extended greater educational opportunities to handicapped children. This act (often referred to as the **mainstreaming** law) specifies extensive due process procedures to guarantee that handicapped children will receive a free, appropriate education. Through the act's provisions, parents are given the opportunity to assist in planning educational programs for their handicapped children.

One controversial provision of PL 94-142 requires that handicapped children be mainstreamed with nonhandicapped children. Mainstreaming is based on the desirability of placing handicapped children in a "least restrictive environment"—handicapped learners may be placed in special classes only when regular classroom instruction (augmented with supplementary materials and aids) is not feasible. Another controversial aspect of the law is the requirement that an Individualized Educational Program (IEP) be developed, with the input of parents or guardians, for each handicapped learner, to be reviewed at least once a year and revised if necessary.

The 1980s

The first half of the 1980s saw a continuation, perhaps even an escalation, of the criticisms aimed at the schools during the two previous decades. With the publication in 1983 of the report by the National Commission on Excellence in Education, *A Nation at Risk: The Imperative for Educational Reform,* a great national debate was begun on how to improve the quality of schools. Education even became a major campaign issue in the presidential election of 1984.

Nation at Risk *A Nation at Risk* and the dozens of other national reports on American schools were interpreted by some as evidence that the schools were failing miserably to achieve their goals. The report claimed that "if an unfriendly foreign power had attempted to impose on America the mediocre educational performance that exists today, we might well have viewed it as an act of war."[49] Specific complaints in the report included the high rate of illiteracy among 17-year-olds and minority youth, a drop in SAT scores, and the need for colleges and businesses to offer remedial reading, writing, and computation.

The evidence presented in the reform literature resulted in a significant erosion of support for public schools. For many parents who could afford alternatives, the flurry of reform reports was the deciding factor in their decision to take their childen out of the public schools and place them in private schools.

Responses to the Great Debate Superintendents, school boards, principals, teachers, and the public eagerly read the reform reports that continued to appear on the national scene during the 1980s. As a result, many recommendations contained in the reports were either implemented or hotly debated in local communities.

Mortimer Adler's *Paideia Proposal* (1982), which called for a rigorous core curriculum based on the Great Books, prompted several schools to revise their curricula. *High School: A Report on Secondary Education in America* (1983), written by Ernest Boyer for the Carnegie Foundation for the Advancement of Teaching, recommended strengthening the academic core curriculum in high schools, a recommendation that was widely adopted. In 1986, former Secretary of the U.S. Department of Education William Bennett advocated an ideal high-school curriculum that he described in *James*

Madison High. Educators at the middle-school level began to consider creating small learning communities, eliminating tracking, and developing new ways to enhance student self-esteem as a result of the Carnegie Foundation's report by its Task Force on Education of Young Adolescents, *Turning Points: Preparing American Youth for the 21st Century* (1989).

These and other reform reports that swept across the nation during the 1980s made a lasting imprint on education in the United States. Whether specific recommendations for reform were actually implemented in their schools or the possibility merely discussed, teachers generally welcomed the heightened national dialogue on how to improve schools. Though it was a period of ferment and controversy, teachers recognized that it could herald an era of greater public support for education and new and exciting opportunities for teachers who wished to grow professionally.

The 1990s

The push to reform schools begun in the 1980s has continued into the 1990s. Currently, bold new steps are being taken to empower teachers and to restructure schools. Across the country, teachers are becoming more involved in making decisions related to curriculum, textbooks, standards for student behavior, staff development, promotion and retention policies, teacher evaluation, school budgets, and the selection of teachers and administrators. Furthermore, as evidenced by their increased participation on professional practice boards in nearly every state, teachers are having a greater say in establishing criteria for entering the profession.

While extrinsic motives such as money, prestige, and power may have only partially motivated teachers during previous decades, today's teachers are finding new opportunities to satisfy these motives and to shape their professional lives. Many school districts are restructuring their schools through the implementation of shared decision-making and/or school-based management models of governance (see Chapter 8). Furthermore, a variety of career ladders, merit pay plans, and teacher-designed staff development programs, is making it clear that teaching is evolving into a full profession. While it is too early to evaluate the push to empower teachers and to restructure schools, it appears that the trend will continue throughout the 1990s.

SUMMARY

We began this chapter by suggesting that professional teachers are able to use their knowledge of educational history to evaluate current proposals for change and to inform their classroom practice. We then journeyed through six time periods of American education, noting for each period its predominant educational concerns and the contributions made by its most influential educators. The aim of this historical voyage, of course, was to illustrate how current problems and opportunities reflect the past.

In spite of the shortcomings of the U.S. system of education, ours is one of the few countries in the world to offer a free public education to *all* of its citizens. When we look to the future and contemplate ways to make our educational system even better, we must acknowledge the debt we owe to those who have shaped the history of American education up to the present moment. We must be willing to be students of our past if we are to improve education in the future.

The United States has set for itself an educational mission of truly ambitious proportions. To realize fully this mission will be difficult, but an examination of our history shows us that it is not impossible. In little more than 370 years, our educational system has grown from one that provided only a minimal education to an advantaged minority to one that now provides maximal educational opportunities to the majority.

KEY TERMS AND CONCEPTS

dame schools, **167**

reading and writing schools, **167**

Latin grammar school, **167**

Primers, **168**

Massachusetts Act of 1642, **170**

Massachusetts Act of 1647, **170**

academies, **171**

common schools, **175**

normal schools, **177**

McGuffey readers, **178**

Morrill Land-Grant Act, **179**

kindergarten, **179**

progressive movement, **182**

G.I. Bill of Rights, **184**

desegregation, **186**

Elementary and Secondary Education Act, **187**

Education for All Handicapped Children Act, **191**

mainstreaming, **191**

ANSWER KEY FOR CONSIDER THIS . . .

"Have Attitudes Toward Teaching Changed?"

1934 Responses: 1—88%, 2—88%, 3—13%, 4—95%, 5—77%, 6—77%, 7—6%, 8—70%, 9—20%, 10—36%.

DISCUSSION QUESTIONS

1. What remnants remain of the Puritan influence on American education? Of the progressive influence?

2. Do you agree with Franklin that a priority should be placed on teaching students those things that will be most useful for their future professions? What disadvantages might such an approach have?

3. Do you agree with Diane Ravitch when she says that "a veteran teacher may be excused for secretly thinking, when confronted by the next campaign to 'save' the schools, 'This too shall pass' "? What historical evidence can you offer to suggest that school reform measures have been successful?

4. To what extent and how well does American education truly provide equal educational opportunity?

5. What has been the actual effect on the schools of the great debate over education that began in the early 1980s? What evidence can you cite to indicate that teachers are becoming more empowered and/or that schools are being restructured?

APPLICATION ACTIVITIES

1. In this chapter we have summarized briefly the contributions of just a few of the educators who have influenced American education. The following list includes their names as well as the names of a few others. Select one of these individuals and prepare a written report on his or her contributions. If possible, share your report with those in your class.

Henry Barnard	Thomas Jefferson
Alfred Binet	William Kilpatrick
James Coleman	William H. McGuffey
James Conant	Horace Mann
John Dewey	Col. Francis Parker
Benjamin Franklin	Noah Webster

2. Trace the significant events in the development of education in your state. Compare your findings with those obtained by your classmates.

3. Examine several textbooks currently in use at the level of education that interests you the most. Now try to locate some texts that were used at that level several decades ago. What differences do you notice? Report your findings to your classmates.

4. After forming six small groups, have each group prepare a brief presentation on what it was like to teach during one of the six time periods identified in this chapter. If possible, presentations should be based on written accounts by teachers from each period.

5. Read one of the educational reform reports mentioned in this chapter. Present a brief oral summary to the rest of your class. Include in your comments an assessment of whether the report's recommendations have been implemented.

FIELD EXPERIENCES

1. Interview a retired, lifelong teacher about the changes he or she has seen over the years. Also, visit with several elderly people and ask about their school experiences. Do any of their recollections coincide with the descriptions of the time periods discussed in this chapter?

2. Arrange a brief interview with a professor of American history on your campus. Ask him or her to comment on the history of American education. Share your findings with the rest of the class.

3. Visit a museum in your area for the purpose of examining some artifacts from our country's early educational history. Take notes on what you find and describe several of the artifacts to the rest of your class.

4. Interview a teacher or administrator at a private school in your area. Ask him or her to comment on the role of the private school in our educational history.

SUGGESTED READINGS

Button, H. Warren, and Eugene F. Provenzo, Jr. *History of Education and Culture in America,* 2nd ed. Englewood Cliffs, N.J.: Prentice-Hall, 1989. *A thoughtful, well-written account of the interrelationships between American education and American culture.*

Cremin, Lawrence A. *The Transformation of the School: Progressivism in American Education, 1876–1957.* New York: Knopf, 1961. *A classic, award-winning book on the development of progressive education in the United States.*

Johanningmeier, Erwin. *Americans and Their Schools.* Chicago: Rand McNally, 1980. *A thoughtful discussion of how schools have been an integral part of the cultural, social, and intellectual history of our nation.*

Ravitch, Diane. *The Troubled Crusade: American Education, 1945–1980.* New York: Basic Books, 1983. *A very readable, authoritative account of education in the United States between 1945 and 1980.*

Rippa, S. Alexander. *Education in a Free Society: An American History.* New York: Longman, 1984. *A well-organized account of the major events in the history of American education.*

TEACHERS . . .

What is the most important change in education that has taken place during your lifetime, and why was it important?

I believe the most important changes are whole language and curriculum integration. The concept of integrating rather than isolating individual parts of learning is an idea that makes sense! Life is not isolated and fragmented, so why should learning and teaching be?

—Julie A. Addison
Rock Ridge Elementary School, Castle Rock, Colorado

One of the most important changes that has taken place in education in my lifetime is the teachers' freedom to teach the way they want to teach within the curriculum guidelines. I had much stiffer guidelines imposed on me when I first started teaching in the mid-1960s. I even had to follow a strict dress code in my first teaching assignment. The change is important because teachers need flexibility to be effective. They need to feel that they are important to the educational system to do their best job of teaching students.

—Rose Ann Blaschke
Vivian Elementary School, Lakewood, Colorado

One important change in education in my lifetime has been the shift from competitive to cooperative classrooms. In the former, students are motivated by competing for individual stakes, which implies the failure of others. In the latter, however, team victories are the rule and the possibility exists that all can be winners. The cooperative approach also implies that the tasks facing our world in the future are too great for individual problem solvers. Since it is more fun to work as a team, it may also be the most attractive option for the future.

—Olive Ann Slotta
Fred N. Thomas Career Education Center, Denver, Colorado

One of the most important changes . . . [that has] taken place in the classroom in my lifetime is the use of computers in school. As an elementary student I was introduced to the use of calculator[s] in class. This was a new idea to bring it down to an elementary level. My brother, who was a high school student at the time, would bring home stacks of computer cards and would spend many hours filling in little squares on each card so he could feed it through the computer as part of a larger program. Each card would have only one line of a program on it! When I got to high school, I also filled out cards, which were fed by phone to a local university computer room.

Today computers are in the classroom and software has replaced the cards. Children have computer labs where they are taught early how to keyboard and program the computer themselves. Computers are used for everything from language to science and not just math. We have come to live in a computerized world, a great addition and change from the world I grew up in.

—Allyson Briggs
Rosamond Elementary School, Riverton, Utah

Do you think teachers should be expected to model higher standards of virtue?

Teachers are human and have the same strengths and weaknesses as others. They should be allowed to be themselves as long as what they directly teach is not unlawful or immoral.

—Anita Dollar
Mitchell Elementary School, Denver, Colorado

I feel that if you want to teach our young people you need to be willing to model the behaviors you are trying to teach. I feel that if we are preaching not to use drugs, not to drink and drive, to always strive to do one's best, to be motivated to learn, then we need to live by these same principles. Society has every right to expect this from a teacher.

—Amy Orcutt
Green Gables Elementary School, Jefferson County, Colorado

I'm not sure it would be classified as a higher level of virtue, but I do believe that teachers are role models. We spend a great deal of time with children throughout the school year and I think we should respect ourselves and our profession to be a quality citizen. We should live what we preach! If we support drug-free programs, for example, then we should have our personal lives reflect what our professional life is selling to our young people.

—Suzanne Neal
William Woods College, Fulton, Missouri

Philosophical Foundations
of American Education

*I*t might seem a
hard thing to expect
educators to be
philosophers. But can
they be anything
else?

Max Black
*Harvard Educational
Review* (1956)

Southside Middle School has ranked lowest among the city's middle schools on the annual standardized test of basic skills for the last four years. Southside is in a poor area of the city, and few people thought the school could do much better—until Miss Hartford, Southside's new principal, arrived. She has a dream for Southside, and she is about to reveal it to her new faculty at a Monday morning workshop held in the library, three days before the start of the new school year.

"As you know, we have for some time now had scores on the annual basic skills test that place us at the bottom compared to other middle schools in the city. Our immediate goal this year will be to increase the basic skills achievement of every student. *Every* teacher, regardless of subject or level, will stress the basics. To accomplish this, I am instituting several procedures." She then outlines the components of her plan and opens up the meeting for comments and questions.

Mrs. Watkins, a science teacher, speaks first. A 15-year veteran at Southside, she has lived through many programs designed to improve the school. "I'm not against the basics," she begins, "but there's more to education than reading, writing, and arithmetic. If we emphasize only the basics, we'll turn out kids who can't think and can't apply what they've learned." Several teachers murmur their approval at her last remark.

Mr. Harrington, an eighth-grade language arts teacher, then rises to speak. "Our curricula have been weakened by having to teach nonacademic subjects—typing, how to do the family budget, sex and drug education, and so on. If kids were exposed to more great literature, the ideas of great scientists and mathematicians, we wouldn't have a problem with the basic skills." A few teachers nod their approval, but even more express their disagreement. "That's unrealistic," says one. "That's not what our kids need," adds another. "An elitist view, if I ever heard one," says another.

Miss Hartford recognizes the next speaker, Mr. Draper, a seventh-grade language arts teacher. He stands a moment, waiting for the teachers to be quiet.

"The purpose of education is to help kids grow," he says. "We should stress positive, growth-promoting teacher-student relationships—not tests to measure bits of information most kids probably won't use anyway."

As several groans of disagreement indicate, Mr. Draper's position is not popular. Obviously surprised, Mr. Draper quickly sits down.

Miss Hartford now expertly refocuses the group's attention on her plans for the year. "I realize everyone has his or her idea about what the purposes of education ought to be. Such diversity is professionally healthy. I'd like to point out, though, that the program we'll follow this year is compatible with all of the views that have been expressed."

 FIVE-MINUTE FOCUS   Imagine that you are a teacher on Miss Hartford's faculty. What would you tell her the purposes of education ought to be? Date your journal entry and write for five minutes.

FOCUS QUESTIONS

1. How can philosophy contribute to a teacher's effectiveness?
2. What philosophical questions do all teachers have to answer?
3. What determines a teacher's educational philosophy?
4. In what ways have major philosophical ideas influenced education?
5. How can a teacher begin to build a more carefully thought-out educational philosophy?

As the above hypothetical scenario suggests, all teachers must answer several vital questions about their work. What should the purpose(s) of education be? What is the nature of knowledge? Are students inherently good or evil—or somewhere in between? What is teaching? What knowledge is of most worth? How should learning be evaluated? To find answers to these and similar questions, teachers must make use of philosophy. "All serious discussion of educational problems, no matter how specific, soon leads to consideration of educational *aims,* and becomes a conversation about the good life, the nature of man, the varieties of experience. . . . These are the perennial themes of philosophical investigation."[1]

THE NATURE OF PHILOSOPHY

Philosophy is concerned with identifying the basic truths about being, knowledge, and conduct. While the religions of the world arrive at these truths based on supernatural revelations, philosophers use their reasoning powers to search out answers to the fundamental questions of life. Philosophers use a careful, step-by-step, question-and-answer technique to extend their understanding of the world. Through very exacting use of language and techniques of linguistic and conceptual analysis, philosophers attempt to describe the world we live in.

The word *philosophy* may be literally translated from the original Greek as "love of wisdom." In particular, a philosophy is a set of ideas formulated to comprehend the world. Among the world's great philosophers have been Socrates, Plato, Aristotle, St. Thomas Aquinas, René Descartes, John Locke, David Hume, Jean-Jacques Rousseau, Immanuel Kant, Georg Hegel, John Stuart Mill, Karl Marx, John Dewey, Jean-Paul Sartre, and Mortimer Adler. They devoted their lives to pondering the significant questions of life: What is truth? What is reality? What life is worth living?

THE IMPORTANCE OF PHILOSOPHY TO TEACHERS

For the teacher, philosophy can reveal principles that may be used as a guide for professional action. Every teacher, whether he or she recognizes it, has a philosophy of education—a set of beliefs about how human beings learn and grow and what one should learn in order to live the good life. Teachers differ, of course, in regard to the amount of effort they devote to the development of their personal philosophy or educational platform. Some feel that philosophical reflections have nothing to contribute to the actual act of teaching (this stance, of course, is itself a philosophy of education). Other teachers recognize that teaching, because it is concerned with *what ought to be,* is basically a philosophical enterprise. As the great educational philosopher John Dewey put it, to be concerned with education is to be concerned with philosophy: "If we are willing to conceive education as the process of forming fundamental dispositions, intellectual and emotional, toward nature and fellow men, philosophy may even be defined as *the general theory of education.*"[2]

Philosophy is also important to schools. Most schools have a statement of philosophy that serves to focus the efforts of teachers, administrators, students, and parents in a desired direction. A school's philosophy is actually a public statement of what a school values, a description of the educational goals it seeks to attain. So important is a school's philosophy that school accrediting agencies evaluate schools partially on the basis of whether they achieve the goals set forth in their statements of philosophy.

YOUR EDUCATIONAL PHILOSOPHY

In simplest terms, your **educational philosophy** consists of what you believe about education. It includes "the assumptions, theories, and beliefs one holds for key aspects of effective teaching, such as the purpose of schooling, perceptions of students, what knowledge is of most worth, and the value of certain teaching techniques and pedagogical principles."[3] Educational philosophy is also vitally concerned with improving all aspects of teaching. By putting into practice their educational philosophy, teachers can discover the solutions to many educational problems. Five purposes that have been identified for educational philosophy clarify how it can contribute to these solutions:

1. Educational philosophy is committed to laying down a plan for what is considered to be the best education absolutely.
2. Educational philosophy undertakes to give directions with respect to the kind of education that is best in a certain political, social, and economic context.
3. Educational philosophy is preoccupied with correcting violations of educational principle and policy.
4. Educational philosophy centers attention on those issues in educational policy and practice that require resolution either by empirical research or rational reexamination.
5. Educational philosophy conducts an inquiry into the whole of the educational enterprise with a view toward assessing, justifying, and reforming the body of experience essential to superior learning.[4]

There is a strong connection between your behavior as a teacher and your beliefs about teaching and learning, students, knowledge, and what is worth knowing (see Figure 7.1). Regardless of where you stand in regard to these four dimensions of teaching, you should be aware of the need to reflect continually on *what* you do believe and *why* you believe it.

Beliefs about Teaching and Learning

One of the most important components of your educational philosophy is how you view teaching and learning. In other words, what is the teacher's primary role? Is the teacher a subject matter expert who can efficiently and effectively impart knowledge to students? Is the teacher a helpful adult who establishes caring relationships with students and nurtures their growth in needed areas? Or is the teacher a skilled technician who can manage the learning of many students at once?

How each of us views the role of the teacher says a lot about our basic conception of teaching. As we pointed out in Chapter 2, some people view teaching as a science—a complex activity that is, nevertheless, reducible to a specified set of discrete, objectively

FIGURE 7.1

The Influence of the Teacher's Educational Beliefs on Teaching Behavior

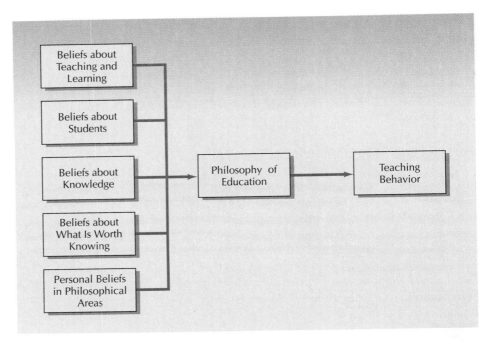

determined behaviors. For others, teaching is viewed as an art—a spontaneous, unrehearsed, and creative encounter between teacher and student. And for others, still, teaching is an activity that is both science and art; it requires the artistic (or intuitive) implementation of scientifically determined procedures.

In regard to learning, some teachers emphasize the individual student's experiences and cognitions; others stress the student's behavior. Learning, according to the first viewpoint, is seen as the changes in thoughts or actions that result from personal experience; learning is largely the result of internal forces within the individual. In contrast, the other view defines learning as the associations between various stimuli and responses; here, learning results from forces that are external to the individual.

Beliefs about Students

Your beliefs about students will have a great influence on how you teach. Every teacher formulates an image in his or her mind about what students are like—their dispositions, skills, motivation levels, and expectations. What you believe students are like is based on your unique life experiences, particularly your observations of young people and your knowledge of human growth and development.

At one extreme are those teachers who come to have largely negative views of students, viewing them as less than full human beings. Young people are not okay as they are but must be made into adults (forcibly, if necessary) as quickly as possible. These teachers believe that the child's natural inclination is not to learn and grow but to resist any and all efforts of the adult to move the child in that direction. As a result, such teachers typically cultivate an adversarial relationship with students. Though such attitudes are often beyond the awareness of teachers who hold them, students are quite perceptive in identifying how their teachers really feel about them.

FACT FINDING

What Do New Teachers Expect of Themselves and Their Students?

New teachers begin their work with optimism and idealism, according to a Metropolitan Life survey of 1,002 teachers who began teaching in the fall of 1990. Ninety-nine percent agree that "all children can learn."

	Percentage						
	Strongly Agree	Somewhat Agree	Somewhat Disagree	Disagree Strongly	Not Sure	Total Agree	Total Disagree
All children can learn	93	6	*	*	*	99	1
I can really make a difference in the lives of my students	83	16	1	*	*	99	1
If I do my job well, my students will benefit regardless of how the rest of the school functions	42	47	10	1	*	89	10
Many children come to school with so many problems that it's very difficult for them to be good students	28	47	18	6	—	75	25
Even the best teachers will find it difficult to really teach more than two-thirds of their students	8	38	39	15	1	45	54

*Less than 0.5%

Source: Louis Harris and Associates, *The Metropolitan Life Survey of the American Teacher 1990: New Teachers: Expectations and Ideals, Part I: Entering the Classroom* (New York: Louis Harris and Associates, 1990), p. 1. Used with permission.

In contrast, other teachers' views of children are almost entirely positive. Children are seen as basically good rather than bad or evil. These teachers believe that, fundamentally, all children want to grow and learn in healthy, socially acceptable ways. Those children who become antisocial do so not because of any innate badness but because of the insidious influence of experiences or hereditary predispositions, both of which are beyond the child's control.

In regard to these diametrically opposed views of children, most teachers would position themselves somewhere between the two—that is, children are neither totally bad nor totally good. We would also add that neither view is correct, rather more or less helpful for bringing about the education of students. The first view of students may promote teacher-student relationships based on fear and coercion rather than trust and helpfulness. The second view runs the risk of not providing students with sufficient structure and direction and not communicating sufficiently high expectations. In the final analysis, the truly professional teacher—the one who has a carefully thought-out educational philosophy—recognizes that children differ in regard to their predisposition to learn and grow. One child, for example, may have knowledge and experiences that suit her for advanced work in small groups; however, she is somewhat lazy and needs to be prodded to get involved. Another child needs gentle support and encouragement in order to feel secure enough to participate in large-group discussions. Yet another child is somewhat of a bully, a low achiever with almost no desire to learn; he requires structure and continuous, firm guidance from the teacher.

Beliefs about Knowledge

Though it may not seem immediately obvious, how a teacher views knowledge is directly related to how he or she goes about teaching. If knowledge is viewed as the sum total of small bits of subject matter or discrete facts, students will most likely spend a great deal of time learning that information in a straightforward, rote manner. As students, we have all, at one time or another, been directed to memorize certain information: the capitals of the 50 states, definitions for the eight parts of speech, the exact contents of the periodic table in chemistry, and so on.

Other teachers view knowledge more conceptually, that is, as consisting of the big ideas that enable us to understand and influence our environment. Such a teacher would want students to be able to explain how legislative decisions are made in the state capital, how an understanding of the eight parts of speech can empower the writer and vitalize one's writing, and how chemical elements are grouped according to their atomic numbers.

Finally, teachers differ in regard to whether they consider students' increased understanding of their own experiences a legitimate form of knowledge. Knowledge of self and one's experiences in the world is clearly not the same as knowledge about a particular subject, yet such knowledge is essential if one is to live a full, satisfying life. Teachers who primarily view knowledge as that which enables the individual to confront and interpret the meaning of experience will present students with opportunities to develop that ability. Thus, students would be required to reflect on how they might use the disciplines of social studies, English grammar, or chemistry to further their understanding of the world.

Beliefs about What Is Worth Knowing

It is obvious that teachers want students to learn as a result of their efforts, though teachers differ in regard to what they believe should be taught. Teacher A feels that it is most important that students learn the basic skills of reading, writing, computation, and oral communication. These are the skills they will need to be successful in their chosen occupations, and it is the school's responsibility to prepare students for the world of work. Teacher B believes that the most worthwhile content is to be found in the classics or the Great Books. Through mastering the great ideas from the sciences, mathematics, literature, and history, students will be well prepared to deal with the world of the future. Teacher C is most concerned with students learning how to reason, communicate effectively, and solve problems. Students who master these cognitive processes will have learned how to learn—and this is the most realistic preparation for an unknown future. Finally, Teacher D is concerned with developing the whole child, teaching students to become self-actualizing persons. Thus, the content of the curriculum should be meaningful to the student; it should contribute as much as possible to the student's efforts to become a mature, well-integrated person.

Your beliefs about teaching and learning, students, knowledge, and what knowledge is worth knowing, then, are the foundation of your educational philosophy. These beliefs will guide your practice as a professional teacher, and it is important that you develop the mental habit of continually reviewing your philosophy.

✓ CONSIDER THIS . . .

What Are Your Views on Educational Goals?

After studying the following list, cross out the ten educational goals that you regard as least important. Then rank the remaining ten items in the order of their importance to you by numbering them from 1 to 10 from the most to the least important. To learn where you stand among the six philosophical orientations to teaching, compare your results with the key at the end of the chapter.

me = exist + behavior

a. Practical preparation for life and work _____

b. The fostering of curiosity and creativity _____5_____

c. The teaching of cognitive and critical thinking skills _____

d. Self-actualization of the whole person _____1_____

e. The teaching of basic communication skills _____8_____

f. Behavior modification _____10_____

g. Moral education _____6_____

h. Exposure to great ideas and enduring truths _____

i. Preparation for whatever the future holds _____

j. The search for truth _____

k. The teaching of problem-solving skills _____9_____

l. Exposure to great works in the humanities _____

m. The fostering of positive values and citizenship _____

n. The mastery of facts and scientific information _____

o. Transmission of a common core of knowledge _____4_____

p. Cultivation of the intellect _____

q. The development of rational, well-rounded individuals _____2_____

r. The search for personal meaning _____3_____

s. Values clarification _____

t. The global improvement of the quality of life _____7_____

Nope

more than one = eclectic

BRANCHES OF PHILOSOPHY

To provide you with further tools to use in formulating and clarifying your educational philosophy, this section will present brief overviews of six areas of philosophy that are of central concern to teachers: metaphysics, epistemology, axiology, ethics, aesthetics, and logic. Each of these areas focuses on one of the questions that have concerned the world's greatest philosophers for centuries: What is the nature of reality? What is the nature of knowledge and is truth ever attainable? According to what values should one live life? What is good and what is evil? What is the nature of beauty? and finally, What processes of reasoning will yield consistently valid results? While we readily admit that answers to these questions are not easily found (indeed, these questions continue to challenge the world's sharpest minds), as a teacher you do need to arrive at *your own* answers to these questions.

Metaphysics

Metaphysics is concerned with explaining, as rationally and as comprehensively as possible, the nature of reality (in contrast to how reality appears). What is reality? What is the world made of? These are metaphysical questions. Metaphysics is sometimes used interchangeably with ontology, which derives from the Latin term *onto* (to be) and *ology* (the study of). Ontology is concerned with the nature of being and explores questions such as, What does it mean to exist? What is humankind's place in the scheme of things?

Since anything that is real must exist, and anything that exists must be real, we will not make the fine distinctions between metaphysics and ontology that some philosophers do. What we wish to stress, however, is that such metaphysical questions are at the very heart of educational philosophy. As one educational philosopher put it, "nothing short of the fullest awareness possible of 'man's place in the cosmos' is the constant problem of the philosopher of education."[5] Or, as others put it: "Our ultimate preoccupation in educational theory is with the most primary of all philosophic problems: metaphysics, the study of ultimate reality."[6]

To some, it may seem a waste of time to speculate about what is real. After all, isn't it possible to care not one whit about such problems and still live quite satisfactorily from day to day? We would point out, however, that most of humankind's great technological advances have come about because of our dogged determination to understand the world better. We have gone far beyond the metaphysics of the early Greeks, who believed that reality consisted of earth, air, fire, and water. Our quest for answers to metaphysical questions has made possible, for example, our dramatic breakthroughs in the exploration of space. The continuing press to answer such questions places humankind on the verge of looking back in time to the very origins of the universe. It is the engine that drives many ventures—formulating tentative explanations of such mind-boggling phenomena as black holes, pulsars, quarks, and quasars, and sending people to the moon.

Metaphysics has important implications for education because the school curriculum is based on what we know about reality. And what we know about reality is driven by the kinds of questions we ask about the world. We would not, for example, teach students about neutrons and protons inside the nucleus of atoms had others not been driven to discover the tiniest bit of matter, the ultimate stuff of which reality is composed. In fact, any position regarding what the schools should teach has behind it a particular view of reality, a particular set of responses to metaphysical questions.

Even though definitive answers to metaphysical questions are ultimately beyond human intelligence, teachers do convey, implicitly as well as explicitly, their views of reality to students. It is important, then, that you give serious consideration to the major metaphysical questions that confront all humankind: What is the meaning of life? Do events in the universe occur randomly or according to a purpose? Is our behavior determined or the result of our free will? If you honestly and openly search out your own answers to questions such as these, you will increase the likelihood that your students will, in turn, become earnest, open seekers of knowledge.

Epistemology

The next major set of philosophical questions that concerns teachers is called **epistemology.** These questions all focus on knowledge: What knowledge is true? How does knowing take place? How do we know that we know? How do we decide between opposing views of knowledge (for example, creationist versus evolutionary explanations for the beginning of life on our planet)? Is truth constant, or does it change from situation to situation? and finally, What knowledge is of most worth?

Epistemology is of central concern to teachers since a school's main task is to present knowledge of the world to students. Schools, first of all, must be confident that the knowledge presented to students is true, and, secondly, the school must understand as much as possible how it is that students come to know. The school's major function as a transmitter of knowledge is illuminated effectively by Van Cleve Morris and Young Pai, who suggest an intriguing simile for the school.

> The school can be likened to a store whose stock in trade is knowledge. Knowledge of all types lines its shelves, and its principal task is to retail this knowledge to each wave of customers, and succeeding generation. But as an epistemological retail establishment it has two fundamental problems. One concerns the authenticity and accuracy of the stock itself. Can we have confidence that all of the items on the "shelf of knowledge" are really true? In order to be sure, we must inquire into how these things were first found out. If we have confidence in such-and-such a method of finding something out, then we can return to the "store," tag the "merchandise" as authentic, and proceed to retail it as true. . . .
>
> Our second concern in the epistemological retail establishment concerns the "customers": How do they come to know things? If we understood how knowing-in-general takes place, perhaps we could get a better idea of how boys' and girls' knowing in the classroom takes place. Especially would this be true if we could discover a similarity between the knowing process of the research scholar, standing at the frontier of knowledge and probing the unknown, and the knowing process of youngsters standing at their own "frontier" and being taken by their teacher in successive stages into wider and wider spheres of thought and action.[7]

How you answer the epistemological questions that confront all teachers will have significant implications for your approach to curriculum and instruction. First, you will need to determine what is true about the content you will teach, then you must decide on the most appropriate means of conveying this content to students. Even a casual consideration of epistemological questions reveals that there are many ways of knowing about the world. We believe that there are at least five different ways of knowing that are of interest to teachers.

1. *Knowing based on authority:* People acquire knowledge from the sage, the poet, the priest, or the ruler. In schools, the textbook, the teacher, the administrator are the sources of authority for students. In everyday conversations, we refer to unnamed "experts" as sources of authoritative knowledge: *They* say we'll have a manned flight to Mars by the turn of the century.

2. *Knowing based on divine revelation:* Throughout human history, supernatural revelations have been a major source of knowledge about the world. Whether it be the sun god of early man, the many gods of the ancient Greeks, or the Judeo-Christian god, divine revelations have provided humans with knowledge about life.

3. *Knowing based on empiricism (experience):* The term *empirical* refers to knowledge acquired through the senses. When we state that experience is the best teacher, we refer to this mode of knowing. Informally gathered empirical data direct most of our daily behavior.

4. *Knowing based on reason:* We can also come to know things as a result of our ability to reason and use logical analysis. In schools, students learn to apply rational thought to such tasks as solving mathematical problems, distinguishing facts from opinions, or defending or refuting a particular argument. Many students also learn a method of reasoning and analyzing empirical data known as the scientific method. Through this method a problem is identified, relevant data are gathered, a hypothesis is formulated based on these data, and the hypothesis is empirically tested.

5. *Knowing based on intuition:* Just about everyone has at some time acquired knowledge through intuition, a nondiscursive (beyond reason) form of knowing. Intuition draws from our prior knowledge and experience and gives us an immediate understanding of the situation at hand. Our intuition convinces us that we know something, but we don't know how we know. Our intuitive sense would seem to be a mixture of instinct, emotion, and imagination.

As a teacher, you should remember that there is no right way to acquire knowledge. A particular mode of acquiring knowledge that works for one student may not work for another.

Axiology

The next set of philosophical problems concerns values. What values should teachers encourage students to adopt? What values raise the human race to its highest levels of humaneness? What values does a truly educated person hold? These are a few of the axiological questions that teachers must answer for themselves.

In essence, **axiology** highlights the fact that the teacher has an interest not only in the *quantity* of knowledge that students acquire but also in the *quality* of life that becomes possible because of that knowledge. Extensive knowledge of the basic skills, the Great Books of the Western World, or trigonometry, for example, may not benefit the individual if he or she is unable to put that knowledge to good use. This, of course, raises additional questions: How do we define quality of life? What curricular experiences contribute most to that quality of life? All teachers must deal with the issues raised by these questions.

Ethics   The term **ethics** is sometimes used interchangeably with axiology. While axiology addresses the question "What is valuable?" ethics focuses on "What is good and evil, right and wrong?"

A knowledge of ethics can help the teacher solve many of the dilemmas that arise in the classroom. Frequently, teachers must take action in situations where they are unable to gather all of the relevant facts and where no single course of action is totally right or wrong. A student whose previous work was above average is known—by the teacher and several classmates—to have plagiarized a term paper: Should the teacher fail the student for the course if the example of swift, decisive punishment will likely prevent other students from plagiarizing? Or should the teacher, following her hunches about what would be in the student's long-term interest, have the student redo the term paper and risk the possibility that other students might get the mistaken notion that plagiarism has no negative consequences? Another ethical dilemma: Is an elementary mathematics teacher justified in trying to increase achievement for the whole class by separating two disruptive girls and placing one in a mathematics group beneath her level?

Ethics can provide the teacher with ways of thinking about problems where it is difficult to determine the right course of action. This branch of philosophy also helps the teacher to understand that "ethical thinking and decision making are not just following the rules."[8]

Aesthetics The branch of axiology known as **aesthetics** is concerned with values related to beauty and art. While we expect that teachers of music, art, drama, literature, and writing regularly have students make judgments about the quality of works of art, we can easily overlook the role that aesthetics ought to play in *all* areas of the curriculum. Harry Broudy, a well-known educational philosopher, said that the arts are "necessary," not "just nice."[9] Through the heightening of their aesthetic perceptions, students can find increased meaning to all aspects of life.

Aesthetics can also help the teacher increase his or her effectiveness. Teaching, because it may be viewed as a form of artistic expression, can be judged according to artistic standards of beauty and quality.[10] In this regard, the teacher is an artist and continually tries to improve the quality of his or her work.

Logic

If all the parties who have a genuine interest in education were to decide on a single goal that schools ought to strive for, it would most likely be to teach students how to think. Our extensive ability for various kinds of thinking is, after all, one of the major differences between us and other forms of animal life. Even a casual reflection on the great advances of civilization during the last several centuries reveals that such progress has been the result of our ability to think with ever-increasing degrees of clarity, insight, and creativity. **Logic** is the area of philosophy that deals with the process of reasoning and identifies rules that will enable the thinker to reach valid conclusions.

One hallmark of the teacher as a professional is his or her familiarity with the processes of logical thinking. Such a teacher makes regular use of logical reasoning in four important ways. First, the teacher employs logic to present ideas to students in a sequential, well-organized manner. Students are made to feel the power of the teacher's reasoning ability as he or she transforms the subject matter in such a way that students learn more effectively. Second, the teacher employs logic as a tool for the problem solving and decision making that are part of the teacher's daily life in the classroom. Third, the teacher uses logic to provide feedback to students who use fallacious reasoning and therefore arrive at erroneous conclusions. Finally, the teacher uses logic to evaluate the validity of new methods, materials, and subject-matter content. In this regard, the teacher uses hypothetical thinking to explore the probable outcomes of new approaches.

The two kinds of logical thinking processes that teachers most frequently have students master are *deductive* and *inductive* thinking. The deductive approach requires the thinker to move from a general principle or proposition to a specific conclusion that is valid. An example of deductive thinking would be the following: All dogs are animals; this is a dog; therefore, this is an animal. A social studies teacher using a deductive approach to instruction might first inform students that people are social beings (the general principle) and then point out that people voluntarily form numerous social interaction groups in the areas of work and play (the specific conclusion).

Inductive reasoning, on the other hand, moves from the particular to the general rather than from the general to the particular. Here, the student begins by examining particular examples that eventually lead to the acceptance of a general proposition. For example, if the above social studies teacher used an inductive approach, students would first consider several specific examples of social interaction groups and then, with or without the teacher's assistance, arrive at the general principle that people are social beings. This form of inductive teaching is often referred to as discovery teaching—where students discover, or create, their own knowledge of a topic.

The six areas of philosophy that we have examined briefly in the preceding pages—metaphysics, epistemology, axiology, ethics, aesthetics, and logic—represent the mental tools that teachers can use for thinking about various aspects of teaching. Though the six areas pose many very difficult questions, each also offers a strategy that the teacher can use to become more aware of the complexities of the educative process. Teachers who appreciate the inherent philosophical nature of teaching understand *why* they act as they do in the classroom; other teachers mechanically employ methods and materials without such insight.

FIVE-MINUTE FOCUS   Of the six branches of philosophy discussed in this chapter (metaphysics, epistemology, axiology, ethics, aesthetics, and logic), which one concerns you most in regard to your future as a teacher? Write a paragraph or two expressing your concerns. Date your journal entry and write for five minutes.

SIX PHILOSOPHICAL ORIENTATIONS TO TEACHING

As we previously mentioned, there are no correct answers to the many difficult philosophical questions raised by metaphysics, epistemology, axiology, ethics, aesthetics, and logic. There have been, however, six major coherent philosophical orientations to teaching that have been developed in response to the questions with which all teachers must grapple. These orientations, or schools of thought, are perennialism, progressivism, essentialism, existentialism, behaviorism, and reconstructionism. A brief description of each of these orientations is presented in the following sections. At the end of each description, we present a sample portrait of a teacher whose behavior illustrates that philosophical orientation in action.

Perennialism — TEN Eyck

Perennialism, as the term implies, views truth as constant, or perennial. The aim of education, according to perennialist thinking, is to ensure that students acquire knowledge of these unchanging principles or great ideas. Perennialists also believe that the natural world and human nature have remained basically unchanged over the centuries; thus, the great ideas continue to have the most potential for solving the problems of any era. Furthermore, the perennialist philosophy emphasizes the rational thinking abilities of human beings; it is the cultivation of the intellect that makes human beings truly human and differentiates them from other forms of animals.

The curriculum, according to the perennialists, should stress students' intellectual growth in the arts and sciences. Students should encounter in these areas the best, most significant works that humans have created. In regard to any area of the curriculum, only one question needs to be asked: Are students acquiring content that represents the human race's most lofty accomplishments in that area? Thus, a high school English teacher would require students to read Melville's *Moby Dick* or any of Shakespeare's plays rather than a novel on the current best-seller list. Similarly, science students would learn about the three laws of motion or the three laws of thermodynamics rather than build a model of the space shuttle.

Perennialist Educational Philosophers   Two of the best known advocates of the perennialist philosophy have been Robert Maynard Hutchins and, more recently, Mortimer Adler. As president of the University of Chicago, Hutchins developed an undergraduate curriculum based on the study of the Great Books and discussions of these classics in small seminars. Hutchins's perennialist curriculum was based on three assumptions about education,[11] which are summarized below:

1. Education must promote humankind's continuing search for truth. Whatever is true will always, and everywhere, be true; in short, truth is universal and timeless.
2. Since the mind's work is intellectual and focuses on ideas, education must also focus on ideas. The cultivation of human rationality is the essential function of education.
3. Education should stimulate students to think thoughtfully about significant ideas. Teachers should use correct and critical thinking as their primary method, and they should require the same of students.

characteristics?
Humanities

Noted educational philosopher Mortimer Adler, along with Hutchins, was instrumental in organizing the Great Books of the Western World curriculum. Through the study of over 100 enduring classics, from Plato to Einstein, the Great Books

Perennialist teachers often inspire students to seek the truth, to discover the universalities of human experience, and to celebrate the greatest of human achievements.

Cheer up Mr. Green... just'cause the new text says Washington was a snob doesn't mean it's true...

SIPRESS

approach aims at the major perennialist goal of teaching students to become independent and critical thinkers. It is a demanding curriculum, and it focuses on the enduring disciplines of knowledge rather than on current events or student interests.

One of the most influential recent works in support of perennialism is Adler's *Paideia Proposal* released in 1982. Adler's approach stresses the humanities and literature and reiterates Hutchins's idea that "The best education for the best is the best education for all."

Portrait of a Perennialist Teacher   Mrs. Bernstein, a heavy-set lady in her late fifties, has been teaching English at the high school since the mid 1960s. Among students and teachers as well, she has a reputation for demanding a lot. As one student put it, "You don't waste time in Mrs. Bernstein's classes."

During the 1960s, she had a difficult time dealing with students who aggressively insisted on being taught subjects that were "relevant." As a graduate of a top-notch university in the East where she received a classical, liberal education, Mrs. Bernstein refused to lessen the emphasis in her classes on great works of literature that she felt students needed to know, such as Beowolf, Chaucer, Dickens, and Shakespeare.

Now that the permissive, personally relevant approaches of the sixties and seventies have waned, Mrs. Bernstein feels less conflict related to her job. Most of her students appreciate the fact that she has high expectations of them and pushes them to think critically. She is proud of the number of her students who have gone on to good colleges and universities. She is especially pleased when former students return to thank her for giving them a solid foundation in English language and literature.

As far as her approach to classroom management is concerned, one student sums it up this way: "She doesn't let you get by with a thing; she never slacks off on the pressure. She lets you know that she's there to teach and you're there to learn." Mrs. Bernstein believes that hard work and effort are necessary if one is to get a good education. As a result, she gives students very few opportunities to misbehave, and she appears to be immune to the grumblings of students who do complain openly about the workload.

She becomes very animated when she talks about the value of the classics to students who are preparing to live as adults in the twenty-first century:

The classics are unequaled in terms of the insights they can give students into the major problems that they will have to deal with during their lifetimes. Though our civilization has made impressive technological advances during the last two centuries, we have not really progressed that much in terms of improving the quality of our lives as human beings. The observations of a Shakespeare or a Dickens on the human condition are just as relevant today as they were when they were alive.

Mrs. Bernstein welcomed the educational reform reports of the early 1980s that called for a renewed commitment to excellence in education. In her words,

> The greatest challenge that teachers face today is to restore standards of excellence and quality to the curriculum. As educators, we need to teach students what we know they need to know—not what they want to know. Students might object today if we don't give them what they want, but tomorrow they'll thank us for giving them a good, solid education—one that is well grounded in the arts and sciences.

Progressivism

Progressivism differs in many significant respects from perennialism. The greatest difference is that progressive education begins with the child rather than with the subject-matter discipline. As we learned in the previous chapter, John Dewey's writings in the twenties and thirties contributed a great deal to the spread of progressive ideas. Briefly, Deweyian progressivism is based on the following six assumptions:

Child centered not subject centered

1. The content of the curriculum ought to be derived from students' interests rather than from the academic disciplines.
2. Effective teaching takes into account the whole child, his or her interests and needs in regard to cognitive, affective, and psychomotor areas.
3. Learning is essentially active rather than passive; effective teachers provide students with experiences that enable them to learn by doing.
4. The aim of education is to teach students to think rationally so that they may become intelligent, contributing members of society.
5. At school, students learn personal, as well as social, values.
6. Humankind is in a constant state of change, and education makes possible a future that is better than the past.

Progressive Strategies   The progressive philosophy also contends that knowledge that is true in the present may not be true in the future. Hence, the best way to prepare students for an unknown future is to equip them with problem-solving strategies that will enable them to cope with new challenges in life and to discover what truths are relevant to the present. Through continual self-analysis and reflection, the individual can identify values that are appropriate for the immediate moment.

Progressives feel that life is evolving in a positive direction and that human beings, young as well as adult, are good and may be trusted to act in their own best interests. In this regard, educators with a progressive orientation give students a considerable amount of freedom in determining their school experiences. Contrary to the perceptions of many, though, progressive education does not mean that teachers do not provide structure or that students are free to do whatever they wish. Progressive teachers begin with where students are and, through the daily give-and-take of the classroom, lead students to see that the subject to be learned can enhance their lives.

The teacher's role in a progressively oriented classroom is to serve as a guide or resource person whose primary responsibility is to facilitate student learning. The teacher is concerned with helping students learn what is important to them rather than passing on a set of so-called enduring truths. Toward this end, the progressive teacher tries to provide students with experiences that replicate everyday life as much as possible. Students are given many opportunities to work cooperatively in groups, often solving problems the group, not the teacher, has identified as important.

Portrait of a Progressive Teacher   Mr. Barkan teaches social studies at a middle school in a well-to-do part of the city. Boyishly handsome and in his mid-thirties, Mr. Barkan usually works in casual attire—khaki pants, soft-soled shoes, and a sports shirt. He seems to get along well with students. Mr. Barkan likes to give students as much freedom of choice in the classroom as possible. Accordingly, his room is divided up into interest and activity centers, and much of the time students are free to choose where they want to spend their time. One corner at the back of the room has a library collection of paperback and hardcover books, an easy chair, and an area rug; the other back corner of the room is set up as a project area and has a worktable on which are several globes, maps, large sheets of newsprint, and assorted drawing materials. At the front of the room in one corner is a small media center with three cassette tape recorders with headphones, a phonograph, and a slide-viewing machine about the size of a small portable television.

Mr. Barkan makes it a point to establish warm, supportive relationships with his students. He is proud of the fact that he is a friend to his students. "I really like the kids I teach," he says in a soft, gentle voice. "They're basically good kids, and they really want to learn if we . . . teachers, I mean . . . can just keep their curiosity alive and not try to force them to learn. It's up to us as teachers to capitalize on their interests."

The visitor to Mr. Barkan's class today can sense his obvious regard for students. He is genuinely concerned about the growth and nurturance of each one. As his students spend most of their time working in small groups at the various activity centers in the room, Mr. Barkan divides his time among the groups. He moves from group to group and truly seems to immerse himself, as an equal participant, in each group's task. One group, for example, has been working this term on making a papier-mâché globe. Right now, several students are animatedly explaining to him how they plan to transfer the flat map of the world they have drawn to the surprisingly smooth sphere they have fashioned out of the papier-mâché. Mr. Barkan listens carefully to what his students have to say and then congratulates the group on how cleverly they have engineered the project. When he speaks to his students he does so in a matter-of-fact, conversational tone, as though speaking to other adults.

Though Mr. Barkan uses the social studies textbook approved by the board of education, he makes it a point to go beyond the text and help students to identify problems that they can get excited about and involved in. During a recent unit on world hunger, for example, one group of students presented to the class its findings on local provisions to feed the hungry. Another group looked at population trends in the state during the last hundred years and then, based on its findings, wrote a skit on what life would be like in their city during the year 2020.

As much as possible he likes to bring textbook knowledge to life by providing his students with appropriate experiences—field trips, small-group projects, simulation activities, role-playing, and so on. Mr. Barkan believes that his primary function as a teacher is to prepare his students for an unknown future. Learning to solve problems at an early age is the best preparation for this future, he feels.

Progressive teachers often establish informal relationships with students and bring textbook knowledge to life by engaging students in creative problem-solving activities.

The increase in the amount of knowledge each decade is absolutely astounding. What we teach students as true today will most likely not be true tomorrow. Therefore, students have to learn how to learn and become active problem solvers. In addition, students need to learn how to identify problems that are meaningful to them. It doesn't make much sense to learn to solve problems that belong to someone else.

To accomplish these things in the classroom, teachers have to be willing to take the lead from the students themselves . . . to use their lives as a point of departure for learning about the subject. What this requires of the teacher is that he or she be willing to set up the classroom along the lines of a democracy, a close community of learners whose major purpose for being there is to learn. You can't create that kind of classroom atmosphere by being a taskmaster and trying to force kids to learn. If you can trust them and let them set their own directions, they'll respond.

Essentialism

Essentialism is a conservative philosophy of education that was originally formulated as a response to progressive trends in schools. William C. Bagley (1874–1946), a professor of education at Teachers College, Columbia University, was the founder of the Essentialistic Education Society. To promote the essentialist philosophy, he founded the educational journal, *School and Society*.

Bagley and several other like-minded educators had become very critical of progressive educational practices, contending that the movement had damaged intellectual and moral standards among young people.[12] Following World War II, criticism of progressive education became even more widespread and seemed to point to one

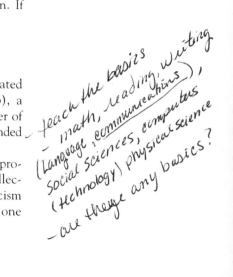

(handwritten margin note) teach the basics — math, reading, writing (Language, communications), Social Sciences, computers (Technology) physical science — are there any basics?

conclusion: schools were failing in their task of transmitting the country's social and intellectual heritage.

Essentialism, which has some similarities to perennialism, holds that our culture has a core of common knowledge that the schools are obligated to transmit to students in a systematic, disciplined way. Unlike perennialism, which emphasizes a set of external truths, essentialism stresses what advocates believe to be the essential knowledge and skills that productive members of our society need to know. Several books have been written that lament the decline of rigorous schooling in the United States and call for an essentialist approach to schooling. Among them have been James D. Koerner's *The Case for Basic Education* (1959), H. G. Rickover's *Education and Freedom* (1959), and Paul Copperman's *The Literacy Hoax: The Decline of Reading, Writing, and Learning in the Public Schools and What We Can Do About It* (1978).

According to essentialist philosophy, schooling should be practical and provide children with sound instruction that prepares them to live life; schools should not try to influence or set social policies. Critics of essentialism, however, charge that such a tradition-bound orientation to schooling will indoctrinate students and rule out the possibility of change. Essentialists respond that, without an essentialist approach, students will be indoctrinated in humanistic and/or behavioral curricula that run counter to society's accepted standards and need for order.

The Back-to-Basics Movement   The back-to-basics movement that began in the mid-seventies is the most recent large-scale push to install essentialist programs in the schools. Above all else, the essentialists contend, the schools must train students to communicate clearly and logically. The core skills in the curriculum should be reading, writing, and speaking, and the school has the responsibility for seeing that all students master these skills.

Essentialists are critical of many innovations in the schools, citing them as examples of pedagogy gone soft, a trend, they claim, that has led to a lowering of standards and a dramatic decline in achievement. In support of this view, they are able to point to low scores on state-mandated tests of basic skills and declining scores on college board examinations. What schools need to do, according to essentialist thinking, is get rid of fads and frills in the schools and restore sound, traditional teaching to the classroom. Schools should also provide special programs for talented youth whose needs are not met by curricula that have been reduced to a level of common mediocrity.

The essentialist curriculum emphasizes the teaching of facts; it has little patience with the indirect, introspective approaches promoted by progressivism. Some essentialists even view the arts and humanities as frills and feel that the hard sciences and technical and vocational courses are the true essentials that students need in order to contribute to society.

Though the essentialist educator does not view the child as evil, neither does he or she view the child as naturally good. Unless children are actively and vigorously taught the value of discipline, hard work, and respect for authority, they will not become valuable members of society. The teacher's role, then, is to shape children, to hold their natural, nonproductive instincts (e.g., aggression, mindless gratification of the senses, etc.) in check until their education has been completed.

Portrait of an Essentialist Teacher   Mr. Samuels teaches mathematics at a junior high school in a poor section of a major urban area. Prior to coming to this school six years ago, he taught at a rural elementary school.

Middle-aged and highly energetic, Mr. Samuels is known around the school as a hardworking, dedicated teacher. His commitment to children is especially evident when he talks about preparing "his" children for life in high school and beyond. "A lot of teachers nowadays have given up on kids," he says with a touch of sadness to his voice. "They don't demand much of them. If we don't push kids now to get the knowledge and skills they're going to need later in life, we've failed them. My main purpose here is to see that my kids get the basics they're going to need."

Mr. Samuels has made it known that he does not approve of the methods used by some of the younger, more humanistically oriented teachers in the school. At a recent faculty meeting, for example, he was openly critical of some teachers' tendency to let students do their own thing and spend time expressing their feelings. He called for all teachers to focus their energies on getting students to master subject-matter content, "the things kids will need to know," rather than on helping students adjust to the interpersonal aspects of school life. He also reminded everyone that "kids come to school to learn." All students would learn, he pointed out, if "teachers based their methods on good, sound approaches that have always worked—not on the so-called innovative approaches that are based on fads and frills."

Mr. Samuels's students have accepted his no-nonsense approach to teaching. With few exceptions, his classes are orderly, business-like operations. Each class period follows a standard routine. Students enter the room quietly and take their seats with a minimum of the foolishness and horseplay that mark the start of many other classes in the school. As the first order of business, the previous day's homework is returned and reviewed. Following this, Mr. Samuels presents the day's lesson, usually a 15–20 minute explanation of how to solve a particular kind of math problem. His min-ilectures are lively, and his wide-ranging tone of voice and animated, spontaneous delivery convey his excitement about the material and his belief that students can learn. During large-group instruction, Mr. Samuels also makes ample use of the blackboard, overhead transparencies, and various manipulatives such as a large abacus and colored blocks of different sizes and shapes.

Following the presentation of the day's new material, Mr. Samuels has students work through several practice problems. At this time, he has four to five students work their practice problems at the board. Using the work that students have displayed on the board, Mr. Samuels comments on the correct procedures to be followed. During the final 15 mintues or so of class, students begin to work on their homework as-signment, usually a set of problems in the textbook or on a dittoed worksheet. As students work at their desks, the room takes on an atmosphere of subdued, yet earnest industriousness. Without exception, all students address themselves to the task at hand. Mr. Samuels moves about the room, stopping here and there to check on a student's work or to answer a question.

Existentialism

Existential philosophy is unique in that it focuses on the experiences of the individual. Other philosophies are concerned with developing systems of thought for identifying and understanding what is common to *all* reality, human existence, and values. **Existentialism,** on the other hand, offers the individual a way of thinking about *my* life, what has meaning for *me*, what is true for *me*. In general, existentialism emphasizes creative choice, the subjectivity of human experiences, and concrete acts of human existence over any rational scheme for human nature or reality.

The writings of Jean-Paul Sartre (1905–1980), well-known French philosopher, novelist, and playwright, have been most responsible for the widespread dissemination of existential ideas. According to Sartre, every individual first exists and then he or she must decide what that existence is to mean. The task of assigning meaning to that existence is the individual's alone; no preformulated belief system of philosophy can tell one who one is. It is up to each of us to decide who we are. According to Sartre, "Existence precedes essence. . . . First of all, man exists, turns up, appears on the scene, and, only afterwards, defines himself."[13]

Two Existentialist Views   There are two schools of existential thought—one *theistic,* the other *atheistic.* Most of those belonging to the first school refer to themselves as Christian Existentialists and point out that humankind has a longing for an ultimate being, for God. Though this longing does not prove the eixstence of God, people can freely choose to live their lives as if there was a God.[14] The Spanish philosopher Miguel de Unamuno expresses this position well: "Let life be lived in such a way, with such dedication to goodness and the highest values, that if, after all, it is annihilation which finally awaits us, that will be an injustice."[15]

Most existentialists, however, point out that it is demeaning to the human condition to say that we must entertain a fantasy in order to live a life of moral responsibility. Such a stance absolves humans of the responsibility for dealing with the complete freedom of choice that we all have. It also causes them to avoid the inescapable fact that "we are alone, with no excuses," and that "we are condemned to be free."[16]

Life, according to existential thought, has no meaning, and the universe is indifferent to the situation humankind finds itself in. With the freedom that we have, however, each of us must commit ourselves to assign meaning to *our* life. The human enterprise that can be most helpful in promoting this personal quest for meaning is the educative process. Teachers, therefore, must allow students freedom of choice and provide them with experiences that will help them find the meaning of their lives. This approach, contrary to the belief of many, does not mean that students may do whatever they please; logic indicates that freedom has rules, and respect for the freedom of others is essential.

Existentialists judge the curriculum according to whether or not it contributes to the individual's quest for meaning. The ideal curriculum is one that provides students with extensive individual freedom and requires them to ask their own questions, conduct their own inquiries, and draw their own conclusions.

Portrait of an Existentialist Teacher   Right after he first started teaching English eight years ago at a suburban high school, Fred Winston began to have doubts about the value of what he was teaching students. While he could see a limited, practical use for the knowledge and skills he was teaching, he felt he was doing little to help his students answer the most pressing questions of their lives. Also, Fred had to admit to himself that he had grown somewhat bored with following the narrow, unimaginative Board of Education curriculum guides.

During the next eight years Fred gradually developed a style of teaching that placed emphasis on students finding out who they are. He continued to teach the knowledge and skills he was required to teach, but he made it clear that what students learned from him they should use to answer questions that were important to them. Now, for example, he often gives writing assignments that encourage students to look within in order to develop greater self-knowledge. He often uses assigned literature as a springboard for values clarification discussions. And, whenever possible, he gives his students the freedom to pursue individual reading and writing projects. His only requirement is that students be meaningfully involved in whatever they do.

Fred is also keenly aware of how the questions his students are just beginning to grapple with are questions that he is still, even in his mid-thirties, trying to answer for himself. Thoughtfully and with obvious care for selecting the correct words, he sums up the goals that he has for his students:

> I think kids should realize that the really important questions in life are beyond definitive answers, and they should be very suspicious of anyone—teacher, philosopher, or member of organized religion—who purports to have *the* answers. As human beings, each of us faces the central task of finding *our own* answers to such questions. My students know that I'm wrestling with the same questions they're working on. But I think I've taught them well enough so that they know that my answers can't be their answers.

Fred's approach to teaching is perhaps summed up by the bumper sticker on the sports car he drives: "Question authority." Unlike many of his fellow teachers, he wants his students to react critically and skeptically to what he teaches them. He also presses them to think thoughtfully and courageously about the meaning of life, beauty, love, and death. He judges his effectiveness by the extent to which students are able and willing to become more aware of the choices that are open to them.

Behaviorism

Behaviorism is based upon the principle that desirable human behavior can be the product of design, rather than accident. According to behaviorists, it is an illusion to say that humans have a free will. While we may act as if we are free, our behavior is really *determined* by forces in the environment that shape our behavior. "We are what we are and we do what we do, not because of any mysterious power of human volition, but because outside forces over which we lack any semblance of control have us caught in an inflexible web. Whatever else we may be, we are not the captains of our fate or the masters of our soul."[17]

While behaviorists are quick to point out that their beliefs are a psychological system based on science, not philosophy, we include behaviorism in our discussion of philosophical orientations to teaching because it is a comprehensive world view that serves as the basis for the way many teachers approach teaching.

Founders of Behavioristic Psychology John B. Watson (1878–1958) was the principal originator of behavioristic psychology and B. F. Skinner (1904–1990) its best-known promoter. Watson first claimed that human behavior consisted of specific stimuli that resulted in certain responses. In part, he based this new conception of learning on the classic experiment conducted by Russian psychologist Ivan Pavlov (1849–1936). Pavlov had noticed that a dog he was working with would salivate when it was about to be given food. By introducing the sound of a bell when food was offered and repeating this several times, Pavlov discovered that the sound of the bell alone (a conditioned stimulus) would make the dog salivate (a conditioned response). Watson was so confident that all learning conformed to this basic stimulus-response model (now termed classical or type S conditioning) that he once boasted, "Give me a dozen healthy infants, well-formed, and my own specified world to bring them up in, and I'll guarantee to take any one at random and train him to become any type of specialist I might select—doctor, lawyer, artist, merchant-chief and, yes, even beggar-man and thief, regardless of his talents, penchants, tendencies, abilities, vocations, and race of his ancestors."[18]

Skinner went beyond Watson's basic stimulus-response model and developed a more comprehensive view of conditioning known as operant (or type R) conditioning. Operant conditioning is based on the idea that satisfying responses are conditioned, unsatisfying ones are not. In other words, "The things we call pleasant have an energizing or strengthening effect on our behaviour."[19] For the teacher, this means that desired student behavior should be reinforced, undesired behavior should not. Also, the teacher should be concerned with changing students' behavior rather than trying to alter their mental states.

In his novel *Walden Two* (1962), Skinner portrayed how "behavioral engineering" could lead to the creation of a utopian society. The book describes how a community with a desirable social order was created by design rather than by accident. In much the same way, educators can create learners who exhibit desired behaviors by carefully and scientifically controlling the educative process. The teacher need merely recognize that all learning is conditioning and adhere to the following four steps:

1. Identify desired behaviors in concrete (observable and measurable) terms.
2. Establish a procedure for recording specific behaviors and counting their frequencies.
3. For each behavior, identify an appropriate reinforcer.
4. Ensure that students receive the reinforcer as soon as possible after displaying a desired behavior.

Portrait of a Behaviorist Teacher   Jane Day teaches fourth grade at a school with an enrollment of about 500 in a small midwestern town. Now in her fifth year at the school, Jane has spent the last three years developing and refining a systematic approach to teaching. Last year, the success of her methods was confirmed when her students received the highest scores on the state's annual basic skills test.

Her primary method is individualized instruction wherein students proceed at their own pace through modules she has put together. The modules cover five major areas: reading, writing, mathematics, general science, and spelling. She is working on a sixth module, geography, but it won't be ready until next year. She has developed a complex point system to keep track of students' progress and to motivate them to higher levels of achievement. The points students accumulate entitle them to participate in various in-class activities: free reading, playing with the many games and puzzles in the room, drawing or painting in the art corner, or playing video games on one of the two personal computers in the room.

Jane has tried to convert several other teachers at the school to her behavioristic approach, and she is eager to talk to anyone who will listen about the effectiveness of her systematic approach to instruction. When addressing this topic, her exuberance is truly exceptional. She smiles a great deal and speaks rapidly, traits that reflect a genuine, almost childlike excitement about her work rather than nervous energy:

It's really quite simple . . . students just do much better if you tell them exactly what you want them to know and then reward them for learning it. So, for every subject I teach I've got a set number of behavioral objectives that students have to master. Each subject has a certain number of modules with anywhere from 10 to 20 objectives in each module.

For completing the activities in each module and passing the module's test, a student will get a certain number of points. For each 100 points a student gets so much time to spend on a special activity in class. Right now, the video games are real popular, so the kids have to get 200 points before they can do that.

In regard to the methods employed by some of her colleagues, Jane can be rather critical. She knows some teachers in the school who teach by a trial-and-error method and "aren't clear about where they're going." She is also impatient with those who talk about the "art" of teaching; in contrast, everything that she does as a teacher is done with precision and a clear sense of purpose. "Through careful design and management of the learning environment," she says, "a teacher can get the results that he or she wants."

Although Jane enjoys positive relationships with her students, she does not feel that teachers should necessarily strive to be friends to students. As she puts it, "The teacher's main role is clear: to manage the important business of students learning what they need to know in order to become productive members of society. A teacher who is effective and efficient serves students better than one who is merely a friend."

As a behaviorist, Jane does not recognize a separation between knowledge and action, or knowing from doing. She is single-minded in her emphasis on changing behavior. Her success is measured only in terms of whether students achieve clearly stated learning outcomes. "Students get frustrated with teachers who want them to 'know,' to 'appreciate,' or to 'understand' the material," she says. "That's too vague, and kids don't know what you want them to do."

Reconstructionism

As the name implies, **reconstructionism** holds that schools should take the lead in reconstructing the current social order. Theodore Brameld (b. 1904), acknowledged as the founder of reconstructionism, bases his philosophy on two fundamental premises about the present: (1) we live in a period of great crisis, most evident in the fact that humans now have the capability of destroying civilization overnight, and (2) humankind also has the intellectual, technological, and moral potential to create a world civilization of "abundance, health, and humane capacity."[20] In this time of great need, then, the schools should become the primary agent for planning and directing social change. In short, the schools should not only *transmit* knowledge about the existing social order; they should seek to *reconstruct* it as well.

Reconstructionism and Progressivism Reconstructionism has clear ties to progressive educational philosophy. Both attach primary importance to the kind of experiences students have. The classroom should be characterized by extensive interactions between teacher and students and among students themselves. Furthermore, both philosophies place a premium on bringing the community, if not the entire world, into the classroom. Student experiences often include field trips, community-based projects of various sorts, and opportunities to interact with persons beyond the four walls of the classroom.

Through a reconstructionist approach to education, students would learn appropriate methods for dealing with the significant crises that confront the world: war, depression, international terrorism, hunger, inflation, and ever-accelerating technological advances. The curriculum would be arranged to highlight the need for various social reforms and, whenever possible, allow students to have firsthand experiences in reform activities. Teachers would realize that they can play a significant role in the control and resolution of these problems, that they and their students need not be buffeted about like pawns by these crises.

According to Brameld, the educative process should be based upon a continuous quest for a better society. The logical outcome of this quest would be the eventual realization of a world-wide democracy.[21] Unless we actively seek to create this kind of world through the intelligent application of present knowledge, we run the risk that the destructive forces of the world will determine the conditions under which humans will live in the future.

Portrait of a Reconstructionist Teacher   At the urban high school where she teaches social studies and history, Martha Perkins has the reputation for being a social activist. Upon first meeting her, she presents a casual and laid-back demeanor. Her soft voice and warm smile belie the intensity of her convictions about pressing world issues, from international terrorism and hunger to peaceful uses of space and the need for all humans to work toward a global community.

During the late 1960s, Martha participated as a high school student in several protests against the war in Vietnam. This also marked the beginning of her increased awareness of social injustice in general. Like many young people of that era, Martha vigorously supported a curriculum that focused on students understanding these inequities and identifying resources that might eliminate them from society. Before she graduated from high school, Martha had formulated a vision of a healthier, more just society, and she vowed to do what she could to make that vision become a reality during her lifetime.

In her teaching, Martha takes every appropriate opportunity to confront her students with social problems and then help them work toward solutions. Within the last few months, for example, her students have spearheaded an in-school drug education program, written letters to the governor expressing their views on capital punishment, and completed 10-hour service projects at a nearby nursing home. When she can, Martha also likes to arrange field trips for her classes and guest speakers.

Martha feels strongly about the importance of having students learn about social problems as well as discovering what they can *do* about them. "It's really almost immoral if I confront my students with a social problem and then we fail to do anything about it," she says. "Part of my responsibility as a teacher is to raise the consciousness level of my students in regard to the problems that confront all human beings. I want them to leave my class with the realization that they *can* make a difference when it comes to making the world a more humane place."

For Martha to achieve her goals as a teacher, she frequently has to tackle controversial issues—issues that many of her colleagues avoid in the classroom. She feels that students would not learn how to cope with problems or controversy if she were to avoid them.

> I'm not afraid of controversy. When confronted with controversy, some teachers do retreat to the safety of the more "neutral" academic discipline. However, I try to get my students to see how they can use the knowledge of the discipline to attack the problem. So far, I've gotten good support from the principal. She's backed me up on several controversial issues that we've looked at in class: the nuclear energy plant that was to be built here in this county, the right to die, and absentee landlords who own property in the poorer sections of the city.

Keepers of the Dream

Socrates

(c. 469–399 B.C.)
Greek Philosopher and Teacher

A Greek philosopher and teacher, Socrates devoted his life to a quest for truth and goodness, and became one of the most admired teachers in history. Much of our knowledge about Socrates' life and teachings comes from the writings of his most famous student, the philosopher Plato.

Socrates taught by questioning his pupils in a manner that led them to see errors and inconsistencies in their thinking. His questions and his unorthodox views on religion and politics angered powerful Athenians, and he was charged with heresy and corrupting the youth. A jury found him guilty and sentenced him to death. Although he could have chosen exile or escaped from prison, he calmly carried out the sentence by drinking a cup of hemlock poison.

Socrates' method of teaching, known today as the Socratic method, consisted of holding philosophical conversations ("dialectics") with his pupils. By using an inductive approach—reasoning from specific facts to general principles—Socrates believed that the truth could be discovered. In the following dialogue about government, Socrates and Glaucon have just determined that the guardians of Athens must have both a gentle nature and a fierce spirit in order to do their job well—a seemingly impossible combination.

"Your Dog Is a True Philosopher."

"Yet there do exist natures gifted with those opposite qualities."

"Where do you find them?"

"Our friend the dog is a good example; you know that well-bred dogs are perfectly gentle to their familiars and acquaintances, and the reverse to strangers."

"Yes, I know."

"Then there is nothing impossible or unnatural in finding a guardian who has a similar combination of qualities?"

"Certainly not."

"Would not he who is fitted to be a guardian also need to have the qualities of a philosopher?"

"I do not understand your meaning."

"The trait I am speaking of may also be seen in the dog."

"What trait?"

"Why, a dog, whenever he sees a stranger, is angry; when he sees an acquaintance, he welcomes him, although the one has never done him any harm, nor the other any good. Did this never strike you as curious?"

"The matter never struck me before; but I recognize the truth of your remark."

"And surely this instinct of the dog is very charming—your dog is a true philosopher."

"Why?"

"Why, because he distinguishes the face of a friend and of an enemy only by the criterion of knowing and not knowing. And must not an animal be a lover of learning who determines what he likes and dislikes by the test of knowledge and ignorance?"

"Most assuredly."

"And is not the love of learning the love of wisdom, which is philosophy?"*

Socrates concludes that the best guardian of Athens would combine wisdom with strength. The legacy of Socrates lives on in all teachers who recognize that encouraging students to think for themselves is the ultimate aim of teaching.

*Source: (Abridged from Plato, The Republic, Book II, Chicago, Ill.: Great Books Foundation, 1948, pp. 109–112). Reprinted with permission of Oxford University Press.

EDUCATION
in the
N E W S

The Right Choice

"School choice" has become a catchall term for a wide variety of policies. In some "open enrollment" plans students within a district are permitted to attend any school. New York City's District 4, for example, has allowed this form of open enrollment since 1975. In a community known as East Harlem, the district has more than 12,000 students, mainly from low-income Latino and African-American families, and 19 school buildings. Over the last 15 years the district has gradually created 50 different small schools from the elementary to high school level in the same 19 buildings. The schools range in size from less than 100 to more than 300 students. Although most elementary students attend their local school, they are allowed to attend another school in the district as space permits. Six alternative elementary schools attract students from all over the district and city. Beginning with sixth grade, students must choose which post-elementary school in the district they wish to attend.

The nation's first interdistrict, or statewide, open enrollment plans are being implemented in Minnesota, Ohio, Nebraska, Arkansas, Iowa, and Washington. Although the states mandate that all school districts allow interdistrict transfers by students, various restrictions are imposed, largely in response to criticisms of early school choice programs.

In Washington, for example, students who wish to leave their resident district must show that their school of choice is more accessible to a parent's place of work or to child care, or that they are experiencing "a special hardship or detrimental condition" in their present school. In other cases, a parent must show that the student's financial, educational, safety, or health condition will be "reasonably improved" as a result of the transfer. Resident school districts are allowed to prevent students from leaving if greater racial segregation, or some other harm to remaining students, would result. Parents can appeal the district's decision.

Districts accepting transfer students can charge a "transfer fee" based on differences in local school-tax rates, with the state legislature paying the transfer fees of students from low-income families. Provisions for funding transportation and informing parents of their options are included in the plan.

Supporters of the open enrollment concept say it is a cost-free reform that inspires greater parental involvement and improved curricula through free market forces. Critics point out, however, that the many variations of "school choice" must satisfactorily address the same fundamental issues of providing all students with both quality and equity in education.

Sources: Rogers Worthington, "Students' Right to Switch Puts Schools to the Test," *Chicago Tribune* (March 4, 1990).

William Snider, "Washington Lawmakers Adopt School-Choice Package," *Education Week* (April 11, 1990).

Deborah Meier and Ruth Jordan, "The Right 'Choice' for Teachers," *Teacher Magazine* (December 1989).

FIVE-MINUTE FOCUS   Recall one of your favorite teachers in grades K–12. Which of the six educational philosophies you have just read about (perennialism, progressivism, essentialism, existentialism, behaviorism, or reconstructionism) captures best that teacher's approach to teaching? Write your own portrait of that teacher. Date your journal entry and write for five minutes.

BUILDING YOUR OWN EDUCATIONAL PHILOSOPHY

As you read the preceding brief descriptions of six philosophical orientations to teaching, perhaps you felt that no single approach fit perfectly the kind of teacher you want to become. Or, there may have been some element of each approach that seemed compatible with your own emerging philosophy of education. In either case, don't feel that you need to identify a single educational philosophy around which you will build your teaching career; in reality, few teachers follow only one educational philosophy. Remember that our portraits of six teachers were drawn with purposefully bold, one-dimensional contrasts in order to illustrate the different orientations.

It has been our observation that most teachers develop an *eclectic* philosophy of education, which means they have developed their own unique blending of two or more philosophies. Many effective combinations are possible. One might be a perennialist when it comes to selecting content and a behaviorist in regard to motivating students to learn that content. Or, one might be both a progressivist and an existentialist, one who pays particular attention to the needs of the whole child as well as the child's need to develop a personal meaning for life.

We encourage you to reflect on the philosophies we have discussed, incorporating from each the features that are most congruent with your personality and the kind of teacher you wish to become. Be cautioned, however, that your choices should be based on clear, hard thinking about the important philosophical questions raised in the beginning of this chapter. To develop a meaningful, workable philosophy of education requires more than just the random piecing together of ideas that seem attractive at the moment. It requires hard work and time. Remember, the philosophers we have discussed in this chapter have devoted most of their lifetimes to the study of the same questions and issues that confront us all.

In addition, you may expect your educational philosophy to change over time. As you mature professionally, acquiring greater knowledge about teaching and developing a fund of experiences as a teacher, you will undoubtedly refine and sharpen your philosophy. In fact, one characteristic of the professional teacher is that he or she continually tries to arrive at a clearer, more comprehensive answer to one basic philosophical question: Why do I teach the way I do?

SUMMARY

In this chapter we learned how philosophy is vital to the work of the teacher. A teacher's educational philosophy, we suggested, is made up of personal beliefs about teaching and learning, students, knowledge, and what is worth knowing. For the teacher who wishes to formulate sound, well thought-out beliefs in these four areas, familiarity with the following main currents of philosophical thought is essential: metaphysics, epistemology, axiology, ethics, aesthetics, and logic. These branches of philosophy are concerned with answering six fundamental questions that are central to teaching: What is the nature of reality? What is the nature of knowledge? What values should guide one's life? What is good and evil, right and wrong? What is beautiful? and, What processes of reasoning will yield optimum results for the individual? We concluded the chapter by examining six philosophical orientations to teaching, each representing a unique stance toward life and the educative process.

KEY TERMS AND CONCEPTS

philosophy, 200	logic, 209
educational philosophy, 201	perennialism, 210
metaphysics, 206	progressivism, 213
epistemology, 207	essentialism, 215
axiology, 208	existentialism, 217
ethics, 208	behaviorism, 219
aesthetics, 209	reconstructionism, 221

ANSWER KEY FOR CONSIDER THIS . . .

"What Are Your Views on Educational Goals?"
KEY—Items most closely associated with each philosophical orientation to teaching: perennialism—*c, h, j, l, p;* progressivism—*b, i, k, m, q;* essentialism—*a, e, g, n, o;* existentialism—*d, r;* behaviorism—*f;* reconstructionism: *s, t.*

DISCUSSION QUESTIONS

1. Do you agree with Miss Hartford's comment in the opening scenario that a basic skills program could be made compatible with the diverse views expressed by her teachers? Explain.
2. Think back to the teachers you had during your elementary through secondary years. Which ones would you classify as being predominantly perennialist? progressive? essentialist? existentialist? behaviorist? reconstructionist?
3. Of the six philosophical orientations to teaching, which do you believe are most popular among teachers today? Why? Least popular?
4. Do you imagine that teachers on the elementary, middle/junior, and senior-high levels differ in regard to their preferred philosophical orientation to teaching?
5. What specific steps will you take throughout your teaching career to ensure that your philosophical orientation to teaching remains dynamic and growing rather than becoming static and limited?
6. Of the six philosophical orientations to teaching we have examined, which one is most attractive to you? Least attractive? If you look ahead 10 years, do you anticipate any shift in your preference?

APPLICATION ACTIVITIES

1. In this chapter we made reference to the work of several educational philosophers. Select one of them and prepare a written report on the contributions he or she has made to education.
2. Conduct a survey of current journals in education and try to locate articles that reflect the six philosophical orientations discussed in this chapter. Which orientations appear to have the greatest representation?
3. Conduct a comparative survey of an education journal at 10-year intervals and try to determine if there have been any significant changes over the years in regard to the philosophical orientations to teaching reflected in the journal.

4. Imagine that Socrates was alive today, teaching in the subject area and at the level for which you are preparing. Describe the activities that would be occurring in his classes. How might his teaching be viewed by students? By other teachers? By administrators? By parents?

FIELD EXPERIENCES

1. Interview a teacher for the purpose of clarifying his or her educational philosophy. Formulate your interview questions in light of the philosophical concepts discussed in this chapter. Report your findings to the rest of the class.
2. If possible, arrange a short interview with a professor of philosophy on your campus. Ask him or her to comment on the contributions that philosophy can make to education. Give the rest of the class a report on your visit.
3. Observe the classes of two different teachers at the level at which you plan to teach. Which *one* of the six philosophical orientations to teaching discussed in this chapter most characterizes each teacher? Share your findings with the rest of your class.
4. Visit a school and interview the principal about the school's educational philosophy. Ask him or her to comment on what is expected of teachers in regard to achieving the goals contained in the statement of philosophy.

SUGGESTED READINGS

Adler, Mortimer J. *Reforming Education: The Opening of the American Mind.* New York: MacMillan, 1990. *A set of thought-provoking essays by one of America's best-known philosophers.*

Barrow, Robin and Ronald Woods. *An Introduction to Philosophy of Education.* London: Routledge Chapman and Hall, 1989. *A concise, informative introduction to educational philosophy that examines the relationship between philosophy and topics such as curriculum and creative thinking.*

de Nicholas, Antonio T. *Habits of Mind: An Introduction to the Philosophy of Education.* New York: Paragon House, 1989. *A comprehensive look at the role that philosophy plays in education.*

Ozman, Howard and Samuel Craver. *Philosophical Foundations of Education.* New York: Merrill, 1986. *An authoritative, readable introduction to educational philosophy. Explains different philosophical positions according to best-known schools of thought.*

Power, Edward J. *Philosophy of Education: Studies in Philosophies, Schooling, and Educational Politics.* Englewood Cliffs, N.J.: Prentice-Hall, 1982. *This perceptive and well-written book deals with principal systematic educational philosophies and concludes with a look at frequently disputed issues in contemporary educational policy.*

TEACHERS . . .

What is your educational philosophy?
What do you believe the aims of education should be?

Education is a lifelong process of learning. To be productive citizens, people must learn how to learn. It is the primary function of educators to teach this skill and to inspire a love for learning.

—Mark Kincaid
Leander High School, Liberty Hill, Texas

The aims of education should be the self-fulfillment of every child to the best of his inner needs. I strongly follow the Montessori philosophy. Maria Montessori was a physician and educator who was years ahead of her time. The ideas she generated through the observation of children [are] having an impact on us today. I strive to live up to her ideals.

—Anita Dollar
Mitchell Elementary School, Denver, Colorado

I believe that all children can learn. I also believe that learning is easier when children feel safe, secure and loved. All students should be treated with dignity, respect and understanding. The aim of education should be to instill in our students a burning desire to learn. Children should be taught that learning is an ongoing process that never ends.

—Dolores Ramón
Montgomery Drive Elementary School, San Antonio, Texas

My educational philosophy is existentialism. I believe the freedom to choose lies within the individual. The teacher is to be a facilitator, not an instrument to fill up empty vessels. Since finding out that I have multiple sclerosis, I "seize the day" (*carpe diem*). In my teaching I am less concerned about making waves and taking risks; rather, I try to make a difference.

—Julie A. Addison
Rock Ridge Elementary School, Castle Rock, Colorado

My philosophy of education includes wanting a classroom that projects a supporting atmosphere, one that fosters respect and self-esteem. The class and lessons should be flexible and creative and should promote individual freedom. Each student will be held responsible and accountable for his or her learning. I believe the chief aim of school should be to encourage students to think and live independently.

—Jennifer Cronk
Rocky Mountain Hebrew Academy, Denver, Colorado

ON TEACHING

Education is not simply the development of the mind. I feel that a complete education develops the complete individual—academically, socially, emotionally and physically. It is the responsibility of educators to supply an environment in which children are motivated to learn and to think. Realizing that educators cannot be responsible for raising every child . . . [who] comes through the classroom, it is important that they influence them to the point that the children will take responsibility for their own futures. The demands on education are great, but with sincere, caring, educated and motivated people in the profession, the goal of developing a well-rounded, balanced person is quite within our grasp.

—Amy Orcutt
Green Gables Elementary School, Jefferson County, Colorado

My educational philosophy is based on creating a warm learning environment where my students feel free to take risks and responsibility for their learning. My teaching has to have meaning for my students. I strongly agree that it is not just what they learn, but how. . . . It is not the product, but the process!

—Elizabeth Hudson
Clyde Miller Elementary School, Aurora, Colorado

I believe the aim of education should be to give students the tools to seek out knowledge that will ensure their success in the future. Education should expose students not only to the three R's, but also to the arts so they will become well-rounded, contributing members of our society.

—Rose Ann Blaschke
Vivian Elementary School, Lakewood, Colorado

I believe the aim of education should be . . . [to motivate] students . . . [to learn] how to learn. A person needs to learn how to think, reason, ask questions, inquire, and solve problems. Educators need to motivate students to use their minds by becoming aware of ideas, issues, problem-solving techniques, [and] conceptual understanding, and to have high expectations [of students].

   Educators need to provide opportunities for students to become effective in discussing ideas and issues, making decisions, and setting goals for themselves. Students should develop imagination and a sense of curiosity. They should learn that they can make changes and that even a failure can give them an opportunity to begin again. Most importantly, students need to develop self-awareness and acceptance of their own capacities, interests, and needs. Hopefully, they will be motivated for high education and a continual desire for further learning, independence, and self-direction.

—Rosanne Newell
Twin Peaks Elementary School, Salt Lake City, Utah

Governance and Support of American Education

Man is by nature
a political animal.

Aristotle
Politics, Book III

Y ou've just entered the teachers' lounge on your planning period. It's obvious that the three teachers in the room have been having a heated discussion.

"I don't see how you can say that we make those kinds of decisions," says Kim, a language arts teacher who came to the school two years ago. "The books I can select from are chosen by a district textbook selection committee. Next April all my kids have to take a test mandated by the state. And. . . ."

"Hold it," says Betty, raising her hand to silence her. "How can you say that we don't control the schools? Unless I'm mistaken, I was the only one teaching in my classroom just before I came in here. I've been here eight years and no one's ever told me what to do." Betty takes a quick sip of her diet soda.

"It's the politicians; they're starting to run the schools more and more," says Lara, looking up from the mathematics book she is evaluating. "Look," she continues, "the politicians even set up a beginning teacher program to try to tell this new teacher how to teach and what to teach." She motions for you to have a seat at the table. Feeling a bit uncomfortable, but anxious to fit in with your new colleagues, you take a seat.

"Lara's right," says Kim. "The other day, Robin Matthews, who teaches over at Crestview, told me that someone at his school figured out that teachers there have a total of over 100 federal, state, and local guidelines they have to follow. Can you imagine that!" She rolls her eyes to emphasize the point.

"Right," Lara says. "I'm surprised the number isn't higher—not only do you have state tests, you've got mandated standards for grading, for graduation, for athletic eligibility, for placement in special programs, for suspending kids, for just about anything you can think of."

"That's an exaggeration," says Betty. "We've got the freedom to decide what we want to teach and how we want to teach it. Sure, there are guidelines, but they're there to help us and the kids."

"Help us?" says Kim, rolling her eyes again in a pained expression of disbelief. "How can you say that?"

"We've got a difficult enough job to do without the politicians making it harder," says Lara.

"I hear what you're both saying," says Betty, "but you've got to remember why we're here—for the kids. The Feds, our legislators, the school board . . . they're just looking out for the kids."

"Well, who's looking out for us?" asks Kim. "If we meet all their guidelines, then we've got less time to teach the kids. Is that helping kids?"

"Well, I still think you're over-reacting," says Betty. "Why don't we ask the new teacher here. What do you think?"

The three teachers look at you, awaiting your response. What do you say?

FOCUS QUESTIONS

1. What are the local, state, and federal influences on education?
2. In what ways are the educational concerns of various interest groups within our society in conflict?
3. How do state and local boards of education function?
4. What are the three main sources of funding for schools?
5. What steps are being taken to equalize disparities in school funding?

In preparing to become a teacher, your primary concern is most likely how to become effective in dealing with the six realities of teaching discussed in Chapter 2. Compared to these realities, an understanding of how schools are governed and supported may not seem very important. Though teachers must acquire the specific knowledge and skills that will enable them to survive their first months of teaching, true professionals also recognize the need to understand the political forces that influence their work. An appreciation for the political dimensions of teaching can have positive results, as the following examples suggest:

- Three high school English teachers awarded a state grant to develop a humanities program had submitted letters of endorsement for their project from the president of the board of education and the superintendent.
- A group of concerned teachers was instrumental in getting a local bond issue passed in order to fund a much-needed remodeling and expansion project at their school.

POLITICAL TURBULENCE AND U.S. SCHOOLS

Before we look at how political events influence schools, we wish to point out that education is not (and never will be) apolitical. Our discussion of the historical foundations of American education in Chapter 6, for example, showed how political forces have shaped the character of our schools since their early beginnings.

Some teachers might prefer not to dirty their hands with politics, but it is a fact of life that school policies are developed in a political milieu. Whenever educators try to enlist governmental support for a particular approach to schooling, they are acting politically. In fact, some educators feel that it is quite appropriate to act in this way: "Each time educators or lay leaders take action to influence educational policy, or policies in other areas of society, they are involved in politics. Thus, educational leadership to upgrade educational standards is political. And if educators and citizens desire changes in school programs, they must be good politicians. Performing as a politician to develop quality schools is a perfectly legitimate, statesmanlike activity."[1]

There are many complex political forces that currently shape schools in the United States (see Figure 8.1). During the 1980s, for example, numerous groups pressed to have school policies reflect their special, often conflicting, interests. In the 1990s we see a continuation of this struggle to control various aspects of the educational enterprise. Among the groups that will continue to have a keen concern for shaping educational policies, at least nine can be identified:

1. *Parents*—concerned with controlling local schools so that quality educational programs are available to their children.
2. *Students*—concerned with policies related to freedom of expression, dress, behavior, and curricular offerings.
3. *Teachers*—concerned with improving conditions of the workplace, terms of employment, and other professional issues.
4. *Administrators*—concerned with providing leadership so that the constructive energies of various interest groups are channeled into the development of quality educational programs.
5. *Taxpayers*—concerned with maintaining an appropriate formula for determining local, state, and federal financial support of schools.

FIGURE 8.1 **Political Influences on the Schools**

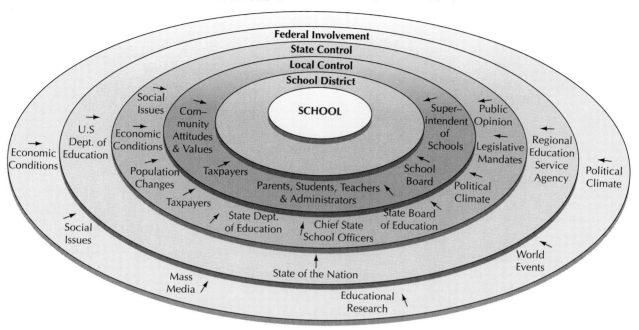

6. *State and federal authorities*—concerned with the implementation of court orders, guidelines, and legislative mandates related to the operation of schools.
7. *Minorities and women*—concerned with the availability of equal educational opportunity for all and with legal issues surrounding administrative certification, terms of employment, and evaluation.
8. *Educational theorists and researchers*—concerned with using theoretical and research-based insights as the bases for improving schools at all levels.
9. *Businesses and corporations*—concerned with receiving from the schools graduates who have the knowledge, skills, attitudes, and values to help an organization realize its goals.

Out of the complex and often turbulent interactions of these groups school policies are developed. And, as strange as it may seem, no one of these groups can be said to control today's schools. In fact, some observers suggest that the period since 1960 might be characterized as the "era of nobody in charge."[2] Those who we might imagine control schools—principals, superintendents, and boards of education—are in reality responding to shifting sets of conditions created by those who have an interest in the schools. In addition, schools are influenced by several out-of-school factors—what sociologists have termed *environmental press*. Because schools are a reflection of the society they serve, they are influenced directly and indirectly by an almost infinite number of factors. Some of the more obvious factors that exert their press upon the schools are listed below.

mass media	political climate	religion
legislative mandates	educational research	technology
growth of minorities	international events	economics
demographic shifts	community attitudes	social issues

FIVE-MINUTE FOCUS   Select one of the factors listed at the bottom of page 233 and describe how it is currently influencing education in a school district with which you are familiar. Date your journal entry and write for five minutes.

Clearly, it is difficult to untangle the web of political forces that influence schools. Figure 8.2 shows graphically how school authorities are confronted with the difficult task of funneling the input from various sources into unified, coherent school programs.

FIGURE 8.2   **School Politics**

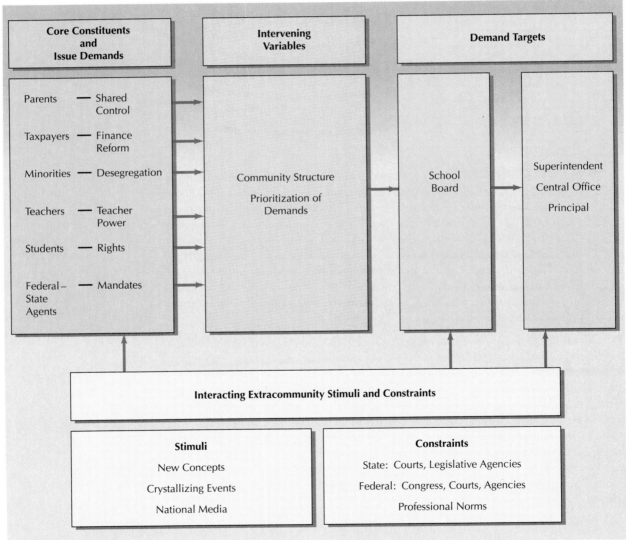

Source: Adapted from Frederick M. Wirt, "Political Turbulence and Administrative Authority in the Schools," in *The New Urban Politics,* ed. Louis H. Masotti and Robert L. Lineberry (Cambridge: Ballinger, 1976): 63. Used with permission.

FACT FINDING

How Has the Number of School Districts Changed?

Since 1930, the consolidation of school districts in the United States has been a steady trend. In 1987–88, the number of school districts was less than one-eighth the number that existed in 1931–32.

Number of U.S. Public School Systems: 1931–32 to 1987–88

Year	Number	Year	Number
1931–32	127,531	1970–71	17,995
1941–42	115,493	1980–91	15,912
1951–52	71,094	1987–88	15,577
1961–62	35,676		

Source: Based on data from *Digest of Education Statistics 1989*, Twenty-Fifth Edition, National Center for Education Statistics, U.S. Department of Education.

In the next four sections of this chapter, we will examine the many political forces that impinge upon the schools by looking at how they are influenced at the local, state, federal, and intermediate levels.

LOCAL CONTROL OF SCHOOLS

The Constitution does not address the issue of public education, but the Tenth Amendment is used as the basis for giving states the responsibility for the governance of education, that is, the legal authority to create and manage school systems. In addition, as we saw in Figure 8.2, various individuals and groups, though not legally empowered, do exercise local control over schools by trying to influence those legally entitled to operate the schools.

The Tenth Amendment gives to the states all powers not reserved for the federal government and not prohibited to the states. The states have, in turn, created local school districts, giving them responsibility for the daily operation of public schools. As a result of efforts to consolidate districts, the number of local school districts has declined steadily during the last half century.

Local School District

Local school districts vary greatly in regard to demographics such as number of school-age children; educational, occupational, and income levels of parents; operating budget; number of teachers; economic resources; and number of school buildings. Some serve ultrawealthy communities, others impoverished ghetto neighborhoods or rural areas. Their operations include 729 one-teacher schools in this country[3] as well as scores of modern, multibuilding campuses in heavily populated areas. The largest school districts are exceedingly complex operations with multimillion-dollar-a-year operating budgets (see Table 8.1). The largest—the New York City school system—

[handwritten margin note: an agency at the local level that has the authority to operate schools in the district.]

TABLE 8.1   Selected Data for the Ten Largest Public School Systems, 1987–88

School System	Total Enrollment	Number of Teachers	Pupils per Teacher	Number of Schools	Total Expenditures	Expenditures per Pupil
New York City	939,933	52,953	17.8	993	$4,486,907,000	$4,584
Los Angeles Unified	568,754	21,177*	—	703*	$2,284,966,000	$3,886
City of Chicago	419,537	21,753	19.3	597	$1,621,231,000	$3,637
Dade County, FL Schools	253,720	14,014	18.1	292	$1,018,743,000	$3,965
Philadelphia City	194,698	10,756	18.1	255	$871,675,000	$4,014
Houston Independent School District	191,708	10,499	18.3	239	$642,129,000	$3,018
Detroit City	181,583	8,775*	—	280	$744,369,000	$3,511
Hawaii Dept. of Education	166,160	9,270	17.9	229	$536,251,000	$3,019
Broward County, FL	137,336	7,104	19.3	165	$538,235,000	$3,800
Dallas Independent School District	130,885	6,904	19.0	188	$468,456,000	$3,219

*Data for 1981–82.

— Data not available.

Source: Adapted from *Digest of Education Statistics 1989,* Twenty-Fifth Edition, National Center for Education Statistics, U.S. Department of Education.

has nearly a million pupils, 53,000 teachers, 1,000 schools, and total annual expenditures of nearly 4.5 billion dollars.

School districts have varying influences on the conditions under which teachers work. Some of these differences are readily apparent. For example, in many districts the central office determines how funds will be spent. In others, principals and teachers have a considerable say in how money will be spent. Also, many districts are decentralizing and giving their schools greater freedom to determine policies and how resources will be allocated.

School districts also differ in regard to their organizational structures. Large districts in urban areas, for example, tend to have a more complex distribution of roles and responsibilities than do smaller school districts. The larger the district, the more office administrators and support personnel. The Teacher's Resource Guide shows the "Typical Organizational Structure for a Medium-Sized School District" (about 20,000 students) and the "Organizational Chart for a Large Metropolitan School District," the Jefferson County Public School System in Louisville, Kentucky. This district, the twentieth largest in the country, serves over 93,000 students and employs more than 5,000 teachers.

FIVE-MINUTE FOCUS   Would you prefer working in a large, medium, or small school district? Discuss the reasons for your choice. Date your journal entry and write for five minutes.

School Board

The primary governing body of a district is the **school board.** The board, acting as an agent of the state, is responsible for the following important activities: approving the teachers, administrators, and other school personnel hired by the superintendent; developing organizational and educational policies; and determining procedures for the evaluation of programs and personnel.

In most communities, school board members are elected in general elections. In some urban areas, however, board members are selected by the mayor. Board members typically serve a minimum of three to five years, and their terms of office are usually staggered. School boards usually range in size from five to fifteen members, with five or seven frequently suggested as the optimum size. While board members in urban areas are usually paid, board members in most other areas are not.

In their 1990 national survey of school board members, the *American School Board Journal* and Virginia Tech reported that women on school boards constituted 33.7 percent. The survey also revealed that minority membership on school boards was 6.5 percent, with the South reporting the greatest minority representation (16.7 percent African American). School board members are somewhat atypical of the general population in other ways: they are older—77.1 percent are over 40; and they are more affluent—56.9 percent have total family incomes of $50,000 or more, with 25.1 percent earning more than $80,000 per year.[4]

Nearly all school board meetings are open to the public; in fact, many communities even provide radio and television coverage. Open meetings allow parents and interested citizens an opportunity to express their concerns and to get more information about problems in the district.

Because school boards are made up of unique individuals, each board meets its responsibility for controlling local schools in various ways. To continue to receive state and federal support, however, school boards must abide by guidelines set by those branches of government. One study of the communication and decision-making processes at board of education meetings concluded that school board meetings differ in the following six areas:[5]

1. Topics on the agenda—curriculum, finances, student services, discrimination, performance evaluation, etc.
2. Individual or group who sets the agenda—school board, superintendent, staff experts, the public
3. Participants in the discussion
4. How participation varies according to topic of discussion
5. Individual or group who proposes policy
6. The degree to which the board defers to the recommendations of the superintendent of schools

Superintendent of Schools

Though school boards operate very differently, the **superintendent** is invariably the key figure in determining a district's educational policy. The superintendent is the chief administrator of the school district, the person charged with the responsibility of seeing to it that schools operate in accord with federal and state guidelines as well as policies set by the local school board. Though the board of education delegates broad powers to the superintendent, his or her policies require board approval.

The specific responsibilities of the superintendent are many. Among the most important are:

1. To serve as professional advisor to the board of education and to make policy recommendations for improving curricular and instructional programs
2. To act as employer and supervisor of professional and nonteaching personnel (janitors, cafeteria workers, etc.)
3. To represent the schools in their relations with the community and to explain board of education policies to the community
4. To develop policies for the placement and transportation of students within the district
5. To prepare an annual school budget and adhere to the budget adopted by the school board

How the superintendent and his or her board work together appears to be related to the size of the school district, with superintendents and school boards in larger districts more likely to be in conflict. Schools boards in smaller districts, however, are more effective when they do oppose the superintendent. In large districts, the board's own divisiveness makes it less likely that the board will successfully oppose the superintendent.[6] Superintendents have also observed how widely the political climate of school districts can vary. "In some schools, changing the location of a bicycle rack will cause parents to call the principal. In other schools, we can cut the school day from seven periods to six periods without neighborhood reaction."[7]

Superintendents must have a great deal of skill in order to respond appropriately to the many external political forces that demand their attention. As one observer has put it, "Conflict is the DNA of the superintendency," and effective superintendents demonstrate that they are able to play three roles simultaneously: politician, manager, and teacher.[8] It is a demanding position, and turnover is high. Research has shown that the average tenure in office for superintendents is between three and four years.[9] During the early 1970s, 22 out of 25 urban superintendents were replaced,[10] and during the 1980s, several cities (New York, Chicago, Cleveland, Boston, Seattle, and Denver) had three different superintendents in less than three years.[11] In an environment characterized by political turbulence and demands from competing interest groups, the superintendent cannot be an omnipotent, insensitive figure; he or she must be a "negotiator-statesman."[12]

Optimally, the Superintendent of Schools and the elected or appointed school board work together to decide and implement educational policies. Budget issues and school-community relations are often the superintendent's greatest challenges.

Parents

Parents may not be involved legally in the governance of schools, but they do play an important role in American education. As we learned in Chapter 5, for example, one characteristic of successful schools is that they have developed close working relationships with parents. Children whose parents or guardians support and encourage school activities have a definite advantage in school.

Groups such as the Parent-Teacher Association (PTA), Parent-Teacher Organization (PTO), or Parent Advisory Council (PAC) give parents the opportunity to communicate with teachers on matters of interest and importance to them. Through these groups, parents can become involved in the life of the school in a variety of ways—from making recommendations regarding school policies to providing much-needed volunteer services, or to initiating school-improvement activities such as fund-raising drives.

The National PTA—the National Congress of Parents and Teachers—is the nation's largest parent-teacher organization. Founded in 1897, the PTA now has more than 6.1 million members, and sponsors many activities and publications to support schools, protect children, and help parents learn to be better parents. Ann P. Kahn, past president of the National Congress of Parents and Teachers, points out, for example, that the PTA has played a key role in

> supporting compulsory public education, including kindergarten; establishing the juvenile-justice system; starting hot lunch programs in schools in order that all children would have at least one nutritious meal a day; field testing the Salk polio vaccine; leading the fight against drug and alcohol abuse by young people; speaking out for adequate funding for public education; and challenging the use of public funds for nonpublic schools. [13]

SCHOOL RESTRUCTURING

At many schools across the country exciting changes are taking place in regard to how schools are controlled locally. To improve the performance of schools, to decentralize the system of governance, and to enhance the professional status of teachers, some districts are **restructuring** their school systems. Restructuring goes by several names: shared governance, administrative decentralization, teacher empowerment, professionalization, bottom-up policy-making, school-based planning, school-based management, and shared decision making. What all these approaches to school governance have in common is allowing those who know students best—teachers, principals, aides, custodians, librarians, secretaries, and parents—the freedom to decide how to meet students' needs.

School-Based Management

One of the most frequently used approaches to restructuring schools is **school-based management** (SBM). Most programs have three components in common:

1. Power and decisions formerly made by the superintendent and school board are delegated to teachers, principals, parents, community members, and students at local schools. At SBM schools, teachers can become directly involved in making decisions about curriculum, textbooks, standards for student behavior, staff development, promotion and retention policies, teacher evaluation, school budgets, and the selection of teachers and administrators.

2. At each school, a decision-making body (known as a board, cabinet, site-based team, or council)—made up of teachers, the principal, and parents—implements the SBM plan.
3. SBM programs operate with the whole-hearted endorsement of the superintendent of schools.[14]

The primary aim of school-based management is to provide teachers, administrators, staff, and, indeed, the entire school community with a greater sense of ownership and efficacy in the operation of schools. Such empowerment, it is believed, will result in greater cooperation, satisfaction, and pride among those directly involved with educating children. The assumption is that if people have a greater say in the decisions that affect them, they will become more involved and, ultimately, their schools will become more successful. In the words of the president of the local teachers' union that helped implement an SBM program in Dade County, Florida:

> We are convinced that kids are going to get a better education when the decisions that affect them are made in the schools they're attending, by the people who are there in the classroom.[15]

The restructuring of programs increases communication among teachers, principals, parents, students, and other groups concerned with the operation of schools. With increased communication comes a greater awareness of what needs to be done to improve education at the local school site. As a middle school teacher involved in restructuring said: "We were convinced that what we wanted to change was possible. . . . The thing we learned is that communication is very, very important."[16]

The range of management decisions that can be made by teachers is very broad. As Joseph A. Fernandez, superintendent of New York City schools, said of his approach to implementing school-based management in Dade County, Florida, his former district: "The instructions to schools were very simple. We told them the sky is the limit."[17]

Among the changes implemented at some SBM schools are the following:

- Offering Saturday classes to teach students in a more informal setting
- Initiating various before- and after-school programs
- Hiring aides instead of assistant principals
- Creating new positions, such as "discipline manager" and "enrichment coordinator"
- Having teachers give up some of their planning time to reduce class size during basic-skills instruction
- Creating a developmental program for 5-year-olds that includes monthly "hands-on" workshops for parents
- Having teachers create their own report card to give parents more detailed information about their children
- Instituting a high school "teacher-as-advisor" program in the middle of the day to counsel students about suicide, drug abuse, and stress-related problems[18]

Three Pioneers in School-Based Management

Three school districts that have pioneered SBM programs are the Dade County, Florida, Public Schools; the City of Chicago Public Schools; and the Rochester, New York, Public Schools. In the following paragraphs, we describe the SBM programs in these districts. The description of the Dade County program is based on the experiences of one of the authors of this textbook, who assisted with the implementation of SBM programs. Descriptions of the Chicago and Rochester programs are based on extensive media coverage.

Dade County, Florida As part of its "professionalization of education" movement, Dade County invited faculties at its 292 schools to prepare school-based management proposals in 1987. Teachers and administrators were given permission by the Board of Education to develop their own approaches to self-governance. At each site, SBM proposals were developed and approved by at least two-thirds of the teachers. Each proposal was unique and reflected the specific needs of students, teachers, and administrators. To facilitate the SBM program, existing requirements concerning maximum class size, length of school day, number of minutes per subject, and so on were waived. Similarly, the Dade County Federation of Teachers agreed to waive contract provisions concerning teachers working additional hours without more pay and evaluating other teachers.

Initially, 32 schools were identified as SBM schools and were given unprecedented control over their budgets, allocation of staff, and approaches to instruction. Currently, almost half of the county's schools are participating in the program. According to Dade County's assistant superintendent in charge of SBM programs, "Any kind of program you can think of, we've got it here."[19]

Although the Dade County school-based management program has resulted in several positive changes—higher teacher morale, a variety of programs to meet students' special needs, improved student attendance, and a lower dropout rate, for example—change has not come easily. At one school, for example, SBM tended to increase divisiveness and polarization among the faculty. Among the barriers to implementing the program were (1) resentment over additional time needed to meet new responsibilities, (2) fear of taking risks, (3) resistance to change, and (4) concern with loss of power in a setting where new roles and responsibilities are being developed.[20]

Chicago, Illinois For years, the Chicago Public School System has been beset by an array of problems: low student achievement, periodic teacher strikes, budget crises, a top-heavy central bureaucracy, and schools in the decaying inner city that seemed beyond most improvement efforts. In response to these problems, the late Mayor Harold Washington appointed a 55-member committee of business, education, and community leaders to develop a school reform proposal. Among the group's recommendations was the creation of a local school council for each of the city's 597 schools, with the majority of council members being parents of school children.

In July 1989, the Chicago School Reform Act was enacted by the state. The Act gave extensive policy-making powers to the local school councils. Among the provisions of the Act were the following:

- School budgets would be controlled by a local school council made up of six parents, two community members, two school employees, and the principal.
- The council had the authority to hire and fire the principal.
- The council, with input from teachers and the principal, had the authority to develop an improvement plan for the local school.
- New teachers would be hired on the basis of merit, not seniority.
- Principals could remove teachers 45 days after serving them official notice of unsatisfactory performance.

CONSIDER THIS . . .

How Would You Do in a School-Based Management School?

According to a national survey of educators, released in 1990 by Southwest Educational Development Laboratory, certain aspects of working in school-based management schools may be difficult for some teachers. The following self-assessment is based on that survey and on the authors' experiences assisting with the implementation of SBM programs. It is designed to give you an opportunity to determine how suited you might be for working in an SBM school. For each item, circle a number to indicate to what extent each listed behavior would be difficult or easy for you to do.

	Very Difficult for Me To Do				*Very Easy for Me To Do*
1. Taking new risks	1	2	3	4	5
2. Sharing power with others	1	2	3	4	5
3. Willingly changing roles and responsibilities	1	2	3	4	5
4. Learning to trust others	1	2	3	4	5
5. Working in situations that may lack definition and clarity	1	2	3	4	5
6. Being willing to learn new skills	1	2	3	4	5
7. Doing more than is specified in a teaching contract	1	2	3	4	5
8. Assuming a leadership role	1	2	3	4	5
9. Being patient while waiting to see the results of one's efforts	1	2	3	4	5
10. Listening carefully to the opinions of those with whom I disagree	1	2	3	4	5

Total Score _____

Now add up your total score, which will range from 10 to 50. A score of 50 suggests that you would be "perfectly" suited for working at a school-based management school. High scores on some items and low scores on others show your areas of strength and weakness in adapting and contributing to school-based management programs.

While it is too early to evaluate the effectiveness of the Chicago program, it is clearly one of the more dramatic efforts to empower parents and make them full partners in the educative process.

Rochester, New York   The Rochester, New York, schools—like many schools in Chicago and other urban areas—have had to deal with a high student dropout rate, low achievement, discipline problems, and lack of motivation among students who, increasingly, were from low socioeconomic backgrounds. Rochester's approach to restructuring (known locally as school-based planning) is based on the Carnegie Foundation's "career ladder" model. Rochester teachers now participate in a career ladder comprised of the following four levels:

1. *Intern teacher*—beginning teachers who are supervised by experienced teachers
2. *Resident teacher*—teachers who have completed their internship and have a provisional certificate
3. *Professional teacher*—teachers who have a permanent certificate
4. *Lead teacher*—teachers who have 10 or more years of experience and devote 10 percent more time to such activities as mentoring other teachers, developing school improvement activities, and other leadership roles

In the Rochester school system, lead teachers can make as much as $70,000 a year. These increases in salary and decision-making opportunities, of course, do not come without increased responsibility, and methods for holding teachers more accountable for student outcomes such as achievement and attendance have been developed.

STATE CONTROL OF SCHOOLS

Above the level of local control, states have a great influence on the governance of schools. Throughout the seventies and eighties, the influence of the state on educational policy increased steadily. Sparked by numerous national reports critical of American education in the early 1980s, many states took extensive initiatives to improve education, such as:

- Tougher requirements for graduation from high school
- Longer school days and years
- Career ladders for teachers and master teacher programs
- Higher expectations for students, including testing of basic skills
- Testing graduates of teacher education programs prior to certification

As mentioned earlier, the Tenth Amendment to the Constitution allows the states to organize and to administer education within their boundaries. In their interpretation of this amendment, some states have typically been more aggressive (California and Florida, for example), while others (New Hampshire and Colorado, for example) have been less aggressive.[21]

To meet the responsibility of maintaining and supporting schools, the states have assumed several powers:

- The power to levy taxes for the support of schools and to determine state aid to local school districts
- The power to set the curriculum and, in some states, to identify approved textbooks
- The power to determine minimum standards for teacher certification
- The power to establish standards for accrediting schools
- The power to pass legislation necessary for the proper maintenance and support of schools

To carry out the tasks implied by these powers, the states have adopted a number of different organizational structures. Most states, however, have adopted a hierarchical structure similar to that shown in the Teacher's Resource Guide, "Organizational Structure of a Typical State School System."

The Roles of State Government in Education

Various persons and agencies within each state government play a role in operating the educational system within that state. Though state governments differ in many respects, the state legislature, the state courts, and the governor have a direct, critical impact on education in their state.

The Legislature   In nearly every state, the legislature is responsible for establishing and maintaining public schools and for determining basic educational policies within the state. To accomplish these ends, the legislature has the power to enact laws related to education.

Among the policies that the state legislature may determine are

- How the state boards of education will be selected and what their responsibilities will be
- How the chief state school officer will be selected and what his or her duties will be
- How the state department of education will function
- How the state will be divided into local and regional districts
- How higher education will be organized and financed
- How local school boards will be selected and what their powers will be

In addition, the legislature may determine how taxes will be used to support schools, what will or will not be taught, the length of the school day and school year, how many years of compulsory education will be required, and whether or not the state will have community colleges and/or vocational/technical schools. Legislatures may also make policies that apply to such matters as pupil attendance, admission, promotion, teacher certification, teacher tenure and retirement, and collective bargaining.

Other policies developed by the state legislature may also apply to nonpublic schools in the state—policies related to health services, building construction, safety, school lunch services, textbooks, and testing of pupils, for example. In general, state legislatures may pass laws that provide for the reasonable supervision of nonpublic educational institutions.

The Courts   From time to time, state courts are called upon to uphold the power of the legislature to develop laws that apply to schools. The state courts must determine, however, that this power does not conflict with the state or federal constitution. It is important to remember, too, that the role of state courts is not to develop laws but to rule on the reasonableness of laws that apply to specific educational situations. In the following chapter we will examine several state court rulings that have influenced schools.

The Governor   Though the powers of governors vary greatly from state to state, a governor can, if he or she chooses, have a far-reaching impact on education within the state. The governor may appoint and/or remove educators at the state level, and in some states the governor may even appoint the chief state school officer. Furthermore, in every state except North Carolina, the governor may use his or her veto power to influence the legislature to pass certain laws related to education. Governors are also extremely influential because they make educational budget recommendations to legislatures, and, in many states, they may elect to use any accumulated balances in the state treasury for education.

State Board of Education

The **state board of education,** acting under the authority of the state legislature, is the highest educational agency in a state. Every state, with the exception of Wisconsin, has a state board of education. In most states there are two separate boards, one responsible for elementary through secondary education, the other for higher education.

The method of determining board members varies from state to state. Some members are appointed by the governor; in other states members are selected through general elections. Two states have *ex officio* members who, by virtue of the positions they hold, automatically serve on the board. Most states have either seven- or nine-member boards.[22]

People disagree on which is better: electing or appointing board members. Some believe that election to the state board may cause members to be more concerned with politics than with education. Others argue that elected board members are more aware of the wishes of the public whom the schools are supposed to serve. People in favor of appointing members to the state board suggest that appointment increases the likelihood that individuals will be chosen on the basis of merit rather than politics.

There is no uniformity when it comes to the exact functions of state boards of education, but just about every board is charged with several regulatory and advisory functions. The regulatory functions held by state boards are, generally:

- Ensuring that local school districts adhere to legislation concerning educational policies, rules, and regulations
- Setting standards for issuing and revoking teaching and administrative certificates
- Establishing standards for accrediting schools
- Managing state monies appropriated for education
- Developing and implementing a system for collecting educational data needed for reporting and program evaluation

State boards of education also perform several important advisory functions, which include:

- Advising the governor and/or the state legislature on educational issues
- Identifying both short- and long-range educational needs in the state and developing plans to meet those needs
- Hearing all disputes arising from the implementation of its educational policies

In addition, some state boards of education have instituted a statewide textbook adoption system. In the adoption system, boards choose a small number of titles for each subject area and grade level for all the state's schools. Individual schools and teachers then select their textbooks from this list. Textbook adoptions have had a significant effect on the content of textbooks. Publishers have been responsive to the recommendations of textbook adoption states, such as Texas and California, because of the attraction of statewide sales.

State Department of Education

The educational program of each state is implemented by the state's department of education, under the leadership of the chief state school officer. State departments of education have a broad set of responsibilities, and they affect literally every school, school district, and teacher education program in a state. In general, the state board of education is concerned with policy-making, the **state department of education** with the day-to-day implementation of those policies.

Until the 1950s, state departments of education primarily gathered evaluative data on educational programs within the state. Since that time, an increasing number of proposals at the federal level for school reform have led to greatly expanded responsibilities for state departments of education. Perhaps the greatest boost for the development of state departments of education came with the federal government's Elementary and Secondary Education Act of 1965 (see Chapter 6). This act and its subsequent amendments required that local applications for federal funds to be used for innovative programs and for the education of disadvantaged, handicapped, bilingual, and migrant students first receive approval from state departments of education.

Today, the responsibilities of state departments of education include (1) certifying teachers, (2) distributing state and federal funds to school districts, (3) reporting to the public the condition of education within the state, (4) ensuring that school districts adhere to state and federal guidelines, (5) accrediting schools, (6) monitoring student transportation and safety, and (7) sponsoring research and evaluation projects to improve education within the state.

Throughout the 1990s, the power and influence of state departments of education will continue to be extensive. Perhaps the most significant index of the steady increase in state control during the 1980s is the fact that the states now supply the majority of funding for schools.

Chief State School Officer

The **chief state school officer** (known as the commissioner of education or superintendent of public instruction in many states) is the chief administrator of the state department of education and the head of the state board of education. In 27 states, the state board of education appoints the chief state school officer; in 18, the office is filled through a general election; and in the remaining 5, the governor appoints an individual to that position.[23] It is generally acknowledged that states with chief state school officers appointed by the board of education are more likely to attract individuals to that position who have the professional background and expertise necessary to provide effective leadership. In states where the office is filled through elections, the likelihood is increased that political considerations, not professional qualifications, will determine who occupies the office.

Though the specific responsibilities of the chief state school officer vary from state to state, Kimbrough and Nunnery have identified several responsibilities that most persons in this position hold in common:

1. Serving as chief administrator of the state department of education
2. Selecting and recommending to the state board candidates for the state department of education
3. Recommending policies, rules, and regulations to the state board deemed necessary for efficient governance of the schools
4. Interpreting state school laws and state board of education policies, rules, and regulations
5. Ensuring compliance with applicable laws, policies, rules, and regulations

6. Arranging for studies, committees, and task forces as necessary to study educational problems and recommend plans for improvement
7. Reporting on the status of education within the state to the governor, legislature, state board, and public[24]

As the aforementioned responsibilities indicate, the chief state school officer is a very influential person. He or she is frequently called upon to tell the governor, the legislature, the state board of education, and the people of the state what steps should be taken to improve education.

FIVE-MINUTE FOCUS If you were able to arrange a 15-minute meeting with the chief state school officer in your state, what would you tell him or her about the concerns of prospective teachers? Date your journal entry and write for five minutes.

REGIONAL CONTROL OF SCHOOLS

When we think of how schools are governed and the sources of political pressure applied to them, we typically think of influences originating at three levels: local, state, and federal. There is, however, an additional source of control—the regional, or intermediate, unit. The intermediate unit of educational administration, or the **Regional Educational Service Agency** (RESA), is the least understood branch of the state public school system. The intermediate unit "provides certain administrative and supervisory functions as well as supplementary educational programs and services to a cluster of two or more local school districts. . . . It is the middle echelon in a state system of education that includes the local school district and the state education agency as well."[25] Through the intermediate unit, local school districts can receive supportive services that, economically and logistically, they could not provide for themselves.

Presently, 27 states and Puerto Rico have some form of intermediate or regional unit. Ohio and Arkansas have the most units, with 87 and 75, respectively; Alaska, Idaho, and Missouri have the fewest, with two each.[26] The average unit is made up of 20 to 30 local school districts and covers a 50-square-mile area. The intermediate or regional unit has many different names: education service center (in Texas), intermediate school district (in Michigan), multicounty educational service unit (in Nebraska), board of cooperative educational services (in New York), and educational service region (in Illinois).[27]

The primary role of the intermediate unit is to provide assistance directly to districts in the areas of staff development, curriculum development, instructional media, and program evaluation. Intermediate or regional units also help school districts with their school improvement efforts by providing help in targeted areas such as bilingual education, vocational education, computer education, and the education of gifted and talented and handicapped students.[28] While intermediate units do monitor local school districts to see that they follow state educational guidelines, "local districts [actually] exert more influence over the intermediate unit and often specify what services shall or shall not be rendered by the regional unit."[29]

FEDERAL INVOLVEMENT IN THE SCHOOLS

Since the birth of our nation, the federal government has played a major role in shaping the character of our schools. This branch of government has always recognized that the strength and well-being of our country are directly related to the quality of our schools. Just before winning the 1988 presidential election, George Bush said, "More than 2,200 years ago, Aristotle wrote, 'All who have meditated on the art of governing mankind have been convinced that the fate of empires depends on the education of youth.' "[30] As we look to the twenty-first century it is clear that as a nation we will face unprecedented levels of both global competition and the need for greater international cooperation. Our rapidly changing, increasingly complex society will require a better-educated workforce if we are to compete and cooperate successfully.

The federal government has taken aggressive initiatives to influence education at several points in our history. Whether it be the allocation of federal money to improve science, mathematics, and foreign language education after Russia launched the world's first satellite or the appointment of a presidential commission to prepare the *Nation at Risk* report, the federal government has had a far-reaching impact.

Frederick M. Wirt and Michael W. Kirst have identified the following six modes of federal influence on the public schools:

1. *General aid*—Provide no-strings aid to state and local education agencies or minimal earmarks such as teacher salaries. [Federal expenditures for education during 1990–1991, for example, topped $21 billion.]
2. *Stimulate through differential funding*—Earmark categories of aid, provide financial incentives through matching grants, fund demonstrations projects, and purchase specific services.
3. *Regulate*—Legally specify behavior, impose standards, certify and license, enforce accountability procedures.
4. *Discover knowledge and make it available*—Have research performed; gather and make other statistical data available [for example, ERIC].
5. *Provide services*—Furnish technical assistance and consultants in specialized areas or subjects. [For example, the Office of Civil Rights will advise school districts that wish to design voluntary desegregation plans.]
6. *Exert moral suasion*—Develop vision and question assumptions through publications, speeches by top officials. [Ronald Reagan, for example, signed a proclamation naming 1984–85 the Year of Excellence in Education.][31]

The federal government also disseminates research results and descriptions of exemplary educational programs. In addition, various branches of the federal government operate educational programs—for example, the Department of Defense schools for children of military personnel, the Bureau of Indian Affairs schools on reservations, and educational programs for the Department of Labor's Job Corps. Perhaps the federal government's most important role is to ensure, often through the intervention of the federal courts, that all Americans receive the equal educational opportunity guaranteed by the United States Constitution and federal laws.

U.S. Department of Education

In 1979 President Carter increased the potential for a larger, more clearly defined federal role in education when he signed a law creating the Department of Education. This new cabinet-level department assumed the responsibilities of the U.S. Office of Education, which had been formed in 1953 as a branch of the Department of Health,

Education, and Welfare. Shirley Hufstedler, a Supreme Court judge, became the first Secretary of Education when the new department opened in mid-1980.

The continued representation of education in the president's cabinet was threatened momentarily in 1983 when President Reagan suggested that the Department of Education be dismantled and replaced with a Foundation for Education Assistance. However, the response of the American public to *A Nation at Risk* convinced the President that education was too important an issue not to be represented at the cabinet level. In addition, a proposal to eliminate the Department of Education was soundly defeated at the 1984 Republican National Convention. So solid was the rejection of the proposal to eliminate the department that former Secretary of Education Terrel H. Bell was moved to comment in 1986 that "dissolution of the department will not, in my opinion, ever again be a serious issue. Diehards may mount feeble attempts to do away with it, but I do not anticipate any real threats to the department's existence. The Education Department is here to stay."[32]

In addition to supporting educational research, disseminating the results of much of that research, and administering federal grants, the U.S. Department of Education provides the President with a platform for promoting and/or implementing his educational agenda. For example, Secretary of Education Lamar Alexander was a spokesman in the early 1990s for the following components of President Bush's controversial educational platform:

- Restoring voluntary prayer in the schools
- Setting national goals for education
- Providing vouchers or tuition tax credits for parents who wished to send their children to private schools
- Making the United States number one among countries in mathematics and science achievement
- Increasing parental choice in education
- Contributing educational funding to states in the form of consolidated grants that could be managed free from federal regulations

The Impact of Federal Policies

Presidential platforms on education often have a profound effect on education. President Reagan's two terms of office (1980–1988), for example, saw a significant shift in the federal government's role in education. In general, the Reagan administration sought to scale back what it viewed as excessive federal involvement in education. Wirt and Kirst have identified six basic changes that characterized this federal educational policy:

1. From minimal support of private education to significant support
2. From a prime concern with equity to more concern with efficiency and state and local freedom to choose
3. From a larger and more influential federal role to a mitigated federal role
4. From mistrust of the motives and capacity of state and local educators to a renewed faith in governing units outside of Washington
5. From categorical grants [i.e., funding earmarked at the federal level for specific programs] to more unrestricted types of financial aid [to the states]
6. From detailed and prescriptive regulations to deregulation[33]

With the election of George Bush as the 41st president, many hoped that the federal government would assume a more active role in education during the 1990s.

Bush, who stated during the 1988 campaign that he wished to be known as the "Education President," set the following education-related goals for his administration:

- Creation of a new $500 million federal program for National Merit Schools
- Significantly increased funding for a variety of educational programs, including Head Start, the National Assessment of Educational Progress, and the Fund for Improvement and Reform of Schools and Teaching
- Increased federal assistance for at-risk students and the development of magnet schools
- Greater emphasis on teaching moral values in the schools

Those who wished to see increased federal involvement in and support for education were further encouraged when the Cold War ended in 1990. Improved relations between the United States and the Soviet Union, they reasoned, would result in a "peace dividend" for education; that is, money previously spent on defense could be redirected to education. However, an economic recession at home and the costs of the Persian Gulf War in 1991 delayed any increased funding that might have resulted from the end of the Cold War.

FINANCING U.S. SCHOOLS

To provide free public education to all school-age children in our nation is a costly undertaking. Schools must provide services and facilities to students from a wide range of ethnic, racial, social, cultural, linguistic and individual backgrounds. Expenditures

FIGURE 8.3
Total Current Expenditures per Pupil in 1989 Constant Dollars: 1950–1989

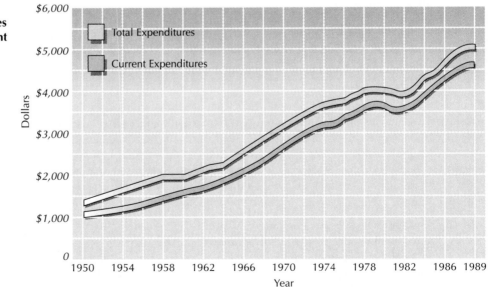

Note: Current expenditure includes expenditures for operating local public schools, excluding capital outlay, and interest on debt.

Source: U.S. Department of Education, National Center for Education Statistics, *Statistics of State School Systems,* various years; *Revenues and Expenditures for Public Elementary and Secondary Education,* Common Core of Data survey, various years; and unpublished tabulations. Reprinted from National Center for Education Statistics, *The Condition of Education 1990: Volume 1, Elementary and Secondary Education,* p. 83.

for these services and facilities have been rising rapidly. In 1950, the total **expenditure per pupil** was $1,396; by 1989, this figure had risen to $5,172, almost four times the amount spent in 1950 (see Figure 8.3). The total estimated expenditure for public elementary and secondary schools in the United States for 1988–89 was $167,324,897,000.

Financing an enterprise as vast and ambitious as our system of free public schools has not been easy. It has proven difficult both to devise a system that equitably distributes the tax burden for supporting schools and to provide equal educational services and facilities for all students. Moreover, there has been a tendency for the financial support of schools to be outpaced by factors that continually increase the cost of operating schools, such as inflation, rising enrollments, and the need to update aging facilities, for example.

A combination of revenues from local, state, and federal sources is used to finance public elementary and secondary schools in the United States. As Table 8.2 shows, schools received almost half of their 1987 school-year funding from the state, 44.1 percent from local and other sources, and 6.3 percent from the federal government.

TABLE 8.2   Public School Revenues and Sources: Selected Years, 1920–1988

School Year Ending	Gross National Product[1]	Total Revenue[1]	Revenues as a Percent of GNP	Sources (Percent of total)		
				Local[2]	State	Federal
1920	—	—	—	83.2	16.5	0.3
1930	—	—	—	82.7	16.9	0.4
1940	—	—	—	68.0	30.3	1.8
1950	—	—	—	57.3	39.8	2.9
1960	—	—	—	56.5	39.1	4.4
1970	$3,106	$129	4.2	52.1	39.9	8.0
1972	3,253	149	4.6	52.8	38.3	8.9
1974	3,533	143	4.0	50.1	41.4	8.5
1976	3,564	154	4.3	46.5	44.6	8.9
1978	3,897	151	3.9	47.6	43.0	9.4
1980	4,110	142	3.5	43.4	46.8	9.8
1982	4,122	143	3.5	45.0	47.6	7.4
1984	4,375	151	3.5	45.4	47.8	6.8
1986	4,729	170	3.6	43.9	49.4	6.7
1987	4,835	174	3.6	43.9	49.8	6.4
1988	—	—	—	44.1	49.5	6.3

— Not available.

[1]In billions of 1989 constant dollars.

[2]Includes intermediate sources (e.g., gifts and tuition and transportation fees from patrons).

Note: Percents may not add up to 100 due to rounding. Some figures are revised from previously published data.

Source: U.S. Department of Education, National Center for Education Statistics, *Digest of Education Statistics, 1989* (based on the Common Core of Data and its predecessors); Executive Office of the President, *Economic Report of the President, 1989;* Council of Economic Advisors, "Economic Indicators," January 1989. Reprinted from National Center for Education Statistics, *The Condition of Education: Volume 1, Elementary and Secondary Education,* p. 80.

Prior to the 1979–80 school year, however, schools received most of their revenues from local sources, and early in the twentieth century, nearly all school revenues were generated from local property taxes.

Such revenues are influenced by many factors, among them the apportionment of taxes among the local, state, and federal levels; the size of the tax bases at each level; and competing demands for allocating funds at each level. In addition, funding for education is influenced by the following factors:

- The rate of inflation
- The health of the national economy
- The size of the national budget deficit
- Taxpayer revolts to limit the use of property taxes to raise money, such as Proposition 13 in California, Proposition 2½ in Massachusetts, and Oregon's property tax limitation passed in 1990
- Changes in the size and distribution of the population
- Legislation for equalizing educational opportunity and increasing the accountability of schools

Local Funding

At the local level, most funding for schools comes from **property taxes** that are determined by the value of property in the school district. Property taxes are assessed against real estate and, in some districts, personal property such as cars, household furniture and appliances, and stocks and bonds.

The Challenge of Equitable Taxation   Though property taxes provide a steady source of revenue for local school districts, there are inequities in the ways in which they are determined. By locating in areas where taxes are lowest, businesses and industries often avoid paying higher taxes while they continue to draw upon local resources and services. However, the main problem of using property taxes to fund education is that not all districts have the same tax base. A poor district, for example,

During the 1980s, teachers, parents, and concerned citizens in many states protested against budget constraints that cost jobs, cut valuable programs, and left public education underfunded. The issues of tax equity, equity in educational opportunity, and the funding of excellence in education remain unresolved.

may have to tax its residents disproportionately compared to residents in a wealthier district.

An additional challenge for local funding is the development of guidelines for assessing the value of property. The fair market value of property is difficult to determine, and the qualifications and training of assessors vary greatly. Moreover, individuals and groups in a community sometimes pressure assessors to keep taxes on their property as low as possible.

Most states specify by law the minimum property tax rate for local school districts to set. In many districts, an increase in the tax rate must have the approval of voters. Some states place no cap, or upper limit, on tax rates, while other states set a maximum limit.

Community-School Partnerships   To develop additional sources of funding, many local school districts have established partnerships with community groups interested in improving educational opportunities in the schools. Some groups raise money for schools. The American Jewish Committee and the Urban League raised funds for schools in Pittsburgh, for example. Other "partners," such as a major airline based in Miami, "adopt" or "sponsor" schools and enrich their educational programs by providing funding as well as other resources and services.

In Fairfax County, Virginia, 25 local and multinational businesses raised almost a million dollars for a new college preparatory school of science and technology—Thomas Jefferson High School in Annandale, Virginia. This school with state-of-the-art facilities was made possible through the efforts of such companies as AT&T, Mobil, Boeing, Honeywell, and Exxon. Facilities include a $600,000 telecommunications lab with a television studio, radio station, weather station, and a satellite earth station. The school has a biotech laboratory for genetic engineering experiments in cloning and cell fission as well as labs for research on energy and computers.

Business-school partnerships take many forms. Businesses may contribute funds or materials needed by a school or may give employees release time to visit classrooms. In some dropout prevention programs, businessmen and businesswomen adopt individual students, visiting them at school, eating lunch with them once a week, meeting their families, and taking them on personal field trips. Community groups may also provide a variety of special services, such as "museum-in-the-schools" programs, outdoor education, local history projects, and model government activities. Community-based fraternal, civic, and service organizations also provide valuable support. They may sponsor sports teams, recognize student achievement, or award scholarships.

State Funding

Most state revenues for education come from sales taxes and income taxes. Sales taxes are added to the cost of items such as general goods, gasoline, amusements, alcohol, and insurance. Income taxes are placed on individuals (in many states) and on business and industry.

Some states, such as Florida, set aside for education a percentage of the revenue from state lotteries. However, such schemes may not meet the funding needs of education. In Florida, for example, legislators have used lottery revenues to *replace* rather than augment education dollars that previously came from state taxes. The assumption that high lottery sales would mean less need to raise money for education through taxes proved false.

TABLE 8.3   Total Expenditures for Public Elementary and Secondary Schools and Revenues by Source for Selected States and the District of Columbia

State	1988–89 Expenditures[1]	Percent of Total Revenues 1987–88		
		Federal	State	Local
Alaska	$869,879,000	11.2	63.3	25.5
Colorado	$2,397,958,000	4.9	39.2	56.0
Delaware	$457,464,000	7.6	68.5	23.9
District of Columbia	$526,941,000	10.6	0.6	88.8
Florida	$6,864,156,000	6.7	55.0	38.4
Kansas	$1,631,870,000	5.0	43.2	51.9
Missouri	$2,761,369,000	5.9	40.7	53.5
Ohio	$7,000,000,000	5.1	48.5	46.4
Texas	$11,168,859,000	7.8	44.5	45.0
Washington	$3,312,436,000	6.0	75.4	18.6

[1]Date estimated by state education agencies.

Note: Percent may not add up to 100 due to rounding.

Source: National Center for Education Statistics, *Digest of Education Statistics 1989,* Twenty-Fifth Edition, U.S. Department of Education, pp. 149, 153.

As mentioned previously, states contribute nearly 50 percent of the resources needed to operate the public schools. The money that is given to cities and towns by a state is known as **state aid.** Table 8.3 compares selected states on the percent of education funds received from local, state, and federal sources in relation to total expenditures for 1988–89. The table also shows how expenditures per pupil may vary widely from state to state. Between 1969 and 1987, for example, Alaska's per pupil expenditures increased by 142 percent, while Utah's increased by only 31 percent.

Trends in Federal Funding

The role of the federal government in providing resources for education has been limited. From 1950 to 1980, however, the federal contribution to education rose from less than 4 percent of the gross national product to almost 10 percent. Prior to 1980 the federal government had in effect bypassed the states and provided funding for local programs that were administered through various federal agencies, such as the Office of Economic Opportunity (Head Start, migrant education, and Follow Through) and the Department of Labor (Job Corps and the Comprehensive Employment Training Act [CETA]). Since 1980, the federal contribution to education has declined to 6.3 percent of the GNP (gross national product). Federal aid has increasingly been given directly to the states in the form of **block grants,** which a state or local education agency may spend as it wishes with few limitations. The 1981 **Education Consolidation and Improvement Act** (ECIA) gave the states a broad range of choices in spending federal money. The ECIA significantly reduced federal aid to education, however, thus making state aid to education even more critical.

FIGURE 8.4 **Spending on Grades K–12: An International Comparison**

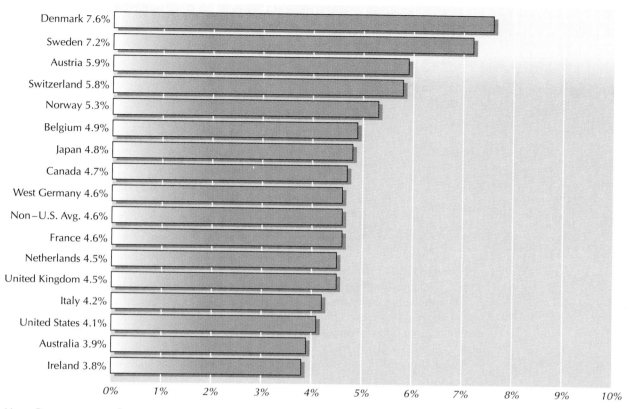

Note: Percentages are of countries' 1985 gross domestic products.
Source: Reprinted with permission from the Economic Policy Institute in their EPI Briefing Paper.
As originally reproduced in *Teacher Magazine*, March 1990, p. 22.

Compared to other industrialized nations, the amount of money the United States spends on education is significantly less. Figure 8.4 shows the percentage of the 1985 gross domestic product spent on grades K–12 in 15 countries other than the United States.

Funding Equal Education and Excellent Schools

The fact that schools have had to rely heavily on property taxes for support has resulted in fiscal inequities for schools. Districts with a high level of property wealth are able to generate more money per pupil than districts with less. The degree of inequity between the wealthiest and the poorest districts, therefore, can be quite large. In some states, for example, the ability of one district to generate local property tax revenues may be as much as seven times greater than another district's.[34]

Schemes for Achieving Equity To correct these inequities, several court suits were initiated during the 1970s. In the 1971 *Serrano* v. *Priest* case in California, it was successfully argued that the relationship between spending and property wealth violated the state's obligation to provide equal protection and education. The California

"Today in math class we learned all about negative numbers from a guest lecturer who works in the federal budget office."

Supreme Court ruled in a 6–1 decision that the quality of a child's education should not be dependent upon the "wealth of his parents and neighbors." The court also recognized that communities with a poor tax base could not be expected to generate the revenues of more affluent districts. Nevertheless, the Court did not forbid the use of property taxes to fund education.

Then, in 1973, the U.S. Supreme Court decided in *San Antonio Independent School District* v. *Rodriguez* that fiscal inequities stemming from unequal tax bases did not violate the Constitution. That court's decision reversed a lower court's ruling claiming that school financing on the basis of local property taxes was unconstitutional.

Regardless of the mixed outcomes of court challenges, many state legislatures have enacted school finance equity reforms during the last 15 years. A few states (California and Hawaii, for example) have led the way by developing programs to ensure statewide financial equality. These states have "full funding programs" in which the state sets the same per-pupil expenditure level for all schools and districts.

Other states have developed various mechanisms for providing **"vertical equity,"** that is, for allocating funds according to legitimate educational needs. Thus, additional support is given to programs that serve students from low-income backgrounds; those with limited English proficiency, handicapping conditions, or special gifts and talents; and those who need special vocational programs. In addition, funding adjustments are made to compensate for differences in costs within a state—higher expenses due to rural isolation or the higher cost of living in urban areas, for example.

Though a small proportion of the funds for schools comes from the federal level, the federal government has enacted supplemental programs to help meet the educational needs of special populations. Such programs are often referred to collectively as **entitlements.** The most significant is the Elementary and Secondary Education Act of 1965. Title I of the Act allocates a billion dollars annually to school districts with large numbers of students from low-income families. Among the other funded entitlement programs are the Servicemen's Readjustment Act (G.I. Bill of Rights, 1944), the Vocational Education Act (1963), the Manpower Development and Training Act (1963), the Economic Opportunity Act (1964), Project Head Start (1964), the Bilingual Education Act (1968), the Indian Education Act (1972), and the Education for All Handicapped Children Act (1975).

Keepers of the Dream

Mary McLeod Bethune
(1875–1955)
Teacher and Activist for
African-American Education

Born as the fifteenth child of former slaves in South Carolina, Mary McLeod Bethune went on to become one of our country's most outstanding educational leaders and a champion of the educational rights of African Americans. Few educators have had such a profound impact on education in the United States.

Bethune attended a school operated by the Presbyterian Board of Missions for Freedmen and Barber-Scotia College in Concord, North Carolina. She then went on to study at the Moody Bible Institute in Chicago. One of the first teaching positions she held was at Haines Institute in Augusta, Georgia.

After the death of her husband, Bethune decided to go to Florida where she had heard that African Americans were denied educational opportunities. She went to Daytona Beach in 1904 where, with only $1.50 in savings, she founded a school for girls. The school was called the Daytona Normal and Industrial School for Training Negro Girls.

The school was in a run-down building Bethune rented. At first, she had only six students, including her son. To keep the school open, Bethune and her students sold sweet potato pies and fried fish and gave concerts in nearby resort hotels. In 1923, the school merged with an all-boys school in Jacksonville, Florida, and became Bethune-Cookman College a year later.

Mary McLeod Bethune was an eloquent spokesperson for the educational rights of African-American youth. In 1935 during the Great Depression she was appointed to the Advisory Board of the National Youth Administration

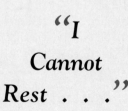

"I Cannot Rest . . ."

(NYA). That year almost 24 percent of the 21 million youths between 16 and 24 years of age were out of school and jobless. When Bethune spoke eloquently and passionately on behalf of the educational needs of African-American youths, President Franklin Roosevelt added an office of minority affairs to the NYA and asked Bethune to direct it. As director of the NYA, she developed a friendship with Eleanor Roosevelt, who personally supported Bethune's campaigns to improve the quality of life for African Americans.

The level of Bethune's commitment to education is reflected in a comment of hers that appeared in the *Journal of Negro Education* (Summer 1982, p. 290): "I cannot rest while there is a single Negro boy or girl lacking a chance to prove his worth." As director of the NYA, she made it possible for 150,000 African-American young people to attend high school and for 60,000 to graduate from college with NYA student aid programs.

Mary McLeod Bethune received many honors during her lifetime in an era when racial segregation and discrimination were commonplace. Eleven universities granted her honorary degrees for her pioneering work in education. She was elected to positions of responsibility in many organizations, including the National Association of Colored Women, of which she was president. For her courage, determination, and achievements, Mary McLeod Bethune is remembered today as an inspiration to all teachers.

The Voucher System   One approach to providing educational equity that has generated considerable controversy is the **voucher system** of distributing educational funds. While various plans have been proposed, one of the most common would give states the freedom to distribute money directly to parents in the form of "vouchers." Parents would then use the vouchers to enroll their children in schools of their choice. Some voucher proposals would allow parents to choose from among public as well as private (secular and parochial) schools; others would limit parents' choice to public schools.

People in favor of the voucher system of distributing funds say that it would make available to students from low socioeconomic backgrounds the same educational opportunities available to students from more advantaged backgrounds. Furthermore, the voucher system would be a direct, powerful way to make schools accountable to local citizens. In open competition, schools that were not excellent would not survive.

Opponents of the voucher system point out that allowing parents to choose where to send their children to school will not necessarily improve education. It could lead to the creation of segregated schools and schools that would be more committed to competing for education dollars than providing quality education.

FIVE-MINUTE FOCUS   Imagine that you have vouchers to send your child to any school in your state. What factors would you consider in making your choice? Date your journal entry and write for five minutes.

Parents choose their children's school

Interest has grown in proposals that would allow students to attend schools based on **school choice,** especially after President Bush made parental choice a part of his education platform. According to the 1990 Gallup Poll of the Public's Attitudes Toward the Public Schools, 62 percent were in favor of parental choice. Currently, legislators in more than 20 states are considering public school choice for parents, while parents in Minnesota, Arkansas, and Iowa have that option now. If experiments in parental choice prove successful in providing excellent schools for all students, it is likely that this trend will increase in the future.

SUMMARY

In the first part of this chapter we examined the political forces that influence education in America. A knowledge of how schools and teachers fit into the educational power structure can increase your effectiveness and job satisfaction. As the educational reform movement begun in the early 1980s continues to be played out in the 1990s, a complex and often contradictory assortment of political forces are at work, generating new challenges, opportunities, and rewards for teachers. As we move into this exciting, unknown educational future, it will be professionals such as yourself who will use their knowledge of the political dimensions of teaching to provide children with the best education possible.

The last part of this chapter examined how schools are financed in the United States. Schools are supported with revenues from the local, state, and federal levels, with most funding now coming from the state level. Two critical challenges to financing schools have been the development of an equitable means of taxation for the support of education and the equitable distribution of funds to schools. Though great strides have been made in these two areas during the last two decades, much remains to be done before both excellence and equity characterize all schools in the United States.

KEY TERMS AND CONCEPTS

local school districts, 235
school board, 237
superintendent, 237
restructuring, 239
school-based management, 239
state board of education, 245
state department of education, 246
chief state school officer, 246
Regional Educational
    Service Agency, 247

expenditure per pupil, 251
property taxes, 252
state aid, 254
block grants, 254
Education Consolidation and
    Improvement Act, 254
vertical equity, 256
entitlements, 256
voucher system, 258
school choice, 258

DISCUSSION QUESTIONS

1. What are some changes you feel should be made at the local, state, and federal levels of education?
2. What do you think should be the federal government's role in education? Do you support the new federalism as it is applied to the support and governance of education? Why or why not?
3. What role should teachers take in influencing education at the local level?
4. Are the most effective local school board members selected through appointments or through elections? Why?
5. Some people object to the use of lottery revenues for the support of education. Do you agree or disagree with their position? Explain.
6. What are some arguments for and against providing "vertical equity" in school funding—that is, basing levels of funding on educational need?

APPLICATION ACTIVITIES

1. Obtain an organizational chart for the local school district in your home town. Compare the organizational structure of that district with the charts obtained by your classmates.
2. Examine the organizational structure of the state department of education in your state. What are its strengths and weaknesses?
3. Examine Figure 8.2. What "issue demands" are being expressed in a school district with which you are familiar? How is the local board of education responding to these issues?
4. Think of businesses and groups in your community that may make good candidates for a partnership with a school. Select one of them and develop a proposal outlining the nature, activities, and benefits of the partnership you envision.

5. Help your instructor arrange a "town meeting" in your class on the topic of vouchers and parental choice.
6. Write a "letter to the editor" in which you make a case for increased funding of local schools.

FIELD EXPERIENCES

1. Attend a meeting of the local school board and observe the communication and decision-making processes at that meeting. Note the following: topics on the agenda, who set the agenda, who participates in the discussion, how participation varies according to topic, who proposes policy, and the extent of agreement between superintendent and board. Note also the harmony or lack of harmony among board members. Finally, do you see evidence of single-issue interests?
2. Interview a school superintendent and ask him or her to comment on how federal, state, and local forces impact education in the district. To what extent do influences at these three levels help (and/or hinder) the district in accomplishing its goals?
3. Interview a teacher and ask how legislation at the federal and state levels affects the teacher's work. Would the teacher like to see the federal government more or less involved in education? Report your findings to the rest of the class.
4. Develop and administer a questionnaire to teachers on the subject of restructuring and school-based management. Design your questions to discover what teachers think about shared decision making and local governance of schools, and share your findings with classmates.
5. Interview a local school principal to find out which budget items are at the principal's discretion and which are not. Ask the principal what criteria he or she uses when asked to propose cuts in the school budget.
6. Conduct a newspaper survey to trace the history of tax equity issues in your community over the past few years. What are those issues? What trends do you see?

SUGGESTED READINGS

Campbell, Roald, et al. *The Organization and Control of American Schools*, 5th ed. Columbus, Ohio: Merrill, 1985. *A comprehensive, insightful discussion of how schools in the United States are organized and controlled.*

Gutherie, James W.; Walter I. Garms; and Lawrence C. Pierce. *School Finance and Educational Policy: Enhancing Educational Efficiency, Equality, and Choice*, 2nd ed. Boston: Allyn and Bacon, 1988. *A thorough explanation of the financing of public schools and higher education.*

Kimbrough, Ralph B., and Michael Y. Nunnery. *Educational Administration: An Introduction*, 3rd ed. New York: Macmillan, 1988. *An excellent survey of the principles of educational administration and the organization of schools in this country. Stresses the role of the superintendent as educational leader.*

Kindred, Leslie W.; Don Bagin; and Donald R. Gallagher. *The School and Community Relations*, 4th ed. Boston: Allyn and Bacon, 1990. *A comprehensive guide to school and community relations. Provides a step-by-step approach for creating a positive school-community PR program.*

Knezevich, Stephen J. *Administration of Public Education: A Sourcebook for the Leadership and Management of Educational Institutions,* 4th ed. New York: Harper and Row, 1984. *A comprehensive treatment of the art and science of educational administration. Includes a review of the administrative process, principles of educational policy-making, and theories of systems management and instructional leadership.*

Writ, Frederick M., and Michael W. Kirst, *Schools in Conflict.* Berkeley, Calif.: McCutchan, 1982. *An astute analysis of the political forces that contribute to the turbulence in contemporary American education.*

TEACHERS . . .

What impact have state and federal legislation had on your teaching?

Do you support the trend for teachers to be more involved in making decisions about the schools?
What changes have you helped to bring about at your school?

Although the state and federal governments have a financial impact on the educational system, the main impact on my teaching is the use of standardized tests. These tests are outdated and do not evaluate the process of learning, only the outcomes. The question of more or less state and federal involvement is complex. I have not taken a stand—there are pros and cons to both sides.
—Julie A. Addison
Rock Ridge Elementary School, Castle Rock, Colorado

It seems to me that only the federal government can provide national recognition for excellence and the funding to ensure equity among the states. Because there are some topics with regional uniqueness, state departments of education need to draft minimal curriculum guidelines. State programs that showcase effective methods and teachers are also helpful in the reform process. Implementation is always most effective at the grassroots, or local, level where the energy and incentive resides.
—Olive Ann Slotta
Fred N. Thomas Career Education Center, Denver, Colorado

I support the idea of teachers being involved in the academic areas of our profession. I believe that we have the expertise to make decisions for the benefit of the students. The students have to be the main reason(s) we change the elements of the learning process. They are the core of what the teaching profession is all about.

Administrators and teachers need to cooperate when making decisions that affect student behavior, school budgets, teacher salaries and evaluations. Both are going to have to support the final decision, so input would help them become better members of a working team. I believe that if a stalemate exists, then the administrator should make the final decision for the good of all parties involved.
—Suzanne Neal
William Woods College, Fulton, Missouri

ON TEACHING

I greatly support the new trend toward involving teachers in more of the decision making in each school. Teachers know what the students need to be successful. I also think teachers will work harder at their jobs if they know their input is taken to heart. I would not support this trend if the decision makers became political to the extent that teachers . . . [had] to fight through mounds of paperwork in order to see their suggestions implemented.

One of the changes I've helped to promote at my school is the realization that music is as important to a child's education as any academic subject is. I did this by incorporating music into the various social studies units being taught by classroom teachers. One teacher commented to me that his class had learned more about colonial America through the music program they did for parents than through anything she had taught them during that entire quarter.

—Rose Ann Blaschke
Vivian Elementary School, Lakewood, Colorado

I fully support increased teacher involvement in the decision-making process. I also want to see more community control in education—a real grassroots program. I want to see less adherence to standardized testing and more emphasis on cultural respect and awareness.

—Anita Dollar
Mitchell Elementary School, Denver, Colorado

I feel that the more ownership a teacher has in the operation and design of the working environment, the more pride and production will take place. I definitely support the trend of teachers having more pull in the many different decisions dealing with education.

I have been directly involved with many student discipline problems. We have implemented a community service program, both in and out of the school, which has been very successful. I have also been involved with student mediation programs where students help other students work out problems. It has also been a success.

—Amy Orcutt
Green Gables Elementary School, Jefferson County, Colorado

Putting my professional reputation on the line, I took a stand on an issue that affected student health in my district. My independent action forced administrators to deal openly with the issue to the students' benefit. I now have an even greater commitment to the students with whom I work. I believe that the students should be at the center of the decision-making process.

—Marc Gray
Highland Middle School, Louisville, Kentucky

Legal Concerns in American Education

*F*irst Amendment rights, applied in light of the special characteristics of the school environment, are available to teacher and students. It can hardly be argued that either students or teachers shed their constitutional rights to freedom of speech or expression at the schoolhouse gate.

Justice Abe Fortas
U.S. Supreme Court,
1969

Carol, a student in your class in the middle school where you teach, idolizes several punk rock stars and has begun to dress like them. Her once-pretty long black hair is now cut short except for several random strands that hang down to her shoulders. Lately, she's been applying a sweet-smelling, gooey, pink gel to her hair, which seems to be changing gradually from black to red.

Today, she is wearing black-checked stockings and an old evening dress that she bought at a local second-hand clothing store. The heavy makeup that encircles her brown eyes and the ruby red lipstick applied recklessly to her thin lips give her face a hardened, almost grotesque, look.

Since she began dressing like this, other students have started to tease her. She's resilient and seems to be handling the situation well enough, but she has created a commotion in your class that gets worse by the day.

Other girls have started to copy her style. Today, you notice that Judy is dressed in a similar manner. Her short blond hair is slicked back, as though she just stepped out of a shower. She is wearing a tight black skirt that is several inches above the knee and a bright green polyester blouse that looks as though it might glow in the dark.

Judy strolls around the room, taking her time, and, if her smile is any indication, delighting in the fact that everyone's eyes are on her. Several students laugh at her hysterically and point. Judy stares menacingly at them and finally slides into a seat right behind Carol. Their classmates continue to giggle and squirm in their seats.

"All right, class," you begin. "Let's settle down. Take out the homework you did last night."

But, it's more difficult than usual to get your students' attention this Monday. It's obvious that Carol's and Judy's appearance has unsettled the whole class.

As you continue with the lesson, you wonder if you have the right to speak to Carol and Judy and request that they change their appearance. Or, do they have the right to wear whatever they want to school?

FOCUS QUESTIONS

1. What are the legal rights and responsibilities of teachers?
2. What are the legal rights of students?
3. Under what circumstances can teachers be charged with negligent behavior?
4. What can teachers do to reduce the risk of getting into legal difficulties?
5. Under what conditions can school authorities abridge First Amendment rights?
6. What is the legal status of student teachers or teaching interns?

In this chapter we examine significant legal decisions that affect the rights and responsibilities of teachers, administrators, and students. Teachers must act in accordance with a wide range of federal and state legislation and court decisions. As a teacher, you may need to deal with such legal issues as the teacher's responsibility for accidents, discriminatory employment practices, freedom of speech, desegregation, student rights, and circumstances related to termination or dismissal. Without a knowledge of the legal dimensions of such issues, you will be ill-equipped to protect your rights and the rights of your students.

WHAT DO YOU KNOW ABOUT EDUCATION AND THE LAW?

Our country has a long history of protecting human rights through the enactment of specific laws. From the early colonists who sought religious freedom to African Americans involved in the Civil Rights movement, Americans have sought protection under the law. During the last two decades, increased attention has been devoted to various legal aspects of the educative process, particularly the rights of teachers and students.

Like many students who are preparing to teach, you are limited in terms of your knowledge of the law and education. At this point in your professional preparation, this is understandable. To continue to be unaware of the rights and responsibilities of teachers and students, however, would be to ignore an important part of the professional challenge of teaching. Such a lack of knowledge also increases the likelihood that you and your students might be denied freedoms guaranteed by law.

A PROFESSIONAL CODE OF ETHICS

The actions of professional teachers are determined not only by what is legally required of them, but by what they know they *ought* to do. They do what is legally right, and they *do the right thing*. A specific set of values guides them. A deep and lasting commitment to professional practice characterizes their work. They have adopted a high standard of professional ethics and they model behaviors that are in accord with that code of ethics.

At present, the teaching profession does not have a uniform **code of ethics** similar to the Hippocratic oath, which all doctors are legally required to take when they begin practice. We have, however, discovered an "Educator's Oath," which graduates of the College of Education at Michigan State University have used since 1983. As it captures the professional commitment all teachers should make, we include it here.

a set of guidelines that defines appropriate behavior for professionals.

266

The Educator's Oath

I hereby affirm my dedication to the profession of education. With this affirmation I embrace the obligations of professional educators to improve the general welfare, to advance human understanding and competence, and to bring honor to the endeavors of teaching and learning. I accept these obligations for myself and will be vigilant and responsible in supporting their acceptance by my colleagues.

I will be always mindful of my responsibility to increase the intelligence of students through the disciplined pursuit of knowledge. I will be steadfast in this commitment, even when weary and tempted to abdicate such responsibility or blame failure on obstacles that make the task difficult. I will be persistent in my commitment to foster respect for a life of learning and respect for all students.

To perform faithfully these professional duties, I promise to work always to better understand my content, my instructional practice, and the students who come under my tutelage. I promise to seek and support policies that promote quality in teaching and learning and to provide all engaged in education the opportunity to achieve excellence. I promise to emulate personally the qualities I wish to foster, and to hold and forever honor a democratic way of life that cannot exist without disciplined, cultivated, and free minds.

I recognize that at times my endeavors will offend privilege and status, that I will be opposed by bias and defenders of inequality, and that I will have to confront arguments that seek to discourage my efforts and diminish my hope. But I will remain faithful to the belief that these endeavors and the pursuit of these goals make me worthy of my profession, and my profession worthy of a free people.

In the presence of this gathering, I bind myself to this oath.[1]

FIVE-MINUTE FOCUS Reread carefully the third paragraph of "The Educator's Oath." What specific steps will you take as a teacher to live up to these promises? Date your journal entry and write for five minutes.

Ethical Teaching Attitudes and Practices

Teaching is an ethical enterprise—that is, a teacher has an obligation to act ethically, to follow what he or she knows to be the most appropriate professional action to take. The best interests of students, not the teacher, provide the rule of thumb for determining what is ethical and what is not. Behaving ethically is more than a matter of following the rules or not breaking the law—it means acting in a way that promotes the learning and growth of students and helps them realize their potential.

Unethical acts break the trust and respect on which good student-teacher relationships are based. An example of unethical conduct would be public ridicule of the appearance of Carol and Judy, the two students described in this chapter's opening vignette. Other examples would be using grades as a form of punishment, expressing rage in the classroom, or intentionally tricking students on tests. You could no doubt think of other examples from your own experience as a student. The "NEA Code of Ethics" in the Teacher's Resource Guide identifies specific behaviors a teacher should avoid. Examine this code carefully. Do you disagree with any of the items? Should any be added?

Ethical Dilemmas in Classroom and School

Teachers routinely encounter **ethical dilemmas** in the classroom and in the school. They often have to take action in situations in which all the facts are not known or for which no single course of action can be called "right" or "wrong." At these times it can be quite difficult to decide what an ethical response might be. Dealing satisfactorily with ethical dilemmas in teaching often requires the ability to see beyond short-range consequences to consider long-range consequences.

Consider, for example, the following three questions based on actual case studies. On the basis of the information given, how would you respond to each situation?

1. Should the sponsor of the high school literary magazine refuse to print a well-written story by a budding writer if the piece appears to satirize a teacher and a student?
2. Is a reading teacher justified in trying to increase achievement for an entire class by separating two disruptive students and placing one in a reading group beneath his reading level?
3. Should a chemistry teacher punish a student (on the basis of circumstantial, inconclusive evidence) for a laboratory explosion if the example of decisive, swift punishment will likely prevent the recurrence of a similar event and thereby ensure the safety of all students?[2]

As these cases suggest, responding ethically to a dilemma can be difficult. The first case poses a choice between censorship and disrespect, the second between class disruption and individual low achievement, and the third between inappropriate punishment and the possibility of accidents. Teachers must be prepared to go beyond their first impulse, to carefully weigh alternatives and consider possible consequences.

THE TEACHER'S LEGAL RIGHTS

It is frequently observed that with each freedom comes a corresponding responsibility to others and to the community in which we live. As long as there is more than one individual inhabiting this planet, there is a need for laws to clarify individual rights and responsibilities. This necessary balance between rights and responsibilities is perhaps more critical to teaching than to any other profession. As one observer put it, the "rights of teachers are simultaneously simple yet complex; straightforward yet convoluted; and, clearly established yet little understood. These apparently mutually exclusive qualities exist because there are two sources of the rights that teachers enjoy: (1) their general rights as individual citizens, and (2) adjustments in those rights required by the special nature of their occupation."[3]

While there are "adjustments" that apply to the legal rights of teachers, their right to **due process** cannot be violated. Teachers, like all citizens, are protected from being treated arbitrarily by those in authority. A principal who disagrees with a teacher's methods cannot suddenly fire that teacher. A school board cannot ask a teacher who demonstrated against the Persian Gulf War to resign. A teacher cannot be dismissed for "poor" performance without ample documentation that the performance was, in fact, "poor" and without sufficient time to meet clearly stated performance evaluation criteria. As the Fifth Amendment to the Constitution states: "no person shall . . . be deprived of life, liberty, or property without due process of law," and the Fourteenth Amendment: "nor shall any State deprive any person of life, liberty, or property, without due process of law."

In addition to the right of due process, there are several specific legal rights that concern prospective teachers. These rights are in the areas of certification; contracts, tenure, and dismissal; and academic freedom. The following sections address these rights; each includes a brief case study designed to illustrate the legal issue discussed. Immediately after reading each case study ask yourself how you would resolve the issue. Then read on to find out if your solution agrees with the legal resolution.

Certification

Frank Smith is a high school mathematics teacher who lives in a state with a law that specifies that a teacher must show proof of five years of successful teaching experience for a teaching certificate to be renewed. Last year was Frank's fifth year of teaching, and his principal gave him an unsatisfactory performance rating. Frank's principal has stated that Frank's teaching certificate cannot be renewed. Is the principal correct?

Frank's principal is mistaken about the grounds for nonrenewal of a teaching certificate. According to that state's law, *unsuccessful* performance, or a failure to complete the school year, is grounds for nonrenewal of a certificate—not performance that is judged to be *unsatisfactory*.

No teacher who meets all of a state's requirements for initial certification can arbitrarily be denied a certificate. And once obtained, a certificate may not be revoked without due process of law. For a certificate to be revoked, the reason must be job-related and demonstrably impair the teacher's ability to perform satisfactorily. In this regard, the case of a California teacher whose certificate was revoked because someone admitted to having a homosexual relationship with the teacher is often cited. The court determined that the teacher's homosexual conduct was not an impairment to the teacher's performance and ordered the certificate restored.[4] However, the courts do consider whether the individual's conduct represents a publicly held stance for a certain position. For example, the courts ruled in favor of the California State Board of Education that had revoked the certificate of a teacher who had committed a homosexual act on a public beach.[5]

Teachers' Rights to Nondiscrimination

Mary Briggs has met all the qualifications for teaching but is denied certification because she has a prison record. Once as a young woman she was convicted of a felony. Mary claims she is being discriminated against because of her past. Is she right?

States may impose certain limitations on initial certification as long as those limitations are not discriminatory in regard to race, religion, ethnic origin, sex, or age. Nearly four-fifths of the states, for example, require that applicants for a teaching certificate pass a test that covers basic skills, professional knowledge, or academic subject areas.[6] Qualifications for initial certification may also legally include certain personal qualities. The case at the beginning of this section, for example, is based on an Oregon case involving a man who had successfully completed a teacher training program but was denied a certificate because he had once been found guilty of a felony and served a term in prison. The Oregon State Board of Education raised some legitimate questions regarding the moral character of the applicant.[7] As a result, he was unable to obtain the teaching certificate he needed to be hired as a teacher.

**How Have Supreme Court Decisions
Affected the Public Schools?**

For each of the following practices, check whether the Supreme Court has held that practice to be mandatory ("Must"), permitted ("May"), or prohibited ("Must Not"). The correct answers, based on minimum federal legal requirements, are given in the answer key at the end of this chapter.

	Must	May	Must Not
1. A school district _____ require . . . the posting in each classroom of a copy of the Ten Commandments which has been obtained via private contributions and which is expressly labeled as nonreligious material.	☐	☒	☐
2. A school district _____ provide classes to nonpublic school students in classrooms located in nonpublic schools.	☒	☐	☐
3. A school district _____ dismiss a teacher for expressing criticism of school policies or practices that are not of public interest.	☐	☐	☒
4. A school district _____ dismiss teachers who engage in an illegal strike unless the teachers can show the board's decision was based on personal, pecuniary, or antiunion bias.	☒	☐	☐
5. A school district _____ allow the union that is the exclusive bargaining agent sole access to its interschool mail system and teacher mailboxes, limiting access by rival unions and other groups.	☐	☐	☐
6. A school district _____ permit nonexcessive corporal punishment of students under the authorization or in the absence of a state statute.	☐	☐	☐
7. A school district _____ conduct a search of a student, without the assistance of police, if the school authorities have reasonable suspicion . . . that the student has violated or is violating the law or school rules.	☐	☐	☐
8. A school district _____ refuse to provide clean-intermittent-catheterization for handicapped students who need this service to attend school.	☐	☐	☐
9. A school district _____ deny enrollment in their public schools to children who are "illegal aliens" in the United States.	☐	☐	☐
10. A school district _____ discipline students for using lewd and offensive language that does not cause a substantial disruption in the school.	☐	☐	☐

Source: Perry A Zirkel and Faith MacMurtrie, "A Quick Quiz on Supreme Court Decisions Affecting Public Schools," *Kappa Delta Pi Record* (Spring 1988): 93. Reprinted by permission of Kappa Delta Pi, An International Honor Society in Education.

Protection against discrimination in regard to employment is provided by Title VII of the Civil Rights Act of 1964, which states:

> It shall be an unlawful employment practice for an employer (1) to fail or refuse to hire or to discharge any individual, or otherwise to discriminate against any individual with respect to his compensation, terms, conditions, or privileges of employment, because of such individual's race, color, religion, sex, or national origin; or (2) to limit, segregate, or classify his employees or applicants for employment in any way which would deprive or tend to deprive any individual of employment opportunities or otherwise adversely affect his status as an employee, because of such individual's race, color, religion, sex, or national origin.

Contracts, Tenure, and Dismissal

Public school teachers have a set of legal obligations to the local board of education that hires them. In the case of teachers in private schools, these obligations are to the board of trustees or the executive committee responsible for hiring them. These obligations are spelled out in the contract to teach, a document that usually outlines the rights and responsibilites of teachers, criteria to be met for the granting of tenure, and conditions under which a teacher may be dismissed.

Contracts   A **teaching contract** represents an agreement between the teacher and a board of education. For a contract to be valid, it must meet these five criteria:

1. *Competency*—the parties entering into the contract with the school board must be competent; the board cannot enter into contracts beyond the authority given to it by the state, and the teacher must meet the criteria for employment.
2. *Mutual assent*—there must be a formal offer and acceptance of the terms of the contract by the employee.
3. *Consideration*—the teacher must receive valid and adequate consideration for his or her services.
4. *Specificity*—the contract must be sufficiently specific in spelling out the rights and obligations of each party.
5. *Legality*—the contract must not be illegal or against public policy.[8]

Before you sign your teaching contract, it is important that you read it carefully and be certain that it is signed by the appropriate member(s) of the board of education or board of trustees. Ask for clarification of any sections you don't understand. It is preferable that any additional nonteaching duties be spelled out in writing rather than left to an oral agreement. Since all board of education policies and regulations will be part of your contract, you should also read any available teacher handbook or school policy handbook.

The importance of carefully reading a contract and asking for clarification is illustrated in the following case study:

> Martha Smith had just begun her first year as a science teacher at a middle school in a city of about 100,000. Martha became quite upset when she learned that she had been assigned by her principal to sponsor the science club. The club was to meet once a week after school. Martha refused to sponsor the club, saying that the contract she had signed referred only to her teaching duties during regular school hours. Could Martha be compelled to sponsor the club?

Certain assignments, though not specified in a contract, may be required of teachers in addition to their regular teaching load, as long as there is a reasonable relationship between the teacher's classroom duties and the additional assignment. Though Martha's contract did not make specific reference to club sponsorship, such a duty would be a reasonable addition to her regular teaching assignment.

When school authorities have assigned teachers to additional duties not reasonably related to their teaching, the courts have tended to rule in favor of teachers who file suit. For example, a directive to one teacher to supervise an off-campus, after-school group of student bowlers was held to be beyond the teacher's obligations.[9] In a similar case, a New York court ruled that coaching a team did not fall within the implied duties of a mathematics teacher.[10]

Tenure   Tenure is a policy that provides the individual teacher with job security by (1) preventing his or her dismissal on insufficient grounds and (2) providing him or her with due process in the event of dismissal. Tenure is granted to teachers by the local school district after a period of satisfactory teaching, usually two to five years. In most cases, tenure may not be transferred from one school district to another.

The following case study highlights the importance of tenure to a teacher's professional career:

A teacher was dismissed from his teaching position by the school board after it learned that the teacher was a homosexual. The teacher filed suit in court, claiming that his firing was arbitrary and violated the provisions of tenure that he had been granted. The school board, on the other hand, maintained that his conduct was inappropriate for a teacher. Was the school board justified in dismissing the teacher?

The events in this case were actually heard by a court, which ruled that the teacher was unfairly dismissed.[11] The court said that the board violated the teacher's rights as a tenured employee by failing to show "good and just cause" for dismissal. The teacher was awarded the balance due under his contract and an additional one-half year's salary.

The practice of providing teachers with tenure is not without controversy. Some critics point out that tenure policies make it too difficult to dismiss incompetent teachers and that performance standards are high in many other fields that do not provide employees with job security. They also contend that tenure perpetuates the status quo and makes it more difficult for new people to enter the profession.

In spite of these objections, it is clear that tenure (1) protects effective teachers from arbitrary dismissal and (2) specifies procedures to be followed in the dismissal of those who are incompetent. The courts have held that, overall, "tenure is for the improvement of education and not for the special benefit of any one class [of teachers]."[12]

Dismissal   Just about every state today has a tenure law that specifies that a teacher may be dismissed with good cause; what counts as a good clause varies from state to state. The courts have ruled on a variety of reasons for **dismissal:** (1) insubordination, (2) incompetence or inefficiency, (3) neglect of duty, (4) conduct unbecoming a teacher, (5) subversive activities, (6) retrenchment or decreased need for services, (7) physical and/or mental health, (8) age, (9) causing or encouraging disruption, (10) engaging in illegal activities, (11) using offensive language, (12) personal appearance, (13) sex-related activities, (14) political activities, and (15) use of drugs or intoxicants.[13]

For a tenured teacher to be dismissed, a systematic series of steps must be followed so that the teacher receives due process and his or her constitutionally guaranteed rights are not violated. Due process involves a careful, step-by-step examination of the charges brought against a teacher. Most states have outlined procedures that adhere to the following nine steps:

1. The teacher must be notified of the list of charges.
2. Adequate time must be provided for the teacher to prepare a rebuttal to the charges.
3. The teacher must be given the names of witnesses and access to evidence.
4. The hearing must be conducted before an impartial tribunal.
5. The teacher has the right to representation by legal counsel.
6. The teacher (or legal counsel) can introduce evidence and cross-examine adverse witnesses.
7. The school board's decision must be based on the evidence and findings of the hearing.
8. A transcript or record must be maintained of the hearing.
9. The teacher has the right to appeal an adverse decision.[14]

The procedures a school board must adhere to in seeking to dismiss a teacher are highlighted in the case study that follows:

Near the start of his fifth year of teaching at an elementary school in a small city, and two years after earning tenure, Mr. Mitchell went through a sudden and painful divorce. A few months later a woman whom he had met around the time of his divorce moved into the house he was renting.

For the remainder of the school year he and the woman lived together. During this time, he received no indication that his lifestyle was professionally unacceptable, and his teaching performance remained satisfactory.

At the end of the year, however, Mr. Mitchell was notified that he was being dismissed because of immoral conduct, that is, he was living with a woman he was not married to. The school board called for a hearing and Mr. Mitchell presented his side of the case. The board, nevertheless, decided to follow through with its decision to dismiss him. Was the school board justified in dismissing Mr. Mitchell?

Though at one time teachers could readily be dismissed for living, unmarried, with a member of the opposite sex, a lifestyle such as Mr. Mitchell's is not that unusual today. Since the board had not shown that Mr. Mitchell's alleged immoral conduct had a negative effect on his teaching, his dismissal would probably not hold up in court. Moreover, Mr. Mitchell could charge that his right to privacy as guaranteed by the Ninth Amendment to the Constitution had been violated. Overall, it appears that the decision to dismiss Mr. Mitchell was arbitrary and based on the collective bias of the board.

Teachers also have the right to organize and to join teacher organizations without fear of dismissal. In addition, most states have passed **collective bargaining** laws that require school boards to negotiate contracts with teacher organizations. Usually, the teacher organization with the most members in a district is given the right to represent teachers in the collective bargaining process.

An important part of most collective bargaining agreements is the right of a teacher to file a **grievance,** a formal complaint against his or her employer. A teacher may not be dismissed for filing a grievance, and he or she is entitled to have the grievance heard by a neutral third party. Often, the teachers' union or professional association that negotiated the collective bargaining agreement will provide a teacher who has filed a grievance with free legal counsel.

One right that teachers are not granted by collective bargaining agreements is the right to strike. Like other public employees, teachers do not have the legal right to strike. Teachers who do strike run the risk of dismissal, though when teacher strikes occur a school board cannot possibly replace all the striking teachers.

Academic Freedom

A male high school English teacher assigned his students an article in the *Atlantic Monthly* that employed and explored the uses of a well-known vulgar term for an incestuous son. Several parents who learned of the assignment protested, and the school board ordered the teacher not to use the term in class again. The teacher refused and was suspended. Was the teacher acting within his rights?

The above case is based on actual events involving a teacher in Massachusetts. The teacher brought suit against the board to prevent it from carrying out its threat to fire him. In his suit the teacher cited the principle of **academic freedom** and said that the assignment called for a legitimate analysis of a serious piece of writing. The First Circuit Court of Appeal, pointing out that the term was widely used and could be found in some books in the library, ruled in favor of the teacher. The board was prevented from firing the teacher.[15]

The concept of academic freedom may be traced back to its origins in higher education. Scholars at colleges and universities have long been concerned that they have the freedom to carry out their academic inquiries without constraint. During the last few decades, however, teachers of younger students have increasingly demanded the freedom to decide what and how to teach.

the right of teachers to teach, free from external constraint, censorship or interference.

Famous Cases   A landmark court ruling in support of academic freedom was *Pickering* v. *Board of Education* (1968). Pickering was an Illinois teacher who had a letter published in the local newspaper that was critical of the school board's allocation of funds between academic and athletic programs. The school board dismissed Pickering, alleging that the letter contained false statements and damaged the reputations of board members. After the Illinois courts denied Pickering's claim, the U.S. Supreme Court reversed the lower court's ruling. The Court concluded that Pickering's letter did not have a detrimental effect on his teaching. Furthermore, the Court pointed out that the role of teacher provides a special vantage point from which to make an "informed and definite opinion" on the allocation of district funds and that the false statements in Pickering's letter were not "knowingly or recklessly" made.

Several recent cases concerning academic freedom have focused on the teacher's use of instructional materials. In *Mozert* v. *Hawkins County Public Schools* (1986), for example, a group of Tennessee parents objected to "secular humanist" reading materials used by their children's teachers. In *Smith* v. *Board of School Commissioners of Mobile County* (1987), 624 parents and teachers initiated a court suit alleging that 45 history, social studies, and home economics texts used in the Mobile County, Alabama, public schools encouraged immorality, undermined parental authority, and were imbued with the "humanist" faith.

States' Rights   The preceding cases notwithstanding, the courts have not set down specific guidelines to reconcile the teacher's freedom with the state's right to require

"Now that we know how to read, they're banning all the good stuff."

teachers to follow certain curricular guidelines. The same federal court, for example, heard a similar case regarding a high school teacher who wrote a vulgar word for sexual intercourse on the blackboard during a discussion of socially taboo words. The court actually sidestepped the issue of academic freedom and ruled instead that the regulations authorizing teacher discipline were unconstitutionally vague and, therefore, the teacher could not be dismissed. The court did, however, observe that a public school teacher's right to traditional academic freedom is "qualified," at best, and the "teacher's right must yield to compelling public interests of greater constitutional significance." In reviewing its decision, the court also said, "Nothing herein suggests that school authorities are not free after they have learned that the teacher is using a teaching method of which they disapprove, and which is not appropriate to the proper teaching of the subject, to suspend him [or her] until he [or she] agrees to cease using the method."[16]

While some teachers have been successful in citing academic freedom as the basis for teaching controversial subjects, others have been unsuccessful. Teachers have been dismissed for ignoring directives regarding the teaching of controversial topics related to sex, polygamy, race, and religion. Though the courts have not been able to clarify just where academic freedom begins and ends, they have made it clear that the state does have a legitimate interest in what is taught to impressionable children. For the most part, teachers have the greatest protection when the material they discuss is related to course material and assigned readings.

FIVE-MINUTE FOCUS   What limits do you believe should be placed on *what* teachers teach? On *how* they teach? Date your journal entry and write for five minutes.

Keepers of the Dream

John T. Scopes
1901–1970
Biology Teacher, Tennessee

A famous case involving a teacher's academic freedom involved John Scopes, a biology teacher. In 1925 Scopes challenged the Butler Act, a Tennessee law that made it illegal to teach in a public school "any theory which denies the story of the Divine Creation of man as taught in the Bible, and to teach instead that man is descended from a lower order of animals." Scopes maintained that Darwin's theory about human origins had scientific merit and that the state's requirement that he teach the Biblical account of creation violated his academic freedom.

Scopes's trial, which came to be known as the Monkey Trial, attracted national attention. Prosecuting Scopes was the "silver-tongued" William Jennings Bryan, a famous lawyer, politician, and presidential candidate. The defending attorney was Clarence Darrow.

Scopes believed strongly in academic freedom and his students' right to know about scientific theories. He expressed his views in his memoirs, *Center of the Storm* (New York: Holt, Rinehart, & Winston, 1966, p. 277):

Especially repulsive are laws restricting the constitutional freedom of teachers. The mere presence of such a law is a club held over the heads of the timid. Legislation that tampers with academic freedom is not protecting society, as its authors piously proclaim. By limiting freedom they are helping to make robot factories out of schools; ultimately, this produces nonthinking robots rather than the individualistic citizens we desperately need—now more than ever before.

The Monkey Trial ended after 11 days of heated, eloquent testimony. Scopes was found guilty of violating the Butler Act and was fined $100. The decision was later reversed by the Tennessee Supreme Court on a technicality.

John Scopes returned to teaching, but the issue on which he had staked his career was not resolved for all time. To this day controversies perennially arise over academic freedom and the place of religious teachings in public school education. During the 1980s, for example, in many states religious fundamentalists won rulings that required science teachers to give equal time to both Creationism and Evolutionism in the classroom. Reformers representing religious groups also called for the elimination of "secular humanism" from the curriculum, a world view perceived as undermining religious faith.

"Freedom Demands an Unending Struggle."

"Freedom demands an unending struggle," Scopes wrote in *Center of the Storm*. But in conflicts between citizens' religious freedom, teachers' academic freedom, and students' freedom of inquiry, whose freedom should we struggle for the most? Which freedom should the laws protect above all others? However the courts decide and redecide these questions, teachers who act on their courage and convictions, like John Scopes, are also keepers of the dream.

FACT FINDING

How Many Children Are Taught at Home?

In the 10 years between 1980 and 1990, the number of children receiving a home education increased tenfold from about 50,000 to about 500,000. The trend is for advocates of home schooling to win their cases in the state legislatures, but to lose in the courts.

Source: Perry Zirkel, "Home Schooling," *Phi Delta Kappan*, January 1991: 409.

Parents' Rights   One spinoff of the heightened awareness during the 1980s of the problems that schools face has been the decision by some parents to educate their children in the home. Many of these parents also view home schooling as an opportunity to provide their children with a curriculum based on religious values. According to a 1984 report by the Education Commission of the States, 38 states have statutory provisions for education in the home. In five states that have no law, current policies or court decisions do in fact permit the practice: Illinois, Kentucky, Michigan, New Hampshire, and Washington. Of the remaining states, only New Mexico has a statute that specifically prohibits home instruction.[17]

When parents do teach their children in the home, in almost all cases, they must demonstrate to local officials that the home curriculum is comparable to that offered by the local schools. Frequently, parents will be required to show proof of their children's adequate progress by submitting test results and periodic progress reports.

Some parents decide to educate their children at home because the public school curriculum is incompatible with their religious beliefs. One such case involved the DeJonges, a Michigan couple who taught their children at home using materials published by the Christian Liberty Academy of Arlington Heights, Illinois. Michigan law allowed children to attend a "state approved nonpublic school," as long as the teachers were certified and the curriculum comparable to that of the public schools. Since their home school did not meet these conditions, the DeJonges were convicted of truancy. They appealed on several grounds, but in 1989 Michigan's court of appeals upheld the conviction.[18]

THE TEACHER'S LEGAL RESPONSIBILITIES

Teachers are, of course, responsible for meeting the terms of their teaching contracts. As noted earlier, teachers are responsible for duties not covered in the contract if they are reasonably related to teaching. Among these duties may be club sponsorship; lunchroom, study hall, or playground duty; academic counseling of students; and record keeping.

Teachers are also legally responsible for the safety and well-being of students assigned to them. While it is not expected that a teacher be able to control completely the behavior of young, energetic students, a teacher can be held liable for any injury to a student if it is shown that the teacher's negligence contributed to the injury.

Avoiding Tort Liability

An eighth-grade science teacher in Louisiana left her class for a few moments to go to the school office to pick up some forms. While she was gone, her students continued to do some laboratory work that involved the use of alcohol-burning devices. Unfortunately, one girl was injured when she tried to relight a defective burner. Could the teacher be held liable for the girl's injuries?

The events described above actually occurred in 1974.[19] The court that heard the case determined that the teacher failed to provide adequate supervision while the students were exposed to dangerous conditions. Considerable care is required, the court observed, when students handle inherently dangerous objects, and the need for this care is magnified when students are exposed to dangers they don't appreciate.

"Technically defined, *a tort is a civil* (as distinguished from criminal) *wrong arising out of a breach of duty that is imposed by law* and not by contract."[20] According to tort law, an individual who is negligent and at fault in the exercise of his or her legal duty may be required to pay money damages to an injured party. "Torts arise from negligence, i.e., failure to exercise the degree of care for the safety of others that a reasonable and prudent person would have exercised under similar circumstances."[21] Specific laws on negligence exist in about half the states.

Negligence   In contrast to the decision reached by the Louisiana court mentioned above, the courts have made it clear that there are many accidents that teachers cannot reasonably foresee that do result in student injuries. For example, a Michigan teacher was found to be not negligent when a pupil was injured while watering plants used in a nature study class. With the teacher's knowledge, the student stood on a chair to water some plants and was badly cut when she fell off the chair and landed on the broken bottle in which she carried water. The Supreme Court of Michigan ruled that a "reasonably careful and prudent person" would not have anticipated that the student's safety would have been endangered in performing the act.[22] In another case, the court ruled that a New York teacher could not have anticipated that the paper bag she asked a student to pick up contained a broken bottle upon which the student cut herself.[23] In two almost identical cases, the courts ruled that a teacher of a class with a good behavior record could not reasonably be expected to anticipate that a student would be injured by a pencil thrown by a classmate while the teacher was momentarily out of the room attending to her usual duties.[24]

When a court considers a case involving **tort liability,** evidence is examined to determine whether the responsible party (the school district, the administrator, or the teacher) acted negligently. For a school official to be considered liable, the following must be shown to exist:

1. A duty or obligation requiring one to conform to a certain standard of conduct so as to protect others against unreasonable risk
2. A failure on one's part to act in a manner which conforms to the standard of conduct required
3. The breach of duty by the defendant was the proximate cause of the complainant's injury, i.e., that a direct and unbroken chain of events existed between the breach of duty complained of and the injury to the complainant
4. Injury, loss, or damage to another caused by one's failure to act in the manner required[25]

(handwritten margin note: Conditions that would permit the filing of legal charges against a professional for breach of duty and/or behaving in a negligent manner)

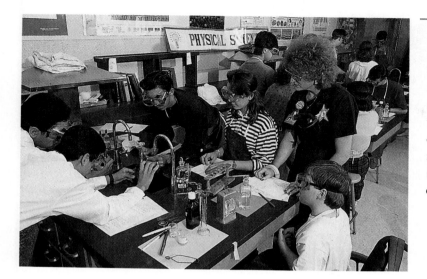

Teachers are responsible for the safety and well-being of students assigned to them and can be sued for damages if their negligence can be proven. Many state-mandated and school rules reflect teachers' liability, such as the safe use of corridors and stairways and the required use of safety goggles by individuals performing science experiments.

As a teacher, you should be especially alert when conditions exist that might lead to accidental injury of one or more students. You will have a duty in regard to your pupils, and you could be held liable for injuries that students incur as a result of your **negligence.** This does not mean, however, that your liability extends to any and all injuries your students might suffer; only if you fail to provide the same degree of care for pupils that a reasonable and prudent person would have shown in similar circumstances can you be held liable. Our review of court cases involving the tort liability of teachers suggests that most cases involve at least one of the following:

[handwritten margin note: failure to exercise reasonable prudent care in providing for the safety of others]

- Inadequate supervision
- Inadequate instruction
- Lack of or improper medical treatment of pupils
- Improper disclosure of defamatory information concerning pupils

Educational Malpractice   Since the mid-1970s the possibility of school districts and school personnel being held liable for an unusual kind of injury has increased. Several plaintiffs have charged in their **educational malpractice** suits that schools should be responsible for a pupil whose failure to achieve is significant. In the first of such cases, the parents of Peter W. Doe charged that the San Francisco Unified School District was negligent because it allowed him to graduate from high school with a fifth-grade reading level and this handicap would not enable him to function in adult society. In particular, they charged that the "defendant school district, its agents and employees, negligently and carelessly failed to provide plaintiff with adequate instruction, guidance, counseling and/or supervision in basic academic skills such as reading and writing, although said school district had the authority, responsibility, and ability [to do so]." They sought $500,000 for the negligent work of the teachers who taught Peter.

[handwritten margin note: liability for injury that results from the failure of a teacher school, school district to provide a student w/ adequate instruction, guidance, counseling, and/or supervision]

In evaluating the claim of Peter W. Doe and his parents, the court pointed out that the alleged injury was not within the realm of tort law and that many factors beyond a school's responsibility or control can account for lack of achievement. The court did not hold the school responsible for Peter's lack of achievement and made it clear that to do so would be to set a precedent with potentially drastic consequences:

"To hold [schools] to an actionable duty of care, in the discharge of their academic functions, would expose them to the tort claims—real or imagined—of disaffected students and parents in countless numbers. . . . The ultimate consequences, in terms of public time and money, would burden them—and society—beyond calculation."[26]

While no suit charging the schools with educational malpractice has been successful, such cases raise troubling issues that school personnel cannot ignore. As Robert C. O'Reilly and Edward T. Green have observed, many parents view malpractice suits as one means of ensuring that their children are educated:

> To the extent that parents have felt shunted aside by an educational bureaucracy, an angry alienation is likely to be one result. When, additionally, they then see their children coming through a thirteen-year education experience with only modest academic achievements; or when they see their child placed for instruction in a manner to which they object, but for which they can discover no real recourse, frustration often drives them to ask, "What can I do to change the system?" Clearly, legal recourse comes forward as a possible solution, and many parents pursue it.[27]

Reporting Child Abuse

Teachers, who are now *required* by law to report any suspected child abuse, are in positions to monitor and work against the physical, emotional, and sexual abuse and the neglect and exploitation of children. Teachers' professional journals and information from local, state, and federal child welfare agencies encourage teachers to be more observant of children's appearance and behavior in order to detect symptoms of child abuse. Such sources often provide lists of indicators of potential child abuse, similar to that shown in Table 9.1. Many communities, through their police departments or other public and private agencies, provide programs adapted for children to educate them about their rights in child abuse situations and to show them how to obtain help. Teachers in school systems that do not take advantage of these services may encourage their administrators to do so.

Schools usually have a specific process for dealing with suspected abuse cases, involving the school principal and nurse as well as the reporting teacher. Because a child's physical welfare may be further endangered when abuse is reported, caution and sensitivity are required. Before the school year begins teachers need to know the procedural expectations for their school. Teachers are in a unique position to help students who are victims of child abuse, both because they have daily contact with them and because children learn to trust them. It is therefore imperative that they be informed about this problem and alert to signs of abuse in their children.

Observing Copyright Laws

The continuing rapid development of technology has resulted in a new set of responsibilities for teachers in regard to observing **copyright laws** pertaining to the use of photocopies, videotapes, and computer software programs. In 1976 Congress revised the Copyright Act by adding the doctrine of **fair use.** While the fair use doctrine cannot be precisely defined, it is generally taken to mean that one may "use the copyrighted material in a reasonable manner without [the copyright holder's] consent"[28] as long as that use does not reduce the demand for the work or the author's income.

To clarify the fair use doctrine as it pertained to teachers photocopying instructional materials from books and magazines, Congress endorsed a set of guidelines

TABLE 9.1   Signs of Child Abuse

Physical Abuse	Sexual Abuse	Neglect
Unexplained bruises, black eyes, burns, frequent injuries	Sexually-transmitted disease in young child	Frequent truancy
Children who do not want to sit down	Complaints of pain/itching in genital area	Obvious malnourishment
Children who do not want to change clothes for physical education	Evidence of trauma in genital area	3–4 standard deviations below normal height/weight
Wearing long sleeves even in hot weather	Unusual odors around genital area	Child is given inappropriate food, drink, or medicine
Complaints about pain without obvious injury	Torn, stained, or bloody underclothing	Obvious and uncorrected medical/dental problems
Frequent absences or tardiness without reasonable explanations	Difficulty in walking or sitting	Inappropriate dress for weather
Aggressive, disruptive, destructive behavior	Pregnancy in young child	Torn, dirty clothing
Passive, withdrawn, fearful of other children or adults	Unusual seductive behavior	Body and hair dirty, offensive body odor
Manipulative or distrustful attitude	Drawings or writings may have strong, often bizarre sexual theme	Fatigue, listlessness
Absence of joy	Overly sophisticated knowledge and interest in sexual acts and vocabulary	"Failure to thrive"
Lack of expression of anger or pain	Expression by child or other children of his/her being sexually involved with an adult	
Complaints of beatings or other harsh treatment	Repeated attempts to run away from home	
Child is "too eager" to please	Poor peer relationships	
There is a significant change in the child's attitude or behavior at school	Overly mature appearance or behavior	

Source: From *The Abused Child,* pamphlet developed by the Texas State Teachers Association, Instruction and Professional Development Committee (Austin, Tex.: TSTA/NEA, 1984).

developed by educators, authors, and publishers. These guidelines allow teachers to make single copies of copyrighted material for teaching or research but are more restrictive regarding the use of multiple copies. The use of multiple copies of a work must meet the tests of brevity, spontaneity, and cumulative effect.

- *Brevity* means that short works can be copied. Poems or excerpts cannot be longer than 250 words, and copies of longer works cannot exceed 1,000 words or 10 percent of the work (whichever is less). Only one chart or drawing can be reproduced from a book or an article.
- The criterion of *spontaneity* means that the teacher doing the copying would not have time to request permission from the copyright holder.
- The criterion of *cumulative effect* limits the use of copies to one course and limits the material copied from the same author, book, or magazine during the semester. Also, no more than nine instances of multiple copying per class are allowed during a semester.

Guidelines for the use of videotapes made by teachers of television broadcasts were issued by Congress in 1981. Videotaped material may be used in the classroom only once by the teacher within the first 10 days of taping. Additional use is limited to reinforcing instruction or evaluation of student learning, and the tape must be erased within 45 days.

Computer software publishers have become concerned about the abuse of their copyrighted material. Limited school budgets and the high cost of computer software have led to the unauthorized reproduction of software. To address the problem, the Copyright Act was amended in 1980 to apply the fair use doctrine to software. Accordingly, a teacher may now make one backup copy of a program. If a teacher were to make multiple copies of software, the fair use doctrine would be violated because the software is readily accessible for purchase and making multiple copies would substantially reduce the market for the software.

THE LEGAL RIGHTS OF STUDENTS

As a prospective teacher, you have an obligation to become familiar with the rights of students. Since the 1960s students have increasingly confronted teachers and school districts with what they perceived to be illegal restrictions on their behavior. In this section we will discuss briefly some of the major court decisions that have clarified students' rights related to freedom of expression, suspension and expulsion, physical punishment, search and seizure, privacy, and nondiscrimination.

Freedom of Expression

The case of *Tinker* v. *Des Moines Independent Community School District* (1969) is perhaps the most frequently cited case concerning students' **freedom of expression.** The Supreme Court ruled in *Tinker* that three students, ages 13, 15, and 16, had been denied their First Amendment freedom of expression when they were suspended from school for wearing black arm bands in protest of the Vietnam War. The court ruled that neither teachers nor students "shed their rights to freedom of speech or expression at the schoolhouse gate." In addition, the court found no evidence that the exercise of such a right interfered with the school's operation.[29]

Freedom of expression applies to the various means people may use to express their beliefs. In addition to using speech and writing, people may express themselves through their appearance and dress and the wearing of symbols or insignia. Generally, the courts have ruled against students' freedom of expression only when it results in (or has the potential to result in) "substantial disruption" of the educative process.

Censorship   One area of student expression that has generated frequent controversy is that of student publications. Prior to 1988, the courts generally made it clear that student literature enjoyed constitutional protection, and it could only be regulated if it posed a substantial threat of school disruption, if it was libelous, or if it was judged vulgar or obscene *after publication.* However, school officials could use "prior restraints" or "prior **censorship**" and require students to submit literature before publication if such controls were necessary to maintain order in the school. Some courts issued the following guidelines for controlling student literature prior to publication:

1. Schools must issue clear and narrowly drawn regulations in advance to notify students of what is required.

freedom granted by the first amendment to the Constitution, to express one's beliefs

the act of removing from circulation printed material judged to be libelous, vulgar, or obscene.

2. School procedures must ensure a prompt decision by school authorities on submitted materials.
3. Timely and fair (informal) hearings and a prompt appeal to higher authority on decisions to censor must be ensured.[30]

Within these guidelines, students frequently successfully defended their right to freedom of expression. For example, the right of high school students to place in the school newspaper an advertisement against the war in Vietnam was upheld.[31] Students were also upheld in their right to distribute information on birth control and on laws regarding marijuana.[32] And other cases upheld the right of students to public literature that was critical of teachers, administrators, and other school personnel.[33]

In January of 1988, however, the Supreme Court, in a 5–3 ruling in *Hazelwood School District* v. *Kuhlmeier,* departed from the earlier *Tinker* decision and gave public school officials considerable authority to censor school-sponsored student publications. The case involved a Missouri high school principal's censorship of articles in the school newspaper, the *Spectrum,* on teenage pregnancy and the impact of divorce on students. The principal believed the articles were inappropriate because they might identify pregnant students and because references to sexual activity and birth control were inappropriate for younger students. Several students on the newspaper staff distributed copies of the articles on their own and later sued the school district, claiming that their First Amendment rights had been violated.

Writing for the majority in *Hazelwood School District* v. *Kuhlmeier,* Justice Byron White (who had voted with the majority in *Tinker*) said school officials could bar "speech that is ungrammatical, poorly written, inadequately researched, biased or prejudiced, vulgar or profane, or unsuitable for immature audiences."[34] White also pointed out that *Tinker* focused on a student's right of "personal expression," while the Missouri case dealt with school-sponsored publications that were part of the curriculum and bore the "imprimatur of the school." According to White, "Educators do not offend the First Amendment by exercising editorial control over the style and content of student speech in school-sponsored expressive activities so long as their actions are reasonably related to legitimate pedagogical concerns."[35]

A case involving an attempt to regulate an "underground" student newspaper entitled *Bad Astra,* however, had a different outcome. Five high school students in Renton, Washington, produced a four-page newspaper at their expense, off school property, and without the knowledge of school authorities. *Bad Astra* contained articles that criticized school policies, a mock poll evaluating teachers, and several poetry selections. The students distributed 350 copies of the paper at a senior class barbecue held on school grounds.

After the paper was distributed, the principal placed letters of reprimand in the five students' files, and the district established a new policy whereby student-written, non-school-sponsored materials with an intended distribution of more than 10 were subject to predistribution review. The students filed suit in federal district court, claiming a violation of their First Amendment rights. The court, however, ruled that the new policy was "substantially constitutional." Maintaining that the policy was unconstitutional, the students filed an appeal in 1988 in the Ninth Circuit Court and won. The court ruled that *Bad Astra* was not "within the purview of the school's exercise of reasonable editorial control."[36]

Dress Codes   Few issues related to the rights of students have generated as many court cases as have dress codes and hairstyles. The demand on the courts to hear such cases prompted Supreme Court Justice Hugo L. Black to observe that he did not believe "the federal Constitution imposed on the United States Courts the burden of supervising the length of hair that public school students should wear."[37] In line with Justice Black's observation, the Supreme Court has repeatedly refused to review the decisions reached by the lower courts.[38]

In general, the courts have suggested that schools may have dress codes as long as such codes are clear, reasonable, and students are notified. However, when the legality of such codes has been challenged, the rulings have largely indicated that schools may not control what students wear unless it is immodest or is disruptive of the educational process. (Recall, for example, how the appearance of Carol and Judy, described in the opening vignette at the start of this chapter, disrupted learning.) Rulings on hairstyles have been inconsistent and vary from location to location. Recent cases, however, indicate that students are being granted greater freedom regarding their choice of hairstyle, as long as the hairstyle in question does not pose a health hazard or disrupt learning.

Suspension and Expulsion

In February and March of 1971, a total of nine students received 10-day suspensions from the Columbus, Ohio, public school system during a period of city-wide unrest. One student, in the presence of his principal, physically attacked a police officer who was trying to remove a disruptive student from a high school auditorium. Four others were suspended for similar conduct. Another student was suspended for his involvement in a lunchroom disturbance that resulted in damage to school property. All nine students were suspended in accordance with Ohio law. Some of the students and their parents were offered the opportunity to attend conferences prior to the start of the suspensions, but none of the nine was given a hearing. Asserting that their constitutional rights had been denied, all nine students brought suit against the school system.

In a sharply divided 5–4 decision, the Supreme Court ruled that the students had a legal right to an education, and that this "property right" could be removed only through the application of procedural due process. The court maintained that suspension is a "serious event" in the life of a suspended child and may not be imposed by the school in an arbitrary manner.[39]

A similar case involved the expulsion of two sophomore girls from an Arkansas school for spiking the punch at a school party, an act in violation of a school board rule forbidding "any intoxicating beverage" at such affairs. The girls admitted to the act, and, without a hearing, the board expelled them for three months. (A suspension is usually defined as a temporary exclusion, 10 days or less; an expulsion refers to exclusion from school for a period of 10 days or more and may be as long as a semester or a school year.)

The parents brought suit against the school board, the school district, and the superintendent. In response to the suit, school officials maintained that they were unaware of the need to follow due process procedures in expelling the girls. The court, however, asserted that ignorance of the law did not justify the violation of constitutional rights. Thus, any school official who knows, or *should know,* that he or she is violating the constitutional rights of a student may be held liable for such behavior.[40]

As a result of cases such as the preceding two, every state has outlined procedures for school officials to follow in the suspension and expulsion of students. In cases of suspension, the due process steps are somewhat flexible and determined by the nature of the infraction and the length of the suspension. Expulsion, because it is more severe than suspension, requires a more extensive due process procedure. Generally, the following 10 criteria are adhered to in most cases of expulsion:

1. Notice of charges.
2. Right to counsel.
3. Right to a hearing before an impartial tribunal.
4. The individual has the right to avoid self-incrimination.
5. Evidence must be presented against the accused.
6. The accused has the right to cross-examine the witnesses.
7. Witnesses are compelled to testify.
8. There is a standard (burden) of proof on the part of the accused.
9. A record of the hearings must be kept.
10. The accused has the right to appeal.[41]

Physical Punishment

The practice of **corporal punishment** has had a long and controversial history in American education. Recall, for example, our reference in Chapter 7 to seventeenth-century Latin grammar school teachers who routinely hit students for unsatisfactory recitations. Currently, policies regarding the use of corporal punishment vary widely from state to state, and even from district to district.

Physical punishment applied to a student by a school employee as a disciplinary measure.

There is considerable evidence to suggest that corporal punishment is an ineffective means for controlling student behavior. Critics have shown that

> corporal punishment inhibits learning, interferes with the accomplishment of each of the important developmental tasks of children, and has the potential for physical harm to the child. The practice has been labeled anachronistic, counterproductive, and most damaging to children who are already emotionally disturbed. Moreover, children who witness physically punitive adult behavior are more likely themselves to behave aggressively and antisocially.[42]

In spite of such arguments against its effectiveness, corporal punishment continues to be widespread. Only three states, Hawaii, Massachusetts, and New Jersey, have statutes prohibiting corporal punishment.[43]

The most influential Supreme Court case involving corporal punishment is *Ingraham* v. *Wright*, decided in 1977. In Dade County, Florida, in October 1970, junior high school students James Ingraham and Roosevelt Andrews were paddled with a wooden paddle. Both students received injuries as a result of the paddlings, with Ingraham's being the most severe. Ingraham, who was being punished for being slow to respond to a teacher's directions, refused to assume the "paddling position" and had to be held over a desk by two assistant principals while the principal administered twenty "licks." "As a result, Ingraham was severely bruised, suffered a hematoma, and required compresses, laxatives, sleeping pills, pain pills, 10 days of rest, and suffered discomfort for three weeks."[44]

The court had two significant questions to rule on in *Ingraham:* Does the Eighth Amendment's prohibition of cruel and unusual punishment apply to corporal punishment in the schools? And, if it does not, should the due process clause of the Fourteenth Amendment provide any protection to students before punishment is administered? In regard to the first question, the Court, in a sharply divided 5–4 decision, ruled that the Eighth Amendment was not applicable to students being disciplined in school, only to persons convicted of crimes. On the question of due process, the Court said, "We conclude that the Due Process clause does not require notice and a hearing prior to the imposition of corporal punishment in the public schools, as that practice is authorized and limited by the common law." The Court also commented on the severity of the paddlings in *Ingraham* and said that, in such cases, school personnel "may be held liable in damages to the child and, if malice is shown, they may be subject to criminal penalties."[45]

Though the Supreme Court has upheld the constitutionality of corporal punishment, many districts around the country have instituted policies banning its use. Where corporal punishment is used, school personnel are careful to see that it meets criteria that have emerged from other court cases involving corporal punishment:

1. It is consistent with the existing statutes.
2. It is a corrective remedy for undesirable behavior.
3. It is neither cruel nor excessive.
4. There is no permanent or lasting injury.
5. Malice is not present.
6. The punishment is suitable for the age and sex of the child.
7. An appropriate instrument is used.[46]

FIVE-MINUTE FOCUS   What is your position regarding corporal punishment? Are there circumstances under which its use is justified? Date your journal entry and write for five minutes.

Beyond the issue of corporal punishment, teachers should also recognize the need to be careful about any form of physical contact with students. A casual pat on the head, a hand placed on the shoulder, or an encouraging hug can reassure or motivate a student, but for some individuals and groups and in some contexts such behavior can be easily misinterpreted as threatening, demeaning, or suggestive. In light of recent increases in reported instances of child exploitation and molestation, teachers would be wise to exercise reasonable caution.

Search and Seizure

As a teacher you have reason to believe that a student has drugs, and possibly a dangerous weapon, in his locker. Do you have the right to search the student's locker and seize any illegal or dangerous items? According to the Fourth Amendment, citizens are protected from **search and seizure** conducted without a search warrant. With the escalation of drug use in schools and school-related violence, however, cases involving the legality of search and seizure in schools have increased. These cases suggest guidelines that you can follow if confronted with a situation such as that described above.

One case focused on the use of trained dogs to conduct searches of 2,780 junior and senior high school students in Highland, Indiana. During a two-and-a-half to three-hour period, six teams with trained German shepherds sniffed the students. The

the process of searching an individual and/or his or her property if that person is suspected of an illegal act; reasonable or probable cause to suspect the individual must be present.

dogs alerted their handlers a total of 50 times. Seventeen of the searches initiated by the dogs turned up beer, drug paraphernalia, or marijuana. Another 11 students singled out by the dogs, including 13-year-old Diane Doe, were strip searched in the nurse's office. It turned out that Diane had played with her dog, who was in heat, that morning and that the police dog had responded to the smell of the other dog on Diane's clothing.

Diane's parents later filed suit, charging that their daughter was searched illegally. The court ruled that the use of dogs did not constitute an unreasonable search, nor did holding students in their homerooms constitute a mass detention in violation of the Fourth Amendment. The court did, however, hold that the strip searches of the students were unreasonable. The court pointed out that the school personnel did not have any evidence to suggest that Diane possessed contraband because, prior to the strip search, she had emptied her pockets as requested. Diane was awarded $7,500 in damages.[47]

Another case concerns a Kentucky high school, where for some time students had been setting off firecrackers in the school. According to reports from several students, a freshman girl was supplying students with firecrackers. When confronted with a request from school officials to empty the contents of her purse, the girl refused. She was then suspended for five days. The court hearing the case noted that the request to search the girl was based on a reasonable cause and even met the higher standard of probable cause that applies to searches conducted by police officers. Since the request to search was justified, the suspension was also justified.[48]

For the most part, court cases involving search and seizure in school settings have upheld the following three points:

1. School lockers are the property of the schools, not students, and may be searched by school authorities if reasonable cause exists.
2. Students may be sniffed by police dogs if school authorities have a reasonable suspicion that illegal or dangerous items may be found. Strip searches, however, are unconstitutional.
3. Since school authorities are acting *in loco parentis* (in the place of parents), they have a responsibility to take steps to protect students under their care.

In legal matters concerning the needs and rights of students, schools increasingly rely on outside support. In many schools, principals, teachers, social workers, and law enforcement officers work together to help keep students safe and law-abiding.

Closing the Gap

Our traditional system of financing education has led to many inequities between rich and poor school districts. Nationwide, bold moves to close the gap between "have" and "have not" schools have made headlines. Often, broad-based educational reforms calling for greater school accountability go hand in hand with new tax packages or redistricting schemes.

The Rockcastle County school system, for example, based in Mount Vernon, Kentucky, was until recently a "have not" school district. Many students in the district are considered socioeconomically disadvantaged, with 65 percent of the 3,000 enrolled qualifying for federally funded free lunches. Students have lacked the facilities and services that those in wealthier districts take for granted.

Then, in 1985, the Rockcastle County school system joined 65 other school districts in a lawsuit asking the state courts to rule Kentucky's school-financing system unconstitutional. The courts not only struck down the school-financing system, but also mandated sweeping educational reform.

In 1990 Kentucky's governor signed into law a bill increasing state education funding by 23 percent through increases in the state sales tax and corporate taxes. Today, Rockcastle County students are the beneficiaries of an additional one million dollars in their school system's budget. Like other Kentucky schools, however, Rockcastle County schools must do well in performance evaluations.

Kentucky's new law creates a system of rewards and sanctions to address issues of educational adequacy and excellence. Schools are evaluated on student performance, student health, dropout rates, and attendance, for example. The law also changes the role of the state education department, calling for school-based management. As movements for school-financing reforms gain momentum, other states will find, as Kentucky has, that equity issues often lead to changes in school governance and that equity and accountability go hand in hand.

Source: Reagan Walker, "From the Backwater to the Cutting Edge," from *Education Week,* in *Teacher Magazine* (June/July 1990): 12–14.

As schools have taken on broader powers in response to the continued prevalence of drugs in our society, new issues related to search and seizure have been raised. One of the most controversial of these is drug testing of students. Some schools use drug testing as a requirement for either attendance or interscholastic participation, including sports competition, or as a means of discipline. A 1987 federal district court case rejected a urinalysis test for marijuana use because the test did not prove possession or use during school and amounted to a strip search.[49] However, a similar drug-testing program for randomly selected student athletes was upheld since those who tested positively were suspended only from participating in sports for a period of time and no disciplinary or academic penalties were imposed.[50] A few schools have attempted to implement mandatory drug testing of teachers. So far these programs have been struck down as violations of the Fourth Amendment's prohibition of unreasonable searches.[51]

Privacy

Prior to 1974 students and parents were not allowed to examine school records. On November 19, 1974, Congress passed the Family Educational Rights and Privacy Act (FERPA), which gave parents of students under 18 and students 18 and older the right to examine their school records. Every public or private educational institution must adhere to the law, known as the **Buckley Amendment,** or lose federal money.

Under the Buckley Amendment, schools must

1. Inform parents or eligible students of their rights.
2. Facilitate access to records by parents or eligible students by providing information on the types of educational records that exist and the procedures for gaining access to them.
3. Permit parents or eligible students to review educational records, request changes, request a hearing if the changes are disallowed, and add their own statement by way of explanation, if necessary.
4. Insure that the institution does not give out personally identifiable information without the prior written informed consent of a parent or an eligible student.
5. Allow parents and eligible students to see the school's record of disclosures.[52]

The Buckley Amendment actually sets forth the minimum requirements that schools must adhere to, and many states and school districts have gone beyond these minimum guidelines in granting students access to their records. Most high schools, for example, now grant students under 18 access to their educational records, and all students in Virginia, elementary through secondary, are guaranteed access to their records.[53]

A number of exceptions are allowed by the Buckley Amendment. The teacher's gradebook, psychiatric or treatment records, notes or records written by the teacher for his or her exclusive use or to be shared with a substitute teacher, or the private notes of school law enforcement units, for example, are not normally subject to examination.[54]

Students' Rights to Nondiscrimination

Schools are legally bound to avoid discriminating against students on the basis of race, sex, religion, handicap, marital status, or infection with a noncommunicable disease such as AIDS. One trend of the 1980s and 1990s that has confronted schools with the need to develop more thoughtful and fair policies has been the epidemic in teenage pregnancies.

In regard to students who are married, pregnant, or parents, the courts have been quite clear: students in these categories may not be treated differently. A 1966 case in Texas involving a 16-year-old mother established that schools may provide separate classes or alternative schools on a *voluntary* basis for married and/or pregnant students. However, the district may not *require* such students to attend separate schools, nor may they be made to attend adult or evening schools.[55]

The courts have made an about-face in their positions on whether students who are married, pregnant, or parents can participate in extracurricular activities. Prior to 1972 participation in these activities was considered a privilege rather than a right, and restrictions on those who could participate were upheld. In 1972, however, cases in Tennessee, Ohio, Montana, and Texas established the right of married students (and, in one case, a divorced student) to participate.[56] Since then, restrictions applicable to extracurricular activities have been universally struck down.

Since the mid-1980s, many school districts have become embroiled in controversy over the issue of how to provide for the schooling of young people with AIDS and whether school employees with AIDS should be allowed to continue working. Thomas Flygare commented in his 1986 legal column in *Phi Delta Kappan,* "Teachers, principals, and superintendents are caught in the intense crossfire between state school officials who issue policies to protect victims of AIDS and parents who demand decisive action to prevent the spread of the dread disease."[57]

In their rulings on AIDS-related cases, the courts have sided with the overwhelming medical evidence that students with AIDS pose no "significant risk" of spreading the disease. Furthermore, " . . . the courts have been quite consistent in rejecting exclusion as the automatic answer."[58] In 1987 a judge prevented a Florida school district from requiring that three hemophiliac brothers who were exposed to AIDS through transfusions be restricted to homebound instruction.

FIVE-MINUTE FOCUS   Now that you have read the section on the legal rights of students, describe a time when you believe your rights as a student (or the rights of a classmate) were denied. Date your journal entry and write for five minutes.

YOUR RIGHTS AND RESPONSIBILITIES AS A STUDENT TEACHER

Do student teachers have the same legal status as certified teachers? Read the following case study:

> Meg Grant had really looked forward to the eight weeks she would spend as a student teacher in Mrs. Walker's high school English classes. Meg knew that Mrs. Walker was one of the best supervising teachers she might have been paired with, and she was anxious to do her best.
>
> In Mrs. Walker's senior class, Meg planned to teach *Brave New World.* Mrs. Walker pointed out to Meg that this book was controversial and some parents might object. She asked Meg to think about selecting an additional title that students could read if their parents objected to *Brave New World.* Meg, however, felt that Mrs. Walker was bowing to pressure from conservative parents, so she decided to go ahead and teach the book.
>
> Two weeks later Meg was called down to the principal's office where she was confronted by an angry father who said, "You have no right to be teaching my daughter this Communist trash; you're just a student teacher." What should Meg do? Does she have the same rights as a fully certified teacher?

In some states, a student teacher such as Meg might have the same rights and responsibilities as a fully certified teacher; in others her legal status might be that of an unlicensed visitor. The most prudent action for Meg to take would be to apologize to the father and assure him that if any controversial books are assigned in the future, alternative titles would be provided. In addition, Meg should learn how important it is for a student teacher to take the advice of his or her supervising teacher.

The exact status of student teachers has been the subject of controversy in many states. In fact, a 1976 study found that the authority of student teachers to teach was established by law in only 36 states, and no state had a statutory provision regulating the dismissal of a student teacher, the assignment of a student teacher, or the denial of the right to student teach.[59] Given the ambiguous status of student teachers, it is important that you begin your student teaching assignment with a clear idea of your rights and responsibilities. To help you do this we have included a "Bill of Rights for Student Teachers" in the Teacher's Resource section at the end of this textbook.

SUMMARY

This chapter began with a discussion of the ethical dimensions of teaching followed by a description of the ethical dilemmas teachers may encounter. Next, we looked at the teacher's legal rights in regard to certification; nondiscrimination; contracts, tenure, and dismissal; and academic freedom. Then we examined three legal responsibilities that concern teachers: avoiding tort liability, reporting child abuse, and observing copyright laws.

Next, we examined recent court rulings on students' legal rights in several areas: freedom of expression, suspension and expulsion, physical punishment, search and seizure, privacy, and nondiscrimination. Finally, we considered your rights and responsibilities as a student teacher and pointed out that, in most states, the legal status of student teachers has not been clarified.

The issues we have just examined make it very clear that the law touches just about every aspect of the teacher's professional life. Daily, the media remind us that ours is an age of litigation, and the teacher is no longer quite as free as in the past to determine what happens behind the closed classroom door. A complex array of court decisions and local, state, and federal laws must be taken into account. While our brief review of school law has answered some of the more common questions students have about their rights and responsibilities as a teacher, it may have made you aware of other questions you need to answer. Because school law is constantly changing and is interpreted and applied differently from state to state, you may wish to consult some current publications on school law in your state.

KEY TERMS AND CONCEPTS

code of ethics, **266**

ethical dilemmas, **268**

due process, **268**

nondiscrimination, **269**

teaching contract, **271**

tenure, **272**

dismissal, **272**

collective bargaining, **273**

grievance, **273**

academic freedom, **274**

tort liability, **278**

negligence, **279**

educational malpractice, **279**

copyright laws, **280**

fair use, **280**

freedom of expression, **282**

censorship, **282**

corporal punishment, **285**

search and seizure, **286**

Buckley Amendment, **289**

ANSWER KEY FOR CONSIDER THIS . . .

"How Have Supreme Court Decisions Affected the Schools?"

The answers to the quiz items are at follows: 1—*must not,* 2—*must not,* 3—*may,* 4—*may,* 5—*may,* 6—*may,* 7—*may,* 8—*must not,* 9—*must not,* 10—*may.* The primarily relevant citation for each item is: 1—*Stone* v. *Graham,* 449 U.S. 39 (1980); 2—

School District of Grand Rapids v. Ball, 105 S. Ct. 3216 (1985); 3—*Connick v. Myers*, 461 U.S. 138 (1983); 4—*Hortonville Joint School District No. 1 v. Hortonville Education Association*, 426 U.S. 482 (1976); 5—*Perry Education Association v. Perry Local Educator's Association*, 460 U.S. 37 (1983); 6—*Ingraham v. Wright*, 430 U.S. 651 (1977); 7—*New Jersey v. T.L.O.*, 469 U.S. 325 (1985); 8—*Irving Independent School District v. Tatro*, 468 U.S. 883 (1984); 9—*Plyler v. Doe*, 457 U.S. 202 (1982); 10—*Bethel School District v. Fraser*, 106 S. Ct. 3159 (1986).

DISCUSSION QUESTIONS

1. Do you disagree with any of the court decisions that are presented in this chapter? For each case, explain your reasons for arriving at a different decision.
2. Are there circumstances under which a student might be justified in filing an educational malpractice suit? Explain your answer.
3. Discuss the advantages and disadvantages of teacher tenure.
4. What guidelines can the teacher use to exercise his or her academic freedom and yet avoid overstepping its boundaries?
5. Do copyright laws as they apply to teachers seem fair? Do they deprive students of educational opportunities?
6. In *Hazelwood School District v. Kuhlmeier*, what rationale did the Supreme Court use in upholding the right of a school district to censor school-sponsored publications?
7. What are the pros and cons of student dress codes? Teacher dress codes?
8. What is your position regarding corporal punishment? Can you imagine circumstances under which you might use it? If so, describe.
9. What are the pros and cons of drug testing for students? For teachers?

APPLICATION ACTIVITIES

1. Obtain copies of teacher and student handbooks for your local school district. What do these documents say about the rights and responsibilities of teachers and students?
2. Select one of the court cases summarized in this chapter and locate additional information on the case in the library. Present your findings to the rest of your class in a brief oral report. Poll your classmates to determine how many of them agree with the court's ruling in the case.
3. With the assistance of your instructor, set up several role-plays based on hypothetical conflicts related to the rights of teachers. At the end of each role-play, those who did not participate should provide feedback to those who did. If time permits, do some role-plays that focus on the rights of students.
4. Examine the "Bill of Rights for Student Teachers" in The Teacher's Resource Guide. What steps can you take to ensure that these rights will apply to your student teaching or internship experience?

FIELD EXPERIENCES

1. Interview a lawyer and ask him or her to comment on the legal dimensions of teaching that should be of concern to teachers. Present your findings to your classmates in the form of a brief oral report.

2. For a group project, develop a questionnaire to find out how teachers feel about academic freedom, corporal punishment, freedom of expression, and other issues discussed in this chapter. Arrange to have a representative sample of teachers in your community respond to the questionnaire. When you and your classmates analyze the results, look for differences among teachers at various levels (elementary, middle, secondary). Also note differences related to other variables such as sex, years of experience, age, and so on.

3. Interview several students at a middle school or high school to get their views regarding the legal rights of students discussed in this chapter. Present the results of these interviews to your class in the form of a brief oral report.

4. Interview a school superintendent or principal to find out how much litigation occurred in the district during the last year or so. Also, ask him or her to identify procedures the district has in place to ensure due process for teachers and students. Report your findings to the class.

SUGGESTED READINGS

La Morte, Michael W. *School Law: Cases and Concepts*, 3d ed. Englewood Cliffs, N.J.: Prentice-Hall, 1990. *A practical guide to school law for teachers.*

McCarthy, Martha and Nelda H. Cambron-McCabe. *Public School Law: Teachers' and Students' Rights*, 2d ed. Boston: Allyn and Bacon, 1987. *A comprehensive book that emphasizes legal principles for elementary through secondary teachers. Presents court cases selected for their applicability to the problems teachers are likely to encounter.*

1986 Deskbook Encyclopedia of American School Law. Rosemount, Minn.: Data Research, 1986. *This reference book provides a comprehensive, detailed summary of school law. Includes a chapter on legal issues related to private schools and the rights of handicapped students.*

Strike, Kenneth A. and Jonas F. Soltis. *The Ethics of Teaching*. New York: Teachers College Press, 1985. *Describes two approaches teachers can use to resolve ethical dilemmas in the classroom. Part III contains excellent case studies on such topics as censorship, segregation, grading policies, plagiarism, and lying.*

Thomas, Stephen B. (ed.). *The Yearbook of Education Law 1991*. Topeka, Kans.: National Organization on Legal Problems of Education. *A helpful annual publication that provides an up-to-date interpretation of trends and issues in school law.*

Valente, William D. *Law in the Schools*, 2d ed. Columbus, Ohio: Merrill Publishing, 1987. *A practical, well organized reference on school law for teachers, administrators, and counselors. Includes illustrative excerpts from leading court opinions.*

Zirkel, Perry A. "De Jure." A monthly column on school law in *Phi Delta Kappan*. *Zirkel's excellent, readable column interprets the larger patterns and current trends in school law.*

TEACHERS . . . .

Have you handled situations that concerned your legal rights or responsibilities as a teacher?

What would you do if you were threatened with a lawsuit by the parents of a child you disciplined for misbehavior?

When potentially legal issues arise in the classroom, there is little time to evaluate the legal consequences of a particular action or response by the teacher. In the heat of a situation, legal rights consideration is not foremost on my mind. I have had many situations in which physical restraints have been used to ensure students' safety. I feel judgment in verbal exchanges is fairly safe in my school because of the academic freedoms given to teachers.

—Marc Gray
Highland Middle School, Louisville, Kentucky

I would ask the parents to come into my room and discuss their concerns. We would sit at a group table and I first would tell them that I appreciate their coming to me with their concerns. I would tell them how much I enjoy something about their child. I would ask them to tell me specifically why they are concerned. (I would have contacted each parent with positive comments about their child by the end of the first month of school.) After hearing their concerns, I would deal with each one, explaining the discipline procedure I use (the one that was sent home at the beginning of the year). I would question them about their child's attitude before leaving for school that day. I would explain that I was worried about the child's response on the day I disciplined him because he usually complied with classroom rules after being reminded.

Most of all I would listen to the parents and let them air their feelings. I would be supportive of their efforts to make learning pleasant for their child and let them know that I also want the best for the child. I would listen to any suggestion they may have and work with them to make a better working relationship among parents, child, and teacher. Upon summarizing our plan of action, I would ask if they feel good about our conclusion or . . . [if they would] feel better if I ask[ed] the principal to talk with us. Regardless of their response, I would communicate to the principal their report to me.

—June L. Wilhoit
Chase Street Elementary School, Athens, Georgia

I would wait. Hot heads usually cool down. Parents who respond in this manner are usually the ones who react to all situations with anger and accusations which, once vented, disappear. Instead of fearing their reactions, feel sorry for their child. This is who he or she has as role models [*sic*]. With this in mind you can focus on possible ways in which the child can be helped to recognize more productive ways of venting . . . [his or her] own emotions. If, however, a parent is able to convince the superintendent of the validity of their complaint, I would go to the meeting armed with documentation of past behavioral outbursts and my interventions. I would probably take along someone experienced in confrontational management—for example, my principal or local association representative.

—Susan S. Reid
Chattanooga High School, Chattanooga, Tennessee

What do you do to maintain control when students are disruptive in your class?

With a disruptive student, first I would talk to the student to let him know that I did not like his behavior in my class. If he did not settle down and act as a student should, I would have to talk to his or her parents. If after this warning the behavior persisted, I would follow through with a phone call to the parents. If after another week nothing changed, I would ask the guidance department to set up a conference with the parents. If it proved necessary, I would finally have the student removed from my class until the parents could guarantee that the behavior would stop.

—Ricardo Cortez Morris
Hixson High School, Hixson, Tennessee

Adolescents strive to be independent and will often go to extremes to test authority and take initiative. It is important to allow students the freedom to express themselves in a nonjudgmental environment. It is not important that they always respond as the teacher expects, but that they be given opportunities and freedom to express what is inside their own hearts and minds.

I try to accept students for who they are and to allow them to have thoughts and views that differ from the conforming norms education often breeds. A good teacher does not feel that his or her authority is threatened by the intellectual curiosity of the students. Give students the impression that you are investing in them and see them as capable and mature adults who can be responsible for their own actions. Don't call their parents or the vice-principal with every little skirmish that represents the testing of your authority; just realize that it is developmentally appropriate for adolescents to be at times totally unresponsive, unreliable, physically out of control (hormones are raging!), intellectually curious and emotionally immature.

—Barbara Arnold
Valencia High School, Placentia, California

Students: The Focus of Our Teaching

I had learned to respect the intelligence, integrity, creativity, and capacity for deep thought and hard work latent somewhere in every child.

Sybil Marshall
An Experiment in Education

At a crowded, noisy party you bump into someone you remember seeing in the education building a few semesters ago. You introduce yourself and discover that she's in the midst of her first year as a high school English teacher. When you mention your own plans to teach, she seems eager to talk, so you launch a series of questions: Did she feel prepared when she started? What surprises has she run into? What so far is the hardest part of her job as a teacher? The best?

Her answer to most of the questions is basically the same: the students. "They're the reason I feel great going to work every day . . . and they're the reason I sometimes think about quitting. Actually, there are times when I feel more like a counselor than a teacher . . . and in some respects I suppose I like that, like their trust in me and the potential I have to help them in significant ways.

"But that's where I get discouraged. What am I supposed to do with a student who's on drugs? Or the one who stops coming to school because she's pregnant? Or the students in the back of the room who do nothing—absolutely nothing!

"But then there are the ones who tug at your heart and remind you of how important you can be. For instance, there's this student who told me that he didn't see any point in living any more. I managed to keep him talking while I frantically tried to remember the people I know who counsel depressed or suicidal people. He agreed to let me make an appointment for him the next day with a counselor we both know and left reassuring me that he'd call after their meeting. But of course he never even showed up for it, and I spent the weekend worrying about him and blaming myself for not handling things better. On Monday he arrived in class looking tired, pale, and a bit sheepish. I'm still puzzled about what happened, but he avoids talking to me now.

"You asked how good my teacher preparation was. My courses taught me a lot about lesson plans, state mandates, test design, curriculum planning, and classroom management strategies, but they never showed me how to deal with real students. Actually I didn't learn much about students in any of my education classes. Nothing about all the ways they differ from each other, in their talents, needs, and intelligence. Nothing about how their family situations influence their development and education. Nothing about what motivates, stresses, or concerns them. That probably was my biggest surprise when I started teaching. I didn't realize I knew so little about the students.

"It's ironic, isn't it? Students are the focus of our teaching and yet so little is taught about them. Sometimes we miss the most obvious. What about your courses? Are you learning anything about students in them?"

FOCUS QUESTIONS

1. How do students differ from one another?
2. What kinds of special challenges may students face as exceptional learners?
3. What are the seven intelligences proposed by Howard Gardner?
4. What are some of the psychosocial developmental issues of students in childhood, early adolescence, and late adolescence?
5. How can teachers help students with problems such as drug addiction, teen pregnancy, dropping out, and suicide?

$\mathbb{W}$ith a class of 26 students ranging in age from five to ten, Sybil Marshall, a teacher in one of England's last one-room schoolhouses, experienced an ongoing course in human development—six age levels at once—and was forced to respond to the varying needs of each individual. Fortunately, she had the spirit and temperament to do so, and not only survived the experience but also wrote the engaging account of it referenced in the chapter-opening quote.

We begin this chapter by considering students' individuality and exploring how they differ. Next, we consider the unique needs of students with special challenges. Then we discuss the special issues and concerns of students at three broad developmental levels—childhood, early adolescence, and late adolescence. The need to learn about the intellectual and psychological growth of students at the age level you plan to teach is obvious. In addition, understanding how their interests, quests, and problems change throughout their school years will better equip you to serve them in the present. Finally, we look at how teachers can help students grow and develop during their school years.

HOW STUDENTS DIFFER

Though you are well aware that people differ, as a teacher you will discover how extensive and challenging the variation can be. Your students may be approximately the same age, live in the same area, be exposed to similar community values, and even dress alike, but this does not mean that their abilities, interests, and concerns will be the same. In addition, as Figure 10.1 illustrates, individual students belong to many different **microcultural groups,** that is, subgroups within the larger American culture.[1] Your students will probably have diverse racial, cultural, ethnic, and linguistic backgrounds, and some may be members of a special population, such as the handicapped or gifted.

To begin exploring how students vary as individuals, let us look at six areas of difference among students: family life, sex role development, intelligence, cognitive development, learning styles, and special needs and talents.

FIGURE 10.1
Individuals Belong to Many Different Microcultural Groups

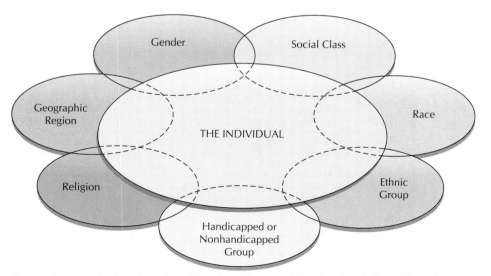

Source: James A. Banks, *Multiethnic Education: Theory and Practice,* 2d ed. Copyright © 1988 by Allyn and Bacon. Reprinted with permission.

Family Life

In some schools during certain periods in our history, teachers had to make home visits at the beginning of the school year and at various times thereafter. What they gained in those visits was a special and intimate understanding of their students, which many contemporary teachers miss. Today's school open houses and parent conferences are formal, somewhat awkward, and school-oriented. Teachers take advantage of school open houses to outline the school curriculum, explain testing programs, and communicate their expectations of student behavior and performance. Overlooked in these sessions, or at least considerably deemphasized, are the lives of the students in the context of their families. The focus in parent-teacher encounters has clearly shifted from a discussion of how the school is meeting the students' needs (home-visit orientation) to how the student is meeting the school's expectations (parent-conference orientation). The consequences of this shift can be significant, especially for students who are at risk of dropping out.

Family Structures   Teachers need to deliberately seek out information about their students in terms of their families. For instance, teachers may learn much simply by being informed about their students' family structures. With the high rate of divorce and women's entry into the workforce, family constellations have changed dramatically. No longer is there a typical American family in the form of a working father, a mother who stays at home, and two or three children. In its place is a mixture of structures:

- Single-parent families, with parents (who may be widowed, divorced, separated, or never married) living alone with their children or with other single parents to share expenses
- Stepparent families, with children living with their natural parent and a stepparent
- Blended families, with two single-parent families blended by a remarriage that creates various combinations of step-siblings and half-siblings
- Extended families, which include relatives such as aunts, uncles, and grandparents
- Nuclear families, which consist of two parents living alone with their own children, adopted children, or providing a foster home
- Families headed by unmarried couples, lesbians, homosexuals, older siblings, or grandparents

Each family's structure and economic arrangement places different demands and expectations on the children in them. Also, changes in family structure can bring about subtle or obvious changes in students' behaviors and attitudes at school. When their parents divorce, they may suddenly be burdened with adult responsibilities and concerns, along with their own grief over the breakup of their family, the real or imagined loss of the noncustodial parent, and the reduction in attention received from either parent. School may seem irrelevant, and performances and grades may plummet. In other cases, the arrival of new siblings or stepsiblings will shift students' positions in their family, changing their roles at home and their attitudes at school.

Belief Systems   The beliefs of students' families also influence their lives at school. For instance, while some families value schools and education, others may be suspicious and resentful of all outsiders. Strong religious beliefs that are integral to a family's daily life can often affect a student's actions at school. Similarly, ethnicity may determine many families' basic values and their relationships to others.

Perhaps the most obvious example of how family beliefs may influence students is when they are prevented from studying certain topics or from participating in holiday activities, parties, and dances. More subtly, family beliefs affect students' attitudes toward teachers, toward the process of learning, and toward their fellow students. The way students address and regard their teachers, their willingness to risk making a mistake, their openness to new ideas, their concern for saving face for their family as well as themselves, and their reluctance or desire to compete with a classmate are attitudes that are shaped by the values of each family. These attitudes, in turn, affect teachers' modes of instruction and interaction with students.

Sibling Positions   Of particular interest to researchers and educators are the sibling positions that students hold in their families. As psychologist Rudolph Dreikurs has written, "It is upon this one fact—the child's subjective impression of his place within the family constellation—that much of his future attitude toward life depends."[2] Some personality theorists believe that individuals are influenced more by their siblings—especially the sibling most unlike them—than by their parents.

FIVE-MINUTE FOCUS   What is your sibling position and how has it affected you in your schooling? Note that if a sibling is five or more years older than you, you are more like an only child than the youngest. Date your journal entry and write for five minutes.

According to Dreikurs, because parents tend to have high expectations for their firstborns, these children in turn tend to be responsible, serious, and achieving.[3] Interestingly, firstborns are overrepresented in Supreme Court Justices, in National Merit finalists, and in *Who's Who* listings. Dreikurs also speculated that another common characteristic of firstborns—being conservative—can be attributed to their experience of being dethroned by the arrival of a younger sibling. The family constellation shift that results when a new sibling enters the family can give the firstborn feelings of insecurity and an overall conservative resistance to change.

Dreikurs noted that second and middle children are more outgoing than firstborns. Second-born children may also be more competitive and aggressive, attempting to catch up with the firstborn. Middle children may feel left out in the family and turn to their peers for support. In large families middle children learn to be interdependent and cooperative.

Youngest children may attempt to catch up with their older siblings, striving for achievement and success. They may expect a lot from the world and be more adventurous, which is indicative of their sense of security, so often the result of parents' increased experience and reduced anxiety about parenting.

The influence of sibling position on the development of students can be a significant contributing factor to individual differences. Teachers may find explanations for students' incongruous behavior by considering their family constellations. Knowledge about family constellations can offer teachers clues, if not clear insights, into the thinking and behavior of the complex and unique individuals who are their students.

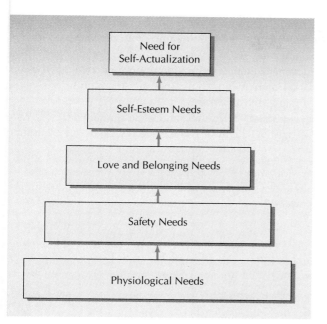

FIGURE 10.2
Maslow's Hierarchy of Needs

Satisfaction of Needs   Families vary in their abilities and inclinations to satisfy the basic and psychological needs of their children. These may best be considered by reviewing the model of a **hierarchy of needs,** formulated by psychologist Abraham Maslow (see Figure 10.2). In his extensive study of motivation, much of which focused on successful and satisfied people, Maslow examined the role that needs and desires play in an individual's behavior and development. He concluded that people are motivated by their most basic needs first, and when they feel these have been met, they naturally seek higher needs, the highest of which is self-actualization—the desire to use one's talents, abilities, and potentialities to the fullest. The hierarchical sequence of needs originally proposed by Maslow—physiological safety, love, esteem, and self-actualization—is of special significance, because the gratification of the needs at one stage brings about the emergence of needs at the next.[4] Individuals whose needs for safety have been fairly well satisfied will discover strong needs for friendship, affection, and love, for example. Similarly, if efforts to satisfy the various needs are thwarted, the result can be maladjustment and an interruption in the individual's full and healthy development.

For teachers this information has particular relevance, because students differ markedly in terms of where they are on Maslow's hierarchy of needs. Many families lack the resources to provide adequately for their most basic needs. Children from families that are concerned with day-to-day survival may not receive the support that could help them succeed in school:

> The family must have sufficient emotional strength remaining after dealing with survival issues, to care for and nurture its children. In practical terms, this means access to food, shelter, physical safety and economic stability. As these resources diminish, stress increases and the outcomes in terms of the children become less acceptable.[5]

Life Settings of Students at Risk   Many children in the United States live in families that help them grow up healthy, confident, and skilled, but many do not. Instead, their life settings are characterized by problems of alcoholism or other substance abuse, family or gang violence, unemployment, poverty, poor nutrition, teenage parenthood, and a history of school failure. They live in "multiproblem" families and communities that frequently become dysfunctional, unable to provide their children with the support and guidance they need. With their futures dimmed by such conditions, these young people are at risk of dropping out of school.

Children at risk are from families of all ethnic and racial groups and all socioeconomic levels. As Marian Wright Edelman of the Children's Defense Fund said:

> Millions of children are not safe physically, educationally, economically, or spiritually. . . . The poor black youths who shoot up drugs on street corners and the rich white youths who do the same thing in their mansions share a common disconnectedness from any hope or purpose.[6]

Many youths leave their immediate families in search of a better life, placing themselves at greater risk of becoming a dropout statistic. The girl quoted below, for example, was married at 14 and divorced at 15. Separated from her mother, she lost the parental nurturing and guidance that are so necessary for success in school:

> My mother, she's in Austin, and she'll call once in a while, like every couple of months because, you know, she's already got her own life, and she's used to being without children. She's more like a friend than a mother now, because she's been gone so long.[7]

As the following excerpt from an essay written by a 12-year-old boy illustrates, other youths must cope with homelessness:

> As I lay in bed crying myself to sleep in the Prince George Hotel, the largest hotel used to house homeless families in New York City, I could not bring myself to overcome the fear of what was happening to me. Over and over again I keep telling myself that I don't deserve this. I'm only 12 years old. I feel so alone. People in school call me a hotel kid. . . . It seems like people are so afraid of ending up where I'm at that they want to punish me for reminding them that being homeless is possible. . . . [8]

A deeper understanding of students can be brought about by becoming aware of students' family structures, belief systems, and sibling positions, and by paying attention to how well the family provides for the satisfaction of the various levels of needs. Clearly, the challenges of meeting the educational needs of students at risk are many. By becoming aware of their life settings, however, teachers can help students at risk learn and can give them a sense of belonging, hope, and purpose. Teachers who do that have taught their students the greatest lesson of all—that education can improve the quality of their lives.

Gender and Sex Role Socialization

Students differ not only by sex but also by society's traditional expectations of them as males and females. Families, the media, the schools, and other powerful social forces condition, or socialize, boys and girls to act differently. Moreover, as part of the American heritage, males have traditionally been accorded higher status. This heritage has created many inequities. The feminist movement and sociological research of the past few decades drew attention to the problems of **sex role stereotyping** and sex discrimination in our society.

Evidence abounds that schools significantly contributed to these problems. From kindergarten on, girls often were reinforced for "feminine" behaviors and roles (such

FACT FINDING

What Risks Do Today's Children Face?

A 1991 report by the Center for the Study of Social Policy revealed the following alarming data about today's youth:

- Violent death rate for teens (ages 15–19) increased by 12 percent between 1984 and 1988
- Percent of teen out-of-wedlock births increased by 10 percent between 1980 and 1988
- Juvenile incarceration rate increased by 41 percent between 1979 and 1987
- 19.5 percent of children are not covered by health insurance; 40 percent live with a single parent; 30 percent are latchkey children; 15 percent have physical or mental handicaps

Source: Kids Count Data Book (Washington, D.C.: The Center for the Study of Social Policy, The Annie E. Casey Foundation, 1991).

as playing with dolls and preparing for careers as homemakers) and boys for "masculine" ones (such as playing with trucks and preparing to become executives or to run their own businesses). In the not-so-distant past, if girls were planning careers other than homemaking, they were encouraged to become nurses or secretaries rather than doctors or senators. Girls are still often subtly encouraged to be passive, dependent, unassertive, and unambitious.

While Title IX of the Educational Amendments of 1972 guaranteed equality of educational opportunity to both sexes, girls and boys today still experience inequities in school. Unlike other ways in which students differ, gender differences should not affect what and how you teach. Because the needs of boys and girls as students ideally are the same, teachers face the challenge of providing an education that is free from gender bias and fair in encouraging all students to develop their capabilities to the fullest extent.

FIVE-MINUTE FOCUS Recall an example of sexist behavior or sex-role stereotyping that you have observed in a school setting. Describe the events that took place and discuss how you felt. Date your journal entry and write for five minutes.

Intelligence

Students differ also in terms of their intellectual capacity. Unfortunately, test scores, and sometimes IQ scores, are treated as accurate measurements of students' intellectual development, because of their convenience and long-time use. What is intelligence and how has it been redefined to account for the many ways in which it is expressed? Though many definitions of intelligence have been proposed, the term has yet to be completely defined. One view is that **intelligence** is the ability to learn. As David Wechsler, the developer of the most widely used intelligence scales for children and adults, said: "Intelligence, operationally defined, is the aggregate or global capacity to act purposefully, to think rationally, and to deal effectively with the environment."[9]

Origins of Intelligence Testing   The intelligence tests that we now use can be traced to the 1905 Metrical Scale of Intelligence designed by French psychologists Alfred Binet and Theodore Simon, who were part of a Paris-based commission for "dealing with the problem of subnormal children in the public schools."[10] Their scale was a set of increasingly difficult subtests that had successfully distinguished between below-average and bright children and between younger and older children in their research.

Binet revised the scale in 1908 and established the use of mental ages for scores, indicating how children perform in terms of the performance of others in their age group. He originally regarded children as being mentally retarded if they scored two or more years behind the average score for others in their age group.[11] This interpretation was not appropriate as children matured, however, because 6-year-olds who performed as 4-year-olds were presenting more serious lags behind their age group than 16-year-olds performing at the level of 14-year-olds. To correct this, a German psychologist, William Stern, in 1916 devised the **IQ** formula, dividing the mental age by the chronological age and multiplying by 100.

$$IQ = \frac{MA}{CA} \times 100$$

MA = Mental Age—average performance of individuals of that chronological age on IQ test

CA = Chronological Age

Binet's test was translated and adapted for American children in 1916 by Lewis Terman, a psychologist at Stanford University. Terman's test was, in turn, further adapted, especially by the U.S. Army, which transformed it into a paper and pencil test that could be administered to large groups. The use of such intelligence tests has continued throughout the years.

Criticism of Reliance on IQ Scores   Individual intelligence tests are presently valued by psychologists and those in the field of special education because they can be helpful in diagnosing a student's strengths and weaknesses. However, group intelligence tests given for the purpose of classifying students into like-score groups have received an increasing amount of criticism. Think for a moment about what the criticisms would be.

FIVE-MINUTE FOCUS   Think about why group IQ tests are criticized by some. What is unfair about them? Who might not do well on such tests? How could these test scores hurt students? Date your journal entry and write for five minutes.

The most significant and dramatic criticism of group IQ tests has been that test items and tasks are culturally biased, drawn mostly from white middle-class experience. Thus, the tests are more assessments of how informed students are about features in a specific class or culture than of how intelligent they are in general. This complaint became a formal, legal challenge when, on the basis of their IQ test scores, a group of African-American children were put into special classes for mentally retarded children. Their parents brought the complaint to the courts in 1971 and persisted with it all the way to the Supreme Court, where a decision was made in their favor in 1979. In that well-known case, *Larry P.* v. *Riles,* the court decided that IQ tests were discriminatory and culturally biased.[12] However, within a year, another case, *PASE* v. *Hannon,* softened that decision by adding that when IQ tests were used in conjunction with other forms of assessment, such as teacher observation, they were not discriminatory for placement purposes.[13] While the criticism continues, a number of psychometricians are seeking other solutions by attempting to design culture-free intelligence tests.[14]

Another criticism of intelligence tests is that they are timed and thus rely heavily on students' abilities to work quickly, to withstand the press of time, and to be motivated to do well. Students who are not so motivated and students who experience test anxiety take their time answering questions and consequently, score poorly. Emotional factors may also influence how well a student performs. If self-esteem is low, or if the student is upset, sick, or tired, performance on an IQ test may be lower than normal. The one-time, one-sitting score is a recognized drawback.

Intelligence tests have also been regarded as inadequate measures of intelligence because they tap only students' "crystallized" rather than "fluid" knowledge. According to one critic, the tasks in the tests "are decidedly microscopic, are often unrelated to one another, and seemingly represent a 'shotgun' approach to the assessment of human intellect."[15]

Cognitive Development

Although some students clearly seem smarter than others, because of the difficulty of measuring intelligence accurately and fairly, educators need perspectives on intellectual ability that are more flexible, dynamic, and complex. Two such perspectives are Piaget's theory of **cognitive development** and Gardner's theory of **multiple intelligences.**

Piaget's Model Jean Piaget, the noted Swiss biologist and epistemologist, made extensive observational studies of children. He concluded that children reason differently from adults and even have different perceptions of the world. Piaget surmised that children learn through actively interacting with their environments, much as scientists do, and proposed that a child's thinking progresses through a sequence of four cognitive stages. (See Figure 10.3.) According to Piaget's theory of cognitive development, the rate of progress through the four stages varies from individual to individual.

During the school years, students move through the **preoperational stage,** the **concrete operations stage,** and the **formal operations stage;** yet, because of individual interaction with the total environment, each student's perceptions and learnings will be unique. According to Piaget,

> A student who achieves a certain knowledge through free investigations and spontaneous effort will later be able to regain it; he will have acquired a methodology that can serve him for the rest of his life. . . . At the very least, instead of . . . subjugating his mind to exercise imposed from outside, he will make his reason function by himself and will build his own ideas freely.[16]

FIGURE 10.3
**Piaget's Stages of Cogni-
tive Growth**

1. *Sensorimotor Intelligence (birth to 2 years):* Behavior is primarily sensory and motor. The child does not yet "think" conceptually; however, "cognitive" development can be observed.

2. *Preoperational Thought (2–7 years):* Development of language and rapid conceptual development are evident. Children begin to use symbols to think of objects and people outside of their immediate environment. Fantasy and imaginative play are natural modes of thinking.

3. *Concrete Operations (7–11 years):* Children develop ability to use logical thought to solve concrete problems. Basic concepts of objects, numbers, time, space, and causality are explored and mastered. Through use of concrete objects to manipulate, children are able to draw conclusions.

4. *Formal Operations (11–15 years):* Cognitive abilities reach their highest level of development. Children can make predictions, think about hypothetical situations, think about thinking, and appreciate the structure of language as well as use it to communicate. Sarcasm, puns, argumentation, and slang are aspects of adolescents' speech that reflect their ability to think abstractly about language.

Multiple Intelligences   While appreciating the flexibility of Piaget's theory of cognitive development, Howard Gardner found it limited to only one form of knowledge—the logical-mathematical or scientific intelligence especially valued in Western culture. Gardner proposes that "there is persuasive evidence for the existence of several relatively autonomous human intellectual competences, [referred to] as 'human intelligences' . . . [The] exact nature and breadth of each has not so far been satisfactorily established, nor has the precise number of intelligences been fixed."[17] Drawing on the theories of others and research findings on *idiots savants*, stroke cases, child prodigies, and so-called "normal" children and adults, Gardner suggests that there are at least seven human intelligences: logical-mathematical, linguistic, musical, spatial, bodily-kinesthetic, intrapersonal, and interpersonal. (See Table 10.1.)

Though this is not the place to examine and critique Gardner's theory of multiple intelligences, we mention it because it is valuable in helping teachers recognize that their students differ not only in their logical-mathematical or linguistic abilities—the ones traditionally assessed in intelligence tests—but also in a variety of other intelligences. Some students are talented in terms of their interpersonal relations and exhibit natural leadership abilities. Others seem remarkably in touch with their own feelings, thinking, and development, revealing intrapersonal strengths. Differences in musical, athletic, and mechanical abilities can be recognized by even the minimally informed observer. Because these intelligences are not tested or highlighted, they may go unnoticed, with the possible consequence of their being wasted. We encourage you to guide students' intellectual growth by recognizing and promoting all forms of intelligence and adapting your teaching to their interests and stages of cognitive development.

Learning Styles

Students vary greatly in regard to their learning styles, that is, the approaches to learning that work best for them. The National Task Force on Learning Style and Brain Behavior suggests the following definition of **learning style:**

a set of cog, affective, physiological behaviors through which an individual learns most effectively; determined by a combination of hereditary and environmental influences

(defn)

TABLE 10.1　The Seven Intelligences

Intelligence	End-States	Core Components
Logical-mathematical	Scientist Mathematician	Sensitivity to, and capacity to discern, logical or numerical patterns; ability to handle long chains of reasoning.
Linguistic	Poet Journalist	Sensitivity to the sounds, rhythms, and meanings of words; sensitivity to the different functions of language.
Musical	Composer Violinist	Abilities to produce and appreciate rhythm, pitch, and timbre; appreciation of the forms of musical expressiveness.
Spatial	Navigator Sculptor	Capacities to perceive the visual-spatial world accurately and to perform transformations on one's initial perceptions.
Bodily-kinesthetic	Dancer Athlete	Abilities to control one's body movements and to handle objects skillfully.
Interpersonal	Therapist Salesman	Capacities to discern and respond appropriately to the moods, temperaments, motivations, and desires of other people.
Intrapersonal	Person with detailed, accurate self-knowledge	Access to one's own feelings and the ability to discriminate among them and draw upon them to guide behavior; knowledge of one's own strengths, weaknesses, desires, and intelligences.

Source: H. Gardner and T. Hatch, "Multiple Intelligences Go to School: Educational Implications of the Theory of Multiple Intelligences," *Educational Researcher,* 18(8) (1989): 6. Copyright © 1989 by the American Educational Research Association. Reprinted by permission of the publisher.

Learning style is that consistent pattern of behavior and performance by which an individual approaches educational experiences. It is the composite of characteristic cognitive, affective, and physiological behaviors that serve as relatively stable indicators of how a learner perceives, interacts with, and responds to the learning environment. It is formed in the deep structure of neural organization and personality [that] molds and is molded by human development and the cultural experiences of home, school, and society.[18]

Students' learning styles are determined by a combination of hereditary and environmental influences. Some quickly learn things they hear; others learn best when they see material in writing. Some need a lot of structure; others learn best when they can be independent and follow their desires. Some learn best in formal settings; others learn best in informal, relaxed environments. Some need almost total silence to concentrate; others learn well in noisy, active environments. Some are intuitive learners; some prefer to learn by following logical, sequential steps.

While learning style preferences can be quite strong, they do change as the individual matures. During the last decade, much research has been conducted on students' learning styles, and dozens of conceptual models and accompanying learning-style assessment instruments have been proposed.

Learning-Style Models　For example, David Hunt has pointed out that students differ in the amount of structure they require in their learning activities.[19] Rita Dunn, Kenneth Dunn, and Gary Price have suggested that an individual's learning style reflects "the manner in which at least eighteen different elements from four basic stimuli [environmental, emotional, sociological, and physical] affect a person's ability

FIGURE 10.4   **Diagnosing Learning Style**

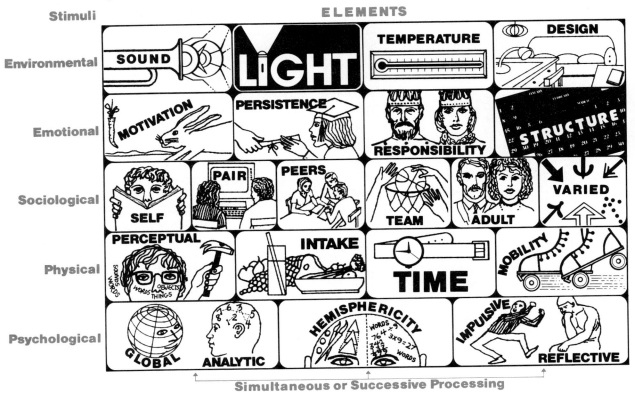

to absorb and retain."[20] (See Figure 10.4.) They have developed a Learning Style Inventory that identifies a student's peak learning time, degree of motivation, and preferences for informal or formal classroom arrangements, perceptual modality (the extent to which the student prefers to perceive through sight, smell, hearing, touch, or movement), and structure (the student's preference for sequentially and hierarchically arranged learning tasks).

Anthony Gregorc suggests that learners prefer activities that are either abstract or concrete and either sequential or random. Combinations of these preferences create four distinct learning modes that characterize individual learning styles. Bernice McCarthy proposes four learning styles based on how people perceive the world and how they process information. She characterizes learners as innovative, analytical, commonsensical, or dynamic.[21] Table 10.2 describes these four kinds of learners and suggests appropriate teacher responses.

FIVE-MINUTE FOCUS   Describe your learning style. Refer to the material presented in this section and in Figure 10.4 and Table 10.2. Date your journal entry and write for five minutes.

TABLE 10.2 Four Learning Styles: The McCarthy 4-Mat

Style	Characteristics of the Learner	Teacher Response
Imaginative/ Innovative Learner	• Seeks meaning • Wants reasons for learning new material • Needs to be personally involved in the learning process • Desires to work with people • Is highly imaginative • Has good divergent thinking skills • Perceives information concretely, processes it reflectively	• Is a motivator • Uses the discussion approach • Incorporates a great deal of teacher-student interaction
Analytic Learner	• Wants to know the facts • Perceives information abstractly, processes it reflectively • Can create concepts and build models • Enjoys collecting data • Needs to know what the experts think • Values sequential thinking	• Provides information by direct instruction • Sees knowledge as increasing comprehension
Common-Sense Learner	• Needs to know how things work • Seeks usability • Enjoys solving problems • Desires hands-on experiences • Wants ideas to be practical • Needs to know how things that they are asked to do will help in real life • Likes to practice ideas • Perceives information abstractly, processes it actively	• Becomes a coach • Models • Involves the student • Gives immediate feedback
Dynamic Learner	• Needs to use the self-discovery method • Takes risks • Is flexible • Relishes change • Seeks action • Follows through with plans • Enjoys the trial-and-error method • Receives information concretely, processes it actively	• Is a resource • Becomes an evaluator • Serves as a facilitator • Encourages a variety of learning approaches

Source: Adapted from Bernice McCarthy, *The 4-Mat System: Teaching & Learning Styles with Right/Left Techniques* (Barrington, Ill.: EXCEL, 1980).

Impact of Culture on Learning Styles   Research suggested that social class has the greatest influence on how much students learn. Though less powerful than social class, culture also influences learning styles. It has been suggested that youths who grow up outside the dominant larger culture "tend to process information differently from the predominant way it is processed in schools. Their learning styles are often described as relational, as opposed to the analytical style rewarded in schools."[22] Evidence indicates, for example, that Native-American students "approach tasks visually, seem to prefer to learn by careful observation which precedes performance, and seem to learn in their natural settings experientially."[23] Research also suggests that African-American students tend to be "field-dependent" learners, that is, they

As a teacher, you will quickly learn that no one instructional approach matches the learning styles and needs of every child. Knowing your students and providing a variety of learning experiences is a good way to lessen the uncertainty of teaching outcomes.

are more attuned to the social environment and motivated by external factors in that environment. Also, it has been shown that bilingual individuals, such as fluent speakers of both Spanish and English, tend to have greater cognitive flexibility than those who have learned only one language.[24]

There is no one "correct" view of learning styles to guide teachers in their daily decision making. Culture-based differences in learning styles are subtle, variable, and difficult to describe. Moreover, critics have pointed out flaws in many learning-style schemes that have been proposed. Nevertheless, you should be aware of the concept of learning styles and realize that any given classroom activity may be more effective for some students than for others. Knowledge of your own and your students' learning styles will help you to individualize instruction and motivate your students.

Special Challenges

Students also differ according to their special needs and talents. Some enter the world with exceptional abilities or disabilities; others encounter life experiences that change their capabilities significantly, and still others struggle with conditions that medical scientists have yet to understand. Where possible, all of these exceptional children and youth are given a public education in America. This has been assured by several federal laws, among them the Education for All Handicapped Children Act, the Gifted and Talented Children's Act, and the Education Consolidation and Improvement Act.

Exceptional Children   Children "who require special education and related services if they are to realize their full human potential"[25] are referred to as **exceptional learners.** They are taught by special education teachers (perhaps you or some teacher

[handwritten marginal note:] Students whose growth and dev deviate from the norm to the extent that their ed. needs can be met more effectively through a mod of regular school programs.

education students you know are seeking certification in special education) and by regular teachers into whose classrooms they have been integrated or "mainstreamed." Among the many exceptional children that teachers may encounter in the classroom are students who are physically, mentally, or emotionally handicapped; students who are gifted or talented; and students who speak English as a second language.

Handicapped Students Table 10.3 shows that the percentage of all students participating in federally supported education programs for **handicapped students** increased from 8.6 percent in 1978 to 11.1 percent in 1988. In 1988 almost 4.5 million students participated in these programs.

Various tests and other forms of assessment are used to identify individuals with handicapping conditions. A system of classification, though imperfect, helps educators determine the special needs of exceptional learners. "Learning-disabled" (LD), for example, includes slow learners and students with dyslexia, a severe impairment of reading ability. "Speech-impaired" includes students who stutter, for example, or have difficulty articulating words. "Mentally retarded" children are usually classified as "educable" if they have an IQ between 75 and 70 and "trainable" if they have an IQ between 50 and 25. Students classified as "emotionally disturbed" include children and adolescents who are schizophrenic, autistic, chronically depressed, or clinically diagnosed with some other mental or emotional condition. "Hearing-impaired" and "visually impaired" students include those who are hard of hearing, deaf, partially sighted, blind, and both deaf and blind. Physical disabilities include, for example, congenital abnormalities, cerebral palsy, epilepsy, and health impairments such as AIDS, sickle cell anemia, and diabetes.

TABLE 10.3 **Percent of Elementary and Secondary Students Served by Federal Programs for the Handicapped, 1978–1988***

Type of Handicap	1978	1980	1982	1984	1986	1988
All conditions	8.6	9.6	10.5	10.9	10.9	11.1
Learning-disabled	2.2	3.1	4.0	4.6	4.7	4.8
Speech-impaired	2.8	2.9	2.8	2.9	2.9	2.4
Mentally retarded	2.1	2.1	2.0	1.9	1.7	1.5
Seriously emotionally disturbed	0.7	0.8	0.9	0.9	1.0	0.9
Hard of hearing and deaf	0.2	0.2	0.2	0.2	0.2	0.1
Orthopedically handicapped	0.2	0.2	0.1	0.1	0.1	0.1
Other health-impaired	0.3	0.3	0.2	0.1	0.1	0.1
Visually impaired	0.1	0.1	0.1	0.1	0.1	0.1
Multihandicapped	**	0.1	0.2	0.2	0.2	0.2
Deaf-blind	**	***	***	***	***	***

* Includes students served under Chapter 1 and Education of the Handicapped Act (EHA). Based on enrollment in public schools, kindergarten through 12th grade, including a relatively small number of prekindergarten students.

** No data available.

*** Less than 0.1 percent.

Source: U.S. Department of Education, Office of Special Education and Rehabilitative Services, Annual Report to Congress on the Implementation of the Education of the Handicapped Act, various years; National Center for Education Statistics, Common Core of Data survey; and unpublished data. Taken from National Center for Education Statistics, *The Condition of Education 1990: Volume 1, Elementary and Secondary Education*, p. 131.

Gifted and Talented Students In addition to students with handicapping conditions, you may find students with exceptional abilities in your classroom. Some may be **gifted and talented**, that is, have exceptional abilities in one or more of the following areas: general intellectual ability, academic aptitude, creative thinking, leadership ability, or visual and performing arts. To ignore or limit the potential of this special population, our most talented young people and children, is a grave mistake for them and the country. Teachers need to become attuned to these students, recognizing their strengths and promoting their growth, talents, and productivity.

Educators disagree on the best criteria for identifying gifted and talented students. Some rely exclusively on IQ scores and set a score of 130 and above for identifying the gifted and talented. Others believe that the cutoff IQ score should be 160 or above. Broader criteria identify students with exceptional abilities in the performing arts, visual arts, and sports. Depending on the criteria used, estimates of the number of gifted and talented students range from 2 to 5 percent of the total population.

In general, Joseph Renzulli and C. H. Smith believe that gifted and talented persons exhibit the following characteristics:

1. High ability (including but not limited to intelligence)
2. High creativity
3. High task orientation (the motivation to initiate and complete a task)[26]

Linguistically Challenged Students Another special group of students you may encounter in your classroom is **linguistically challenged students,** that is, students with limited ability to understand, speak, and write English. Since these students do not know the standard American English of the dominant culture, they may experience learning problems in school. As Christine Bennett points out,

> Areas of potential conflict related to verbal communication are dialect differences, especially grammar and semantics, and discussion modes. Students who speak "country," Black vernacular, or any nonstandard dialect are often perceived as uneducated or less intelligent. Many White students and some upper- and middle-income Black students who have grown up in ethnically encapsulated environments cannot understand their Black or Latino peers, or incorrectly assume they do understand.[27]

Educators debate the best way to teach linguistically challenged learners. Research has shown, however, that no matter what program of instruction is used, bilingual students at first make slower progress in their second language.

Labeling Exceptional Learners Special-needs students are often referred to synonymously as "handicapped" or "disabled." However, it is important for teachers to understand the following distinction between a disability and a handicap:

> A disability is an inability to do something, a diminished capacity to perform in a specific way. A handicap, on the other hand, is a disadvantage imposed on an individual. A disability may or may not be a handicap, depending on the circumstances. Likewise, a handicap may or may not be caused by a disability. For example, blindness is a disability that can be anything but a handicap in the dark. In fact, in the dark the person who has sight is the one who is handicapped. . . . When working and living with exceptional individuals who have disabilities, we must constantly strive to separate the disability from the handicap. That is, our goal should be to confine their handicap to those characteristics that cannot be changed and to make sure that we impose no further handicap by our attitudes or our unwillingness to accommodate their disability.[28]

Teachers should also become aware that the definitions for the disabilities are generalized, open to change, and significantly influenced by the current cultural perception of normalcy. For example, note the nonspecificity of the definition of mental retardation proposed by the American Association of Mental Deficiency (AAMD), the one most widely accepted: "Mental retardation refers to significantly subaverage general intellectual functioning resulting in or associated with impairments in adaptive behavior and manifested during the developmental period."[29] The definition attempts to encompass the many forms and degrees of retardation, those with clear biological causes as well as those of unknown origin, those that are temporary as well as those that are more permanent in nature. Significantly, the AAMD at one time placed the cutoff point for retarded intellectual functioning at an IQ of 84 or less. When they made the revision to an IQ of 70, a large group of individuals was suddenly no longer regarded as mentally retarded.

Even though specific descriptors for disorders may change, the students who are affected by them still need special treatment and programs. Teachers can best serve such students by seeking a better understanding of their disabilities and handicaps and by regarding them, and all of their students, as unique individuals with varying needs.

STAGES OF DEVELOPMENT

After reviewing some of the ways that students differ, we turn now to issues and concerns that students at each level of schooling have in common. Regardless of the level you plan to teach, knowledge of the development of your students before or after you work with them will help you to better understand and appreciate them in the present. For this reason, we now focus our discussion on three specific age groups— childhood, early adolescence, and late adolescence.

Our discussion of students' concerns at the three age levels draws upon Erik Erikson's theory of personality development. His developmental model delineates eight

TABLE 10.4   Erikson's Eight Stages of Man

Stage	Psychosocial Crisis	Virtue
Infancy	Trust vs. Mistrust	Hope
Early Childhood	Autonomy vs. Shame and Doubt	Will
Play Age	Initiative vs. Guilt	Purpose
School Age	Industry vs. Inferiority	Competence
Adolescence	Identity vs. Role Confusion	Fidelity
Young Adult	Intimacy vs. Isolation	Love
Adulthood	Generativity vs. Rejectivity	Care
Mature Love	Integrity vs. Despair	Wisdom

Source: Adapted from *Childhood and Society*, 2d ed. by Erik H. Erikson, by permission of W. W. Norton & Co., Inc. Copyright 1950, © 1963 by W. W. Norton & Company, Inc. Copyright renewed 1978 by Erik H. Erikson.

stages, from infancy to old age (see Table 10.4). For each stage a **psychosocial crisis** is central in the individual's emotional and social growth. Erikson expresses these crises in polar terms; for instance, in the first stage, that of infancy, the psychosocial crisis is trust versus mistrust. Erikson explains that the major psychosocial task for the infant is to develop a sense of trust in the world but not to give up totally a sense of distrust. In the tension between the poles of trust and mistrust, a greater pull toward the more positive pole is considered healthy and is accompanied by a virtue. In this case, if trust prevails, the virtue is hope. For further information on this significant and useful theory of development, we recommend that you read Erikson's first book, *Childhood in Society.* [30]

Students in Childhood

According to Erikson, elementary school students are concerned with the psychosocial issue of industry versus inferiority and developing competence. Of special concern to teachers are the challenges and consequences of **childhood** stress. 2-10yrs

Developing Competence   During Erikson's "School Age" stage, children strive for a sense of industry and struggle against feelings of inferiority. If they are successful, they gain the virtue of competence, believing in their abilities to do things. The self-confidence and sense of control that come with the mastery of new skills and the production of acceptable projects is self-generating. Successes build on success and promote a positive attitude toward learning and participating actively and enthusiastically in their worlds.

If, on the other hand, children find evidence that they are inferior to others, if they experience failure when they try new tasks, and if they struggle without ever gaining a sense of mastery, then they feel incompetent. These negative feelings also perpetuate themselves, and the children experiencing them will protectively pull back from learning opportunities, regarding them as unpleasant and threatening.

Children gain the sense of industry needed at this age by playing seriously, mastering new skills, producing products, and being workers. When they first go to school they are oriented toward accomplishing new things (some kindergartners expect to learn to read their first day of school and are disappointed when they don't). For young schoolchildren, the idea of work is attractive; it means that they are doing something grown-up. They may hope to have homework (until they really do) and enjoy bragging about having lots of work to do in school.

Older elementary students, who have encountered some of the unpleasant realities of schoolwork, can still lose themselves in their own learning endeavors—designing and building a science project, reading a series of books by the same author, studying the biographies of famous people, writing their own books. Unless thwarted by unpleasant school experiences, boring exercises, or the pressure of anxious parents, elementary students have a natural inclination for industry and an inner desire to gain competence.

Coping with Childhood Stress What are some of the areas of concern for elementary school children? Though a wide range of concerns exist, we will confine our discussion to the general area of childhood stress. Is childhood a time of carefree play or a period of stress? Certainly the answer depends upon the life circumstances and personalities of the individual child. Many adults are surprised to learn that stress is a common feature in the lives of most children. We are prone to look back on our own childhoods nostalgically, recalling the happy times and forgetting the anxieties we felt.

FIVE-MINUTE FOCUS   Think back to your elementary school days. What things worried you? What things made you afraid and which life events were stressful to you? Date your journal entry and write for five minutes.

A few researchers have explored the worries and fears of children and young people. One particularly interesting series of studies was conducted by Kaoru Yamamoto, an educational psychologist who explored the sources of stress for children in the fourth, fifth, and sixth grades in the United States and other countries.[31] He and his associates found greater similarity between American children and children from other countries than between American children and American child development professionals in their perceptions of stressful events. What does this tell us about how well adults understand the concerns of children?

A common source of stress for children is the pressure applied on them by parents, teachers, and the media to grow up quickly, even bypassing childhood in their fast-paced journey into adulthood. Children seem to be pushed today: pushed away by parents who are too busy with jobs or careers to spend time with them; pushed to assume adult responsibilities in single-parent or two-career families; and pushed ahead to perform earlier and better in school. As Elkind observes in his popular book *Hurried Child,* many parents today seem more concerned about having the smartest child in school rather than the happiest.

Serious stress is experienced by latchkey children, who are left on their own or in each others' care for part or all of the day without adult supervision. These children are placed at risk in terms of their physical safety as well as their emotional sense of well-being. Their parents, often single, may be equally stressed, feeling guilty and anxious about their children's lack of supervision; yet they see no alternatives because of their economic situation.

CONSIDER THIS . . .

How Do Children View Stressful Events?

Below are 20 stressful events Kaoru Yamamoto asked fourth-, fifth-, and sixth-grade students in the United States and Japan to rate on a scale from 1 (least upsetting) to 7 (most upsetting). Guess how they responded by ranking the items from 1 (rated as most upsetting) to 20 (rated as least upsetting) for both groups. Compare your ranking with the one presented in the answer key at the end of this chapter.

	USA	U.S. Students	Japanese Students
1. Having a new baby sister or brother	20	15	
2. Getting lost in some strange place	11	4	
3. Receiving a poor report card	8	8	
4. Being caught stealing something	6	2	
5. Going to a dentist	18	19	
6. Telling the truth, but no one believing me	7	14	
7. Losing my mother or father	1	1	
8. Being picked last on a team	16	20	
9. Moving to a new school	13	13	
10. Going blind	2	7	
11. Being laughed at in front of the class	12	12	
12. Losing in any game or sport	17	18	
13. Being kept in the same grade next year	3	9	
14. Wetting pants in class	4	5	
15. Going to a hospital for an operation	10	3	
16. Having a scary dream	14	16	
17. Being sent to the principal's office	9	10	
18. Not making a perfect score (100) on a test	15	17	
19. Getting up in front of the class to give a report	19	11	
20. Hearing my parents quarrel and fight	5	6	

Source: Items prepared by Kaoru Yamamoto. Used with permission.

Children are subject to many other forms of stress. An alarming number of children must endure, for example, the stress of coping with physical, sexual, and/or psychological abuse. As a teacher you must be alert for signs of child abuse and, as the law requires, report any incidence of suspected abuse.

The pressures to handle situations beyond their abilities, whether at home or in a classroom, can deprive children of their childhoods and darken the years when they should be feeling cared for and secure. Parents, teachers, and community leaders need to make certain that children have physically and psychologically safe settings in which to grow.

Students in Adolescence

Before we can consider today's adolescents in terms of their psychosocial development, we need to regard them from the broad perspective of their place in the contemporary world and along the continuum of their development. We thus begin our exploration of adolescence today by recognizing two dimensions: the changed world in which they live and the existence of substages of **adolescence**. *10–19yrs*

The list of alarming concerns in adolescence includes academic failure and retention, accidents, anorexia, assaultive behavior, criminal activity, cultism, depression, discipline problems, dropouts, drug abuse, homicides, incest, prostitution, runaways, school absenteeism, suicide, teenage pregnancy, vandalism, and the contraction of sexually transmitted diseases. Clearly, all of these concerns merit our attention and study, but an extensive examination of them is beyond the scope of this text. In addition, we must remind ourselves that these problems often occur in conjunction—and are not limited to only one stage of adolescence.

The Adolescent's Changing World   The world of today's adolescents is markedly different from the one their parents experienced at the same age. Technological changes, a multiplicity of social options and values, the media's intrusion and influence, and the blurring of the lines separating adults and children are features of the contemporary American landscape that influence all Americans regardless of age.[32] As the authors of *How to Survive Your Adolescent's Adolescence* point out vividly, today's adolescents confront challenges unknown to their parents and most of their teachers when they were growing up:

> Do we grasp what it means for kids today to be able to buy marijuana or cocaine or heroin at school or in their neighborhood hangouts just as easily as we purchase a loaf of bread at the store? Can we relate to the nonchalance of the thirteen-year-old who knows his best friend overdosed on PCP? . . . Teenagers today have a drastically different set of sexual values and a greater amount of sexual knowledge than we did when we were teens. . . .[33]

To promote a positive and healthy passage through adolescence, then, we must consider today's adolescents within the context of their changed world.

Stages of Adolescence   An increasing number of psychologists believe that adolescence contains two distinct stages: an early period covering the ages of 10–12 through the ages of 14–16, and a late period from approximately 15–16 through 19. While a continuity exists in each individual's life, the psychosocial issues of adolescence—coping with change and seeking identity—vary in form and importance as individuals progress through the transition from childhood to adulthood. In early adolescence changes are multiple and rapid, peers are paramount, and vulnerabilities are high; whereas in late adolescence a quest for personal meaning supersedes the regard of peers, moving one toward the establishment of a feeling of efficacy and a more integrated sense of identity.

In Erik Erikson's model of the eight stages of man identity versus role diffusion is the psychosocial crisis for the adolescent years. While the quest for identity is a key psychosocial issue for both early and late adolescence, many believe that Erikson's identity vs. role diffusion stage fits best for early adolescence. During this time, young adolescents, using their new thinking abilities, begin integrating a clearer sense of identity. Erikson's role diffusion refers to the variety of roles that adolescents have available to them.

The most important psychosocial tasks of early adolescence are developing self-acceptance, strategies for coping with rapid changes, and positive relations with peers.

According to Erikson's theory, when adolescents do identify themselves with a group, with a school, or with a cause, their sense of fidelity—the "virtue" of this stage—is clear and strong. At this stage adolescents are loyal and committed, sometimes to people or ideas that may dismay or alarm their parents, sometimes to high ideals and dreams.

The hazard of this stage, according to Erikson, is being overwhelmed by the options and roles open to them. Some may respond by overidentifying with other people, developing crushes, and losing a sense of themselves in their imitation of others. Still other young people may respond by doing nothing, making no decisions or commitments, or dropping out of school.

Developments during Early Adolescence

Young people in early adolescence are especially vulnerable to a full range of life stresses because they mature more quickly physically than they do cognitively or socially. In the United States the average age of menarche has dropped from 16 years of age 150 years ago to 12½ today, with a similar trend in boys' reproductive maturity. This fact, coupled with the freedom given to young people in our society, places early adolescents in positions where they "are able to, and do, make many fateful decisions that affect the entire life course, even though they are immature in cognitive development, knowledge, and social experience."[34]

Coping with Change   Young adolescents have a paramount need to cope with physical, cognitive, and emotional changes that occur concurrently and at a rapid pace. Contributing to some of the confusion caused by this state of transition is the fact that their friends are no longer predictably the same either, since they too are undergoing dramatic changes. Further, young adolescents ascend to a new level of freedom and independence in school and at home, where they have substantially more control over their time and activities than during their childhood years. Adjusting to new situations at any age is challenging, but the multiple transitions that confront students in their middle school years magnify the problem.

The newness of so many features in their lives and the confusion or insecurity caused by the pace of personal change contribute to adolescents' drive to be accepted by their peers. Looking outward rather than inward, they latch onto superficial behaviors that seem to guarantee them a place in their peer group. Thus, wearing the right clothes in the right way, using the current slang correctly, and presenting the physical image that's valued (i.e., the "in" posture, weight, walk, gestures, complexion, hairstyle, and makeup) become issues of concern and ways that young adolescents seek acceptance and security.

Relating to Self and Others   Two interesting consequences that stem from new cognitive abilities and the stress of adjusting to change are what David Elkind refers to as the "imaginary audience" and the "personal fable." In his book *All Grown Up and No Place to Go,* he explains the concept of the imaginary audience as the belief that others are preoccupied with one's appearance and behavior.[35] Though there is a real basis for their concern, since adolescents can reject each other cruelly and unfairly simply on the basis of impressions, to believe that others are always watching and thinking about them, noticing their mistakes and sources of embarrassment, is a distortion of reality.

Elkind describes the personal fable concept as adolescents' belief that they are somehow special or immortal and not subject to the laws of nature. This too could be regarded as a means of adjusting to change, since having unique powers is one way to gain a sense of security amidst a confusing array of changes and choices. The sense of omnipotence may also result from the exhilaration that comes with the discovery that they can make their own life-changing decisions. Not surprisingly, the concept of personal fable may well explain why adolescents participate in behaviors that risk life and limb, such as driving too fast and recklessly, or why they engage in odds-defying behaviors that lead to pregnancy and drug addiction.

Developments during Late Adolescence

In late adolescence, the period between the ages of 15–16 and 19 years, the quest for identity shifts from others to self. Eliot Wigginton, a high school teacher and author, writes about the relationship between the first and second stages of adolescence: "Even though the early needs [for affection, esteem, security, recognition, and belonging] are never completely outgrown by any of us, the extent to which the needs of the second phase can emerge and be satisfied depends largely on the extent to which those of the first have been dealt with. The need that bridges both phases is self-importance."[36] Without that sense of self-importance, the move to the identity issues of the second stage is hampered.

Seeking Identity   Young people continue to work on strengthening their sense of identity in late adolescence, but as they do so they draw less on the reactions of their peers and more on their own regard for what matters. During this stage, the needs of the adolescent are best met by allowing them "to do things of importance—to do real work of real consequence in the real world."[37] Wigginton complains that we force late adolescents to remain in early adolescence by applying unneeded restrictions and direction that are more appropriate in the earlier stage. Instead, we need to grant the older adolescent opportunities to make significant contributions, respecting their new abilities to handle responsibilities and to think and work independently. To do otherwise is to risk their experiencing school and life as meaningless and to turn instead to self-destructive escape activities.

Achieving Independence   While young people in late adolescence possess an array of interests, talents, and goals in life, they share a desire to achieve independence. More like adults than children, late adolescents are anxious to use newly acquired strengths, skills, and knowledge to achieve their own purposes. Whether through marriage, parenthood, full-time employment, education beyond high school, or military service, late adolescents are eager to prove to others and to themselves that they are independent.

Many late adolescents gain their independence only after working through a period of conflict with parents, teachers, and other adults. Some late adolescents, for example, are in conflict with their parents over such matters as earning money for clothes and personal expenses, using the family car, dating, and staying out late. As we learned in Chapter 5, however, an alarming number of adolescents express their rebellion against and defiance of parents, authorities, and the law by turning to substance abuse, crime, and other antisocial acts.

Teachers of late adolescents must be aware of their strong need to become independent and must provide them with appropriate ways to express that independence. While occasionally challenging and stressful, helping youth to make the transition between late adolescence and early adulthood can be very rewarding for teachers.

HOW TEACHERS CAN HELP

Because we believe that students and their needs are central to an understanding of teaching, we encourage you to take courses in child and adolescent development as part of your preparation for becoming a teacher. Here we look at how teachers can help from the perspective of the counseling role, paying attention to an all-encompassing quality that teachers who are sensitive counselors have and develop: regard for their students. Teachers who have regard for their students believe in them and encourage them with that belief. Kaoru Yamamoto explains the counseling concept of regard in this way: "Basically, what is sought is not praise, reward, or pity, but *regard*. The former is an accounting for past deeds, while the latter is an acknowledgment of one's personhood and trust in what is and is to come."[38]

The psychologist Rudolph Dreikurs suggested that teachers show their regard for their students through an attitude toward them that he called *encouragement*.[39] He observed that teachers can be quite skilled in criticizing and discouraging students, but that they seem to be awkward in giving students encouragement. Encouragement, according to Dreikurs, is a *belief in* the child, not in what he or she will become, or in what he or she is doing, but in who the child is at that moment and any other. Dreikurs cautioned against an extensive use of praise. "Praise, necessary as it is, must be used with caution or it may lead to a dependency on approval. Overdone, it promotes insecurity as the child becomes frightened at the prospect of not being able to live up to expectations."[40]

The counseling role of teaching is the essential human role. In it, teachers must first strengthen their regard for themselves, confronting the emotional challenges in teaching and growing through them. Then they must show the same quality of regard for their students, tuning their guidance to individual needs. When teachers attend to both, the quality of their lives and their students' lives will be enriched.

Keepers of the Dream

Gloria Marino
Special Needs Teacher
Simon Lake School, Jonathan Law High School
Milford, Connecticut

After 20 years as a special-needs teacher, Gloria Marino says, "It's wonderful. I'm as excited about teaching today as I was when I started. It's so much fun to teach these students."

Gloria teaches language skills to students with severe and moderate mental retardation (IQ scores 38–59) at Jonathan Law High School in Milford, Connecticut. Most of her students, who are now 14 to 20 years old, have been with her since 1985. In 1990, she moved with them from Simon Lake School, also in Milford, to the high school. "That way I get to see their success continue," she says.

Gloria, who earned her bachelor's and master's degrees at Southern Connecticut University, decided to become a special education teacher in college. "For a report in an introductory psychology course, I read an article on special education. Once I got a taste of it, I couldn't get enough."

Applying her knowledge, Gloria introduced a total communication reading program at Simon Lake School. She used a multisensory approach that combined spoken words with gestural signs and printed words on flashcards. Gloria explains, "Conventional pictures and words were too abstract for the children to learn." Most of the eight students who began Gloria's program had difficulty expressing themselves verbally. Five had Down's syndrome, two were totally nonverbal, and one had a hearing impairment. One nonverbal student frequently became aggressive and destructive.

> ## "Some People Had No Hope for Them."

After two years in Gloria's program, five students could read and sign more than 100 words, two could read and sign 90 words, and the hearing-impaired student could read and sign more than 60 words. After four years, her students could express their basic needs and read at the first-grade level. In June 1987, six of eight students in the intermediate special-needs class could read at the fourth-grade level.

At first, parents feared that Gloria's total communication program might encourage their children to depend on signing rather than on spoken communication. Their doubts vanished, however, when, for the first time, their children read aloud to them from books Gloria had created. Gloria even formed a weekly evening class to teach parents the total communication language approach.

"Some people had no hope for them," Gloria says. "But I saw those students grow and blossom and keep their heads up and feel so good about themselves. A teacher can make all the difference in the world."

The total communication reading program Gloria developed is still in use. Gloria's advice to new teachers, in both regular and special-needs classrooms, is the same: "Try new ways of teaching. Don't be afraid to be creative. You can show students books of fruits and vegetables, but take them into a grocery store and let them feel, smell, and taste. That means so much more. That's how they learn."

Addressing Students' Needs

In addition to being sensitive counselors, effective teachers address the needs of their students. As we have seen throughout this chapter, the needs of special students and students at different stages of development are many and varied. Though no single approach is appropriate for meeting such a diverse array of needs, it is important for teachers to individualize instruction as much as conditions will allow. Through the application of such concepts as learning styles, for example, teachers can provide each student with learning experiences appropriate to his or her needs and interests.

Teachers also better serve students by providing assistance in a variety of appropriate ways. To help students whose basic needs are not being met, for example, teachers can help them apply for free breakfast or lunch programs, bring in snacks, or assist them in finding after-school jobs. Furthermore, teachers have the power to establish a safe and supportive classroom climate, to encourage social interaction and acceptance, to contribute to a student's sense of self-esteem, and to offer leadership opportunities and intellectual challenges to those who are self-actualizing.

After-school programs, flexible scheduling for working parents, day-care facilities in the workplace, and high-quality, low-cost, extended day care are some of the solutions being explored to reduce the number of latchkey children. Also, many parents and teachers are teaching children life-survival skills (i.e., how to answer the telephone or door when no adult is home) so that they will have a greater sense of control and confidence when they are on their own.

Teachers can ease the stress of growing up too fast by deemphasizing grades and tests, by incorporating enjoyable activities into the daily schedule, and by sharing a positive attitude and good sense of humor with their students. A relaxed and supportive classroom climate can provide a haven for students who are under too much pressure at home. For children who seem especially hurried, teachers can be available to calm, reassure, and support them. Being accessible to students and having time to listen to their concerns takes some planning in the full schedule of the school day, but teachers can incorporate a visiting period at the beginning of the school day or breaks during the day to accommodate these needs. They can join students during lunch and recess periods or make appointments with individual students they are concerned about.

Understanding Developmental Stages

Teachers at all levels, from preschool through college, can better serve and teach their students by understanding some of the basic developmental issues and related areas of concern. For example, what can teachers do to help children develop competence? First, teachers need to be attuned to the importance of their students' struggles to avoid feeling inferior and incompetent. One effective way to directly promote a sense of competence in students is providing a climate in which children are so secure that they will risk making mistakes. Another way is assigning work that children can perform successfully while still being challenged. Praising more than criticizing, taking students and their work seriously, respecting their dignity, and encouraging them by expressing genuine belief in them are sound teaching practices.

Teachers can also focus directly on promoting students' sense of self-esteem by planning activities that boost morale. Games that require students to compliment each other, certificates awarded for particularly fine work, and bulletin boards and interviews devoted to "student of the week" are a few examples of exercises that teachers can use to enhance students' self-concepts.

School spirit, opportunities to participate actively in school life in and out of the classroom, and practical problem-solving skills all contribute to students' self-esteem and social adjustment. By addressing students' needs and understanding their developmental stages, and by taking preventive action or intervening when necessary, teachers can help provide optimum conditions for all children to succeed.

Teachers can promote a sense of industry and competence by providing opportunities for elementary school students to do projects of their own—to compose stories and poems, create and perform dramas, build models of historical sites, prepare science experiments, photograph and edit films, design and use computer programs, and plan and produce art pieces. In addition, teachers can give students a greater sense of importance by arranging for older students to assist younger ones in tutoring situations or by having their class adopt a younger class. For the children, a sense of competence is gained by helping those less competent and by assuming responsibilities.

Teachers who work with adolescents can better appreciate the young adolescent's experience if they recall their own feelings when they encounter a major life change, such as a geographical move, a new position at work, or a status change, such as marriage, parenthood, or divorce. In both cases—youths going through adolescence and adults encountering new experiences—individuals must cope with change, concern themselves with impression management, and establish an identity in a new situation. To recall their own feelings related to change may help adults be more respectful, sympathetic, and helpful in their interactions with young adolescents.

Taking Preventive Action

Those who teach children and youths must be prepared on occasion to intervene and take preventive action. Young people in adolescence are especially vulnerable to life stresses because they are maturing more quickly physically than they are cognitively or socially. To help prevent the problems that place young people at risk, an energetic, creative, and multifaceted approach is recommended. On a practical, day-to-day basis, teachers can provide a structured classroom environment where students feel secure, as well as have opportunities for discussion about values, morals, consequences, preferences, and so on. You can guide students to practice problem-solving skills and learn methods of avoiding unwanted activities without losing face or alienating others. In addition, you can gather and convey current information on subjects of special concern to students. On a broader scale, groups and individuals in all sectors of our society—businesses, schools, churches, and government agencies—need to join in the effort to seek solutions to the damaging problems that affect too many of our young people.

In the Teacher's Resource Guide at the end of this book, "Resources for Meeting the Challenges of Teaching At-Risk and Exceptional Students" lists organizations, publications, video productions, and telephone hotlines that are good sources of information on the problems adolescents may encounter. On the following pages, we discuss the important role teachers can play in responding to four specific problems of adolescence: drug abuse, teenage pregnancy, dropping out of school, and suicide.

Preventing Drug Abuse   Adolescents' use of drugs varies from community to community and year to year, but overall it is disturbingly high. A wide range of mind-altering substances is used commonly by adolescents, from the easily accessible glue, liquid correction fluid, and felt marker, to alcohol, tobacco, marijuana, amphetamines, and cocaine.[41] Parents and teachers rightly fear the use and abuse of drugs because of the risk of addiction and overdosing, but also because of the possibility that their use could lead to related problems such as teenage pregnancy, depression, suicide, automobile accidents, criminal activity, dropping out, and, indeed, the full range of adolescent problems noted earlier. Especially frightening is the possibility of teens being exposed to AIDS through the sharing of contaminated needles or sexual intercourse.

Teachers are in an ideal position to note unusual behavior in their students because they are around them for considerable periods of time. In addition, teachers who gain their students' respect are often entrusted with personal confidences and thus obtain information about drug problems directly from the students or their friends.

What specifically can teachers do? In a 1985 essay, David Hamburg of the Carnegie Corporation, gives sound guidance for the development of prevention programs.[42] First, "prevention through education for health must be actively explored."[43] Second, rather than pointing to long-term health hazards, adults need to show adolescents the short-term risks of drug use so that they can better resist the apparent attractions of the drug culture. Third, Hamburg emphasizes the need to have a network approach to the problem, involving parents, the schools, and the whole community.[44]

One drug prevention program, Texans' War on Drugs, uses the network strategy Hamburg describes. Especially important in this program is the youth contingent, based on the knowledge that youths listen to and influence one another both negatively and positively: "Young people who have a history of drug involvement tell us that the initial reason for experimentation was so their friends would not forsake them. . . . Part of the answer to keeping straight kids straight is to provide a straight or drug-free group to which they can belong."[45]

Teachers can be helpful in detecting problems and in helping to set up drug prevention programs in their schools. As a future teacher, prepare yourself to assist in the prevention process by becoming informed about drugs and their effects on your students, by learning about the drug activity in your community, and by discovering the programs and resources available to you and your students.

Preventing Teenage Pregnancy   Teenage pregnancy has been increasing in the last decade. Elkind tells us that the number of sexually active teenage girls has tripled over the last two decades.[46] The statistics regarding teenage pregnancy in America reported in the 1986 Annual Report of the Carnegie Corporation should concern all teachers: (1) the teenage pregnancy rate for white Americans is twice as high as that of any other industrialized country, (2) the rate for African Americans is twice as high as that of whites; and (3) though the pregnancy rate has declined for American girls over 14, it has increased for those younger.[47] The problem is a dramatic and significant one simply in terms of the young girls and boys whose lives are affected, but it reaches alarming proportions when we consider the consequences for the children of these children.

Experts recognize the seriousness of the problem, but they see no simple solutions for preventing teen pregnancies. Sex education and the availability of contraceptives have not markedly reduced teen pregnancies. One author refers to this fact as "one of the most puzzling aspects surrounding teenage pregnancy."[48] One possible explanation may be that teenagers are influenced by current disputes between right-to-life supporters and those who support contraception and abortion rights. Another sad explanation is offered by Marian Wright Edelman, the president of the Children's Defense Fund, who observes that because of poverty, school failure, and disrupted home lives some young women are very much in need of love.[49] Their low self-esteem causes them to seek love in any form, even a casual sexual encounter. Even more profound is the love they expect to gain from the child they will bear.

Each ethnic group has its own attitudes and problems. For example, teenage pregnancy among African Americans may be due to the dearth of marriageable males who can support a family, which is related to the high unemployment rate for African Americans, which, in turn, may relate to the lack of educational equity. In addition to recognizing the complexity of the teenage pregnancy problem, Edelman stressed the need to avoid turning the work toward solutions into an arena for the debate over abortion. Too often, efforts to deal with the teen pregnancy problem have bogged down in angry religious and ethical arguments.

Researchers studying teenage pregnancy stress the importance of not overlooking the ways that young men contribute to the problem, especially through their attitudes toward sexual activity. The following findings of a leading researcher in the field, Joy Dryfoos, make this need obvious:

- Premarital sex is a norm for American male adolescents; in some communities, the average age of first sexual intercourse is 12 years old.
- More than half of first sexual acts for boys were without benefit of contraception. . . .
- Peers exert a heavy influence on boys to lose their virginity.
- Parents have more difficulty talking with their sons about sex than with their daughters.
- Males are more ignorant about sexuality, contraception, and pregnancy than females. . . .
- There are more than 16 million young men in the U.S. ages 14–21, of whom 10 million are sexually active.[50]

In a majority of communities, information and courses on sex education are regarded as appropriate responses to the epidemic of teenage pregnancies. In addition, elementary teachers, especially in first and second grade, are called on to pay particular attention to disadvantaged girls in their classes to see that they gain the basic skills of reading, writing, and computing, so that they will have options other than parenting in their teen years. Finally, pregnant teenagers need to be encouraged to continue their education, to get prenatal care, and to learn parenting skills through classes provided by the school or community.

Helping to Keep Kids in School   A few startling statistics: "Nationally, one in four students does not graduate from high school";[51] boredom was the most frequently given reason for dropping out;[52] and 85–90 percent of the prisoners in the United States are school dropouts.[53] Less surprising is the fact that dropouts are "disproportionately from poor, urban, and minority backgrounds, [and] have a history of failure in school and a low opinion of themselves."[54] In their report published by the National Coalition of Advocates for Students, Harold Howe II and Marian Wright Edelman warn that the United States cannot afford to lose "the talents of millions of children who happen to be born different by virtue of race, language, sex, or income status. Nor can it ignore, under the pretense of educational excellence, the unfinished national task of offering every child . . . a fair chance to learn and become a self-sufficient citizen."[55]

As with drug abuse and teenage pregnancy, the dropout problem has no single quick solution. Similarly, a multifaceted approach to dealing with the problem is required, since the causes of dropping out are variable and compounded. Teachers can contribute to the effort by learning about dropout prevention programs in their communities and the options available to them for helping to redirect their students who are at risk for dropping out.

Preventing Suicide   While still relatively rare, suicide needs to be a major concern for all who care about today's young people. Even though the number of students affected is relatively low, we discuss suicide here because of its seriousness and because when these tragedies do occur, teachers often realize that they overlooked signs of distress and wish that they had intervened in some way.

In his book *The Urge to Die,* psychiatrist Peter Giovacchini explains that there is no set of clues, no formula for recognizing incipient suicides.[56] He does, however, offer some broad categories of behaviors and life events that can precede suicides and some guidance for responding to those who may be suicidal.

1. Take all talk of suicide seriously. Often the talk is a cry for help. Not all youths who plan to commit suicide tell others, but some do.
2. Be alert if you note a dramatic mood swing. It is not uncommon for adolescents to experience a drastic shift in mood—often from despair to exhilaration—shortly before attempting suicide.
3. Changes in an adolescent's environment that force changes on the adolescent are worth noting. The most common traumatic changes are separation, disillusionment, and adult insensitivity.[57]

Of special concern is the occurrence of multiple suicides that result from suicide pacts, imitative behavior, or the influence of role models. What should be done at such times? People in the community—parents, teachers, school administrators, therapists, religious leaders, and other young people—need to be alert to the potential for additional suicides and should take preventive action. Group counseling sessions conducted by therapists and psychologists trained in suicide prevention should be arranged. Efforts should also be made to educate parents, teachers, and students in the signs and appropriate treatment of people who show suicidal tendencies. As general preventive measures, creative problem-solving strategies and opportunities for mainstreaming self-esteem should be stressed.

In addition, difficult questions should be asked. Are students encouraged in school and at home to make decisions for themselves? Are they recognized and valued for who they are? Did the use of drugs contribute to the suicides? Are there groups of adolescents or individuals who are rejected by their peers, families, or the community as a whole? Do adolescents in general feel valued by the community? In what ways are adolescents aided in their quest for identity? Are older adolescents being frustrated by treatment more appropriate for early adolescents and thereby kept from experiencing their own importance and significance? The answers to these questions should help you as a teacher to guide youths away from self-destructive behavior and toward meaningful lives.

SUMMARY

In this chapter we sought a better understanding of students, the focus of our teaching. We began by looking at how students differ from one another in the following areas: family life, gender and sex role socialization, intelligence, cognitive development, and learning styles.

Next, we examined characteristics of exceptional learners: handicapped students, gifted and talented students, and linguistically challenged students. We concluded this section by urging teachers to be cautious in labeling exceptional students.

In the next section, we regarded students from a developmental perspective and looked at the major psychosocial issues and areas of concern during childhood and adolescence. The section on elementary school students highlighted their desire to gain a sense of competence through industrious behavior. Older students were then discussed, first in terms of the challenges they face during the two stages of adolescence and then in terms of the psychosocial issues of coping with change and seeking identity in early and late adolescence.

We concluded the chapter with a discussion of how teachers can assist students in their growth and development and help prevent common problems of childhood and adolescence. Specifically, we looked at the importance of addressing students' needs, understanding the developmental stages through which students grow, and taking preventive action against drug abuse, teenage pregnancy, dropping out, and suicide.

KEY CONCEPTS AND TERMS

microcultural groups, 298
hierarchy of needs, 301
sex role stereotyping, 302
intelligence, 303
IQ, 304
cognitive development, 305
preoperational stage, 305
concrete operations stage, 305
formal operations stage, 305

multiple intelligences, 305
learning style, 306
exceptional learners, 310
handicapped students, 311
gifted and talented, 312
linguistically challenged students, 312
psychosocial crisis, 314
childhood, 314
adolescence, 317

ANSWER KEY FOR CONSIDER THIS . . .

"How Do Children View Stressful Events?"

Children represented in sample: U.S.A.—367 Phoenix children in fourth, fifth, sixth grades; Japan—248 Tokyo children in fourth, fifth, sixth grades. The U.S.A. ranking is first followed by a slash and then the Japanese ranking: Losing my mother or father—*1 / 1*; Going blind—*2 / 6*; Being kept in the same grade next year—*3 / 2*; Wetting pants in class—*4 / 4*; Hearing my parents quarrel and fight—*5 / 9*; Being caught stealing something—*6 / 4*; Telling the truth, but no one believing me—*7 / 4*; Receiving a poor report card—*8 / 8*; Being sent to the principal's office—*9 / 7*; Going to a hospital for an operation—*10 / 12*; Getting lost in some strange place—*11 / 16*; Being laughed at in front of the class—*12 / 10*; Moving to a new school—*13 / 13*; Having a scary dream—*14 / 14*; Not making a perfect score (100) on a test—*15 / 15*; Being picked last on a team—*16 / 11*; Losing in any game or sport—*17 / 17*; Going to a dentist—*18 / 18*; Getting up in front of the class to give a report—*19 / 19*; Having a new baby sister or brother—*20 / 20*. *Source:* Karou Yamamoto. Used with permission.

DISCUSSION QUESTIONS

1. What are the positive influences a student's family life can have on his or her performance in school? Negative influences?
2. To what extent are children and young people in your community content, stressed, or overindulged? What advice would you give their parents and teachers?
3. Why is the labeling and diagnosing of exceptional students a problem?
4. Compare and contrast Piaget's and Erikson's developmental stages. How useful are they to teachers?
5. Do the two stages of adolescence fit with your own experience of those years and your observations of young people today? Explain.
6. Which of the areas of concern discussed in this chapter do you consider to be most important in your community? Childhood stress, drug abuse, teenage pregnancy, dropping out, or suicide? Which do you believe is most prevalent?

APPLICATION ACTIVITIES

1. Contact a high school teacher or guidance counselor and ask him or her to bring into your class a group of students who have been at risk of dropping out of school. Interview the students to determine what factors might have caused them to consider dropping out. What factors convinced them to stay in school?
2. Survey several other education classes, using the Yamamoto questionnaire, to see if college students are able to predict children's perceptions of the stressfulness of the 20 life events.
3. Have everyone in the class write a description of a student in early adolescence and one in late adolescence, drawing on personal memories and adding specific experiences where possible. Analyze the set of descriptions in terms of the psychosocial issues and concerns present in each stage.
4. Invite several school counselors from the elementary and secondary school levels to your class. Have them discuss the most frequent student needs they encounter and suggest ways that teachers can help students with those needs.

FIELD EXPERIENCES

1. Visit an agency in your community that offers substance abuse counseling, remedial tutoring, training in job employment skills, or family planning and parenting information to at-risk youth. Ask a staff member to explain the services that are offered. Report your findings to the rest of your class.
2. Observe and interview a student in the age group you wish to teach to conduct a brief case study that focuses on common developmental tasks for that age group and the areas of individual differences highlighted in this chapter. Then prepare a written portrait of the student.
3. Visit a school at the level you plan to teach. Interview the counselor, asking questions about the problems that bring students to the counselor most often. If possible, shadow the counselor for a day.
4. Attend an extracurricular event such as a high school basketball game or Little League soccer game. Observe the students on the field as well as any students watching the players. Notice the differences between the students in terms of their physical appearance, clothing and hairstyles, athletic abilities, social skills, and evidence of personal interests and confidence. Share your observations in class.

SUGGESTED READINGS

Brendtro, Larry K., Martin Brokenleg, and Steve Van Bockern. *Reclaiming Youth at Risk: Our Hope for the Future.* Bloomington, Ind.: National Educational Service, 1990. *A unique book that draws on the wisdom of Native Americans and suggests how to create environments in which children can grow.*

Elkind, David. *Hurried Child: Growing Up Too Fast Too Soon.* Reading, Mass.: Addison-Wesley, 1989. *An engaging, thought-provoking discussion of how parents push their children to achieve.*

The Forgotten Half: Pathways to Success for America's Youth and Young Families, Final Report. Washington, D.C.: The William T. Grant Commission on Work, Family and Citizenship, 1988. *An authoritative overview of the problems confronting America's youth. Contains extensive data, descriptions of exemplary programs, and resources.*

Guild, Pat Burke and Stephen Garger. *Marching to Different Drummers.* Alexandria, Va.: Association of Supervision and Curriculum Development, 1985. *Presents clear explanations of several approaches to instruction based on students' learning styles.*

"Helping Youngsters Cope with Life." *Educational Leadership* 45 (March 1988): 3–75. *This issue (18 articles) of the journal of the Association for Supervision and Curriculum Development is on life skills for coping with substance abuse, smoking, etc.*

Hicks, Barbara Barrett. *Youth Suicide: A Comprehensive Manual for Prevention and Intervention.* Bloomington, Ind.: National Educational Service, 1990. *An excellent guide for all professionals interested in preventing suicide among youth.*

Kershner, Keith M. and John A. Connolly, eds. *At-Risk Students and School Restructuring.* Philadelphia, Pa.: Research for Better Schools, 1991. *A comprehensive set of strategies for meeting the learning needs of at-risk students.*

Sander, Daryl. *Focus on Teens in Trouble: A Reference Handbook.* Santa Barbara, Calif.: ABC–CLIO, 1991. *Discusses gangs and violence, substance abuse, runaways, adolescent crime, and the juvenile justice system. Lists books, films, videos, organizations, agencies, etc.*

Yamamoto, Kaoru, ed. *The Child and His Image: Self-Concept in the Early Years.* Boston: Houghton Mifflin, 1972. *An exploration of self-concept in the early years.*

TEACHERS . . .

What strategies do you use for motivating students and convincing them that learning can make a positive difference in their lives?

What other challenges do you face as a teacher?

To motivate an unmotivated class, I would find out their interests through talking and brainstorming. We would discuss the objectives or goals we had to accomplish and I would let them help decide what activities we could use to satisfy the goals. I would convince them that learning can make a positive difference in their lives by actually letting them accomplish activities that are meaningful and useful to them. This is why I would let them share in the decision-making process.

—June L. Wilhoit
Chase Street Elementary School, Athens, Georgia

At the beginning of the school year I always make my students aware of my grading system. I grade most assignments with a participation grade. All classwork and homework completed, even if errors are present, are worth a grade of 100 percent. Partially completed assignments are graded as a percentage of completeness. Tests are graded in the standard way, the percent correct. Projects, reports and published pieces are graded holistically with a focus on positive responses and questions to elicit more information.

Once students see that I grade in exactly that manner, they are willing to try, for they do not fear the dreaded F or the deadly teacher comment. I devised my system when I began working with inner-city high school students who had mainly given up because their attempts to do their work always ended up in failure because of errors. I felt that if I would give a concrete value to effort, the positive effects of being rewarded for simply trying might shift the students into a more positive mindset. This method of grading seems to reinforce the self-motivated and parent-motivated students and causes most of the nonmotivated students to realize they *can* succeed if they try.

—Susan S. Reid
Chattanooga High School, Chattanooga, Tennessee

I always maintain a sense of calm, keep my humor, and stay flexible. Working with children is unpredictable, and although I continue to achieve specific goals academically with the class, my daily routine is adaptable to their needs. Each day I enter the class overprepared, with more lessons and activities than time permits. That way if one plan is not effective, I can immediately use another.

ON TEACHING

My main challenge in teaching 35 kindergarteners is to give each child the individual time and attention necessary to adequately teach them. Each day I spend at least two minutes with each child, and I read to them or use number or alphabet flashcards. This year I have also implemented eighth-grade "Big Brothers/ Big Sisters" once a week and the cross-age tutoring has been quite successful.

—Sherry Reeve
Acacia Academy, West Covina, California

Having pride in oneself and in one's work is something I try to stress with my students. I praise them for any worthwhile contribution they make to the class. I also try to acknowledge even the smallest effort made by each student. Children need to feel pride in themselves so they can instill pride in others. They also need to learn that both hard work and perseverance are important to their future success as individuals and to the well-being of our country as a whole.

—Rose Ann Blaschke
Vivian Elementary School, Lakewood, Colorado

Each day is a challenge emotionally, physically, and mentally. The greatest concerns I deal with have to do with the expanding curriculum and the lack of student preparation. Our students come from less prepared and disciplined homes, unstable emotional situations, and an overly stimulated audiovisual world.

What can I do as a teacher to meet these challenges? Learning the technology becomes secondary to the acceptance and security each child needs from me. A touch, a laugh, a listening ear to boost self-esteem is all I can give to some; skills to deal with an ever-changing complex society may help others.

—Charlotte McDonald
Canyon Rim Elementary School, Salt Lake City, Utah

The biggest challenge I face as a teacher is trying to reach every student. Teachers often have a grandiose idea that every student will make progress while in their classrooms. In reality this does not happen and it is hard to deal with. To create a motivating environment and to spend the time to enable each student to succeed is a wonderful challenge that never ends.

—Amy Orcutt
Green Gables Elementary School, Jefferson County, Colorado

Dynamics of Classroom Life

Smoothly running classrooms whose students are highly involved in learning activities and which are free from disruption and chronic misbehavior are not accidental.

Edmund T. Emmer, Carolyn M. Evertson, Julie P. Sanford, Barbara S. Clements, and Murray E. Worsham
Classroom Management for Secondary Teachers

Y ou enter the classroom at the scheduled time, ready to do your first "miniteaching," as your professor calls it. Immediately, you're struck by the presence of students. When you met with the teacher earlier in the week the room was a quiet place in which to discuss your lesson plan. Now that it is filled with moving, energetic bodies, you feel a bit unnerved.

You feel like a foreigner in a strange culture and envy the students for their apparent nonchalance. They seem so comfortable—almost smug—knowing exactly how to behave and what to expect. In contrast, you feel awkward and wonder if you'll have enough confidence to stay in control of the group and do a decent job with the miniteaching. No one ever told you teaching would be like this! The theories you learned at the university and the carefully prepared and practiced lessons suddenly seem lifeless and irrelevant in this dynamic setting.

From this new and uneasy perspective, you wish you knew more about the dynamics of classroom life. You'd like to know more about how classrooms are organized, how students are grouped, and how classroom activities are structured. Realizing that in a minute or two you'll begin speaking to these students, you also wish you had a grasp of group dynamics. Now you know what your instructors meant when they referred to teaching as a live performance in a dynamic setting. You're about to discover what being a classroom teacher is all about.

FOCUS QUESTIONS

1. What are the environmental factors that affect the culture of the classroom?
2. How does the structure of activity affect classroom life?
3. What aspects of group dynamics affect the culture of the classroom?
4. How can teachers develop effective classroom management?
5. What are the characteristics of effective teaching?

Making the transition between the study of teaching and actual teaching can be a challenge. A unit plan or course design that is perfect in theory could fail completely in the classroom because of its inappropriateness for a particular group of students or its being presented at the wrong time in terms of the group's development or the school's schedule of vacations. The more teachers know about "the types of classroom conditions and student behaviors that provide good learning environments," the better prepared they will be to make the transition smoothly.[1]

To help you better understand these conditions and behaviors, we look first at the culture of the classroom and then discuss how theories of group dynamics can help you function more effectively in this culture. Then, we discuss classroom management and other essential teaching skills and the characteristics of effective teachers.

WHAT TO EXPECT

A beginning teacher has spent many years in classrooms, and may imagine that he or she knows what to expect as a teacher. However, adjusting to the role of being solely responsible for student learning in the classroom setting can be difficult. Evidence indicates that for many teachers it is not easy to "learn the ropes."

One study of beginning elementary teachers revealed that they commonly experience "reality shock", since the real world of the students violates so many of the teachers' expectations.[2] It may take time to adjust to the fact that some students can be rude, lazy, hostile, or unreceptive to adult guidance. Depending upon your personality, you may experience a degree of "psychological buffeting"—attempts by students to weaken the teacher's self-esteem through such behaviors as complaining that the class is boring, failing to cooperate, or being critical of the class in general.[3] Estelle Fuchs found that some teachers experience symptoms similar to those anthropologists have found in people suffering from "culture shock."[4]

Of course, no two individuals experience the early days of teaching in quite the same way. The following comments of beginning teachers, however, are common:

> I'm overwhelmed at the amount of work. My internship was nothing. Now, so many needs to meet and no matter what, you can't meet all their needs.

> Teaching itself is what I expected; it was the other stuff, however. I'm 40 percent teacher and 60 percent social worker. I didn't expect that. So many kids, even ones from middle-class families, come with no values. They don't sit down when asked, show respect, and so on.

While it is impossible to predict exactly what the experience of beginning to teach will be like for you, remember that anxiety is normal for anyone just entering a profession. As you acquire the knowledge and skills necessary to master the challenges of teaching, you will begin to enjoy teaching's many rewards.

I went into the classroom with some confidence and left with lots of confidence. I felt good about what was going on. I established a comfortable rapport with the kids and was more relaxed. Each week I grew more confident. When you first go in you are not sure how you'll do. When you know you are doing o.k., your confidence improves.

THE CULTURE OF THE CLASSROOM

As we learned in Chapter 5, one definition of *culture* is the way of life common to a group of people. In much the same way, each classroom develops its own culture. The culture of a classroom is determined by the manner in which teachers and students participate in common activities.

The activities that teachers and students engage in are influenced by several factors. "There are characteristics of the physical milieu (building, materials, resources, etc.) and social milieu (norms, rules, expectations, grouping, climate, distribution of power, accountability structure) that affect life in . . . classroom[s]."[5] Anita Woolfolk and Charles Galloway have identified the following six "interdependent and interacting sources of influence" on classroom culture:

1. The activity format, procedure, or delivery system for instruction
2. The academic content itself
3. The physical, spatial, and temporal constraints of the particular classroom
4. The accountability structure: how, when, where, against what standards, and by whom student responses (oral and written) will be evaluated
5. The players in the classroom drama
6. The dynamic interaction among participants, activities, content, materials, etc.[6]

Let us use these six influences on classroom culture to analyze a discussion in a high-school English class of Ralph Waldo Emerson's essay on self-reliance. What is the activity format? A discussion, directed by the teacher. And the academic content? Two or three themes in Emerson's essay and their application to students' lives. What are the physical, spatial, and temporal constraints of the classroom? An arrangement conductive to discussion is a small classroom with chairs and tables set up in a circle, square, or U-shaped pattern so that students can see each other as they talk.

What is the accountability structure that determines how students will be evaluated? Student performances in class discussions are difficult to measure, but teachers can note on their rosters the students who are particularly active, engaged, or insightful in their contributions.

Who are the players in the classroom drama and what are their expectations? In our example of the discussion on Emerson's essay, the students and the teacher are the participants. Expectations are fairly clear: students are supposed to reveal their understanding of the themes in the essay and to engage in critical thinking: the teacher is expected to motivate students to analyze, critique, and evaluate concepts presented in the essay.

What is the dynamic interaction among participants, activities, and content? This question refers to the live dimension of the discussion, which in turn raises more questions: How are the students responding to Emerson's ideas? Are many students participating in the discussion? How interested is the teacher in what is happening? How lively and relevant is the discussion?

How would the lesson change if one of the six aspects of classroom culture was changed? Imagine that the activity format was a lecture instead of a discussion or substitute a test as the accountability structure, and consider how the dynamics of the class would be changed as a result.

Classroom Organization

A factor in the culture of the classroom is **classroom organization**—the way teachers and students are grouped for instruction and the way time is scheduled in the classroom. As explained in Chapter 5, teachers and students are grouped in several ways. At the elementary-school level, the self-contained classroom is the traditional arrangement. The teacher and students remain in the same classroom for the entire day and the teacher teaches all the main subjects. Elementary teachers in self-contained classrooms often organize all the day's activities around a unifying theme.

In contrast, team teaching arrangements divide responsibility for two or more classes, among two or more teachers who specialize in different subject areas, skills, or ability groupings of students.

In less-structured open-space classrooms where open-concept education is practiced, students work independently, with a number of teachers providing individual guidance.

Middle schools and junior and senior high schools typically have departmentalized classrooms. Students study four or five academic subjects taught by teachers who specialize in them and move from classroom to classroom for their lessons. Departmentalized arrangements require a more structured schedule of blocks of time, a series of separate periods lasting 45 to 55 minutes.

The Classroom Environment

However your classroom is organized, you will need to be concerned with the quality of the classroom environment. When you become a teacher, the physical environment you must work in will probably be similar to that of the school where you were educated. However, we encourage you, with the help of your students, to make your surroundings as pleasant as possible. Plants; clean, painted walls; displays of students' work; a comfortable reading or resource area; and a few prints or posters can enhance the quality of teacher-student relationships.

Seating arrangements and the placement of other classroom furniture can do much to shape the classroom environment. While seating by rows may be very appropriate for whole-group instruction or examinations, other arrangements may be more beneficial for other activities. For example, you can enhance small-group activities by moving desks into small clusters in different parts of the room. Figure 11.1 shows the arrangement of a classroom at an exemplary elementary school. The room is designed to encourage students to learn through discovery at learning centers located around the room.

However you design your classroom, take care to ensure that seating arrangements do not reduce the opportunity of some students to learn. For example, students in some classrooms receive more attention if they are seated in the "action zone," the middle front-row seats and seats on the middle aisle.[7] Teachers often stand near this area and unknowingly give students seated there more opportunities to speak. Teachers also may group students by ability to instruct them more effectively. However, such arrangements often have a negative impact on relationships among students because

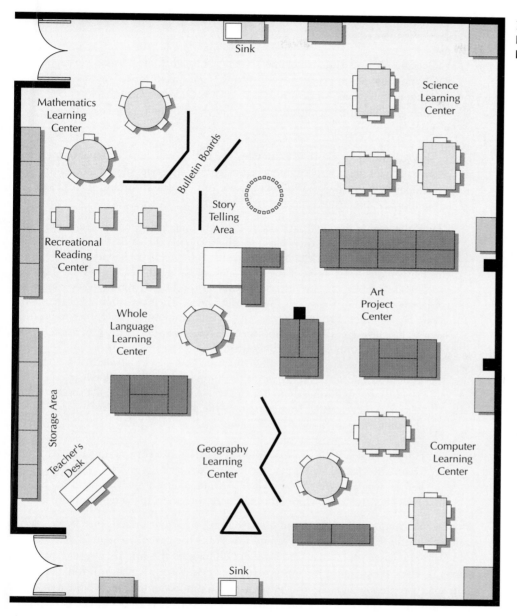

FIGURE 11.1
Learning Centers in an Elementary Classroom

low-ability students who are seated together, for example, may believe they have lower status than other students.

Classroom Climate

Part of the environment of the classroom is **classroom climate**—"the ways in which the people within the classroom interact with each other."[8] Differences in classroom climates are readily apparent: some appear to be relaxed, safe, and even homelike; others suggest businesses, efficiently productive; still others present the impression of armed camps, with teachers and students, or cliques of students, suspicious, aggressive, and defensive in their interactions. The following eight dimensions have been used to describe classroom climates:

- Openness versus Defensiveness
- Confidence versus Fear
- Acceptance versus Rejection
- Belonging versus Alienation
- Trust versus Suspicion

- High Expectations versus Low Expectations
- Order versus Chaos
- Control versus Frustration[9]

The positive qualities of classroom climates are within teachers' spheres of influence and are promoted, consciously or unconsciously, by their styles of communicating and treating students. Consider the following description of a classroom in terms of the preceding climate dimensions:

> The front room is alive with activity. David and Maurice are building a runway with wooden blocks. Darlene, their teacher, sits in the middle of the block pile offering support and assistance. "Beautiful, David. It's going really well. Here, Maurice, use this big one, get some more of the long ones from over there."
>
> David and Maurice are intent on building the longest runway they can make. Carl comes and joins them, but they hardly notice. Their attention is on the task at hand. Shaquan and Ebony occupy a small block building in one corner where they seem to be putting dolls to bed and then waking them up. "This is my hotel," says Ebony. "And it's only for me and my friends."
>
> Maurice pushes a perilously high stack of long blocks slowly across the room toward the runway. Just as it arrives at its destination, it crashes loudly to the floor, and David laughs and rushes up to untangle the wreckage and keep the runway going.
>
> "Teacher," Pete wails. "Someone took my glue."
>
> "Doesn't everyone have a cup?" Marilyn asks.
>
> "Yea, but she dipped in mine."
>
> "Okay, Natika. This is yours. And Pete, there's more if you run out." Changing directions, she asks, "Doesn't glue feel funny on your fingers?"
>
> Pete frowns and says, "It's yukky." Afrinique dips her whole hand in the glue and, watching the thick white drops fall back into the cup, smiles contentedly.[10]

How would you rate this classroom climate using the eight dimensions above? What changes in the teacher's behavior could transform the overall climate?

While teachers influence the classroom climate by the way they regard and treat students, they also shape it by their instructional decisions. David Johnson and Roger Johnson, two researchers in the area of classroom communication and dynamics, delineate three types of interactions promoted by instructional decisions: cooperative or positive interdependence, competitive or negative interdependence, and individualistic or no interdependence.[11] To illustrate the three types, Johnson and Johnson suggest that a group project to measure classroom furniture would promote cooperative interdependence; a race to be the first student to measure the furniture would call for competitive interdependence; and having a student measure the furniture independently would be an example of no interdependence. Johnson and Johnson believe that teachers should use strategies that foster all three forms of interactions, depending upon their instructional goals, but that, ideally, the emphasis should be on furthering cooperative interdependence. As teachers increase their awareness of their influence on classroom climate, they become empowered to create the climates they prefer for themselves and their students.

This dynamic kindergarten class exhibits many of the characteristics of a positive classroom climate. Relations are open and trusting; everyone is accepted and actively engaged; and a sense of order prevails even in an activity format that calls for self-expression.

For development of the classroom group, Schmuck and Schmuck describe their ideal classroom climate as

> one in which the students share high amounts of potential influence—both with one another and with the teacher; where high levels of attraction exist for the group as a whole and between classmates; where norms are supportive for getting academic work done, as well as for maximizing individual differences; where communication is open and featured by dialogue; and where the processes of working and developing together as a group are considered relevant in themselves for study.[12]

How do the classrooms you have experienced or observed compare to their ideal? When you have been in a class with a great deal of cohesiveness and spirit, was the climate similar to the ideal one they describe?

Student Groupings

Classroom culture is also affected by student groupings. In Chapter 10, we explored the unique needs of different groups of students. A widespread method of addressing these needs is to group students on the basis of shared characteristics. Two commonly used approaches are between-class ability grouping (often called tracking) and within-class ability grouping. Between-class grouping is used at the middle and high school levels, and within-class grouping is used at the elementary level.

Students who attend schools where **between-class ability grouping** is practiced are assigned to classes on the basis of ability or achievement (usually determined by scores on standardized tests). Another form of between-class ability grouping, especially at the high school level, is based on students' curricular interests. Many high schools, for example, have a college preparatory track, a vocational track, and a business education track.

Research on between-class ability grouping suggests that, for the most part, it does not contribute to greater achievement.[13] Its supporters nevertheless claim that teachers are better able to meet the needs of students in homogeneous groupings.

EDUCATION
in the
N   E   W   S

Sherman Indian High

Schools in the news include those that are successful in helping at-risk students overcome socioeconomic and cultural barriers to academic achievement. One such school is Sherman Indian High School in Riverside, California, the nation's first college preparatory school for Native Americans. Four hundred students representing 77 tribes of the southwestern United States attend.

Native Americans may be regarded as the least educated ethnic group in the United States. Only 55 percent of children raised on a reservation ever complete high school, and of those only 5 percent go on to college. Experts point to two main sources of this problem: cultural barriers to academic success and the failure of schools to address the particular needs of Native-American students.

The cultural barriers stem not from traditional Indian ways, but from reservation life, which engenders an array of historically entrenched social problems. It is a culture of poverty, and too often a culture of idleness, apathy, and despair. In a climate of few opportunities and low expectations, alcoholism and other forms of addiction claim many lives.

The failure of schools both on and off the reservations also relates to poor opportunity structure and low expectations. Curricula and instruction traditionally focus on remediation and, in the process, often ignore or even attack the culture-based learning styles of Native-American students. A report of the Center for American Indian Studies at Montana State University stated that Native Americans in the United States routinely receive a substandard education.

Sherman Indian High School, an off-reservation boarding school operated by the Federal Bureau of Indian Affairs, is a step toward change. With the help of southern California colleges and universities, educators developed an integrated, nonremedial, college-track curriculum. The program includes opportunities for advanced placement courses and is well equipped with educational support technology. Teachers and staff include Native Americans with a special stake in their students' futures.

What makes Sherman High—as well as other schools with "come-from behind" student populations—successful is the commitment of teachers to excellence. Refusing to lower their expectations for their disadvantaged students, these teachers instill in them the self-confidence to master difficult subjects and the sense of self-worth to have—and to achieve—high ambitions.

Source: CNN news broadcast, May 22, 1990.

Within-class ability grouping is often used for instruction in reading and mathematics within a class, where a teacher instructs students in homogeneous, small groups. Within-class grouping is used widely on the elementary level. Perhaps you can recall learning to read in a small group with a name such as the Eagles, the Redbirds, or the Mustangs. Like tracking, within-class ability grouping can heighten preexisting differences in achievement between groups of students if teachers give high-achieving groups more attention. Also, once students are grouped, they tend not to be regrouped, even when differences in achievement have been reduced.

At best, evidence to support student groupings is mixed. Whether students are grouped on the basis of ability, curricular interests, or handicapping condition, there is a danger that some group labels can evoke negative expectations, causing teachers to "underteach" certain students, and their peers to isolate or reject them. The most serious consequence, of course, is that students so labeled are taught to feel inadequate, inferior, and limited in their options for growth.

The Structure of Activity

Of the eight dimensions of classroom culture mentioned at the beginning of this section, perhaps the most significant is the "activity format, procedure, or delivery system for instruction." In short, what the teacher does and what students do has a powerful influence on the quality of classroom life.

The following excerpt from an essay written by two elementary school teachers captures the rich diversity of activities found in most classrooms.

> Our classrooms are complicated and complex . . . The images that shape our talk about classroom life are of beehives of activity; popcorn poppers, with ideas bouncing off walls; workshop/laboratories where students and teachers engage in serious, purposeful work; tapestries of interwoven lives.[14]

Activity Formats   Perhaps the most common **activity format** in elementary schools consists of students doing seatwork on their own or listening to their teachers and participating in whole-class recitations. In addition, however, students participate in reading groups, games, and discussions; take tests; check work; view films; give reports; and help clean up the classroom.[15]

One of the most important decisions a teacher makes is how to answer the following question: "What activity will enable me to accomplish my instructional goals?" A teacher may choose to emphasize discussion one day and lecture the next. He or she may decide to arrange a class field trip or a visit from a local businessperson or to use a popular television quiz show format to conduct a review rather than a teacher-led drill-and-practice format.

"Jim claims it triples their attention span."

Use of Time   How teachers use time affects both the culture of the classroom and student learning. An important use of time is **allocated time,** the time teachers allocate for instruction in various areas of the curriculum. Teachers vary widely in their instructional use of time. Educational researchers Tom Good and Jere Brophy, for example, report that "some students may receive as much as four times more instructional time in a given subject than other students in the same grade."[16]

Perhaps even more important than the amount of allocated time is the *quality* of use, or how time is actually used. Several researchers have shown that **time on task**— the amount of time students are actively engaged in learning activities—is directly related to learning. As anyone who has ever daydreamed while appearing to pay attention to a teacher can confirm, time on task is difficult to measure. In response to this difficulty, Charles Fisher and his colleagues introduced the concept of **academic learning time**—the amount of time a student spends working on academic tasks with a high level of success (80 percent or higher).[17] Not surprisingly, learning time, like allocated time, varies greatly from classroom to classroom. For example, Fisher found that some second-grade students spend between 3 and 42 minutes a day successfully engaged in reading.[18]

Cooperative Learning   An important use of learning time is **cooperative learning,** which can be integrated into instruction at any level of school. In cooperative arrangements, students work in small groups as teams, teaching each other, sometimes sharing the work, and completing assignments together. A fifth-grade science teacher describes her approach to cooperative learning in the following account:

> I have the class divided into groups of five students and each group works as a team. The job duties are as follows: principle investigator (PI), materials manager (MM), reader, recorder, and reporter. The PI is the leader of the group and helps mediate when problems occur. The PI is the only student that can come to me with questions during the actual procedure. This rule enables me to monitor the groups and also teaches the group to work independently.
>
> Students change job duties within their group each activity and every six weeks students change groups. This plan gives each student the experience of working with different classmates as well as learning the responsibility of group participation through performing the different job duties.

Team Learning is a form of cooperative learning that incorporates competition into the design.[19] Robert Slavin of the Student Team Learning project believes that fair team competition offers students benefits similar to those found in sports competition. In this design a teacher instructs the whole class in one skill (e.g., how to use guide words in a dictionary) and then divides the class into fairly equivalent teams of students with different ability levels. The teams practice and drill together to prepare for a tournamentlike competition using the skill.

The contribution that cooperative learning arrangements can make to the culture of the classroom is expressed by Craig Pearson: "The best rewards for the teacher are those signs that cooperation is becoming second nature with the children. I'm always impressed when a group finishes its work and then, without being told or even asked, goes to help other groups."[20] In addition, cooperative learning is a form of student grouping that can enhance the interpersonal skills of all students. When students from different racial, ethnic, and cultural backgrounds and mainstreamed special needs students all contribute to a common group goal, friendships increase and group members tend to view one another as more equal in status and worth.

GROUP DYNAMICS IN THE CLASSROOM

Cooperative learning is an example of positive group dynamics among students and between students and teacher. Some teachers seem to have a magic touch that gives them easy rapport with individual students, an enjoyable and productive classroom climate, and problem-free interactions with the class as a whole. Are they unusually talented or do they know some strategies for handling classroom groups? In most cases, the teachers have learned basic group dynamics skills for achieving effective and harmonious group interactions. In this section we examine the importance of group dynamics in the classroom, beginning with a look at stages of group development.

Stages of Group Development

Richard Schmuck and Patricia Schmuck, leading theorists in the study of classroom group processes, describe four sequential **stages of group development,** shown in Figure 11.2. Schmuck and Schmuck relate their theory of group development to Erik Erikson's eight-stage theory of human development, discussed in Chapter 10. The first stage in both theories is the establishment of trust, and subsequent stages build on the satisfactory completion of that human and group need. In addition, the Schmucks' theory parallels Erikson's in the belief that development may stop at any stage when the issues of that stage are not resolved. In such a case, the group, like the individual, fails to mature.

During Stage 1 of a class's group development, students are on their best behavior. As Schmuck and Schmuck note, "The first weeks of the class's life are critical times for finding out who one is in relation to the others."[21] Teachers who are aware of this "honeymoon period" use it to their advantage: they discuss and teach classroom rules and procedures, outline their goals, and deliberately set the classroom tone and standards they want.

During Stage 2, teachers seeking to promote group development are advised to encourage student participation and communication and to discourage the formation of cliques. To help detect the subgroup patterns in their classes, teachers can draw on sociometrics, a graphic means of describing the relationships among people in groups. A common sociometric device is a questionnaire to gather data on students' preferences for classmates they would choose to be with for various activities—studying, working on a class project, attending social events—and then charting the information on a diagram, called a **sociogram.** The relationship patterns that emerge indicate which students are sought by their peers, which are isolates, and which are members of subgroups.[22] Teachers can use the information from the sociogram to make new classroom groupings if they choose.

Groups that have met the requirements of the preceding stages move into Stage 3, which lasts for the majority of the expected life of the group—the semester or the school year. Stage 4, the final stage, is described by Schmuck and Schmuck as "the ideal level of maturity . . . when [the group's] norms allow for a variety of individual learning styles to be expressed and accepted, and when the group has the power to change itself toward a more effective state."[23] Classroom groups can arrive at the final cohesive stage more quickly if clear and motivating group goals are set. A class newsletter, dramatic presentations, academic or athletic competitions, fund drives, class trips, and community service work can spur on a group's development.

FIGURE 11.2
Hierarchy of Group Development

Stage 4

- Flexible group norms allow for the expression of a variety of individual learning styles
- The group renews itself and has the power to change toward ever greater cohesion and effectiveness
- Effective and lasting group academic learning takes place

↑

Stage 3

- The group sets common goals and procedures for attaining them, and enters a stage of high productivity
- Group identity increases through a sense of shared history
- Group cohesiveness increases through the processes of evaluation, reevaluation, and conflict resolution
- Conflicts are resolved through discussion, negotiation, compromise, and team effort

↑

Stage 2

- Subgroups or cliques develop, based on members' characteristics, interests, or concerns
- Conflicts tend to arise between subgroups, between individuals and their subgroups, and between subgroups and the teacher or the class as a whole
- Communication patterns develop along with influence patterns concerning task performance and the maintenance of the group

↑

Stage 1

- Individual students seek acceptance by their teacher and peers
- Students develop a sense of inclusion or membership in a group
- Students establish a basic sense of trust in the teacher and in one another

---

Source: Adapted from Richard A. Schmuck and Patricia A. Schmuck, *Group Processes in the Classroom*, 5th ed., pp. 51–62. (Dubuque, Iowa: William C. Brown, 1988).

FIVE-MINUTE FOCUS   Recall the group projects that you participated in during your school career. Analyze the success or failure of one group project in terms of the stages of group development described in Figure 11.2. Date your journal entry and write for five minutes.

Classroom Norms and Sanctions

An important aspect of group life is the establishment of norms and sanctions. People in groups behave according to **norms,** the stated or unstated expectations of behavior that group members agree to follow. Expectations of appropriate school attire, procedures for handing in homework, and values such as disapproval of cheating are examples of school norms. **Sanctions** are the rewards and punishments a group develops to encourage members to behave in desired ways. Sanctions may be formal (e.g., detention or public recognition) or informal (e.g., the negative or positive comments students direct at one another).

According to Schmuck and Schmuck, norms may also be static or dynamic. A norm is static if group members adhere to it without much pressure being applied; it is dynamic if it requires occasional enforcement. Figure 11.3 illustrates the types of classroom norms and gives several examples.

Effective teachers recognize and act upon a group's need for clear norms and sanctions. Research on classroom management shows that effective teachers establish their expectations early and clearly and encourage students' acceptance of norms by positively reinforcing appropriate behavior.

Classroom groups with shared norms have a sense of cohesiveness or spirit and work together like a team or family. Others are attracted to such a group—its members, its interests and goals, and its prestige.[24]

	Formal	*Informal*
	Rules abided by without much discussion:	Procedures and routines:
Static	a) no cheating b) asking permission to leave the room c) addressing teacher when seeking permission to change something in the room	a) how students enter the room b) who talks to whom for how long c) saying "Good morning," "Thank you," etc., to the teacher
	Rules in need of at least occasional enforcement:	Interpersonal actions about which there is active monitoring:
Dynamic	a) no talking during story time or individual study time b) turning work in on time c) using correct grammar in talking and writing	a) addressing teacher in a nasty fashion b) wearing hair quite differently than other students do c) acting abusively toward others

FIGURE 11.3
Types of Classroom Norms

Source: From Richard A. Schmuck and Patricia A. Schmuck, *Group Processes in the Classroom,* 5th ed. Copyright © 1988 Wm. C. Brown Publishers, Dubuque, Iowa. All Rights Reserved.

Teachers can make their classes more attractive by (1) recognizing and building students' self-esteem; (2) developing common group goals and class projects; and (3) giving the class recognition for its achievements. Successes should be reported to the local newspaper or to the principal for school or community recognition; this reflects on the individual students while encouraging them to live up to the class reputation.

FIVE-MINUTE FOCUS   Describe some informal norms and sanctions you learned as a member of classroom groups in middle school or high school. Date your journal entry and write for five minutes.

Leadership in the Classroom

The ability to provide leadership in the classroom may lie with the teacher, the students, or both. For good or ill, students as well as teachers exert leadership in classrooms. Wise teachers quickly identify student leaders and develop ways to focus their leadership abilities on the attainment of goals that benefit the entire class.

Negative student leaders, those who pull their followers away from schoolwork or destroy class spirit and cohesiveness, present challenges. If such leaders are motivated by a desire for power, teachers can grant them acceptable forms of influence, which may turn negative leadership into more positive avenues. However, if they simply seek to frustrate teachers and interfere with the progress of other students, the matter is more serious, requiring a search for the causes of the behavior and to work out ways of improving the situation. Whatever the circumstances, teachers benefit by getting to know the student leaders in their classes.

Teachers should also encourage their students to develop leadership skills. Our goal as teachers is not to train good soldiers who follow orders obediently; rather, it is to educate good citizens competent at making wise decisions and willing to be accountable for their actions. By providing leadership practice, teachers guide students toward the important life goals of becoming autonomous, accepting responsibility, and influencing others to respect their opinions.

The Teacher's Leadership Style   Teachers vary in their leadership styles and the amount of authority they exert over their classes. Some, regarded as authoritarian, keep most of the power and expect students to abide by their rules; others share their power with the group and establish a democratic classroom climate; and still others, usually labeled permissive, exert little power and allow their students free rein.

Which of these approaches should you use? Opinions are divided between the first two: the authoritarian, "don't smile until Christmas," camp and the democratic, "involve the learners in the process," camp. Unquestionably, the circumstances of schools and the makeup of student populations may necessitate specific leadership styles, but, optimally, the democratic approach is the preference. In an examination of the literature on leadership styles in classrooms, Jere Brophy and Thomas Good noted that "teachers with democratic styles generally were preferred to those with authoritarian styles, and they generally created more positive classroom atmospheres characterized by greater student enjoyment and cooperation and less competitiveness and frustration."[25]

TABLE 11.1 Comparison of Leadership Styles

Autocratic	*Democratic*
Boss	Leader
Sharp voice	Friendly voice
Command	Invitation
Power	Influence
Pressure	Stimulation
Demands cooperation	Wins cooperation
"I tell you what you should do"	"I tell you what I would like to do"
Imposes ideas	Sells ideas
Dominates	Guides
Criticizes	Encourages
Finding fault	Acknowledges achievement
Punishes	Helps
"I tell you"	Discusses
"I decide; you obey"	"I suggest and help you to decide"
Has sole responsibility of group	Shares responsibility of team

Source: Rudolph Dreikurs, Bernice Bronia Grunwald, and Floy C. Pepper, *Maintaining Sanity in the Classroom: Classroom Management Techniques,* 2nd ed., p. 76. Copyright © 1982 by the Estate of Rudolph Dreikurs, Bernice Bronia Grunwald, and Floy C. Pepper. Reprinted by permission of HarperCollins Publishers.

Teachers must be alert to the impact and consequences of the type of leadership they choose to exert. Autocratic and democratic teachers exhibit strikingly different characteristics, and they elicit noticeably different responses from students (see Table 11.1). According to one study, "hostility, competitiveness, and high dependency marked the autocratic group, while openness, friendly communication, and independence typified the democratically led group."[26] Teachers' leadership styles unquestionably affect the climate and the quality of human interactions in their classrooms.

The Democratic Classroom In democratic classrooms and schools, students are given more power and responsibility than in autocratic systems. If they are to learn how to live in a democracy, students must be able to manage freedom responsibly.

Student councils, student judicial systems, class officers, class meetings, and school assemblies planned by students are forms of student government that offer leadership opportunities and a means of practicing democracy. Some schools provide leadership conferences, enlisting the help of members of the community.

Teachers model democracy by giving their students some choices and control over some of the events that occur in their classrooms. For instance, consider the reflections of one teacher who promotes democratic decision making when a class is small enough:

> This past year my P.E. classes ranged in size from 11 to 25. This size allows for relatively easy management and allowing the students to participate in the decision making increases participation and dedication. As part of the system, two different

captains are selected each week, rotating alphabetically. . . . They also choose teams at the first of the week. Two or three times a week students are allowed to vote on which activities to have. An example would be voting on having a kickball game or softball game, both of which would obtain the desired objectives for that day.

To create a **democratic classroom** is not easy. It takes time, patience, skill, and a willingness to share power. However, the rewards for teachers who implement democratic principles can be significant. Group spirit and school pride are often enhanced; student attitudes toward learning improve; and achievement can soar.

Interpersonal Interaction

Interactions between teachers and students are the very core of teaching. The quality of these interactions reveals to students how the teacher feels about them. Teachers who empathize with students, genuinely respect them, and expect them to learn are more likely to develop a positive classroom climate. In classrooms with positive group interactions, teachers and students work toward a common goal—learning. In classrooms with negative interactions, the energy of teachers and students may be channeled into conflict rather than into learning.

There is no precise formula to guarantee success in the classroom; however, Robert Rosenthal has suggested four rules of thumb that teachers can follow to increase student achievement through positive interactions:

1. Establish warm social-emotional relationships with students
2. Give students more feedback about their performance
3. Teach students more (and more difficult) material
4. Give students more opportunities to respond and to ask questions[27]

Speaking and Listening   Interactions between teachers and students involve the communication skills of speaking and listening. It has been estimated that in the "typical" classroom someone is speaking about 75 percent of the time, and, not surprisingly, it is the teacher who speaks about three-quarters of this time. Knowledge about the speaking and listening that occurs in classes taught by effective teachers was increased greatly by the Beginning Teacher Evaluation Study (BTES), a pioneering long-term study that in one phase focused on 20 second-grade and 20 fifth-grade classrooms. On the basis of student achievement during two-week units of instruction in reading and mathematics, the researchers identified 10 "more effective" and 10 "less effective" teachers at each grade level and in each subject area.

The researchers found that the behaviors of the more effective teachers created a positive climate.

> [They] enjoyed teaching and were generally polite and pleasant in their daily interactions. They were more likely to call their students by name, attend carefully to what they said, accept their statements of feeling, praise their successes, and involve them in decision making.[28]

Furthermore, the more effective teachers treated students with greater respect and were less likely to criticize students.

> The more effective teachers were less likely to ignore, belittle, harass, shame, put down, or exclude their students. Their students were less likely to defy or manipulate the teachers. Thus, the more effective classes were characterized by mutual respect, whereas the less effective classes sometimes showed evidence of conflict.[29]

Finally, the more effective teachers did not hesitate to make demands on students.

They encouraged them to work hard and take personal responsibility for academic progress, and they monitored that progress carefully and were consistent in following through on directions and demands. Thus, these teachers were pleasant but also businesslike in their interactions with students.[30]

In addition to verbal behavior that promotes a positive classroom climate, teachers should give special attention to the questions they ask of students. Research indicates that most questions teachers ask are **lower-order questions,** those that assess a student's ability to recall specific information. Effective teachers, however, also ask **higher-order questions** that demand more critical thinking and answers to questions such as, Why? What if . . .?

In their interactions with students, teachers should also avoid treating high-achieving and low-achieving students differently. Jere Brophy and Thomas Good reviewed the research in this area and found that several teacher behaviors may indicate unequal treatment of students (see Table 11.2).

TABLE 11.2   How Teachers Treat Low Achievers Differently

1. Giving low achievers less time
   - Waiting less time for them to answer questions
   - Paying less attention to them and interacting with them less frequently
   - Avoiding the use of effective but time-consuming instructional methods with them when time is limited

2. Showing low achievers less patience
   - Giving them answers or calling on others rather than improving their responses by giving clues or by repeating or rephrasing questions
   - Giving briefer and less informative feedback to their questions
   - Calling on them less often to respond to questions

3. Excluding low achievers
   - Seating them farther away from the teacher
   - Failing to accept and use their ideas
   - Interacting with them more privately than publicly; failing to give feedback about their public responses

4. Communicating less positively with low achievers
   - Acting less friendly toward them; smiling at them less
   - Making less eye contact
   - Giving them fewer nonverbal indicators of support, attention, and responsiveness

5. Discriminating against low achievers
   - Praising them less frequently than others for success; criticizing them more often for failure
   - Demanding less from them
   - Monitoring and structuring their activities more closely
   - Administering or grading their tests or assignments differently; failing to give them benefit of the doubt
   - Rewarding inappropriate behavior or incorrect answers

Source: Adapted from Thomas L. Good and Jere E. Brophy, *Looking in Classrooms,* 4th ed. (New York: Harper and Row, 1987), pp. 128–129. Copyright © 1987 by Harper & Row, Publishers, Inc. Reprinted by permission of HarperCollins Publishers.

The quality of interaction between teachers and students is vital to student achievement. Effective teachers establish respectful relationships, listen to their students, give frequent feedback and opportunities to ask questions, and demand higher-level performance.

Student Games   In addition to understanding key aspects of interpersonal interaction, teachers should be aware of the nonproductive, often self-defeating games students can play and the strategies they use to cover their failure or unwillingness to learn. Perhaps you played some of these roles and games yourself, but soon you will need to respond to them from the other side of the teacher's desk.

One study of seventh-graders and their teacher in an inner-city school, for example, identified the following stereotypical names for various nonproductive roles students assumed:

- The class clown
- The isolate or loner
- The nonworker or do-nothing student
- The reject or outcast[31]

Teachers often unwittingly reinforce nonproductive roles by responding appreciatively or sympathetically to aspects of the students' role behavior—for example, by chuckling at the class clown's imitation of Bart Simpson or by letting the loner work alone when everyone else is working in groups.

In his book *How Children Fail,* the late John Holt described some of the games that elementary school children play to avoid appearing to be school failures.[32] Holt outlined several school survival strategies that students use to cover their lack of learning. One method is to avoid being called on during recitation periods. Referring to one child who had a need to be always right, Holt wrote:

She also knows the teacher's strategy of asking questions of students who seem confused, or not paying attention. She therefore feels safe waving her hand in the air, as if she were bursting to tell the answer, whether she really knows it or not. . . . When someone else answers correctly she nods her head in emphatic agreement. . . . It is also interesting to note that she does not raise her hand unless there are at least half a dozen other hands up.[33]

Another method of fooling the teacher when the answer to a question is unknown is what Holt described as the strategy of "guess-and-look, in which you start to say a word, all the while scrutinizing the teacher's face to see whether you are on the right track or not."[34]

Another view of the games students play is offered by Ken Ernst, the high school teacher who wrote *Games Students Play*. Using transactional analysis, a psychological approach to analyzing verbal communication, Ernst describes the interactional games students can play. In one game called "Do Me Something," for example, an unmotivated student "challenges" the teacher to teach something to him or her. Whenever the teacher complies, the student insists that the effort is a failure, whereupon the teacher is compelled to either perpetuate the game or give up trying to teach that student. The student's message is, "You can't win." The teacher's response may also comprise a game—for example, one that could be called, "Well, I tried," implying, "but I know I can't win."

Games are destructive because they are manipulative and require a winner and a loser. An awareness of destructive games and nonproductive roles in the classroom can help you minimize their effects and find countermeasures. When enlightened about the psychology of group dynamics, students themselves can be allies in helping to make your classroom a place where everyone is a winner.

FIVE-MINUTE FOCUS   Give names to some of the roles and games you and your classmates played as younger students and list them in your journal. Add to the list games teachers played that you observed as a member of their classes. Which nonproductive student roles and games do you think would be most upsetting to you as a teacher? Which teacher games are you determined to avoid? Date your journal entry and write for five minutes.

CLASSROOM MANAGEMENT

For most new teachers **classroom management** is a significant concern. How can you control misbehaving students so that you can teach? Unfortunately, effective classroom management cannot be reduced to a cookbook recipe. And, until recently, the best advice new teachers could find was to "use whatever works." Today, however, "research in classrooms has established clearly that some approaches [to classroom management] are more effective than others and in particular that *the key to successful classroom management is preventing problems before they occur.*"[35]

Problem Prevention

How can teachers prevent discipline problems from occurring? The key to preventive discipline is excellent planning and an understanding of group dynamics. In addition, teachers who have mastered the essential teaching skills have fewer discipline problems because students recognize that such teachers are prepared, well organized, and have a sense of purpose. They are confident of their ability to teach all students, and their task-oriented manner tends to discourage most classroom management problems.

Jacob Kounin has conducted extensive research on how teachers prevent discipline problems. In one study Kounin looked at two sets of teachers: those who managed their classrooms smoothly and productively with few disruptions and those who seemed to be plagued with discipline problems and chaotic working conditions. He found that the teachers who managed their classrooms successfully had certain teaching behaviors in common: (1) on the first day of school they established and discussed several clear comprehensive rules for behavior, (2) they displayed the proverbial "eyes in the back of their head" quality of alertness, a quality Kounin referred to as *withitness*, (3) they used individual students and incidences as models to communicate to the rest of the class their conduct expectations, Kounin's *ripple effect*, (4) they supervised several situations at once effectively, and (5) they were adept at handling transitions smoothly.[36] In addition, you will need to adjust discipline approaches to particular students and situations. For instance, older students may be embarrassed by teacher praise, and behavior modification techniques may be offensive to the gifted student.

Effective Problem Solving

When management problems do emerge in the classroom, effective teachers draw from a repertoire of problem-solving skills. Two of the most widely used structured approaches to classroom management are the LEAST approach and behavior modification.

The LEAST Approach   Especially helpful for secondary teachers is a sequence of discipline steps outlined in the LEAST program, which can be found in *A Design for Discipline: The LEAST Approach.*[37] The acronym spells out the steps:

1. **L**eave it alone. Decide first of all if the misbehavior is worth noticing. Often it is not.
2. **E**nd the action indirectly. Have the student run an errand for you or assist a fellow student with a problem. Direct the student toward an alternative, correct behavior without a confrontation over the misbehavior.
3. **A**ttend more fully. This is the counseling component of teaching. You need to get to know the student better before you decide what to do.
4. **S**pell out directions. Specify the problem and tell them what you want them to do. Avoid using negatives. Instead say what they should start doing. At times you may need to also tell them what the consequences will be if they do not start doing what you have specified.
5. **T**rack the behavior. Keep records on how the students are doing. In this step you may have to follow through on the consequences.

Many experienced teachers recognize this sequence as the approach they have used for years. Spelled out, however, the **LEAST approach** offers the beginning teacher clear and effective procedures to follow.

Behavior Modification Strategies   Another approach to classroom management that many teachers have used with success is **behavior modification.** Based primarily on the theories of the late B.F. Skinner, a well-known psychologist, behavior modification calls for teachers to reinforce (or reward) only desired student behaviors. Teachers can reward students with effective praise, a smile, or tokens can use to "buy" time for activities they enjoy (see Table 11.3). Behaviors that are reinforced will tend to be repeated, and those that are not reinforced will tend to be extinguished. By reinforcing only desired behaviors, the teacher can "shape" students' behavior, because students soon associate the desired behavior with the pleasure of being rewarded. Those who advocate behavior modification point out that negative reinforcement makes undesired behavior disappear only temporarily.

An Individualized Approach   Rudolf Dreikurs, a psychologist and author of several books on discipline, developed an approach to individual problems that can be used for dealing with classroom management. According to Dreikurs, there are four "mistaken" goals for children's misbehavior: "(1) to gain attention, (2) to seek power, (3) to seek revenge, (4) to display inadequacy (real or imagined)."[38] Teachers can recognize when a child is acting with the goal of gaining attention if they feel annoyed and/or frustrated by the child's behavior. The "treatment" for students who misbehave

TABLE 11.3   Guidelines for Effective Praise

Effective Praise	*Ineffective Praise*
1. Is delivered contingently	1. Is delivered randomly or unsystematically
2. Specifies the particulars of the accomplishment	2. Is restricted to global positive reactions
3. Shows spontaneity, variety, and other signs of credibility; suggests clear attention to the student's accomplishment	3. Shows a bland uniformity that suggests a conditioned response made with minimal attention
4. Rewards attainment of specified performance criteria (which can include effort criteria, however)	4. Rewards mere participation, without consideration of performance processes or outcomes
5. Provides information to students about their competence or the value of their accomplishments	5. Provides no information at all or gives students information about their status
6. Orients students toward better appreciation of their own task-related behavior and thinking about problem solving	6. Orients students toward comparing themselves with others and thinking about competing
7. Uses student's own prior accomplishments as the context for describing present accomplishments	7. Uses the accomplishments of peers as the context for describing student's present accomplishments
8. Is given in recognition of noteworthy effort or success at difficult (for this student) tasks	8. Is given without regard to the effort expended or the meaning of the accomplishment
9. Attributes success to effort and ability, implying that similar success can be expected in the future.	9. Attributes success to ability alone or to external factors such as luck or (easy) task difficulty
10. Fosters endogenous attributions (students believe that they expend effort on the task because they enjoy the task and/or want to develop task-relevant skills)	10. Fosters exogenous attributions (students believe that they expend effort on the task for external reasons—to please the teacher, win a competition or reward, etc.)
11. Focuses students' attention on their own task-relevant behavior	11. Focuses students' attention on the teacher as an external authority figure who is manipulating them
12. Fosters appreciation of, and desirable attributions about, task-relevant behavior after the process is completed	12. Intrudes into the ongoing process, distracting attention from task-relevant behavior

Source: Thomas L. Good and Jere E. Brophy, *Looking in Classrooms*, 4th ed. (New York: Harper & Row, 1987), p. 241. Reprinted by permission of Harper & Row Publishers, Inc.

for this reason is to ignore the bad behavior and pay attention to the good. If the teacher feels threatened, the student is probably misbehaving with the goal of seeking power. Dreikurs suggests that teachers should avoid engaging in power confrontations and, instead, seek ways to provide opportunities for students to use power productively.

When the teacher feels hurt, it is a sign that students may be misbehaving to seek revenge. Dreikurs urges teachers to cover up their hurt and show instead a caring regard for the students, for those who hurt others are often deeply hurt themselves.

The most serious of the goals for misbehavior is to display real or imagined helplessness. These students have become convinced that they cannot do what is expected of them, and so they do not even try. Teachers can recognize this motivation by their own discouragement, as they wonder if they can do anything that can help. For these students, Dreikurs tells teachers to give encouragement and never give up on the student.

Dreikurs' approach is based on three key ideas: (1) students misbehave for different reasons, (2) teachers can use their own emotional reactions to help determine the student's motivation to misbehave, and (3) different corrective strategies need to be used for misbehavior caused by different motivations.

ESSENTIAL TEACHING SKILLS

As we pointed out in Chapter 1, along with essential knowledge teachers must possess two types of essential skills: (1) teaching skills and techniques and (2) interpersonal skills. Unfortunately, the complexities of teaching and the widely varying cultures of schools and classrooms make it difficult to identify precisely the skills teachers need in these two areas. However, one broad helpful view of essential teaching skills was presented by the late B. Othanel Smith in *Teachers for the Real World.* According to Smith, students preparing to teach should be able to do the following things:

1. Perform stimulant operations—question, structure, probe [i.e., find ways to attract students' attention, motivate their learning, and maintain a high interest level]
2. Manipulate the different kinds of knowledge [i.e., encourage critical and creative thinking as well as the recall and comprehension of facts and concepts]
3. Perform reinforcement operations [i.e., use frequent and extensive positive reinforcement in the form of genuine praise, privileges, rewards, and other forms of recognition. Learn to use negative reinforcement and behavior modification techniques to guide discouraged, reluctant, or recalcitrant students]
4. Negotiate interpersonal relations [teach conflict resolution strategies and promote cooperative learning]
5. Diagnose student needs and learning difficulties
6. Communicate and empathize with students, parents, and others
7. Perform in and with small and large groups
8. Utilize technological equipment
9. Evaluate student achievement
10. Judge appropriateness of instructional materials[39]

While it is difficult to identify *all* of the skills you will need as a future teacher, you will minimally need to acquire skills in organization and planning, evaluation, communication, and instruction.

Keepers of the Dream

Shirley A. Hopkinson
1991 Teacher of the Year
Brightwood Elementary School, Washington, D.C.

"Teaching is about taking chances, taking risks. It means allowing failure to happen, even if it is you who fails," says Shirley Hopkinson, a teacher of three- and four-year-olds at Brightwood Elementary School in Washington, D.C. A native of Guyana, South America, Hopkinson has taught students of all ages, from prekindergarten to adults.

Hopkinson has been so successful teaching at-risk students that she was named Washington D.C.'s Teacher of the Year in 1991. Her style of teaching is based on what she calls a "tri-combination program." She uses a combination of music, movement, and story-telling to motivate students.

When I tell a story, I light a candle. I begin with a high energy activity and then calm them down with stories that relate to basic skills and physical movement. Then we move into activities at learning centers. I have 20 kids and 20 centers in my classroom.

Hopkinson developed and implemented Project CAPABLE (Children and Parents Are Becoming Learning-Empowered) to involve parents in the education of their children. At potluck meetings every other week, Hopkinson helps parents learn to interact more positively with their children. During "lap time," for example, Hopkinson tells stories while children sit in their parents' laps.

Parents don't know how to sit with their children. It's always "Shoo, child." At first, some parents don't let

their children sit in their laps. But, gradually, they get a little closer to their children.

Hopkinson's high level of energy and her determination to find creative ways to motivate students have enabled her to develop strategies for teaching students of drug-abusing parents.

It all started with one student I had in 1987 whose mother had been on crack. By the end of the day, I was exhausted! He would fall and hurt himself. You'd put a band-aid on and he'd pick it off and just look at the blood. I couldn't understand it.

To get some understanding of children with these problems, I joined PRIDE (Parent Resource Institute for Drug Education). I've learned that you have to take risks trying to teach these children. Also, you have to be patient. If things don't work today, you try tomorrow.

> ## "You Have To Go with the Flow."

Hopkinson encourages the student teachers who are frequently assigned to her to "go with the flow" of the children. "At first, they don't understand, but after a week or so they know what I mean.

Teaching at the Early Childhood level has to go beyond the ABCs and Mother Goose into the time and societal conditions in which children now live. We must help kids develop powerful, positive values and choices as antidotes against violence and hate.

Organization and Planning

The ability to organize time, materials, and activities, and to plan carefully are among the most important skills of teaching. In the following words, a first-year junior high school teacher tells how organization and planning helped her to have a successful first day of teaching.

> All I could think about all the way home [after the first day of school] was just that it was as smooth as it could be. I was prepared. . . . I guess I just planned well enough. I knew what I was going to say.[40]

Six months later, the same teacher comments on how she came to realize that planning for control and management is also an essential teaching skill.

> I thought that if you planned the *curriculum* really well, the management just falls into place. I really thought that when I was student teaching. If you are not well planned you are *going* to have problems. . . . Now [after six months], I plan a lot more things, like transition time and walking into the other room [to check on the students].[41]

Before planning a course, designing a unit, or teaching a lesson, teachers need to know what they intend to do, how they want to do it, why they want to do it, and how they will know that they have been successful. Recent studies of teachers' thinking and planning have yielded interesting findings. Christopher Clark and Penelope Peterson conclude that teachers engage in eight types of planning: lesson, daily, weekly, unit, long-range, short-range, term, and yearly, with the unit plan being considered most important.[42] Early in the school year, planning is focused on "establishing the physical environment and social system of the classroom" according to a study of elementary teachers.[43] In a study of British secondary teachers, planning was found to focus on (in order of importance) "(1) pupil needs, abilities, and interests; (2) subject matter; (3) goals; (4) teaching methods."[44]

How teachers go about making lesson plans and how college students are taught to do so may vary. A standard procedure for writing lesson plans is taught in most colleges of education, but student teachers and new teachers often discover that many experienced teachers do not use written lesson plans. Why? Some experienced teachers have internalized the process, skipping steps in the paperwork of the lesson plan but not in their thinking. Others have simply taken too many planning shortcuts and their teaching suffers in the process. On the sequence experienced teachers follow in preparing their lesson plans, The *Harvard Education Letter* reports:

> For three decades supervisors have told student teachers to plan each lesson in four steps: first specify objectives ("the students will be able to multiply improper fractions"); then select learning activities; then organize these activities; and finally, design a way to evaluate what students have learned.
>
> In fact, however, few teachers seem to proceed in this way. About a dozen studies have asked teachers to think aloud as they plan, to talk about their planning, or to keep a planning journal. For most of the teachers studied, planning was a cyclical process, which started either with what they knew about students' needs and interests or with the content to be taught. Teachers specified formal objectives only after the lesson began to take shape.[45]

Figure 11.4 illustrates the two approaches to planning described above.

Though time-consuming, planning is beneficial not only for the quality of teaching that students will experience but also for the state of mind of the teacher. As Clark

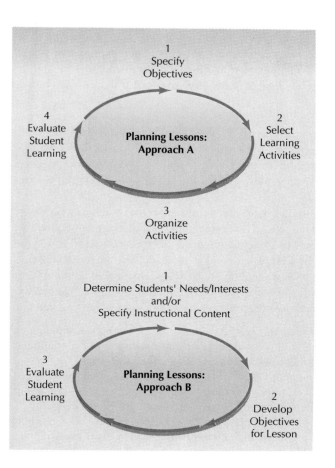

FIGURE 11.4

Two Approaches to Planning Lessons

and Peterson note, teachers find that "the planning process produces immediate psychic rewards in the form of feelings of confidence and reduction of uncertainty."[46]

Evaluation

Evaluation is a critical teaching skill. As evaluators, teachers make judgments about the performance of students *and* about their own performance as teachers. Successful teachers continually evaluate the effectiveness of their teaching because they recognize that how well students learn depends on how well they teach.

Teachers use two approaches to evaluating student learning: formative and summative evaluation. **Formative evaluation** occurs when the teacher measures students' learning for the purpose of planning for teaching. For example, as an aid to planning for a new unit of instruction, a teacher may assess students' understanding of a subject. **Summative evaluation,** on the other hand, is used by teachers to determine grades at the end of a unit, semester, or year and to decide whether students are ready to proceed to the next phase of their education. At some point in your teacher education program, you will learn about **measurement,** that is, the different techniques for assessing student learning. Also, you will be introduced to basic statistical methods for comparing the learning of students within a group and between groups of students.

Communication

Successful teachers possess effective communication skills. They express themselves verbally and nonverbally in a manner that is clear, concise, and interesting. In addition, they are good listeners. Their students feel that not only are they heard, they are understood.

Effective teachers relish the live, thinking-on-your-feet dimensions of classroom communication. Their communication skills enable them to respond appropriately to events that could sabotage the plans of less effective teachers: a student's clowning, announcements on the p.a. (public address system), interruptions by other teachers or parents, students' private arguments or romances, or simply the mood of the class at that particular time.

One of the findings in the studies of teachers' thinking is that teachers who ignore student reactions and continue to focus on the lesson plan objectives are not as effective as those who attend to and adjust to students' responses. Closely related to this is the finding that experienced teachers were better able to read their students and thus could adjust the content of the lessons according to their students' abilities and interest levels. The *Harvard Education Letter*'s summary of this finding applies to elementary teachers, but it should be considered when observing secondary teachers as well:

> Experienced teachers, compared to beginners, know a great deal about children in general—what they do outside of school, how many are likely to need special help, and so on—and analyze classroom events in a more sophisticated way. . . .
>
> While all teachers reprimanded the unruly and aided the confused, experienced teachers were *five times* as likely as novices to respond to "positive cues"—a giggle of excitement, an item of news, a nod of comprehension, or an unexpected insight. . . .
>
> At all points in the processes of planning and teaching, experienced teachers keep the responses of their particular students near the center of their minds.[47]

How can new teachers use these research findings? Perhaps the best lessons to be gained are: (1) to know students well, in terms of their lives outside of school as well as in; (2) to know the subject(s) thoroughly, so well that they can be adapted to the ongoing responses of students; and (3) whenever in a position to do so, to ask teachers what they are thinking and how they are making their decisions as they plan and teach.

Instruction

As we pointed out in our discussion of educational philosophy in Chapter 7, beliefs about teaching and learning, students, knowledge, and what is worth knowing influence the instructional methods a teacher uses. In addition, instruction is influenced by variables such as the teacher's personality and learning style, the learners' characteristics, the culture of the school and surrounding community, and the resources available. All of these components contribute to the "model" of teaching the teacher uses in the classroom. In *Methods of Teaching,* Bruce Joyce and Marsha Weil define a **model of teaching** as "a plan or pattern that we can use to design face-to-face teaching in classrooms or tutorial settings and to shape instructional materials—including books, films, tapes, and computer-mediated programs and curriculums (long-term courses of study)."[48] Table 11.4 presents brief descriptions of five widely used models of teaching.

TABLE 11.4   Five Instructional Models

	Goals and Rationale	*Methods*
Mastery Learning	Virtually all students can learn material if given enough time and taught in the appropriate manner. Students learn best when they participate in a structured, systematic program of learning that enables them to progress in small, sequenced steps.	• Set objectives and standards for mastery. • Teach content directly to students. • Provide corrective feedback to students on their learning. • Provide additional time and help in correcting errors. • Follow cycle of teaching, testing, reteaching, and retesting.
Cooperative Learning	Students can be motivated to learn by working cooperatively in small groups if rewards are made available to the group as a whole and to individual members of the group.	• Small groups (4–6 students) work together on learning activities. • Assignments require that students help one another while working on a group project. • In competitive arrangements, groups may compete against one another. • Group members contribute to group goals according to their talents, interests, and abilities.
Theory into Practice	Teachers make decisions in three primary areas: content to be taught, how students will learn, and the behaviors the teacher will use in the classroom. The effectiveness of teaching is related to the quality of decisions the teacher makes in these areas.	The teacher follows seven steps in the classroom: 1. Orients students to material to be learned. 2. Tells students what they will learn and why it is important. 3. Presents new material that consists of knowledge, skills, or processes students are to learn. 4. Models what students are expected to do. 5. Checks for student understanding. 6. Gives students opportunity for practice under the teacher's guidance. 7. Makes assignments that give students opportunity to practice what they have learned on their own.
Behavior Modification	Teachers can "shape" student learning by using various forms of reinforcement. Human behavior is learned, and behaviors that are positively reinforced (rewarded) tend to increase while those that are not reinforced tend to decrease.	• Teacher begins by presenting stimulus in the form of new material. • The behavior of students is observed by the teacher. • Appropriate behaviors are reinforced by the teacher as quickly as possible.
Nondirective Teaching	Learning can be facilitated if teachers focus on personal development of students and create opportunities for students to increase their self-understanding and self-concepts. The key to effective teaching is the teacher's ability to understand students and to involve them in a teaching-learning partnership.	• Teacher acts as a facilitator of learning. • Teacher creates learning environments that support personal growth and development. • Teacher acts in the role of a counselor who helps students to understand themselves, clarify their goals, and accept responsibility for their behavior.

CONSIDER THIS . . .

What Teaching Models Do You Prefer?

Rate yourself in terms of whether you agree or disagree with the following statements (place an X in the appropriate space). Then turn to the answer key at the end of this chapter to learn how your answers suggest the kinds of instructional models you probably prefer as a teacher.

	Agree Strongly	Agree	Disagree	Disagree Strongly
1. Teachers should tell students what they will learn and why it is important.	X			
2. Students should proceed through learning activities in small, sequential steps.	X			
3. Students can help one another learn and should be encouraged to do so.		X		
4. Teachers are primarily decision makers.		X		
5. Competition among small groups can promote individual learning.			X	
6. Teachers should reward desired student behavior.	X			
7. Students should be given as much time as they need to learn new material.			X	
8. Teachers are primarily concerned with changing the behavior of students.			X	
9. The teacher should establish warm, caring relationships with his or her students.	X			
10. By working in small groups, students learn important social skills.		X		
11. In addition to pointing out "errors" in students' work, teachers should reteach the material as often as necessary.			X	
12. Teachers should be concerned with improving students' self-concepts.		X		
13. Observing student behavior is the best way for teachers to evaluate student learning.				X
14. During instruction, teachers should periodically check students' level of understanding.	X			
15. The teacher's primary role is to create an environment that facilitates learning.	X			

Developing Your Own Instructional Model

Rather than selecting and rigidly following only one instructional model, we encourage you to experiment with several. Joyce and Weil's *Models of Teaching,* for example, provides concise, well-organized descriptions of more than two dozen models of teaching.

Effective teachers use a "repertoire" of teaching models, depending upon their situations and the goals they wish to attain. Your teaching strategies in the classroom will most likely be eclectic, that is, a combination of several models. Also, as you gain classroom experience and acquire new skills, your personal model of teaching will evolve, enabling you to respond appropriately to a wider range of teaching situations.

CHARACTERISTICS OF EFFECTIVE TEACHING

Whatever model of teaching you practice, there are several behaviors that researchers have identified as characteristic of effective teaching. Research on teacher effectiveness has moved through two eras, according to educational researcher Donald Cruickshank.[49] In the first era, roughly 1900 to 1960, the search for effectiveness focused on teachers' personality traits, which proved unworkable because of shortcomings in the research methods and the complexity and human dimension of the phenomenon of teaching. In the second era, from the 1960s to the present, researchers have been more successful in correlating teacher behaviors and students' achievements.

Research Findings on Effective Teaching

A summary of the findings for effective teaching of well-structured subjects is provided by Barak Rosenshine and Robert Stevens in the *Handbook of Research on Teaching,* edited in 1986 for the American Educational Research Association. Rosenshine and Stevens note that the procedures are ideal for step-by-step knowledge and skill development, but are not appropriate for less structured areas such as composition, literary criticism, discussion of social issues, and problem solving in specific subject areas. To help teachers be more successful with the structured type of instruction, Rosenshine and Stevens provide the following summary of the research findings from seven major studies conducted with students ranging in age from elementary to senior high school:

- Begin a lesson with a short review of previous, prerequisite learning.
- Begin a lesson with a short statement of goals.
- Present new material in small steps, with student practice after each step.
- Give clear and detailed instructions and explanations.
- Provide a high level of active practice for all students.
- Ask a large number of questions, check for student understanding, and obtain responses from all students.
- Guide students during initial practice.
- Provide systematic feedback and corrections.
- Provide explicit instruction and practice for seatwork exercises and, where necessary, monitor students during seatwork.[50]

The above findings can help make field observations more instructive and can act as guides for the preparation of lessons calling for step-by-step knowledge. Similarly, descriptions of effective teachers can aid in initial observing and planning experiences.

One such description, based on observations in British primary schools, is provided by researchers M. Galton and B. Simon:

> The successful teachers all engage in above-average levels of interaction with the pupils. They appear to devote considerable effort to ensuring that the routine activities proceed smoothly; they engage in high levels of task statements and questions, and provide regular feedback. At the same time, they also encourage the children to work by themselves toward solutions to problems . . . [and] make above-average use of higher-order interactions, including . . . more open-ended types of questioning.[51]

Most colleges of education offer courses in the strategies of teaching and on methods and materials for instruction in specific subject areas. Studying these skills will help prevent future teachers from becoming overwhelmed in their first year of teaching, thus avoiding an educationally wasteful year for students breaking in a new, unprepared teacher.

FIVE-MINUTE FOCUS   In which areas of teacher effectiveness do you feel the most and the least confident? What might you do, or what program might you undertake, to strengthen your effectiveness in areas in which you feel you lack confidence? Date your journal entry and write for five minutes.

Two Portraits of Effectiveness

What do effective teachers do when they are teaching? How do they communicate with students? How do they manage classroom activities? What models of teaching do they use? The following sections provide answers to these questions by presenting brief portraits of two effective teachers in action. As you read each portrait, look for evidence that shows how the teachers use the essential teaching skills discussed earlier in this chapter.

Case 1: A Middle School Teacher   Mr. Gebhart is a seventh- and eighth-grade art teacher at a middle school on the West Coast. Notice how he is able to create what he calls a "delicate balance between control and freedom" in a ceramics class.

> At first no teacher is visible. Then he can be discerned in his open-necked shirt and clay-streaked pants, bending over one student's project discussing the aesthetic quality of the glaze, then over another's to suggest how to solve the problem of reattaching pieces that fell off in the first firing. Two minutes after the bell has summoned the faithful, Mr. Gebhart stands up. He has already had individual consultation with five students.
> "Bo, turn off the radio please, till everyone is working."
> A boy from the non-working table silences the music. Most of the students look up for a moment, then resume work. Some approach him with questions concerning evaluation of their work, further directions, or technical or aesthetic problems demanding solution. Mr. Gebhart attends briefly to them, but directs his attention to the back table where a girl is wrapping her scarf around Bo's head, talking.
> "Penny, what are you working on?" She shrugs. "Don't just sit there and chat. You've had enough time to get started." Mr. Gebhart turns to somebody else. Penny pulls out a lacy clay shoe and starts smoothing out its high heel.

FACT FINDING

What Teacher Behaviors Promote Student Achievement?

According to the Stanford Studies:

- Using an overview or analogy to introduce material
- Reviewing, repeating
- Praising or repeating pupil answers
- Being patient in waiting for responses
- Integrating the responses into the lesson
- Making clear presentations
- Providing feedback to students and improving responses that are incomplete or incorrect
- Using lower-order questions

According to the Beginning Teacher Evaluation Study (BTES):

- Good organization
- Maximizing time devoted to instruction
- Minimizing time spent on preparation, procedures, or discipline
- Spending most time actively instructing and monitoring seatwork

According to Stalling's Study on Teaching Basic Skills in Secondary Schools:

- Quantity of instruction
- Reviewing or discussing assignments
- Having students read aloud
- Praising success
- Providing support and corrective feedback

Source: Donald Cruickshank, "Profile of an Effective Teacher," *Educational Horizons* (Winter 1986): 14.

The radio is turned on. "Leave that off till everyone is working. I'll say when everyone is working." The radio is turned off. Students admonish one another to get to work. Fifteen minutes into the period Mr. Gebhart turns the music on. Another work-day is in progress.

Every two weeks or so Mr. Gebhart introduces a new lesson. He asks the students to gather round, which they do, some perched on the front tables, one on crutches, balanced dangerously between two tables. This lesson involves sculpting a figure, "doing something, not looking like it just died," from a small block of clay. Mr. Gebhart demonstrates the basic cuts and twists which produce a human form, telling students to attend to proportion, not detail. He shows them how to use their bodies to determine arm length. The students seem captivated by the emerging figure. Working quickly, Mr. Gebhart notes that the figure should be posed after its basic form is established, and then brings forth a seated figure, torso twisted, knee raised.

Having given basic directions, Mr. Gebhart shows the students illustrations in *Sports and Games in Art*—Bellows' boxers, Moore's abstractions, Greek wrestlers. He brings the pictures to life: "This one was probably made in clay first like you're doing." "We call this 'abstracted.' Just put in what you think is essential." "Notice how this conveys a feeling of movement." He throws his body forward to walk. "In art we create the same process by throwing the whole body off center."

Pointing to a Giacometti with slender legs, "What's the problem with this one if you were making it out of clay?" ("It wouldn't stand.") "How could you solve that problem?" With no hesitations solutions are offered, "put wire inside and clay around it"; "a platform"; "support."

Mr. Gebhart expands on the students' answers, showing further illustrations and reminding them to think about how they will present their figure. Then he recaps several tips adapting ideas from existing art pieces, planning before starting, using one's body as a guide, adding details last.

During the fourteen-minute lecture, Mr. Gebhart has the students' attention. Barb, chin on hands, has her eyes riveted to him and the book, nodding to herself. Valerie is unobtrusively observing from behind some more assertive students. Even Bo and Penny watch. "Continue with your work," concludes Mr. Gebhart. The students disperse, and the day continues in the usual manner of individual instruction. Seven or eight different types of projects are underway.[52]

Case 2: An Elementary School Teacher   Maya Dawson teaches kindergarten at a private school in New York City. As you read the following portrait, notice how effectively Maya communicates with her students.

Maya articulates with precision. Her voice is warm and soft, with a reminder of the rural South only in the slowness and sweetness of her speech. She is trim and energetic, a medium Afro forming a black halo around her open, friendly face. Her hands are in motion as she talks, softly hammering home a point, underlining a word, sweeping away an argument.

"Listen to the plans now," she says. "Yesterday you painted some wonderful penguins. And the day before we painted a beautiful Antarctic background. Today I want some of you to cut out penguins and paste them on the background in the hall."

"Me!"

"Me!"

"Me!"

Maya holds up her hand. "Wait a minute. Quiet now. We'll talk first and then we'll decide who will do what. So some of you will make a mural of millions and millions of penguins. Now, who didn't make a card for Spring [a student who is moving to Italy]?"

"I did!"

"I made a red one."

"No," Maya smiles. "No, my question is who did *not* make a card?"

Not a hand goes up. "Good. Everyone made one."

"I did."

"Yes!"

"Yes."

"Okay, good. Now, I wrote a message on the chalkboard, and I'd like someone to read it." About a half dozen hands shoot up, and these children go to the board one at a time to read out loud: "Dear Spring. We Will Miss You."

Maya selects five volunteers to cut out penguins.

"There's a lot of work to do there so you better get right to it. And don't forget to get scissors and paste." Off they go.

"We haven't done little books in a long time. Who wants to do little books at the table?" Ben, Vanessa, and Angola raise their hands and troop off to get supplies. "I'll be over in a minute," Maya calls after them.

"Who wants to play at the water table? Okay, Thomas and Aisha. And remember, one definite rule about the water table is you have to keep the water in the water table," she says with emphasis. "Now, you three can start working with blocks. I'll be there to see how you're doing in a short while."

The room begins to hum, and Maya moves around checking on each little group. She smiles at the block builders as they transform themselves quickly into doctors in a hospital emergency room.[53]

As the portraits of Gebhart and Dawson show, effective teachers are well organized, they create a positive classroom climate, and they establish meaningful, authentic relationships with students. While Gebhart and Dawson use different models of teaching, they share a commitment to working hard to promote the learning and growth of students.

SUMMARY

In this chapter we examined the dynamics of classroom life to help you anticipate the live teaching situation. We first discussed the culture of the classroom and reviewed the types of classrooms and common activities that take place in them.

Next, we examined how group dynamics can be applied in the classroom. We considered four aspects of group life: stages of group development, classroom norms and sanctions, leadership, and interpersonal interactions. Our discussion of classroom management pointed out that the key to effective management is problem prevention. As examples of strategies that can be used when management problems arise, we considered the LEAST approach, behavior modification strategies, and an individualized approach.

We then looked at several essential teaching skills: organization and planning, evaluation, and communication. These skills, we pointed out, are critical components of the instructional model a teacher uses. Finally, we identified several characteristics of effective teaching and illustrated these with two portraits of effective teachers.

ANSWER KEY FOR CONSIDER THIS . . .

"What Teaching Models Do You Prefer?" If you agreed with items 2, 7, and 11, you chose characteristics of the *Mastery Learning Model*. Other items you agreed with indicate the following preferences: Items 3, 5, and 10—*the Cooperative Learning Model*; Items 1, 4, and 14—*the Theory-into-Practice Model*; Items 6, 8, and 13—*the Behavior Modification Model*; and Items 9, 12, and 15—*the Nondirective Teaching Model*.

KEY TERMS AND CONCEPTS

classroom organization, 336
classroom climate, 337
between-class ability grouping, 339
within-class ability grouping, 340
activity format, 341
allocated time, 342
time on task, 342
academic learning time, 342
cooperative learning, 342
stages of group development, 343
sociogram, 343
norms, 345

sanctions, 345
democratic classroom, 348
lower-order questions, 349
higher-order questions, 349
classroom management, 351
LEAST approach, 352
behavior modification, 352
formative evaluation, 357
summative evaluation, 357
measurement, 357
model of teaching, 358

DISCUSSION QUESTIONS

1. Which of the approaches to classroom organization described in this chapter do you prefer? Why?
2. Do you agree with the Schmucks' description of the ideal classroom climate? Suggest an alternative climate that would also be effective.
3. Which student roles (i.e., class clown, isolate or loner, nonworker or do-nothing student, and reject or outcast) seem most challenging to you? What are some suggestions you have for working with these students?
4. Which student games have you seen used? Are these strategies ever of value?
5. Why are some teachers more successful than others at managing their classrooms?
6. When evaluating students, to what extent should teachers consider the effort students have applied to their learning?

APPLICATION ACTIVITIES

1. Analyze a course you are taking using the six sources of influence on classroom culture identified by Woolfolk and Galloway.
2. Determine the norms for the class for which you are reading this text. Use the format in Figure 11.3 to guide your analysis. Compare your perceptions with those of your classmates.
3. For any four of the guidelines for effective praise presented in Table 11.3 write hypothetical examples of praise you might give students after you have become a teacher.

FIELD EXPERIENCES

1. Observe several teachers at the level for which you are preparing to teach. To what extent does each teacher use the behaviors Rosenshine and Stevens present in their summary of research findings on teaching (see page 361)?
2. Form a team with several other classmates and analyze three to five classrooms in terms of the eight dimensions of effective and ineffective classroom climates. When you do so, apply a 10-point scale to the continuum between the negative and positive qualities (e.g., let 10 stand for order and 0 stand for chaos) and estimate where each class fits along the continuum. Discuss your answers and report your observations to the rest of the class.
3. After observing in a classroom for several days, offer to collect data for a sociogram for the teacher. (Use the description of a sociogram in this chapter to guide you. If you need further direction, refer to pages 166–171 in Alfred Gorman's book *Teachers and Learners: The Interactive Process of Education.*) Share the sociogram with the teacher and discuss with your class what you learned from the experience.

SUGGESTED READINGS

Canfield, J., and H. C. Wells. *100 Ways to Enhance Self-Concept in the Classroom: A Handbook for Teachers and Parents.* Englewood Cliffs, N.J.: Prentice-Hall, 1976. *This handbook provides many tips and strategies for enhancing student's self-esteem.*

Doyle, Walter. "Classroom Organization and Management." In *Handbook of Research on Teaching,* 3d ed., ed. Merlin C. Wittrock. New York: Macmillan, 1986. *In this chapter, Doyle includes his own extensive research on classroom organization and thoroughly reviews the findings of other researchers who have studied elementary and secondary classroom dynamics.*

Jackson, Philip. *Life in Classrooms,* 2d ed. New York: Teachers College Press, 1990. *This book is regarded as a classic in the field. It is a readable, perceptive look into elementary classroom life.*

Johnson, David W., Roger T. Johnson, Edythe Johnson Holubec, and Patricia Roy. *Circles of Learning.* Washington, D.C.: Association for Supervision and Curriculum Development, 1984. *A step-by-step guide to cooperative learning.*

Lightfoot, Sara Lawrence. *The Good High School: Portraits of Character and Culture.* New York: Basic Books, 1983. *A beautifully written view of several exemplary high schools and the students, administrators, and teachers in them.*

Waxman, Hersholt C., and Herbert J. Walberg, eds. *Effective Teaching: Current Research.* Berkeley, Calif.: McCutchan, 1991. *A comprehensive review of current research on effective teaching. Includes chapters on motivating students, cooperative learning, and research on "expert" teachers.*

TEACHERS . . .

What have you found is the best way to begin the school year?

My most successful years of teaching are attributed to organization and motivation. Organization is essential in planning, scheduling, setting up your room, establishing guidelines for the class to follow, and creating materials for each unit. It is also important to show your enthusiasm and excitement for the new school year. This way you are modeling the attitude you expect in your classroom.

—Amy Orcutt
Green Gables Elementary School, Jefferson Country, Colorado

The best way to "set the tone" for the year does not happen the first day. It actually takes a week. I let the students have an active role in this process. Together we set the standards, behaviors, and consequences that will mold the classroom.

—Julie A. Addison
Rock Ridge Elementary School, Castle Rock, Colorado

On the first day I believe teachers and students need to bond. Making introductions and setting the tone by helping students to communicate interpersonally can be helpful. This tends to set the stage.

A technique to begin the year: let the students know they matter as students and as human beings—very special human beings. I let my students know the class can be fun—exciting and enjoyable.

—Gail Grau
Southwest State Texas University, San Marcos, Texas

The first day of class!!!@@***!!! The impressions that are made in the first fifteen minutes of each class set the tone for the entire semester. Students note the way you greet them, say their names, call roll, identify class expectations and deal with the first actions of the designated class troublemaker. With calculated knowledge, they size up the personality of the class within minutes and decide immediately if it will be a drag—or totally awesome. They know who will get the A's and who will get the F's. They can tell just how tardy they can be before you'll notice and mark it in the book.

ON TEACHING

The only way to handle the first day of class is to do the unexpected. Grab their attention and their enthusiasm. Students can sense when you love what you're doing. Greet them at the door with handshakes, put candy kisses on each seat—anything that captures their attention. Let them know you care about them and what they can contribute to the class. Ask their opinions about things, and don't give needless busy work just because you have a homework policy.

—Barbara Arnold
Valencia High School, Placentia, California

The best way to begin any school year is to be thoroughly prepared. The entire month of August is devoted to preparing for that very first day. When my students walk into the classroom, they can see that their new room has been carefully and thoughtfully prepared. The bulletin boards, the lesson plans, the seating arrangement, the name tags, the polished furniture, and even the sharpened pencils. The room says, "I'm ready for you!" I dazzle the children by knowing their names, I warm them by sharing personal stories, and I challenge them by setting goals and expectations. The first day does say it all. It says, "I love teaching and I'm glad that you're here."

—Raelene Waddell
Leonard G. Westhoff Elementary School, Walnut, California

Since I teach kindergarten, I send out a letter to my students and parents welcoming them to my classroom and telling them how excited I am about our year together. Then I do an "open house" before the first day of school in which the parents bring their children and I introduce myself and show the children around my classroom. I have them walk over to their desk and their cubby with me; then I have their mom and dad let them play outside for awhile to become comfortable and acquainted with our schoolyard. Then the parents bring the child back and I ask them to show me where they sit and where their cubby is. If they forgot, I show them again. Before they leave I give them a new pencil and a special sticker. I strive to make this day as positive as possible.

—Sherry Reeve
Acacia Academy, West Covina, California

CHAPTER 12

The School Curriculum

*T*o the growth of the child all studies are subservient; they are instruments valued as they serve the needs of growth.

John Dewey
The Child and the Curriculum

As a beginning teacher, you are attending your school's open house held one evening during the early fall. From 7:30 to 8:30, teachers stay in their classrooms and visit with parents as they drop by. Several parents have already visited your classroom and heard you explain your curriculum. Based on their comments and questions, they appear to be pleased with what their children are learning.

Near the end of the evening, the parents of one of your students enter the room. After greeting them, you outline the goals and objectives of your curriculum. They listen attentively; the father even jots down a few notes on the cover of the open house program he was given when he signed in at the office.

After a few minutes, you begin to conclude. "Overall, one of the main goals of my curriculum is for students to go beyond the basics. I want them to know how to use the material they learn, how to solve problems."

At this point, your student's mother says, "I'm not sure I agree. The purpose of the curriculum should be to learn the basics. We want our child to do well on the state's test of basic skills."

"Right," her husband says. "If kids don't do well on the test, they're less likely to continue their education. To focus on anything other than the basics is to emphasize needless frills. That may sound harsh, but that's the way I feel."

How do you justify your curriculum to these parents?

FOCUS QUESTIONS

1. What is the ultimate aim of the curriculum?
2. What kinds of curricula do all students experience?
3. What factors influence what is taught in the schools?
4. How do textbook publishers influence the school curriculum?
5. How has the school curriculum changed during our nation's history?
6. What are some current trends and issues in the subject areas?

Think back to your experiences as a student at the elementary, middle, junior, and secondary schools you attended. What things did you learn? Certainly, the curriculum you experienced included reading, computation, penmanship, spelling, geography, and history. In addition to these topics, though, did you learn something about cooperation, competition, stress, football, video games, popularity, and the opposite sex? Or, perhaps, did you learn to love chemistry and to hate English grammar?

WHAT IS TAUGHT IN THE SCHOOLS?

The countless things you learned in school make up the curriculum that you experienced. Curriculum theorists and researchers have suggested several different definitions for **curriculum,** with no one definition universally accepted. Here are some definitions in current use.

1. A course of study, derived from the Latin *currere,* meaning "to run a course"
2. Course content, the information or knowledge that students are to learn
3. Planned learning experiences
4. Intended learning outcomes, the *results* of instruction as distinguished from the *means* (activities, materials, etc.) of instruction
5. All the experiences that students have while at school

No one of these five is in any sense the "right" definition. How we define curriculum depends on our purposes and the situation we find ourselves in. If, for example, we were advising a high school student on the courses he or she needed to take in order to prepare for college, our operational definition of curriculum would most likely be "a course of study." On the other hand, if we were interviewing sixth-grade students for their views on the K–6 elementary school they had just graduated from, we would probably want to view curriculum as "all the experiences that students have while at school."

For this chapter, let us posit an additional definition of curriculum. *Curriculum refers to the experiences, both planned and unplanned, that enhance (and sometimes impede) the education and growth of students.* According to this definition, the purpose of the curriculum is to educate, to promote growth. Although students have almost limitless experiences at school, not all of these experiences are educative or growth-promoting. One of the challenges you will face as a teacher, then, will be to present your students with a curriculum that contains as many experiences as possible that promote education or growth.

Kinds of Curriculum

Elliot Eisner, a noted educational researcher, has said that "schools teach much more— and much less—than they intend to teach. Although much of what is taught is explicit and public, a great deal is not."[1] For this reason, we need to look at the four curricula that all students experience. The more we understand these curricula and how they influence students, the better we will be able to develop educational programs that do, in fact, educate.

Explicit Curriculum   The explicit, or overt, curriculum refers to what a school intends to teach students. This curriculum is made up of several components: (1) the goals and aims the school has for all students, (2) the actual courses that make up each student's course of study, and (3) the specific knowledge, skills, and attitudes that teachers want students to acquire. If we asked a principal to describe the educational program at his or her school, our inquiry would be in reference to the explicit curriculum. Similarly, if we asked a teacher to describe what he or she wished to accomplish with a particular class, we would be given a description of the explicit curriculum.

In short, the **explicit curriculum** represents the publicly announced expectations the school has for its students. These expectations range from learning how to read, write, and compute to learning to appreciate music, art, and cultures other than one's own. In most instances, the explicit curriculum takes the form of written plans or guides for the education of students. Examples of such written documents are course descriptions, curriculum guides that set forth the goals and objectives for a school or district, texts and other commercially prepared learning materials, and teachers' lesson plans. Through the instructional program of a school, then, these curricular materials are brought to life.

Hidden Curriculum   The hidden, or implicit, curriculum refers to the behaviors, attitudes, and knowledge the culture of the school unintentionally teaches students. The image students formulate of themselves and their beliefs about how they should relate to others and to society in general are strongly influenced by the **hidden curriculum.**

What students learn via the hidden curriculum may be either positive or negative. Some students learn positive behaviors, such as how to cooperate with others, how to postpone gratification for more significant rewards, or how to stay on task in spite of temporary setbacks. Others learn negative behaviors, such as how to manipulate adults, how to get by on the effort of others, or how to cheat. Important attitudes are also acquired through the hidden curriculum: one can trust/mistrust those in authority; hard word does/does not pay off; school is/is not worthwhile; or teachers do/do not care about their students. Finally, the hidden curriculum presents students with knowledge about the way of the world: those in authority have more freedom than those who are not; the appropriateness of one's behavior depends upon the situation and the context; or misbehavior invites certain consequences.

As a result of the hidden curriculum of schools, students learn more than their teachers imagine. Although teachers cannot directly control what students learn through the hidden curriculum, they can increase the likelihood that what it teaches will be positive. By allowing students to help determine the content of the explicit curriculum, by inviting them to help establish classroom rules, and by providing them with challenges appropriate for their stage of development, teachers can ensure that the outcomes of the hidden curriculum are more positive than negative. The key is for teachers not to forget the hidden curriculum, to remember that one of the most important lessons students learn is what to make out of their lives at school.

FIVE-MINUTE FOCUS   Reflect on the 12,000 or so hours that you have spent in classrooms on the K–12 levels. What did the hidden curricula in these classes teach you about yourself? About teachers? Date your journal entry and write for five minutes.

Null Curriculum   Discussing a curriculum that cannot be observed directly is like talking about a black hole, a phenomenon whose proposed existence must be inferred because its incredible denseness and gravitational field does not allow light to escape. In much the same way, we can consider the curriculum that we *do not* find in the schools; it may be as important as what we *do* find. Elliot Eisner has labeled the intellectual processes and content that schools do not teach "the **null curriculum** . . . the options students are not afforded, the perspectives they may never know about, much less be able to use, the concepts and skills that are not a part of their intellectual repertoire."[2]

For example, the kind of thinking that schools foster among students is largely based on manipulations of words and numbers. Thinking that is imaginative, subjective, and poetic is stressed only incidentally. Also, students are seldom taught anthropology, sociology, psychology, law, economics, filmmaking, or architecture.

Eisner points out that "certain subject matters have been traditionally taught in schools not because of a careful analysis of the range of other alternatives that could be offered but rather because they have traditionally been taught. We teach what we teach largely out of habit, and in the process neglect areas of study that could prove to be exceedingly useful to students.[3] Japanese schools, for example, require considerably more art, music, and literature than most American schools. In addition, all Japanese students must study handicrafts and calligraphy. Japanese curricula go beyond verbal and numerical thinking to include the development of aesthetic capabilities. H. Fukushima, education attaché at the Japanese Embassy in Washington, D.C., has said of the school curriculum in his country, "The arts are very important to help people learn to cooperate and become good Japanese."[4] Unlike some of their American counterparts, the Japanese would be reluctant to consider eliminating art, music, or physical education (which includes dance) from the curriculum.

Certainly, American schools do need to emphasize essential skills in reading, writing, computation, and oral communication. However, the fact that so much of the K–12 curriculum in our schools is devoted to unvarying emphasis on these areas suggests that tradition and habit, not the immediate situation and the needs and interests of students, determine what is taught. When you accept the challenge of teaching, then, we ask that you devote your energy not only to clarifying *what* you will teach but *why* you will teach it. You will discover that school systems grant teachers varying degrees of freedom regarding what they teach. Your goal as a professional will be to work within surrounding constraints and offer students the subject matter your professional judgment suggests they need.

Extracurricular/Cocurricular Programs   The curriculum includes school-sponsored activities—music, drama, special interest clubs, sports, student government, and honor societies, to name a few—that students may pursue in addition to their studies in academic subject areas. When such activities are perceived as additions to the academic curriculum, they are termed *extracurricular*. When these activities are seen as having important educational goals—and not merely as "extras" added to the academic curriculum—they are termed *cocurricular*. To reflect the fact that these two labels are commonly used for the same activities, we will use the term *extracurricular/cocurricular activities*.

Though **extracurricular/cocurricular programs** are most extensive on the secondary level, many schools at the elementary, middle, and junior levels also provide their students with a broad assortment of extracurricular/cocurricular activities. For those students who choose to participate, such activities provide an opportunity to use social and academic skills in many different contexts.

Research shows that the larger a school is, the less likely it is that a student will take part in extracurricular/cocurricular activities. At the same time, those who do participate tend to have higher self-concepts than those who do not.[5] The actual effects that extracurricular/cocurricular activities have on students' development, however, are not entirely clear. In their review of research on the topic, Duane Alvin and David Morgan concluded that (1) there is little evidence to suggest that participation in sports is related to improved academic achievement, (2) participation in extracurricular/cocurricular activities does influence subsequent behavior, and (3) participation in extracurricular/cocurricular activities—particularly music, service and leadership activities, and sports—does have a positive influence on the level of education and the occupation one aspires to and eventually attains.[6]

It is clear, however, that students who might benefit the most from participating in extracurricular/cocurricular activities—those below the norm in academic achievement and students at risk—tend not to participate. For example, Table 12.1, based

TABLE 12.1   Participation in Extracurricular/Cocurricular Activities, Grades 7–12

Activities	Total Percent	Percent of Males	Percent of Females
1. Athletic teams/clubs	48.2%	54.3%	43.0%
2. Band/orchestra	20.7	20.9	20.4
3. Choir/choral groups	17.6	9.1	24.9
4. Career-oriented clubs	15.2	10.2	19.5
5. Language clubs	12.0	8.5	15.0
6. Drama/theater	11.8	8.0	15.0
7. Pep club	11.7	6.2	16.4
8. School publications	11.5	9.6	13.1
9. Student council/government	10.6	5.6	15.0
10. Service/volunteer groups	10.2	6.2	13.7
11. National Honor Society	7.9	7.8	7.9
12. Other honorary societies	6.7	4.7	8.5
13. Debate/speech	6.6	4.9	8.1
14. Cheerleading	5.8	0.5	10.4
15. Science clubs	5.2	6.2	4.2
16. None	17.7	20.5	15.2

Source: "The Mood of American Youth" (Reston, Va.: National Association of Secondary School Principals, 1984). Used with permission.

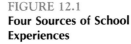

FIGURE 12.1
**Four Sources of School
Experiences**

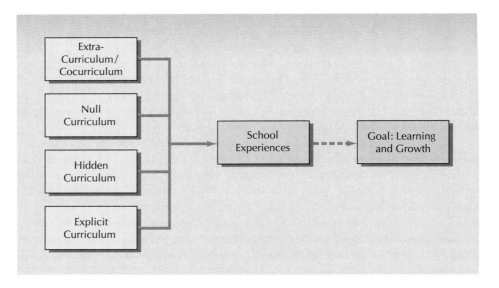

on a 1983 survey of 1,500 students in grades 7 through 12, reveals that nearly 52 percent of all students do *not* participate in athletics; nearly 80 percent do *not* take part in band or orchestra; over 78 percent are *not* involved in their schools' pep clubs; and nearly 18 percent are involved in *no* extracurricular/cocurricular activities at all.[7]

When you become a teacher it is important for you to recognize that all students are influenced by the four sources of school experiences we have just discussed. Figure 12.1 illustrates that the ultimate goal of these experiences is the learning and growth of students. As a professional, your task is to do what you can to ensure that each student has a broad range of school experiences that are truly worthy of being called educative. If you are able to do that, you will have gone a long way toward meeting the challenge of the profession.

Curriculum Content

Our nation's schools teach what the larger society feels young people should learn. Although some curricula reflect local and regional differences, the educational programs of most schools in this country are more alike than different. In fact, Goodlad found that what schools teach is characterized more by uniformity than by diversity: "Our data, whatever the source, reveal not only the curricular dominance of English/ Language arts and mathematics but also the consistent and repetitive attention to basic facts and skills. Developing 'the ability to read, write, and handle basic arithmetical operations' pervades instruction from the first through the ninth grades and the lower tracks of courses beyond."[8]

As we pointed out earlier, the purposes of education go beyond the mere accumulation of facts and skills. However, just about every group that has an interest in the schools—parents, educators, students, and politicians—has its own views regarding what should be taught. For example, in recent years in some states, parents and citizens' groups have demanded that certain content be added to the curriculum, or that certain subjects—such as moral education, women's studies, or environmental protection—receive more emphasis in the curriculum.

CONSIDER THIS . . .

What Subjects Should Students Study?

The 1990 Gallup Poll of the Public's Attitudes Toward the Public Schools asked respondents to identify high school courses that college-bound and noncollege-bound students should be required to take. Below, in alphabetical order, are the 14 subjects respondents were asked to rank.

For both groups of students, rank the courses from the most to the least important as required courses in both your own opinion and public opinion according to your predictions of the 1990 Gallup Poll results (1 = most important; 14 = least important). When you have finished your rankings, compare your results with the Gallup Poll findings presented in the answer key at the end of this chapter.

Most Important for College-Bound Students			Most Important for Noncollege-Bound Students	
Public Opinion	Your Own Opinion		Public Opinion	Your Own Opinion
____	*12*	Art *13*	____	____
____	*5*	Business Education *9*	____	____
____	*6*	Career Education *7*	____	____
____	*7*	Computer Training *5*	____	____
____	*1*	English *2*	____	____
____	*8*	Foreign Language *6*	____	____
____	*9*	Geography *10*	____	____
____	*10*	Health Education *12*	____	____
____	*3*	History/U.S. Government *3*	____	____
____	*2*	Mathematics *1*	____	____
____	*13*	Music *14*	____	____
____	*14*	Physical Education *11*	____	____
____	*4*	Science *4*	____	____
____	*11*	Vocational Training *2*	____	____

CURRICULUM DEVELOPMENT

Clearly, there is no one right approach a teacher can follow in developing the curriculum. Instead, he or she must try to assess sensitively and honestly the many factors that influence students' education, and out of that analysis develop a curriculum that will result in the greatest learning and growth for all.

FIGURE 12.2   **The Tyler Rationale for Curriculum Development**

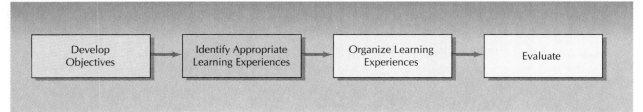

While there is no easy-to-follow set of procedures for developing curriculum, Ralph Tyler has provided four fundamental questions that must be answered in developing any curriculum or plan of instruction. These four questions, known as the **Tyler rationale** (see Figure 12.2), are:

1. What educational purposes should the school seek to attain?
2. What educational experiences can be provided that are likely to attain these purposes?
3. How can these educational experiences by effectively organized?
4. How can we determine whether these purposes are being attained?[9]

Some educators believe that the Tyler rationale underestimates the complexities involved in curriculum development because it advocates a straightforward, step-by-step process that, in reality, is difficult to follow. Nevertheless, Tyler's work has been used by a great number of school systems to bring some degree of order and focus to the curriculum development process.

A key concern in curriculum development is whether greater emphasis should be given to the requirements of the subject area or to the needs of the students. It is helpful to imagine where a school curriculum might be placed on the following continuum.

Student-Centered      Subject-Centered
Curriculum   Curriculum

While no course is entirely subject- or student-centered, curricula vary considerably in the degree to which they emphasize one or the other. The **subject-centered curriculum** places primary emphasis on the logical order of the discipline students are to study. The teacher of such a curriculum is a subject-matter expert and is primarily concerned with helping students understand the facts, laws, and principles of the discipline. Subject-centered curricula are more typical of high school education.

On the other hand, some teachers develop curricula that reflect greater concern for students and their needs. Though teachers of **student-centered curricula** also teach content, they emphasize the growth and development of students. This emphasis is generally more typical of elementary school curricula.

Who Plans the Curriculum?

One perennial issue in American education is who should plan the curriculum. Should planning be done only by the teachers who will be held accountable for implementing the curriculum? Should parents decide what they want their children to learn? Or should government officials, professional associations, or education researchers plan the curriculum?

FIGURE 12.3 **The Curriculum Plans Reservoir**

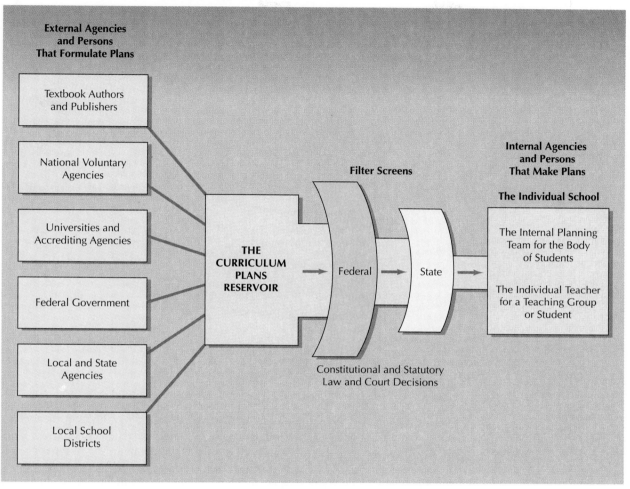

External Agencies and Persons That Formulate Plans

- Textbook Authors and Publishers
- National Voluntary Agencies
- Universities and Accrediting Agencies
- Federal Government
- Local and State Agencies
- Local School Districts

THE CURRICULUM PLANS RESERVOIR

Filter Screens

Federal → State

Constitutional and Statutory Law and Court Decisions

Internal Agencies and Persons That Make Plans

The Individual School

- The Internal Planning Team for the Body of Students
- The Individual Teacher for a Teaching Group or Student

Source: J. Galen Saylor, *Who Planned the Curriculum? A Curriculum Plans Reservoir Model with Historical Examples* (West Lafayette, Ind.: Kappa Delta Pi, 1982), p. 3. Used with permission.

The model presented in Figure 12.3 shows how these and other groups are involved in curriculum planning. Textbook publishers, for example, influence what is taught because many teachers use textbooks as curriculum guides. The federal government contributes to curriculum planning by setting national education goals, and state departments of education develop both broad aims for school curricula and specific minimum competencies for student performance. To ensure that students are mastering minimum competencies, most states have mandated standardized achievement tests at certain grade levels.

Within a given school, the curriculum-planning team and the classroom teacher plan the curriculum that students actually experience. As a teacher you will draw from a reservoir of curriculum plans prepared by others, thus playing a vital role in the curriculum-planning process. Whenever you make decisions about what material to include in your teaching, how to sequence content, and how much time to spend teaching certain material, you are planning the curriculum.

FIGURE 12.4
Influences on the School Curriculum

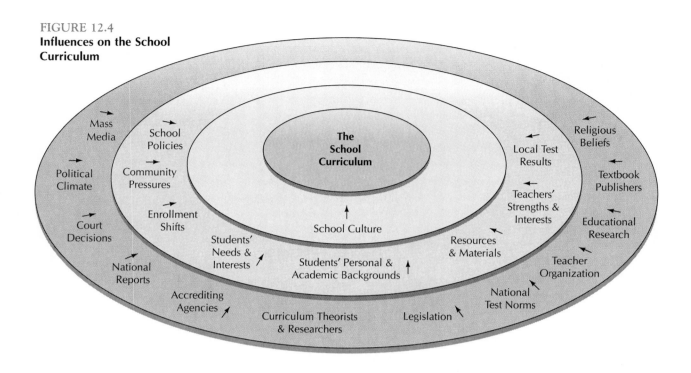

What Influences Curricular Decisions?

From the earliest colonial schools of more than 300 years ago to schools of the 1990s, the curriculum has been broadly influenced by a variety of religious, political, and utilitarian agendas. Figure 12.4 suggests the influence of community pressures, court decisions, students' life situations, testing results, national reports, teachers' professional organizations, research results, and other factors. The inner circle of the figure represents factors that have a more direct influence on curriculum development (such as students' needs and school district policies). The outer circle represents factors that are more removed from the school setting or have less obvious effects on the curriculum. Individual schools respond to all these influences differently, which further affects their curricula. Let us examine some of these influences in greater detail.

Social Issues and Changing Values   Values that affect curriculum planning include prevailing educational theories and teachers' educational philosophies. In addition, curriculum planners respond to social issues and changing values in the wider society. As a result, current social concerns find their way into textbooks, teaching aids, and lesson plans. Often curriculum changes are made in the hope that changing what students learn will help solve social problems or achieve local, statewide, or national goals. Required instructional units on water conservation or earthquake safety may reflect regional realities, for example, while increased recommended instruction in science may reflect beliefs about the national interest. Locally mandated curricula addressing health, safety, and morality issues—such as AIDS, teen pregnancy, substance abuse, and drunk driving—reflect growing public concern about the behaviors and attitudes that ultimately place everyone at risk.

The creative and evaluative tasks of choosing and developing curriculum materials are a source of both empowerment and frustration for teachers. Budget constraints, social and legal issues, and state and local curriculum mandates often determine curriculum choices.

Because the United States is so culturally diverse, proposed curriculum changes also reflect divergent interests and values. This divergence then leads to controversies over curriculum content and conflicting calls for reform. Some groups may demand that Christian teachings and observances be included in the public school curricula, for example, or that materials regarded as objectionable on religious grounds be censored or banned. Other groups may call for the elimination of all activities or symbols that have their origins in organized religion, including even secularized or commercialized ones such as Halloween and the Easter bunny. Curriculum changes to promote greater social integration or equity among racial or ethnic groups may draw complaints of irrelevancy or reverse discrimination. Traditionalists may object to curriculum changes that reflect feminist views.

As you can imagine, consensus on many curriculum reform issues is never achieved. However, because of their public accountability, schools must consider how to respond to those issues. A recent survey revealed that during a one-year period, half the school districts in Florida received complaints about curriculum content. Included were complaints claiming that the schools were undermining family values, overemphasizing globalism, underemphasizing patriotism, permitting profanity and obscenity, and teaching taboo subjects such as satanism and sex.[10]

Textbook Publishing   Textbooks greatly influence the curriculum. According to a survey of 12,000 K–12 teachers, 90 to 95 percent of classroom time is based on commercially published curriculum materials in the form of textbooks, workbooks, and computer software.[11] In addition, publishers influence school curricula by providing teaching objectives, learning activities, tests, audiovisual aids, and other supplements to assist their customers. This influence increases when school districts adopt a series of textbooks by one publisher—usually called a basal series. After adoption these books are used at several grade levels in all the schools in the district.

Like curriculum planners, textbook authors and publishers are influenced by trends in education and by social issues. In response to criticism, for example, publishers now tend to avoid bias in terms of gender, religion, class, race, and culture. However, because the goal of business is profit, publishers are most responsive to market trends

FIGURE 12.5   A Chronology of Major Emphases in the School Curriculum

1620 — Emphasis on basic skills needed to learn religious catechisms and read prayers. Curriculum also includes surveying, navigation, and bookkeeping. Education primarily for the elite.

1636 — Latin grammar (college-prep) schools established and, like Harvard and Yale Colleges, emphasize Latin, Greek, theology, and philosophy for those preparing to enter law or religion.

1647 — Massachusetts Law of 1647 mandates a reading and writing teacher for towns of 50 or more families; a Latin teacher for towns of 100 or more. Females taught basics to enable them to carry out religious and family responsibilities.

Religious Emphasis

1700s — Public schools teach reading, writing, and basic mathematics (counting, adding, and subtracting) to prepare students for jobs and apprenticeships.

Early 1750s — Academies teach secondary students a practical curriculum (drawing, surveying, navigation, merchant's accounting, etc.) to become tradesmen and workers.

Political Emphasis

1821 — First public high school teaches basic skills and history, geography, health, and physical training.

1860 — First English-speaking kindergarten emphasizes growth, activity, play, songs, and stories.

1874 — Free public schooling now includes high schools that place strong emphasis on vocational education and reading, writing, and mathematics.

Utilitarian Emphasis

1893 — Committee of Ten asserts that high schools are for college-bound and curriculum should emphasize mental disciplines in humanities, language, and science.

1918 — Commission on Reorganization of Secondary Education focuses on individual differences. Curriculum to stress Seven Cardinal Principles.

1930s & 1940s — Progressive education movement stresses curriculum based on students' needs and interests. Home economics, health, family living, citizenship, and woodshop added to the curriculum.

Education for Masses

1957 — Russia's Sputnik sparks emphasis on science, mathematics, and languages.

1960s — Calls for relevancy result in expanded course offerings and electives.

Mid-1970s — Back-to-basics movement emphasizes reading, writing, mathematics, and oral communication.

1983 — *Nation at Risk* report calls for "five new basics"—English, mathematics, science, social studies, and computer science.

1985 — Rigorous core curricula advocated at all levels in an effort to increase standards and to ensure quality.

The Excellence Movement

1989 — The Carnegie Council on Adolescent Development report, *Turning Points*, recommends the creation of learning communities and a core academic program for middle-level students.

1990 — President Bush unveils national educational goals in six areas: readiness for school; high school completion; student achievement and citizenship; science and mathematics; adult literacy and lifelong learning; and safe, disciplined, and drug-free schools.

Timeline markers: 1620, 1640, 1660, 1680, 1700, 1720, 1740, 1760, 1780, 1800, 1820, 1840, 1860, 1880, 1900, 1920, 1940, 1960, 1980, 2000 and customer preferences. They are often reluctant to risk losing sales by including subjects that are controversial or that may be offensive to their bigger customers. They may also modify textbooks to appeal to decision makers in populous states that make statewide adoptions of textbooks, such as California and Texas.

Educators have criticized textbooks for inoffensiveness to the point of blandness, for artificially lowered reading levels (called "dumbing down"), and for pedagogically questionable "gimmicks" to hold students' attention. The late child psychologist Bruno Bettelheim and his associate, Karen Zelan, for example, ask the following question about basal readers:

> Why are these primers used to teach reading, when children universally object that they find them boring, when they use an unjustifiably limited vocabulary much too repetitiously, and when they obviously fail in their purpose, since all too few of the children taught by means of these texts become literate?[12]

While the publishing industry continually responds to such criticisms, you would be wise to follow systematic guidelines in evaluating and selecting textbooks and other curriculum materials. One survey reported that 35 percent of teachers spend less than one hour per year on the selection of materials and that 25 percent of them spend an average of only 10 hours per year on the selection process.[13] To assist you in this process we have provided a set of guidelines, "Curriculum Materials Evaluation Criteria," which appear in the Teacher's Resource Guide at the back of this book.

CURRICULUM REFORM

The content of the curricula in America's schools has changed frequently since our colonial period. These modifications came about as the goals of the schools were debated, additional needs of society became evident, and the characteristics of student populations shifted. Over time, schools have had to focus on a wide variety of goals set by society, and through their curricula, they have tried to achieve those goals. The following list is a sampling of goals the schools have set for themselves at different times in our history:

- Prepare students to carry out religious and family responsibilities
- Provide employers with a source of literate workers
- Desegregate society
- Reduce crime, poverty, and injustice
- Help our country maintain its competitive edge in the world economy
- Provide the scientists needed to keep our country strong
- Educate students for intelligent participation in a democracy

It is difficult to sketch a clear picture of how school curricula have changed since our country began. However, curriculum historians J. Minor Gwynn and John Chase, Jr. have suggested that five factors have influenced our schools' curricula at various points in our nation's history: (1) religious sentiments, (2) political factors, (3) utilitarian aims, (4) the push for mass education, and (5) the push for excellence in education.[14] The timeline presented in Figure 12.5 indicates the approximate period during which these five factors exerted their strongest influence on the curriculum. (Each factor, of course, continues to exert at least some influence on today's curricula.) In addition, the timeline shows several of the major shifts in what was actually taught.

Church and School

From 1620 to 1760, the primary aim of the curriculum was to train students in religious beliefs and practices. It was only later that a distinction was made between civil and religious life. Basic skills were taught for the purpose of learning religious catechisms and reading prayers. In addition to taking courses with religious content, students also studied such practical subjects as surveying, navigation, bookkeeping, architecture, and agriculture.

Initially, colonial education was conducted in the home, but by 1647 Massachusetts had passed the Old Deluder Satan Act, which required communities to establish schools. Textbooks were rarely used and usually poor in quality. Most material for instruction came from the Bible or catechisms. The quality of teachers was uneven, and nearly all were judged according to religious criteria. As you have seen, religious views still exert an influence on curriculum, such as the movement during the 1980s to teach creationism along with evolutionism in science courses.

Nation and School

Political motives provided the curriculum's major focus from 1770 to 1860. The United States had just won its independence from England, and many policymakers believed that literacy was essential to the preservation of freedom and a democratic way of life. Accordingly, students were taught history, geography, health, and physical training, as well as the basic skills of reading, writing, and computation. In 1821, the nation's first public high school was opened in Boston, and two years later the first private normal school for teachers opened in Concord, Vermont. The first English-speaking kindergarten, taught by Elizabeth Peabody, opened in Boston in 1860.

By the beginning of the Civil War, the basic skills of reading, writing, and mathematics were well established in the curriculum. Various types of schools had been incorporated into state systems, and in 1852 the first compulsory school attendance law was passed in Massachusetts. Parents in every section of the country wanted more and better opportunities for their children. Through a curriculum that stressed individual virtue, literacy, hard work, and moral development, reformers wished to improve social conditions and to provide more opportunities for the poor.

Political motives continue to influence school life and school curricula. All students, for example, are required to study United States history and the United States Constitution at some time during their school career. Presidents' birthdays and national holidays are built into the school year calendar. Issues concerning civil liberties and the expression of patriotism often become educational issues, as in controversies during the last decades over treatment of the American flag and the recitation of the Pledge of Allegiance in schools.

FIVE-MINUTE FOCUS   What religious and political emphases affected your learning as a student in elementary school or high school? Which experiences do you view as having been positive ones? Which do you view as having been negative for you? Date your journal entry and write for five minutes.

Children and School

Utilitarian goals for the curriculum were most prominent from 1860 to 1920. The turn of the century brought with it many changes that profoundly influenced the curriculum. The dawning of the machine age altered the nature of industry, transportation, and communication. The growth of cities and the influx of millions of immigrants resulted in new functions for all social institutions, and home life was forever changed. As a result, curricula came to be based upon social and individual need rather than upon subject matter divisions. Subjects were judged by the criterion of social utility rather than by their ability to develop the intellect.

During this period, several national committees met for the purpose of deciding what should be taught in elementary and secondary schools. Initially, these communities espoused goals formed by educators at the college and private secondary school levels—that is, uniform curricula with standardized methods of instruction. Gradually, though, these appointed groups began to recommend curricula that were more flexible and based on the needs of children. This shift is seen clearly in the recommendations made by three of the more influential committees during this period: the Committee of Ten, the Committee of Fifteen, and the Commission on Reorganization of Secondary Education.

The Committee of Ten During 1892–93, the directors of the National Education Association appropriated $2,500 for a **Committee of Ten** to hold nine conferences that focused on the following subjects in the high school curriculum: (1) Latin, (2) Greek, (3) English, (4) other modern languages, (5) mathematics, (6) physics, astronomy, and chemistry, (7) natural history (biology, botany, and zoology), (8) history, civil government, and political science, and (9) geography (physical geography, geology, and meteorology). The group's members—five college presidents, one college professor, two headmasters of private schools, one principal of a public high school, and the United States Commissioner of Education—decided that the primary function of high schools was to take intellectually elite students and prepare them for life. Their recommendations stressed mental discipline in the humanities, languages, and science. Table 12.2, for example, shows the number of periods per week that the committee felt high school students should devote to their studies.[15]

The Committee of Fifteen The report of the Committee of Ten sparked such discussion that in 1893 the National Education Association appointed the **Committee of Fifteen** to examine the elementary curriculum. In keeping with the view that high schools were college preparatory institutions, the committee's report, published in 1895, called for the introduction of Latin, the modern languages, and algebra into the elementary curriculum. In addition, the curriculum was to be organized around five basic subjects: grammar, literature, arithmetic, geography, and history.

The Reorganization of Secondary Education In 1913 the National Education Association appointed the Commission on the **Reorganization of Secondary Education.** The commission's report, *Cardinal Principles of Secondary Education,* was released in 1918 and called for a high school curriculum designed to accommodate individual differences in scholastic ability. Seven educational goals were to provide the focus for schooling at all levels: health, command of fundamental processes (reading, writing, and computation), worthy home membership, vocation, citizenship, worthy use of leisure time, and ethical character. Although the report recognized the need to prepare

TABLE 12.2   Recommended Secondary School Subjects, 1894

First Year	
Subject	Periods
Latin	5 p.
English literature, 2 p.	
English composition, 2 p.	4 p.
German (or French)	5 p.
Algebra	4 p.
History of Italy, Spain, and France	3 p.
Applied geography (European political-continental and oceanic flora and fauna)	4 p.
Total	**25 p.**

Second Year	
Subject	Periods
Latin	4 p.
Greek	5 p.
English literature, 2 p.	
English composition, 2 p.	4 p.
German, continued	4 p.
French, begun	5 p.
Algebra,* 2 p.	
Geometry, 2 p.	4 p.
Botany or zoology	4 p.
English history to 1688	* 3 p.
Total	**33 p.**

Third Year	
Subject	Periods
Latin	4 p.
Greek	4 p.
English literature, 2 p.	
English composition, 1 p.	
Rhetoric, 1 p.	4 p.
German	4 p.
French	4 p.
Algebra,* 2 p.	
Geometry, 2 p.	4 p.
Physics	4 p.
History, English and American	3 p.
Astronomy, 3 p. first half year	
Meteorology, 3 p. second half year	3 p.
Total	**34 p.**

Fourth Year	
Subject	Periods
Latin	4 p.
Greek	4 p.
English literature, 2 p.	
English composition, 1 p.	
English grammar, 1 p.	4 p.
German	4 p.
French	4 p.
Trigonometry	
Higher Algebra	2 p.
Chemistry	4 p.
History (intensive) and civil government	3 p.
Geology or physiography, 4 p. first half year	
Anatomy, physiology, and hygiene, 4 p. second half year	4 p.
Total	**33 p.**

*Option of bookkeeping and commercial arithmetic

Source: Report of the Committee of Ten on Secondary School Studies with the Reports of the Conferences Arranged by the Committee (National Education Association, 1894).

able students for college, it also stressed the development of reading and writing abilities for all students. Accordingly, students were to be given writing assignments based on their own experiences rather than on their analyses of great works of literature.

Standards and School

From 1920 to present, schools have become increasingly accountable for providing quality educational experiences to all students. To meet these demands for higher standards, schools have undertaken numerous curricular reforms and used more sophisticated methods for measuring the educational outcomes of these reforms.

The Push for Mass Education Since 1920, schools have been expected to provide educational opportunities for all Americans. During this period, curricula have been developed to meet the needs and differences of many diverse student groups: handicapped, bilingual, gifted, delinquent, and learning disabled students, for example. Moreover, these curricula have been used not only in public and private schools but also in alternative schools: night schoois, schools without walls, summer schools, vocational schools, continuation schools, schools-within-schools, magnet schools, and so on. (One survey conducted in 1973 identified more than 600 alternative public schools;[16] another survey done in 1981 found that the number of public alternative schools had mushroomed to over 10,000, with an estimated three million children enrolled![17])

The Progressive Curriculum The concern in this country for educating all our youth has drawn much of its initial energy from the progressive education movement. During the 1920s, the Progressive Education Association reacted against the earlier emphasis on the mental disciplines and called for elementary schools to develop curricula based on the needs and interests of all students. Throughout the 1930s, progressive ideas were promoted on the secondary level as well.

Though there was no single set of beliefs that united all progressives, there was general agreement that students should be involved in activities that parallel those found in society. Furthermore, those activities should engage students' natural interests. With these guidelines in mind, the progressive education movement expanded the curriculum to include such topics as home economics, health, family living, citizenship, and wood shop. The spirit of the progressive education movement is expressed well in a statement made in 1926 by the Director of the School of Organic Education in Fairhope, Alabama:

> We believe that education is life, growth; that the ends are immediate; that the end and the process are one. We believe that all children should have the fullest opportunity for self-expression, for joy, for delight, for intellectual stimulus through subject matter, but we do not believe that children should be made self-conscious or externalized by making subject matter an end. Our constant thought is not what do the children learn or do, but what are the "learning" and the "doing" doing to them. . . .
>
> We believe that society owes all children guidance, control, instruction, association, and inspiration—right conditions of growth—throughout the growing years until physical growth is completed. No child may know failure—all must succeed. Not "what do you know" but "what do you need," should be asked, and the nature of childhood indicates the answer.[18]

The Eight-Year Study   One of the most ambitious projects of the progressive education movement was the **Eight-Year Study,** which ran from 1932 to 1940. During this period, 30 public and private high schools were given the opportunity to restructure their educational programs according to progressive tenets and without regard for college and university entrance requirements. Over 300 colleges and universities then agreed to accept the graduates of these schools. The aim of the study, according to its director, was "to develop students who regard education as an enduring quest for meanings rather than credit accumulation."[19] The curricula developed by these schools emphasized problem solving, creativity, self-directed study, and more extensive counseling and guidance for students.

Ralph Tyler evaluated the Eight-Year Study by matching nearly 1,500 graduates of the experimental schools who went on to college with an equal number of college freshmen who graduated from other high schools. He found that students in the experimental group received higher grades in every subject area except foreign languages and had slightly higher overall grade point averages. Even more significant, perhaps, was the finding that the experimental group had higher performance in such areas as problem solving, inventiveness, curiosity, and motivation to achieve. Unfortunately, the Eight-Year Study failed to have any lasting impact on American education—possibly because World War II overshadowed the study's results.

The Push for Excellence   Concern with excellence in our schools ran high during the decade that spanned the late 1950s to the late 1960s. More recently, excellence in the curriculum has been a hotly debated issue since the late 1970s. Though schools have always had to strive to accomplish difficult goals, the current excellence movement has attached new meanings to the terms *quality, standards,* and *accountability.*

The Soviet Union's launching of the satellite Sputnik in 1957 marked the beginning of a great concern in this country over the content of the schools' curricula. Admiral Hyman G. Rickover was a leading proponent of an academically rigorous curriculum and urged the public to see that our strength as a nation was virtually linked to the quality of our educational system. He wrote in his 1959 book *Education and Freedom:*

> The past months have been a period of rude awakening for us. Our eyes and ears have been assaulted by the most distressing sort of news about Russia's giant strides in technology, based on the extraordinary success she has had in transforming her educational system. All but in ruins twenty-five years ago, it is today an efficient machine for producing highly competent scientists and engineers—many more than we can hope to train through our own educational system which we have so long regarded with pride and affection.
>
> We are slowly thinking our way through a thicket of bitter disappointment and humiliating truth to the realization that America's predominant educational philosophy is as hopelessly outdated today as the horse and buggy. Nothing short of a complete reorganization of American education, preceded by a revolutionary reversal of educational aims, can equip us for winning the educational race with the Russians.[20]

Fueled by arguments like Rickover's, many curriculum reform movements were begun in the 1950s and 1960s. The federal government became involved and poured great sums of money into developing curricula in mathematics, the sciences, modern languages, and, to a lesser extent, English and history. Once again, the focus of the curriculum was on the mental disciplines and the social and psychological needs of children were secondary. Testing and ability grouping procedures were expanded in an effort to identify and to motivate academically able students.

The Inquiry-Based Curriculum The prevailing view of what should be taught in the schools during this period was influenced significantly by Jerome Bruner's short book, *The Process of Education.* A report on a conference of scientists, scholars, and educators at Woods Hole, Massachusetts, in 1959, Bruner's book synthesized current ideas about intelligence and about how to motivate students to learn. Bruner believed that students should learn the "methods of inquiry" common to the academic disciplines. For example, instead of learning isolated facts about chemistry, students should learn the principles of inquiry common to the discipline of chemistry. In short, students would learn to think like chemists; they would be able to use principles from chemistry to solve problems independently.

Bruner's ideas were used as a rationale for making the curriculum more rigorous at all levels. As he pointed out in an often-quoted statement in *The Process of Education,* "Any subject can be taught effectively in some intellectually honest form to any child at any stage of development."[21] Bruner advocated a "spiral" curriculum wherein children would encounter the disciplines at ever-increasing levels of complexity as they progressed through school. Thus, elementary students could be taught physics in a manner that would pave the way for their learning more complex principles of physics in high school.

The Relevancy-Based Curriculum The push for a rigorous academic core curriculum was offset in the mid-1960s by a call for relevancy in the curriculum. Many educators, student groups, and political activists charged that school curricula were unresponsive to social issues and significant changes in our culture. At some schools, largely high schools, students actually demonstrated against educational programs they felt were not relevant to their needs and concerns. In response to this pressure, educators began to add more courses to the curriculum, increase the number of elective and remedial courses offered, and experiment with new ways of teaching. This concern with relevancy continued until the back-to-basics movement began in the mid 1970s.

The Core Curriculum In the early 1980s, the public was reminded anew that our country's well-being depended upon its system of education, and once again our schools were found lacking in excellence. Several national reports claimed that curriculum standards had eroded. The 1983 report by the National Commission on Excellence in Education asserted, for example, that secondary school curricula had become "homogenized, diluted, and diffused." And even Admiral Rickover, in his characteristically terse, hard-hitting manner, pointed out in 1983 that school curricula had become less rigorous:

> Student performance is lower than in 1957 at the time of Sputnik, when many so-called reforms were initiated. Some curricula involve expensive gimmicks, trivial courses and quick fixes of dubious value. Teachers are often poorly trained and misused on non-academic tasks. Many students have settled for easy, so-called relevant and entertaining courses. They and their parents are deceived by grade inflation. And the lack of national standards of performance blinds everyone to how poor our education system is.
>
> There should be a return to the ideal of a truly liberal education based on the three R's, which results in the ability to speak fluently and to write clearly. Mandatory academic courses must be given priority over electives.[22]

The push for excellence in the high school curriculum received a boost at the end of 1987 when U.S. Secretary of Education William J. Bennett proposed an academically rigorous **core curriculum** for all high school students. In a U.S. Department of Education booklet entitled *James Madison High School: A Curriculum for American Students,* Bennett described what such a curriculum might look like for an imaginary high school. His course of study called for four years of English consisting of four year-long literature courses; three years each of science, mathematics, and social studies; two years of foreign language; two years of physical education; and one semester each of art and music history. Twenty-five percent of his program would be available for students to use for electives.[23]

As we have seen, the content of the curriculum does not remain static. It is continuously refined, added to or subtracted from, based upon the prevailing needs of society and our views of children and how they learn. Decisions regarding what the schools should teach are not easily arrived at. The curriculum must, somehow, reflect the beliefs, values, and needs of widely different groups: liberals and conservatives, rich and poor, gifted and remedial, college-bound and work-bound, and immigrants and native-born.

SUBJECT AREAS: CURRENT TRENDS

The final section of this chapter will examine briefly some of the current trends and issues regarding what is taught in elementary, middle, junior-high, and high schools. (For a list of periodicals that include techniques and materials, see "Subject-Area Curriculum Materials," and for information on obtaining "Free Curriculum Materials," and "Analysis of Educators' Index of Free Materials, 1990," consult the Teachers' Resource Guide at the end of this book.) At each level we typically find the following subjects: language arts (including reading, writing, English, listening, and speaking), mathematics, science, social studies, foreign languages, the arts, and physical education. Though our nation's schools serve many different student populations, commonalities within these subject areas are easily found.

Language Arts

Unlike other areas of the curriculum, the reading and writing abilities of students have been closely monitored by the public. Some critics have suggested that students' skills in the use of the English language are declining. Though there is uncertain evidence that the language arts skills of the current generation of students are any worse than those of previous generations, language arts teachers are under increasing pressure to teach *all* children the skills they need to become literate.

The importance of attaining a minimum level of literacy in our society cannot be underestimated; the language arts are the tools through which students learn in nearly all other areas of the curriculum. Most students who are deficient in reading and writing skills are at a significant disadvantage when it comes to seeking employment or additional education.

Reading   The teaching of reading at all levels should focus on acquiring basic comprehension skills and learning to appreciate literature in its various forms: novels, essays, poetry, short stories, and so on. Reading teachers, however, are currently far from united as to how these aims should be realized. Does instruction in phonics enhance reading comprehension? Is a holistic, "immersion" approach to the teaching of reading superior to teaching isolated decoding and comprehension skills? Should children be taught the alphabet before learning to read?

In spite of such questions, though, reading research has suggested several general guidelines for improving reading instruction. Among them are the following:

1. Reading skills should be taught in context, not in isolation. Students cannot be taught to read outside the context of their expectations, cares, doubts, questions, loves, or hates.
2. Reading instruction should be explicitly structured and organized. While no specific system of reading instruction works with all students, just about any system works with most if it is structured and organized.
3. Questions asked of readers should be changed to promote better understanding. Questions that ask students to predict, to relate the text to prior knowledge, and to evaluate predicted outcomes are superior to more literal and factual questions.
4. Vocabulary instruction should be changed to relate more to students' present knowledge and experience. Instruction that emphasizes where a word fits in a student's present vocabulary is better than methods that emphasize word recognition vocabulary and verbatim definitions.
5. Reading teachers should give frequent, direct, and explicit instruction for comprehension skills. Current approaches to comprehension that stress only practice omit a critical element—the teacher acting as a model, demonstrating how to solve problems and showing what clues to look for in the text in order to find solutions.[24]

Writing In response to pressures to ensure that all students attain at least a minimum level of literacy, researchers in language arts instruction and groups such as the National Council of Teachers of English and the International Reading Association have formulated guidelines for effective instruction in the language arts. For example, Stephen Tchudi, a leading researcher in the writing process, has made four recommendations for writing instruction at all levels:

1. Writing programs must be based on frequent, authentic writing experiences, for all students—basic or advanced—and with a corresponding decrease in isolated drill in so-called language basic skills.
2. Writing-across-the-curriculum projects must be developed by English and other subject matter faculty and put into place so that writing is used in all classes, not just English/language arts classes.
3. Inservice and staff development for English and content-area teachers must be expanded, preferably at the expense of testing programs.
4. Composition teachers must be given more satisfactory teaching conditions, including manageable class sizes and loads.[25]

During the last two decades, several new approaches have been incorporated into the language arts curriculum. Many English teachers have reduced the amount of time spent on grammar, electing instead to teach grammar as needed within the context of a writing program. Since the 1960s, English teachers have generally broadened their view of literature to include more contemporary forms of writing and the literary contributions of minority or ethnic writers. Teaching in the English classroom now frequently includes such techniques as creative writing, drama, journal writing, guided fantasy exercises, and group discussions. In addition, the advent of personal computers, with their word processing capabilities, holds forth promise that even more powerful ways will be found to teach students the art of writing.

Keepers of the Dream

Eric S. McKamey
Learning Disabilities Teacher
Peabody School, Chicago, Illinois

"I get a lot of results because my kids know that they can trust me," says Eric McKamey, a Learning Disabilities Resource teacher at Peabody Elementary School on Chicago's West Side. Most of McKamey's students, who are 9 to 15 years old, are bilingual (English and Spanish). McKamey teaches writing, reading, and comprehension skills to 19 students who are Puerto Rican, Mexican American, African American, and Anglo American. Each day his students leave their regular classrooms and spend about an hour working with McKamey.

"I try to get close to my children so they know I care about them," says McKamey. "We do a lot of talking, and it's rewarding to see them start to feel better about themselves through learning. Every so often I'll have a student who no longer needs special education services, and that's very satisfying."

Motivating learning-disabled students, McKamey reports, is challenging. "I try everything I can. If something doesn't work, I'll try something else. Each child is different, so you have to look at the individual child and his or her particular learning problems."

One of McKamey's most successful techniques is what he calls the "Tell Me a Story . . ." approach. McKamey tells his students a story and then has them repeat the story in their own words. If students can retell the story, McKamey then has them write the story, answer factual questions, or even draw illustrations. For younger students, McKamey transcribes the stories they retell and gives them a

> *"Because They Know I Really Care"*

sense of ownership by having them illustrate the stories he writes.

McKamey also has his students work on visual and auditory perception, memory, music, and art; he relates these areas to reading and language skills. On occasion, he will go into his students' regular classrooms to help them with their assignments.

McKamey's teaching style is based on the close relationships he establishes with his students.

The one thing I've found is that if you're honest with kids and let them know you're human, they'll be more willing to try to learn. They'll want to learn and try harder because they know I really care and am a fair, honest person.

McKamey is truly dedicated to his students and to the teaching profession. His confirmation comes when he sees a student experiencing, perhaps for the first time, a sense of confidence and pride in his or her accomplishments.

I really like my job. Though I have occasional problems, I really like teaching. I hate to miss a day of school. My kids know I don't like to miss a day of school, and I don't like for them to miss school. I've thought about moving into a position that would take me out of the classroom, but at the last minute I couldn't do it. I could never match the rewards I get from teaching.

One promising new approach is known as the **whole language movement.** Advocates of the whole language approach believe that reading is part of general language development, not an isolated skill students learn apart from listening, speaking, and writing. Teachers in whole language classrooms seldom use textbooks; instead, young students write stories and learn to read from their writing, and older students read literature that is closely related to their everyday experiences.

FIVE-MINUTE FOCUS   In light of calls for writing across the curriculum, what kinds of writing activities will you involve your students in when you begin to teach? Date your journal entry and write for five minutes.

Mathematics

As we have mentioned, the public became quite concerned during the late 1950s with the quality of mathematics education in our schools. The launching of Sputnik in 1957 spurred a wave of reform in the mathematics curriculum, and students in the late 1950s and early 1960s were taught the new math. Though the new math, with its emphasis on the structure of mathematics, has since been shown to be too abstract to be easily applied to everyday problem solving, the movement did highlight the need for continuous evaluation of the mathematics curriculum.

In 1977, the National Council of Supervisors of Mathematics issued a position paper that set forth 10 basic skills areas in mathematics. Eleven years later the Council, stating that its earlier position was a response to "an overly-narrow conception of basic skills," revised its stance in a paper entitled *Basic Mathematical Skills for the 21st Century.* This document identified 12 critical mathematics skills and made it clear that the mathematics curriculum should consist of more than computation skills (see Table 12.3).

As has been the case with nearly all areas of the curriculum in the early 1990s, the goals proposed by the Council have not become a reality. Mathematics programs, from the elementary through secondary levels, frequently focus upon the mechanical acquisition of skills identified by a select few textbooks. Using mathematics to think logically and to solve problems, though an ideal end, may be more the exception than the rule. A hopeful indicator that the mathematics curriculum will continue to be updated, however, is the importance that students attach to this subject. A 1983 survey of 1,500 students in grades 7 through 12 revealed that students judge mathematics to be the most important course in the curriculum (see Table 12.4).

TABLE 12.3   Basic Mathematical Skills for the 21st Century

1. ***Problem solving***—posing questions, analyzing situations, translating results, illustrating results, drawing diagrams, and using trial and error.

2. ***Communicating mathematical ideas***—receiving mathematical ideas through listening, reading, and visualizing; presenting mathematical ideas by speaking, writing, drawing pictures and graphs, and demonstrating with concrete models.

3. ***Mathematical reasoning***—being able to distinguish between valid and invalid arguments; using counter-examples to disprove a conjecture and using models, known facts, and logical arguments to validate a conjecture.

4. ***Applying mathematics to everyday situations***—taking everyday situations, translating them into mathematical representations in light of the initial situation.

5. ***Alertness to reasonableness of results***—questioning the reasonableness of a solution or conjecture in relation to the original problem.

6. ***Estimation***—being able to carry out rapid approximate calculations through the use of mental arithmetic and a variety of computational estimation techniques; acquiring simple techniques for estimating measurements such as length, area, volume, and mass (weight).

7. ***Appropriate computational skills***—gaining facility with addition, subtraction, multiplication, and division with whole numbers and decimals.

8. ***Algebraic thinking***—learning to solve practical problems that involve algebraic thinking; for example, solving ratio, proportion, percent, direct variation, and inverse variation problems.

9. ***Measurement***—learning to measure (in both metric and conventional systems) distance, mass (weight), time, capacity, temperature, and angles, as well as calculate simple perimeters, areas, and volumes.

10. ***Geometry***—understanding concepts such as parallelism, perpendicularity, congruence, similarity, and symmetry, as well as the basic properties of simple plane and solid geometric figures.

11. ***Statistics***—knowing how to construct, read, and draw conclusions from simple tables, maps, charts, and graphs; being able to present information about numerical data such as measures of central tendency (mean, median, mode) and measures of dispersion (range, deviation).

12. ***Probability***—understanding elementary notions of probability to determine the likelihood of future events; becoming familiar with how mathematics is used to help make predictions such as election results and business forecasts.

Source: National Council of Supervisors of Mathematics, *Basic Mathematical Skills for the 21st Century* (Houston, Tex.: National Council of Supervisors of Mathematics, draft, March 7, 1988).

Science

We need only pause for a moment to observe the importance and influence of science in daily life. Ours is a highly scientific and technological society, and it is becoming more so. Life in such a society requires an understanding of science and its processes.

Perhaps more than any other area of the curriculum, the teaching of science in the United States has come under increasingly critical scrutiny. A 1980 study by the National Science Foundation concluded that the United States is decidedly behind

TABLE 12.4   Students' Importance Ratings
of Courses, Grades 7–12

Courses	Combined Rating	Males' Rating	Females' Rating	Very Important (percent)	Somewhat Important (percent)
1. Mathematics	3.81	3.78	3.83	80.2%	15.0%
2. English	3.72	3.60	3.82	75.8	16.1
3. Computer usage/ programming	3.47	3.53	3.42	48.2	28.7
4. Driver education	3.44	3.42	3.43	50.1	23.6
5. Science	3.36	3.37	3.35	46.7	38.2
6. Government	3.33	3.25	3.39	39.0	36.8
7. Business/commercial	3.32	3.20	3.41	40.4	38.0
8. History/social studies	3.26	3.21	3.30	40.5	41.8
9. Sex education	3.13	2.95	3.28	30.3	31.3
10. Physical education	2.91	2.94	2.87	29.9	35.5
11. Environment/pollution	2.89	2.93	2.86	14.0	38.7
12. Family living	2.88	2.68	3.03	21.5	34.6
13. Foreign languages	2.83	2.69	2.96	19.3	41.5
14. Shop	2.79	2.94	2.66	16.4	41.9
15. Religion	2.65	2.67	2.64	18.0	22.5
16. Music	2.43	2.31	2.53	11.9	29.6
17. Art	2.36	2.30	2.41	7.2	30.3
18. Black studies	2.27	2.17	2.35	6.0	22.0

Very important   = 4.0   Not so important = 2.0
Somewhat important = 3.0   Not important   = 1.0

Source: "The Mood of American Youth" (Reston, Va.: National Association of Secondary School Principals, 1984). Used by permission.

other nations in regard to the scientific literacy of its students.[26] As a nation, we find ourselves in the embarrassing position of living in an age of science and yet having very little understanding of scientific methods.

On the elementary level, the science curriculum consists of assorted science-related topics: animals, plants, seasons, light, sound, heat, weather, magnets, the stars and planets, basic electricity, nutrition, oceanography, and so on. These topics are often restudied in greater depth at the middle or junior-high level in courses variously titled Earth Science, General Science, Physical Science, or Life Science. At the high-school level, students typically may select from only a limited number of basic science courses: Biology, Chemistry, Physical Science, Anatomy and Physiology, and Physics. Many high schools do, however, distinguish between science courses that are applied (for the noncollege-bound) and those that are academic.

Several leading science educators and national committees have recommended changes in the science curriculum. Nearly all stress the need for students to learn more science and to acquire scientific knowledge, skills, and processes through the inquiry, or discovery, method. The teacher's primary role is to guide students in their search for knowledge rather than to act solely as a source of information and/or right answers. The College Board report of 1983, for example, called for students to understand how scientific methods could be applied to problems in nuclear power, genetic engineering, fertilizers and pesticides, robotics, information and data processing, and organ transplantation.[27] That same year, the National Science Foundation assembled 40 national leaders to develop goals in science and technology education. Their recommendations are grouped into four grade levels.

Goals for Science and Technology Education

- *K–6*—An integrated, hands-on approach is needed to focus on the relationships between humans and the total environment. Problem solving must be emphasized, including acquisition and analysis of data.
- *Grades 7–8*—There should be two primary emphases: (1) on human science, including human biology and personal health; and (2) on development of quantitative skills in science. Computer-based experiences should be used appropriately to assist in developing quantitative skills that will be needed for more complex, applied problem solving in grades 9–10. Skill in quantitative analysis of data, application of probability, and estimating skills are examples.
- *Grades 9–10*—A two-year sequence, required for *all* students, to address science, technology, and society. Emphasis should be on problem solving and scientific reasoning, applied to real-world problems. It should integrate knowledge and methods from physics, biology, earth science, and chemistry, as well as applied mathematics. This is a much higher-level course than is generally recognized as "general science" for nonscience students.
- *Grades 11–12*—One- and two-semester courses in physics, biology, chemistry, and earth sciences should be available for students who wish to go on to further academic study in science-related courses.[28]

In 1990, the American Association for the Advancement of Science issued a set of recommendations based on Project 2061: Education for a Changing Future; (2061 refers to the year Halley's comet returns). The Association recommended (1) integrating science and mathematics with other disciplines, (2) preparing students to become inquirers and critical thinkers rather than sources of right answers, and (3) focusing upon the contributions science can make to current social issues—population growth, environmental pollution, waste disposal, energy, and birth control.[29]

Social Studies

One thing can be said with certainty about the place of the social studies in the curriculum in the early 1990s: there is considerable disagreement about the importance of the social studies and about what should be taught in them. Social studies is a blanket term for several subject areas in the social sciences: history, political science, geography, psychology, sociology, anthropology, and economics. Of these, history is the most frequently offered of the social studies throughout the school years.

Goals for the social studies lack the precision that we find in other subject areas. Consider, for example, Charles Beard's comment in 1938 that the social studies aim at the "creation of rich and many-sided personalities, equipped with practical knowledge and inspired by ideals so that they can make their way and fulfill their mission in a changing society which is part of a world complex."[30] Or the assertion in 1979 by the National Council for the Social Studies that "the basic goal of social studies education is to prepare young people to be humane, rational, participating citizens in a world that is becoming increasingly interdependent."[31] Not surprisingly, such vague and lofty goals have been translated into a patchwork quilt of social studies programs, especially at the elementary level. Here we find a wide assortment of topics addressed in no particular sequence, such as understanding the self, the family, and community; community needs and problems; state history; the interdependencies of nations in regard to food, raw materials, and manufactured goods; America's early exploration and colonization; basic concepts of history, geography, economics, and civics; and use of maps and globes. At the high school level, the social studies curriculum becomes more uniform: United States history, world history, geography, and frequently a course in the history of the state in which the school is located.

The content of traditional social studies courses has remained comparatively unchanged during the last decade. Trends include fewer offerings in ancient history and civics and more offerings in psychology, economics, world cultures, and marriage and the family. Experimental courses or units in subjects such as black studies, Hispanic culture, and women's history have been criticized variously as gratuitous, distorting or misrepresentative, ethnocentric, or defamatory. The development of a truly multicultural curriculum is presently the subject of heated debate.

Foreign Languages

As we become increasingly aware of our interconnectedness with other nations, the small number of students who study foreign languages at the elementary through secondary levels is alarming. Support for foreign languages increased briefly immediately following Russia's launching of Sputnik in 1957, but foreign language enrollments declined dramatically during the 1960s and 1970s. In 1979, President Carter formed the President's Commission on Foreign Language and International Studies to investigate the problem. In its report a year later, the commission contended that "Americans' incompetency in foreign languages is nothing short of scandalous, and it is becoming worse."[32] The commission found that only 15 percent of public high school students were studying a modern foreign language.

The first year of a foreign language, particularly Spanish or French, is sometimes offered at the middle school or junior high-school level. Students typically study the first part of Spanish I, for example, in the sixth or seventh grade and complete the course the next year. As high-school freshmen they are ready for Spanish II. However, rarely are students introduced to foreign language study at the optimal time for learning a second language—as early as second grade.

Since 1980, several states began setting guidelines for foreign language study, and governmental and private groups began working cooperatively with foreign language organizations to promote the need for foreign language study. The success of these and other efforts was apparent when the American Council on the Teaching of Foreign Languages released, early in 1988, the results of a survey that showed that 30.9 percent of the nation's high school students were studying a modern foreign language, the largest proportion in 70 years.

According to the council, successful foreign language programs are characterized by the following factors.

1. Extensive activities integrating language study into the fabric of school life
2. A high incidence of target language usage with special motivational techniques to promote such usage
3. An exploratory language course
4. Unusually long course sequences
5. Study and travel abroad; exchange programs
6. An especially strong, dynamic staff
7. Inservice training
8. A strong public relations effort
9. Special recruiting efforts
10. A resolve to connect language study with the practical and concrete[33]

To meet the needs of the estimated 3.6 million students from non-English-speaking backgrounds who need special assistance in learning the school curriculum, many schools offer various programs. Among the approaches commonly used are:

1. *Immersion programs*—students learn English and other subjects in classrooms where only English is spoken. Aides who speak the first language of students are sometimes available, or students may also listen to equivalent audio-taped lessons in their first language.
2. *Maintenance programs*—To maintain the student's native language and culture, instruction in English and instruction in the native language are provided from kindergarten through twelfth grade.
3. *Pull-out programs*—on a regular basis, students are separated from English-speaking students so that they may receive lessons in English or reading lessons in their first language.
4. *Transition programs*—students receive reading lessons in their first language and lessons in English as a Second Language (ESL). Once they sufficiently master English, students are placed in classrooms where English is spoken.

Some schools have broadened their foreign language offerings to include such languages as Russian, Japanese, and Chinese. At a few schools, foreign language study has even become a central part of the curriculum. La Salle Language Academy in Chicago, for example, provides its K–8 students daily instruction in French, Spanish, Italian, or German. In addition, parents are encouraged to take special morning or evening language classes, and seventh- and eighth-grade students may participate in a foreign exchange program. In Akron, Ohio, a Foreign Languages in Elementary Schools program introduces all sixth graders to French, German, or Spanish. And advanced students at Akron's Buchtel University High School use their foreign language skills in a career exploration program aided by the city's international businesses.

The International School in Washington, D.C., is one of several schools in the country with an international curriculum, student body, and faculty, and international languages of instruction. At the elementary level, students are taught in English 50 percent of the time, and in either Spanish or French for the remainder. Between the ages of 11 and 16, students take two years of Latin. During their last two years at the International School, students participate in the International Baccalaureate, a curriculum developed by a multinational agency based in Switzerland.

The Arts

More than any other area of the curriculum, the arts hold an insecure position. When schools are faced with budgetary cutbacks or pressure to raise scores on basic skills tests, a cost-conscious public often considers the elimination of music and art. Some parents feel that art and music are not essential to the curriculum, that they are just frills. Even students rate art and music as less important than other areas of the curriculum (see Table 12.4).

The arts, however, have much to contribute to the education of students. As Kathryn Bloom points out, "The quality of our individual lives and the quality of our society are directly related to the quality of our artistic life. We need the arts as the key to the higher order of things—our cultural heritage, our gift of expression, our creative faculty, our sense of beauty."[34]

Typically, elementary art and music are limited to one period a week, and this instruction is given either by regular teachers or by special teachers, some of whom may travel from school to school. In addition, most elementary students have occasional opportunities to use crayons, watercolors, clay, and other art materials as they learn in other subject areas. And, from time to time, many children even have the opportunity to experience dance, puppetry, role-playing, pantomime, and crafts.

At the middle and junior high level, instruction in art and music becomes more structured, as well as more voluntary. Students may choose from band, chorus, arts, and crafts. At the high school level, art and music are usually offered as electives. Depending on the school's resources, however, students frequently have a wide assortment of classes to choose from: jazz band, glee club, band, orchestra, drama, girls' and boys' chorus, photography, sculpture, ceramics, and filmmaking, to name a few.

President Kennedy once said that "art establishes the basic human truths which must serve as the touchstone of our judgment." Discipline-based art instruction, however, is underemphasized in most American schools. Art programs are often perceived as frills, the first part of the curriculum to be cut during budget crises.

In addition, middle school and high school students may receive instruction in Practical Arts, such as sewing, cooking, woodworking and metalworking, automotive shop, print shop, and courses teaching agricultural knowledge and skills. A noteworthy trend is for students of both sexes to take courses in all the practical arts rather than follow traditional sex-role stereotypes; that is, you will increasingly find both boys and girls both in the kitchen and in the garage.

In spite of the tenuous position of the arts in the curriculum, art educators are working to create a new awareness of the unique contribution that the arts can make to all areas of the curriculum. Several reform reports of the 1980s underscored the importance of the arts in the curriculum. In its study of the academic preparation that students need for college, the College Board included the visual and performing arts as one of the six essential areas of the basic academic curriculum.[35] The observation team for the Carnegie Foundation's report on high schools in America found the arts "shamefully neglected" and recommended that "all students study the arts to discover how human beings use nonverbal symbols and communicate not only with words but through music, dance, and the visual arts.[36]

Art education in American schools received considerable attention in the mid-1980s when the Getty Center for Education in the Arts, funded by the J. Paul Getty Trust, began to call for a "discipline-based" approach to art education. **Discipline-based art programs** would emphasize art production, art criticism, art history, and aesthetics.[37] The Getty Center spearheaded five major efforts during the late 1980s to influence the quality of art education in the schools:

- Public advocacy for the value of art in education
- Professional development programs for school administrators and teachers
- Development of the theoretical bases of discipline-based art education
- Development of model programs to demonstrate discipline-based art education in the classroom
- Development of discipline-based curricula[38]

Physical Education

The ultimate aim of physical education is to promote physical activities that develop a desire in the individual to maintain physical fitness throughout life. In addition, students in physical education programs may receive instruction in health and nutrition, sex education, and driver education.

During the 1960s, physical education programs consisted largely of highly competitive team sports. Many children, less aggressive and competitive than their peers, did not do well in such programs and experienced a lowered sense of self-esteem. Gradually, instructors began to offer activities designed to meet the needs and abilities of all students, not just the athletically talented. In addition to traditional team sports such as football, baseball, and basketball, and individual sports such as swimming and wrestling, many students in grades K–12 may now participate in a broad array of physical activities, including aerobics, archery, badminton, dodgeball, folk and square dancing, gymnastics, handball, hockey, table tennis, golf, racquetball, shuffleboard, skating, volleyball, soccer, and yoga.

In addition to becoming more sensitive to the needs and abilities of individual students, physical education programs were required by law to provide more opportunities for female students. In 1972, Congress enacted Title IX of the Education

FACT FINDING

How Smart Are Students About Their Health?

According to *The National Adolescent Student Health Survey* administered to 11,000 eighth- and tenth-grade students nationwide in 1987, adolescents are informed about some, but not all, health issues.

Informed	*Uninformed*
91% of students know sharing needles increases risk of AIDS	92% of students who ride bicycles never wear a helmet
85% believe it is acceptable to "say no" to sex	78% believe they should fight if someone hits them
73% know that eating foods high in saturated fat may cause heart problems	63% went during the past year to places known to be dangerous
51% believe there is a great risk associated with smoking one or more packs of cigarettes a day	47% believe donating blood increases risk of AIDS
43% believe their close friends would disapprove of them drinking alcohol occasionally	39% rode during the past month with a driver who had used drugs or alcohol
	14% have attempted suicide
35% usually cross a busy street at the corner	3% used cocaine during the past month

Source: Scott Willis, "Health Education: A Crisis-Driven Field Seeks Coherence," *ASCD Curriculum Update* (Alexandria, Va.: Association for Supervision and Curriculum Development, November 1990): 4–5. Reprinted with permission of the Association of Supervision and Curriculum Development. Copyright 1985 by ASCD. All rights reserved.

Amendments Act, which said, "No person in the United States shall, on the basis of sex, be excluded from participation in, be denied the benefits of, or be subjected to discrimination under any education or activity receiving federal financial assistance." Following Title IX, girls became much more involved in school athletic programs. The National Federation of State High School Associations, for example, found that 1.85 million young women participated in high school athletics in 1980–81 compared to only 240,000 in 1970–71.

SUMMARY

We began this chapter by pointing out how there are four curricula that all students experience. In addition to learning what teachers intend to teach (the explicit curriculum), students learn from the hidden curriculum, the null curriculum, and extracurricular/cocurricular programs. We then painted a broad portrait of the many factors that influence what is taught in the schools—from school policies to national politics and the mass media. We also discussed how there is no one right way to develop the curriculum. Teachers must base their curricula not only on the needs and interests of students but also on a variety of local, state, and national pressures. However, the ultimate criterion for deciding what to teach is whether the planned activities will contribute to students' learning and growth.

Next, we described how the school curriculum has changed during the course of our nation's history. Religion, for example, has played an important role in the development of the school curriculum. The need to train students in religion was reflected in the colonial school curriculum, while today several groups have opposing views about whether religious beliefs should be included in the school curriculum. Similarly, school curricula have been viewed as a way of teaching students the knowledge, skills, and attitudes necessary to maintain our democratic way of life. The content of the curriculum is largely dependent upon the current needs of society and the prevailing beliefs about education.

The chapter concluded with a brief look at current trends and issues in language arts, mathematics, science, social studies, foreign languages, the arts, and physical education. What stands out in our survey of these seven subject areas is that school curricula are not static. Since the ultimate aim of the curriculum is to prepare today's students to solve tomorrow's problems, teachers must be prepared to assume their important role in the curriculum development process.

KEY TERMS AND CONCEPTS

curriculum, 372
explicit curriculum, 373
hidden curriculum, 373
null curriculum, 374
extracurricular/cocurricular
  programs, 375
Tyler rationale, 378
subject-centered curriculum, 378
student-centered curricula, 378
Committee of Ten, 385

Committee of Fifteen, 385
Reorganization of
  Secondary Education, 385
Eight-Year Study, 388
inquiry-based curriculum, 389
relevancy-based curriculum, 389
core curriculum, 389
whole language movement, 393
discipline-based art programs, 400

ANSWER KEY FOR CONSIDER THIS . . .

"What Subjects Should Students Study?"

Rank for College-Bound: 1—*Mathematics*, 2—*English*, 3—*History/U.S. Government*, 4—*Science*, 5—*Computer Training*, 6—*Geography*, 7—*Career Education*, 8—*Business Education*, 9—*Foreign Language*, 10—*Health Education*, 11—*Physical Education*, 12— *Vocational Training*, 13—*Art*, 14—*Music*; Rank for Non-College-Bound: 1—*Mathematics*, 2—*English*, 3—*Vocational Training*, 4—*History/U.S. Government*, 5—*Computer Training*, 6—*Business Education*, 7—*Career Education*, 8—*Science*, 9—*Health Education*, 10—*Geography*, 11—*Physical Education*, 12—*Foreign Language*, 13—*Art*, 14—*Music*.

DISCUSSION QUESTIONS

1. What are the arguments for and against teachers being free to determine what they teach in their classrooms?
2. What could teachers at a particular school do so that the hidden curriculum might make a more positive contribution to student learning?
3. At the level at which you plan to teach, what is the null curriculum (i.e., the subjects that students will *not* have the opportunity to learn)? Which, if any, of these subjects do you feel students should be exposed to?
4. How would you improve the curriculum at the level at which you plan to teach?
5. Review the four questions in the Tyler rationale for curriculum development. What additional questions would need to be asked when developing a curriculum? Give reasons for your choices.
6. To what extent should schools address social issues in their curricula? What issues should be addressed and which should be omitted from the curriculum?
7. How should teachers and schools respond to complaints about the content of instructional materials?
8. In regard to the subject areas discussed in this chapter, what other trends and issues can you identify?

APPLICATION ACTIVITIES

1. Help your instructor set up an exercise wherein four to six students role-play teachers who are meeting for the purpose of revising or updating the curriculum. (The students should focus on a level and subject with which they are most familiar.) The rest of the class should observe and take notes on the educational beliefs expressed by the role-players. After the role-play (about 15–20 minutes), the entire class should discuss the curriculum development process it has just observed.
2. Select a textbook that you are likely to use in your teaching and evaluate it according to the curriculum materials evaluation criteria presented in the Teacher's Resource Guide.
3. For a one-month period, keep a tally of all the comments that are made in the mass media regarding what should be taught in the schools. Compare your list with those of other students and try to identify any trends.
4. Obtain a few public school curriculum guides from your college or university library or from a nearby school district. Evaluate the guides in regard to their appropriateness for students and usefulness for teachers. How would you improve the guides?
5. Examine Figure 12.4 and then identify several additional forces that influence the school curriculum. Which ones exert an immediate, direct influence at the school site? Which ones are more removed and influence the school less directly? List in order of importance the five factors that you believe *actually* have the greatest impact on the curriculum. Then list the five factors that you believe *ideally* should have the greatest influence. What differences do you notice between your actual and ideal lists? What might be done to reduce the differences between the two lists? Compare your lists with those of other students in your class.

FIELD EXPERIENCES

1. Spend a half-day at a school at the level at which you plan to teach. Take note of your impressions regarding that school's hidden curriculum. If possible, chat briefly with administrators, teachers, and students. Share your observations with others in your education class.

2. Observe students outside of the classroom during a school day and record your impressions of the hidden curriculum. For each topic you list, think how it could be made a desirable and effective part of the explicit curriculum. Share your observations and ideas with others in your class.

3. Interview a school superintendent or principal to find out if he or she has dealt with complaints about instructional materials. How did he or she handle the complaints?

4. Conduct an informal survey of 10 people you know, asking them what they think are the four most important subjects to be taught at the elementary, middle, junior-, and senior-high levels. Compare your data with others in your class.

5. Ask your instructor to arrange for a curriculum coordinator from the local school district to visit your class. In addition to finding out about this coordinator's work, ask him or her to describe how the district's curriculum has changed during the last 5–10 years.

SUGGESTED READINGS

Dewey, John. *The Child and the Curriculum*. Chicago: University of Chicago Press, 1902. *A short book that discusses eloquently and insightfully why the curriculum must be based on students' needs and interests. Though written nearly nine decades ago, Dewey's book continues to be timely and relevant.*

Eisner, Elliot W. *The Educational Imagination: On the Design and Evaluation of School Programs*. 2d ed. New York: Macmillan, 1985. *A thoughtful, well-written book in which the author builds a convincing case for the arts of teaching and curriculum development.*

Hass, Glen, ed. *Curriculum Planning: A New Approach*. 5th ed. Boston: Allyn and Bacon, 1987. *An excellent book of readings that explores current problems and issues in curriculum development.*

Hirsch, E. D., Jr. *Cultural Literacy: What Every American Needs to Know*. Boston: Houghton Mifflin, 1987. *In his thought-provoking book, Hirsch contends that many readers, because they have failed to acquire a sufficient level of background knowledge, are unable to comprehend much of what they read.*

McNeil, John D. *Curriculum: A Comprehensive Introduction*, 4th ed. New York: Harper Collins Publishers, 1990. *A readable, well-organized introduction to the curriculum field.*

Posner, George J. and Alan N. Rudnitsky. *Course Design: A Guide to Curriculum Development for Teachers*. 3d ed. New York: Longman, 1986. *A clearly written guide for planning units and courses of study at the elementary through high school levels.*

Schubert, William H. *Curriculum: Perspective, Paradigm, and Possibility.* New York: Macmillan, 1986. *An impressive, scholarly overview of the curriculum field. Schubert does an excellent job of clarifying different orientations to the curriculum.*

Tyler, Ralph W. *Basic Principles of Curriculum and Instruction.* Chicago: University of Chicago Press, 1950. *A short classic that outlines steps for identifying, organizing, and evaluating objectives for a curriculum.*

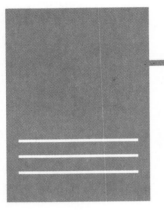

TEACHERS . . .

How is your curriculum decided?
What influences on the curriculum would you like to see expanded or reduced?

The curriculum I teach is decided upon by the central office. There is an urgent need to change this situation. Not only is the curriculum dictated to the system of teachers, but the curriculum in reading is dictated by a textbook. Students are promoted or retained according to the mastery of reading books. The board members have even requested to visit schools to see if the texts are being used. I believe that our curriculum should be correlated to the basic skills that are required by the state. In addition to these, our county should expand this curriculum to enhance student learning. Teachers should be held accountable for these skills, but they should be given a choice of how to accomplish them. We have many teachers who want to use an integrated approach but are hampered because they are also responsible for the textbook tests in each subject area. We have adopted the state-funded SIA, which mandates the developmental approach for K–2 students, yet those students are still required to work in the county-adopted textbooks.

—June L. Wilhoit
Chase Street Elementary School, Athens, Georgia

It seems we have come full circle in regard to curriculum expectations. In the mid-1970s and early 1980s there was little school board focus on curriculum and therefore much teacher independence. Then came tremendous input on curriculum guidelines and high expectations for implementation. Now we see more independence in the middle-school level. With an emphasis on magnet programs, we have noticed not only a loosening of the curriculum, but also an expected and encouraged variation. I like the freedom that our system, school, and department provide.

—Marc Gray
Highland Middle School, Louisville, Kentucky

My curriculum is predetermined by the state. It is not carved in stone, however, and teachers have a good bit of freedom to pick and choose what they teach and how they teach. I feel the curriculum is somewhat unrealistic in the amount they want covered in a school year. I think it should cover less in greater detail.

—Ricardo Cortez Morris
Hixson High School, Hixson, Tennessee

ON TEACHING

To what extent should teachers or students have greater control in determining the curriculum and classroom activities?

Students should have an invested role in determining the curriculum and classroom activities. After all, it is their education. On a scale of one to ten, the teacher's control should be about a five. They should outline students' education but not dictate every aspect of it.

—Julie A. Addison
Rock Ridge Elementary School, Castle Rock, Colorado

I feel that the teacher should have more control. Although the state of Texas mandates the essential elements that need to be taught, I still have control as to the manner and the extent to which I teach these elements. Because students are often unaware of the mandates issued by the state, and because they are not professional educators, I feel that students should be given a minimal amount of control in determining the curriculum and classroom activities.

—Dolores Ramón
Montgomery Drive Elementary School, San Antonio, Texas

On a ten-point scale for teacher control, I am about a six. I am not willing to relinquish half or more of my control over the class, but it is important to include the ideas and thoughts of the students when making decisions. I have no problem with asking for student input, and I certainly would be open to using those suggestions that have merit. I don't think elementary-age students are capable of making all the decisions about what they learn and how.

—Rose Ann Blaschke
Vivian Elementary School, Lakewood, Colorado

On a ten-point scale of teacher control I would average about a four, depending on my objectives for that day. If the lesson is a discovery lesson—for instance, the nature of right triangles—it is student-driven. If the lesson is in theoretical algebra I may be close to total control. Some learning teams in my classes have total determination of their curriculum topics, but I control absolutely the delivery system. It all depends on the situation.

—Olive Ann Slotta
Fred N. Thomas Career Education Center, Denver, Colorado

Teaching: Your Chosen Profession

*T*eaching meets
the basic criterion for
being considered a
profession: it is a
matter of life and
death.

Robert B. Howsam
Educating a Profession

You are near the end of your first month of teaching at an urban school. The board of education has just announced that it is unable to provide the salary increases promised to teachers last year. According to the board, the school system is faced with tremendous financial problems.

Teachers at your school, most of whom belong to the teachers' unions, are very angry about the board's failure to live up to its promise. Many teachers believe that the board can find the money if it really wants to. Your school's union representative has just called a meeting of teachers to discuss the situation and to consider a possible strike. The day before the meeting he stops by your classroom to urge you to attend.

"This is an important meeting," he says. "As a new teacher, you need to find out how the board of education has treated teachers."

"Well," you begin, "I'm not sure. I'd like to make more money like anyone else, but if we go on strike, what about the kids? We have a responsibility to them."

"Just a minute," he says. "This is not just about money. The board has a history of failing to live up to its promises. We're actually doing this for the kids. If the board gets away with this, a lot of good teachers are going to transfer out of the district. And *that's* going to hurt the kids."

You agree to attend the meeting, but you're still not sure how you feel about teacher unions in general. Prior to the meeting, several questions keep coming to mind. If teachers are professionals, should they belong to unions? If teachers decide to go on strike, will I honor the strike? Would I cross the picket line in order to teach?

FOCUS QUESTIONS

1. What are the characteristics of a profession, and to what extent does teaching reflect these characteristics?
2. What distinguishes the behavior of teachers who are truly professional?
3. What opportunities are available for teachers to increase their professional effectiveness?
4. What stages of professional development are common for most preservice and inservice teachers?
5. How do the National Education Association and the American Federation of Teachers differ in regard to their strategies for improving the professional status of teaching?

In previous chapters we referred to teaching as a profession. Indeed, the subtitle of this book points to the fact that you will soon be "accepting the challenge of a profession." However, if we compare teaching with other professions—law and medicine, for example—we find some significant differences. As a result of these differences, current opinion is divided as to whether teaching is actually a profession. We will continue to refer to teaching as a **profession,** though others have labeled teaching a *semi*-profession,[1] an *emerging profession,*[2] an *uncertain* profession,[3] an *imperiled* profession,[4] and an *endangered* profession.[5]

In this chapter we will explore the extent to which teaching is, and is not, a profession. We will take a frank look at some of the realities of teaching that suggest the occupation falls short of having full professional status. We will also discuss the obligation to the profession, stressing how important it is that you make a commitment to becoming a true professional. We will also make several recommendations that will help you become a professional. Finally, we will look at several teacher organizations that are vitally concerned with enhancing the professional status of teachers.

THE MEANING OF PROFESSIONALISM

We use the terms *professional* and *profession* quite frequently, usually without thinking about their meanings. We talk about those who play professional sports, the professional truck driver, the professional exterminator we must call if we want our home or apartment treated for an invasion of insects, or the professional who cares for our lawns and shrubs. In one sense, then, *professional* refers to anyone who does his or her job with skill and understanding. A person attempting that same job without a high degree of competence we would label an amateur. In addition, a professional is paid for the work he or she does, and an amateur is not.

This view of what it is to be a professional is rather limited, however. The differences between professionals and other workers are more extensive. Professionals "possess a high degree of *specialized theoretical knowledge,* along with methods and techniques for applying this knowledge in their day-to-day work, . . . [and they] are united by a high degree of in-group solidarity, stemming from their common training and common adherence to certain doctrines and methods."[6]

From several sociologists and educators who have studied teaching come additional characteristics of occupations that are highly professionalized.[7] As you read each characteristic in Table 13.1, think about the degree to which it applies to teaching.

Characteristics of Teaching as a Profession

Now let us examine the extent to which teaching satisfies each of these commonly agreed upon characteristics of full professions. As we do so, we will see that teaching meets some, but not all, of the criteria. Also, we will understand John Goodlad's conclusion in *Teachers for Our Nation's Schools,* a comprehensive report on teacher education released in 1990, that "teaching remains the not-quite profession."[8]

TABLE 13.1   Characteristics of a Profession

1. Professionals are allowed to institutionalize a monopoly of essential knowledge and services. For example, only lawyers may practice law; only physicians may practice medicine.

2. Professionals are able to practice their occupation with a high degree of autonomy. They are not closely supervised, and they have frequent opportunities to make their own decisions about important aspects of their work. Professional autonomy also implies an obligation to perform responsibly, to self-supervise, and to be dedicated to providing a service rather than meeting minimum requirements of the job.

3. Professionals must typically undergo a lengthy period of education and/or training before they may enter professional practice. Furthermore, professionals usually must undergo a lengthy induction period following their formal education or training.

4. Professionals perform an essential service for their clients and are devoted to continuous development of their ability to deliver this service. This service emphasizes intellectual rather than physical techniques.

5. Professionals have control over their governance, their socialization into the occupation, and research connected with their occupation.

6. Members of a profession form their own vocational associations, which have control over admissions to the profession, educational standards, examinations and licensing, career development, ethical and performance standards, and professional discipline.

7. The knowledge and skills held by professionals are not normally available to nonprofessionals.

8. Professionals enjoy a high level of public trust and are able to deliver services that are clearly superior to those available elsewhere.

9. Professionals are granted a high level of prestige and higher-than-average financial rewards.

Institutional Monopoly of Services   On the one hand, teachers do have a monopoly of services. Only those who are certified members of the profession may teach in public schools. On the other hand, the varied requirements we find for certification and for teaching in private schools weaken this monopoly. (Although state certification and teacher education courses are generally not required to teach in private schools, a college degree is a minimum requirement.) In addition, any claim teachers might have as exclusive providers of a service is being further eroded by the current teacher shortage. As we learned in Chapter 4, many state systems are approving temporary, or emergency, certification measures to deal with these shortages—a move that establishes teaching as the only profession that allows noncertified individuals the right to practice the profession.

Perhaps the most significant argument against teachers claiming to be the exclusive providers of a service, however, is the fact that a great deal of teaching occurs in informal, nonschool settings and is done by people who are not teachers. Every day, thousands of people teach various kinds of how-to-do-it skills: how to water-ski, how to make dogs more obedient, how to make pasta from scratch, how to tune a car's engine, and how to meditate. The teaching of others focuses on the acquisition of knowledge: knowledge about the Bible, knowledge of the stars, knowledge about the Great Books, knowledge about good health, and knowledge about investments. Finally, young people learn a great deal from their parents, so much so that it is no exaggeration to refer to the curriculum as the home and parents as the child's first teachers.

In spite of the fact that young people learn many different things from many different people, teachers are the experts charged with teaching people how to read, write, and compute—the essential skills upon which all later learning depends.

CONSIDER THIS . . .

To What Extent Is Teaching a Profession?

Before reading further in this chapter, indicate to what extent you believe the following statements are "mostly true" or "mostly untrue" about teaching as a profession. For each statement, circle the number in the range that corresponds to your belief. Your score will range from a high of 36 to a low of 9.

	Mostly Untrue			Mostly True
1. Teachers have a monopoly on their services.	1	2	3	4
2. Teachers have a high degree of autonomy.	1	2	3	4
3. Compared to other jobs, teaching requires many years of education and training.	1	2	3	4
4. Teachers provide an essential service to society.	1	2	3	4
5. Teachers are able to govern themselves.	1	2	3	4
6. Professional associations exercise considerable power and influence within the teaching profession.	1	2	3	4
7. Teachers possess knowledge and skills that members of the public do not have.	1	2	3	4
8. Teachers enjoy a high level of public trust.	1	2	3	4
9. For their services, teachers receive substantial prestige, benefits, and pay.	1	2	3	4
	TOTAL* _____			

*If your total score is above 18, you tend to view teaching as a full profession.

Teacher Autonomy   In one sense teachers have considerable autonomy. They usually work behind a closed classroom door, and only seldom is their work observed by another adult. In fact, one of the norms among teachers is that the classroom is a castle of sorts, and teacher privacy a closely guarded right. While the performance of new teachers may be observed and evaluated on a regular basis by supervisors, veteran teachers are observed much less frequently, and they usually enjoy a high degree of autonomy.

Teachers also have extensive freedom regarding how they structure the classroom environment. They may emphasize discussions as opposed to lectures. They may set certain requirements for some students and not for others. They may delegate responsibilities to one class and not another. And, within the guidelines set by local and state authorities, teachers may determine much of the content they teach.

There are, however, constraints placed on teachers and their work. Teachers, unlike doctors and lawyers, must accept all the "clients" who are sent to them. Only infrequently does a teacher actually "reject" a student assigned to him or her. On the other hand, students, unless they choose to attend private schools, must usually accept their assignment to schools and teachers without having much choice. When choosing the services of a physician or lawyer, however, a person has almost total freedom.

Teachers must also agree to teach what state and local officials say they must. Moreover, the work of teachers is subject to a higher level of public scrutiny than that found in other professions. Since the public provides "clients" (students) and pays for schools, it has a significant say regarding the work of teachers. Citizens may judge the quality of services delivered by teachers more readily than that of lawyers, physicians, or members of the ministry.

Teaching also differs from other professions in that teachers are usually evaluated by persons who are not presently teachers: principals and other supervisors appointed by the school districts. The degree of supervision that teachers actually experience varies greatly, with most teachers having considerable autonomy as long as they continue to perform at a reasonable level of effectiveness.

Years of Education and Training   As sociologist Amitai Etzioni points out in his discussion of the "semi-professions," the training of teachers is less lengthy than that required for other professionals—lawyers and physicians, for example.[9] The professional component of teacher education programs is the shortest of all the professions—only 15 percent of the average bachelor's degree program for a high school teacher is devoted to professional courses. However, as we learned in Chapter 3, several colleges and universities have begun five-year teacher education programs. If continued, this trend toward extended programs will decidedly enhance the professional status of teaching.

Many school districts also require that teachers complete a certain number of hours of graduate study within a specified time period as a condition of employment. Still other districts require their teachers to obtain a master's degree within a specified time limit. Figure 13.1 shows the highest degree held by public school teachers and the percent of teachers who earned college credits during the last three years. Clearly, the trend since 1961 has been for teachers to attain higher levels of education.

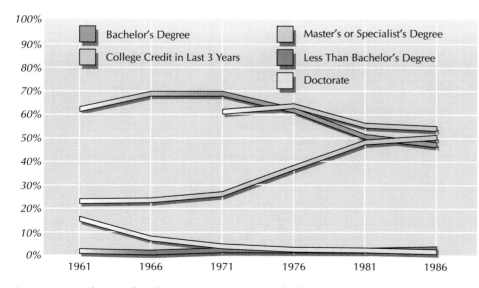

FIGURE 13.1

Highest Degree Held by Public School Teachers and College Credit Earned during Last Three Years, 1961–1986

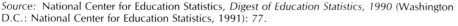

Source: National Center for Education Statistics, *Digest of Education Statistics, 1990* (Washington D.C.: National Center for Education Statistics, 1991): 77.

In most professions, new members must undergo a prescribed induction period. Physicians, for example, must serve an internship or residency before beginning practice, and most lawyers begin as clerks in law firms. Sociologists have termed this process of gradually moving from simple to more complex tasks, small to greater responsibility, as "mediated entry" into a profession. In contrast, teachers do not go through a formal induction period before assuming full responsibility for their work. Practice teaching comes closest to serving as an induction period, but it is often relatively short, informal, and lacking in uniformity. In reality, entry into teaching is abrupt, and, as the saying goes, a new teacher must either sink or swim.

In spite of the anxiety that affects just about anyone who faces a classroom full of students for the first time, teaching has been characterized as an "easy entry" profession.[10] Moreover, the training teachers undergo tends not to be valued by teachers themselves, as sociologist Dan Lortie points out. "Teachers are inclined to talk about their training as easy ('mickey mouse'); I have yet to hear a teacher complain that education courses were too difficult or demanded too much effort. Teachers do not perceive their preparation as conveying something special—as setting them apart from others. . . . Teachers do not consider training the key to their legitimation as teachers. That rests in experience."[11]

Provision of Essential Service   Throughout our nation's history, teachers have been designated by law as the primary providers of instructional services in schools. While it is generally acknowledged that teachers provide a service that is vital to the well-being of individuals and groups, the public does need to be reminded of this fact from time to time. This importance was driven home on a large scale during the early 1980s when several reports calling for school reform linked the strength of our country to the quality of its schools.

The ability to function as the spark that stimulates young people to learn and grow can give teachers a sense of meaning and fulfillment they might not be able to find in other professions. A foreign language teacher, who immigrated to this country several years ago, summed up what many teachers feel about their choice of professions: "I feel that I get satisfaction . . . that I am a useful member of the society. I feel this is the field in which . . . I can contribute more to society than in any other field. . . . I am doing a job which is good [for] the American society."[12]

Indeed, it is no exaggeration to say that teaching is a matter of life and death. Robert B. Howsam and his colleagues point out in their landmark study of the teaching profession that

> every moment in the lives of teachers and pupils brings critical decisions of motivation, reinforcement, reward, ego enhancement and goal direction. Proper professional decisions enhance learning and life; improper decisions send the learner towards incremental death in openness to experience and in ability to learn and contribute. Doctors and lawyers probably have neither more nor less to do with life, death, and freedom than do teachers.[13]

Degree of Self-Governance   The limited freedom of teachers to govern themselves probably detracts from the overall status of the profession more than any other factor. A quick look at the organizational chart for any school district will show that teachers are low on the totem pole (only students are lower) when it comes to decision-making powers. These powers, it turns out, are held by boards of education, largely made up of persons who have never taught. As a result, teachers have little or no say over what they teach, when they teach, whom they teach, and, in extreme instances, *how* they teach. As Albert Shanker, head of the American Federation of Teachers, put it in an article appropriately titled "Why Teachers Are Angry,"

> No group of professionals in American society—other than teachers—has so little to say about how its members discharge their responsibilities. . . .
>
> The basic materials teachers use in their classrooms—from textbooks to chalk— are selected and rationed by others. Teachers rarely are consulted in discussions of the optimum school year, school day, or even class period. Streams of innovations— each one heralded as the century's greatest breakthrough—are imposed on teachers, often with no advance notice whatever, and usually with no chance for teachers either to evaluate them conceptually or even to examine their practicability.[14]

In other, more full, professions, members of the profession, not laypersons, make decisions about practice. Nonmembers are seen as not having sufficient understanding to participate in professional governance. In fact, these professions (most notably, law and medicine) have shown their ability to move swiftly and decisively to squelch any suspected movement toward lay control.

Traditionally, teachers have allowed other parties to make major decisions regarding significant aspects of their work. Occasionally, a teacher, with or without the support of other teachers, will refuse to follow the dictates of a principal or board of education. Such a maverick teacher often faces the prospect of not having a contract renewed, being fired outright, being transferred, or being given an undesirable teaching assignment.

The paths that one follows in becoming socialized into a profession can be, if controlled by members of the profession, another form of governance. To be initiated into a profession by peers enhances professional identity and makes control by nonmembers that much more unlikely.

When we look at teaching we see that socialization into the profession is minimal. Due to the flat career paths of teachers (a veteran of thirty years has essentially the same status as a beginner), experienced teachers usually devote little effort to induct beginning teachers into a professional culture or way of life. Though new teachers may certainly expect veteran teachers to show them the ropes related to working at a particular school, little is done to help them identify with the profession. "Assisting occupational identity formation, encouraging collegial patterns of behavior, fostering generational trust, and enhancing self-esteem," are forms of assistance that experienced teachers tend not to provide to neophytes.[15]

The conduct of research related to practice is yet another way that professionals have of influencing their profession. When we look at research on teaching, we see that most of it is done by persons in higher education or at centers for research and development. Classroom teachers—those most intimately involved in professional practice—are only minimally involved in research efforts aimed at generating a deeper understanding of effective teaching. The development of cadres of teacher-researchers whose task it would be to focus on problems related to professional practice would greatly enhance the overall status of the profession.

Professional Associations   Teachers, like other professionals, have formed a number of vocational associations that are vitally concerned with such issues as admissions to the profession, educational standards, examinations and licensing, career development, ethical and performance standards, and professional discipline. It is clear, though, that the more than 300 national teacher organizations have not progressed as far as other professions have in gaining control of these areas. (Later in this chapter, we will examine the efforts of two of these groups, the National Education Association and the American Federation of Teachers, to influence laws and regulations pertaining to teachers.)

Professional Knowledge and Skills   Professionals are granted a certain status because they possess knowledge and skills not normally held by the general public. When one visits a surgeon, for example, it is with the understanding that the surgeon, by virtue of professional membership, possesses the necessary knowledge and skills. Moreover, for the surgeon or similar professional, the outcomes of practice are specific and easily determined—the patient recovers from the operation, or the judge rules in favor of the defendant, for example.

Within the profession of teaching, however, the requirements for membership are much less precise. In spite of the ongoing efforts of educational researchers, there exists no commonly agreed upon body of knowledge and skills that is considered necessary in order to teach.[16] If we ask what knowledge teachers possess that other occupational groups lack, perhaps the best answer we can come up with is knowledge about education. As we learned in Chapter 2, the outcomes of teaching are unpredictable; therefore, it is much more difficult to develop a stable knowledge base for teachers to operate from.

Further evidence of the vaguely defined knowledge base upon which teaching rests may be found in the varied programs at the 1,300 or so colleges and universities that train teachers. Required courses may, at first glance, appear similar, but closer inspection reveals almost endless differences in content.

Attempts to clarify the knowledge base for teaching are frequently hampered when members of the public routinely feel compelled to offer their usually inexpert opinions on what and how teachers should teach. As a result, discussions of the problems of education include not only observations made by members of the profession but commentaries, often uninformed and conflicting, that appear in newspapers and magazines or are offered up on television and radio talk shows.

"Just pretend we're not here, Ms. Robinson..."

<table>
<tr><td>

E D U C A T I O N
in the
N   E   W   S

</td></tr>
</table>

Corporate Education

Corporate contributions to education, about $2 billion annually, have more than tripled over the past decade for a total of $13.4 billion. About 9 percent goes to elementary and secondary education and the rest to colleges, including grants to improve teacher training.

Business involvement in schools has taken many forms, including, for example, adopt-a-school programs, cash grants for pilot projects and teacher development, educational use of corporate facilities and expertise, employee participation, student scholarship programs, and political lobbying for school reform. Extending beyond advocacy, private sector efforts include job initiatives for disadvantaged youths, inservice programs for teachers, management training for school administrators, minority education and faculty development, and even construction of school buildings.

Corporate investments in education increasingly encourage experimentation and promote school reform. For school restructuring programs of the 1990s, for example, RJR Nabisco pledged $30 million, the Coca-Cola Foundation $50 million, General Electric Company $35 million, and IBM $25 million. Special projects funded by these companies include Hispanic family-literacy programs in Texas, California, and Florida; a pilot peer mentoring program in Atlanta; on-site training for teachers in computer-based instruction; and grants aimed at doubling the number of students from inner-city schools in Albuquerque, Cincinnati, Louisville, and Milwaukee who go on to college.

Business-sponsored school-building experiments focus on creating model schools or laboratory schools or on addressing particular local needs. Minneapolis, for example, boasts two new schools dedicated to improving student performance through nongrouped classes, small class sizes, and high expectations of students. One is the K–6 Public School Academy, sponsored by General Mills, and the other is the Chiron Middle School, founded by a Minneapolis real estate developer and a consortium of local businesspeople, teachers, school administrators, and parents. With the support of Minneapolis's superintendent, school board, and local teachers' union, these innovators have implemented programs in which teachers are chosen on the basis of talent and telephones are installed in the classrooms for greater communication between teachers and parents.

As successful business involvement in education increases, older-style adopt-a-school programs are being augmented by more dynamic and more directive partnerships. Business leaders are becoming more aggressive in promoting educational and school reform, and they are spending more money to that end. As this new style of business-school partnership spreads from community to community and from state to state, the nation's educational system is undergoing a promising transformation.

Sources: Ann Bradley, " 'Take Some Risks'," *Education Week,* in *Teacher Magazine* (January 1990): 23–24.
David Hill, "Making Schools Their Business," *Teacher Magazine* (January 1990): 60 + .
Reagan Walker, "The Education of Business," *Education Week,* in *Teacher Magazine* (January 1990): 66–68.

On May 15, 1987, however, a step was taken to demonstrate that teachers do possess a body of professional knowledge and skills. On that day, the **National Board for Professional Teaching Standards** was established, based on the 1986 Carnegie Foundation report, *A Nation Prepared: Teachers for the 21st Century.* Much as the accounting profession has a system for certifying accountants and the medical profession for certifying physicians, the National Board for Professional Teaching Standards was created to issue certificates to teachers who meet the Board's high standards.

The Board plans to issue its first certificates by 1993. Board certification will be based on professional knowledge and on the ability to perform at a high level. "Assessment techniques [being considered by the Board] include interactive video, simulations of classroom situations, observations of teachers in a school setting, interviews, essays, multiple choice tests, teaching portfolios and various combinations of these technologies."[17]

Level of Public Trust   The level of trust that the public extends to teachers as professionals varies greatly. On the one hand, the public appears to have great confidence in the work that teachers do. Because of its faith in the teaching profession, the public invests teachers with considerable power over its children. For the most part, parents willingly allow their children to be molded and influenced by teachers, and this willingness must be based on a high degree of trust. In addition, most parents expect their children to obey and respect teachers.

On the other hand, it appears that the public's trust of teachers has eroded during the last two decades or so. The profession has received considerable "bad press" during this period. Teachers have been portrayed as incompetent, greedy, unprofessional, unintelligent, immoral, and generally unable to live up to the public's expectations. Just about all of our country's problems—from declining achievement test scores, to our difficulty in meeting economic challenges from abroad, to the lack of respect for authority among youth—have been blamed on teachers.

Though all professions have some members who might be described as unprofessional, teaching is especially vulnerable to such charges. The sheer size of the teaching force makes it difficult to maintain consistently high professional standards. Moreover, teaching is subject to a level of public scrutiny and control that other, more established, professions have traditionally not tolerated. However, the era of widespread public trust may also be running out for these other professions as well. The recent mushrooming of malpractice suits against doctors, for example, may be a sign that here, too, public confidence has significantly eroded.

FIVE-MINUTE FOCUS   In your opinion, what accounts for the erosion of public trust in the teaching profession? What might be the best way to rebuild that trust? Date your journal entry and write for five minutes.

Prestige, Benefits, and Pay   Teachers have typically not been given status and salaries in keeping with other professions. Although considerable salary gains have been made for teachers in most states since the start of the 1980s, teachers still earn less than members of other professional groups. And if comparisons are made with professions requiring approximately the same amount of schooling, the discrepancies are still significant. In 1988, for example, high school teachers averaged $30,300 per year and elementary teachers $28,900, while computer system analysts averaged $35,800, pharmacists $37,336, financial managers $32,800, and architects $32,000.[18]

In spite of relatively low salaries, teachers appear to rank well above average in regard to occupational status. For example, in a 1971 study completed at the University of Chicago, Paul Siegel reported that, compared to more than 500 occupations, teachers were above the 90th percentile in status.[19] The highest score was 81.5 for physicians and surgeons; the lowest was 9.3 for shoe shiners. High-school teachers received a rating of 63.1, and elementary teachers were rated 60.1. However, it is unlikely that such survey results do much to convince teachers that they enjoy high status, given the fact that the salaries the public is willing to grant them communicate a much different perception of the profession. And, until the financial rewards for teaching are brought into line with other professions requiring similar education and training, we may expect teachers to remain dissatisfied and to express this dissatisfaction in militant ways.

In the final analysis, perhaps the most accurate view of the status accorded teachers comes from the teachers themselves. In 1984, 47 percent of the 1,981 teachers responding to the Metropolitan Life Survey of the American Teacher agreed with the statement, "As a teacher I feel respected in today's society." According to the 1989 survey of 2,000 teachers, the number of teachers agreeing with the statement had increased to 53 percent.

Ways to Enhance Professionalism

Our discussion of the characteristics of a profession might at first seem discouraging. In response to the question, Is teaching a full profession? the evidence we have presented thus far would seem to suggest that the answer is Not yet. However, we believe that the current thrust among teachers, teacher educators, policymakers, and the general public is in the direction of making teaching a full profession. Be aware, too, that countless career teachers find teaching immensely satisfying. In spite of problems that confront the profession today, morale among most teachers is high. As one lifelong teacher put it:

> I hope that awareness of the problems . . . will not discourage talented young men and women from entering our profession. Some problems will be solved; the others can be lived with. All professions have their problems. If I were making a career choice in the twenty-first century, I would have no hesitation about becoming a teacher because I firmly believe that teaching, done well, is still the most personally satisfying of all the professions as well as the one offering the greatest long-range service to the human race.[20]

In the remainder of this section we look at four characteristics of teachers who are truly professional. They are committed to professional behavior, lifelong learning, teacher empowerment, and professional involvement and activism. If you strive to acquire each of these characteristics to the best of your abilities, you will have accepted, and met, the professional challenge of teaching.

Professional Behavior   The professional teacher is guided by a specific set of values. He or she has made a deep and lasting commitment to professional practice. He or she has adopted a high standard of professional ethics and models behaviors that are in accord with that code of ethics. The professional teacher also engages in serious, reflective thought about how to teach more effectively. Moreover, he or she does this *while* teaching, continually examining experiences to improve practice.

Donald Shön has described this professional behavior as "reflection-in-action," and he describes how a teacher might use it to solve a problem in the classroom:

> An artful teacher sees a child's difficulty in learning to read not as a defect in the child but as a defect "of his own instruction." So he must find a way of explaining what is bothering the pupil. He must do a piece of experimental research, then and there, in the classroom. And because the child's difficulties may be unique, the teacher

cannot assume that his repertoire of explanations will suffice, even though they are "at the tongue's end." He must be ready to invent new methods and must "endeavor to develop in himself the ability of discovering them."[21]

The professional teacher Shön describes is dedicated to making careful, sensitive observations of classroom events and then reflecting upon the meaning of those observations. In reality, the teacher acts as a researcher—continuously experimenting with ways to become more effective. Such a teacher has the courage and creativity to develop new ways of reaching students, ways that go beyond traditional, often limited, approaches.

For example, the professional teacher has at his or her disposal not only conventional methods and materials but also a store of more effective, and sometimes unconventional, strategies. While the repertoire of less professional teachers may be limited to lecturing, assigning problems at the end of a chapter in the text, using workbooks, and asking factual questions, professional teachers use approaches that reveal creativity and insight: small-group projects designed to prompt students to think rather than to parrot stock responses, and opportunities for students to select topics for independent study. In short, teachers who use reflection-in-action are continuously alert to the differences between routine and ideal practice.

Because of their positions and their encounters with young people, teachers may find opportunities to become **mentors** for some of their students. Accepting this responsibility is another example of professionalism. Awareness of this opportunity can make it more accessible to you when you teach.

The role of mentor is unique in several ways. First, mentorship develops naturally and is not an automatic part of teaching, nor can it be assigned to anyone. True mentorships grow from teaching relationships and cannot be artificially promoted. Second, the role of mentor is a *comprehensive* one: mentors express broad interest in their protégés (those whom they mentor). Third, the role of mentor is *mutually* recognized by student and teacher; both realize that their relationship has a special depth.[22] Fourth, the role of mentor is a significant one and has the potential to change the quality and direction of protégés' lives. And fifth, the opportunity to work with a mentor is free to protégés, mentors' gifts of care.[23]

Mentoring is a key attraction to the teaching profession and a hallmark of professional teachers. In addition, for many teachers the opportunity to mentor students—to make a difference even to only one—is their main source of motivation for furthering their careers as educators.

The longer teachers teach, the more they encounter opportunities for mentorships to develop, discovering that they can mentor younger teachers and student teachers as well as students. The rewards that come from the unique role of mentor may well be the most satisfying of all the teacher's roles because of the significance of the relationship to the lives of protégés.

Lifelong Learning   The professional teacher is dedicated to continuous learning—both about the teaching-learning process and about the subject taught. No longer is it sufficient for career teachers to obtain only a bachelor's degree and a teaching certificate. Professional teachers see themselves as both teachers and learners.

Several states have mandated continuing education for teachers. The content of the curriculum as well as methods and materials for teaching that content are changing so rapidly that teachers must be involved in continuous learning to maintain their professional effectiveness. In addition, we feel that teachers must practice what they preach. A teacher who is not continuously learning raises serious questions for students: If it's not important for our teachers to learn, why should we? The attitude toward learning that teachers model for students may be as important as the content they teach.

Many opportunities are available for teachers to learn new knowledge and skills. Nearly every school district makes provisions for inservice training or staff development. These programs are usually offered on days when students are dismissed early or not required to attend at all. Inservice training is usually given by district personnel or by faculty from a nearby college or university. The topics covered in inservice programs vary and are usually targeted at a particular need of the school. For example, we have led inservice sessions on classroom management, test-taking skills, constructing teacher-made tests, implementing research on effective teaching, and improving student achievement in the basic skills.

One of the most challenging ways to become a more effective professional is to enroll in a graduate program at a nearby college or university. Class schedules are usually developed with teachers in mind, with most courses offered in the evenings, on Saturdays, and during the summer. If you pursue graduate study, not only will you find the professional dialogue with instructors and fellow students stimulating, you'll acquire theories and practical approaches that you can implement in your classroom the following day. Also, you might find some other area of education—administration and supervision, guidance and counseling, special education, or curriculum development—that you want to pursue in your long-term career development.

FIVE-MINUTE FOCUS   As a teacher, what opportunities will be available to you to continue learning? Which ones will you take advantage of? Date your journal entry and write for five minutes.

Teacher Empowerment   The professional teacher welcomes opportunities to share decision-making power concerning education and the schools. From making decisions about the curriculum to implementing new programs designed to meet students' needs, professional teachers want to become empowered. Like other professionals, they welcome the opportunity to make decisions that directly affect their work.

FIGURE 13.2
**Principals and Teachers
Should Plan Together**

Question:
  Should principals and teachers spend time together after the school day to formally plan staff development, curriculum, and management?

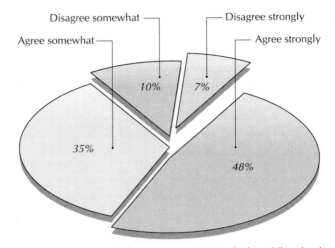

Note: Survey of 2,000 teachers—1,048 elementary, 430 junior high/middle school, and 443 high school teachers (79 taught both junior high and high school).
Source: Louis Harris and Associates, Inc. *The Metropolitan Life Survey of the American Teacher 1989: Preparing Schools for the 1990s* (New York: Louis Harris and Associates, Inc., 1990), p. 80. Used with permission.

Those who have participated in the trend toward **teacher empowerment** often report a renewed zest for teaching. For example, several middle school teachers in Florida, participants in a "faculty-driven" school improvement project since 1986–87, had this to say about becoming empowered:

For the first time inservice is meeting my needs. It's not something decreed from central administration that I don't care about.

Before I didn't feel I had any power to get things done. Having an opportunity to initiate change was something I had never thought possible.

The [improvement] committees have been the most important part of this project. They give us [teachers] an opportunity to sit down and discuss issues and decide what we should do about problems.[24]

As we saw in Chapter 8, teachers around the country are taking a more active role in school governance. In fact, the 1989 Metropolitan Life Survey of the American Teacher showed that 83 percent of teachers believe that "principals and teachers should share time together after the school day to formally plan staff development, curriculum, and management" (see Figure 13.2).

Professional Involvement and Activism   Though we may not associate such terms as *activism* and *militancy* with being a professional, we do feel that they capture well the kind of professional involvement that teaching presently needs if it is ever to become a full profession. The professional teacher is willing to get involved with colleagues and to press not only for increased financial rewards but for better working conditions and a greater role in professional governance.

FACT FINDING

How Involved Are Teachers in Professional Decision Making?

Research shows that the greatest opportunity for most teachers in professional decision making is selecting textbooks. In what area of decision making do most teachers have the least access?

Area of Decision Making	Percent of Teachers*
Choosing textbooks	79
Shaping the curriculum	63
Tracking students into special classes	45
Setting promotion and retention policies	34
Deciding school budgets	20
Evaluating teacher performance	10
Selecting new teachers	7
Selecting new administrators	7

*Based on responses from 11,827 elementary teachers and 11,651 secondary teachers.

Source: The Carnegie Foundation for the Advancement of Teaching, *Teacher Involvement in Decision Making: A State-by-State Profile,* September 1988. Data reported in National Center for Education Statistics, *Digest of Education Statistics 1990* (Washington, D.C.: National Center for Education Statistics, 1991): 80.

Presently, it is clear that teachers have not been given the power they need to improve the profession. As a result, this power will have to be attained in two ways. First, teachers must demonstrate by their behaviors and accomplishments that they *are* professionals. When all members of the profession—not just isolated outstanding teachers—do this, teaching will come to occupy its rightful status.

Second, teachers must more frequently demand—and in some cases even take— this power from parties who presently hold it. Teachers must realize that they have the most important role in the educational enterprise. They must therefore take a broader view of the decisions that, as professionals, they have the right to make. In some instances, power to make these decisions may have to be wrestled away from those who—because of tradition, not competence—have held it.

CONTINUING PROFESSIONAL DEVELOPMENT

Fortunately, changes are taking place in American education during the 1990s that are designed to promote the **professionalization of teaching.** From longer and more rigorous teacher preparation programs, to the creation of shared decision making/ school-based management programs, today's teachers have unprecedented opportunities to enhance their professional status. Therefore, we urge you to take every opportunity to continue your professional development *throughout* your career. Your

Being a professional teacher involves participating in teachers' organizations and professional associations. In addition to working for the enhancement of teaching's professional status, teachers are active in advocacy groups and reform lobbies calling for educational excellence and equity in education funding.

learning and growth, like your students', must not end upon completion of a course of study. We encourage you to be alert for new ideas, to refine your decision-making skills, and to become more effective in integrating theory and practice.

Sources of Motivation

Once an individual becomes certified to teach, the effort to continue learning often stops, a phenomenon that seems to be due more to the prevailing image of teaching as an easy occupation than to any personal lack of initiative. A key source of motivation for professional development is the anticipation of being intellectually challenged in order to enter and then to function effectively in fields such as medicine, engineering, and finance.[25] Because teaching has yet to gain a similar reputation as an intellectually rigorous field, those who enter it must take the initiative to continue to grow professionally. Because of this, new teachers need to overcome a certain inertia. One avenue for professional development is to become a member of professional organizations and to subscribe to one or more professional journals. Continued learning can also be promoted by teachers selecting to use their free periods or professional days to observe reputedly talented and effective veteran teachers in their own and neighboring school districts. They can ask trusted colleagues to observe and critique their teaching or tap their students' perceptions through evaluative, anonymous questionnaires. Experimenting with several teaching strategies and comparing the results, reading books in the field by experts and the growing group of teacher-authors, and attending conferences and workshops to strengthen specific skills are still other ways that those so motivated can learn more about teaching.

Opportunities for Development

After becoming a teacher you should take note of opportunities for professional development. If you are fortunate, you will be able to participate in an induction program or a beginning teacher assistance program such as those described in Chapter 3. In addition, most school systems and universities have in place several other sources for continuing professional education: teacher workshops, teacher centers, the opportunity to supervise student teachers, and graduate programs.

Teacher Workshops   The quality of **inservice workshops** is uneven, varying with the size of school district budgets and the imagination and knowledge of the administrators and teachers who arrange them. For every teacher fortunate enough to participate in an inservice program, there are many more who suffer, too frequently, through boring and irrelevant programs that offer simplistic, inapplicable solutions to complex classroom problems. It is significant that the most effective inservice programs tend to be the ones that teachers request—and often design and conduct.

Some workshops focus on topics that all teachers (regardless of subject or level) can benefit from: classroom management, writing-across-the-curriculum, or strategies of teaching, for example. Other workshops have a sharper focus and are intended for teachers of a subject at a certain level—for example, whole-language techniques for middle school students, discovery learning for high school science students, or student-centered approaches to teaching literature in the high school classroom.

Some inservice programs give teachers the opportunity to meet with other teachers at similar grade levels or with similar subject specializations for the purpose of sharing ideas, strategies, and solutions to problems. A day or part of a day may be devoted to this kind of workshop, often called an "idea exchange." You may even be given released time from your regular duties to visit other schools and observe exemplary programs in action. Such visits are effective because they allow you to see how your peers address the challenges of teaching.

Teacher Centers   **Teacher centers** are quite simply "places where teachers can come together with other teachers, and perhaps with other useful persons . . . to do things that will help them teach better."[26] In contrast to inservice programs, these are more clearly initiated and directed by teachers. Some centers cooperate with a local or neighboring college of education and include members of the faculty on their planning committees. Their goals range from providing a setting for teachers to exchange ideas, to offering information on education products and procedures, to arranging instruction in new areas of responsibility, such as supervision of student teachers and teaching students with special needs.

Many teachers find teacher centers stimulating because they offer opportunities for collegial interaction in a quiet, professionally oriented setting. The busy, hectic pace of life in many schools, teachers often find, provides little time for professional dialogue with peers. Furthermore, in the teacher center teachers are often more willing to discuss openly areas of weakness in their performance. As one teacher put it:

> At the teacher center I can ask for help. I won't be judged. The teachers who have helped me the most have had the same problems. I respect them, and I'm willing to learn from them. They have credibility with me.

Supervision of Student Teachers   After several years in the classroom, teachers may be ready to stretch themselves further by supervising student teachers. Some of the less obvious values of doing so are that teachers must rethink what they are doing so that they can explain and sometimes justify their behaviors to someone else, learning themselves in the process. Furthermore, because they become a model for their student teachers, they continually strive to offer the best example. In exchange, they gain an assistant in the classroom—another pair of eyes, an aid with record keeping—and more than occasionally fresh ideas and a spirit of enthusiasm.

The benefits of supervising a student teacher are evident in the following comments of a junior-high language arts teacher:

> I find that having a student teacher keeps me intellectually alive. It's also very satisfying to pass on what I have learned. To explain to a young teacher why I do certain things in the classroom is not easy. I know what works and why it works, but it can be difficult to communicate that.

Graduate Study   A more traditional form of professional development is to do graduate study. With the recent reforms, most states now require teachers to take some graduate work in order to keep their certifications and knowledge up to date. Some teachers only take courses that are of immediate use to them; others use their graduate study to prepare for new teaching or administrative positions; and still others pursue doctoral work in order to teach prospective teachers or others in their discipline at the college level.

Graduate study can be a catalyst for professional growth. During his second year of teaching at one of Chicago's most difficult inner-city high schools, for example, one of the authors of this book began graduate study in a quest to become more effective:

> With [a] sense of frustration at my professional ineffectiveness and an inability to see order and meaning in my teaching situation, I decided to begin [graduate study] in education at the University of Chicago. Initially, I was motivated largely by a desire to find out if some of the country's leading educators could provide me with the keys to greater effectiveness at a place as crazy as [my school]. Any educational principles I acquired through my study, I reasoned, I would immediately "reality check" back at the school. [The school] would be my "laboratory"—a laboratory where I would endeavor to integrate theory and practice.[27]

Stages of Professional Development as a Teacher

It may be helpful to think of your quest to become a professional teacher as a journey. During this journey, which will span your entire teaching career, you will experience a series of ups, downs, and plateaus. However, over time, you will become increasingly confident, skilled, and able to enjoy the many rewards of teaching.

Throughout the stages of professional development, teachers cultivate professional identities as lifelong learners. Taking advantage of opportunities for continuing teacher education, which are abundant in most states, professional teachers continually upgrade their knowledge and skills and broaden their expertise.

Theorist	Preservice		Inservice	
	Fuller and Bown (1975)	Sacks and Harrington (1982)	Gregorc (1973)	McDonald (1982)
Stages	Preteaching concerns	Anxiety	Becoming	Transition stage
	Early concerns about survival	Entry	Growing	Exploring stage
		Orientation	Maturing	Invention and experimenting stage
	Teaching situation concerns	Trial and error	The fully functioning professional	
		Integration/ consolidation		Professional teaching stage
	Concerns about pupils	Mastery		

FIGURE 13.3
Teachers' Developmental Stages

Theorists
Fuller, F. F. and Bowen, O. H. "Becoming a Teacher." In K. Ryan (Ed.), *Teacher Education* (74th Yearbook of the National Society for the Study of Education, Part II. Chicago: University of Chicago Press, 1975.
Sacks, S. R. and Harrington, C. N. *Student to Teacher: The Process of Role Transition.* Paper presented at the meeting of the American Educational Research Association, New York, March 1982.
Gregorc, A. F. "Developing Plans for Professional Growth." *NASSP Bulletin, 57.* 1973.
McDonald, F. J. *A Theory of the Professional Development of Teachers.* Paper presented at the meeting of the American Educational Research Association, New York, March 1982.
Source: Excerpted from "Teacher Development," by Paul R. Burden. Used with permission of Macmillan Publishing Company from *Handbook of Research on Teacher Education,* W. Robert Houston, Editor, p. 317. Copyright © 1990 by the Association of Teacher Educators.

Several researchers have studied the developmental stages through which preservice and inservice teachers pass. Figure 13.3, for example, shows the stages identified in two studies of preservice teachers and two studies of inservice teachers. Though the studies label the stages somewhat differently, the researchers' overall findings indicate that (1) anxiety is normal for students entering a teacher education program and (2) teachers reach higher levels of mastery as they move through their careers.

In regard to the stages through which preservice teachers pass, Fuller and Bown suggest that individuals move from concerns about teaching to concerns about pupils, while Sacks and Harrington see them moving from anxiety to mastery. For inservice teachers, both Gregorc and McDonald see teachers as moving through stages of growth that culminate in becoming a "fully functioning professional" (Gregorc) or reaching the "professional teaching stage" (McDonald).

TEACHERS' PROFESSIONAL ORGANIZATIONS

The push to make teaching more fully a profession draws much of its strength from the activities of more than 300 teacher organizations.[28] These organizations, and the scores of hardworking teachers who run them, have been responsible for the many gains teachers have made in salaries, benefits, and working conditions during the last few decades. In addition to working for such improvements, teacher organizations also perform the important function of solidifying the professional identity of teachers.

Professional teacher organizations support a variety of activities to improve teaching and schools. Through lobbying in Washington and at state capitols, for example, teacher associations acquaint legislators, policymakers, and politicians with critical issues and problems in the teaching profession. Many associations have staffs of teachers, researchers, and consultants who produce professional publications, hold conferences, prepare grant proposals, engage in school improvement activities, and promote a positive image of teaching to the public. The Teacher's Resource Guide at the end of this book lists 30 professional organizations to which teachers belong.

In the quest to improve the professional lives of all teachers, two national organizations have led the way: the National Education Association (NEA) and the American Federation of Teachers (AFT). These two groups have had a long history of competition for the allegiance of teachers. The hope of many is that one day these two rival organizations will merge, resulting in even greater gains for the profession. Until that day comes, the teaching profession will most likely remain divided, with sporadic organizational conflict characterizing the relationship between the two groups.

The National Education Association

Membership in the **National Education Association,** the oldest and largest of the two organizations, includes both teachers and administrators. Originally called the National Teachers Association when it was founded in 1857, the group was started by 43 educators from a dozen states and the District of Columbia.[29] Although the NEA has grown today to a complex Washington-based organization with 1,600,800 members and a staff of 600,[30] it is still guided by the twofold purpose set by its founders: "to elevate the character and advance the interests of the profession of teaching, and to promote the cause of popular education in the United States."[31]

The NEA has affiliates in every state plus Puerto Rico and the District of Columbia, and its local affiliates number 10,000. About half of the teachers in this country belong to the NEA. More than 78 percent of NEA's members are teachers; about 12 percent are guidance counselors, librarians, and administrators; almost 3 percent are university professors; about 2 percent are college and university students; about 3 percent are support staff (teacher aides, secretaries, cafeteria workers, bus drivers, and custodians); and about 2 percent are retired members.

To improve education in this country, the NEA has standing committees in the following areas: affiliate relationships, higher education, human relations, political action, teacher benefits, and teacher rights. These committees engage in a wide range of activities, among them preparing reports that deal with important educational issues, disseminating the results of educational research, conducting conferences, working with federal agencies on behalf of children, pressing for more rigorous standards for the teaching profession, helping school districts resolve salary disputes, developing ways to improve personnel practices, and enhancing the relationship between the profession and the public.

The Unionization Movement   Prior to World War II, the NEA was more concerned with improving the quality of instruction than with the bread-and-butter issues of teachers' salaries and benefits. Moreover, up until the 1940s it was commonly felt that teaching was a calling similar to the ministry, and that it was therefore inappropriate for teachers to press for higher salaries and better working conditions.

Following World War II, the NEA began to take a more productive stance regarding issues related to teacher welfare. By 1950 the organization had grown to over 400,000 members, and it was capable of making its views widely known. Postwar inflation had caused large numbers of teachers to leave the profession for jobs that kept better pace with rising prices. By the late 1940s, the nation was faced with a critical teacher shortage.

The plight of teachers was made known through publications put out by the NEA, the American Federation of Teachers, and other teacher organizations. During this period, some teachers banded together and began using the strike as a means of securing their demands. Initially, the NEA was staunchly opposed to the use of strikes. It stressed the fact that teachers were professionals, and professionals should not resort to the use of a labor union strategy.

Instead of supporting teacher strikes, the NEA worked to obtain more federal monies for education, part of which would be used to improve teachers' salaries and working conditions. If teacher strikes became more widespread, the NEA leadership reasoned, Congress would be reluctant to provide significant aid to education. Federal aid to education was not significantly increased until after the launching of Sputnik by the Russians in 1957. However, as we learned in the previous chapter, most of the federal money poured into education was used to develop new curricula for mathematics, sciences, and languages. Only a small amount was used to increase teachers' salaries.

Though it was not until the late 1960s that the NEA acknowledged the strike as a legitimate weapon for teachers to use, it did use other means to press for improvements. In 1946, at its annual meeting, the NEA established the National Commission on Teacher Education and Professional Standards (TEPS). The TEPS Commission worked from 1946 until its demise in 1971 to improve teachers' working conditions and to develop a "continuing program of teacher recruitment, selection, preparation, certification, and the advancement of professional standards, including standards for institutions that prepare teachers."[32]

Gains in Teachers' Rights   By the late 1960s and early 1970s, the NEA recognized that it had to become increasingly militant in order to secure much needed improvements in teachers' working conditions. In fact, the NEA entered the 1974 congressional elections with the campaign theme, "Get mad: it matters."

Many teachers had been treated unfairly in the United States because they lacked the resources to obtain legal redress through the courts. One particular case, in 1943, marked the start of NEA-funded legal assistance for teachers. Three teachers in Muskogee, Oklahoma, learned through the local newspaper that they had not been reappointed for the following school year. They were given no written or oral notice. No hearing had been held, and no charges had been made. The Executive Committee of the NEA decided to devote $10,000 to support the teachers in their case against the Muskogee school board. The NEA's Committee on Tenure charged the board with dismissal without just cause, failure to state the charges against the teachers, and failure to exercise due process.

Following the NEA's successful support of the teachers' case, the $984.39 unspent on legal fees was used to begin the Dushane Fund for Teacher Rights. Since the fund's establishment in 1944, the number of legal cases the NEA has supported has mushroomed. In 1957, the NEA spent $82,620 supporting teachers' rights. During 1978–79, expenditures were $2.6 million, not including state and local funds. The number of cases handled has also increased dramatically. From 1975 to 1979, for example, the number of cases increased from 1,743 to 15,614.[33] The increase reflects issues related to collective bargaining, civil rights, pupil violence, the increased exercise of constitutional rights by NEA members, and the increasing trend toward using legal action to resolve disputes.

FIGURE 13.4
Number of Teacher Strikes, 1973–1983

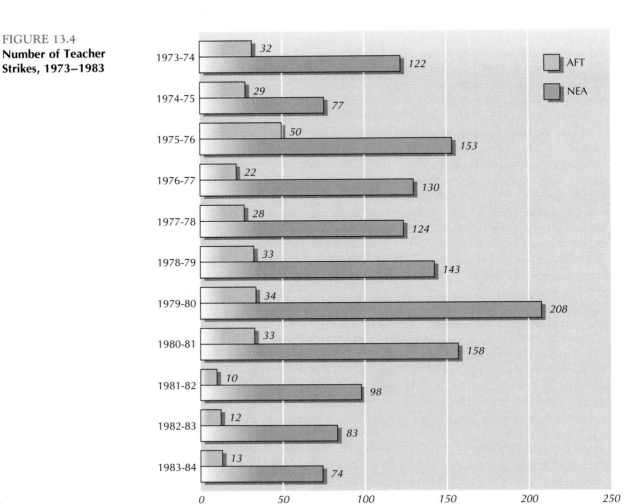

Source: Based on information provided by the National Education Association and the American Federation of Teachers.

Collective Bargaining and Strikes   The NEA officially adopted the practice of collective bargaining (it chose to call it "professional negotiation") at a Representative Assembly meeting in Denver in 1962. Representatives of local NEA affiliates quickly acquired skills in formal collective bargaining so they could best represent the interests of teachers. During the 1970s, the NEA supported an average of over 100 teacher strikes per year (see Figure 13.4). Initially uncomfortable with the label "strike," the NEA used the phrase "withdrawal of services." The number of teacher strikes has declined significantly since 1980, prompted in part by growing antilabor sentiment in the country and by the determination of officials and a tax-conscious public to deny pay increases and to discharge striking workers.

When the NEA became involved in teachers' strikes in the 1960s, strikes were illegal in every state. Teachers who participated in such actions risked losing their jobs and being prosecuted for breaking the law. Though some teachers and strike leaders were jailed in the late 1960s and early 1970s, most settlements included amnesty provisions that allowed teachers to return to work without fear of charges being pressed against them.

The NEA has worked to help pass state laws that would make strikes legal. As of 1980, 31 states had passed some type of collective bargaining laws that applied to teachers. There is little uniformity among these laws, with most of the 31 states permitting strikes only if certain conditions have been met. The NEA has gone on record as supporting a federal statute that would set up uniform procedures for teachers to bargain with their employers.

The NEA continues today to focus on issues of concern to teachers, primarily in the area of professional governance. The organization is supporting proposals that would allow teachers to make more decisions that impact their classroom lives. Efforts are being made to broaden teachers' decision-making powers related to curriculum, extracurricular responsibilities, staff development, and supervision. To promote the status of the profession, the NEA conducts annual research studies and opinion surveys in various areas and publishes *NEA Today*, the *NEA Research Bulletin*, and its major publication, *Today's Education*.

The American Federation of Teachers

The **American Federation of Teachers** (AFT) was founded in 1916. Three teachers' unions in Chicago issued a call for teachers to form a national organization affiliated with organized labor. Teacher unions in Gary, Indiana; New York City; Oklahoma; Scranton, Pennsylvania; and Washington, D.C. joined the three Chicago unions to form the AFT. The newly formed AFT had four objectives:

1. To bring associations of teachers into relations of mutual assistance and cooperation.
2. To obtain for them all the rights to which they are entitled.
3. To raise the standards of the teaching profession by securing the conditions essential to the best professional service.
4. To promote such a democratization of the schools as will enable them better to equip their pupils to take their places in the industrial, social, and political life of the community.[34]

The AFT differs from the NEA in that it is open only to teachers and nonsupervisory school personnel. The AFT is active today in organizing teachers, collective bargaining, public relations, and developing policies related to various educational issues. In addition, the organization conducts research in such areas as educational reform, bilingual education, teacher certification, and evaluation, and it also represents members' concerns through legislative action and technical assistance.

The AFT has 715,000 members who are organized through 2,200 local affiliates.[35] The AFT is affiliated with the American Federation of Labor—Congress of Industrial Organizations (AFL-CIO), which has over 14 million members. To promote the idea that teachers should have the right to speak for themselves on important issues and to be an aggressive, responsive advocate for teachers, the AFT does not allow superintendents, principals, and other administrators to join. As an informational brochure on the AFT states, "Because the AFT believes in action—in 'getting things done' rather than issuing reports, letting someone else do the 'doing'—a powerful, cohesive structure is necessary."

Keepers of the Dream

Thelma Holmes
First-Grade Teacher and Union Leader
Martin Luther King Elementary School
Miami, Florida

Thelma Holmes, a first-grade teacher and Vice President of the 9,000-member United Teachers of Dade County, Florida, says that teaching "is like watching a garden grow. First you plant seeds, but you see nothing. Then after a while the plants come up and you see beautiful flowers."

Holmes has taught for 31 years in Dade County. Four years ago she began teaching at Martin Luther King Elementary School in inner-city Miami. The school has about 350 students, prekindergarten through third grade. "It's a small school, so you really get to know the kids," says Holmes. She loves to share the joy and excitement of her students as they learn to read.

It's so rewarding to hear them begin to read. It's fantastic. I work with the Right to Read program, and to hear them attack words, even big words they haven't had before, is a good feeling.

Holmes realizes how important it is for teachers to continue their professional growth. "When I first started teaching, I didn't have a bachelor's degree," she says. "I was a substitute teacher and went back to school to earn my degree." Since then Holmes has earned a master's degree in administration and supervision and a specialist degree in elementary education.

Today, you just can't get a bachelor's degree and say now I know how to teach. Once you start teaching you are constantly learning. To reach students you have to be willing to try a little bit of everything. You

"So I'm 'On Call' To Help Them"

might be able to motivate one class in a certain way, but when you get to another class it may not work. If you're dedicated, you're constantly trying to find out what's new.

Holmes has been Vice President of the United Teachers of Dade County for eight years, a position that gives her an opportunity to help other teachers grow professionally. "I'm on the legislative committee—we're constantly watching the state legislature so we can pass relevant information on to the teachers," she says. "Sometimes, teachers become frustrated and don't know where to turn for help. So I'm 'on call' to help them."

To enhance the professionalism of Dade County teachers, Holmes frequently attends workshops, seminars, and training programs and then shares her new knowledge with other teachers. "We get the new information that teachers want," she says.

She is also a recruiter for the Dade County Public Schools, and she frequently hosts union teachers from other communities who come to visit her school.

Holmes encourages beginning teachers to become involved in professional organizations.

Beginning teachers should know that they will have some dark days. But they should not become discouraged; they should become more qualified. Find out what's new, find out what will work with your kids. One of the best ways to get new ideas is to become involved professionally.

Unlike the NEA, the AFT has been steadfastly involved throughout its history in securing economic gains and improving working conditions for teachers. Though the AFT has been criticized for being unprofessional and too concerned with bread-and-butter issues, none other than the great educator and philosopher John Dewey took out the first AFT membership card in 1916. After 12 years as a union member, Dewey made his stance on economic issues clear:

> It is said that the Teachers Union, as distinct from the more academic organizations, overemphasizes the economic aspect of teaching. Well, I never had that contempt for the economic aspect of teaching, especially not on the first of the month when I get my salary check. I find that teachers have to pay their grocery and meat bills and house rent just the same as everybody else. I find that the respect in which they individually and collectively are held in the community is closely associated with the degree of economic independence which they enjoy. . . . It is academic folly and mere fantasy to suppose that the conduct of public education can be divorced from the prominence which economic, industrial, and financial questions occupy in all other phases of our social life.[36]

The rivalry between the NEA and the AFT has often been bitter over the years. In various cities and states, both groups have confronted one another in head-to-head battles for the right to represent teachers.

Claiming that teachers should be represented by a professional association, the NEA has condemned the AFT's use of militant union tactics, such as collective bargaining and strikes. The NEA has also stated repeatedly that the AFT's affiliation with labor has damaged the public's perceptions of teachers. On the other hand, the AFT has been critical of the NEA for allowing administrators to join and for using less aggressive negotiating tactics.

The AFT scored its biggest win over the NEA in December 1961, when New York City's teachers voted two to one to have the AFT local, the United Federation of Teachers (UFT), act as the teachers' bargaining agent. With this victory, the UFT won the right to represent the city's more than 50,000 teachers.

Traditionally, the AFT has been strongest in urban areas. Today, the AFT represents teachers not only in Chicago and New York but in Philadelphia, Washington, D.C., Kansas City, Detroit, Boston, Cleveland, and Pittsburgh. NEA membership, on the other hand, has tended to be suburban and rural. The NEA has always been the larger of the two organizations, and it is presently more than twice the size of its rival (see Table 13.2).

In 1968, Charles Cogen, president of the AFT, proposed a merger with the NEA. In the AFT's publication, *The American Teacher*, Cogen wrote:

> There is no use denying that the AFT and the NEA are engaged in dire competition for the membership of the teachers of America. But we must do this without giving aid and power to the governmental authorities, boards of education, and superintendents with whom we are contending. And then, let us keep the door open; let us look forward to the day when AFT–NEA unity may become a reality. Heaven knows, we badly need a strong, unified, militant, and labor-oriented teachers' union to fight the great battles that lie ahead.[37]

The NEA, however, declined the AFT's invitation to explore that possibility and proposed instead that the AFT drop its AFL-CIO affiliation and join the NEA. At that point, talk of a national merger was abandoned. A few local affiliates (Flint, Michigan; Los Angeles; Florida; and New York state), however, did go on to merge.

TABLE 13.2   Membership in the NEA and AFT

Year	NEA	AFT
1857*	43	—
1870	170	—
1880	354	—
1890	5,474	—
1900	2,322	—
1910	6,909	—
1916**	—	1,500
1920	22,850	10,000
1930	216,188	7,000
1940	203,429	30,000
1950	453,797	41,000
1960	713,994	59,000
1970	1,100,000	205,000
1980	1,650,000	550,000
1990	1,600,800	580,000
1991	1,600,800	715,000

*Year the NEA was founded
**Year the AFT was founded
Sources: "Your NEA," *Today's Education* (1983–84): 78–79; "AFT Membership Growing Again," *Annual Report of the American Federation of Teachers, 1982–83* (Washington, D.C.: AFT, 1983): 43; *Encyclopedia of Associations, 1989, 1990, and 1991* (Detroit: Gale Research Inc., 1988, 1989, 1990).

Another attempt was made to merge in 1973–74. Talks begun that October were terminated the following February. Once again, the NEA rejected an AFT request to resume the talks, citing the AFT's insistence on AFL–CIO affiliation as the major stumbling block. Since then, the possibility of a merger has seemed remote. Although both organizations continue to call for a merger in their publications, bitter conflicts between the two groups continue to occur around the country.

FIVE-MINUTE FOCUS   Do you plan to join a teachers' association such as the NEA or AFT? What are your reasons? What advantages and disadvantages of joining are most important to you? Date your journal entry and write for five minutes.

Other Professional Organizations

In addition to the NEA and AFT, teachers' professional interests are represented by more than 300 other national organizations. Several of these are concerned with improving the quality of education at all levels and in all subject areas. Two of the most respected and influential of these groups are Phi Delta Kappa and the Association for Supervision and Curriculum Development.

Phi Delta Kappa A professional and honorary fraternity of educators, **Phi Delta Kappa** is concerned with enhancing quality education through research and leadership activities. Founded in 1906, Phi Delta Kappa now has a membership of 130,000.[38] Members, who are graduate students, teachers, and administrators, belong to one of 650 chapters. To be initiated into Phi Delta Kappa, one must have demonstrated high academic achievement, have completed at least 15 semester hours of graduate work in education, and have made a commitment to a career of educational service. Phi Delta Kappa members receive *Phi Delta Kappan,* an excellent journal of education published 10 times a year.

The Association for Supervision and Curriculum Development A professional organization of teachers, supervisors, curriculum coordinators, education professors, administrators, and others, the **Association for Supervision and Curriculum Development** (ASCD) is interested in school improvement at all levels of education. Founded in 1921, the association has a membership of 120,000.[39] ASCD provides professional development experiences in curriculum and supervision, disseminates information related to educational issues, and encourages research, evaluation, and theory development. ASCD also conducts several National Curriculum Study Institutes around the country each year and provides a free Research Information Service to members. Members receive *Educational Leadership,* a well-respected journal printed eight times a year. ASCD also publishes a yearbook, each one devoted to a particular educational issue, and occasional books in the area of curriculum and supervision.

Subject-Area and Special-Student Associations Many teachers also belong to professional organizations whose primary purpose is to identify and disseminate promising practices in specific subject areas and for special groups of students. See the Teacher's Resource Guide for descriptions of the following "Teachers' Associations."

- American Alliance for Health, Physical Education, Recreation and Dance (AAHPERD)
- American Association of Teachers of French (AATF)
- American Association of Teachers of German (AATG)
- American Association of Teachers of Spanish and Portuguese (AATSP)
- American Classical League (ACL)
- American Council on the Teaching of Foreign Languages (ACTFL)
- Association for Childhood Education International (ACEI)
- Council for Exceptional Children (CEC)
- Division for Early Childhood (DEC)
- Foundation for Exceptional Children (FEC)
- Home Economics Education Association (HEEA)
- International Reading Association (IRA)
- Kappa Delta Pi
- Music Teachers National Association (MTNA)
- National Art Education Association (NAEA)
- National Association for Bilingual Education (NABE)
- National Association of Biology Teachers (NABT)
- National Association for the Education of Young Children (NAEYC)

- National Association for Gifted Children (NAGC)
- National Association for Trade and Industrial Education (NATIE)
- National Business Education Association (NBEA)
- National Council for the Social Studies (NCSS)
- National Council of Teachers of English (NCTE)
- National Council of Teachers of Mathematics (NCTM)
- Reading Is Fundamental (RIF)
- Teachers of English to Speakers of Other Languages (TESOL)

THE IMPACT OF TEACHERS' ASSOCIATIONS ON EDUCATION

Teachers' unions and other organizations can have both a positive and a negative potential impact on education. To the extent that professional teacher organizations put the growth of students before the growth of the organizations themselves, they can have a tremendous positive influence on education. A review of the 30 associations listed in the Teacher's Resource Guide, for example, reveals an impressive array of publications, research projects, and support offered directly to students and teachers. And, as we have pointed out in previous chapters, teacher associations are working diligently to professionalize training and improve schools.

On the other hand, competition among teacher associations can lead to less public support for education. In the case of the NEA and the AFT, their differences over the years have become less apparent. Collective bargaining and the use of strikes, long opposed by the NEA, are now used by both organizations. The major difference between the two groups now is the AFT's affiliation with organized labor, another source of public disaffection in some areas. Disruptions caused by strikes can also erode public support.

Many persons within both the NEA and the AFT believe that the interests of teachers and students could best be served through a merger of the two organizations. One national teachers' union with enormous political strength is the goal. A significant step was made in this direction when the local affiliates of the AFT and the NEA in San Francisco merged in 1989 to become the United Educators of San Francisco.

SUMMARY

For an occupation to be considered a profession, it must satisfy many criteria. Though no occupation meets all the criteria, some occupations meet more of them and therefore have a higher professional status in our society. In regard to the nine criteria examined in this chapter, teaching meets some more fully than others. The general consensus is that teaching is presently not a full profession, but it is rapidly becoming more professionalized.

The most potent force for improving teaching is for teachers to see that their behavior reflects professional practice, ethical conduct, a commitment to lifelong learning, a desire to become empowered, and professional involvement and activism. Among the opportunities available for teachers who wish to grow professionally are teacher workshops, participation in teacher centers, supervision of student teachers, and graduate study. Taking advantage of opportunities for professional development is an important part of your teaching career.

Several teacher organizations work on the national, state, and local levels to improve the teaching profession. Among the most influential are the National Education Association and the American Federation of Teachers. Though initially founded on different approaches to improving the profession, both groups now use militantly proactive strategies to secure greater financial rewards and improved working conditions for teachers. The AFT's affiliation with organized labor has been the major barrier to a merger of the two organizations. The prospect of a united, national teacher organization seems dim, as the two groups continue to wage bitter campaigns around the country for the right to represent teachers.

KEY TERMS AND CONCEPTS

profession, **410**
National Board for Professional
   Teaching Standards, **417**
mentor, **420**
teacher empowerment, **422**
professionalization of teaching, **423**
inservice workshops, **425**

teacher centers, **425**
National Education Association, **428**
American Federation of Teachers, **431**
Phi Delta Kappa, **435**
Association for Supervision and
   Curriculum Development, **435**

DISCUSSION QUESTIONS

1. As a teacher, what specific activities will you become involved in that will promote the overall status of the profession?
2. What do you think should be done to enhance the public's view of teaching as a profession? What can you do to bring this change about?
3. In what ways does the possibility of a future teacher shortage enhance the professional status of teaching? In what ways does it detract from it?
4. What is your position regarding the use of strikes by teachers to attain their professional goals? For the profession, what are the advantages and disadvantages of this strategy?
5. Which group do you find more compatible with your views of teaching as a profession, the NEA or the AFT? Why?
6. Are you in favor of, or against, a united, national teachers' organization? Defend your answer.

APPLICATION ACTIVITIES

1. Do some research to find out whether teacher strikes are legal in your state. What penalties or risks do striking teachers face? If possible, find out what sequence of events led up to any recent nearby teacher strikes. What were the results of those strikes? Share your findings in a brief oral report to the rest of your class.
2. Help your instructor set up a role-play in which members of your class imagine that they are teachers trying to decide whether to join a union that is affiliated with organized labor. Two students should give short talks that are prounion. Two

others should be given equal time to present their reasons for not joining the union. Following these presentations, the class should hold a secret ballot on whether the group will join the union.

3. Review several recent issues of the NEA publication, *Today's Education,* and the AFT publication, *The American Teacher.* Make a list of concerns or issues that each publication addresses. Make a list of the overall differences you find between the NEA and AFT publications.

4. Examine Figure 13.3, "Preservice and Inservice Teachers' Developmental Stages." What stage do you feel you are in now? What steps can you take to move to the next stage of professional development? How will you know when you have reached that stage?

FIELD EXPERIENCES

1. Arrange an interview with a principal in your home town on the topic of teaching as a profession. Take notes regarding his or her views on what teachers could do to enhance the status of the profession. Then present a brief oral report of your findings to your class. Compare your results with those obtained by other students.

2. Visit a nearby school and talk to several teachers about what steps should be taken to improve the professional status of teachers. Take notes regarding their views. Then present a brief oral report of your findings to your class. Compare your results with those obtained by other students.

3. Interview several adults who are not involved in education to get their views on teaching as a profession. What image do these adults have of teaching? What are their suggestions for improving the profession?

4. Visit a school and interview a teacher who is actively involved in a professional association or teachers' union. What benefits does the teacher obtain from his or her professional involvement?

SUGGESTED READINGS

The Commission on Educational Reconstruction. *Organizing the Teaching Profession: The Story of the American Federation of Teachers.* Glencoe, Ill.: Free Press, 1955. *An account of the founding and development of the American Federation of Teachers.*

Goodlad, John I. *Teachers for Our Nation's Schools.* San Francisco: Jossey-Bass, 1990. *Presents 19 postulates for restructuring teacher education. Concludes with the fable of renewal in teacher education at "Northern State University."*

Lieberman, Ann, ed. *Building a Professional Culture in Schools.* New York: Teachers College Press, 1988. *Contains articles by leading educators who examine the nature of professionalism in teaching and offer strategies for increasing collaboration among teachers as well as opportunities for them to exercise leadership in schools.*

Lortie, Dan C. *Schoolteacher: A Sociological Study.* Chicago: University of Chicago Press, 1975. *A renowned educational sociologist provides a look at the social system that characterizes public school teaching.*

Maeroff, Gene I. *The Empowerment of Teachers: Overcoming the Crisis of Confidence.* New York: Teachers College Press, 1988. *This book insightfully and eloquently points out how teachers must be empowered in ways that allow them to increase their status, their knowledge, and their access to decision making.*

West, Allan M. *The National Education Association: The Power Base for Education.* New York: Free Press, 1980. *This book, by an NEA staff member, chronicles the many changes that have occurred in the NEA between 1957 and 1980.*

TEACHERS . . .

What knowledge or experiences have had the greatest influence on the kind of teacher you are today?

Being a parent has had the greatest influence on the kind of teacher I am today. Each day, with every lesson—including discipline—I ask myself, "Would I want me for my child's teacher? Is this how I expect my child to be treated?"

—Dolores Ramón
Montgomery Drive Elementary School, San Antonio, Texas

I had a wonderful lady, Mrs. Shane, as my teacher in grades five through eight. She had only twelve students in that one-room school, but everyone was enthusiastic about learning and was successful. She used the older students as peer tutors, recognized that one student had a musical talent, encouraged another to run daily and to participate in track meets, and insisted that another enter a speaking contest and go to the state finals. Mrs. Shane's memory is still vivid today and I can still hear her encouraging me to "try" and to always do my best.

—Ruby Diepholz
Acacia Middle School, Hemet, California

In my early childhood school was extremely difficult. At the time, in the early 1960s, few people understood dyslexia. I was considered a "slow learner" or just plain "lazy." School was a time of great disappointment. I felt that the other children were smarter than I was. I felt great pain and a sense of extreme inferiority. Fortunately, in the fourth grade (my second year in fourth grade), my teacher taught me to play tennis. This gave me one of the first feelings of being "liked" by a teacher. In sixth grade, and in a Media class and a Psychology class in high school, I also felt that I could be successful in school.

Because of these experiences, the fact that I had learned coping mechanisms to deal with my learning problems, and the need to influence others' lives, I decided to become a teacher. If I could send a message to future teachers, I would say to be considerate of the child with learning difficulties. This child is capable of learning and is worth teaching. The difficult task for the educator is to establish an environment where this child can feel safe to make mistakes and to learn from them. I only hope that through my living the terror of being a child with a learning difficulty, I can be a source of encouragement to other children, letting them know that they can make it!

—Jerry D. Brookshire
Wildomar Elementary School, Wildomar, California

ON TEACHING

In my experience as a PE teacher, there is one instance in particular that has influenced my teaching habits. While I was doing some of my field work, I observed a PE class in a junior high school. The class was not very organized and the teacher seemed uninterested and lethargic. He was an older gentleman, not in very good shape. I asked if I could see his lesson plans for that day. After some fidgeting around in his desk, he pulled out his plans. They were dated 1969! I was appalled that he had not taken the time or energy to update and renew his teaching style and ideas for so many years. That is when I vowed that I would maintain a high level of enthusiasm and would stay up to date in my field.

—Amy Orcutt
Green Gables Elementary School, Jefferson County, Colorado

A creative writing teacher in my high school . . . had a great influence on my teaching. She made each student feel welcome and safe from the laughing taunts and peer pressures other high school students placed on each other. In my class were the very elite of our school: football players, class officers, etc. Among them were shy, awkward, unpopular people like me. She treated each of us the same. We all had the same talent and potential in her eyes. With a smile, a wink, or a warm hand on the shoulder she let us know we were important to her.

—Allyson Briggs
Rosamond Elementary School, Riverton, Utah

The first turning point in my career occurred after I had been teaching for five years. I was tired of making pennies for my efforts, tired of being trapped in a building for eight hours, tired of having a twenty-minute lunch period, tired of not being able to go to the restroom when I needed to go, etc. So, I called a publishing company, went for an interview, and was hired as a language arts consultant. Not only was I making more money for less actual working hours, but I also had a company car, an expense account, an opportunity to travel, and an enormous amount of freedom. After traveling the Southeast for a year, visiting different school systems, observing and talking with other teachers, I realized that *I* was a *good* teacher (I always felt that I wasn't) and that I missed the classroom. So, I resigned and went back to teaching.

The next turning point occurred when I was assigned to a high school as a Chapter I teacher. My certification was K–9 and my experience was in kindergarten and grades 3 and 6. Not only was I assigned to a high school, but it was considered the toughest inner-city school in the city. It was at this school that I received a number of valuable lessons. The discovery that I *loved* teaching high-school-aged kids was the most startling revelation of all.

—Susan S. Reid
Chattanooga High School, Chattanooga, Tennessee

Equalizing Educational Opportunity

Our teachers come
to class,
And they talk and
they talk
Till their faces are
like peaches.
We don't;
We just sit like
cornstalks.

Written by a Navajo
child in New Mexico[1]

A student of yours believes that one day he will become a great Chicano leader. Antonio, who hates to be called Tony, and his older brother are members of every Chicano organization in the community. Antonio frequently misses school so he can attend political functions with his brother. When he does come to school, he is often short-tempered with his Anglo teachers. He has become a nuisance on the playground, where he tries to instruct his "little brothers and sisters" in Chicano culture. Largely because of his irregular attendance, Antonio is barely passing his subjects.

Last month Antonio missed a week of school when he visited relatives in Mexico. That week you phoned his home several times to speak to his mother or father, but no one was home. When Antonio finally returned, you arranged to talk to his mother about Antonio's attendance. She was pleasant but seemed unwilling to acknowledge that Antonio's absence from school was a problem. You also felt that she was not going to put pressure on Antonio to improve his attendance or to work harder at school.

Antonio is deeply committed to his culture and is intent on furthering the Chicano cause. "I wish to become something proud," he says, "an example to my thousands of little brothers and sisters in the barrios across the nation."

What strategies would you use to get Antonio to put more effort into school? What steps could you take to improve the relationship between you and him?

FOCUS QUESTIONS

1. How have certain ethnic groups in our society been denied equal educational opportunities?
2. What are some of the special needs of students from different ethnic and cultural groups?
3. What are the implications of Public Law 94-142 for regular classroom teachers?
4. What knowledge and skills can best equip teachers to work with students from different ethnic and cultural groups?
5. How are female students and students perceived as handicapped treated differently from other students in the classroom?

This chapter looks at equalizing educational opportunity for all students and takes the position that the professional teacher sees cultural diversity as an asset to be preserved and valued, not a liability. This country has always derived strength from the diversity of its people, and *all* students should receive a quality education so that they may make their unique contributions to our society.

All persons have the right to expect that they will be treated equally, that they will be judged on the basis of what they can do rather than who they are. In the classroom, the teacher is confronted with the difficult challenge of being sensitive to differences among students while at the same time treating all equally and fairly. There are no easy recipes to follow to accomplish this. It may help, though, to remember that as human beings we are more alike than different. The requirements for teaching all students, regardless of their ethnic or racial backgrounds or any special needs they might have, are the same. They learn well from teachers who are knowledgeable, energetic, flexible, creative, and committed; they do not learn as well from teachers who lack these characteristics.

YOUR MULTICULTURAL CLASSROOM

As a teacher you will teach students who historically have not received full educational opportunity—students from the more than 100 racial and ethnic groups in America and students who are poor, handicapped, gifted, or female. You will face the challenge of reaching out to all students and teaching them that they are persons of worth and can learn.

You will also need to model an attitude of respect for students from different minority groups and be alert for ways to increase their learning. To achieve this, it may help to remember that the term **minority** refers to a percentage of the population. While the 1980 census revealed that nonwhite ethnic minorities made up about 17 percent of the population, in certain parts of the country minorities are actually in the majority. The census showed, for example, that African Americans and Hispanic Americans constitute majorities in the following cities:

African-American Majority	*Hispanic-American Majority*
Richmond, VA	San Antonio, TX
Gary, IN	Hialeah, FL
Inglewood, CA	Laredo, TX
Newark, NJ	Miami, FL
New Orleans, LA	Brownsville, TX
Atlanta, GA	El Paso, TX
Baltimore, MD	
Birmingham, AL	
Detroit, MI	

In your **multicultural** classroom your aim is not to develop a different curriculum for each group of students—that would be impossible and would place undue emphasis on differences among students. Rather, your curriculum should help increase students' awareness and appreciation of the rich diversity in American culture. As James A. Banks, an authority on multicultural education, suggests:

> The multicultural curriculum should enable students to derive valid generalizations and theories about the characteristics of ethnic groups and to learn how they are alike and different, in both their past and present experiences. . . . *[Each] curriculum should focus on a range of groups that differ in their racial characteristics, cultural experiences, languages, histories, values, and current problems.*[2]

Ethnicity and Race

Your understanding of the distinction between ethnicity and race will enable you to prepare a curriculum that reflects ethnic and racial diversity in meaningful ways.

Ethnic Groups "Ethnicity" is the quality of being a member of an ethnic group. **Ethnic groups** have been defined as

> groups whose members share a unique social and cultural heritage passed on from one generation to the next. . . . Ethnic groups are frequently identified by distinctive patterns of family life, language, recreation, religion, and other customs that cause them to be differentiated from others. Above all else, members of such groups feel a consciousness of kind and "interdependence of fate" with those who share the customs of the ethnic tradition.[3]

Some individuals mistakenly limit their view of ethnicity to people of color. As the above definition suggests, however, all people are members of an ethnic group. The 1980 census revealed that 83 percent of Americans perceived themselves as belonging to at least one ethnic group. The most frequently reported groups were the following:

English	50 million	Scottish	10 million
German	49 million	Polish	8 million
African American	21 million	Mexican	8 million
French	13 million	American Indian	7 million
Italian	12 million	Dutch	6 million

Race The concept of **race** is used to distinguish among human beings on the basis of biological traits and characteristics. Numerous racial categories have been proposed, but because of the diversity among humans and the mixing of genes that has taken place over time, no single set of racial categories is universally accepted. People can be classified into as many as 300 "races," depending on the kind and number of genetic features chosen for measurement. In his book, *Man's Most Dangerous Myth: The Fallacy of Race,* anthropologist Ashley Montagu pointed out that

> It is impossible to make the sort of racial classifications which some anthropologists and others have attempted. The fact is that all human beings are so . . . mixed with regard to origin that between different groups of individuals . . . "overlapping" of physical traits is the rule.[4]

In light of the arbitrariness of the concept of race, James Banks points out: *"In most societies, the social significance of race is much more important than the presumed physical differences among groups."*[5] Unfortunately, many people attach great importance to the concept of race. If you believe "that human groups can be validly grouped on the basis of their biological traits and that these identifiable groups inherit certain mental, personality, and cultural characteristics that determine their behavior"[6] then you hold racist beliefs. When people use such beliefs as a rationale for oppressing other groups, they are practicing **racism.**

As a teacher, you will not be able to eliminate racism in our society. However, you have an obligation to all your students to see that your curriculum and instruction are free of any form of racism and that you model for students the desirability of celebrating human diversity.

Minority Enrollments in the Schools   You may be certain that during your career as a teacher you will have students from diverse ethnic, racial, and cultural groups. In California during the 1988–89 school year, for example, more "students of color" were enrolled than white students.[7] According to *One-Third of a Nation,* a report released by the American Council on Education and the Education Commission of the States, "students of color" will comprise about 46 percent of the student population by 2020, an increase of 19 percent since 1982.[8]

Clearly, the need for teachers to understand students from different cultural backgrounds is critical. Minority students come from all social classes. Because of a history of unequal opportunities, however, they are frequently poor and manifest many of the problems associated with poverty. Data released in 1990 by the National Center for Education Statistics indicate that the percentage of African-American children living below the poverty level was three times that of white children in 1987, while Hispanic Americans were 2.6 times more likely than white children to be living in poverty.[9]

Academic Achievement among Minorities   Minority group students are disproportionately represented among students who have failed to master minimum competencies in reading, writing, and mathematics. In addition, they often have limited abilities in the English language. It has been estimated that ethnic minority students are two to four times more likely than others to drop out of high school. Minority students are also expelled or suspended from school more often than white students.

One of the most extensive studies comparing the academic achievement of minority group students and white students was done by James S. Coleman and his associates in 1966. The Coleman report, *Equality of Educational Opportunity,* looked at the test scores of 600,000 students at 4,000 schools in grades one, three, six, nine, and twelve. For each grade level, achievement for the average Mexican American, Puerto Rican, Native American, and African American was significantly lower than that for the average Asian American or white. Coleman also found that the achievement gap widened at higher grade levels. The reading scores of blacks in the first grade, for example, were about six months behind those of whites; by the twelfth grade, this gap had widened to about three-and-a-half years.[10]

A similar study in 1980, involving a national sample of high school sophomores, explored the relationships among minority group membership, social class, and academic achievement. Data from this study (see Table 14.1) upheld the findings of the Coleman study. With the exception of the math scores of Asian students, the data reveal that as socioeconomic status increases, achievement also increases.[11]

TABLE 14.1   Language and Math Scores and Socioeconomic Status of High School Sophomores According to Racial and Ethnic Group, 1980

Racial/Ethnic Group	*Avg. Language Skills Scores (Vocab., Reading, and Writing)* Maximum Score = 57	*Avg. Math Scores* Maximum Score = 38	*Percent in Lowest 25% SES**	*Percent in College-Bound Programs*
Black	14.5	6.5	45	29
Hispanic	15.6	7.7	43	23
Native American	18.5	7.8	36	23
Asian-Pacific American	25.2	16.6	22	47
White (Non-Hispanic)	27.8	15.5	18	37

*Socioeconomic status based on father's and mother's education, father's occupation, parental income, and household items.
Source: High School and Beyond Study (Washington, D.C.: National Center for Education Statistics, 1980).

One of the most comprehensive, ongoing studies of student achievement has been the **National Assessment of Educational Progress (NAEP).** The NAEP assesses the achievement of students in several subject areas on a four- or five-year cycle. Several thousand youths, ages 9, 13, and 17, have been tested since 1969. Here, too, the data indicate that African-American and Hispanic students are consistently below the national average in their scores in reading, writing, history, mathematics, and science (see Table 14.2).

Data from studies such as these make it clear that minority children are more likely than white children to be at risk in obtaining a good education. Committed, professional teachers, however, can reduce the number of students who fail to receive such an education.

Traditionally Unempowered Groups

Many groups of people have continuously struggled to obtain full educational, economic, political, and social opportunities in our society. Along with minority racial and ethnic groups, others who have traditionally lacked power in American public life are immigrants, the poor, children and the elderly, non-English speakers, members of minority religions, and women. Groups that have been most frequently discriminated against in terms of the quality of education they have received include African Americans, Spanish-speaking Americans, Native Americans, Asian Americans, exceptional learners, and females. There is mounting evidence that many students from these groups continue to receive a substandard education that does not meet their needs or help empower them to participate fully and equally in American life.

People Perceived as Handicapped

As we pointed out in Chapter 10, more than ten percent of our nation's students are classified as exceptional; that is, they have special educational needs because they are physically, mentally, emotionally, socially, or linguistically challenged. In addition, some people are perceived as "different" and presumed to be "handicapped" because of their appearance or physical condition. Evidence suggests, for example, that people

TABLE 14.2   National Assessment of Educational
Progress, by Subject and by Race*

Reading, 1987–88	9-year-olds	13-year-olds	17-year-olds
National Average	211.8	257.5	290.1
White	217.7	261.3	294.7
Black	188.5	242.9	274.4
Hispanic	193.7	240.1	270.8
Writing, 1988	**4th graders**	**8th graders**	**11th graders**
National Average	173.3	208.2	220.7
White	180.0	213.1	225.3
Black	150.7	190.1	206.9
Hispanic	162.2	197.2	202.0
History, 1988	**4th graders**	**8th graders**	**11th graders**
National Average	220.6	263.9	295.0
White	227.5	270.4	301.1
Black	199.5	246.0	274.4
Hispanic	202.7	244.3	273.9
Mathematics, 1985–86	**9-year-olds**	**13-year-olds**	**17-year-olds**
National Average	222.0	269.0	302.0
White	227.0	274.0	308.0
Black	202.0	249.0	279.0
Hispanic	205.0	254.0	283.0
Science, 1985–86	**9-year-olds**	**13-year-olds**	**17-year-olds**
National Average	224.3	251.4	288.5
White	231.9	259.2	297.5
Black	196.2	221.6	252.8
Hispanic	199.4	226.1	259.3

*National Assessment of Educational Progress scales in reading, writing, history, mathematics, and science range from 0 to 500.

Source: National Center for Education Statistics, *Digest of Education Statistics 1990* (Washington, D.C.: National Center for Education Statistics, 1991): 113, 116, 118, 120, 121.

who are short, obese, or unattractive are often victims of discrimination, as are people with such conditions as AIDS, cancer, multiple sclerosis, or epilepsy. Significantly, many individuals with clinically diagnosable and classifiable impairments or disabilities do not perceive themselves as "handicapped." The term itself means permanently unable to be treated equally.

The nation became aware of how "handicapped" students can be denied equal educational opportunity when AIDS patient Ryan White was expelled from the Kokoma, Indiana, school system in 1987. His mother sued the Western School Corporation to have Ryan readmitted. "All I wanted was to go to school and fit in," Ryan said.[12] Eventually, though, Ryan and his mother moved to nearby Cicero,

Ryan White, shown here with his mother, bravely publicized the plight of children with AIDS. His story helped bring national attention to widespread ignorance of this dreaded disease and to school discrimination against children with AIDS.

Indiana. There, with the full support of students, teachers, administrators, and parents, Ryan enrolled at Hamilton Heights High School. Before he died in 1990, he became active in school life and attended ballgames, dances, and the prom. Most importantly, he became an eloquent spokesperson for members of all victims of discrimination when he gracefully and courageously called for the equal treatment of people perceived as handicapped.

Officially labeling students has become a necessity with the passage of the laws that provide education for exceptional students. The labels help determine which students qualify for the special services, educational programs, and individualized instruction provided by the laws, and they bring to educators' attention many exceptional children and youth whose educational needs could be overlooked, neglected, or inadequately served otherwise. Detrimental aspects include the fact that labels tend to evoke negative expectations, which can cause teachers to avoid and underteach these students, and their peers to isolate or reject them, thereby stigmatizing individuals, sometimes permanently. The most serious detriment, however, is that students so labeled are taught to feel inadequate, inferior, and limited in terms of their options for growth.

It has taken our school system years of careful research and tracking to determine these groupings of students...

SIPRESS

FIVE-MINUTE FOCUS   In your school years, did you ever experience discrimination as a member of a "different" or "unempowered" group? What one incident stands out that you feel affected your performance as a student? Date your entry and write for five minutes.

EDUCATION AND ETHNIC GROUPS

In this section we consider the quest of certain racial and ethnic groups for equal educational opportunity and focus on strategies for teaching in multicultural classrooms. Our discussion of each group begins with a brief student portrait that illustrates some of the issues or challenges you might encounter in teaching students from that group. These portraits are based on students we have taught or observed others teach. We present each portrait as if you were the teacher, and we encourage you to think about the steps you would take to be effective in each situation. Try to discover your true feelings about the students presented in these portraits, but guard against using them to reinforce any stereotypes you have about the groups being discussed. Not all children from ethnic minorities are poor or undereducated, for example. Socioeconomic status—not race, language, or culture—has been shown to contribute most strongly to students' achievement in school.

African Americans

> Willie, a fourteen-year-old African-American youth from the ghetto, has been inattentive in your class for several days now. He's even dozed off a few times. You've asked him to stay after class so the two of you can talk about his behavior.
>
> You've always had a good relationship with Willie, though you have not succeeded in getting him to take his studies seriously. He reads at about the third-grade level and isn't motivated to improve. He is outgoing and presents himself to adults in a cocky, streetwise manner.
>
> Today, he tells you quite frankly what he's been up to and why he's been so tired in class. "I be in the streets hangin' out an' gettin' high. I guess I just be tired when school time come."

As a result of being enslaved in this country from the 1600s to 1865, African Americans have had an especially difficult struggle for equality. As we pointed out in Chapter 5, the quest of African Americans to enter the mainstream of American life has been blunted by the burden of having to deal with widespread discrimination, poverty, crime, unemployment, and lack of quality education.

Desegregation   The most blatant form of discrimination against African Americans has been the segregation of schools. This country's first recorded case of school segregation goes back to a decision made by the Massachusetts Supreme Court in 1850. The Roberts family sought to send their daughter, Sarah, to a white school in Boston. The court, however, ruled that "equal, but separate" schools were provided, and therefore the Roberts could claim no injustice."[13]
Although the separate-but-equal doctrine was challenged several times during the next 50 years, whites and African Americans often attended schools that were totally

segregated. It was not until the National Association for the Advancement of Colored People (NAACP) brought suit on behalf of a Kansas family (*Brown v. Board of Education of Topeka, Kansas*[14]) in 1954 that the law was decidedly struck down.

The parents of Linda Brown felt that the education the fourth-grader was receiving in the segregated Topeka schools was inferior. When their request that she be transferred to a white school was turned down, they filed suit. In a landmark decision, the U.S. Supreme Court ruled that segregated schools are "inherently unequal" and violate the equal protection clause of the 14th Amendment. American citizens, the justices asserted, have a right to receive an equal opportunity for education.

One year later, in a decision frequently referred to as *Brown II,*[15] the Court called for all public schools in the country to be desegregated "with all deliberate speed." Relying on extreme interpretations of what the phrase "with all deliberate speed" might mean, southern schools were only gradually desegregated. For example, only 2 percent of African-American students in the south attended school with whites in 1963. Following the stormy civil rights movement, however, most southern schools eventually desegregated. In 1969, the U.S. Supreme Court declared (*Alexander v. Holmes County Board of Education*) that the time for "all deliberate speed" had ended and separate schools would not be allowed. Since that time, however, some schools in the north have experienced de facto segregation as a result of white flight from decaying urban centers.

Since 1969, the greatest progress in desegregating schools has occurred in cities of moderate size and in rural areas. Geographically, the South has made the greatest gains and is now the most integrated region of the country. As of 1980, about one-third of African-American students attended racially isolated minority schools (90 percent or more minority); in 1968, almost two-thirds of African-American students attended such schools.[16]

Though African-Americans have made significant strides toward the realization of equal educational opportunity, much remains to be done. The injustices our society has committed, and continues to commit, against African Americans have resulted in a set of social problems that continue to confound the efforts of schools to adequately educate all African Americans.

Learning Styles of African-American Students   As we saw in Chapter 10, learning style is related to a student's success in school. It has been suggested that our schools are "monoethnic" and do not take into account the diverse learning styles of ethnic minorities.[17] In the case of African-American students, the failure of the school curriculum to address their learning styles may contribute to high dropout rates and below-average achievement.

Though it is risky indeed to characterize the learning style of an entire group of people, the conclusions of an expert on gifted minority children about the learning styles of African Americans are worth considering.

African-American Learners

1. Tend to respond to things in terms of the whole picture instead of its parts. ([Anglo Americans] tend to believe that anything can be divided and subdivided into pieces and that these pieces add up to a whole.) Therefore, art is sometimes taught by numbers, as are dancing and music.
2. Tend to prefer inferential reasoning to deductive or inductive reasoning.
3. Tend to approximate space, numbers, and time rather than stick to accuracy.

4. Tend to prefer to focus on people and their activities rather than on things. This tendency is shown by the fact that so many [African-American] students choose careers in the helping professions, such as teaching, psychology, social work, and so forth. . . .
5. Have a keen sense of justice and are quick to analyze and perceive injustice.
6. Tend to lean toward altruism, a concern for one's fellow man.
7. Tend to prefer novelty, freedom, and personal distinctiveness. This is shown in the development of improvisation in music and styles of clothing.
8. Tend not to be "word-dependent." They tend to be very proficient in non-verbal communications.[18]

These observations may help you to think about how to modify instruction or to periodically evaluate the experiences you offer your students.

Spanish-Speaking Americans

Carmen is an attractive ten-year-old Guatemalan girl who lives with her three older brothers and younger sister in a tenement in the city. Her mother, a seamstress, and her father, a clerk in a grocery store, brought the family to the United States about a year ago.

Carmen transferred into your fifth-grade class about four months ago. You believe her work would improve if she got more involved. She's shy and withdrawn, and you think she's having trouble adjusting to life in this country.

Carmen seems to trust you, so you've decided to talk to her this morning since she usually arrives for the start of school about five minutes before the other children. As she talks, timidly at first then more openly and naturally, you realize that Carmen is depressed because of the stress of adjusting to life in this country. She misses the extended family she lived with in Guatemala. She believes she does not speak English well and is worried that the other children will tease her if she speaks out in class.

The limited English proficiencies of many "Hispanic" children contribute significantly to the difficulties they have in school. Prior to the 1960s, public schools with large populations of Spanish-speaking students frequently enforced a no-Spanish rule that prevented students from speaking Spanish while at school. The goal of such a policy was to replace the students' language and culture with the English language and Anglo culture. It is now illegal for schools to enforce a no-Spanish rule, and federally funded bilingual-bicultural programs have attempted to meet the educational needs of Spanish-speaking students. One of the major thrusts of these programs has been to encourage teachers to view the child's cultural background positively and to use the child's experiences and background knowledge as a bridge to the school's curriculum.[19]

In spite of an increased awareness among educators of the problems Spanish-speaking children encounter when they try to adjust to the culture of American schools, much remains to be done. As the following portrait of José Martinez, a Puerto Rican who immigrated to the United States when he was six, shows, school officials must be very careful and sensitive when deciding how to meet the learning needs of Spanish-speaking students.

At a time when he was ready to learn to read and write his mother tongue, José was instead suddenly thrust into an exclusively English-speaking environment where the only tool he possessed for oral communication was completely useless to him. When he went to school it was as if the teacher were broadcasting in AM but José was equipped to receive her only in FM. He remembers it this way: "My teacher and I could not communicate with each other because each spoke a different language and neither one spoke the language of the other. This made me stupid, or retarded, or at least disadvantaged." Since teachers cannot be expected to "work miracles" on kids who are disadvantaged, José fell victim to the self-fulfilling prophecy, "He won't make it." They agreed, however, to allow him to "sit there" because the law required that he be in school.

For the next two years José "vegetated" in classes he did not understand—praying that the teacher would not call on him. The fact is the teacher rarely called on him and seldom collected his papers on the grounds that she could not expect of José what she demanded of the "more fortunate" children. Reasonable as this notion appears to be, it served only to cause the child's self-concept to deteriorate.

Another Puerto Rican boy in the classroom who spoke English was asked to teach José English and help him in the process of adjustment. They were not permitted, however, to speak Spanish to each other because it would "confuse José and prolong the period of transition"—also because it annoyed the hell out of other people who did not understand what they were saying. The other boy, then, could not translate academic subject matter for José. English was the one and only priority. In other words, he would have to "break the code" before getting the message. By the time he began to understand English, he was so far behind academically that he had to work twice as hard to keep from sinking. . . . The situation became unbearable when, as a result of a test administered in English, José was found to be *academically* retarded and was put in a class for the *mentally* retarded.[20]

Cultural factors that affect the school experience of Hispanic students include values and attitudes that represent a fusion of Spanish colonial and Native-American cultures. A historian describes this fusion as a spiritual and romantic individualism that emphasized soul, honor, self-respect, integrity, and personal self-expression, combined with mutual trust, strong community ties, and a Roman Catholic heritage.[21] It is noteworthy that this cultural heritage, shared by most Spanish-speaking Americans, cuts across all racial distinctions.

Socioeconomic factors also affect the education of Hispanics, especially the children of migrant farm workers. Among the estimated one million or so migrant farm workers in this country, more than 70 percent are Spanish-speaking. The dropout rate among all migrant workers is 90 percent, and 50 percent leave school before finishing the ninth grade.[22] Migrant children are handicapped by the language barrier, deprivation resulting from poverty, and irregular school attendance.

Native Americans

William is an Oglala Sioux who has just moved to town from a village where everything was shared and no emphasis was placed on ownership—everything in the village was community property.

Since William enrolled in your seventh-grade class, things have begun to disappear from student desks, lockers, and teachers' desks. Last week you found some school supplies belonging to other students in William's desk. William has yet to return his overdue library books; he told you that he passed them on to friends and family members.

Other students in the class have begun to complain loudly. "William's a thief—he steals." William clearly has trouble understanding this. Socially, he's become an outcast. When a student can't find something, William is immediately blamed, whether or not he has taken the item.

As we pointed out in Chapter 5, there is great cultural and linguistic diversity among the 1.5 million Native Americans in this country. Native Americans were not granted U.S. citizenship until 1924. By that time, confinement on reservations, followed by decades of forced assimilation, had devastated Native-American cultures. The 1970s saw a resurgence of interest in preserving traditional languages, skills, and land claims.

Education for Native-American children living on reservations is administered by the federal government's Bureau of Indian Affairs (BIA). The **Indian Education Act of 1972** and its 1974 amendments supplement the BIA's educational programs and provide direct educational assistance to tribes. The act seeks to improve native American education by providing funds to school districts to meet the special needs of Native-American youth, to Indian tribes and state and local education agencies to improve education for youth and adults, to colleges and universities for the purpose of training teachers for Indian schools, and to Native-American students to attend college.

The culture-based learning style of many Native Americans differs from that of students from the majority culture. In William's traditional culture, for example, exclusive private ownership was discouraged and individuals "borrowed" whatever they needed at any time. Tribal property was shared. The upbringing of Native-American children generally encourages them to develop a view of the world that is holistic, intimate, and shared. "They approach tasks visually, seem to prefer to learn by careful observation which precedes performance, and seem to learn in their natural settings experientially."[23] J. C. Phillips describes how the preferred mode of learning for Native-American children can place them at odds with the expectations of teachers who are not sensitive to the influence of culture on learning style:

> [Native] American students customarily acquire the various skills of their culture (i.e., hunting, tanning, beadwork) in a sequence of three steps. First, the child over a period of time watches and listens to a competent adult who is performing the skill. Secondly, the child takes over small portions of the task and completes them in cooperation with and under the supervision of the adult, in this way gradually learning all of the component skills involved. Finally, the child goes off and privately tests himself or herself to see whether the skill has been fully learned: a failure is not seen by others and causes no embarrassment, but a success is brought back and exhibited to the teacher and others. The use of speech in this three-step process is minimal.
>
> When these same children go to school they find themselves in a situation where the high value placed on verbal performance is only the first of their cross-cultural hurdles. . . . Acquisition and demonstration of knowledge are no longer separate steps but are expected to occur simultaneously. Furthermore, this single-step process takes place via public recitations, the assumption apparently being that one learns best by making verbal mistakes in front of one's peers and teachers. Finally, the children have little opportunity to observe skilled performers carrying out these tasks, for the other children who perform are as ignorant and unskilled as they. Under these circumstances, it is small wonder that these [Native] American students demonstrate a propensity for silence.[24]

Christine I. Bennett, an authority on multicultural education, suggests a set of general guidelines to ensure that the school experiences of Native-American students are in "harmony" with their cultural backgrounds. "An effective learning environment for Native Americans is one that does not single out the individual but provides frequent opportunities for the teacher to interact privately with individual children and with small groups, as well as opportunities for quiet, persistent exploration."[25]

Keepers of the Dream

Yvonne Wilson
Multicultural Teacher
Talmoon and Deer River, Minnesota

Yvonne Wilson, a first-grade teacher at North Elementary School in Talmoon, Minnesota, says, "I always felt the curriculum was not culturally relevant to the needs of our Indian students. We needed to strengthen the self-concept of Indian students. One way to do this was to help them recognize their heritage and give them a sense of belonging."

Twenty-five percent of students in the Deer River School District are Ojibwe. To acquaint all the students with the art, customs, and values of the Ojibwe Indians who live in the area, Wilson along with several colleagues in the district and their students have developed a curriculum based on material gathered from Ojibwe community members. They call their committee *Nü-maa-moo-chi-ge-min,* Ojibwe for "a coming together."

The new curriculum meets the needs of Ojibwe students who, Wilson found, did not always respond well to traditional methods. "They learn best through hands-on, visual and audio activities," she says. "They also do better if they progress at their own rate."

The curriculum Wilson and her fellow teachers developed also uses state-of-the-art videodisc technology. Members of the Ojibwe tribe are recorded as they talk about their heritage and demonstrate artistic skills that capture the richness of their culture. Outside support for the development of the new curriculum came from the Christa McAuliffe Institute, the Blandin Foundation, and Apple Computer.

Wilson, herself an Ojibwe Indian, helps her students examine and value the cultural differences among people.

I talk with my students about all kinds of people, their differences and similarities. We talk about skin color and how diversity goes beyond skin color. We talk about where we come from, where their parents come from. We talk about how many of their parents went to Indian boarding schools—how they were taken from their homes and taught not to speak their language and learn their culture.

To meet the needs of students from cultures other than their own, Wilson advises teachers to "take an interest in students, learn where they came from." She also stresses the importance of becoming involved in the community and getting to know parents.

People in the community know if you are trying to understand their culture. Students also see it. Becoming involved—going to a powwow or participating in other cultural events—shows people that here is a teacher who is trying to learn about our culture.

Wilson also stresses the importance of emphasizing linguistic diversity in the classroom.

I do a lot of activities with languages. That really seems to spark an interest in the kids. My children learn to count to ten in Ojibwe.

A proponent of the whole language approach, Wilson integrates instruction in language arts, reading, and spelling with writing and telling stories. "I love in the wintertime to tell legends because that was part of the culture; that was how children learned from the elders," she says.

"We must create in schools an awareness of the diversity of all cultures—that's the only way we will be able to respect differences among people."

> " *[We] count to ten in Ojibwe.* "

Asian Americans

Toyohiko, a polite, intelligent high school junior, is in your third-period class. His behavior and performance from a teacher's point of view are exemplary. However, you are concerned that he doesn't fit in with the other students. You've visited with Toyohiko's parents at an open house, and you know that they have high expectations of their son and constantly pressure him to do well in school. They almost seem to equate his worth as a person with his ability to get good grades.

This pressure has caused Toyohiko to spend endless hours studying and to forgo social activities. As a result, he has not learned even the most basic social skills. His formal, rigid behavior is in sharp contrast to the more informal, spontaneous behavior of the other students, who genuinely seem to want his friendship.

There is a widespread perception that Asian students—Japanese, Chinese, Vietnamese, Cambodian, Laotian, Korean, Pacific Islander, and others—come from cultures that strongly support education. Though teachers certainly appreciate cultural values that support their efforts to teach, there is evidence that more and more Asian-American youth are in conflict with their parents' way of life. Leaders in Asian-American communities are concerned about increases in dropout rates, school violence, and declining achievement. Teachers of students from these groups will need to be sensitive to cultural conflicts that may contribute to problems in school adjustment and achievement. Indochinese Americans, for example, face deep cultural conflict in our schools. Values and practices that are accepted in the dominant American culture, such as dating and glorification of the individual, are sources of conflict between Indochinese students and their parents. In addition, school placement by age rather than academic preparation places older and illiterate students at a grave disadvantage. According to V. G. Thuy, "[In] addition to the tremendous language barrier and unfamiliarity with the American educational system, these children are unable to live up to the academic expectations of the teacher."[26]

An authority on the education of Asian Americans, B. H. Suzuki, suggests that the tendency of Asian-American students to try to conform to the expectations of schools and teachers may result in their failure to grow in other ways:

> [Many] teachers stereotype Asian and Pacific American students as quiet, hardworking, and docile, which tends to reinforce conformity and stifle creativity. Asian and Pacific American students, therefore, frequently do not develop the ability to assert and express themselves verbally and are channeled in disproportionate numbers into the technical/scientific fields. As a consequence, many Asian and Pacific American students undergo traumatic family/school discontinuities, suffer from low self-esteem, are overly conforming, and have their academic and social development narrowly circumscribed."[27]

TEACHING MULTICULTURAL GROUPS

The enrollment in our nation's schools of students from diverse cultural backgrounds will continue to increase dramatically during the twenty-first century. As this trend continues, it is vitally important that those entering the teaching profession achieve an understanding of children's different backgrounds. Teachers need to appreciate that children do not learn in a vacuum—their culture predisposes them to learn in certain ways.

In addition, teachers must carefully select the materials they use in their multicultural classrooms, for, as James A. Banks points out, "Many of the books and other materials on each ethnic group are insensitive, inaccurate, and written from mainstream and insensitive perspectives and points of view."[28] (See the Teacher's Resource Guide at the end of this book for "Selected Resources for Multicultural Education.")

Guidelines for Selecting Multicultural Instructional Materials

- Books and other materials should accurately portray the perspectives, attitudes, and feelings of ethnic groups.
- Fictional works should have strong ethnic characters.
- Books should describe settings and experiences with which all students can identify and yet accurately reflect ethnic cultures and life-styles.
- The protagonists in books with ethnic themes should have ethnic characteristics but should face conflicts and problems universal to all cultures and groups.
- The illustrations in books should be accurate, ethnically sensitive, and technically well done.
- Ethnic materials should not contain racist concepts, clichés, phrases, or words.
- Factual materials should be historically accurate.
- Multiethnic resources and basal textbooks should discuss major events and documents related to ethnic history.[29]

In regard to instructional strategies, there is no easy way to develop the ability to be effective with students from cultures different from one's own. We are nevertheless convinced that such ability depends upon being open and willing to learn about other groups. In this regard, we encourage you to seek out experiences during the remainder of your professional training with students who are members of the groups we have discussed in this chapter. If you participate whole-heartedly in these experiences, you will begin to acquire knowledge and skills in eight areas that are essential for successful teaching in a multicultural society:

1. The ability to communicate with students from other cultures
2. Skills in diagnosing the knowledge and abilities of students from other cultures
3. Knowledge about the psychology and impact of prejudice
4. The ability to discover the differences between the value systems of different ethnic and class subcultures in the school setting and to understand their effect on the teaching-learning process
5. A deeper, more sensitive knowledge of one's own and other cultures—leading to the realization that human beings are more alike than they are different
6. An increased capacity for humane, sensitive, and critical inquiry into multicultural issues as they relate to multicultural education
7. An increased willingness and openness to examine and to reassess one's own cultural attitudes and values
8. An increased ability to respond positively and sensitively to a diversity of behavior involved in multicultural settings[30]

FIVE-MINUTE FOCUS As a teacher, what activities and materials might you use to reduce the prejudices of students toward racial or ethnic groups other than their own? Give specific examples. Date your journal entry and write for five minutes.

CONSIDER THIS . . .

What Can You Do About Opposition to Multicultural and Global Education?

Despite the growing body of global and multicultural literature and research, and despite the growing emphasis on global and multicultural perspectives in teacher education and curricula, new teachers actually find little support for this trend. Consider the following case of Lisa, a first-year teacher in the Midwest.

The Case of Lisa Stewart

Lisa has just completed her university course work and student teaching. Academically talented, highly creative, and hard-working, Lisa was an outstanding student teacher with great promise. She took to heart what was taught at the university about the importance of multicultural and global perspectives and the special relationship between their goals and those of the social studies. But there had been little opportunity to act upon these commitments during student teaching since few materials were readily available, and she was expected to "cover the curriculum." Her social studies methods instructor at the university had assured her that once she had her own classroom it would be possible, especially since she has accepted a position in what is considered an enlightened school.

Lisa is visibly nervous as she prepares to greet the parents. Several students and colleagues have alerted her to the fact that a large group will attend tonight's school open house and plan to question what is happening in her social studies classes. A number of parents have already complained to the principal. Several question her use of *Huckleberry Finn* as a resource, some because they feel it belongs in an English course and others because they see it as a racist book. Other parents are outraged over her treatment of apartheid and the showing of *Witness to Apartheid*. Again, their complaints stem from different concerns. Some are angry that the students are encouraged to question U.S. government and corporate policies. Others are upset that Afrikanner perspectives are studied along with the history and viewpoints of the British, Coloreds, and Black South Africans, fearing that students might be led to sympathize with the South African government.

The frantic calls to her university mentor, in the face of brewing parental discontent, have helped her better articulate the goals of her curriculum. She feels nervous but confident that she can clearly explain what her goals are and why they are important. The parents from her first period class file into her room.

What can Lisa say to these parents to reduce opposition to her plans and the materials she has chosen? In the space below, outline her general strategy and specific points she could make.

_____

_____

_____

_____

_____

Source: Christine I. Bennett, *Comprehensive Multicultural Education: Theory and Practice* (Boston: Allyn and Bacon, 1990), p. 274.

EDUCATION AND EXCEPTIONAL LEARNERS

As we pointed out in Chapter 5, exceptional students have made great strides in obtaining equal educational opportunity. The learning needs of exceptional students are provided for through a variety of special education programs. **Special education** refers to "specially designed instruction that meets the unusual needs of an exceptional child."[31] Teachers who are trained in special education become familiar with special materials, techniques, and equipment and facilities for exceptional students.

> For example, children with visual impairment may require reading materials in large print or Braille; students with hearing impairment may require hearing aids and/or instruction in sign language; those with physical disabilities may need special equipment; those with emotional disturbances may need smaller and more highly structured classes; and children with special gifts or talents may require access to working professionals. Related services—special transportation, psychological assessment, physical and occupational therapy, medical treatment, and counseling—may be necessary if special education is to be effective.[32]

Just as there are no easy answers for how teachers should meet the needs of students from diverse cultural backgrounds, there is no single strategy for teachers to follow to ensure that all exceptional students receive an appropriate education. The key, however, lies in "finding and capitalizing on exceptional children's *abilities*."[33] To build on students' strengths, regular classroom teachers must work cooperatively and collaboratively with special education teachers. Furthermore, students in special education programs must not become isolated from other students.

Teaching Linguistically Challenged Students

> Three weeks ago, just after the winter holidays, Hector Ramos transferred into your class from a school in San Juan, Puerto Rico. You know from school records that Hector was an excellent student at his school in San Juan. However, you're concerned because Hector doesn't seem to be adjusting well. He often seems to be sad. He doesn't read English well and is falling behind in his work. Also, the other children have started to tease Hector because he "talks funny."

Linguistically challenged students often have special social, as well as educational, needs. While approaches to bilingual instruction vary, it is more crucial than ever in today's increasingly multicultural classrooms to model respect for all students' cultural, racial, and ethnic differences.

As described in Chapter 12, four types of bilingual education programs (immersion, maintenance, pull-out, and transition) are currently available to provide special assistance to the 3.6 million students in the United States who are linguistically challenged. Unfortunately, only about 315,000 students actually participate in some kind of bilingual program, and the desirability of such programs is a hot issue in many communities. Though most bilingual education programs serve Spanish-speaking students, there are bilingual education programs for the more than 90 other ethnic groups in the United States. Figure 14.1 shows the distribution among the states of persons with non-English mother tongues.

What can easily happen to linguistically challenged students if they are taught by teachers who are not sensitive to their learning needs is illustrated in the following portrait of Josué, a student with **limited English proficiency (LEP).**

FIGURE 14.1

Number of Persons with Non-English Mother Tongues by State

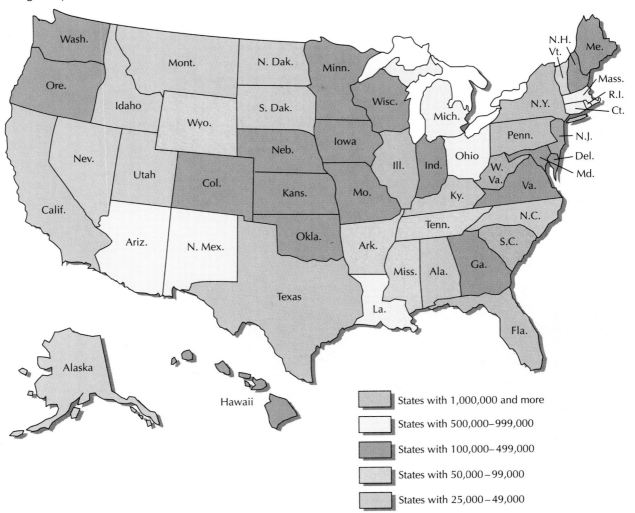

States with 1,000,000 and more

States with 500,000–999,000

States with 100,000–499,000

States with 50,000–99,000

States with 25,000–49,000

Source: Nancy Faires Conklin and Margaret A. Lourie, *A Host of Tongues* (New York: The Free Press, A Division of Macmillan, 1983). Reprinted with permission.

Josué sits silently in the back of the classroom. His book is closed; he stares at his new fifth-grade surroundings. He has mastered the nuances of English. He nods his head appropriately when spoken to in a pleasant tone—looks downcast when an English voice is angry. He displays all the proper nonverbal cues in his new American school. He misses Puerto Rico and the familiar sound of Spanish in the classroom. The teacher likes Josué; thinks he is a good boy, but slow. Without assistance, Josué will become part of a forgotten minority—the Hispanic gifted.[34]

Limited English Proficiency Christine I. Bennett captures well the dilemma that many LEP students find themselves in: "LEP students are often caught up in conflicts between personal language needs—for example, the need to consolidate cognitive skills in the native language—and a sociopolitical climate that views standard English as most desirable and prestigious."[35] The degree to which students from non-English backgrounds are motivated to learn English varies from group to group. Mexican-American students who live in the Southwest, for example, may retain the Spanish language in order to maintain ties with family and friends in Mexico. Recently arrived Laotians, on the other hand, may have a stronger motivation to learn the language of their new country. In regard to what they wish to learn, children, of course, take their cues from the adults around them. If their parents or guardians and friends and relatives have learned English and are bilingual, then they will be similarly motivated.

What Monolingual Teachers Can Do The needs of linguistically challenged students are best met by teachers who speak their native language as well as English. However, this is often not possible, and monolingual teachers will find increasing numbers of LEP students in their classrooms. Bennett offers several general strategies for improving reading skills among LEP students and points out that these can be used whether or not the teacher is bilingual.

1. Become familiar with features of the students' dialect. This will allow the teacher to better understand students and to recognize a reading miscue (a noncomprehension feature) from a comprehension error. Students should not be interrupted during the oral reading process. Correction of comprehension features are best done after the reading segment.
2. Allow students to listen to a passage or story first. This can be done in two ways: (a) finish the story and then ask comprehension questions or (b) interrupt the story at key comprehension segments and ask students to predict the outcome.
3. Use predictable stories, which can be familiar episodes in literature, music, or history. They can be original works or experiential readers.
4. Use visual aids to enhance comprehension. Visual images, whether pictures or words, will aid word recognition and comprehension.
5. Use cloze procedure deletions to focus on vocabulary and meaning. Cloze procedures are simply selected deletions of words from a passage in order to focus on a specific text feature. EXAMPLE: The little red hen found an ear of corn. The little red ———— said, "Who will dry the ear of ————?" (vocabulary focus)
   Today I feel like a *(noun)*. (grammar focus)
   There was a *(pain)* in the pit of his stomach. (semantic focus)
6. Allow students to retell the story or passage in various speech styles. Have students select different people to whom they would like to retell the story

(family member, principal, friend) and assist them in selecting synonyms most appropriate to each audience. This allows both teacher and student to become language authorities.

7. Integrate reading, speaking, and writing skills whenever possible.

8. Use the microcomputer (if available) as a time-on-task exercise. The microcomputer can effectively assist in teaching the reading techniques of skimming (general idea), scanning (focused reference), reading for comprehension (master total message), and critical reading (inference and evaluation). Time on task is extremely important to skills development.[36]

Teaching Physically Challenged Students

It is the first day of school and you're just about to meet your fifth-grade class for the first time. Based on the comments of their teacher from last year, you know that all of the children in the class are bright and eager to learn. However, you are concerned about one of your new students. Fred has slight cerebral palsy and experiences mild motor and speech problems. He walks with a jerky motion, but he can get around on his own. He is academically talented and has always performed well in school.

Like other minority groups, physically challenged students have often not received the kind of education that most effectively meets their needs, though they are beginning to make significant strides toward becoming mainstreamed into regular classrooms. While teaching handicapped students in a regular classroom is challenging, it can also be very rewarding. Consider what Michele Wilson, a teacher in a prekindergarten program in an innovative public elementary school in New York City, has to say about Ashley, the first child she has taught who has Down's Syndrome:

> It's an experiment. Sometimes I think it's not going to work because the demands of the classroom are too great. Other times I think it will work, and everyone will benefit. Sometimes I see her using an area of the room the way I'd planned for it to be used, or I see her respond to something simple and direct, and I get goosebumps.[37]

Prior to the twentieth century, physically challenged youngsters were usually segregated from regular classrooms and taught by special education teachers in state-run and private schools. Around the turn of the century, however, some mildly handicapped students were placed in special education classes in regular schools. This trend toward self-contained special education classes within regular schools continued until 1975, when Congress passed the **Education for All Handicapped Children Act (Public Law 94-142).** This act guarantees to all handicapped children a free and appropriate public education. The law, which applies to every teacher and every school in the country, outlines extensive procedures to ensure that handicapped students are granted due process in regard to identification, placement, and educational services received.

The Law   Public Law 94-142, which is one of the most important and far-reaching pieces of educational legislation ever passed in this country, has several provisions with which all teachers should be familiar.

Least restrictive environment: PL 94-142 requires that all handicapped children be educated in the least restrictive environment. In other words, a handicapped student must be mainstreamed into a regular classroom whenever such integration is feasible and appropriate and the child would receive educational benefit from such placement.

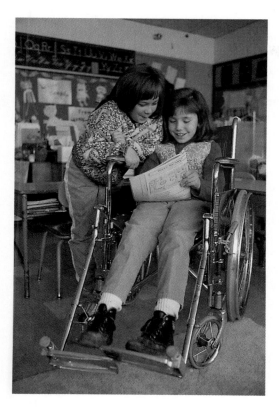

The "mainstreaming law" entitles physically challenged students to equal education opportunity. Peer teaming as part of the Individual Education Programs can aid in the full integration of special needs students in regular classrooms.

Individualized education program: Every handicapped child is to have a written **Individualized Education Program (IEP)** that meets the child's needs and specifies educational goals, methods for achieving those goals, and the number and quality of special educational services to be provided. The IEP must be reviewed annually by five parties: (1) a parent, (2) the child, (3) a teacher, (4) a professional who has recently evaluated the child, and (5) others, usually the principal or a special education resource person from the school district.

Confidentiality of records: PL 94-142 also ensures that records on a handicapped child are kept confidential. Parental permission is required before any official may look at a child's records. Moreover, parents can amend a child's records if they feel information in it is misleading, inaccurate, or violates the child's rights.

Due process: PL 94-142 gives parents the right to disagree with an IEP or an evaluation of their child's abilities. If a disagreement arises, it is settled through an impartial due process hearing presided over by an officer appointed by the state. At the hearing, parents may be represented by a lawyer, give evidence, and cross-examine, and are entitled to receive a transcript of the hearing and a written decision on the case. If either the parents or the school district disagree with the outcome, the case may then be taken to the civil courts.

Meeting the Mainstreaming Challenge To help teachers satisfy the four general provisions of PL 94-142, school districts across the nation have developed inservice programs designed to acquaint regular classroom teachers with the unique needs of handicapped students. In addition, colleges and universities with preservice programs for educators have added courses on teaching students with special needs.

While knowledge of various handicaps and the teaching methods and materials appropriate for each is important, the effective teacher is also characterized by his or her positive attitudes toward special students. In this regard, a recent study of 212 K–12 student teachers found that "developing acceptance and pupil self-confidence" was judged to be the most important competency for teaching mainstreamed students.[38]

In addition, special educators Daniel P. Hallahan and James M. Kauffman suggest that *all* teachers should be prepared to participate in the education of exceptional students. Teachers should be willing to

1. Make maximum effort to accommodate individual students' needs
2. Evaluate academic abilities and disabilities
3. Refer [students] for evaluation [as appropriate]
4. Participate in eligibility conferences [for special education]
5. Participate in writing individualized education programs
6. Communicate with parents or guardians
7. Participate in due process hearings and negotiations
8. Collaborate with other professionals in identifying and making maximum use of exceptional students' abilities[39]

Teaching the Learning-Disabled

Audrey, a twelve-year-old student in your class, puzzles you. She has an adequate vocabulary and doesn't hesitate to express herself; however, her achievement in reading and mathematics doesn't "add up" to what you believe she can do. Audrey is restless and has a short attention span. Often, when you give the class instructions, Audrey seems to get confused about what to do. In working with her one-on-one, you've noticed that she often reverses letters and numbers—she sees a "b" for a "d" or a "6" for a "9."

Learning-disabled (LD) students have problems taking in, organizing, remembering, and expressing information. Like Audrey, LD students usually show a significant difference between their estimated intelligence and their actual achievement in the classroom. Estimates on the number of LD students vary, though perhaps as many as 16 percent of all schoolchildren have learning disabilities and require special instructional strategies.

Identifying Learning Disabilities   Since the term **learning disability** was first introduced in the early 1960s, no universally accepted definition has been arrived at. In part, this confusion has resulted from the fact that there are many different forms a learning disability can take. In 1981 the National Joint Committee for Learning Disabilities proposed the following definition:

Learning disabilities is a generic term that refers to a heterogeneous group of disorders manifested by significant difficulties in the acquisition and use of listening, speaking, reading, writing, reasoning, or mathematics abilities. These disorders are intrinsic to the individual and presumed to be due to central nervous system dysfunction. Even though a learning disability may occur concomitantly with other handicapping conditions (e.g., sensory impairment, mental retardation, social and emotional disturbance) or environmental influences (e.g., cultural differences, insufficient/inappropriate instruction, psychiatric factors), it is not the direct result of these conditions or influences.[40]

Learning-disabled children are generally believed to have an attention deficit disorder, and many are hyperactive or easily distracted. The most common and widely publicized learning disability is **dyslexia**—difficulty in reading. In addition, LD students can have problems in writing (dysgraphia) and mathematics (dyscalculia). Among the well-known, highly successful people who have had learning disabilities are Thomas Edison, Albert Einstein, and Nelson Rockefeller.

What Regular Classroom Teachers Can Do   Regular classroom teachers play an important role in providing for the education of learning-disabled students. By being alert for students who exhibit several of the following symptoms, teachers can help in the early identification of learning-disabled students so that they can receive the special education services they need.

Signs of Learning Dysfunctions

- Short attention span (restless, easily distracted)
- Reverse letters and numbers (sees "b" for "d," "6" for "9")
- Reads poorly, if at all (below age and grade level)
- Often confused about directions and time (right-left, up-down, yesterday-tomorrow)
- Personal disorganization (can't follow simple schedules)
- Impulsive and inappropriate behavior (poor judgment in social situations, talks and acts before thinking)
- Poor coordination (clumsy, has trouble using pencil, scissors, crayons)
- Inconsistent performance (can't remember today what was learned yesterday)
- Fails written tests but scores high on oral exams (or vice versa)
- Speech problems (immature speech development, has trouble expressing ideas)[41]

After an initial referral by a regular classroom teacher, a team consisting of a learning disabilities teacher, psychologist, and social worker or nurse evaluate the student to determine if the child has a learning disability. In the event the child does, he or she is usually placed in a classroom with a teacher trained in learning disabilities. In that classroom, the child is taught through techniques that involve not only the child's sense of hearing and vision but also touch and movement.

Teaching the Gifted and Talented

You are concerned about the poor performance of Paul, a student in your eighth-period high school class. Paul is undeniably a bright young man. When he was ten, he had an IQ of 145 on the Stanford-Binet. Last year, when he was 16, he scored 142.

Paul's father is a physician, and his mother is a professor. Both parents clearly value learning and are willing to give Paul any needed encouragement and help.

Throughout elementary school, Paul had an outstanding record. His teachers reported that he was brilliant and very meticulous in completing his assignments. He entered high school amid expectations by his parents and teachers that he would continue his outstanding performance. Throughout his first two years of high school, Paul never seemed to live up to his promise. Now, halfway through his junior year, Paul is failing English and geometry.

Paul seems to be well adjusted to the social side of school. He has a lot of friends and says he likes school. Paul explains his steadily declining grades by saying that he doesn't like to study.

Gifted and talented students, those who have demonstrated a high level of attainment in intellectual ability, academic achievement, creativity, or visual and performing arts, are evenly distributed across all ethnic and cultural groups and socioeconomic classes. While you might think it is easy to meet the needs of gifted and talented students, you will find that this is not always the case. "Gifted and talented students often challenge the 'system' of the school, and they can be verbally caustic. Their superior abilities and unusual or advanced interests demand teachers who themselves are highly intelligent, creative, and motivated."[42]

Gifted and Talented Teachers   Strategies for teaching the gifted and talented begin with effective teachers. It has been suggested that effective teachers of the gifted have the following characteristics.

- Understands, accepts, respects, trusts, and likes self
- Is sensitive to, supports, respects, and trusts others
- Has high intellectual, cultural, and literary interests
- Is flexible, open to new ideas
- Desires to learn; has high achievement needs and enthusiasm
- Is intuitive, perceptive
- Is committed to excellence
- Is democratic rather than autocratic
- Is innovative and experimental rather than conforming
- Uses problem-solving; doesn't jump to unfounded conclusions
- Seeks involvement of others in discovery
- Develops flexible, individualized programs
- Provides feedback; stimulates higher mental processes
- Respects creativity and imagination[43]

In addition, a study of the differences between outstanding and average teachers of gifted and talented students showed that the outstanding teachers were characterized as

- Having enthusiasm for own work with gifted students
- Having self-confidence in ability to be effective
- Being a facilitator of other people as resources and learners
- Being able to apply knowledge of theory to practice
- Having a strong achievement orientation
- Being committed to the role of educator of gifted students
- Building program support for gifted education programs[44]

Programs for the Gifted and Talented   During the last decade, several innovative ways of meeting the educational needs of gifted students have emerged. Several of these are briefly summarized here.

Acceleration: There seems to be increasing support for various kinds of accelerated programs for intellectually precocious students. One researcher has even advocated "extreme educational acceleration" or "radical acceleration" for gifted youth.[45] Such programs have proven to be successful. For example, one survey that spanned a 50-year period and examined 200 studies of accelerated programs found that two-thirds were beneficial.[46] To meet the educational needs of gifted students who have outgrown the high school curriculum, many colleges and universities now participate in accelerated programs whereby gifted youths may enroll in college courses.[47]

Self-directed or independent study: For some time, self-directed or independent study has been recognized as an appropriate way for teachers to maintain the interest of gifted students in regular classes. Gifted students usually have the academic backgrounds and motivation to do well without constant supervision and the threat or reward of grades.

Individual education programs: Since the passage of PL 94-142 and the mandating of Individual Education Programs (IEPs) for special education students, IEPs have been promoted as an appropriate means for educating gifted students. Most IEPs for gifted students involve various enrichment experiences, self-directed study, and special, concentrated instruction given to individuals or small groups.

Special or magnet schools: During the 1960s and 1970s, several large-city school systems developed magnet schools that were organized around specific disciplines, such as science, mathematics, fine arts, basic skills, and so on. The excellent programs at these schools were designed to attract superior students from all parts of the district. Many of these schools have continued into the 1990s to offer outstanding programs for gifted and talented youth. E. Paul Torrence, a noted researcher in gifted education and children's creative thinking skills, said of such schools: "Students in these schools stayed for hours after school and returned on weekends. They were enthusiastic, intense, and satisfied."[48] A few of the more successful special schools for the gifted are the Bronx High School of Science, the New York City School of Music and Art, the Interlachen Arts Academy and National Music Camp in Michigan, and Prep-Tech in Lexington, Massachusetts.

Weekend and summer programs: Many communities have special weekend and summer programs to meet the needs of gifted and talented youth. These programs often make use of community resources—museums, theaters for the performing arts, businesses, and universities.

EDUCATION AND FEMALES

> The behavior of Anna, an intelligent and precocious first-grader, is starting to disrupt your class. Anna's parents, it seems, are very sensitive about sex-role stereotyping. They actively discourage their daughter from playing with dolls or taking part in activities that others might label "for girls only."
>
> Actually, you agree with Anna's parents. You think she ought to be able to do what she wants. The boys in your class, however, don't share your views. They are really beginning to get upset because Anna wants to be a fireman, policeman, cowboy, or doctor and not a mommy, nurse, or secretary. Several of the boys have complained to you that Anna won't "play right."

Females in our society have been, and still are, discriminated against in the marketplace and in the classroom, victims of **sexism.** Presently, more than 51 percent of our nation's population is female, and projections are that this gap will increase between now and the turn of the century.[49]

It is a well-established fact that women in our society are employed at lower levels than men, and, when they are employed at the same level, they earn less. Since the 1960s, women's groups such as the National Organization for Women (NOW) and an array of feminist publications have alerted all of us to the many forms that sex discrimination takes in our society. The old saying "Boys will be boys" is but one of many clues that powerful forces of socialization condition boys to act one way in our society and girls to act in another.

Evidence abounds that schools have made significant contributions to the divisions between the sexes. From kindergarten on, girls tend to be reinforced for certain behaviors, boys for others. Girls are supposed to play with dolls, boys with trucks.

Girls are supposed to be passive, boys active. Part of the hidden curriculum girls encounter at school makes them feel that they should prepare to become homemakers by learning about home economics and family living. Or, at the very most, they may prepare for clerical positions in business by taking typing, shorthand, and bookkeeping. Boys, on the other hand, learn that there are more options open to them. Girls are conditioned to believe that they may become nurses, while boys may become doctors. Girls may become teachers, but boys may become superintendents. Girls may become legal secretaries, but boys may become lawyers. Girls may become executive secretaries, but boys may become executives.

FIVE-MINUTE FOCUS   Recall an example of sexist behavior or sex-role stereotyping that you have observed in a school setting. Describe the events that took place and discuss how you felt. Date your journal entry and write for five minutes.

It was not until Title IX of the Education Amendments Act was passed in 1972 that women were guaranteed (on paper, at least) equality of educational opportunity. That law states that "no person in the United States shall, on the basis of sex, be excluded from participation in, be denied the benefits of, or be subjected to discrimination under any education program or activity receiving federal financial assistance."

Title IX has had the greatest impact on athletic programs in schools. The law requires that both sexes have equal opportunities to participate and equal benefit in regard to the availability of coaches, equipment, resources, and so on. For contact sports such as football, wrestling, and boxing, separate teams are allowed.

The right of females to equal educational opportunity was further enhanced with the passage of the **Women's Educational Equity Act (WEEA)** of 1974. This act provides the following:

- Expanded math, science, and technology programs for females
- Programs to reduce sex-role stereotyping in curriculum materials
- Programs to increase the number of female educational administrators
- Special programs to extend educational and career opportunities to minority, disabled, and rural women
- Programs to help school personnel increase the educational opportunities and career aspirations for females
- Encouragement for more females to participate in athletics[50]

A clear challenge teachers face is ensuring that girls *and* boys receive an education that is free from **gender bias** and encourages them to develop to the full extent of their capabilities. Unfortunately, evidence such as the following suggests that boys and girls continue to experience inequities in school.

Girls

- Girls start out ahead of boys in speaking, reading, and counting. In the early grades, their academic performance is equal to that of boys in math and science. However, as they progress through school, their achievement test scores show significant decline. The scores of boys, on the other hand, continue to rise and eventually reach and surpass those of their female counterparts, particularly

FACT FINDING

What Percentage of Males and Females Complete High School Courses?

A government survey revealed the following data on the percentage of males and females who enrolled *and then completed* high school courses in several areas.

Courses	Percent Males Completing	Percent Females Completing
Algebra	81.6	76.8
Trigonometry or geometry	60.1	50.3
Chemistry or physics	54.2	42.3
English, 3 years or more	92.8	94.1
Foreign language, 2 years or more	39.1	48.1
Industrial arts, shop, or home economics, 2 years or more	58.1	55.7
Business course, 2 years or more	25.7	56.7

Source: National Center for Education Statistics, *Digest of Education Statistics 1990* (Washington, D.C.: National Center for Education Statistics, 1991): 130.

in the areas of math and science. Girls are the only group in our society that begins school ahead and ends up behind.

- In spite of performance decline on standardized achievement tests, girls frequently receive better grades in school. This may be one of the rewards they get for being more quiet and docile in the classroom. However, their silence may be at the cost of achievement, independence, and self-reliance.
- Girls are more likely to be invisible members of classrooms. They receive fewer academic contacts, less praise and constructive feedback, fewer complex and abstract questions, and less instruction on how to do things for themselves.
- Girls who are gifted are less likely to be identified than are gifted boys. Those girls who *are* identified as gifted are less likely to participate in special or accelerated programs to develop their talent. Girls who suffer from learning disabilities are also less likely to be identified or to participate in special education programs than are learning-disabled boys.

Boys

- Boys are more likely to be scolded and reprimanded in classrooms, even when the observed conduct and behavior of boys and girls does not differ. Also, boys are more likely to be referred to school authorities for disciplinary action than are girls.
- Boys are far more likely to be identified as exhibiting learning disabilities, reading problems, and mental retardation.
- Not only are boys more likely to be identified as having greater learning and reading disabilities, they also receive lower grades, are more likely to be grade repeaters, and are less likely to complete high school.[51]

Following is a list of general guidelines to reduce gender bias in your classroom:

1. Equalize teacher-student interactions.
2. Promote girls' achievements in math and science.
3. Counter young children's self-imposed sexism.
4. Strengthen girls' transitions into early adolescence.
5. Teach about sexism directly.[52]

SUMMARY

We began this chapter by looking at the challenges teachers face in providing equal educational opportunities for special populations of students. We pointed out how schools and classrooms will become increasingly diverse—ethnically and culturally—during the remainder of the 1990s. Therefore, one aim of your curriculum should be to emphasize diversity, thereby enabling students to appreciate different points of view and to see the contributions that persons from all groups have made to our society.

Next, we clarified the distinction between ethnicity and race, after which we looked at the efforts of four ethnic groups to obtain equal educational opportunity in our country: African Americans, Spanish-speaking Americans, Native Americans, and Asian Americans. We concluded this section by presenting several guidelines for selecting instructional materials that contribute to the creation of a multiculturally oriented classroom, and we suggested a set of attitudes and skills necessary for teaching in a multicultural society.

In our examination of education for exceptional learners, we considered how teachers can meet the needs of linguistically challenged, physically challenged, learning-disabled, and gifted and talented students. The key to meeting their needs, we suggested, is to emphasize their abilities and to become a careful observer of students' classroom behavior.

In the final section, we focused on how females, though a majority of our population, have been denied equal educational opportunity. We also pointed out how males, too, have been the victims of gender bias in education.

KEY TERMS AND CONCEPTS

minority, **444**

multicultural, **445**

ethnic groups, **445**

race, **445**

racism, **446**

National Assessment of Educational Progress (NAEP), **447**

Indian Education Act of 1972, **454**

special education, **459**

limited English proficiency (LEP), **460**

Education for All Handicapped Children Act (Public Law 94-142), **462**

Individualized Education Program (IEP), **463**

learning disability (LD), **464**

dyslexia, **465**

sexism, **467**

Women's Educational Equity Act (WEEA), **468**

gender bias, **468**

DISCUSSION QUESTIONS

1. Why do you think long-standing efforts to provide equal educational opportunities to all students in our society have not been more successful? What do you see as the major roadblocks to providing equal opportunity?
2. What should educational leaders and policymakers do in order to improve the quality of education for the various groups discussed in this chapter?

3. With which of the student groups discussed in this chapter do you feel most comfortable? Least comfortable? What reasons do you have for feeling as you do?

4. What stereotypes do you have about the groups of students we have discussed in this chapter? How do you think these stereotypes might influence your teaching?

APPLICATION ACTIVITIES

1. Discuss with your classmates what steps teachers might take to ensure harmonious relationships among students of different cultural groups.

2. Select an ethnic/cultural group in America with which you are unfamiliar and prepare a short report on that group. Report your findings to the rest of the class.

3. Have your instructor arrange several role-plays based on the nine student portraits presented in this chapter. Your instructor may wish to divide the class into three or four small groups. Each student should have the opportunity to role-play both a student and a teacher. Those observing the role-plays can provide helpful feedback to those in the role of the teacher.

FIELD EXPERIENCES

1. Visit a local school that has a large enrollment of students whose cultural backgrounds differ from your own. Note how you respond to the cultural differences between yourself and the students. How might these responses influence your teaching?

2. Interview a teacher at the school identified in the above field experience activity. What special satisfactions does he or she experience from teaching at the school? What significant problems does he or she encounter, and how are they dealt with?

3. Observe in a classroom that has exceptional students. What steps does the teacher take to meet the needs of these students? Interview the teacher to determine what he or she sees as the challenges and rewards of teaching exceptional students.

SUGGESTED READINGS

Banks, James A. *Multiethnic Education: Theory and Practice*, 2d ed. Boston: Allyn and Bacon, 1988. *An excellent, comprehensive resource book for developing curricula that reflect ethnic diversity. Includes a model unit for teaching ethnic content, decision making, and social action skills.*

Coleman, Laurence J. *Schooling the Gifted.* Menlo Park, Calif.: Addison-Wesley, 1985. *An informative survey of the varieties of giftedness and current practices for educating the gifted. Also provides practical steps for teachers to follow in developing their own curricular units for the gifted.*

Hallahan, Daniel P. and James M. Kauffman. *Exceptional Children: Introduction to Special Education*, 5th ed. Englewood Cliffs, N.J.: Prentice-Hall, 1991. *An authoritative, well written introduction to special education—addresses concerns of regular classroom teachers as well as special education teachers.*

National Board of Inquiry into Schools. *Barriers to Excellence: Our Children at Risk.* Boston: National Coalition of Advocates for Students, 1985. *Reviews the different forms of discrimination that can deny students equal educational opportunity. Also presents over 100 strategies for creating quality schools available to all students.*

Tiedt, Pamela L. and Iris M. Tiedt. *Multicultural Teaching: A Handbook of Activities, Information, and Resources*, 3d ed. Boston: Allyn and Bacon, 1990. *An extensive, rich source of ideas for creating an effective multicultural classroom.*

TEACHERS . . . .

How do you meet the needs of at-risk students in your classroom and school?

Our students are statistically measured as 43 percent "at risk." This has been a constant dilemma at my school in that our resources are so few for problems so great. We have continued to offer extensions of our activities academically and socially, but it is difficult to work with large at-risk groups. Recently we have received state money that will be used before school, after the school day, after the school year, and on Saturdays to help alleviate this problem.

Our students are greatly affected by socioeconomic status. I don't think this is new, but our government's ability or interest in attacking the issue inside or outside of school is dwindling. This focus is on more local control and that is good, but local funds are available only to some localities and not to others. Consequently, I think we may be farther than ever from guaranteeing equal rights in the educational process. Changes for meeting the challenge will have to include funding for community outreach. Our housing, medical care, child care, etc. are so lacking in the fundamentals that kids really are not ready for school.

We will also have to provide new alternatives. Our system is now focused mainly on upper-echelon students. Our regular and at-risk students are being pulled down by the inability of the system to cope with the severest of psychosocial problems many students display. Some students will have to be removed from regular settings to allow teachers to accommodate regular students in the mainstream. Public education cannot continue to take the worst of society's problems without lasting and irreversible effects on the whole system.

—Marc Gray
Highland Middle School, Louisville, Kentucky

What can a teacher do? It is difficult to find the right answer. Just as each student is different, each solution must also be considered. I have experienced students with family problems, especially the case of the broken home. Often the student seems to feel responsible for the parents' problems. This student needs reassurance that he or she is not to blame. They also need to know that they are not "bad" and that someone cares about their problem. A student facing this problem needs to feel that [he or she] can attain success. Special consideration may be needed to allow the means to succeed, such as passing a test or handing in work late.

It seems most important that students have help in bolstering their egos. If the teacher does not feel confident in counseling the student, he or she must find help for the student. I would start first with the guidance counselor or an administrator, who can seek further help for the student. Whatever path you follow, remember

ON TEACHING

that the total student is important. As teachers we must not become so self-centered as regards our classroom requirements that we let a problem student slip through the system. They are our clients and we should be there to help them.

—Wanda L. Smith
Bradford High School, Starke, Florida

What strategies, activities and materials would you use to increase cross-cultural communication in a multicultural class?

I have a new student who enrolled late and speaks little English. I have never seen anyone come in with more enthusiasm and interest than this young Mexican girl, but she is still floundering socially in a group of students who have been together for many years. I spend a lot of time talking with her about her homeland, what she has done, and what she will do when she returns. For involvement in school activities, I encourage others to reach out to her and include her in group work. She is well liked, so this low-key approach is working. It is amazing how socially "closed" some of our young people are at such an early age!

—Marc Gray
Highland Middle School, Louisville, Kentucky

This year I asked for tables instead of desks. To break up the socialization patterns I saw forming (old friends, racial groupings, groupings by sex), I developed a seating plan that I hoped would create open lines of communication and understanding among all the students. My curriculum included the study of authors of both sexes and all cultures and backgrounds. The nature of the writing process itself provided ample opportunity for group interaction.

—Susan S. Reid
Chattanooga High School, Chattanooga, Tennessee

Creative problem-solving activities that involve divergent and flexible thinking are wonderful means for crossing cultures. A simple drawing on the board where students identify many uses or purposes of the picture will quickly tear down boundaries. Ideas that surface will point out similarities among groups rather than differences. Group puzzles that demand cooperation among students are also good for eliminating hesitancies to interact and barriers that separate individuals.

—Gale W. Ulmer
P. K. Yonge Lab School, Gainesville, Florida

CHAPTER 15

Teaching and the Challenge of the Future

All education springs from some image of the future. If the image of the future held by a society is grossly inaccurate, its educational system will betray its youth.

Alvin Toffler
Future Shock

Writing in the 1960s, educator Alfred Ellison wrote a fictional account of a guided tour through a futuristic school. A part of his provocative essay follows:

He started me off with a fantastic room with materials which I can liken only to the best type of equipment to be found in our day at the Franklin Institute in Philadelphia, or the Museum of Science and Industry in Chicago. The large room was full of working models of all kinds of operating equipment. This equipment reflected tremendous variety and apparently represents a cross-section of the electronic, mechanical, and natural phenomena of the time.

"How do you teach the content, apart from the skills involved, of a subject like Geography, which was under great criticism in my day?"

"There we use what we like to call our 'Immersion Chamber.' "

"Surely, you don't—" I started.

He laughed. "No, the Immersion Chamber is a room with 360-degree projection of three-dimensional holograph motion pictures. Related to this three-dimensional projection is a kit which provides the realia of the area under consideration. What better way to learn to understand a place than actually to visit it? Since we cannot take all of our children physically to the places we want them to know about, we take them there vicariously, through the Immersion Chamber. Some people like to insist that this is better than a real visit since all the important aspects are dramatically included. The normal visitor rarely would be as systematic or as complete even if he were permitted to visit all the places we present. The realia kits provide opportunities to handle and work with artifacts that come from the place shown and include clothing, products, coins, and copies of original documents, maps, and books."[1]

FOCUS QUESTIONS

1. What significant forces and trends are shaping the future of education?
2. Why is change in education often a slow and difficult process?
3. What developments in neurophysiology and cognitive science contribute to the field of education?
4. In what ways can computers be used to help students learn? What other state-of-the-art instructional media are available for the classroom?
5. How can schools best prepare students to meet the challenges of an unknown future?
6. How can teachers prepare for and shape the future?

Today in the 1990s, classroom experiences like those in Ellison's "Immersion Chamber" do exist, though as the most avant-garde of experiments. The future holds more than amazing new technology for the classroom, however. It promises applications to teaching of new knowledge about thinking and learning, new relationships between teachers and learners, new structures for schools, new relationships between schools and communities, new emphases in the curriculum, and more. In this chapter we explore the future of education. We begin by examining forces and trends in our society that are shaping our future.

EDUCATION AND THE FUTURE

What will teaching become in the twenty-first century? Of course, no one really knows. In spite of the impossibility of answering that question, however, it is important for us to think carefully about the kind of world we want for tomorrow. In that way, the choices we make today will increase the likelihood that tomorrow's future will be the one we prefer. In short, we should recognize the importance of planning for the future and trying to create the future we want. As Alvin Toffler pointed out in his classic book *Future Shock,* we must choose wisely from among several courses of action: "Every society faces not merely a succession of *probable* futures, but an array of *possible* futures, and a conflict over *preferable* futures. The management of change is the effort to convert certain possibles into probables, in pursuit of agreed-on preferables. Determining the probable calls for a science of futurism. Delineating the possible calls for an art of futurism. Defining the preferable calls for a politics of futurism."[2]

The primary aim of **futurism** is to enable a society to enter the future that it prefers. Futurists identify possible futures by analyzing current social, economic, and technological trends and then making forecasts based on those analyses.

The Forces of Change

Using forecasting techniques that John Naisbitt first popularized in his 1982 bestseller *Megatrends* and then updated (with Patricia Aburdene) in the 1990 *Megatrends 2000: The New Directions for the 1990s,* and drawing from the forecasts of other futurists, we have identified a number of forces and trends (see Figure 15.1) that seem to be contributing most to how we will live in the twenty-first century.

Social Forces and Trends While family ties will continue to remain a prominent part of our culture, evidence indicates that far too many marriages end in divorce. In addition, soaring numbers of runaway children and cases of child abuse suggest that the family is in trouble. Teachers will continue to find that more and more of their students are from families that are smaller, have working mothers, have a single parent present, or have unrelated adults living in the home.

There is evidence that crime and delinquency will continue to rise in the future. Much of the crime that occurs in and around schools is related to students' use of

FIGURE 15.1   **Significant Forces and Trends Shaping the Future**

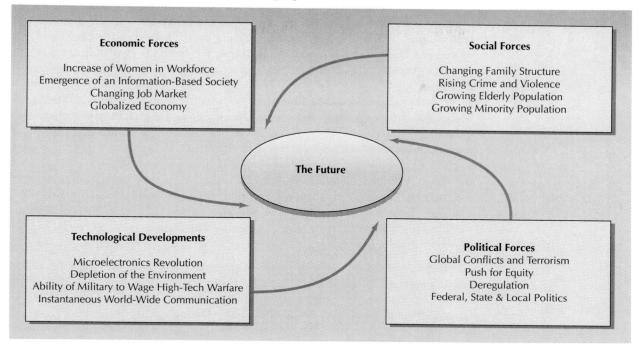

Economic Forces

Increase of Women in Workforce
Emergence of an Information-Based Society
Changing Job Market
Globalized Economy

Social Forces

Changing Family Structure
Rising Crime and Violence
Growing Elderly Population
Growing Minority Population

The Future

Technological Developments

Microelectronics Revolution
Depletion of the Environment
Ability of Military to Wage High-Tech Warfare
Instantaneous World-Wide Communication

Political Forces
Global Conflicts and Terrorism
Push for Equity
Deregulation
Federal, State & Local Politics

drugs. Violence and vandalism in some schools have already reached epidemic proportions. What was originally characterized as an urban problem has now spread to the suburbs and rural areas. Certainly, the reduction of crime is one of the critical challenges of the future.

The United States of the future will be even more culturally diverse than it is today. African Americans, Hispanics, Native Americans, Asian Americans, and others will come to represent an ever-increasing proportion of the total population. Teachers of the future will be responsible for developing curricula and instructional methods that cultivate the potentialities of students from a wide variety of backgrounds.

With computer-age advances in health care, the life span of Americans is steadily being extended. The number of Americans 65 or older will nearly double between 1983 and 2033. More than one out of five Americans in 2033 will be 65 or older.[3] In addition, older Americans of the future will be better educated and more physically, intellectually, and politically active than their predecessors. Tomorrow's elderly will recognize education as one of the keys for a satisfying, productive old age.

Economic Forces and Trends   The jobs we are trained for today may not exist tomorrow. During the last half decade, for example, very few kinds of work have been unaltered by the onrushing developments in computer technology. Today's worker must be able to learn to operate an ever-increasing array of technological devices. Workers who excel are measured not by how much they can produce but by how quickly and well they can learn new skills.

The composition of the work force is also changing. As a result of gains made by the women's movement, for example, more and more women are not only moving out into the work force, they are moving up. Women are obtaining increasing numbers of executive-level positions in the professions, business, and education. In fact, in *Megatrends 2000*, Naisbitt and Aburdene call the 1990s the "decade of women in leadership."[4] Slowly, the workplace is changing to accommodate the career patterns of women. Business and industry, for example, are receiving pressure from women's groups to provide preschool and day-care programs as part of their fringe-benefit packages.

Another major economic force in the United States during the last decade has been the shift from a product-oriented to an information-based, service-oriented economy. Moreover, this "new" economy is not the isolated, self-contained economy of one nation; it is a global economy. Our participation, cooperation, and competition in this global economy depends upon rapid communication of information around the world. As futurist Harold Shane says, "Knowledge and the handling of information have elbowed aside the smokestack and the assembly line as symbols of America's prowess."[5] Information is steadily becoming the critical resource of our age and the ability to learn it and to use it the chief aim of education.

Technological Developments   One of the greatest impacts on education is the mushrooming revolution in microelectronics. Computers, video equipment, and communication devices that employ the awesome powers of tiny silicon microchips are having profound effects on our lifestyles. These technological advances are changing not only how we learn and what we learn; they are forcing us to realize that the future will require all of us to be continuous, lifelong learners.

Technological and scientific advances have given us considerable ability to mold our environment to meet our needs for food, shelter, and safety. However, ecological experts suggest that we are so ravaging the environment that we could one day run out of vital natural resources. Nevertheless, there are signs that we might be able to meet this challenge by harnessing more pollution-free sources of energy, conserving resources, and restoring damaged environments.

Recent technological developments such as fiber-optic cables and communication via satellite have made possible instantaneous, worldwide communication. More than 16 million miles of fiber-optic cable were in place at the start of 1992.[6] Early in 1991, the role that sophisticated communications and space-age technology could play in warfare was illustrated dramatically during the Persian Gulf War.

Clearly, technology is changing the way Americans live and learn. You can now shop by telephone, withdraw money from your bank at any hour by stopping at an automated teller machine, and take high-speed transportation to any part of the world. Similarly, technology has revolutionized the curricular and instructional options open to teachers. Washington state high school students, studying why the ancient loggerhead turtle is becoming extinct, interact with a sophisticated touch-screen computer and "travel" to Florida, the breeding ground of the loggerheads.

Political Forces and Trends   Education in the future will certainly be strongly influenced by political forces at the local, state, and federal levels. For example, the trend at the federal level to grant increasing autonomy to the states in regard to education began with the Reagan administration in the early 1980s. During the Bush administration, a new education agenda was implemented. In February of 1990, President Bush unveiled the following six national goals for American education.

Six National Goals for Education

By the year 2000:

1. All children in America will start school ready to learn.
2. The high school graduation rate will increase to at least 90 percent.
3. American students will leave grades 4, 8, and 12 having demonstrated competency in challenging subject matter, including English, mathematics, science, history, and geography; and every school in America will ensure that all students learn to use their minds well, so that they may be prepared for responsible citizenship, further learning, and productive employment in our modern economy.
4. U.S. students will be first in the world in mathematics and science achievement.
5. Every adult American will be literate and will possess the skills necessary to compete in a global economy and to exercise the rights and responsibilities of citizenship.
6. Every school in America will be free of drugs and violence and will offer a disciplined environment conducive to learning.[7]

FIVE-MINUTE FOCUS In your opinion, what is the likelihood of achieving the six national goals for education by the year 2000? What would it take to achieve each goal? Date your journal entry and write for five minutes.

The role that the federal government is to play in education in the 1990s was extended when President Bush introduced his ambitious *America 2000: An Education Strategy* in April of 1991. That plan included the following components:

America 2000: An Education Strategy

- Strategies for attaining the six national goals President Bush set in 1990
- Funding to create by 1996 a "New Generation of American Schools" (at least 535) around the country
- A 15-point accountability plan for parents, teachers, schools, and communities to measure and compare results among schools
- "New World Standards" in five core subjects for what students need to know and be able to do
- A voluntary system of national testing, the American Achievement Tests, based on the New World Standards
- Incentives to states and local districts to adopt policies for school choice
- Governor's Academies for Teachers designed to assist teachers in helping students pass the American Achievement Tests
- The creation of the New American Schools Development Corporation, a non-profit organization to oversee innovative school-reform efforts
- The creation of electronic networks to serve the New American Schools
- The creation of skill clinics where people can acquire knowledge and skills needed for employment

As a result of the thrust at the federal level to deregulate business and industry, the way has been paved for the corporate sector to become more involved in education.

Companies such as IBM, Coca-Cola, RJR Nabisco, and General Electric, recognizing the stake they have in improving education, are making unprecedented grants to encourage educators to restructure schools.

Another dominant political force during the 1990s will be continued demands for equity in all sectors of American life. In regard to education, the constitutionality of school funding laws will be challenged where inequities are perceived, and tax reform measures will be adopted to promote equitable school funding. As an indicator of the support for need-based school financing, 75 percent of 1,000 kindergarten through 12th-grade teachers who participated in *The Metropolitan Life Survey of the American Teacher, 1991* said they believed that states should provide "greater financial assistance to schools with more poverty and students with more education problems than to schools that have students who are better off."[8]

The Change Process in Education

As you have seen, forces outside and within the educational system continually stimulate changes in education. And changes do occur. However, the modifications, reorganizations, and redirections are relatively slow, complex, and lackluster, especially when compared to the paths of progress in the fields of space, science, and technology, which frequently end with dazzling discoveries. The course of change in American education is often more plodding, progressing undramatically on paths that at times seem circular in nature.

Why is change so difficult to effect in education? Seymour Sarason suggests six answers to this question in his book *The Culture of School and the Problem of Change.* First, he explains, schools are complex social organizations that defy simple, single-approach innovations.[9] In the school culture, a change in one area has consequences in another. For instance, incorporating a new subject such as AIDS education into the curriculum requires all or most of the following actions: (1) obtaining approval from the school board, community, and/or administration regarding the new program; (2) reducing instructional time allotments for existing curriculum to make room for an additional subject; (3) arranging inservice training for teachers; (4) coordinating teachers' efforts in terms of common objectives and their sequence; (5) communicating with parents and the public; (6) maintaining students' skills in other areas of the curriculum; and (7) resolving conflicts that may occur in any of these areas.

A second reason that change is difficult, according to Sarason, is that it is hard to know where to start. Should the agent of change be the principal, the teachers, or the parents?[10] Obviously, all will play a part, but who should begin the process and provide the leadership?

Third, Sarason notes that it is also hard to know which area to target for change (e.g., the administration, the teachers, the community, the teacher-training institutes). If the change process takes the form of parent education, it could be brought about through evening programs sponsored by the parent-teacher association, administration, or school board. In this case the parents are the target for change.

Fourth, participants in the school culture are sometimes skeptical about changes because of previous negative experiences with new programs that had poor results due to the reformers' lack of knowledge of the system. For instance, teachers could be dubious about an AIDS curriculum because an earlier antismoking education effort had been ineffective.

Fifth, change in the school culture is difficult because "each alternative confronts one with a universe of alternatives of action."[11] The leaders initiating the change must care strongly enough about it to create a plan and then carry it through the maze of decisions and adjustments to completion.

And sixth, the time perspective of those seeking improvements often works against the success of the effort. A preference for quick solutions and an impatience with long-term processes frequently cancel innovative programs prematurely.

From Sarason comes a sampling of questions that reformers might ask, which reveals the complexity of the problem of change.

What Reformers Need to Know

- What are the different ways in which pupils can participate in preparing examinations?
- What are the different ways in which a principal can be prepared for his or her position?
- What are the alternative ways of deroutinizing the school day and year?
- What are the different ways [in which] a teacher can generate and utilize question-asking behavior in children?
- What are the different ways in which a neighborhood or community can exercise "control" over schools?[12]

FIVE-MINUTE FOCUS   Read over Sarason's sampling of questions reformers ask. Which one interests you the most? How would you begin to answer that question? What considerations would make your answer complex? Date your journal entry and write for five minutes.

PROMISING INNOVATIONS IN EDUCATION

Recent developments in education range from applications of new scientific knowledge about the human brain to new applications of computer and telecommunications technologies. Other significant changes include new relationships between teachers and learners and between communities and schools.

The innovations in education described in the following sections need to be considered in terms of the complexity of the change process. While none of the innovations is *the* answer to problems in the schools, each represents a departure from the status quo and has the potential for significant, positive change. Each will affect your career as a member of the next generation of teachers.

New Knowledge About Learning

Within the last two decades, educational researchers have increased our understanding of the learning process. **Learning** can be defined as "the information processing, sense making, and comprehension or mastery advances that occur while one is acquiring knowledge or skill."[13] Research into multiple intelligences and multicultural learning styles has broadened our understanding of this definition. In addition, research in the fields of neurophysiology, neuropsychology, and cognitive science promises direct relevance to education by further explaining how people think and learn.[14]

Brain Research   An example of findings from science that have implications for education is the possibility that the brain develops in spurts of physical growth interrupted by plateaus. According to biologist Herman Epstein, growth spurts occur at 3–10 months, 2–4 years, 6–8 years, 10–12 or 13 years, and 14–16 or 17 years. Epstein also observes that "the brain growth spurt of girls at age 11 is about twice that of boys, while something like the converse is true of the brain growth that occurs around age fifteen years."[15]

Epstein proposes that "intensive intellectual input should be situated at the spurt ages."[16] Further, he suggests that intensive intellectual input at the wrong times—

FIGURE 15.2
Brain's Hemispheric Specialization

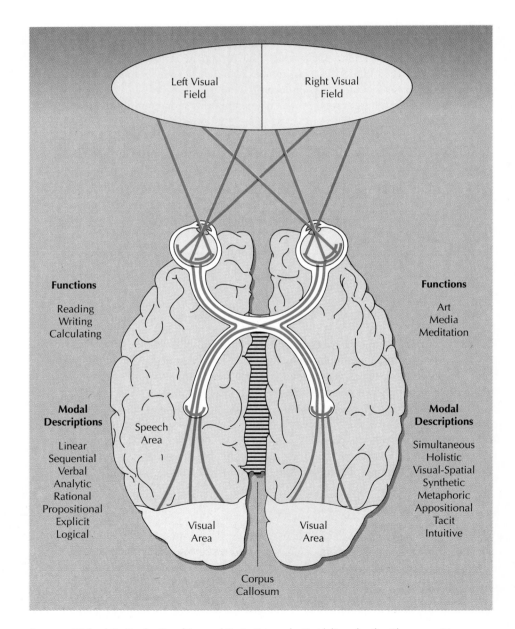

Source: Michael P. Grady, *Teaching and Brain Research: Guidelines for the Classroom* (New York: Longman, 1984).

during plateau periods—could damage the child's ability to absorb that input later at a more appropriate age. He hypothesizes, for example, that "the failure to adapt educational inputs [at 11 years of age] to the far greater capacity of girls might be responsible for the relative lack of females in the more theoretical or abstract professions."[17] A challenge for educators, then, is to match developmental spurts with learning demands—that is, to make the timing and content of learning experiences fit patterns of brain growth.

Also relevant to educators are studies of the brain's **hemispheric specialization** in which "the left hemisphere specializes in linear, sequential, and analytic operations whereas the right hemisphere specializes in simultaneous, holistic, and metaphoric operations."[18] The diagram in Figure 15.2 shows some of the complex relationships between the structure and function of the brain that may affect learning.

Cognitive Studies **Cognitive science** is concerned with the mental processes students use as they learn new material. By drawing from research in linguistics, psychology, anthropology, and computer science, cognitive scientists are developing new models for how people think and learn. For the most part, cognitive scientists focus on students' thought processes while they are learning and attempt to describe how they manipulate symbols and process information. The following excerpt, for example, explains the cognitive model known as **information processing.**

> It is generally assumed that there are three structural levels of the [information processing] system: a sensory or intake register, a working memory, and a long-term memory. All information enters the system through the sensory register, but it can only be held there a short period of time. To remain in the system, information must enter the working memory, where it can be combined with information from the long-term memory. All operations on information occur in the working memory. In other words, this is where conscious thinking occurs. The constraint on the working memory is that it is extremely limited in capacity and can only attend to a few chunks of information at a time. The long-term memory is potentially unlimited in capacity and contains all the information that one knows. The limitation on the long-term memory is the problem of accessing information stored there. In addition to these basic structural features of the system, most information-processing approaches assume the existence of executive or control processes that monitor the operation of the system. These include routines like rehearsal strategies for storing information in long-term memory or possibly general heuristics [strategies] for problem-solving.[19]

— a branch of cognitive science concerned with how individuals use long-term & short-term memory to acquire info and solve problems

The system of rules the cognitive scientist develops are usually presented in the form of a computer simulation program or a flow diagram, such as the one in Figure 15.3.

Trends in Educational Theory and Practice

Research on the thinking and learning processes has contributed to the development of innovative teaching strategies and to new methods of evaluating student performance. An innovative form of instruction that draws from cognitive studies, for example, is **contingent teaching,** which

def. an approach to teaching, sometimes called "scaffolding" in which instruction is based on the student's current level of understanding and ability

> involves pacing the amount of help children are given on the basis of their moment-to-moment understanding. If they do not understand an instruction given at one level, then more help is forthcoming. When they do understand, the teacher steps back and gives the child more room for initiative. In this way, the child is never left alone when he is in difficulty nor is he "held back" by teaching that is too directive and intrusive.[20]

FIGURE 15.3   **An Information Processing Model of Learning**

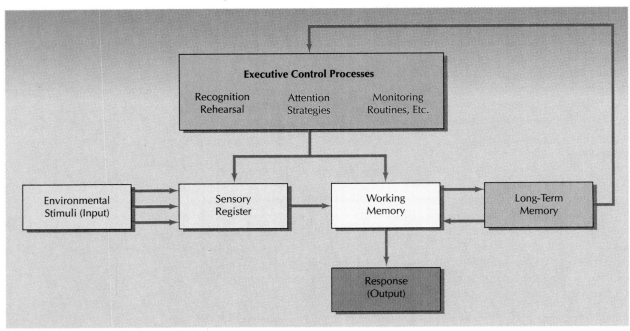

Source: From Anita E. Woolfolk, *Educational Psychology*, 4th ed. Copyright 1990 by Allyn and Bacon. Reprinted with permission. Adapted from R. Gagné, *The Conditions of Learning and Theory of Instruction*, 4th ed., p. 71 (New York: Holt, Rinehart & Winston, 1985); M. Hunt, "How the Mind Works," *The New York Times Magazine*, Jan. 24, 1982, p. 32.

Contingent Teaching   The concept of contingent teaching, sometimes called "scaffolding," is based on the work of L. S. Vygotsky, a well-known Soviet psychologist. Vygotsky coined the term **"zone of proximal development"** to refer to the point at which students need assistance in order to continue learning. The effective teacher is sensitive to the student's zone of development and ensures that instruction neither exceeds the student's current level of understanding nor underestimates the student's ability.

As educational psychologist David Wood points out, contingent teaching is an effective means of increasing students' abilities to process information in more complex ways:

> Contingent teaching helps children to construct local expertise—expertise connected with that particular task or group of tasks—by focusing their attention on relevant and timely aspects of the task, and by highlighting things they need to take account of. It also breaks the task down into a sequence of smaller tasks which children can manage to perform, and orchestrates this sequence so that they eventually manage to construct the completed assembly.[21]

New Ways to Evaluate Performance   For more than a decade, declining test scores, the lack of literacy among many high school graduates, and calls to hold teachers more accountable have fueled a movement to evaluate the performance of students and teachers with ever-increasing numbers of tests. In the 1990s, however, new forms of assessment are being used. Innovations in testing are partly in response to criticisms of the fairness and objectivity of standardized tests, such as the SATs. Educators and the public have criticized college entrance exams not only for class and gender bias in their content but also for failing to measure accurately students' true knowledge, skills, and levels of achievement.

For all these reasons, educators are increasingly going beyond traditional tests and using individual and small-group projects, **portfolios** of work, videotaped demonstrations of skills, and community-based activities to evaluate students' learning. Similarly, the performance of some teachers is being assessed through essay exams that require the analysis of simulated teaching problems, computer simulations of classroom situations, portfolios that document the teacher's work, and videotapes of teaching.

Trends in Teaching-Learning Relationships

Efforts to reform education in the 1980s have led to new teaching relationships that involve teachers, students, parents, and members of the community. These new teaming strategies are based on the premise that everyone involved in the education of the young must work together so that communities serve all students more effectively and schools serve their communities.

Cross-Age Tutoring   Some of the values in **cross-age tutoring** strike us immediately when we hear students speak about the experience. A former ninth-grade dropout who returned to school and became a tutor explained how she felt about the program:

> Right now I feel very good about school and would give it an eight out of ten, but when I was a freshman I would have given it a one. . . . I'm working with third-graders and some of them are passing because I worked with them. . . . I was like a teacher and I know what the teacher goes through and so I don't give them so many problems. . . . I'm so excited about graduating. . . . And I want all of my brothers to finish school also.[22]

Research clearly shows that with proper orientation and training, cross-age tutoring can greatly benefit both "teacher" and learner. Pilot programs teaming students at risk of dropping out of school with younger children and with special needs students have proven especially successful.

The student was a participant in a program in San Antonio, Texas, which was supported by Coca Cola and the Intercultural Development Research Association. The project, which began in 1985, is called the Youth Partnership Dropout Prevention Program. In the program, 100 students at risk, identified by their high school teachers and counselors, are selected to become tutors for younger children. They work for eight hours or more a week and are paid minimum wage for their services. The children being tutored get extra attention, help in their work, and positive role models. A hidden benefit for tutors is that they get to brush up on their academic skills.

Cross-age tutoring programs call for planning, money, and training. Young people cannot be expected to work miracles with children whose teachers have often given up on them. They may indeed become more frustrated. Nor do young people naturally know how to teach skillfully. For these reasons training is imperative.

Peer Counseling   Some schools have initiated student-to-student **peer counseling,** or peer coaching, programs—usually monitored by a school counselor or other specially trained adult. In peer counseling programs, students can address such problems and issues as low academic achievement, interpersonal problems at home and at school, substance abuse, and career planning. Evidence indicates that both peer counselors and students experience increased self-esteem and greater ability to deal with problems.

When peer counseling is combined with cross-age tutoring, younger students can learn about drugs, alcohol, premarital pregnancy, delinquency, dropping out, AIDS, suicide, and other relevant issues. Here the groups are often college-age students meeting with those in high school, or high school students meeting with those in junior high school or middle school. In these preventative programs, older students sometimes perform dramatic episodes that portray students confronting problems and model strategies for handling the situations presented.

Peer coaching is also expanding among teachers. While talented, experienced teachers have always helped novice teachers, recent, more formal programs are designed to extend the benefits of such exchanges to more teachers. Bruce Joyce is a trainer for an approach called *peer coaching,* which encourages teachers to learn together in an emotionally safe environment.

> We enjoy a school where the principal has organized her faculty for peer coaching. She takes over teachers' classes quite a bit so they can get together. Actually, though, the teachers don't spend a lot of time observing each other. . . . A team of her teachers may deal with, say, cooperative learning, and when they get the cooperative learning group going, other teachers go in for a few minutes, more to see the whole setup than to observe a particular lesson.[23]

Master teacher and mentor programs similarly promote teacher-to-teacher support. These approaches to staff development are expected to yield benefits in terms of improved teacher morale and teaching effectiveness.

Faculty Teams   The practice of team teaching is often limited by student enrollments and budget constraints. As integrated curricula and the need for special knowledge and skills increase, however, the use of faculty teams will become more common.

Faculty teams can be created according to subject areas, grade levels, or teacher interests and expertise. The members of a team make wide-ranging decisions about the instruction of students assigned to the team, such as when to use large-group instruction or small-group instruction, how teaching tasks will be divided, and how time, materials, and other resources will be allocated.

Participating on a faculty team requires a willingness to devote extra time to planning and an ability to work collaboratively with others. However, the potential benefits are many: teachers spend more time teaching their areas of expertise and interests, and students are often more motivated to learn when they are taught by a team.

School "Houses"   Faculty teams also participate in school restructuring and school-based management, especially in programs designed to create communities of teachers and learners. For example, to reduce the anonymity that students and teachers can experience in large schools and to create conditions that enhance within-school communication, some schools are restructuring into **school "houses"**—separate, autonomous groups of students and teachers within a single school. One of the authors, for example, taught at a high school that was restructured according to a 45-15 year-round plan. Teachers, students, administrators, counselors, and staff were assigned to one of four houses—A, B, C, or D. On a staggered basis, each house would attend school for 45 days and then take a 15-day mini-vacation. A complete school year consisted of four 45-day sessions and 4 mini-vacations. At any given time, three houses would be in session and one house would be on vacation. As a result of this restructuring, a greater sense of community was created within each house.

FIVE-MINUTE FOCUS   Describe a teaming strategy or partnership you participated in as a student sometime in the past. What aspects of the relationship made your experience helpful, or unhelpful, to you? Date your entry and write for five minutes.

New Relationships between Communities and Schools

In the last decade, the concept of teaming has been extended to include the wider community. From adopt-a-grandparent programs to adopt-a-school projects, teaming between the community and school takes many forms and has great potential. Partnerships with parents and businesses, for example, help make communities valuable resources for schools. Equally important, new directions in restructuring make schools valuable resources for their communities.

The Community as a Resource for Schools   In teamings between communities and schools, individuals, civic organizations, or businesses select a school or are selected by a school to work together for the good of the students. The ultimate goals of such projects are to provide students with better schooling experiences and to assist students at risk.

Adopt-a-grandparent programs can be spiritually uplifting for all concerned, for example, and relatively easy to incorporate into a school, since many older citizens have the time available to serve and the desire to make meaningful contributions to their communities. Students clearly benefit from the perspective, care, and wisdom of the older generation.

Flying KITES

On June 1, 1989, eighth graders in three Massachusetts schools participated in a live, two-way, 90-minute teleconference with ninth graders in Karlsruhe, Germany. The students exchanged information and opinions on such issues as the Chernobyl nuclear disaster, antinuclear protests, the merits of nonfossil fuels, rap music, clothes, and fast foods. These students were part of a multi-organization partnership called KITES—Kids Interactive Telecommunications Experience by Satellite. KITES was initiated in 1988 by the University of Lowell (Massachusetts) College of Education as a way to advance students' cross-cultural sensitivities and infuse the curriculum with the vitality of international perspectives.

The "Experience" was researched, funded, and produced through multiple volunteer partnerships among the University of Lowell, the Massachusetts Corporation for Educational Telecommunications, Massachusetts Educational Television, the Digital Equipment Corporation, VideoStar Connections, PanAmSat, Baden-Wurttemberg's Pedagogische Hochschule Karlsruhe, two German ministries of education, two German banks, Seimens (a high technology company), and countless individuals who donated their time and services.

The students' international video teleconference was a year in the making. Teachers and students in Lowell, Chelmsford, and Dracut, Massachusetts, first used the University of Lowell's interactive video network to receive information and instruction on science topics. Teachers then used a computer conferencing system (CoSy) on a day-to-day basis to jointly develop and integrate their science and social studies curricula in preparation for the main event.

Participants also used various computer networks (such as international electronic mail [e-mail] and C. S. Net—a worldwide network funded by the National Science Foundation—for international data communication and project management. Contact between students, teachers, and planners in the two countries was therefore well established before the live teleconference. Students exchanged photographs, audiocassettes, slides, videotapes, and personal data—such as a "lifestyle survey" on political views; personal relationships; ethnic backgrounds; preferences in sports, food, fashion, and music; and feelings about peer pressure, school life, and parent-child relationships.

KITES was founded on the vision of supporting curriculum and promoting global awareness through joint access to existing community resources: human, material, and electronic. The adoption of this vision by all participating organizations was seen as the single most important element of the partnership. Because of the unqualified success and educational value of the experiment, KITES is expanding to other schools here and abroad.

Source: John LeBaron and Rebecca Warshawsky, "Satellite Teleconferencing Between Massachusetts and Germany," *Educational Leadership* 48, 7 (April 1991): 61–64.

Communities are resources for schools in many other ways. Community organizations may provide special services, for example. Museum in the schools programs, outdoor education, and mock government activities are some enterprises that may emerge from community partnerships. Businesses may contribute funds or materials needed by the school, give employees release time to participate in classroom projects, initiate prevention programs for students at risk, or offer formal career training in conjunction with the school.

Schools as Community Resources   A shift from the more traditional perspective of schools needing support from the community is the view that schools should serve as multipurpose resources *for* the community. Proposals for year-round schools, for example, reflect not only students' educational and developmental needs, but also the needs of parents and the requirements of the work world.

Proposals for making schools community resources include Bettye Caldwell's idea of an **Educare system,** for instance, which would provide day-long, year-round public schooling for children six months through twelve years of age.[24] Ernest Boyer of the Carnegie Foundation for the Advancement of Teaching argues that schools should adapt their schedules to those of the workplace so that parents can become more involved in their children's education, and that businesses, too, should give parents more flexible work schedules. Drawing on the model of Japan, Boyer suggests that the beginning of the school year could be a holiday that frees parents to attend opening day ceremonies, celebrating the launching and continuance of education in the same way that we celebrate its ending.[25]

In response to the increasing number of at-risk students, many schools are also serving their communities by providing an array of health, education, and social services in the school. In 1991, more than 150 **school-based clinics** (SBCs) were operating in schools in this country. Most SBCs are located in high schools and are funded and administered by departments of public health, nonprofit organizations, hospitals, or school districts.

SBCs tend to be in schools that serve low-income areas. According to a survey by the Center for Population Options released in 1988, SBCs provide a wide array of general health services (from immunizations to the diagnosis and treatment of minor injuries) and the following counseling/educational services. Percentages indicate the proportion of SBCs offering the service.

Services Provided by School-Based Clinics

- Health education, 100%
- Counseling on birth control methods, 86%
- Nutrition education, 99%
- Drug and substance abuse programs, 77%
- Mental health counseling, 96%
- Sex education in classroom setting, 73%
- Sexuality counseling, 95%
- Parenting education, 67%
- Weight reduction programs, 95%
- Family counseling, 65%
- Pregnancy counseling, 89%
- Job counseling, 25%[26]

School-based clinics are not without their opponents. Some people believe that schools should act only as a referral point for such services, while others believe that schools have a responsibility to act as direct providers of such services. The debate over the proper role of schools in the twenty-first century is likely to continue as more school-based clinics begin to open their doors.

NEW TECHNOLOGY FOR THE CLASSROOM

Nine-year-old Nancy is seated in front of the computer and color monitor, about to begin a lesson on insects. On the screen is a two-story house. Nancy reaches out to the screen and touches the burnished knob on the front door and it magically opens. The next screen shows the hallway and living room. At various points on the screen are purple bugs. Nancy touches a bug near the bottom of a bookcase. The bookcase fades away and reveals dozens of ants scurrying about. A pleasant-sounding voice comes on and begins to explain how insects and humans coexist. After giving Nancy information about the ants she has discovered, the voice invites her to explore the rest of the house to see what other insects she can find.

To enhance their classroom instruction, today's teachers can draw from a dazzling array of technological devices like the one Nancy was using. Little more than a decade ago, the technology available to teachers who wished to use more than the chalkboard was limited to an overhead projector, a 16-mm movie projector, a tape recorder, and, in a few forward-looking school districts, television sets.

Some Effects of the Television Revolution

Since the 1950s, television has become an omnipresent feature of life in America. Compared to the computer, therefore, television has had a longer and possibly a more predictable impact on education. In fact, the effects of the television revolution—both positive and negative—on all facets of American life are still being studied, and for good cause. Children spend an estimated equivalent of two months of the year watching television.[27] The typical child between six and eleven years of age watches television about 27 hours a week.

Critics of television point out that it encourages passivity in the young, may be linked to increases in violence and crime, often reinforces sexual and ethnic stereotypes, and retards growth and development. Some say that television robs children of the time they need to do homework, to read and reflect, and to build bonds with family members and others through interaction.

On the other hand, television can enhance students' learning. Excellent educational programs are aired by the Public Broadcasting Service and by some cable and other commercial networks. Television has also had a positive impact on how students are taught in schools. With the increased availability of video equipment, many schools have begun to have students produce their own television documentaries, news programs, oral histories, and dramas. Many schools have closed-circuit television systems that teachers use to prepare instructional materials for students in the district.

Whatever the pros and cons, television is a permanent feature of modern life. It represents the explosion and globalization of knowledge and ideas. And it is clearly a primary source of students' orientations to their society and culture.

The Computer Revolution

Chris Held who teaches a fourth- and fifth-grade combination classroom in Bellevue, Washington, a suburb of Seattle, is typical of those whose teaching style has been revolutionized by technology. With the support of his school district, Held removed the desks from his classroom and replaced them with "workstations," a large comfortable sofa, and enough tables for his students on days when he teaches group lessons. His classroom is now filled with computers, printers, videocassette recorders, and video cameras.

FACT FINDING

How Accessible Are Computers to Students?

While computers are becoming more accessible to students, they are not equally so for all students. A survey by Quality Education Data indicated that the ratio of students in grades 6–12 to the number of computers declined from 125 students per computer in 1983–84 to 22 students per computer in 1989–90.

In addition, a 1989 survey by the Census Bureau revealed that:

- Fifteen percent of households had computers, compared with 8 percent in 1984.
- Forty-six percent of children ages 3 to 17 used a computer either at home or at school, up from 30 percent in 1984.
- White students were more likely to use computers at school than African Americans, and private schools provided greater access to computers than public schools.

At a given time, six or seven kids may be pounding furiously at laptop computers in the writing center, while four or five others are building models with Lego bricks, and still others are using computer graphics to "paint" pictures that will illustrate their written work. Meanwhile, another group of five or six students may be practicing math with Microsoft *Excel* or scripting and preparing to tape a classroom news show."[28]

According to Held, "Electronic technology is one of the richest resources to support learning that I've ever encountered. It offers students such a rich classroom environment. Computers and these other machines provide a perfect springboard for all kinds of learning."[29]

Instructional Uses of Computers   Since the early 1980s, the **microcomputer** has revolutionized classroom instruction in the nation's schools. According to Henry Jay Becker, a Johns Hopkins University researcher, about 96 percent of the nation's schools had computers in at least some classrooms at the end of the 1989–90 school year. And in 1991 estimates were that more than two million computers dotted the nation's classrooms.[30]

Instructional uses of computers include 1) recordkeeping through data banks and spread sheets; 2) electronic workbooks for drill and practice; 3) interactive simulations for self-directed study or problem solving; 4) word processing, involving all stages of the writing process; 5) programming, involving the development of logic and other higher cognitive functions; and 6) networking, in which teachers and students access information and communicate with others through telephone-linked computers.

Computer simulations and **networking** are particularly fascinating forms for instruction. Simulations range from the lemonade stand that elementary school students can plan and run vicariously, practicing basic arithmetic and problem-solving skills, to a mock trial, which Harvard Law students can participate in via videodisc and computer. Recently available are computer-based simulations that give students direct learning experiences, such as visiting the great museums of the world or the bottom of the Pacific Ocean.

Through networking, your students may create community electronic bulletin boards of their own and conduct computer conferences within the classroom or between different classes. Your students may even "talk" to students in other schools or different countries. Data bases and on-line experts in many fields also change the way your students conduct research, as more computerized reference works—such as directories, dictionaries, and encyclopedias—become available.

FIVE-MINUTE FOCUS   In your opinion, what is the most important benefit of the computer revolution for education, and what is the most important potential drawback? Date your entry and write for five minutes.

Criticisms of Computer-Based Instruction   Clearly, the computer "revolution" has had an impact on education. Just how widespread and positive the effects have been is the subject of some debate. The Association for Supervision and Curriculum Development, for example, had this to say in late 1990:

> Ten years after large numbers of microcomputers began appearing in U.S. classrooms, they have neither sparked a broad revolution in teaching and learning, as some advocates predicted, nor quietly faded into disuse. Instead, experts say the computer "revolution" some predicted at the beginning of the 1980s is on hold; more computers are available and are integrated in some curriculum areas, but the organization and climate of most schools have yet to be changed in ways that allow teachers and students to truly take advantage of the technology's potential. . . .
>
> For those attempting to use computers in their classrooms, the obstacles are legion: sporadic opportunities for training, a shortage of quality hardware and software, and relatively little time to think about how computers might serve to make learning more productive or better.[31]

Widespread excitement over the promise of the Computer Age is tempered, therefore, by practical concerns and growing criticism.

Implications of Computers for the Future   Concerns about the impact of the computer revolution on education have included images of dehumanized computer addicts—hackers—and fears of robots replacing teachers. However, computers probably have greater potential to transform education and society for the better. Following are some of the many predictions experts have offered about the likely or potential impacts of computers on teaching and learning.

- Greater individualization of instruction
- Advances in the education of children with special needs
- Diagnostic use of computers by teachers to identify learning problems
- Computer use for teacher-designed curriculum materials
- Computer use for routine tasks, giving teachers more time for students
- New teacher responsibilities as planners, coordinators, programmers, and managers

- Earlier development of competence in students as independent learners
- Stronger development of problem-solving and communication skills
- Greater development of cooperative learning modes
- Greater accumulation of, access to, and sharing of information
- Greater interest in linking together knowledge from different fields
- A democratization of the information explosion and the learning process

After all is said, we cannot underestimate the significance of the human dimension in the successes in computer instruction. With any instructional media—textbooks, television, or computers—teachers have the power and opportunity to evaluate, select, and then use creatively and masterfully the media that best suit the needs of their students and the goals of their educational programs.

Classroom Media Magic

Personal computers have so revolutionized the instructional media available to teachers that today it is no exaggeration to refer to the "magic" of media. At schools around the country, students are involved in innovative activities made possible by computers. One sixth-grade class, for example, built a greenhouse, monitored the light, water, and temperature, and then used a computer to plot the data on a graph. Another class used a computer to exchange information on the French Revolution with students in France. Yet another class plotted the position of the stars with the aid of a computer and learned about black holes in space through computer graphics. Some of the most exciting forms of media "magic" involve CD-ROMs, videodiscs, and interactive multimedia.

Today's book buyer can select from more than 800,000 titles. This enormous amount of information might prove overwhelming to anyone who wished to remain informed were it not for small compact discs known as **CD-ROMs.** One 5.25-inch CD-ROM can hold the equivalent of about 270,000 pages of text, or about nine hundred 300-page books. References to any topic in the 270,000 pages can be found in less than 30 seconds. Currently, most CD-ROMs contain reference works such as encyclopedias, dictionaries, and the works of William Shakespeare, but new titles are rapidly becoming available.

I'd like to discuss my test score...

SIPRESS

Instead of traditional seating arrangements and a teacher-at-the-chalkboard focus, elementary classrooms of the future will have work stations for computer-aided instruction. Microelectronics and interactive multimedia will enable students to focus more on self-learning and cooperative learning, and the teacher to focus more on individual students.

Videodiscs are 12-inch discs and resemble the smaller CD-ROMs. Videodiscs show still and moving pictures on a television screen and have much higher quality sound and image than videotapes. A disc can hold the equivalent of 54,000 photographic slides on each side, and the user can freeze frame any of the images. In early 1991, an estimated 7,000 videodisc textbooks were in use in U.S. schools, and Texas was the first state to allow school districts to use textbook money to buy videodiscs. In a science classroom in Texas in which the teacher was using a laser videodisc textbook, "a fourth grade class was studying electricity and the image of a lightning bolt was frozen on the TV screen. Then teacher Rodelle Tompkins touched the remote control and zapped the bolt to life, and her science class was off on an energetic discussion."[32]

Computer-supported **interactive multimedia** allow the user to integrate huge libraries of text, audio, and video information.

> Imagine a classroom with a window on all the world's knowledge. Imagine a teacher with the capability to bring to life any image, any sound, any event. Imagine a student with the power to visit any place on earth at any time in history. Imagine a screen that can display in vivid color the inner workings of a cell, the births and deaths of stars, the clashes of armies, and the triumphs of art. And then imagine that you have access to all of this and more by exerting little more effort than simply asking that it appear.[33]

As in the following example, interactive multimedia systems consist of a computer-controlled videodisc and/or a CD-ROM player.

> A high school history teacher is preparing a lecture on civil rights. Instead of just lecturing to his students about civil rights, the teacher really makes the subject come alive with a multimedia videodisc that includes video news clips of the civil rights marches of the sixties, and Dr. Martin Luther King's famous "I have a dream" speech. The teacher selects the text of relevant court cases from a CD-ROM, and visual and audio information from a videodisc, to create a powerful, animated educational experience for students.[34]

FUTURES PLANNING

When you think about your future as a teacher, that future may seem at once exciting and frightening, enticing and threatening. How, you may ask, can I meet the many educational challenges identified in this book? Much of the knowledge and skills needed to accomplish this you will, of course, acquire in the courses that remain in your teacher education program. In addition, you should remember that the future of teaching will not just happen. In a very real sense, it is in the hands of persons such as yourself to shape with vision and commitment the profession of tomorrow. Teachers must not let the future happen and merely react to emerging conditions; instead, you must work toward the future you desire.

Experiments in futures planning and futures curricula are already underway. In 1988, for example, the Association for Supervision and Curriculum Development created a High School Futures Planning Consortium. The overall aim of the consortium is to train teams from the 26 participating schools in "strategic planning, a system for analyzing societal trends and issues and anticipating their consequences for schools."[35] A consortium school in Pittsburgh, for example, developed a program that features new scheduling patterns, interdisciplinary teacher teams, mentoring sessions, and community involvement.

In a futures curriculum program, students at Burnsville High School in Burnsville, Minnesota, may take two 12-week elective courses oriented toward the future: "Futures: Thinking About Tomorrow" and "Futures: Issues." The first course requires students to "create and evaluate alternative images of themselves and the worlds in which they might live."[36] The second course addresses nine topics: science fiction, energy, biotechnology, megatrends, education, space, terrorism, ecology, and avant-garde thinkers.

FIVE-MINUTE FOCUS Think about two children you know and project them into the future, 20 years from now. What skills are they likely to need? Which talents should help them? List three of these and then consider the ways that today's schools can better promote their development. Date your journal entry and write for five minutes.

Tomorrow's Students: What Will They Need to Know?

In light of the new patterns and trends discussed in this chapter, what knowledge and skills will prepare students to respond intelligently to an unknown future? It is not an easy task for schools to prepare students for an unknown future. Previously, it may have been sufficient to acquaint students with the past and then assume that they would transfer that knowledge appropriately as they responded to future events. However, many schools have recognized that we cannot afford just to let the future happen; we must plan for it and, when possible, make decisions about the kind of future we prefer. New curricula must reflect those decisions. In particular, teachers of the future will need to dedicate themselves to ensuring that all students address eight educational priorities (see Figure 15.4). Though these eight areas of learning will not be all that students will need, these learnings will best enable them to meet the challenges of the future.

FIGURE 15.4   **Educational Priorities for the Future**

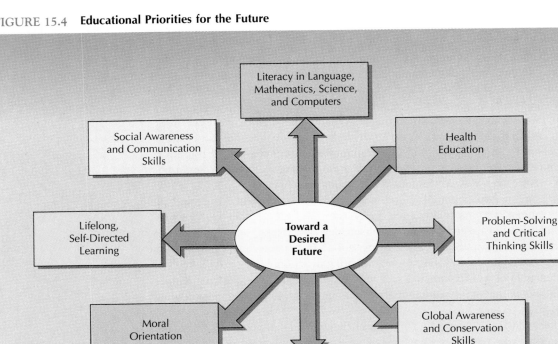

Literacy in Language, Math, Science, and Computers   To solve the problems of the future, students will need to be able to use written and spoken language to communicate clearly and succinctly. Moreover, students will continue to need to be able to read the printed word with a high degree of comprehension. Americans who cannot read will contribute most to the ranks of the unemployed.

The mathematics and science skills needed by students of the future go beyond mere computation and knowledge of scientific facts. Students will also need to be able to apply mathematical and scientific concepts to the solving of new problems. For example, they will need to be able to pose questions, analyze situations, translate results, illustrate results, draw diagrams, and use appropriate trial-and-error methods. Students of the future will also need to understand the awesome potentialities (as well as limitations) of computers. All students should acquire skills in accessing the vast stores of information that computer capabilities routinely handle today. Rather than be shrouded in mystique, "The computer can and should come to be as commonplace as the pencil."[37]

Problem-Solving and Critical Thinking Skills   Students of the future will need to be able to think rather than to remember. While the information that students learn in schools may become outdated or useless, the thinking processes they acquire will not. These processes focus on the ability to find, obtain, and use information resources for solving problems or taking advantage of opportunities. Students will need to learn how to cope with change, how to anticipate alternative future developments, how to think critically and creatively, and how to analyze and synthesize large amounts of complex data. As futurist Harold Shane puts it, tomorrow's students will need to have "minds that are nimble enough to cope with exponential change."[38]

Social Awareness and Communication Skills   Tomorrow's students must be able to communicate with people from diverse cultures. The United States "has the richest mix . . . of ethnic groups and global experience that the world has ever known."[39] The ability to create a better world in the future, then, will surely depend on our willingness to celebrate our rich diversity through the kind of communication that leads to understanding and friendly social relations.

An important lesson for students will be to learn that poverty, discrimination, crime, and unequal opportunities, wherever they occur, affect us all. To solve these and other social problems, students will need to become socially aware, politically active, and skilled in conflict resolution strategies.

Global Awareness and Conservation Skills   Tomorrow's students will need to recognize the interconnectedness they share with all countries and with all people. Our survival may depend on being able to participate intelligently in a global economy and respond intelligently to global threats to security, health, environmental quality, and other factors affecting the quality of human life.

> The realities of interdependence are with us all. Interdependence is not so much an ideal as a very simple fact. Even those who fear it must learn to understand it, if only to set limits to it. At issue is whether we shall manage interdependence effectively, not whether we have the collective capability to wish it away.[40]

One of the most important tasks facing the schools of tomorrow, then, is to give students an understanding of other cultures, both within our country and beyond our borders. The curriculum of the future must emphasize cultural diversity, interdependence, respect for the views and values held by others, an orientation toward international cooperation for resolving global issues, and practical knowledge and skills on, for example, the conservation of natural energy resources.

Health Education   With ever-increasing health care costs, the spread of diseases such as AIDS, increased risks of cancer, and longer life spans, it is imperative that students of the future acquire appropriate knowledge, skills, and attitudes in the area of health education. The health care delivery system is becoming more complex, and high technology (artificial heart implantations or magnetic resonance imaging, for example) is being used ever more widely. To live healthy lives, then, students of tomorrow will need consumer education to select from among an increasingly complex array of health care services. In addition, they will need to be able to make informed choices among alternatives for the prevention or treatment of problems relating to substance abuse, nutrition, fitness, and mental health. Sex education, still a matter for debate in some communities, seems more critical today than at any time in the past.

Moral Orientation   As we pointed out in Chapter 5, schools unavoidably teach values, both directly and indirectly. The school culture and the curriculum reflect both national and community values. The traditional practice of using "values clar-ification" activities in the classroom, however, has been criticized by some for pro-moting relativism at the expense of family values or religious doctrines. Yet, as we witness the effects of gang warfare, racial violence, sexual exploitation of children, drunk driving, white-collar crime, false advertising, unethical business practices, ex-cessive litigation, and so on, many Americans are calling for schools to pay more attention to issues of public morality.

The continuing challenge for teachers and schools will be to find ways to address those issues that are both effective with students and acceptable to their parents. At the very least, teachers help students develop a moral orientation by modeling be-havior, encouraging students to clarify their values, and giving students opportunities to learn respect for themselves and others, as well as for property and laws.

Aesthetics Awareness   Another challenge for teachers and schools is to encourage creativity and greater appreciation for the arts. Many observers of American education point out that emotional, spiritual, aesthetic, and reflective, or meditative, dimensions of life receive less emphasis than analytical thinking and practical life skills. While literature and drama are standard fare in curricula, most students know little, for example, about music, painting, and sculpture. Public school students are rarely taught art history or principles of design or other criteria for evaluating creative works. As a result, students may lack the concepts and experiences that lead to an appreciation of beauty and the development of aesthetic judgment.

Lifelong, Self-Directed Learning   The key educational priority that should guide teachers of the future is to create within each student the ability, and the desire, to continue self-directed learning throughout his or her life. Ironically, one mark of a truly effective teacher is that he or she is needed less and less by students as they assume greater responsibility for their learning.

It has often been said that one of the primary purposes of schooling is for students to learn how to learn. In a world characterized by rapid social, technological, eco-nomic, and political changes, all persons must take responsibility for their own learn-ing. Career changes will be the norm, and continuing education over a lifetime will be necessary. We must, as President Bush said in 1991, become a "nation of students."

A Vision of the Future

Imagine that it is the year 2020, and we are visiting Harrington High, a school in a large city on the West Coast. All of the teachers at Harrington have been certified by the National Teachers Board, a licensing agency similar to those established to certify that lawyers and medical doctors are competent to practice. The salaries of board-certified teachers are on a par with those of other professionals with comparable education and training. About half of the 120 teachers at Harrington have also earned the Advanced Certificate offered by the board. These teachers are known as "lead" teachers and may earn as much as $75,000 per year. Harrington has no principal; the school is run by an executive committee of five lead teachers elected by all teachers at the school. One of these lead teachers is elected to serve as committee chair for a two-year period.

Teachers run Harrington High. All other school personnel are in subordinate positions and have as their primary task supporting the efforts of teachers. Teacher aides, technicians, and clerical workers, for example, are available for all teachers.

✓ CONSIDER THIS . . .

What Does the Future Hold for Education in Your State?

Predict the future of education in your state in terms of the following list of developments. Rate each development according to whether it already exists in your state or when you think it will become common practice in the schools—within the next five or the next fifteen years. If you don't know the status of a particular development in your state, find out. Add at least one new item representing a trend in your state that does not appear on the list. When you have finished rating the items, share your results with your classmates. What reasons or evidence will you give for your predictions?

Developments	Now	Within 5 Yrs.	Within 15 Yrs.	Not Likely
1. Alternative student evaluation	____	____	____	____
2. Cross-age tutoring/mentoring	____	____	____	____
3. Peer counseling	____	____	____	____
4. Faculty teams/team teaching	____	____	____	____
5. School "houses"	____	____	____	____
6. Business-school partnerships	____	____	____	____
7. Community-school teaming	____	____	____	____
8. School-based clinics/counseling centers	____	____	____	____
9. Year-round schools	____	____	____	____
10. School restructuring	____	____	____	____
11. Equity in school funding	____	____	____	____
12. Open enrollment/school choice	____	____	____	____
13. School desegregation	____	____	____	____
14. Telephones in the classroom	____	____	____	____
15. Student computer networking	____	____	____	____
16. Video teleconferencing	____	____	____	____
17. CD-ROMs/videodiscs	____	____	____	____
18. Interactive multimedia	____	____	____	____
19. Sex education	____	____	____	____
20. AIDS education	____	____	____	____
21. Moral orientation in curricula	____	____	____	____
22. Globalism/multiculturalism	____	____	____	____
23. Aesthetics orientation	____	____	____	____
24. Alcohol and drug intervention	____	____	____	____
25. Reduction of gender bias	____	____	____	____
26. Reduction of racial/ethnic prejudice	____	____	____	____
27. Teacher empowerment	____	____	____	____
28. _____	____	____	____	____
29. _____	____	____	____	____
30. _____	____	____	____	____

Keepers of the Dream

Karin Marchant
Second-Grade Teacher
Midway Elementary School, Colbert, Washington

"It's important to give students a global awareness, to help them see beyond their immediate world," says Karin Marchant, a second-grade teacher at Midway Elementary School in Colbert, Washington, a suburb of Spokane. "Seven- and eight-year-olds can focus just on themselves, or they can become positive, caring citizens of the world."

To expand their global awareness, Marchant's students have visited with foreign exchange students at a nearby high school, exchanged letters and gifts with military personnel during the Persian Gulf War, and updated their world map to reflect changes such as the dismantling of the Berlin Wall. "People are often amazed at what second-graders are capable of learning," says Marchant.

Marchant, who earned her bachelor's and master's degrees in elementary education from Washington State University, began teaching in 1979. Since childhood, Marchant knew she wanted to become a teacher. "Everyone has a gift," she says, "and mine is teaching. The classroom is definitely where I'm supposed to be. I've always been interested in children and education."

Teaching requires a deep professional commitment and a willingness to make a substantial investment in students' lives, Marchant believes.

Teaching has to be something that you want to do. It's not just a job you do to fill your working hours. It's something you have a burning desire to do. It's a calling.

The outstanding teachers in our building put a lot of time and effort into teaching. They're not just clock punchers. They're always thinking of ways to change and improve. As a teacher, I don't think I've ever done anything the same way during the 12 years I've been teaching. Students change, and you have to meet their needs.

Marchant enjoys teaching second grade because of the "breakthroughs" she is able to see. "I get to see kids go from being nonreaders to readers. I can see the lights go on when a child says 'I get it!' That's very exciting."

Teachers have an important responsibility for shaping the lives of young people, Marchant believes. The impact teachers can have on students' lives is far-reaching. "You have to think about how you are impacting each life in the classroom. The meaning of every word, every gesture, and every facial expression can impact a student's self-esteem."

"I can see the lights go on . . ."

The key to effective teaching, according to Marchant, is to develop students' self-esteem and their ability to get along with one another. "My students and I talk about how we are a family and we don't always get along. 'You don't have to like everyone,' I tell them, 'but you have to be nice to everyone.' "

Marchant's influence on the lives of her students was illustrated recently when two of her former students, now graduating from high school, told her of their decision to become teachers.

They want to contribute something positive to other people's lives. They both told me "I'm going to become a teacher, and it's because of you."

In addition, the school has several paid interns and residents who are assigned to lead teachers as part of their graduate-level teacher preparation program. Each intern and resident has a bachelor's degree in the arts and sciences.

The logistical operation of the school is handled by several personnel who are accountable to the executive committee. These persons include a business manager, school accountant, and program administrator. Finally, teachers are assisted by such ancillary staff as a learning-style diagnostician; computer specialist; video specialist; social worker; school psychologist; four counselors; special remediation teachers in the areas of reading, writing, mathematics, and oral communication; bilingual and ESL teachers; and special needs teachers.

Harrington High operates many programs that illustrate the close ties the school has developed with parents and the community. The school houses a day-care center that not only gives students an opportunity to learn about child care but provides after-school employment for some. On weekends and on Monday, Wednesday, and Friday evenings the school is used for adult education and for various community group activities. Executives from three local industries spend one day a month at the school visiting with classes, telling students about opportunities in their companies, and conducting career awareness seminars. Two nearby colleges are involved in a tutoring program at Harrington, and both have an on-campus summer enrichment program for high school students who need special help with their studies or who plan to go to college.

Harrington High has a school-based health clinic that offers health care services and a counseling center that provides individual and family counseling. In addition, from time to time Harrington High teachers and students work closely on special programs with community agencies such as the neighborhood improvement association, the city's housing authority, the police and fire departments, and the two hospitals in the area. At the present time, for example, students in social studies, biology, chemistry, and English classes are assisting the city's environmental services department in preparing a report on air pollution in the city.

All the facilities at Harrington High—classrooms, library, multimedia learning center, gymnasiums, vocational shops, the cafeteria, and private offices for teachers—have been designed to create a teaching/learning environment free of all health and safety hazards. The cafeteria, for example, serves meals based on findings from nutrition research about the best foods and methods of cooking. The school is carpeted, and classrooms are soundproofed and well lit. Throughout, the walls are painted in soft pastels tastefully accented with potted plants, paintings, wall hangings, and large murals depicting life in different cultures.

The dress, language, and behaviors of teachers, students, administrators, and staff at Harrington High reflect a rich array of cultural backgrounds. Between classes it is impossible not to hear several languages being spoken and to see at least a few students and teachers wearing non-Western clothing. From displays of students' work on bulletin boards in hallways and in classrooms; to the African-American Heritage Club, Japanese watercolor classes, Mexican pottery making, and other extracurricular/co-curricular activities available after school; to the international menu offered in the cafeteria; to the backgrounds of students who serve on the Student Government Council, there is ample evidence that Harrington High is truly a multiracial, multicultural school and that gender, race, and class biases have been eliminated.

Each teacher at Harrington is a member of a teaching team and spends at least part of his or her teaching time working with other members of the team. Furthermore, teachers determine their schedules, and every effort is made to assign teachers according to their particular teaching expertise. Likewise students are assigned to learning groups according to their preferred modes of learning. Those teachers who work well with large groups, for example, are assigned students who learn well in such situations. Other teachers, whose strengths lie in organizing and managing small-group experiences, work with students who learn best in small groups that give them opportunities for student-teacher and student-student interactions. Students attend Harrington High by choice for its excellent teachers; its curriculum emphasis on problem solving, human relations, creative thinking, and critical thinking; and its programs for helping at-risk students achieve academic success.

Instruction at Harrington High is supplemented by the latest technology. Interactive video disc programs are used frequently by history, English, music, art, psychology, and business teachers. The school subscribes to several computer data bases and cable television services, which teachers and students use regularly. The multimedia learning center has an extensive collection of video cassettes and excellent computer software, much of it written by Harrington teachers. The center also has "virtual reality" interactive videodisc systems, workstations equipped with the latest robotics, and an extensive computer lab, including several voice-activated computers. The computer-supported interactive multimedia in the center use the CD-ROM format and the more advanced Integrated Services Digital Network (ISDN) delivery system.

Every classroom has a video camera and telephone that, in addition to everyday use, are used frequently for satellite video teleconferences with business executives, artists, scientists, scholars, and students at schools in other states and countries. Each classroom also has ten computers that students use routinely for drill and practice, problem-solving exercises, simulations, and networking. Harrington High's technological capabilities permit students to move their education beyond the classroom walls, as they determine much of how, when, where, and what they learn.

Tomorrow's Teacher

Teaching and the conditions under which teachers work may change in some fundamental and positive ways during the next two decades. Teaching will become increasingly professionalized, for example, through such changes as more lengthy and rigorous preprofessional training programs, salary increases that put teaching on a par with other professions requiring similar education, and greater teacher autonomy and an expanded role for teachers in educational policy-making. There will be more male teachers who are African Americans, Hispanics, or members of other minority groups. There will be greater recognition for high-performing teachers and schools through such mechanisms as merit pay plans, master teacher programs, and career ladders; and there will be improvements in working conditions that contribute to teacher stress and burnout. Teachers will commit themselves to professional development and learning throughout their careers.

Though we don't know what the future holds, it will certainly require teachers to use new methods, new materials, and new technologies. According to Forecasting International, Ltd., tomorrow's teachers will achieve new and higher levels of specialization:

> The educator of the future will have extensive experience with such topics as brain development chemistry, learning environment alternatives, cognitive and psychosomatic evaluation, and affective development.

The traditional teaching job will be divided into parts. . . . Some of the new jobs may be:

- Learning diagnostician
- Researcher for software programs
- Courseware writer
- Curriculum designer
- Mental-health diagnostician
- Evaluator of learning performances
- Evaluator of social skills
- Small-group learning facilitator
- Large-group learning facilitator
- Media-instruction producer
- Home-based instruction designer
- Home-based instruction monitor[41]

Though we cannot claim to have handed you an educational crystal ball so that you can ready yourself for the future, we hope you have gained both knowledge and inspiration from our observations in this chapter. Certainly, visions of the future, such as the one of Harrington High presented above, will not become a reality without a lot of dedication and hard work. The creation of schools like Harrington High will require commitment and vision on the part of professional teachers like you—teachers who have a firm grasp of subject matter and high expectations of their students, teachers who are sensitive to the individual differences and needs of their students, teachers who welcome opportunities for empowerment and conduct themselves according to the highest ethical standards.

SUMMARY

To present you with a realistic view of possible futures in teaching, we began this chapter with an analysis of the social, economic, technological, and political forces and trends that are shaping changes in our educational system. We then explored the complexities and requirements of implementing the change process in schools.

After suggesting applications of brain research and cognitive studies to curriculum planning and instruction, we looked at promising innovations in educational theory and methods, such as contingent teaching and portfolio evaluation. Cross-age tutoring, peer counseling, faculty teams, and school "houses" were discussed as innovations in teaching-learning relationships. We also called attention to promising new relationships between communities and schools and new roles for schools in their communities.

Our look at new technology for the classroom included consideration of the effects of the television and computer revolutions on teaching and learning in an Information Age. We also shared the exciting possibilities of computer-assisted technologies, such as CD-Roms, videodiscs, and interactive multimedia.

In our section on futures planning we explored the curriculum of tomorrow in terms of what we think students will need to know, and we presented a vision of how schools could be. The chapter ended with words of inspiration, we hope, to tomorrow's teachers, who will be the architects of change.

KEY TERMS AND CONCEPTS

futurism, **476**

learning, **481**

hemispheric specialization, **483**

cognitive science, **483**

information processing, **483**

contingent teaching, **483**

zone of proximal development, **484**

portfolios, **485**

cross-age tutoring, **485**

peer counseling, **486**

faculty teams, **486**

school houses, **487**

Educare system, **489**

school-based clinics, **489**

microcomputer, **491**

computer simulations, **491**

networking, **491**

CD-ROMS, **493**

videodiscs, **494**

interactive multimedia, **494**

DISCUSSION QUESTIONS

1. How do past events influence the future? What forces and trends are affecting the future of education?
2. What do you feel will be the main problems schools will face in the year 2020? What steps could be taken today to minimize those problems?
3. In terms of long-term impact on education, which innovation presented in this chapter do you believe is the most significant?
4. How should the role of public schools be extended in relation to their communities? What do you think, for example, of the Educare concept and school-based clinics?
5. How can computers be better used in your school? What are some obstacles to their optimum use?
6. What is the future of teaching? Why is it important for teachers to become lifelong learners?

APPLICATION ACTIVITIES

1. Write a scenario forecasting how the teaching profession will change during the next two decades.
2. Select one of the following areas and develop several forecasts for changes that will occur during the next two decades: energy, environment, food, the economy, governance, family structure, demographics, global relations, media, and technology. Upon what current data are your forecasts based?
3. Read recent professional journals to discover current areas of innovation in education. Select one innovation that especially interests you to examine more fully, and report to the class what you learn.
4. Taking turns with a partner as teacher and learner, develop role-plays illustrating the new teaching techniques and teacher-learner relationships described in this chapter. Present your role-plays to the class.
5. Working with a small group of classmates, choose specific instructional content, such as map reading or cell biology, and brainstorm ideas for alternative, nontraditional ways in which to evaluate student learning in that subject.

FIELD EXPERIENCES

1. Interview the principal at a local or nearby school and ask him or her to describe the school in ten years. Now interview several teachers at the school. Compare the forecasts of the principal with those of the teachers. What might account for any differences you find?
2. Observe children of different ages and notice differences between boys and girls in their cognitive development, behavior, and self-concepts. Relate your observations to information in this chapter about development.
3. Survey teachers in the local school district about their experiences on faculty teams. Using the information you gain, develop a list of ten criteria or guidelines for effective team teaching at any grade level.
4. Search for examples of school-community partnership arrangements in the local school district. Find out how these partnerships are progressing, and propose a specific new one based on your knowledge of the community.
5. Sample computer software in a subject area and grade level that interest you. Which programs would you prefer to use in your classroom, and why?

SUGGESTED READINGS

Ambron, Sueann and Kristina Hooper, eds. *Learning with Interactive Multimedia: Developing and Using Multimedia in Education*. Redmond, Wash.: Microsoft Press, 1990. *A comprehensive set of articles that provide an excellent introduction to computer-controlled multimedia for the educator.*

Bloom, Benjamin. *All Our Children Learning*. New York: McGraw-Hill, 1981. *A clear, thorough explanation of the mastery learning approach to teaching children, by the theorist who designed it.*

Cetron, Marvin J., Barbara Soriano, and Margaret Gayle. *Schools of the Future: Education into the 21st Century*. New York: McGraw-Hill, 1985. *A fascinating portrait of schools of the future painted by three forecasters with an impressive record for accurate predictions.*

Flake, Janice L., C. Edwin McClintock, and Sandra Turner. *Fundamentals of Computer Education*, 2d ed. Belmont, Calif.: Wadsworth Publishing Company, 1990. *A readable, practical guide for teachers who wish to enhance their teaching with the power of the computer. Includes excellent computer-based classroom activities and lesson plans.*

Fullan, Michael G., with Suzanne M. Stiegelbauer. *The New Meaning of Educational Change*, 2d ed. New York: Teachers College Press, 1991. *An incisive, up-to-date analysis of the content and process of educational change.*

Hart, Leslie. *Human Brain and Human Learning*. Oak Creek, Ariz.: 1990. *A summary of brain research relevant to education and the author's suggestions for creating a brain-compatible environment.*

Naisbitt, John and Patricia Aburdene. *Megatrends 2000: Ten New Directions for the 1990s*. New York: Avon Books, 1990. *An exciting, readable discussion of ten trends that are shaping our society as we enter the 21st century.*

Wood, David. *How Children Think and Learn*. New York: Basil Blackwell, 1988. *A comprehensive, intriguing discussion of how children think and learn.*

TEACHERS . . .

What is the most significant challenge for education in the twenty-first century, and how should that challenge be met?

In the ideal future, there would be no textbooks, but real-life materials. Students would interact with the community, especially the business community. Teachers would have more time to plan. There would be writing labs with computers at all work stations and a telephone in each classroom. High-tech equipment everywhere! Classrooms would be carpeted and well-lighted, with no desks—only whatever type of work station matches the class needs.

—Susan S. Reid
Chattanooga High School, Chattanooga, Tennessee

The professional status of teachers should be enhanced. First and foremost, teachers should be paid as professionals. Our status in the community needs to be higher. We are often treated like "big" kids. People think, why be a teacher when you can make more money doing something else? We need to be given credit for the contributions we make to the world.

—Ricardo Cortez Morris
Hixson High School, Hixson, Tennessee

While it has always been the school's responsibility to help solve social problems, to teach and nurture the whole child in hopes of countering society's woes, today's problems are so vast that the system is overloaded. Schools need the assistance of other organizations—home, church, business and government—if society's ills are to be cured.

The school, however, should play a vital role in bringing these institutions together. In addition to monitoring the progress of its students, the school must be a watchdog of this networking system. Teachers are trained to understand our changing world and environment, and it is our role to continually learn and develop new skills to work within our increasingly diverse culture.

Education remains the foundation for our future, and teachers must be in the forefront of remolding our lost sense of community.

—Gale W. Ulmer
P. K. Yonge Lab School, Gainesville, Florida

ON TEACHING

What advice would you give to a prospective teacher?

I would advise someone who is considering becoming a teacher to expect to make instantaneous decisions, to be organized, and to be prepared to work harder than they have ever worked.

—Julie Addison
Rock Ridge Elementary School, Castle Rock, Colorado

Work to be the best you can at whatever level you'd like to teach; that is, be well prepared. Also, enter the field with an open mind and consider all of the options and opportunities that teaching can offer.

—Rose Ann Blaschke
Vivian Elementary School, Lakewood Colorado

Anyone can teach; however, I think there are certain traits that separate the good teachers from the best. I may not have all of them, but being aware of them influences the kind of teacher I am today. You have to have a love of children, an enthusiasm for learning, patience, good communication skills, a concern for meaning and relevance in instruction, creativity, flexibility, organization, willingness to take on extra duties and participate in decision making, and knowledge to impart.

—Elizabeth Hudson
Clyde Miller Elementary School, Aurora, Colorado

Realize that you must love your job and love what you are doing. When you leave the building you never leave your job. Your students never leave your mind. Their problems and concerns become yours. Also, you must learn to be a team player with other employees of the school. Aim for the heavens and be thankful if your feet leave the ground!

—Jennifer Cronk
Rocky Mountain Hebrew Academy, Denver, Colorado

Give of yourself in order for the children in your classes to succeed. Try to find a way into each child so he or she will learn what is expected for that grade level and beyond. It is a much harder job than it appears on the surface—so be ready for total commitment to excellence, not mediocrity.

—Suzanne Neal
William Woods College, Fulton, Missouri

Notes

Chapter 1

1. Lucianne Bond Carmichael, *McDonogh 15: The Making of a School* (New York: Avon Books, 1981), p. 113.
2. John Godar, *Teachers Talk* (Macomb, Ill.: Glenbridge Publishing, 1990), p. 15.
3. Cecelia Traugh, Rhoda Kanevsky, Anne Martin, Alice Seletsky, Karen Woolf, and Lynne Strieb, *Speaking Out: Teachers on Teaching* (Grand Forks, N.Dak.: University of North Dakota, 1986), p. 53.
4. John Barth, "Teacher," in *An Apple for My Teacher*, ed. Louis Rubin (Chapel Hill, N.C.: Algonquin Books, 1987), p. 166.
5. John Godar, *Teachers Talk*, p. 244.
6. Eliot Wigginton, *Sometimes a Shining Moment* (Garden City, N.Y.: Anchor Press, 1985).
7. Benjamin Wright and Shirley Tuska, "From Dream to Life in the Psychology of Becoming a Teacher," *School Review* (September 1968): 253–293.
8. Benjamin Wright and Shirley Tuska, "How Does Childhood Make a Teacher?" *The Elementary School Journal* (February 1965): 235–246.
9. Dan C. Lortie, "Observations on Teaching as Work," in *Second Handbook of Research on Teaching*, ed. R. M. W. Travers (Chicago: Rand McNally, 1973), pp. 474–497.
10. Dan C. Lortie, *Schoolteacher: A Sociological Study* (Chicago: University of Chicago Press, 1975), p. 39.
11. Ibid., p. 39.
12. Albert Shanker, "Why Teachers are Angry," *The American School Board Journal* (January 1975): 23.
13. Jack Dunham, *Stress in Teaching* (London: Croom Helm, 1984).
14. Sara Lawrence Lightfoot, *Worlds Apart: Relationships Between Families and Schools* (New York: Basic Books, 1978) p. 65.
15. Stanley M. Elam, "The 22nd Annual Gallup Poll of the Public's Attitudes Toward the Public Schools," *Phi Delta Kappan*, (September 1990): 47.
16. *The Metropolitan Life Survey of the American Teacher, 1986: Restructuring the Teaching Profession* (New York: Louis Harris and Associates, Inc.).
17. Arthur W. Combs, *A Personal Approach to Teaching: Beliefs That Make a Difference* (Boston: Allyn and Bacon, 1982), p. 75.
18. Arthur Jersild, *When Teachers Face Themselves* (New York: Teachers College Press, 1955), p. 83.
19. For an interesting discussion of how people can hide behind various roles, see Erving Goffman, *The Presentation of Self in Everyday Life* (Garden City, N.Y.: Doubleday, 1950).
20. "Job Relatedness Analysis Report for the Position of Elementary Teacher in Washington County" (Washington County School District, Chipley, Fla., n.d., mimeographed).
21. American Association of Colleges for Teacher Education, *Educating a Profession: Profile of a Beginning Teacher* (Washington, D.C.: American Association of Colleges for Teacher Education, 1983).

Chapter 2

1. Haim Ginott, *Teacher and Child* (New York: Avon Books, 1972), p. 15.
2. Roland Barth, *Improving Schools from Within* (San Francisco: Jossey-Bass, 1990), p. 211.
3. Tom Peters and Nancy Austin, *A Passion for Excellence* (New York: Random House, 1984), p. 414.
4. David E. Denton, *Existential Reflections on Teaching* (North Quincy, Mass.: Christopher Publishing House, 1972), p. 37.
5. Eliot Wigginton, from transcript of "An Evening with Eliot Wigginton." LBJ Library, Austin, Texas, April 24, 1986.
6. Eliot Wigginton, *Sometimes a Shining Moment: The Foxfire Experience* (Garden City, N.Y.: Anchor Press, 1985), p. xi.
7. Ann Lieberman and Lynne Miller, *Teachers, Their World, and Their Work* (Alexandria, Va.: Association for Supervision and Curriculum Development, 1984), pp. 4–5.
8. Sybil Marshall, *An Experiment in Education* (London: Cambridge University Press, 1963), p. 41.
9. John Holt, *How Children Fail* (New York: Dell, 1982), p. 281.
10. Eliot Wigginton, *Sometimes a Shining Moment: The Foxfire Experience*, pp. 196–197.
11. Herbert Kohl, *36 Children* (New York: New American Library, 1967).
12. Herbert Kohl, *Growing Minds: On Becoming a Teacher* (New York: Harper and Row, 1984), p. 7.
13. Torey Hayden, *Somebody Else's Kids* (New York: Avon Books, 1981), p. 314.
14. Sara Lawrence Lightfoot, *The Good High School* (New York: Basic Books, 1983), pp. 355–356.
15. As reported in *Chicago Union Teacher* (March 1978).
16. Philip Jackson, "The Way Teaching Is," *NEA Journal* (November 1965): 62.
17. John Canfield, "White Teacher, Black School," in *Don't Smile Until Christmas: Accounts of the First Year of Teaching*, ed. Kevin Ryan (Chicago: University of Chicago Press, 1970), p. 43.

18.   Philip Jackson, *Life in Classrooms* (New York: Holt, Rinehart and Winston, 1968), p. 166.

19.   Arthur L. Costa, "A Reaction to Hunter's Knowing, Teaching, and Supervising," in *Using What We Know About Teaching,* ed. Philip L. Hosford (Alexandria, Va.: Association for Supervision and Curriculum Development, 1984), p. 202.

20.   John Dewey, "The Relation of Theory to Practice in Education," in *The Third Yearbook of the National Society for the Scientific Study of Education,* Part I (Bloomington, Ind.: Public School Publishing Company, 1904), pp. 13–14.

21.   Arthur Combs, *Myths in Education: Beliefs That Hinder Progress and Their Alternatives* (Boston: Allyn and Bacon, 1979), pp. 234–235.

22.   Walter Doyle, "Classroom Organization and Management," in *Handbook of Research on Teaching,* 3rd ed., ed. Merlin C. Wittrock (New York: Macmillan, 1986), p. 395.

23.   John Dewey, *How We Think: A Restatement of the Relation of Reflective Thinking to the Educative Process* (Boston: D.C. Heath, 1933), pp. 35–36.

24.   Bruce Joyce and Marsha Weil, *Models of Teaching,* 3rd ed. (Englewood Cliffs, N.J.: Prentice-Hall, 1986), p. 404.

25.   Albert Bandura, *Social Learning Theory* (Englewood Cliffs, N.J.: Prentice-Hall, 1977), p. 12.

26.   See Chapter 12 for a discussion of the hidden curriculum in classrooms.

27.   Inscription on public building in India.

28.   Philip Jackson, *Life in Classrooms* (New York: Holt, Rinehart and Winston, 1968), p. 152.

29.   Forrest W. Parkay, *White Teacher, Black School: The Professional Growth of a Ghetto Teacher* (New York: Praeger, 1983), p. 47.

30.   Jackson, *Life in Classrooms,* p. 119.

31.   Carl A. Grant and Walter G. Secada, "Preparing Teachers for Diversity," in *Handbook of Research on Teacher Education,* ed. W. Robert Houston (New York: Macmillan, 1990), p. 403.

32.   Parkay, *White Teacher, Black School,* pp. 49–51.

Chapter 3

1.   Karen Kilgore, Dorene Ross, and John Zbikowski, "Understanding the Teaching Perspectives of First-Year Teachers," *Journal of Teacher Education* (January-February 1990): 30–31.

2.   "A Call for Change in Teacher Education," (Washington, D.C.: American Association of Colleges for Teacher Education, 1985): 11.

3.   See John Barth, "Teacher: The Making of a Good One," *Harpers Magazine* (November 1986): 60.

4.   "A Call for Change in Teacher Education," 11.

5.   Ibid., p. 12.

6.   Ibid.

7.   Reprinted by permission of the publisher from Michael W. Sedlak, "Tomorrow's Teachers: The Essential Arguments of the Holmes Group Report," in Soltis, Jonas F., ed., *Reforming Teacher Education: The Impact of the Holmes Group Report* (New York: Teachers College Press, Columbia University. All rights reserved.), pp. 4–6.

8.   John Godar, *Teachers Talk* (Macomb, Ill.: Glenbridge Publishing, 1990), p. 264.

9.   Ibid., p. 115.

10.   Arthur Jersild, *When Teachers Face Themselves* (New York: Teachers College Press, 1955), p. 3.

11.   Anne Lieberman and Lynne Miller, *Teachers, Their World, and Their Work* (Alexandria, Va.: Association for Supervision and Curriculum Development, 1984), pp. 43–44.

12.   Jean V. Carew and Sara Lawrence Lightfoot, *Beyond Bias: Perspectives on Classrooms* (Cambridge, Mass.: Harvard University Press, 1979), p. 19.

13.   James Conant, *The Education of American Teachers* (New York: McGraw-Hill, 1963), p. 93.

14.   Maxine Greene, "Perspectives and Imperatives: Reflection and Passion in Teaching," *Journal of Curriculum and Supervision,* vol. 2 (no. 1, 1986): 72.

15.   Henry A. Giroux and Peter McLaren, "Teacher Education and the Politics of Engagement: The Case for Democratic Schooling," *Harvard Educational Review,* vol. 53 (no. 3, 1986).

16.   Kenneth Zeichner, "Alternative Paradigms of Teacher Education," *Journal of Teacher Education,* 34 (1983): 8.

17.   Barth, "Teacher: The Making of a Good One," 64.

18.   From transcript of "An Evening with Eliot Wigginton," LBJ Library, Austin, Texas, April 24, 1986.

19.   See Mark D. Danner, "How Not to Fix the Schools," *Harpers Magazine* (February 1986): 41.

20.   Ibid., p. 45.

21.   Ibid., p. 51.

22.   Quoted in A. J. Marrow, *The Practical Theorist: The Life and Work of Kurt Lewin* (New York: Basic Books, 1969).

23.   Chester E. Finn, Jr., *What Works: Research about Teaching and Learning,* 2d ed. (Washington, D.C.: U.S. Department of Education, 1987).

24.   Robert V. Bullough, Jr., *First-Year Teacher: A Case Study* (New York: Teachers College Press, 1989), p. 141.

25.   John Dewey, "The Relation of Theory to Practice in Education," in *The Relation of Theory to Practice in Education,* the Third Yearbook of the National Society for the Scientific Study of Education, Part I (Bloomington, Ind.: Public School Publishing Co., 1904), p. 15.

26.   For more information see "The Making of a Teacher: A Report on Teacher Education and Certification" (The National Center for Education Information, 1901 Pennsylvania Avenue, N.W., Suite 707, Washington, D.C. 20006).

27.   Judith Lanier and Judith Little, "Research on Teacher Education" in Merlin C. Wittrock (Ed.), *Handbook of Research on Teaching* (New York: Macmillan, 1986), p. 547.

28.   "Issue: Should Undergraduate Teacher Education Be Discontinued?" *ASCD Update* (September 1986): 4.

29.   Donald R. Cruickshank, *Reflective Teaching: The Preparation of Students of Teaching* (Reston, Va.: Association of Teacher Educators), p. 3.

30.   George J. Posner, *Field Experience: Methods of Reflective Teaching, Second Edition* (New York: Longman, 1989), p. 34.

31.   Leslie Huling-Austin, "Teacher Induction Programs and Internships," in W. Robert Houston (Ed.), *Handbook of Research on Teacher Education* (New York: Macmillan, 1990), p. 539.

Chapter 4

1.   *Estimates of School Statistics 1989–90* (Washington, D.C.: National Education Association, 1990), p. 14.

2.   Roger E. Goddard, ed., *1984 Teacher Certification Requirements* (Grover Hill, Ohio: Teacher Certification Publications, 1984).

3.   John William Zehring, "How to Get Another Teaching Job and What to Do If You Can't," *Learning* (February 1978): 49.

4. Excerpted from *The 1985 Annual Report of the Commissioner of Education: Getting Ready for 1989* (Tallahassee, Fla.: Department of Education, 1985), p. 15.

5. *Gainesville Sun* (22 December 1985), p. 14G.

6. Claude N. Goldberg, "Parents' Effects on Academic Grouping for Reading: Three Case Studies," *American Education Research Journal* (Fall 1989): 329–352.

7. *What Works: Research About Teaching and Learning* (Washington, D.C.: U.S. Department of Education, 1986), p. 19.

8. Rita A. Weathersby, Patricia R. Allen, and Alan R. Blackmer, Jr. *New Roles for Educators: A Sourcebook of Career Information* (Cambridge, Mass.: Harvard Graduate School of Education Placement Office, 1970), p. 6.

9. Anne Miller, "Those who Teach Also Can Sell, Organize, Compute, Write, Market, Design, Manage. . . ." *Instructor* (May 1983): 42.

10. Richard N. Bolles, *What Color Is Your Parachute? 1991* (Berkeley, Calif.: Ten Speed Press, 1991); Bureau of Labor Statistics, *Occupational Outlook Handbook* (Washington, D.C.: U.S. Department of Labor, published annually); Richard Irish, *Go Hire Yourself an Employer*, 3d, rev. & expanded ed. (New York: Anchor Books, 1987); and Sandy Pollack, *Alternative Careers for Teachers*, rev. ed. (Cambridge, Mass.: Harvard Common Press, 1984).

Chapter 5

1. Aristotle, *Politics* (Book VIII), in *The Basic Works of Aristotle*, ed. Richard McKoen (New York: Random House, 1941), p. 1306.

2. *National Goals for Education* (Washington, D.C.: U.S. Department of Education, July 1990), p. 5.

3. Ibid.

4. Ernest L. Boyer, *High School: A Report on Secondary Education in America* (New York: Harper & Row, 1983), pp. 209–210.

5. Charles Silberman, *Crisis in the Classroom: The Remaking of American Education* (New York: Random House, 1970), p. 53.

6. Harold L. Hodgkinson, "The Changing Face of Tomorrow's Student," *Change* (May/June 1985): 38.

7. The Commission on Minority Participation in Education and American Life, *One-Third of a Nation* (Washington, D.C.: American Council on Education and Education Commission of the States, 1988).

8. *A Survey of Public Education in the Nation's Urban School Districts, 1983* (Washington, D.C.: National School Boards Association).

9. Forrest W. Parkay and Henry T. Fillmer, "Improving Teachers' Attitudes Toward Minority-Group Students: An Experiential Approach to Multicultural Inservice," *New Horizons* (November 1984): 177.

10. James A. Banks, *Teaching Strategies for Ethnic Studies*, 5th ed. (Boston: Allyn and Bacon, 1991), p. 5.

11. J. P. Spradley and D. W. McCurdy, *Anthropology: The Cultural Perspective* (New York: John Wiley and Sons, 1975), p. 5.

12. W. H. Goodenough, *Cultural Anthropology and Linguistics*, Georgetown University Monograph Series on Language and Linguistics, no. 9 (1957), p. 167.

13. R. A. LeVine, "Properties of Culture: An Ethnographic View," in *Culture Theory: Essays on Mind; Self and Emotion*, R. A. Sweder and R. A. LeVine, eds. (Cambridge, England: Cambridge University Press, 1986).

14. H. C. Triandis, "Culture Training, Cognitive Complexity and Interpersonal Attitudes," in *Cross-Cultural Perspectives on Learning*, R. W. Brislin, Stephen Bachner, and Walter J. Lonner, eds. (New York: John Wiley and Sons, 1975).

15. James A. Banks, *Teaching Strategies for Ethnic Studies*, 5th ed. (Boston: Allyn and Bacon, 1991).

16. Ibid., p. 8.

17. Ibid., p. 12.

18. Christine I. Bennett, *Comprehensive Multicultural Education: Theory and Practice*, 2nd ed. (Boston: Allyn and Bacon, 1990), p. 42.

19. United States Commission on Civil Rights, *Fulfilling the Letter and Spirit of the Law: Desegregation of the Nation's Public Schools* (Washington, D.C.: U.S. Government Printing Office, 1976), p. 2.

20. Thomas R. Hopkins, "American Indians and the English Language Arts," *The Florida FL Reporter: A Language Education Journal* (Spring/Summer 1969): 145–146.

21. Gerald Gipp, "Help for Dana Fast Horse and Friends," *American Education* 15 (August-September 1979): 19.

22. Harold L. Hodgkinson, "What's Ahead for Education?" *Principal* (January 1986): 11.

23. *The American Heritage Dictionary of the English Language*, William Morris, ed. (Boston: American Heritage Publishing Co., Inc. and Houghton Mifflin Co., 1970), p. 680.

24. Gerald Grant, *The World We Created at Hamilton High* (Cambridge, Mass.: Harvard University Press, 1988), pp. 188–189.

25. John I. Goodlad, *A Place Called School: Prospects for the Future* (New York: McGraw-Hill, 1984), p. 227.

26. Jack Frymier, Catherine Cornbleth, Robert Donmoyer, Bruce M. Gansneder, Jan T. Jeter, M. Frances Klein, Marian Schwab, and William M. Alexander, *One Hundred Good Schools* (West Lafayette, Ind.: Kappa Delta Pi, 1984), p. 162.

27. John Godar, *Teachers Talk* (Macomb, Ill.: Glenbridge Publishing, 1990), p. 24.

28. Arthur Powell, Eleanor Farrar, and David K. Cohen, *The Shopping Mall High School: Winners and Losers in the Educational Marketplace* (Boston: Houghton Mifflin, 1985).

29. Jean Anyon, "Social Class and the Hidden Curriculum of Work," in *Curriculum & Instruction: Alternatives in Education*, Henry A. Giroux, Anthony N. Penn, and William F. Pinar, eds. (Berkeley, Calif.: McCutchan, 1981), pp. 317–341.

30. Ibid., pp. 328–329.

31. Ibid., p. 330.

32. Ibid., p. 333.

33. George S. Counts, *Dare the School Build a New Social Order?* (New York: The John Day Co., 1932), p. 12.

34. As reported by Harold Howe II, "The Prospect for Children in the United States," *Phi Delta Kappan* (November 1986): 195.

35. John Godar, *Teachers Talk*, p. 9.

36. G. G. Wehlage and R. A. Rutter, "Dropping Out: How Do Schools Contribute to the Problem?" in G. Natriello (Ed.), *School Dropouts: Patterns and Policies* (New York: Teachers College Press, 1986), pp. 70–88.

37. As reported in *The Gainesville Sun*, 16 September 1986, p. 3A.

38. As reported in *People Weekly*, 28 October 1985, p. 39.

39. David A. Hamburg, "Preparing for Life: The Critical Transition of Adolescence," *1985 Annual Report* (New York: Carnegie Corporation of New York, 1985): 16.

40. "Adolescent Pregnancy: Testing Prevention Strategies," *Carnegie Quarterly* (Summer/Fall 1986): 2.

41. "Preventing Adolescent Suicide," *The Harvard Education Letter* (November 1987): 3.

42. Edwin Farrell, *Hanging In and Dropping Out: Voices of At-Risk High School Students* (New York: Teachers College Press, 1990), p. 49.

43. Ibid., p. 125.

44. Louis A. Fliegler, *Curriculum Planning for the Gifted* (Englewood Cliffs, N.J.: Prentice-Hall, 1961).

45. Sidney P. Marland, ed., *Education of the Gifted and Talented: Report to the Congress of the United States* (Washington, D.C.: U.S. Government Printing Office, 1972), p. 2.

46. Laurence J. Coleman, *Schooling the Gifted* (Menlo Park, Calif.: Addison-Wesley, 1985), p. 5.

47. Forrest W. Parkay, *White Teacher, Black School: The Professional Growth of a Ghetto Teacher* (New York: Praeger, 1983), p. 73.

48. *The Metropolitan Life Survey of the American Teacher 1989, Preparing Schools for the 1990s* (New York: Louis Harris and Associates, 1990), p. 91.

49. See, for example, Gary Davis and Margaret Thomas, *Effective Schools and Effective Teachers* (Boston: Allyn and Bacon, 1989); Sara Lawrence Lightfoot, *The Good High School: Portraits of Character and Culture* (New York: Basic Books, 1983); and Jack Frymier et al., *One Hundred Good Schools* (West Lafayette, Ind.: Kappa Delta Pi, 1984).

Chapter 6

1. H. Warren Button and Eugene F. Provenzo, Jr., *History of Education and Culture in America* (Englewood Cliffs, N.J.: Prentice-Hall, 1983), p. 35.

2. Dan Lortie, *Schoolteacher* (Chicago: University of Chicago Press, 1975).

3. Ibid., p. 11.

4. Sara Lawrence Lightfoot, *Worlds Apart: Relationships Between Families and Schools* (New York: Basic Books, 1978), p. 47.

5. H. Warren Button and Eugene F. Provenzo, Jr., *History of Education and Culture in America* (Englewood Cliffs, N.J.: Prentice-Hall, 1983), p. 17.

6. S. Alexander Rippa, *Education in a Free Society* (New York: Longman, 1984), p. 43.

7. H. Warren Button and Eugene F. Provenzo, Jr., *History of Education and Culture in America*, p. 12.

8. S. Alexander Rippa, *Education in a Free Society*, p. 37.

9. Ibid., pp. 39–40.

10. Ibid., p. 45.

11. "Massachusetts School Law of 1648," reprinted in *Education in the United States*, ed. Sol Cohen (New York: Random House, 1974), pp. 394–395.

12. S. Alexander Rippa, *Education in a Free Society*, p. 45.

13. David Ramsay, *The History of the American Revolution*, vol. II (1789; New York: Russell and Russell, 1968), pp. 323–324.

14. H. Warren Button and Eugene F. Provenzo, Jr., *History of Education and Culture in America*, p. 38.

15. Benjamin Franklin, "Proposals Relating to the Education of Youth in Pennsylvania," in *Educational Views of Benjamin Franklin*, ed. Thomas Woody (New York: McGraw-Hill, 1931), p. 151.

16. Ibid., p. 158.

17. R. Freeman Butts and Lawrence A. Cremin, *A History of Education in American Culture* (New York: Holt, Rinehart and Winston, 1953), p. 260.

18. S. Alexander Rippa, *Education in a Free Society*, p. 68.

19. Ibid., p. 68.

20. H. Warren Button and Eugene F. Provenzo, Jr., *History of Education and Culture in America*, p. 57.

21. Henry Steele Commager, ed., *Noah Webster's American Spelling Book* (New York: Teachers College Press, 1962), pp. 61–63.

22. Henry Steele Commager, "Noah Webster, 1758–1958," *Saturday Review* 41 (18 October 1958): 12.

23. Erwin V. Johanningmeier, *Americans and Their Schools* (Chicago: Rand McNally, 1980), p. 65.

24. Horace Mann, *Annual Reports on Education*, vol. 3 of *The Life and Works of Horace Mann*, ed. Mary Mann (Boston: Horace B. Fuller, 1868), p. 754.

25. S. Alexander Rippa, *Education in a Free Society*, p. 118.

26. Ibid., p. 120.

27. Quoted in Erwin V. Johanningmeier, *Americans and Their Schools*, p. 140.

28. S. Alexander Rippa, *Education in a Free Society*, p. 119.

29. Ibid., p. 121.

30. Ibid., p. 122.

31. Horace Mann, *Twelfth Annual Report*, in *The Republic and the School: Horace Mann on the Education of Free Men*, ed. Lawrence A. Cremin (New York: Teachers College Press, 1957), p. 87.

32. R. Freeman Butts and Lawrence A. Cremin, *A History of Education in American Culture*, p. 408.

33. Merritt M. Thompson, *The History of Education* (New York: Barnes & Noble, 1951), p. 90.

34. H. Warren Button and Eugene F. Provenzo, Jr., *History of Education and Culture in America*, p. 177.

35. Willard Waller, *The Sociology of Teaching* (New York: J. Wiley, 1932), p. 49.

36. Samuel D. Andrews, Robert R. Sherman, and Rodman B. Webb, "Teaching: The Isolated Profession," *Journal of Thought* (Winter 1983): 53.

37. Diane Ravitch, *The Troubled Crusade: American Education, 1945–1980* (New York: Basic Books, 1983), p. 47.

38. Lawrence A. Cremin, *The Transformation of the School: Progressivism in American Education, 1876–1957* (New York: Alfred A. Knopf, 1961), p. 136.

39. Katherine Camp Mayhew and Anna Camp Edwards, *The Dewey School: The University Laboratory School of the University of Chicago, 1896–1903* (New York: D. Appleton-Century, 1936), p. 3.

40. Patricia A. Graham, *Progressive Education: From Arcady to Academe: A History of the Progressive Education Association, 1919–1955* (New York: Teachers College Press, 1967), p. 145.

41. Diane Ravitch, *The Troubled Crusade: American Education, 1945–1980* (New York: Basic Books, 1983), p. 229.

42. H. G. Rickover, *Education and Freedom* (New York: E. P. Dutton, 1959).

43. *Brown v. Board of Education of Topeka et al.*, 347 U.S. 483 (1954).

44. Quoted in Daniel M. Berman, *It Is So Ordered: The Supreme Court Rules on School Segregation* (New York: W. W. Norton, 1966), pp. 139–140.

45. S. Alexander Rippa, *Education in a Free Society*, p. 377.

46. Diane Ravitch, *The Schools We Deserve: Reflections on the Educational Crises of Our Times* (New York: Basic Books, 1985), p. 303.

47. George H. Gallup, "The 11th Annual Gallup Poll of the Public's Attitudes Toward the Public Schools," *Phi Delta Kappan* (September 1975).

48.   U.S. Department of Commerce, Bureau of the Census, *Statistical Abstract of the United States 1982–83*, p. 135.

49.   National Commission on Excellence in Education, *A Nation at Risk: Imperative for Educational Reform* (Washington, D.C.: GPO, 1983).

Chapter 7

1.   Max Black, "A Note on 'Philosophy of Education,' " *Harvard Educational Review* 26 (1956): 154.

2.   John Dewey, *Democracy and Education: An Introduction to the Philosophy of Education* (New York: Macmillan, 1916), p. 383.

3.   Thomas J. Sergiovanni and Robert J. Starratt, *Supervision: Human Perspectives* (New York: McGraw-Hill, 1983), p. 304.

4.   Edward J. Power, *Philosophy of Education: Studies in Philosophies, Schooling, and Educational Policies* (Englewood Cliffs, N.J.: Prentice-Hall, 1982), pp. 15–16.

5.   Peter A. Bertocci, "Unless Educators Be Philosophers, and Philosophers Be Educators . . ." *Harvard Educational Review* 26 (1956): 158.

6.   Van Cleve Morris and Young Pai, *Philosophy and the American School: An Introduction to the Philosophy of Education* (Boston: Houghton Mifflin, 1976), p. 28.

7.   Ibid., pp. 103–104.

8.   Kenneth A. Strike and Jonas F. Soltis, *The Ethics of Teaching* (New York: Teachers College Press, 1985), p. 3.

9.   Harry S. Broudy, "Arts Education: Necessary or Just Nice?" *Phi Delta Kappan* 60 (1979): 347–350.

10.   Forrest W. Parkay, "A General Theory of Aesthetics for the Conduct of Educational Research" (paper presented at the Annual Meeting of the American Educational Research Association, Montreal, 1983), p. 2.

11.   Robert M. Hutchins, *A Conversation on Education* (Santa Barbara, Calif.: The Fund for the Republic, 1963).

12.   William C. Bagley, *Education and Emergent Man* (New York: Ronald Press, 1934).

13.   Jean-Paul Sartre, "Existentialism," in *Readings in the Philosophy of Education*, ed. John Martin Rich (Belmont, Calif.: Wadsworth, 1972), p. 98.

14.   Van Cleve Morris and Young Pai, *Philosophy and the American School*, pp. 259–260.

15.   Quoted in Van Cleve Morris and Young Pai, *Philosophy and the American School*, p. 260.

16.   Jean-Paul Sartre, "Existentialism," p. 101.

17.   Edward J. Power, *Philosophy of Education*, p. 168.

18.   John B. Watson, *Behaviorism*, 2d ed. (New York: People's Institute, 1925), p. 82.

19.   B. F. Skinner, "Utopia through the Control of Human Behavior," in *Readings in the Philosophy of Education*, p. 74.

20.   Theodore Brameld, "Imperatives for a Reconstructed Philosophy of Education," *School and Society* 87 (1959): 19.

21.   Theodore Brameld, *Toward a Reconstructed Philosophy of Education* (New York: Holt, Rinehart and Winston, 1956).

Chapter 8

1.   Michael Y. Nunnery and Ralph B. Kimbrough, *Politics, Power, Polls, and School Elections* (Berkeley, Calif.: McCutchan Publishing, 1971), p. 1.

2.   Frederick M. Wirt and Michael W. Kirst, *Schools in Conflict: The Politics of Education* (Berkeley, Calif.: McCutchan Publishing, 1982), p. 20.

3.   U.S. Department of Education, National Center for Education Statistics, *Digest of Education Statistics, 1989* (Washington, D.C.: U.S. Government Printing Office, 1989).

4.   Jesse L. Freeman, Kenneth E. Underwood, and Jim C. Fortune, "What Boards Value: Exclusive School Board Survey," *The American School Board Journal* (January 1991): 32–36, 39.

5.   Harmon Zeigler, Harvey J. Tucker, and L. A. Wilson, II, "Communication and Decision Making in American Public Education: A Longitudinal and Comparative Study," in *The Politics of Education: The Seventy-sixth Yearbook of the National Society for the Study of Education*, ed. Jay D. Scribner (Chicago: University of Chicago Press, 1977), pp. 218–254.

6.   Frederick M. Wirt and Michael W. Kirst, *Schools in Conflict: The Politics of Education*, pp. 142–143.

7.   Ibid., p. 145.

8.   Larry Cuban, "Conflict and Leadership in the Superintendency," *Phi Delta Kappan* (September 1985): 28–30.

9.   Ralph B. Kimbrough and Michael Y. Nunnery, *Educational Administration*, 2d ed. (New York: Macmillan, 1983).

10.   Frederick M. Wirt and Michael W. Kirst, *Schools in Conflict: The Politics of Education*, p. 144.

11.   Larry Cuban, "Conflict and Leadership in the Superintendency," p. 28.

12.   Frederick M. Wirt and Michael W. Kirst, *Schools in Conflict: The Politics of Education*, p. 144.

13.   Ann P. Kahn, "Parent Teacher Association, National Congress of Parents and Teachers," in Richard A. Gorton, Gail T. Schneider, and James C. Fisher (eds.), *Encyclopedia of School Administration & Supervision.* (Phoenix, Ariz.: Oryx Press, 1988), p. 189.

14.   For a comprehensive set of articles on school-based management/shared decision making, see the special theme issue of *Education and Urban Society*, August 1989.

15.   Lynn Olson, "The Sky's the Limit: Dade Venture Self-Governance," *Education Week* (2 December 1987): 18.

16.   "Leading School-Based Reform: The Voices of Principals and Teachers," *Doubt & Certainties: Newsletter of the NEA Mastery In Learning Project* (June 1990): 1.

17.   Lynn Olson, "The Sky's the Limit," p. 18.

18.   Ibid.

19.   "Miami Schools to Be Pattern for New York," *The Gainesville Sun* (2 January 1990): 1B.

20.   Forrest W. Parkay and Sandy Damico, "Barriers to School Improvement: The Anatomy of a Failed Effort at Shared-Decision Making." Paper presented at the Annual Meeting of the American Educational Research Association, April 4, 1991, Chicago, Ill.

21.   Michael W. Kirst, "The Changing Balance in State and Local Power to Control Education," *Phi Delta Kappan* (November 1984): 189–191.

22.   *Educational Governance in the States: A Status Report on State Boards of Education, Chief State School Officers, and State Education Agencies* (Washington, D.C.: Council of Chief State School Officers, Department of Education, February 1983).

23.   *Educational Governance in the States*, pp. 23–25.

24.   Ralph B. Kimbrough and Michael Y. Nunnery, *Educational Administration*, p. 138.

25.   Stephen J. Knezevich, *Administration of Public Education: A Sourcebook for the Leadership and Management of Educational Institutions*, 4th ed. (New York: Harper and Row, 1984), p. 198.

26.   *Educational Governance in the States*, p. 92.

27.   William A. Firestone, Gretchen B. Rossman, and Bruce L.

Wilson, *The Study of Regional Educational Service Agencies* (Philadelphia: Research for Better Schools, 1983).
28. Carolyn Moran and Larry Hutchins, "Intermediate Service Agencies and School Improvement," in *Dissemination and School Improvement in Education Organizations*, ed. S. McKibbin and M. Malkas (Berkeley, Calif.: Far West Laboratory for Educational Research and Development, 1982), pp. 57–80.
29. Stephen J. Knezevich, *Administration of Public Education*, p. 190.
30. George Bush, "The Bush Strategy for Excellence in Education," *Phi Delta Kappan* (October 1988): 112.
31. Frederick M. Wirt and Michael W. Kirst, *Schools in Conflict: The Politics of Education*, pp. 278–279.
32. Terrel H. Bell, "Education Policy Development in the Reagan Administration," *Phi Delta Kappan* (March 1986): 492.
33. Ibid., pp. 279–280.
34. Allan Odden, "Financing of Schools," in Richard A. Gorton, Gail T. Schneider, and James C. Fisher (eds.), *Encyclopedia of School Administration & Supervision*. (Phoenix, Ariz.: Oryx Press, 1988), p. 121.

Chapter 9
1. Judith Lanier and Philip Cusick, "An Oath for Professional Educators," *Phi Delta Kappan* (June 1985): 712.
2. Forrest W. Parkay, review of Kenneth A. Strike and Jonas F. Soltis, *The Ethics of Teaching*. (New York, Teachers College Press, 1985), *The Educational Forum* (Fall 1985): 105.
3. Delbert Clear, "Rights of Teachers," in *Educators, Children and the Law*, ed. Lynn Sametz and Caven S. Mcloughlin (Springfield, Ill.: Charles C. Thomas, 1985), p. 60.
4. *Morrison v. State Board of Education*, 461 P.2d 375 (1969).
5. *Sarac v. State Board of Education*, 1 Cal. ed 214–34, 82 Cal. Rptr. 175–91, 461 P.2d 375–91 (1969).
6. *Educational Governance in the States: A Status Report on State Boards of Education, Chief State School Officers, and State Education Agencies* (Washington, D.C.: Council of Chief State School Officers, Department of Education, February 1983), pp. 116–118.
7. *Bay v. State Board of Education*, 378 P.2d 558 (1963).
8. M. Chester Nolte, *How to Survive in Teaching: The Legal Dimension* (Chicago: Teach Em, 1978), p. 32; Stan Ratliff and Carole Veir, *The Nightmare of Being Sued as a Teacher: Handbook on the Legal Aspects of Education for Teachers and Student Teachers* (Westminster, Colo.: SEJI Publications, 1984), p. 24; Leroy J. Peterson, Richard A. Rossmiller, and Martin M. Volz, *The Law and Public School Operation*, 2d ed. (New York: Harper and Row, 1978), pp. 132–135.
9. *Pease v. Millcreek Township School District*, 195 A.2d 104 (1963).
10. *Parrish v. Moss*, 106 N.Y.S.2d 577 (1951).
11. *Burton v. Cascade School Dist. Union High School* No. 5, 512 F.2d 850 (9th Cir. 1975).
12. Leroy J. Peterson, Richard A. Rossmiller, and Marlin M. Volz, *The Law and Public School Operation*, p. 470.
13. Ibid.
14. Joseph Beckham and Perry A. Zirkel, *Legal Issues in Public School Employment* (Bloomington, Ind.: Phi Delta Kappa, 1983), p. 85.
15. *Keefe v. Geanakos*, 418 F.2d 359 (1st Cir.) (1970).
16. *Mailloux v. Kiley*, 323 F.Supp. 1387 (1971), 1393.
17. Patricia M. Lines, "Home Instruction," *Issuegram No. 49*, Education Commission of the States, August 1984.
18. *People v. DeJonge*, 449 N.W. 2d 899 (Mich. App. 1989).

19. *Station v. Travelers Insurance Co.*, 292 So. 2d 289 (1974).
20. William D. Valente, *Law in the Schools*, 2d ed. (Columbus, Ohio: Merrill Publishing, 1987), p. 426.
21. Leroy J. Peterson, Richard A. Rossmiller, and Marlin M. Volz, *The Law and Public School Operation*, p. 281.
22. *Gaincott v. Davis*, 275 N.W. 229 (1937).
23. *West v. Board of Education of City of New York*, 187 N.Y.S. 2d 88 (1959).
24. *Ohman v. Board of Education*, 93 N.E. 2nd 927 (1950); *Simonetti v. School District of Philadelphia*, 454 A. 2d 1038 (1983).
25. Leroy J. Peterson, Richard A. Rossmiller, and Martin M. Volz, *The Law and Public School Operation*, p. 252.
26. *Petwer W. v. San Francisco Unified School District*, 131 Cal. Rptr. 854 (1976).
27. Robert C. O'Reilly and Edward T. Green, *School Law for the Practitioner* (Westport, Conn.: Greenwood Press, 1983), p. 57.
28. *Marcus v. Rowley*, 695 F.2d 1171, 1174 (9th Cir. 1983).
29. *Tinker v. Des Moines Independent Community School District*, 393 U.S. 503 (1969).
30. William D. Valente, *Law in the Schools*, p. 317.
31. *Zucker v. Panitz*, 299 F.Supp. 102 (1969).
32. *Shanley v. Northeast Independent School District*, 462 F.2d 960 (1972).
33. *Scoville v. Board of Education of Joliet Township High School District 204*, 452 F.2d 54 (1971); *Sullivan v. Houston Independent School District*, 305 F. Supp. 1328 (1969).
34. *Hazelwood School District v. Kuhlmeier*, 56 U.S.L.W. 4079, 4082 (1988).
35. Ibid.
36. *Burch v. Barker*, 651 F. Supp. 1149 (W.D. Wash. 1987) and *Burch v. Barker*, 861 F. 2d 1149 (9th Cir. 1988).
37. *Karr v. Schmidt*, 401 U.S. 1201, 91 S.Ct. 592, 27 L. Ed.2d 797 (1972).
38. Leroy J. Peterson, Richard A. Rossmiller, and Marlin M. Volz, *The Law and Public School Operation*, p. 360.
39. *Goss v. Lopez*, 419 U.S. 565 (1975).
40. *Wood v. Strickland* 420 U.S. 308 (1975).
41. Robert C. O'Reilly and Edward T. Green, *School Law for the Practitioner*, pp. 148–150.
42. Forrest W. Parkay and Colleen Conoley, "Characteristics of Educators Who Advocate Corporal Punishment: A Brief Report," *Journal of Humanistic Education and Development* (September 1982): 33–34.
43. Louis Fischer and Gail Paulus Sorenson, *School Law for Counselors, Psychologists, and Social Workers* (New York: Longman, 1985), p. 170.
44. Robert C. O'Reilly and Edward T. Green, *School Law for the Practitioner*, p. 144.
45. *Ingraham v. Wright*, 430 U.S. 651 (1977).
46. Robert C. O'Reilly and Edward T. Green, *School Law for the Practitioner*, pp. 144–145.
47. *Doe v. Renfrow*, 635 F.2d 582 (1980), cert. denied, 101 U.S. 3015 (1981).
48. *Bahr v. Jenkins*, 539 F.Supp. 483 (1982).
49. *Anable v. Ford*, 663 F. Supp. 149 (Ark. 1987).
50. *Schaill v. Tippecanoe School Corporation*, 679 F. Supp. 833 (Ind. 1988).
51. See, for example, *Patchogue-Medford Congress of Teachers v. Board of Education of Patchogue-Medford Union Free School District*, 119 A.D.2d 35, 505 N.Y.S.2d 88 (1986).

52. Louis Fischer and Gail Paulus Sorenson, *School Law for Counselors, Psychologists, and Social Workers,* p. 82.

53. Ibid., pp. 82–83.

54. Eugenia H. Berger and G. R. Berger, "Parents and Law: Rights and Responsibilities," in *Educators, Children and the Law,* ed. Lynn Sametz and Caven S. Mcloughlin (Springfield, Ill.: Charles C. Thomas, 1985), pp. 38–58; Louis Fischer and Gail Paulus Sorenson, *School Law for Counselors, Psychologists, and Social Workers.*

55. *Alvin Independent School District* v. *Cooper,* 404 S.W.2d 76 (1966).

56. *Holt* v. *Shelton,* 341 F.Supp. 821 (1972); *Davis* v. *Meek,* 344 F.Supp. 298 (1972); *Moran* v. *School District No. 7,* 350 F.Supp. 1180 (1972); *Romans* v. *Crenshaw,* 354 F.Supp. 868 (1972).

57. Thomas J. Flygare, "Are Victims of AIDS 'Handicapped' Under Federal Law?" *Phi Delta Kappan* (February 1986): 466–467.

58. Perry A. Zirkel, "AIDS: Students in Glass Houses?" *Phi Delta Kappan* (April 1989): 647.

59. Fred Swalls, *The Law on Student Teaching in the United States* (Danville, Ill.: Interstate Printers and Publishers, 1976).

Chapter 10

1. James A. Banks, *Multiethnic Education: Theory and Practice,* 2d ed. (Boston: Allyn and Bacon, 1988), p. 78.

2. Rudolf Dreikurs, Bernice Bronia Grunwald, and Floy C. Pepper, *Maintaining Sanity in the Classroom: Classroom Management Techniques,* 2d ed. (New York: Harper and Row, 1982), p. 58.

3. The sibling position profiles discussed in this section are based on Dreikurs's descriptions in *Maintaining Sanity in the Classroom,* pp. 58–62.

4. Abraham Maslow, "A Theory of Human Motivation," *Psychological Review* 50/4 (1943): 394.

5. Philip J. Schwartz, Isadora Hare, Peter J. Pecora, Joan H. Slotnick, "Children at Risk: A Social Work Perspective," paper presented at the 2nd Annual National Leadership Symposium of the National Consortium on Interprofessional Education and Practice, Airlie, Va. June 1–3, 1988, p. 1.

6. Marian Wright Edelman, "Children at Risk," *Proceedings of the Academy of Political Science,* 27 (2) (1989), pp. 20–30. Quoted in Larry K. Brendtro, Martin Brokenieg, and Steve Van Bockern, *Reclaiming Youth at Risk: Our Hopes for the Future* (Bloomington, Ind.: National Education Service, 1990), p. 26.

7. From "All Our Children with Bill Moyers," PBS Television, April 10, 1991.

8. William Ayers, *The Good Preschool Teacher: Six Teachers Reflect on Their Lives* (New York: Teachers College Press, 1989), p. 103.

9. David Wechsler, *The Measurement and Appraisal of Adult Intelligence,* 4th ed. (Baltimore: Williams and Wilkins, 1958), p. 7.

10. George A. Miller, "The Test," *Science* (November 1984): 55.

11. Ibid., 56.

12. Paul S. Kaplan, *A Child's Odyssey: Child and Adolescent Development* (St. Paul, Minn.: West, 1986), p. 434.

13. Ibid.

14. For instance, see a description of the Kaufman Assessment Battery for Children in Elliot A. Weiner and Barbara J. Stewart, *Assessing Individuals: Psychological and Educational Tests and Measurements* (Boston: Little, Brown, 1984) and the work of Reuven Feuerstein described by Paul Chance in "The Remedial Thinker," *Psychology Today* (October 1981): 62–65.

15. Howard Gardner, *Frames of Mind: The Theory of Multiple Intelligences* (New York: Basic Books, 1983), p. 18.

16. Jean Piaget, *To Understand Is to Invent* (New York: Penguin Books, 1980), p. 93.

17. Howard Gardner, *Frames of Mind,* p. 8.

18. Quoted in Christine I. Bennett, *Comprehensive Multicultural Education: Theory and Practice,* 2d ed. (Boston: Allyn and Bacon, 1990), p. 140.

19. David E. Hunt, "Learning Style and Student Needs: An Introduction to Conceptual Level," in *Student Learning Styles: Diagnosing and Prescribing Programs* (Reston, Va.: National Association of Secondary School Principals, 1979).

20. Rita Dunn and Kenneth Dunn, "Learning Styles/Teaching Styles: Should They . . . Can They . . . Be Matched?" *Educational Leadership* (January 1979), pp. 238–244.

21. Bernice McCarthy, *The 4MAT System: Teaching to Learning Styles with Right/Left Mode Techniques* (Barrington, Ill.: EXCEL, 1980).

22. Christine I. Bennett, *Comprehensive Multicultural Education,* p. 158.

23. Ibid., p. 159.

24. Ibid., p. 144.

25. Daniel P. Hallahan and James M. Kauffman, *Exceptional Children: Introduction to Special Education,* 5th ed. (Englewood Cliffs, N.J.: Prentice-Hall, 1991), p. 6.

26. Joseph Renzulli and Linda H. Smith, "Two Approaches to Identification of Gifted Students," *Exceptional Children,* 43/8 (May 1977): 512–518.

27. Christine I. Bennett, *Comprehensive Multicultural Education,* p. 58.

28. Daniel P. Hallahan and James M. Kauffman, *Exceptional Children,* p. 6.

29. H. J. Grossman, ed., *Classification in Mental Retardation* (Washington, D.C.: American Association on Mental Deficiency, 1983), p. 11.

30. Erik H. Erikson, *Childhood and Society* (New York: W. W. Norton, 1963).

31. See Kaoru Yamamoto, "Children's Ratings of the Stressfulness of Experiences," *Developmental Psychology* 15/5 (1979): 581–582; Kaoru Yamamoto and James A. Phillips, "Filipinio Children's Ratings of the Stressfulness of Experiences," *Journal of Early Adolescence* 1/4 (1981): 397–406; and Kaoru Yamamoto and O. L. Davis, "Views of Japanese and American Children Concerning Stressful Experiences," *The Journal of Social Psychology* 116 (1982): 163–171.

32. Joshua Meyrowitz, *No Sense of Place: The Impact of Electronic Media on Social Behavior* (New York: Oxford University Press, 1985).

33. Robert C. Kolodny, Nancy J. Kolodny, Thomas E. Bratter, and Cheryl Deep, *How to Survive Your Adolescent's Adolescence* (Boston: Little, Brown, 1984), p. 16.

34. David A. Hamburg, "Reducing the Casualties of Early Life: A Preventive Orientation," *1985 Annual Report* (New York: Carnegie Corporation of New York, 1985), p. 13.

35. David Elkind, *All Grown Up and No Place to Go: Teenagers in Crisis* (Reading, Mass.: Addison-Wesley, 1984).

36. Eliot Wigginton, *Sometimes a Shining Moment: The Foxfire Experience* (Garden City, N.Y.: Anchor Press/Doubleday, 1985), p. 236.

37. Ibid.

38. Kaoru Yamamoto, "To See Life Grow: The Meaning of Mentorship," *Theory Into Practice* (Summer 1988): 183–189.

39. See the books of Rudolf Dreikurs, such as *Coping with Children's*

Misbehavior (New York: Hawthorn Books, 1972) and *Discipline Without Tears* (New York: Hawthorn Books, 1972).

40. Rudolf Dreikurs, *Psychology in the Classroom* (New York: Harper and Row, 1988), p. 66.

41. David A. Hamburg, "Reducing the Casualties of Early Life: A Preventive Orientation," *1985 Annual Report* (New York: Carnegie Corporation of New York, 1985), p. 13.

42. Ibid.

43. Ibid.

44. Ibid., p. 31.

45. "Texans' War on Drugs and You: Models for Drug and Abuse Prevention" (Austin, Tex.: Texans' War on Drugs, 1985), p. 29.

46. David Elkind, *All Grown Up and No Place to Go.*

47. David A. Hamburg, "Preparing for Life: The Critical Transition of Adolescence," *1986 Annual Report* (New York: Carnegie Corporation of New York, 1986), p. 6.

48. Kathleen Stassen Berger, *The Developing Person* (New York: Worth Publishers, 1980), p. 496.

49. Marian Wright Edelman, "Barriers to Excellence: Children at Risk" (Invited Lecture, Annual Meeting of the American Educational Research Association, Washington, D.C., 1987).

50. *Carnegie Quarterly* (Summer/Fall 1986): 5.

51. David A. Hamburg, *1986 Annual Report*, p. 5.

52. Ibid., p. 6.

53. Margaret Dunn, director of the Texas conference, "At the Crossroad: Planning for At-Risk Students," Southwest Texas State University, San Marcos, Tex., March 4–5, 1988.

54. "Drawing in Dropouts," *The Harvard Education Letter* (January 1986): 5.

55. Harold Howe II and Marian Wright Edelman, *Barriers to Excellence: Our Children at Risk* (Boston, Mass.: The National Coalition of Advocates for Students, 1985), p. v.

56. Peter Giovacchini, *The Urge to Die* (New York: Penguin Books, 1981), pp. 9–10.

57. Ibid., pp. 165–169.

Chapter 11

1. Edmund T. Emmer, Carolyn M. Evertson, Julie P. Sanford, Barbara S. Clements, and Murray E. Worsham, *Classroom Management for Secondary Teachers* (Englewood Cliffs, N.J.: Prentice-Hall, 1984), p. xi.

2. M. Wagenschein, "Reality Shock: A Study of Beginning Elementary School Teachers" (Master's thesis, University of Chicago, 1950).

3. J. Gabriel, *An Analysis of the Emotional Problems of Teachers in the Classroom* (London: Angus and Robertson, 1957).

4. Estelle Fuchs, *Teachers Talk: Views from Inside City Schools* (Garden City, N.Y.: Anchor, Doubleday, 1969).

5. Anita E. Woolfolk and Charles M. Galloway, "Nonverbal Communication and the Study of Teaching," *Theory Into Practice* 24/1 (1985): 80.

6. Ibid., pp. 80–81.

7. R. Adams and B. Biddle, *Realities of Teaching: Explorations with Video Tape* (New York: Holt, Rinehart and Winston, 1970).

8. David W. Johnson and Roger T. Johnson, *Learning Together and Alone: Cooperation, Competition, and Individualization* (Englewood Cliffs, N.J.: Prentice-Hall, 1975), p. 26.

9. William J. Seiler, L. David Schuelke, and Barbara Lieb-Brilhart, *Communication for the Contemporary Classroom* (New York: Holt, Rinehart and Winston, 1984), p. 18.

10. William Ayers, *The Good Preschool Teacher: Six Teachers Reflect on Their Lives* (New York: Teachers College Press, 1989), p. 98.

11. David W. Johnson and Roger T. Johnson, *Learning Together and Alone.*

12. Richard A. Schmuck and Patricia A. Schmuck, *Group Processes in the Classroom* (Dubuque, Iowa: William C. Brown, 1971), p. 18.

13. See, for example, Robert Slavin's review of research: *Ability Grouping and Student Achievement in Elementary Schools: A Best-Evidence Analysis*, unpublished manuscript (Baltimore: Center for Effective Elementary and Middle Schools, The Johns Hopkins University, 1986) and S. Rowin and A. Miracle, "Systems of Ability Grouping and the Stratification of Achievement in Elementary Schools," *Sociology of Education* 56 (1983): 133–144.

14. Rhoda Kanevsky and Cecelia Traugh, "Classroom Life: Some Interpretations," in Cecelia Traugh, Alice Seletsky, Rhoda Kanevsky, Karen Woolf, Anne Martin, and Lynne Strieb, *Speaking Out: Teachers on Teaching* (Grand Forks, N.D.: University of North Dakota, 1986), p. 6.

15. Walter Doyle, "Classroom Organization and Management," in *Handbook for Research on Teaching,* 3rd ed., ed. Merlin C. Wittrock (New York: Macmillan, 1986), pp. 398–402.

16. Thomas L. Good and Jere E. Brophy, *Looking in Classrooms,* 4th ed. (New York: Harper and Row, 1987), p. 34.

17. C. Fisher, N. Filby, R. Marliave, L. Cahen, M. Dishaw, J. Moore, and D. Berliner, *Teaching Behaviors, Academic Learning Time, and Student Achievement,* Final report of Phase III-B Beginning Teacher Evaluation Study (San Francisco: Far West Laboratory for Educational Research and Development, 1978).

18. Ibid.

19. For more information write the Johns Hopkins Student Team Learning Project, Center for Social Organization of Schools, Johns Hopkins University, 3505 N. Charles St., Baltimore, MD 21238.

20. Craig Pearson, "Cooperative Learning: An Alternative to Cheating and Failure," *Learning* (March 1979): 36.

21. Richard A. Schmuck and Patricia A. Schmuck, *Group Processes in the Classroom,* p. 120.

22. For information on using a sociogram, see Alfred H. Gorman, *Teachers and Learners: The Interactive Process of Education,* 2d ed. (Boston: Allyn and Bacon, 1974), pp. 166–171.

23. Richard A. Schmuck and Patricia A. Schmuck, *Group Processes in the Classroom,* p. 122.

24. Ibid., p. 29.

25. Jere Brophy and Thomas Good, *Teacher-Student Relationships* (New York: Holt, Rinehart and Winston, 1974), p. 244.

26. K. Benne and P. Sheats, "Functional Roles of Group Members," *Journal of Social Issues* 4 (1948): 41–49.

27. R. Rosenthal, *On the Social Psychology of the Self-Fulfilling Prophecy: Further Evidence for Pygmalion Effects and Their Mediating Mechanisms* (New York: MSS Modular Publications, 1974).

28. Jere Brophy and Thomas L. Good, "Teacher Behavior and Student Achievement," in Merlin C. Wittrock (ed.), *Handbook of Research on Teaching,* 3d ed. (New York: Macmillan, 1986), pp. 350–351.

29. Ibid., p. 351.

30. Ibid.

31. Louis M. Smith and William Geoffrey, *The Complexities of an*

Urban Classroom (New York: Holt, Rinehart and Winston, 1968), pp. 54–55.

32. John Holt, *How Children Fail* (New York: Dell Publishing, 1964).

33. Ibid., pp. 33–34.

34. Ibid., p. 37.

35. Thomas L. Good and Jere E. Brophy, *Looking in Classrooms*, p. 226.

36. Jacob Kounin, *Discipline and Group Management in Classrooms* (New York: Holt, Rinehart and Winston, 1970).

37. Robert Carkhuff, *A Design for Discipline: The LEAST Approach* (Washington, D.C.: National Education Association, 1983).

38. Rudolf Dreikurs, Bernice Bronia Grunwald, and Floy C. Pepper, *Maintaining Sanity in the Classroom: Classroom Management Techniques,* 2d ed. (New York: Harper and Row, 1982), p. 11.

39. B. Othanel Smith, *Teachers for the Real World* (Washington, D.C.: American Association of Colleges for Teacher Education, 1969), p. 71.

40. Robert V. Bullough, Jr., *First-Year Teacher: A Case Study* (New York: Teachers College Press, 1989), p. 23.

41. Ibid., p. 25.

42. Christopher M. Clark and Penelope L. Peterson, "Teachers' Thought Processes," in *Handbook of Research on Teaching,* ed. Merlin C. Wittrock (New York: Macmillan, 1986), pp. 255–296.

43. Ibid., p. 261.

44. Ibid., p. 264.

45. *Harvard Education Letter,* vol. II. (no. 4): 7.

46. Christopher M. Clark and Penelope L. Peterson, "Teachers' Thought Processes," p. 268.

47. *Harvard Education Letter,* vol. II. (no. 4): 7.

48. Bruce Joyce and Marsha Weil, *Models of Teaching,* 3d ed. (Englewood Cliffs, N.J.: Prentice-Hall, 1986), p. 2.

49. Donald Cruickshank, "Profile of an Effective Teacher," *Educational Horizons* (Winter 1986): 90–92.

50. Barak Rosenshine and Robert Stevens, "Teaching Functions," in *Handbook on Research of Teaching* (New York: Macmillan, 1986), p. 377.

51. M. Galton, and B. Simon, *Progress and Performance in the Primary Classroom* (London: Routledge & Kegan Paul, 1980), p. 199.

52. Lorna Catford, "Portrait of a Ceramics Class: Control and Freedom in a Delicate Balance," in Elliot W. Eisner, *The Educational Imagination: On the Design and Evaluation of School Programs,* 2d ed. (New York: Macmillan, 1985), pp. 304–306. Reprinted with permission of Macmillan Publishing Company. Copyright © 1985 by Elliott W. Eisner.

53. Reprinted by permission of the publisher from Ayer, William, *The Good Preschool Teacher.* (New York: Teachers College Press, © 1989 by Teachers College, Columbia University. All rights reserved.), pp. 107, 122–123.

Chapter 12

1. Elliot W. Eisner, *The Educational Imagination: On the Design and Evaluation of School Programs,* 2d ed. (New York: Macmillan, 1985), p. 87.

2. Ibid., p. 107.

3. Ibid., p. 103.

4. "Arts and Humanities Education Undergirds Japanese Success," *ASCD Curriculum Update* (Alexandria, Va.: Association for Supervision and Curriculum Development, March 1984): 6.

5. John I. Goodlad, *A Place Called School,* p. 225.

6. Duane F. Alvin and David L. Morgan, "Extracurricular Activities: Review and Discussion of the Research on Educational Practices" (State of Georgia Department of Education, 1979).

7. "The Mood of American Youth," (Reston, Va.: National Association of Secondary School Principals, 1984).

8. John I. Goodlad, "What Some Schools and Classrooms Teach," *Educational Leadership* (April 1983): 14–15.

9. Ralph W. Tyler, *Basic Principles of Curriculum and Instruction* (Chicago: University of Chicago Press, 1949), p. 1.

10. Daniel T. Scheuerer and Forrest W. Parkay, "The New Christian Right and the Public School Curriculum: A Florida Report," paper presented at the Annual Meeting of the American Educational Research Association, Chicago, Ill., April 3, 1991.

11. Carol B. Daniels, "Quality of Educational Materials: A Marketing Perspective," in *Quest for Quality: Improving Basic Skills Instruction in the 1980s,* ed. Forrest W. Parkay, Sharon O'Bryan, and Michael Hennessy (Lanham, Md.: University Press of America, 1984), p. 100.

12. Bruno Bettelheim and Karen Zelan, *On Learning to Read: The Child's Fascination with Meaning* (New York: Vintage Books, 1981), p. 262.

13. Carol B. Daniels, "Quality of Educational Materials," p. 101.

14. J. Minor Gwynn and John Chase, Jr., eds., *Curriculum Principles and Social Trends* (New York: Macmillan, 1969), pp. 1–29.

15. *Report of the Committee of Ten on Secondary School Studies With the Reports of the Conferences Arranged by the Committee* (National Education Association, 1894).

16. *Changing Schools,* nos. 001, 008 (1972, 1973). (Newsletter published by the Educational Alternatives Project of Indiana University.)

17. May Anne Raywid, "The First Decade of Public School Alternatives," *Phi Delta Kappan* 62 (April 1981): 551–554.

18. Marietta Johnson, "The Educational Principles of the School of Organic Education, Fairhope, Alabama," in *The Twenty-Sixth Yearbook of the National Society for the Study of Education: The Foundations and Technique of Curriculum-Construction,* ed. Guy Montrose Whipple (Bloomington, Ill.: Public School Publishing Company, 1926), pp. 350–351.

19. Wilford M. Aiken, *The Story of the Eight-Year Study* (New York: Harper and Row, 1942), p. 23.

20. Hyman G. Rickover, *Education and Freedom* (New York: E. P. Dutton, 1959), p. 188.

21. Jerome S. Bruner, *The Process of Education* (New York: Random House, 1960), p. 33.

22. Hyman G. Rickover, "Educating for Excellence," *Houston Chronicle,* 3 February 1983.

23. William J. Bennett, *James Madison High School: A Curriculum for American Students* (Washington, D.C.: United States Department of Education, 1987).

24. Forrest W. Parkay and Sharon O'Bryan, "Focus for Basic Skills Instruction in the 1980s," in *Quest for Quality,* pp. 3–4.

25. Stephen N. Tchudi, "Recent Research and New Directions in the Teaching of Writing," in *Quest for Quality: Improving Basic Skills Instruction in the 1980s,* ed. Forrest W. Parkay, Sharon O'Bryan, and Michael Hennessy (Lanham, Md.: University Press of America, 1984), pp. 21–22.

26. National Science Foundation, *Science and Engineering Education for the 1980s and Beyond* (Washington, D.C.: U.S. Government Printing Office, October 1980).

27. College Board, *Academic Preparation for College: What Students Need to Know and Be Able to Do* (New York: College Board, 1983).

28. Robert E. Yager, "Toward New Meaning for School Science," *Educational Leadership* (December 1983/January 1984): 18.

29. F. James Rutherford and Andrew Ahlgren, *Science for All Americans* (New York: Oxford University Press, 1990).

30. Charles Beard, *The Nature of the Social Sciences* (New York: Charles Scribner's Sons, 1938), p. 179.

31. National Council for the Social Studies, "Revisions of the NCSS Social Studies Guidelines," *Social Education* (April 1979): 262.

32. The President's Commission on Foreign Language and International Studies, *Strength Through Wisdom* (Washington, D.C.: U.S. Government Printing Office, November 1979), pp. 5–7.

33. William D. Sims and Sandra B. Hammond, *Award Winning Foreign Language Programs: Prescriptions for Success* (Skokie, Ill.: National Textbook Co., 1981), pp. 1–2.

34. Kathryn Bloom, "Defining the Task," in *An Arts in Education Source Book*, ed. Charles Fowler (New York: American Council for the Arts, 1980), p. 5.

35. College Board, *Academic Preparation for College: What Students Need to Know and Be Able to Do* (New York: College Board, 1983).

36. Ernest L. Boyer, *High School: A Report on Secondary Education in America* (New York: Harper and Row, 1983), p. 98.

37. Ron Brandt, "On Discipline-Based Art Education: A Conversation with Elliot Eisner," *Educational Leadership* (December 1987/January 1988): 6–9. (This issue contains several articles on new approaches to education in the arts.)

38. Leilani Lattin Duke, "The Getty Center for Education in the Arts: A Progress Report," *Phi Delta Kappan* (February 1988): 445.

Chapter 13

1. Amitai Etzioni, *The Semi-Professions and Their Organization: Teachers, Nurses, Social Workers* (New York: Free Press, 1969).

2. Robert B. Howsam et al., *Educating a Profession* (Washington, D.C.: American Association of Colleges for Teacher Education, 1976).

3. Arthur G. Powell, *The Uncertain Profession: Harvard and the Search for Educational Authority* (Cambridge, Mass.: Harvard University Press, 1980).

4. Daniel L. Duke, *Teaching—The Imperiled Profession* (Albany, N.Y.: State University of New York Press, 1984); Gary Sykes, "Contradictions, Ironies, and Promises Unfulfilled: A Contemporary Account of the Status of Teaching," *Phi Delta Kappan* (October 1983): 87–93; and S. Freedman, J. Jackson, and K. Boles, "Teaching: An Imperiled Profession," in *Handbook of Teaching and Policy*, ed. Lee Shulman and Gary Sykes (New York: Longman, 1983): 261–299.

5. John Goodlad, "Teaching: An Endangered Profession," *Teachers College Record* (Spring 1983): 575–578.

6. Bengt Abrahamsson, *Military Professionalization and Political Power* (Stockholm: Allmanna Forlagret, 1971), pp. 11–12.

7. We have gleaned these characteristics from the following excellent sources: Robert B. Howsam et al., *Educating a Profession*; Gunnar Berg, "Developing the Teaching Profession: Autonomy, Professional Code, Knowledge Base," *The Australian Journal of Education*, vol. 27, no. 2 (1983): 173–186; Wilbert E. Moore, *The Professions: Roles and Rules* (New York: Russell Sage Foundation, 1970); Myron Lieberman, *Education as a Profession* (Englewood Cliffs, N.J.: Prentice-Hall, 1956); and Amitai Etzioni, *The Semi-Professions and Their Organization*.

8. John I. Goodlad, *Teachers for Our Nation's Schools* (San Francisco: Jossey-Bass, 1990), p. 71.

9. Etzioni, *The Semi-Professions and Their Organization*, p. v.

10. Dan Lortie, *Schoolteacher: A Sociological Study* (Chicago: University of Chicago Press, 1975).

11. Ibid., p. 160.

12. Forrest W. Parkay, *White Teacher, Black School: The Professional Growth of a Ghetto Teacher* (New York: Praeger, 1983), pp. 114–115.

13. Robert B. Howsam, et al., *Educating a Profession*, p. 15.

14. Albert Shanker, "Why Teachers Are Angry," *The American School Board Journal* (January 1975): 23–24.

15. Dan Lortie, *Schoolteacher*, pp. 160–161.

16. Dan Lortie, *Schoolteacher*; Henrick D. Gideonse, "The Necessary Revolution in Teacher Education," *Phi Delta Kappan* (September 1982): 15–18; and Paul Woodring, *The Persistent Problems of Education* (Bloomington, Ind.: Phi Delta Kappa, 1983).

17. National Board for Professional Teaching Standards, *President's 1987/88 Annual Report*, (Detroit: National Board for Professional Teaching Standards, 1988), p. 7.

18. *Occupational Outlook Handbook, 1990–91 Edition* (Washington, D.C.: U.S. Department of Labor and Bureau of Labor Statistics, 1988), pp. 31, 72, 79, 133, 137, 155.

19. Paul M. Siegel, "Prestige in the American Occupational Structure" (Ph.D. dissertation, University of Chicago, 1971).

20. Paul Woodring, *The Persistent Problems of Education*, p. 121.

21. Donald A. Shön, *The Reflective Practitioner: How Professionals Think in Action* (New York: Basic Books, 1983), p. 66.

22. The terms *comprehensiveness* and *mutuality* come from James G. Clawson, "Mentoring in Managerial Careers," in *Work, Family, and Career*, ed. C. Brooklyn Dorr (New York: Praeger, 1980).

23. For a fuller discussion of the gift-giving concept of mentorships see Nathalie Gehrke, "Toward a Definition of Mentoring," *Theory Into Practice* (Summer 1988): 190–194.

24. Forrest W. Parkay and Sandra Bowman Damico, "Empowering Teachers for Change Through Faculty-Driven School Improvement," *Journal of Staff Development* (Spring 1989): 12–13.

25. Judith Lanier and Judith Little, "Research on Teacher Education" in *Handbook of Research on Teaching*, Merlin C. Wittrock (Ed.) (New York: Macmillan, 1986), p. 543.

26. N. L. Gage, *The Scientific Basis of the Art of Teaching* (New York: Teachers College Press, 1978), p. 57.

27. Forrest W. Parkay, *White Teacher, Black School: The Professional Growth of a Ghetto Teacher* (New York: Praeger, 1983), p. 38.

28. *Directory of Education Associations 1980–81*, comp. Lois V. Lopez (Washington, D.C.: U.S. Department of Education, 1981).

29. Allan M. West, *The National Education Association: The Power Base for Education* (New York: Free Press, 1980), p. 1.

30. *Encyclopedia of Associations, 1991* (Detroit: Gale Research Inc., 1990).

31. Allan M. West, *The National Education Association*, p. 1.

32. Ibid., p. 211.

33. Ibid., p. 113.

34. The Commission on Educational Reconstruction, *Organizing the Teaching Profession: The Story of the American Federation of Teachers* (Glencoe, Ill.: Free Press, 1955), pp. 28, 60–61.

35. *Encyclopedia of Associations, 1991*.

36. The Commission on Educational Reconstruction, *Organizing the Teaching Profession*, pp. 60–61.

37. Charles Cogen, "Teacher Militancy: Bridge to AFT–NEA Unity?" *American Teacher* (March, 1968): 2.

38. *Encyclopedia of Associations, 1991*.

39. Ibid.

Chapter 14

1. Reprinted from Jane Miller, *Many Voices: Bilingualism, Culture, and Education* (London: Routledge & Kegan Paul, 1983), p. 1.

2. James A. Banks, *Teaching Strategies for Ethnic Studies*, 5th ed. (Boston, Mass.: Allyn and Bacon, 1991), p. 14.

3. Peter I. Rose, *They and We: Racial and Ethnic Relations in the United States*, 2d ed. (New York: Random House, 1974), p. 13.

4. Ashley Montagu, *Man's Most Dangerous Myth: The Fallacy of Race*, 5th ed. (New York: Oxford University Press, 1974), p. 9.

5. James A. Banks, *Teaching Strategies for Ethnic Studies*, p. 74.

6. Ibid, pp. 74–75.

7. Ibid, p. 5.

8. The Commission on Minority Participation in Education and American Life, *One-Third of a Nation* (Washington, D.C.: American Council on Education and Education Commission of the States, 1988).

9. *The Condition of Education 1990: Volume 1, Elementary and Secondary Education* (Washington, D.C.: National Center for Education Statistics, 1990), p. 65.

10. James S. Coleman et al., *Equality of Educational Opportunity* (Washington, D.C.: U.S. Government Printing Office, 1966).

11. National Center for Education Statistics, *High School and Beyond Study* (Washington, D.C.: National Center for Education Statistics, 1980).

12. Jack Friedman (with Bill Shaw), "The Quiet Victories of Ryan White," *People Magazine* (May 30, 1988): 89.

13. *Roberts v. City of Boston*, 59 Mass. (5 Cush.) 198 (1850).

14. *Brown v. Board of Education of Topeka, Kansas*, 347, U.S. 483, 74 S.Ct. 686 (1954).

15. *Brown v. Board of Education of Topeka, Kansas*, 349, U.S. 294, 75 S.Ct. 753 (1955).

16. Gary Orfield, *Desegregation of Black and Hispanic Students from 1968 to 1980* (Washington, D.C.: Joint Center for Political Studies, 1982).

17. Christine I. Bennett. *Comprehensive Multicultural Education: Theory and Practice*, 2d ed. (Boston: Allyn and Bacon, 1990), p. 158.

18. A. Hilliard, "Alternatives to IQ Testing: An Approach to the Identification of Gifted Minority Children" (Final report to the California State Department of Education, 1976).

19. Rosalinda Barrera, "The Teaching of Reading to Language-Minority Students: Some Basic Guidelines," in *Quest for Quality: Improving Basic Skills Instruction in the 1980s*, ed. Forrest W. Parkay, Sharon O'Bryan, and Michael Hennessy (Washington, D.C.: University Press of America, 1984).

20. F. Cordasco and D. Castellanos, "Teaching the Puerto Rican Experience," in *Teaching Ethnic Studies*, James A. Banks, ed. (Washington, D.C.: National Council for the Social Studies, 1973), pp. 227–228. Used by permission of National Council for the Social Studies.

21. J. S. Olson, *The Ethnic Dimension in American History*, vol. 2 (New York: St. Martins Press, 1979), pp. 377–378.

22. Christine I. Bennett, *Comprehensive Multicultural Education*, p. 118.

23. Karen S. Deyhle and D. Deyhle, "Styles of Learning and Learning Styles: Educational Conflicts for American Indian/Alaskan Native Youth," *Journal of Multilingual and Multicultural Development*, 8, no. 4 (1987): 350.

24. J. C. Phillips, "College of, by and for Navajo Indians," *Chronicle of Higher Education*, 15 (January 16, 1978): 10–12.

25. Christine I. Bennett, *Comprehensive Multicultural Education*, p. 165.

26. V. G. Thuy, "The Indochinese in America: Who Are They and How Are They Doing" in *The Education of Asian and Pacific Americans: Historical Perspectives and Prescriptions for the Future*, Don T. Nakanishi and Marsha Hirano-Nakanishi, eds. (Phoenix, Ariz.: Oryx Press, 1983), p. 107.

27. B. H. Suzuki, "The Education of Asian and Pacific Americans: An Introductory Overview," *The Education of Asian and Pacific Americans: Historical Perspectives and Prescriptions for the Future*, Don T. Nakanishi and Marsha Hirano-Nakanishi, eds. (Phoenix, Ariz.: Oryx Press, 1983), p. 9.

28. James A. Banks, *Teaching Strategies for Ethnic Studies*, p. 118.

29. Ibid, pp. 119–120.

30. Forrest W. Parkay and Henry T. Fillmer, "Improving Teachers' Attitudes Toward Minority-Group Students: An Experiential Approach to Multicultural Inservice," *New Horizons* (November 1984): 178–179.

31. Daniel P. Hallahan and James M. Kauffman, *Exceptional Children: Introduction to Special Education*, 5th ed. (Englewood Cliffs, N.J.: Prentice-Hall, 1991), p. 8.

32. Ibid.

33. Ibid.

34. Christine I. Bennett, *Comprehensive Multicultural Education*, Second Edition. Copyright © 1990 by Allyn and Bacon. Reprinted with permission.

35. Ibid.

36. Ibid.

37. William Ayers, *The Good Preschool Teacher: Six Teachers Reflect on Their Lives* (New York: Teachers College Press, 1989), p. 87.

38. Yona Leyser, "Competencies Needed for Teaching Individuals with Special Needs," *Clearing House* (December 1985): 179–181.

39. Daniel P. Hallahan and James M. Kauffman, *Exceptional Children*, pp. 15–16.

40. D. D. Hammill, J. E. Leigh, G. McNutt, and S. C. Larsen, "A New Definition of Learning Disabilities," *Learning Disability Quarterly*, 4, no. 4 (1981): 336–342.

41. S. Bever, *Building a Child's Self-Image* (St. Paul: Minnesota Association for Children and Adults with Learning Disabilities, 1980).

42. Daniel P. Hallahan and James M. Kauffman, *Exceptional Children*, p. 432.

43. Julian C. Stanley, "The Case for Extreme Educational Acceleration of Intellectually Brilliant Youths," *Gifted Child Quarterly*, 20 (1976): 66–75; and "Radical Acceleration: Recent Educational Innovation at Johns Hopkins University," *Gifted Child Quarterly* 22 (1978): 62–67.

44. Stephen P. Daurio, "Educational Enrichment Versus Acceleration: A Review of the Literature," in *Educating the Gifted: Acceleration and Enrichment*, ed. William C. George, Sanford J. Cohn, and Julian C. Stanley (Baltimore, Md.: Johns Hopkins University Press, 1979), pp. 13–63.

45. Howard H. Spiker, ed., "University-Based Programs for Gifted Children," *Journal for the Education of the Gifted* 5 (1982): 153–224.

46. E. Paul Torrence, "Teaching Creative and Gifted Learners," in *Handbook of Research on Teaching*, 3d ed., Merlin C. Wittrock, ed. (New York: Macmillan, 1986), p. 634.

47. M. Lindsey, *Training Teachers of the Gifted and Talented* (New York: Teachers College Press, 1980), cited in Daniel P. Hallahan and James M. Kauffman, *Exceptional Children*, p. 432.

48. M. S. Whitlock and J. P. DuCette, "Outstanding and Average Teachers of the Gifted: A Comparative Study," *Gifted Child Quarterly* 33 (1989): 15–21, cited in Daniel P. Hallahan and James M. Kauffman, *Exceptional Children*, p. 433.

49. *Sourcebook of Equal Educational Opportunity* (Chicago: Marquis Who's Who, 1977), p. 584.

50. Joy R. Simonson and Jeffrey A. Menzer, *Catching Up: A Review of the Women's Educational Equity Act Program* (Washington, D.C.: Citizens Council on Women's Education, 1984).

51. Myra Sadker, David Sadker, and Lynette Long, "Gender and Educational Equity," in *Multicultural Education: Issues and Perspectives*, James A. Banks, ed. (Boston: Allyn and Bacon, 1989), pp. 114–115.

52. Beverly Hardcastle, "Gender Equity in the Classroom" (unpublished paper), 1990, pp. 14–18.

Chapter 15

1. Alfred Ellison, "A School for the Day After Tomorrow," in *The Elementary School: Principles and Problems*, ed. J. L. Frost and G. T. Rowland (Boston: Houghton Mifflin, 1969), pp. 520, 538.

2. Alvin Toffler, *Future Shock* (New York: Bantam, 1971), p. 460.

3. "If You Live to Be 100—It Won't Be Unusual," *U.S. News & World Report*, May 1983: A10.

4. John Naisbitt and Patricia Aburdene, *Megatrends 2000: Ten New Directions for the 1990s* (New York: Avon Books, 1990), p. 228.

5. Harold G. Shane, "The Silicon Age II: Living and Learning in an Information Epoch," *Phi Delta Kappan* (October 1983): 126.

6. John Naisbitt and Patricia Aburdene, *Megatrends 2000*, p. 8.

7. *National Goals for Education*, U.S. Department of Education, Washington, D.C., July 1990.

8. The Metropolitan Life Survey of the American Teacher, 1991, *Coming to Terms: Teachers' Views on Current Issues in Education* (New York: Louis Harris and Associates, 1991), p. 2.

9. Seymour B. Sarason, *The Culture of School and the Problem of Change* (Boston: Allyn and Bacon, 1971).

10. Ibid., p. 224; see also Gene E. Hall and Shirley M. Hord, *Change in Schools: Facilitating the Process* (New York: State University of New York Press, 1987).

11. Seymour B. Sarason, *The Culture of School and the Problem of Change*, p. 224.

12. Ibid.

13. Thomas L. Good and Jere E. Brophy, *Looking in Classrooms*, 4th ed. (New York: Harper & Row, 1987), p. 328.

14. Jeanne S. Chall and Allan F. Mirsky, "The Implications for Education," in *Education and the Brain*, ed. Jeanne S. Chall and Allan F. Mirsky, The 77th Yearbook of the National Society for the Study of Education, Part II (Chicago: University of Chicago Press, 1978), p. 377.

15. Herman T. Epstein, "Growth Spurts During Brain Development: Implications for Educational Policy and Practice," in *Education and the Brain*, ed. Jeanne S. Chall and Allan F. Mirsky, The 77th Yearbook of the National Society for the Study of Education, Part II (Chicago: University of Chicago Press, 1978), p. 367.

16. Ibid., p. 362.

17. Ibid., p. 367.

18. Michael P. Grady, *Teaching and Brain Research: Guidelines for the Classroom* (New York: Longman, 1984), p. 20.

19. Thomas A. Romberg and Thomas P. Carpenter, "Research on Teaching and Learning Mathematics: Two Disciplines of Scientific Inquiry," in Merlin C. Wittrock, ed., *Handbook of Research on Teaching*, 3d ed. (New York: Macmillan, 1986), p. 853.

20. David Wood, *How Children Think and Learn* (New York: Basil Blackwell, 1988), p. 81.

21. Ibid, p. 82.

22. "Some Third Graders Are Passing Because I Work With Them," *Harvard Education Letter*, March 1987, 2. Excerpted from Aurelio Montemayor, *Valued Youth Speak* (San Antonio: Intercultural Development Research Association, 1986).

23. Ronald S. Brandt, "On Teachers Coaching Teachers: A Conversation with Bruce Joyce," *Educational Leadership*, vol. 44, no. 5 (February 1987): 15.

24. Bettye Caldwell, "Demographic Relevance—A New Challenge for Tomorrow's Schools" (address to the Kappa Delta Pi 1988 Convocation, New Orleans, April 1988).

25. Ernest Boyer, "Partners in Excellence" (address to the Kappa Delta Pi 1988 Convocation, New Orleans, April 1988).

26. *School-Based Clinics 1988 Update* (Houston: The Support Center for School-Based Clinics, 1988).

27. John Merrow, "Children and Television: Natural Partners," *Phi Delta Kappan* (November 1985): 212.

28. Susan Mernit, "Teaching and Computers: The Guide on the Side," *Instructor* (September 1990): 77–78.

29. Ibid., 78.

30. "Computer 'Revolution' On Hold," *ASCD Update* (November 1990): 4.

31. Ibid.

32. "Classes Turn on to High Tech Texts," *The Gainesville Sun* (28 December 1990): 4A.

33. Sueann Ambron and Kristina Hooper, eds., *Interactive Multimedia: Visions of Multimedia for Developers, Educators, & Information Providers* (Redmond, Wash.: Microsoft, 1988), p. vii.

34. Ibid., p. 7.

35. "Unlocking the Secrets of the Future: ASCD Consortium Plans for 21st Century," *ASCD Update* (September 1988): p. 1.

36. As quoted in Ronald T. LaConte, "Teaching the Future," *Educational Leadership* (September 1983): p. 41.

37. Seymour Papert, "Society Will Balk, but the Future May Demand a Computer for Each Child," *Electronic Education* (September 1981): 5.

38. Sandra M. Long, "Reflections on the Past and Visions of the Future: An Interview With Harold G. Shane," *Phi Delta Kappan* (March 1986): 531.

39. John Naisbitt and Patricia Aburdene, *Megatrends 2000*, p. 24.

40. Humphrey Tonkin and Jane Edwards, *The World in the Curriculum: Curriculum Strategies for the 21st Century* (New Rochelle, N.Y.: Change Magazine Press, 1981), p. 24.

41. Marvin J. Cetron, Barbara Soriano, and Margaret Gayle, "Schools of the Future: Education Approaches the Twenty-First Century," *The Futurist* (August 1985): 22.

Glossary

A

Academic freedom (p. 274): the right of teachers to teach, free from external constraint, censorship, or interference.

Academic learning time (p. 342): the amount of time students spend working on academic tasks with a high level of success (80 percent or higher).

Academies (p. 171): early secondary schools with broader and more practical curricula than those found in grammar schools of the previous era.

Activity format (p. 341): one of many types of activity classroom teachers can use to accomplish an instructional goal.

Adolescence (p. 317): the period of life (10 to 19 years of age) between childhood and young adulthood.

Aesthetics (p. 209): a branch of philosophy concerned with making value judgments about beauty and art.

Aims of education (p. 128): what a society believes the broad, general purposes of education should be—for example, socialization, achievement, personal growth, and social improvement.

Allocated time (p. 342): the amount of time teachers allocate for instruction in various areas of the curriculum.

Alternative certification (p. 101): a provision allowing people who have completed college but not a teacher education program to become certified teachers.

American Federation of Teachers (p. 431): a national professional association for teachers, affiliated with the AFL-CIO.

Association for Supervision and Curriculum Development (p. 435): a professional organization for educators interested in school improvement at all levels.

Axiology (p. 208): the study of values, including the identification of criteria for determining what is valuable.

B

Behavior modification (p. 352): an approach to classroom management in which the teacher reinforces (or rewards) only desired student behaviors.

Behaviorism (p. 219): based on behavioristic psychology, this philosophical orientation maintains that environmental factors shape the behavior of human beings.

Between-class ability grouping (p. 339): the practice of grouping students at the middle and high school levels for instruction on the basis of ability or achievement, often called *tracking*.

Bilingual education (p. 135): a curriculum for nonEnglish-speaking and English-speaking students in which two languages are used for instruction and biculturalism is emphasized.

Block grants (p. 254): federal money for education in the states that is targeted for broad, general purposes, thereby giving states and local school districts greater flexibility in how federal money is spent.

Buckley Amendment (p. 289): a 1974 law, the Family Educational Rights and Privacy Act, granting parents of students under 18 and students over 18 the right to examine their school records.

C

Carnegie Forum on Education and the Economy (p. 64): a forum established in 1985 by the Carnegie Foundation to examine the relationship between economic growth and education.

CD-ROMs (p. 493): small plastic disks (usually 4.72 or 5.25 inches in diameter) that hold 600 or more megabytes of information that can be read by a computer.

Censorship (p. 282): the act of removing from circulation printed material judged to be libelous, vulgar, or obscene.

Chief state school officer (p. 246): the chief administrator of a state department of education and head of the state board of education, often called the commissioner of education or superintendent of public instruction.

Childhood (p. 314): the period of life (2 to 10 years of age) between infancy and early adolescence.

Classroom climate (p. 337): the atmosphere or quality of life in a classroom, determined by how individuals interact with one another.

Classroom management (p. 351): day-to-day teacher control of student behavior and learning, including discipline.

Classroom organization (p. 336): how teachers and students in a school are grouped for instruction and how time is allocated in classrooms.

Code of ethics (p. 266): a set of guidelines that defines appropriate behavior for professionals.

Cognitive development (p. 305): the process of acquiring the intellectual ability to learn from interaction with one's environment.

Cognitive science (p. 483): the study of the learning process that focuses on how individuals manipulate symbols and process information.

Collaborative approach (p. 77): an approach to teacher education in which school-based professionals collaborate in the on-site training of teachers.

Collective bargaining (p. 273): a process followed by employers and employees in negotiating salaries, hours, and working conditions; in most states, school boards must negotiate contracts with teacher organizations.

Committee of Ten (p. 385): an NEA committee that recommended an academically rigorous curriculum for high-school students (1893).

Committee of Fifteen (p. 385): an NEA committee that recommended an academically oriented elementary curriculum (1895).

Common schools (p. 175): free state-supported schools that provide education for all students.

Computer-based simulations (p. 491): computer programs that present the user with multifaceted problem situations similar to those they will encounter in real life.

Concrete operations stage (p. 305): the stage of cognitive development (7 to 11 years of age) proposed by Jean Piaget in which the individual develops the ability to use logical thought to solve concrete problems.

Contingent teaching (p. 483): an approach to teaching, sometimes called "scaffolding," in which instruction is based on (or "contingent" upon) the student's current level of understanding and ability.

Cooperative learning (p. 342): an approach to education in which students work in small groups, or teams, sharing the work and helping one another complete assignments.

Copyright laws (p. 280): laws limiting the use of photocopies, videotapes, and computer software programs.

Core curriculum (p. 389): a set of fundamental courses or learning experiences that are part of the curriculum for all students at a school.

Corporal punishment (p. 285): physical punishment applied to a student by a school employee as a disciplinary measure.

Credentials file (p. 104): a file set up for students registered in a teacher placement office at a college or university, which includes background information on the applicant, the type of position desired, transcripts, performance evaluations, and letters of recommendation.

Cross-age tutoring (p. 485): a tutoring arrangement in which older students tutor younger students; evidence indicates that cross-age tutoring has positive effects on the attitudes and achievement of tutee and tutor.

Cultural lag (p. 12): a mismatch or delay between the perceptions and expectations of reality held by people in a culture and a change in the reality itself.

Culture (p. 134): the way of life common to a group of people; includes knowledge deemed important, shared meanings, norms, values, attitudes, ideals, and view of the world.

Curriculum (p. 372): the school experiences, both planned and unplanned, that enhance (and sometimes impede) the education and growth of students.

D

Dame schools (p. 167): colonial schools, usually held in the homes of widows or housewives, for teaching children basic reading, writing, and mathematical skills.

Democratic classroom (p. 348): a classroom in which the teacher's leadership style encourages students to take more power and responsibility for their learning.

Departmentalization (p. 141): an organizational arrangement for schools in which students move from classroom to classroom for instruction in different subject areas.

Desegregation (p. 186): the process of eliminating schooling practices based on the separation of racial groups.

Discipline-based art programs (p. 400): art education in which students learn art production, art criticism, art history, and aesthetics.

Dismissal (p. 272): the involuntary termination of a teacher's employment; termination must be made for a legally defensible reason with the protection of due process.

Due process (p. 268): a set of specific guidelines that must be followed to protect individuals from arbitrary, capricious treatment by those in authority.

Dyslexia (p. 465): a form of learning disability in which an individual has difficulty reading.

E

Educare system (p. 489): a proposal that would "combine" education and day care to provide day-long, year-round schooling for children 6 months through 12 years of age.

Education Consolidation and Improvement Act (p. 254): a 1981 federal law giving the states a broad range of choices for spending federal aid to education.

Education for All Handicapped Children Act (pp. 191, 462): a 1975 federal act that guarantees a free and appropriate education to all handicapped children (often referred to as the mainstreaming law or **Public Law 94–142**).

Educational malpractice (p. 279): liability for injury that results from the failure of a teacher, school, or school district to provide a student with adequate instruction, guidance, counseling, and/or supervision.

Educational philosophy (p. 201): a set of ideas and beliefs about education that guide the professional behavior of educators.

Educational reform movement (p. 62): a comprehensive effort made during the 1980s and into the 1990s to improve schools and the preparation of teachers.

Educational Resources Information Center (ERIC) (p. 51): a national information system made up of 16 "clearinghouses" that disseminate descriptions of exemplary programs, results of research and development efforts, and related information.

Eight-Year Study (p. 388): an experiment in which 30 high schools were allowed to develop curricula that did not meet college entrance requirements (1932–1940).

Elementary and Secondary Education Act (p. 187): part of President Lyndon B. Johnson's Great Society Program, this act allocated federal funds on the basis of the number of poor children in school districts.

Entitlements (p. 256): federal programs to meet the educational needs of special populations.

Epistemology (p. 207): a branch of philosophy concerned with the nature of knowledge and what it means to know something.

Equity (p. 146): the fair provision of equal opportunity (particularly educational, economic, and social) for all groups of people in a society.

ERIC Clearinghouses (p. 51): 16 Educational Resources Information Centers Clearinghouses that disseminate descriptions of exemplary educational programs, the results of research and development efforts, and related information.

Essentialism (p. 215): formulated in part as a response to progressivism, this philosophical orientation holds that a core of common knowledge about the real world should be transmitted to students in a systematic, disciplined way.

Ethical dilemmas (p. 268): problem situations in which an ethical response is difficult to determine; i.e., no single response can be called "right" or "wrong."

Ethics (p. 208): a branch of philosophy concerned with principles of conduct and determining what is good and evil, right and wrong, in human behavior.

Ethnic group (pp. 136, 445): individuals within a larger culture who share a racial or cultural identity and a set of beliefs, values, and attitudes and who consider themselves members of a distinct group or subculture.

Exceptional learners (pp. 153, 310): students whose growth and development deviate from the norm to the extent that their educational needs can be met more effectively through a modification of regular school programs.

Existentialism (p. 217): a philosophical orientation that emphasizes the individual's experiences and maintains that each individual must determine his or her own meaning of existence.

Expenditure per pupil (p. 251): the amount of money spent on each pupil in a school, school district, state, or nation; usually computed according to average daily attendance.

Explicit curriculum (p. 373): the behavior, attitudes, and knowledge that a school intends to teach students.

Extended preparation programs (p. 75): approaches to teacher education involving additional semesters of study in preparation for becoming a professional teacher.

Extracurricular/cocurricular programs (p. 375): school-sponsored activities students may pursue outside of, or in addition to, academic study.

F

Faculty teams (p. 486): a small number of teachers, brought together on the basis of interests and expertise, who teach a group of students equal in number to what the teachers would have in their self-contained classrooms.

Fair use (p. 280): the right of an individual to use copyrighted material in a reasonable manner without the copyright holder's consent, provided that use meets certain criteria.

Field experiences (p. 77): opportunities for teachers-in-training to experience first-hand the world of the teacher, by observing, tutoring, and instructing small groups.

Focused observations (p. 78): classroom observations that focus on a particular aspect (or aspects) of teaching—e.g., students' interests and ability levels, the teacher's approach to classroom management, or the teacher's questioning strategies.

Formal operations stage (p. 305): the stage of cognitive development (11 to 15 years of age) proposed by Jean Piaget in which cognitive abilities reach their highest level of development.

Formative evaluation (p. 357): an assessment, or diagnosis, of students' learning for the purpose of planning instruction.

Freedom of expression (p. 282): freedom, granted by the First Amendment to the Constitution, to express one's beliefs.

Fringe benefits (p. 97): benefits (i.e., medical insurance, retirement, and tax-deferred investment opportunities) that are given to teachers in addition to base salary.

Futurism (p. 476): the process of making forecasts about the future based on analyses of current social, economic, and technological trends.

G

Gender bias (p. 468): subtle bias or discrimination on the basis of gender; reduces the likelihood that the target of the bias will develop to the full extent of his or her capabilities.

G.I. Bill of Rights (p. 184): a 1944 federal law that provides veterans with payments for tuition and room and board at colleges and universities and special schools; formally known as the Servicemen's Readjustment Act.

Gifted and talented (pp. 154, 312): exceptional learners who demonstrate high intelligence, high creativity, high achievement, or special talent(s).

Grievance (p. 273): a formal complaint filed by an employee against his or her employer or supervisor.

H

Handicapped students (p. 311): students with one or more physical, emotional, or mental disabilities or exceptionalities who may have special educational needs.

Hemispheric specialization (p. 483): the mental operations performed by the left and right hemispheres of the brain—the left specializing in linear, sequential, and analytic operations and the right in simultaneous, holistic, and metaphoric operations.

Hidden curriculum (pp. 142, 373): the behaviors, attitudes, and knowledge the school culture unintentionally teaches students.

Hierarchy of needs (p. 301): a model for understanding a sequence of human needs, proposed by psychologist Abraham Maslow.

Higher-order questions (p. 349): questions that require the ability to engage in complex modes of thought (synthesis, analysis, and evaluation, for example).

Holmes Group (p. 64): a group of 96 colleges of education that prepared *Tomorrow's Teachers,* a 1986 report calling for all teachers to have a bachelor's degree in an academic field and a master's degree in education.

I

Indian Education Act of 1972 (p. 454): a federal law designed to provide direct educational assistance to Native-American tribes and nations.

Individual Education Program (IEP) (p. 463): plans for meeting special needs students' educational needs, specifying goals, objectives, services, and procedures for evaluating progress.

Induction programs (p. 86): programs of support for beginning teachers, usually during their first year of teaching.

Information processing (p. 483): a branch of cognitive science concerned with how individuals use long- and short-term memory to acquire information and solve problems.

Inquiry-based curriculum (p. 389): a curriculum that teaches not only the content but also the thought processes of a discipline.

Inservice workshops (p. 425): on-site professional development programs in which teachers meet to learn new techniques, develop curricular materials, share ideas, or solve problems.

Institution (p. 139): any organization a society establishes to maintain, and improve, its way of life.

Instructional theory into practice (p. 76): a systematic approach to developing lessons that contain seven essential elements: anticipatory set, objective and purpose, input, modeling, check for understanding, guided practice, and independent practice.

Intelligence (p. 303): the ability to learn; the cognitive capacity for thinking.

Interactive multimedia (p. 494): computer-supported media that allow the user to interact with a vast nonlinear, multimedia data base to combine textual, audio, video information.

Interactive teaching (p. 47): teaching characterized by face-to-face interactions between teachers and students in contrast to preactive teaching.

Internship programs (p. 86): programs of assistance and training for beginning teachers, usually for those who have not gone through a teacher education program.

Interstate Certification Compact (p. 101): a reciprocity agreement whereby a teaching certificate obtained in one state will be honored in another; currently, more than half of the states and the District of Columbia are members of the Compact.

IQ (p. 304): Intelligence quotient, a numerical formulation of *intelligence* based on standardized testing results in relation to chronological age.

J

Job analysis (p. 19): a procedure for determining the knowledge and skills needed for a job.

K

Kindergarten (p. 179): a school for children before they begin formal schooling at the elementary level; based on the ideas of German educator Friedrich Fröebel, *kindergarten* means "garden where children grow."

Knowledge base (p. 17): the body of knowledge that represents what teachers need to know and to be able to do.

L

Latin grammar schools (p. 167): colonial schools established to provide male students a precollege education; comparable to today's high schools.

Learning (p. 481): changes in behavior the individual makes in response to environmental stimuli; the acquisition and organization of knowledge and skills.

Learning disability (LD) (p. 464): a limitation in one's ability to take in, organize, remember, and express information.

Learning style (p. 306): a set of cognitive, affective, and physiological behaviors through which an individual learns most effectively; determined by a combination of hereditary and environmental influences.

LEAST approach (p. 352): a sequence of steps teachers can follow to maintain discipline in the classroom.

Letter of application (p. 108): a letter written in application for a specific teaching vacancy in a school district.

Letter of inquiry (p. 107): a letter written to a school district inquiring about teaching vacancies.

Limited English Proficiency (LEP) (p. 460): a designation for students with limited ability to understand, read, or speak English and who have a first language other than English.

Linguistically challenged students (p. 312): students with limited ability to understand, speak, and write English.

Local school district (p. 235): an agency at the local level that has the authority to operate schools in the district.

Logic (p. 209): a branch of philosophy concerned with the processes of reasoning and the identification of rules that will enable thinkers to reach valid conclusions.

Lower-order questions (p. 349): questions that require students to recall specific information.

M

Mainstreaming (p. 191): the policy and process of integrating handicapped or otherwise exceptional learners into regular classrooms with nonexceptional students.

Massachusetts Act of 1642 (p. 170): a law requiring each town to determine whether its young people could read and write.

Massachusetts Act of 1647 (p. 170): a law mandating the establishment and support of schools; often referred to as the "Old Deluder Satan Act" because education was seen as the best protection against the wiles of the devil.

McGuffey readers (p. 178): an immensely popular series of reading books for students in grades 1 through 6, written in the 1830s by Reverend William Holmes McGuffey.

Measurement (p. 357): the gathering of data that indicate how much students have learned.

Mentor (p. 420): a wise, knowledgeable individual who provides guidance and encouragement to someone, a protégé.

Metaphysics (p. 206): a branch of philosophy concerned with the nature of reality.

Microcomputer (p. 491): a small, yet powerful computer with a wide variety of educational applications including computer-aided instruction, data analysis, and simulations.

Microcultural groups (p. 298): cultural subgroups within a larger (macro) culture.

Microteaching (p. 79): a brief, single-concept lesson taught by a teacher education student to a small group of students; usually designed to give the "teacher" an opportunity to practice a specific teaching skill.

Minority (p. 444): any group of people who shares certain characteristics and is smaller in number than the majority of a population.

Model of teaching (p. 358): a coherent pattern of instructional strategies teachers may develop to obtain particular results in the classroom.

Modes of teaching (p. 37): different aspects of the teaching function—e.g., teaching as a way of being, as a creative endeavor, as a live performance, etc.

Morrill Land-Grant Act (p. 179): an 1862 act that provided federal land that states could sell or rent to raise funds to establish colleges of agriculture and mechanical arts.

Multicultural (pp. 132, 445): a term used to describe a group whose members are from several different cultures; **Multiculturalism** refers to diversity among students in classrooms in regard to their race, first language, religion, values, ethnicity, sex, and social class; reflections of concern with this diversity in curricula.

Multiple intelligences (p. 305): a perspective on intellectual ability, proposed by Howard Gardner, suggesting that there are at least seven types of human intelligence.

N

National Assessment of Educational Progress (NAEP) (p. 447): an ongoing, large-scale national testing program to assess the effectiveness of American education.

National Board for Professional Teaching Standards (p. 417): a board established in 1987 that will begin issuing professional certificates in 1993 to teachers who possess a high degree of professional knowledge and the ability to perform at a high level.

National Commission for Excellence in Teacher Education (p. 63): a 17-member group that prepared *A Call for Change in Teacher Education*, a 1985 report that urged the adoption of higher, more specific standards for preparing teachers.

National Education Association (NEA) (p. 428): the oldest and largest professional association for teachers and administrators.

National Teacher Examination (NTE) (p. 101): an examination (prepared by Educational Testing Service) that covers communication skills, general knowledge, and professional knowledge; currently required for teacher certification in most states.

Negligence (p. 279): failure to exercise reasonable, prudent care in providing for the safety of others.

Networking (p. 491): the process of using computers to communicate—e.g., exchanging information through electronic bulletin boards and electronic mail (e-mail).

Nondiscrimination (p. 269): conditions characterized by the absence of discrimination; e.g., employees receive compensation, privileges, and opportunities for advancement without regard for race, color, religion, sex, or national origin.

Normal schools (p. 177): schools that focus on the preparation of teachers.

Norms (p. 345): stated or unstated expectations for behavior that members of a group agree to follow.

Null curriculum (p. 374): the intellectual processes and subject content that schools do not teach.

O

Office of Educational Research and Improvement (OERI) (p. 53): a federal agency that promotes educational research and improving schools through the application of research results.

Open-concept education (p. 141): an approach to education based on individualizing instruction for students and allowing them considerable freedom to learn at their own rate and according to their interests and learning styles.

Open-space schools (p. 141): schools that have large instructional areas with movable walls and furniture that can be rearranged easily.

P

Peer counseling (p. 486): an arrangement whereby students, monitored by a school counselor or teacher, counsel one another in such areas as low achievement, interpersonal problems, substance abuse, and career planning.

Perennialism (p. 210): a philosophical orientation that emphasizes the ideas contained in the Great Books and maintains that the true purpose of education is the discovery of the universal, or perennial, truths of life.

Personal-development view (p. 18): the belief that teachers become more effective by increasing their self-knowledge and developing themselves as persons.

Phi Delta Kappa (p. 435): a professional and honorary fraternity of educators with 650 chapters and 130,000 members.

Philosophy (p. 200): a field of study concerned with identifying basic truths about being, knowledge, and conduct.

Placement service (p. 104): a school, government, or commercial service that matches job applicants with job openings and arranges contacts between employers and prospective employees.

Portfolios (p. 485): a collection of various kinds of evidence (e.g., projects, written work, and video demonstrations of skills) documenting the achievement and performance of teachers or students.

Preactive teaching (p. 48): the stage of teaching when a teacher prepares to teach or reflects upon previous teaching experiences in contrast with interactive teaching.

Preoperational stage (p. 305): the stage of cognitive development (2 to 7 years of age) proposed by Jean Piaget in which the individual begins to use language and symbols to think of objects and people outside of the immediate environment.

Primers (p. 168): books with very explicit religious and moral messages about the proper conduct of life that colonial children used to learn to read.

Problem-solving orientation (p. 21): an approach to teaching that places primary emphasis on the teacher's role as a decision maker and problem solver.

Profession (p. 410): an occupation that requires a high level of expertise, including advanced study in a specialized field, adherence to a code of ethics, and the ability to work without close supervision.

Professionalization of teaching (p. 423): changes taking place in education that are enhancing the professional status of teachers; e.g., longer and more rigorous preparation programs, higher salaries, and more opportunities to share in the governance of schools.

Progressive movement (p. 182): a movement during the 1920s and 1930s to create schools that emphasized democracy, children's interests and needs, and closer connections between school and community.

Progressivism (p. 213): a philosophical orientation based on the belief that life is evolving in a positive direction, that people may be trusted to act in their own best interests, and that education should focus on the needs and interests of students.

Property taxes (p. 252): local taxes assessed against real estate and, in some areas against personal property in the form of cars, household furniture and appliances, and stocks and bonds.

Psychosocial crisis (p. 314): a life "crisis" at one of eight different stages of growth and development, according to psychologist Erik Erikson, individuals must resolve each crisis to reach the next stage.

R

Race (p. 445): a concept of human variation used to distinguish people on the basis of biological traits and characteristics.

Racism (p. 446): the prejudicial belief that one's ethnic or racial group is superior to others.

Reading and writing schools (p. 167): colonial schools, supported by public funds and fees paid by parents, that used a religiously oriented curriculum to teach boys reading and writing skills and, to a lesser degree, mathematics.

Realities of teaching (p. 40): actual conditions teachers face in the classroom, the demands as well as the rewards.

Reconstructionism (p. 221): a philosophical orientation that maintains that a better, more just society can be created by identifying, then correcting, social ills.

Reflection (p. 21): the process of thinking carefully and deliberately about the outcomes of one's teaching.

Reflective teaching (p. 76): an approach to teaching that encourages the teacher to use careful, deliberate reflection as the primary means of decision making.

Reflective teaching log (p. 82): a journal of classroom observations in which the teacher education student systematically analyzes specific episodes of teaching.

Regional Educational Laboratories (p. 51): nine federally supported, nonprofit agencies that serve a region of the country and work directly with educators to improve schools.

Regional Educational Service Agency (p. 247): a state educational agency that provides supportive services to two or more school districts; known in some states as education service centers, intermediate school districts, multicounty education service units, board of cooperative educational services, or educational service regions.

Relevancy-based curriculum (p. 389): a curriculum that is relevant to students' needs, interests, and concerns with social issues.

Reorganization of Secondary Education (p. 385): An NEA commission that recommended a high-school curriculum based on individual differences (1913).

Research and Development Centers (p. 51): 14 federally supported university-based centers, each conducting research and development activities in a different area of education.

Restructuring (p. 239): reorganizing how schools are controlled at the local level so that teachers, principals, parents, and community members have greater authority.

S

Sanctions (p. 345): the rewards and punishments a group develops to encourage members to behave in desired ways.

School-based clinics (p. 489): health and counseling/educational services offered on the school premises.

School-based management (p. 239): various approaches to school improvement in which teachers, principals, students, parents, and community members manage individual schools and share in the decision-making processes.

School board (p. 237): the primary governing body of a local school district.

School choice (p. 258): various proposals that would allow parents to choose the schools their children attend.

School houses (p. 487): a method of organization in which teachers and students at a school are assigned to one of several "houses" within the school; sometimes referred to as the "school-within-a-school" concept.

School traditions (p. 141): the elements of a school's culture that reflect what the school wishes to be known for; e.g., activities that emphasize academic excellence, accomplishments in the arts, or close school-community relations.

Search and seizure (p. 286): the process of searching an individual and/or his or her property if that person is suspected of an illegal act; reasonable or probable cause to suspect the individual must be present.

Self-assessment (p. 23): the process of measuring one's growth in regard to the knowledge, skills, and attitudes possessed by professional teachers.

Self-contained classroom (p. 141): an organizational structure for schools in which one teacher instructs a group of students (typically, 20 to 30) in a single classroom.

Sexism (p. 467): the belief that one's sex is superior to the other, used to justify discrimination.

Sex role stereotyping (p. 302): beliefs that subtly encourage males and females to conform to certain behavioral norms regardless of abilities and interests.

Sociogram (p. 343): a graphic representation of the social relationships among members of a group based on the attitudes of members toward one another.

Special education (p. 459): a teaching specialty for meeting the special educational needs of exceptional learners.

Stages of group development (p. 343): identifiable stages through which a group passes as its members learn to work together.

State aid (p. 254): money given to local school districts that comes from tax revenues raised by a state.

State board of education (p. 245): the highest educational agency in a state, charged with regulating the state's system of education.

State department of education (p. 246): the branch of state government, headed by the chief state school officer, charged with implementing the state's educational policies.

Stereotypes (p. 139): behavioral characteristics attributed to all members of a group; formulated on the basis of limited experiences with and information about the group coupled with an unwillingness to examine prejudices.

Student-centered curricula (p. 378): curricula that are organized around students' needs and interests.

Students at risk (p. 151): students whose living conditions and backgrounds place them "at risk" for dropping out of school.

Subject-centered curriculum (p. 378): a curriculum that emphasizes learning an academic discipline.

Summative evaluation (p. 357): an assessment of student learning made for the purpose of assigning grades at the end of a unit, semester, or year and deciding whether students are ready to proceed to the next phase of their education.

Superintendent (p. 237): the chief administrator of a school district.

T

Task Force on Teaching as a Profession (p. 65): created by the Carnegie Forum on Education and the Economy to prepare *A Nation Prepared: Teachers for the 21st Century,* a 1986 report containing six sweeping recommendations for improving American education.

Teacher centers (p. 425): centers where teachers provide other teachers with instructional materials and new methods and where teachers can exchange ideas.

Teacher effectiveness research (p. 49): educational research focused on identifying the significant differences between more and less effective teachers.

Teacher empowerment (p. 422): the trend to grant teachers greater power and more opportunities to make decisions that affect their professional lives.

Teacher supply and demand (p. 94): the number of school-age students compared to the number of available teachers; may also be projected based on estimated numbers of students and teachers.

Teaching certificate (p. 100): a license to teach issued by a state or, in a few cases, a large city.

Teaching contract (p. 271): an agreement between a teacher and a board of education that the teacher will provide specific services in return for a certain salary, benefits, and privileges.

Teaching simulations (p. 80): an activity in which teacher education students participate in role-plays designed to create situations comparable to those actually encountered by teachers.

Team teaching (p. 141): an arrangement whereby a team of teachers teaches a group of students equal in number to what the teachers would have in their self-contained classrooms.

Tenure (p. 272): an employment policy in which teachers, after serving a probationary period, retain their positions indefinitely and can be dismissed only on legally defensible grounds.

Time on task (p. 342): the amount of time students are actively and directly engaged in learning tasks.

Tort liability (p. 278): conditions that would permit the filing of legal charges against a professional for breach of duty and/or behaving in a negligent manner.

Tyler rationale (p. 378): a four-step model for curriculum development in which teachers identify purposes, select learning experiences, organize experiences, and evaluate.

V

Vertical equity (p. 256): an effort to provide equal educational opportunity within a state by providing different levels of funding based on economic needs within school districts.

Videodiscs (p. 494): 12-inch plastic discs, each side of which holds about 30 minutes of motion video, or 54,000 frames of video; each frame can be "frozen" with a high degree of clarity.

Voucher system (p. 258): funds allocated to parents which they may use to purchase education for their children from public or private schools in the area.

W

Whole language movement (p. 393): the practice of teaching language skills (listening, reading, and writing) as part of students' everyday experiences rather than as isolated experiences.

Within-class ability grouping (p. 340): the practice of creating small, homogeneous groups of students within a single classroom for the purpose of instruction, usually in reading or mathematics, at the elementary level.

Women's Educational Equity Act (WEEA) (p. 468): a 1974 federal law that guarantees equal educational opportunity for females.

Z

Zone of proximal development (p. 484): a term coined by Soviet psychologist L. S. Vygotsky to refer to the point at which students need assistance to continue learning.

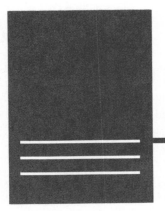

Teacher's Resource Guide

RESOURCES IN EDUCATIONAL RESEARCH

Periodicals and Publications

Academic Computing
Action in Teacher Education
Adolescence
American Biology Teacher
American Educational Research Journal
American Educator: The Professional
    Journal of the American Federation of
    Teachers
American Journal of Education
American School Board Journal
Arithmetic Teacher
Art Education
Bilingual Review
Black Scholar
Business Education Forum
Career Development for Exceptional
    Individuals
Career Development Quarterly
Child Abuse and Neglect: The
    International Journal
Child Development
Child Study Journal
Child Welfare
Childhood Education
Children Today
Children's Literature in Education
Classroom Computer Learning
Clearing House
Communication Education
Comparative Education
Computers and Education
Computers and the Humanities
Computers in the Schools
Computing Teacher
Contemporary Education
Curriculum and Teaching
Early Childhood Research Quarterly
Education and Computing
Education and Urban Society
Educational Forum
Educational Horizons
Educational Leadership
Educational Record
Educational Research
Educational Research Quarterly
Educational Researcher
Educational Review
Educational Technology
Educational Theory
Electronic Learning
Elementary School Journal
English Education
English Journal
English Language Teaching Journal (ETL
    Journal)
Equity and Choice
Equity and Excellence
Exceptional Children
Focus on Exceptional Children
Focus on Learning Problems in
    Mathematics
Forum for Reading

Geographical Education
Gifted Child Quarterly
Gifted Child Today
Gifted Education International
Harvard Educational Review
Health Education
Health Education Quarterly
High School Journal
History and Social Science Teacher
History Teacher
Home Economic Research Journal
Industrial Education
Instructor
International Journal of Early Childhood
International Journal of Educational
    Research
Journal for Research in Mathematics
    Education
Journal for Vocational Special Needs
    Education
Journal of Adolescence
Journal of Alcohol and Drug Education
Journal of American Indian Education
Journal of Black Studies
Journal of Classroom Interaction
Journal of Computer-Assisted Learning
Journal of Computer-Based Instruction
Journal of Computers in Mathematics
    and Science Teaching
Journal of Curriculum and Supervision
Journal of Curriculum Studies
Journal of Developmental Education
Journal of Drug Education
Journal of Early Intervention
Journal of Education
Journal of Educational Computing
    Research
Journal of Educational Research
Journal of Environmental Education
Journal of Home Economics
Journal of Humanistic Education and
    Development
Journal of Learning Disabilities
Journal of Negro Education
Journal of Physical Education,
    Recreation, and Dance
Journal of Reading
Journal of Reading Behavior
Journal of Research in Childhood
    Education
Journal of Research in Computing in
    Education
Journal of Research in Music Education
Journal of Research in Reading
Journal of Research in Science Teaching
Journal of Rural and Small Schools
Journal of Social Studies Research
Journal of Special Education
Journal of Teacher Education
Journal of Teaching in Physical
    Education
Journal of Youth and Adolescence

Kappa Delta Pi Record
Language Arts
Language, Speech, and Hearing Services
    in Schools
Learning
Learning Disabilities Focus
Learning Disabilities Research
Learning Disability Quarterly
Mathematics and Computer Education
Mathematics Teacher
Music Educators Journal
NABE: The Journal for the National
    Association for Bilingual Education
NASSP Bulletin
Negro Educational Review
New Directions for Child Development
New Directions for Teaching and
    Learning
Peabody Journal of Education
Phi Delta Kappan
Physical Educator
Physics Teacher
Preventing School Failure
Programmed Learning and Educational
    Technology
Psychology in the Schools
PTA Today
Reading Horizons
Reading Improvement
Reading Research and Instruction
Reading Research Quarterly
Reading Teacher
Remedial and Special Education
Research in Rural Education
Research in the Teaching of English
Review of Educational Research
Rural Educator
School Arts
School Science and Mathematics
Science and Children
Science Education
Science Teacher
Social Studies and the Young Learner
Social Studies Journal
Social Studies Professional
Sociology of Education
Studies in Art Education
Teacher Magazine
Teachers College Record
Teaching Exceptional Children
TESOL Quarterly
T.H.E. Journal (Technological Horizons
    in Education)
Theory and Research in Social Education
Theory into Practice
Topics in Early Childhood Special
    Education
Urban Education
Vocational Education Journal
Young Children
Youth and Society

Adjunct ERIC Clearinghouse for Art Education
Indiana University
Social Studies Development Center
2805 East 10th Street, Suite 120
Bloomington, IN 47408-2373

Adjunct ERIC Clearinghouse for United States-Japan Studies
Indiana University
Social Studies Development Center
2805 East 10th Street, Suite 120
Bloomington, IN 47408-2373

Adjunct ERIC Clearinghouse on Chapter 1
Chapter 1 Technical Assistance Center
Advanced Technology, Inc.
2601 Fortune Circle East, Suite 300-A
Indianapolis, IN 46241

Adjunct ERIC Clearinghouse on Literacy Education for Limited-English-Proficient Adults
Center for Applied Linguistics (CAL)
1118 22nd Street, NW
Washington, DC 20037

Adult, Career, and Vocational Education
Ohio State University
1900 Kenny Road
Columbus, OH 43210-1090
(614) 292-4353; (800) 848-4815

Counseling and Personnel Services
University of Michigan
School of Education, Room 2108
610 East University St.
Ann Arbor, MI 48109-1259
(313) 764-9492

Educational Management
University of Oregon
1787 Agate Street
Eugene, OR 97403-5207
(503) 346-5043

Elementary and Early Childhood Education
University of Illinois
College of Education
805 West Pennsylvania Avenue
Urbana, IL 61801-4897
(217) 333-1386

Handicapped and Gifted Children
Council for Exceptional Children
1920 Association Drive
Reston, VA 22091-1589
(703) 620-3660

Higher Education
The George Washington University
One Dupont Circle, N.W., Suite 630
Washington, DC 20036-1183
(202) 296-2597

Information Resources
Syracuse University
School of Education
Huntington Hall, Room 030
Syracuse, NY 13244-2340
(315) 443-3640

Junior Colleges
University of California at Los Angeles
Mathematical Science Building, Room 8118
405 Hillgard Ave.
Los Angeles, CA 90024-1564
(213) 825-3931

Languages and Linguistics
Center for Applied Linguistics
1118 22nd St., N.W.
Washington, DC 20037-0037
(202) 429-9551

Reading and Communication Skills
Indiana University, Smith Research Ctr.
2805 East 10th St., Suite 150
Bloomington, IN 47408-2698
(812) 855-5847

Rural Education and Small Schools
Appalachia Educational Laboratory
1031 Quarrier Street, P.O. Box 1348
Charleston, WV 25325-1348
(800) 624-9120; (304) 347-0400

Science, Mathematics, and Environmental Education
Ohio State University
1200 Chambers Road, Room 310
Columbus, OH 43212-1792
(614) 292-6717

Social Studies/Social Science Education
Indiana University
Social Studies Development Center
2805 East 10th St., Suite 120
Bloomington, IN 47408-2698
(812) 855-3838

Teacher Education
American Association of Colleges for Teacher Education
One Dupont Circle, N.W., Suite 610
Washington, DC 20036-2412
(202) 293-2450

Tests, Measurement, and Evaluation
American Institutes for Research (AIR)
3333 K Street, NW
Washington, DC 20007-3893
(202) 342-5060

Urban Education
Teachers College, Columbia University
Main Hall, Room 300, Box 40
525 West 120th Street
New York, NY 10027-9998
(212) 678-3433

Regional Education Laboratories

Appalachia Educational Laboratory (AEL)
P.O. Box 1348
Charleston, WV 25325,
Phone: (304) 347-0400

Far West Laboratory for Educational Research and Development (FWL)
1855 Folsom St.
San Francisco, CA 94103,
Phone: (415) 565-3000

Mid-Continent Regional Educational Laboratory (McREL)
12500 E. Iliff
Aurora, CO 80014,
Phone: (303) 337-0990

North Central Regional Educational Laboratory (NCREL)
295 Emroy Ave.
Elmhurst, IL 60126,
Phone: (312) 941-7677

Northwest Regional Educational Laboratory
300 S.W. Sixth Ave.
Portland, OR 97204,
Phone: (503) 248-6800

Regional Laboratory for Educational Improvement of the Northeast and Islands
The NETWORK, Inc.
290 S. Main St.
Andover, MA 01810,
Phone: (617) 470-1080

Research for Better Schools, Inc. (RBS)
444 N. Third St.
Philadelphia, PA 19123,
Phone: (215) 574-9300

Southeastern Educational Improvement Laboratory (SEIL)
200 Park Offices, Suite 204
P.O. Box 12746
Research Triangle Park, NC 27709,
Phone: (919) 549-8216

Southwest Educational Development Laboratory (SEDL)
211 E. Seventh St.
Austin, TX 78701,
Phone: (512) 476-6861

Educational Research and Improvement Centers (OERI)

Center for Bilingual Research and Second Language Education (CBSLE)
University of California
1100 Glendon Ave., Rm. 1740
Los Angeles, CA 90024,
Phone: (213) 206-1486

Center for Effective Elementary and Middle Schools
Johns Hopkins University
Center for Social Organization of Schools
3505 N. Charles St.
Baltimore, MD 21218,
Phone: (301) 338-7570

Center for Improving Postsecondary Learning and Teaching
University of Michigan
School of Education
Ann Arbor, MI 48109-1259,
Phone: (313) 764-9472

Center for Postsecondary Governance and Finance
University of Maryland, College of Education
Institute for Research in Higher and Adult Education
College Park, MD 20742,
Phone: (301) 454-5766

Center for Student Testing, Evaluation, and Standards (CSTES)
UCLA Graduate School of Education
Center for the Study of Evaluation
Los Angeles, CA 90024,
Phone: (213) 825-4711

Center for the Study of Learning (CSL)
University of Pittsburgh
Learning Research and Development Center
3939 O'Hara St.
Pittsburgh, PA 15260,
Phone: (412) 624-4895

Center for the Study of Reading (CSR)
University of Illinois—Urbana Champaign
51 Gerty Dr.
Champaign, IL 61820,
Phone: (217) 333-2552

Center for the Study of Writing (CSW)
University of California—Berkeley
School of Education
Berkeley, CA 94820,
Phone: (415) 642-2757

Center on Education and Employment
Columbia University
Teachers College
P.O. Box 174
New York, NY 10027,
Phone: (212) 678-3091

Center on Effective Secondary Schools
University of Wisconsin
Wisconsin Center for Education Research
1025 W. Johnson St.
Madison, WI 53706,
Phone: (608) 263-4216

Center on State and Local Policy Development and Leadership
Rutgers—the State University of New Jersey
Eagleton Institute of Politics
Wood Lawn-Neilson Campus
New Brunswick, NJ 08901,
Phone: (201) 828-2210

Center on Teacher Education
Michigan State University
College of Education
Erickson Hall
East Lansing, MI 48824,
Phone: (517) 353-1716

Educational Technology Center (ETC)
Harvard University
College of Education
15 Appian Way
Cambridge, MA 02138,
Phone: (617) 495-9373

Institute for Research on Teaching (IRT)
Michigan State University
Erickson Hall
East Lansing, MI 48824,
Phone: (517) 353-6413

*Job Search—
A Sequence of
Planned Strategies*

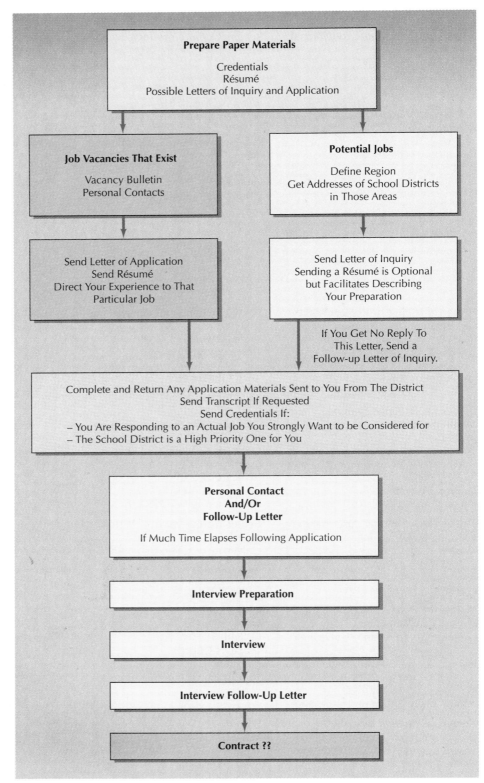

Prepare Paper Materials

Credentials
Résumé
Possible Letters of Inquiry and Application

Job Vacancies That Exist

Vacancy Bulletin
Personal Contacts

Potential Jobs

Define Region
Get Addresses of School Districts
in Those Areas

Send Letter of Application
Send Résumé
Direct Your Experience to That
Particular Job

Send Letter of Inquiry
Sending a Résumé is Optional
but Facilitates Describing
Your Preparation

If You Get No Reply To
This Letter, Send a
Follow-up Letter of Inquiry.

Complete and Return Any Application Materials Sent to You From The District
Send Transcript If Requested
Send Credentials If:
– You Are Responding to an Actual Job You Strongly Want to be Considered for
– The School District is a High Priority One for You

**Personal Contact
And/Or
Follow-Up Letter**

If Much Time Elapses Following Application

Interview Preparation

Interview

Interview Follow-Up Letter

Contract ??

Source: Jan E. Kilby, "Job Search—A Sequence of Planned Strategies," *The ASCUS Annual 1988: A Job Search Handbook for Educators* (Addison, Ill.: Association for School, College and University Staffing), 3. Used with permission.

Job Search—A Timetable Checklist

Presented below is a job-search timetable checklist designed to help most graduating students seeking teaching positions make the best use of their time as they conduct a job search. This timetable checklist should be a helpful tool—especially when it is used in conjunction with services and resources available from your college placement office.

August/September
(12 months prior to employment)
_____ Attend any applicable orientations/workshops offered by your college placement office.
_____ Register with your college placement office and inquire about career services.
_____ Begin to define career goals by determining the types, sizes, and geographic locations of school systems in which you have an interest.

October
(11 months prior to employment)
_____ Begin to identify references and ask them to prepare a letter of recommendation for your credential or placement file.
_____ See a counselor at your college placement office to discuss your job-search plan.

November
(10 months prior to employment)
_____ Check to see that you are properly registered at your college placement office.
_____ Begin developing a résumé and basic cover letter.
_____ Begin networking by contacting friends, faculty members, etc. to inform them of your career plans. If possible, give them a copy of your résumé.

December/January
(8–9 months prior to employment)
_____ Finalize your résumé and make arrangements for it to be reproduced. You may want to get some tips on résumé reproduction from your college placement office.
_____ Attend any career planning and placement workshops designed for education majors.
_____ Use the directories available at your college placement office to develop a list of school systems in which you have an interest.
_____ Contact school systems to request application materials.
_____ If applying to out-of-state school systems, contact the appropriate State Departments of Education to determine testing requirements. Addresses are listed in the ASCUS *Annual.*

February
(7 months prior to employment)
_____ Check on the status of your credential or placement file at your college placement office.
_____ Send completed application materials to school systems along with a résumé and cover letter.
_____ Inquire about school systems who will be recruiting at your college placement office and about the procedures for interviewing with them.

March/April
(5–6 months prior to employment)
_____ Research school systems with which you will be interviewing.
_____ Interview on campus and follow up with thank you letters.
_____ Continue to follow up by phone with school systems of interest.
_____ Begin monitoring the job vacancy listings available at your college placement office.

May/June
(3–4 months prior to employment)
_____ Just before graduation, check to be sure you are completely registered with your college placement office and that your credential or placement file is in good order.
_____ Maintain communication with your network of contacts.
_____ Subscribe to your college placement office's job vacancy bulletin.
_____ Revise your résumé and cover letter if necessary.
_____ Interview off campus and follow up with thank you letters.
_____ If relocating away from campus, contact a college placement office in the area to which you are moving and inquire about available services.

July/August
(1–2 months prior to employment)
_____ Continue to monitor job vacancy listings and apply when qualified and interested.
_____ Begin considering offers. Ask for more time to consider offers, if necessary.
_____ Select the best job offer. Inform individuals associated with your job search of your acceptance.

Source: 1991 ASCUS Annual: A Job Search Handbook for Educators (Evanston, Ill.: Association for School, College and University Staffing, Inc.), p. 5.

Résumés have one purpose: to get an interview. The interview, not the résumé, leads to the job. Jobs come through people, not through paper. If you can get an interview any other way, skip the paperwork.

There is no right or wrong way to write a résumé, although some ways are more effective and sophisticated than others. All rules are broken in this business, sometimes successfully. But each detail of the résumé-writing process should have your meticulous attention because people often are screened *out* on the basis of a poor letter and résumé. The following serve as guidelines and are based on books, articles, and the comments and preferences of hundreds of employers.

1. Résumés should be copied, preferably by offset printing. This is important because it will make your résumé stand out as professional looking. It's not expensive—about $4 for 100 copies. The *copy* of your résumé should always be accompanied by an *individually typed* cover letter.

2. Think of your résumé more as a piece of advertising than as a comprehensive data sheet. Use wide margins and plenty of spacing to make it easy to skim.

3. A listing of coursework does not belong on the résumé because it looks amateurish. If coursework is called for, send a transcript (or send a copy of your unofficial transcript).

4. Don't use a lot of dates or numbers that make the résumé hard to skim. Eliminate dates or place them at the end of a paragraph when describing experience. Don't use them for headlines.

5. Use action verbs. Avoid using forms of "to be." Use verbs such as *initiated, created, instructed, developed, supervised, managed, counseled, negotiated, maintained.*

6. Emphasize skills, especially those that transfer from one situation to another. The fact that you *coordinated* a fifth grade field trip to Washington leads one to believe that you could coordinate other things as well.

7. Forget your best prose. Use short, choppy phrases. Short is sweet.

8. Use positive words. Don't apologize for lack of experience or for weaknesses. This is not the place to hang out your dirty laundry. Be positive, capitalize on strengths, and leave out the negative or neutral words. If your health is "excellent," then don't say "not bad." Avoid negative prefixes or suffixes.

9. Résumés should be one or two pages. Never more. Anything longer is an autobiography, not a résumé.

10. Expound on your relevant experiences and condense descriptions of jobs or experiences that are not directly related to the work you're seeking. This means that you slant your résumé to the type of job you are seeking. Hence, you will need more than one résumé if you are applying for different types of jobs.

11. Make every word count. Use the K.I.S.S. system of writing: **K**eep **I**t **S**hort and **S**imple.

12. Omit "professional objective" or "job objective" unless you know exactly what it is and are closed to all other possibilities. Your job objective doesn't add that much to the résumé, but it can serve to screen you out. The cover letter is the best place to detail your objectives.

13. List your telephone number, including area code. Employers usually call to set up an interview.

14. At the bottom of your résumé, write: "Credentials and references available upon request." Have prospective employers request your credentials from you, not from your placement office. Don't list your references on your résumé.

15. Proofread your résumé. Then have a friend (or better, a professional proofreader) proofread your résumé. Even the pros have been known to send out résumés with humorous and embarrassing mistakes.

Source: John William Zehring, "How to Get Another Teaching Job and What to Do If You Can't," *Learning* (February 1978): 48. Used by permission of the publisher.

In your interviews with K–12 school district administrators, it is very important that you know as much as possible about the school, district, and community in which you might be employed. Also, you should be prepared to ask about concerns and issues related to your employment that are of interest to you.

The following are topics about which job applicants typically have questions.

District

- Type of district (elementary, high school, or unit)
- History and development of the district
- Characteristics of the student population and community
- Size of the district (number of elementary, junior high/middle, and high schools)
- Central office administrators and their roles
- Grades included at each level of education

Curriculum

- Courses in the curriculum in your discipline and their content, sequence, prerequisites, and status as electives or required courses
- Typical schedule of courses in the curriculum (first and/or second semester courses)
- Textbook and supplementary materials, the recency of their adoption, and district adoption procedures
- Availability of AV materials and equipment for classroom use
- New and/or innovative curriculum developments in your discipline in recent years
- Curriculum developments currently being planned

Students

- Type and size of student body in which a position is available
- Typical class size
- Procedures for student placement
- Characteristics of entering and exiting students (i.e., number or percentage who are enrolled in vocational and college preparatory curricula and the number or percentage who enroll in college upon graduation)

Instructional Assignment

- Reasons why the position is available (enrollment increase, retirement, resignation, etc.). Number and type of teaching preparations (i.e., self-contained classes or team-taught classes)
- Other instructional assignments
- Methods and frequency of teacher evaluation
- Availability of summer employment
- Assignments on department, school, or district committees

- Duties in the supervision/sponsorship of student activities
- Starting and ending dates of employment
- Contract length

Faculty

- Number of administrators in the building and their responsibilities
- Size of the faculty within departments and the building
- Number of new teachers hired each year
- Special interests and/or expertise of faculty

Student Services

- Student clubs, organizations, and sports
- Counseling and guidance personnel and services
- Social worker, school nurse, librarian, and other support staff and their roles

Community

- Community support for education
- Involvement of parents and other community members in the school program
- Recreational and other facilities in the community
- Demographic information about community residents
- Cost of living and housing in the community

Salary and Fringe Benefits

- District salary schedule
- Pay for extracurricular responsibilities
- Reimbursement policies for graduate study
- District requirements for continuing professional education
- Vacation and sick leave, personal leave, and other leave policies
- Substitute teacher procedures
- Payroll schedule
- Medical insurance

Selection Procedures

- Number and type of interviews that job candidates can expect
- Individuals involved in the preliminary screening of candidates, interviews, and the final selection
- District requirements for residency of staff

Final Suggestions

- Be certain to read your employment contract carefully before signing it.

You might want to visit the district while classes are in session to visit the department and building in which you might be working. If at all possible, try to meet the department head and/or building principal by whom you would be supervised.

Source: Jan E. Kilby, *The ASCUS Annual 1988: A Job Search Handbook for Educators* (Addison, Ill.: Association for School, College and University Staffing), 16. Used with permission.

States Requiring Testing for Initial Certification of Teachers

State	Authority[1]	Enacted	Effective	Test Used[2]
1	2	3	4	5
*Alabama	St. Bd.	1980	1981	State
Arizona	Leg.	1980	1980	State
Arkansas	Leg.	1979	1983	NTE
*California	Leg.	1981	1982	State
Colorado	Leg.	1981	1983	California Achievement
*Connecticut	St. Bd.	1982	1985	State
*Delaware	St. Bd.	1982	1983	Preprofessional Skills
*Florida	Leg.	1978	1980	State
Georgia	St. Bd.	1975	1980	State
*Hawaii	St. Bd.	1986	1986	NTE
*Idaho	Leg.	1987	1988	NTE
Illinois	Leg.	1985	1988	State
*Indiana	Leg.	1984	1985	NTE
*Kansas	Leg.	1984	1986	NTE
*Kentucky	Leg.	1984	1985	NTE
Louisiana	Leg.	1977	1978	NTE
*Maine	Leg.	1984	1988	NTE
*Maryland	St. Bd.	1986	1986	NTE
*Massachusetts	Leg.	1985	1988	State
*Michigan	Leg.	1986	1991	To be determined[3]
Mississippi	Leg.	1975	1977	NTE
Missouri	Leg.	1985	1988	To be determined

[1]St. Bd. = State Board of Education; Leg. = Legislature; B.P.E. = Board of Public Education; O.T.S.P.C. = Oregon Teacher Standards and Practice Commission; S.P.I. = Superintendent of Public Instruction.

[2]NTE = National Teacher Examination; State = State developed test; C.B.E.S.T. = California Basic Education Skills Test.

[3]For basic skills and subject-matter competencies.

*As of 1989, these states plus Utah, Vermont, and the District of Columbia were members of the Interstate Certification Compact. A "fully certified" teacher in one of these states may be issued a certificate for a minimum of one year by another state in the Compact.

State	Authority[1]	Enacted	Effective	Test Used[2]
1	2	3	4	5
*Montana	B.P.E.	1985	1986	NTE
*Nebraska	Leg.	1984	1989	State
Nevada	St. Bd.	1984	[4]	To be determined
*New Hampshire	St. Bd.	1984	1985	NTE
*New Jersey	St. Bd.	1984	1985	NTE
New Mexico	St. Bd.	1981	1983	NTE
*New York	St. Bd.	1980	1984	NTE
*North Carolina	St. Bd.	1964	1964	NTE
*Ohio[5]	St. Bd.	1986	1987	NTE
*Oklahoma	Leg.	1980	1982	State
Oregon	O.T.S.P.C.	1984	1985	C.B.E.S.T.
*Pennsylvania	St. Bd.	1985	1987	State
*Rhode Island	St. Bd.	1985	1986	NTE Core Battery
*South Carolina	Leg.	1979	1982	NTE and State
*South Dakota	St. Bd.	1985	1986	NTE
Tennessee	St. Bd.	1980	1981	NTE
Texas	Leg.	1981	1986	State
*Virginia	Leg.	1979	1980	NTE
*Washington	St. Bd.	1984	[3]	To be determined[6]
*West Virginia[7]	St. Bd.	1982	1985	State
*Wisconsin	S.P.I.	1986	1990	To be determined

[4]Effective year is yet to be determined.

[5]Required for individuals entering Ohio-approved education programs after July 1987.

[6]State and undetermined tests will be used.

[7]Required for individuals entering West Virginia-approved education programs as of fall 1985.

*As of 1989, these states plus Utah, Vermont, and the District of Columbia were members of the Interstate Certification Compact. A "fully certified" teacher in one of these states may be issued a certificate for a minimum of one year by another state in the Compact.

Source: Based on data from *Digest of Education Statistics 1989,* National Center for Education Statistics, 146, and Roger E. Goddard, ed., *1989 Teacher Certification Requirements* (Lake Placid, Fla.: Teacher Certification Publications, 1989), 118–119.

A certificate is valid only in the state for which it is issued. Therefore, applicants who wish to move to another state are advised to contact the certification office listed below for additional information, application procedures and forms.

Alabama
Division of Professional Services
Department of Education
404 State Office Building
Montgomery 36130-3901,
 (205) 261-5290

Alaska
Department of Education
Teacher Education and Certification
PO Box F
Goldbelt Building
Juneau 99811-0500,
 (907) 465-2810

Arizona
Teacher Certification Unit
Department of Education
1535 W. Jefferson
P.O. Box 85002
Phoenix 85007, (602) 542-4368

Arkansas
Department of Education
Teacher Certification & Education
#4 Capitol Mall, Rooms 106B/107B
Little Rock 72201, (501) 682-4342

California
Commission on Teacher
 Credentialing
1812 9th Street
Sacramento 94244-2700,
 (916) 445-7254

Colorado
Teacher Certification
Colorado Department of Education
201 East Colfax Ave
Denver 80203, (303) 866-6628

Connecticut
State Department of Education
Division of Curriculum and
 Professional Development
P.O. Box 2219
Hartford 06115, (203) 566-4561

Delaware
Department of Public Instruction
Supervisor of Certification and
 Personnel
Townsend Building
PO Box 1402
Dover 19903, (302) 736-4688

District of Columbia
Division of Teacher Services
District of Columbia Public Schools
415 12th Street, N.W.
Room 1013
Washington 20004-1994,
 (202) 724-4250

Florida
Department of Education
Division of Human Resource
 Development
Teacher Certification Offices
325 W. Gaines Street
Tallahassee 32399-0400,
 (904) 488-5724

Georgia
Georgia Department of Education
Division of Teachers Certification
1452 Twin Towers East
Atlanta 30334, (404) 656-2604

Hawaii
State Department of Education
Office of Personnel Services
P.O. Box 2360
Honolulu 96804, (808) 548-5802

Idaho
State Department of Education
Teacher Education and Certification
Len B. Jordan Office Building
Boise 83720, (208) 334-3475

Illinois
Illinois State Board of Education
100 North First Street
Springfield 62777, (217) 782-2805

Indiana
Department of Education
Center for Professional Development
Room 229, State House
Indianapolis 46204, (317) 232-9010

Iowa
Board of Education Examiners
State of Iowa
Grimes State Office Building
Des Moines 50319-0146,
 (515) 281-3245

Kansas
State Department of Education
Certification, Teacher Education &
 Accreditation
120 East 10th Street
Topeka 66612, (913) 296-2288

Kentucky
State Department of Education
Teacher Education and Certification
18th Floor, Capital Plaza Tower
Frankfort 40601, (502) 564-4606

Louisiana
State Department of Education
Bureau of Higher Education and
 Teacher Certification
P.O. Box 94064
Baton Rouge 70804-9064,
 (504) 342-3490

Maine
Department of Education and
 Cultural Services
Teacher Education and Higher
 Education
State House Station 23
Augusta 04333, (207) 289-5992

Maryland
State Department of Education
Division of Certification and
 Accreditation
200 West Baltimore Street
Baltimore 21201-2595,
 (301) 333-2142

Massachusetts
Division of Educational Personnel
Department of Education
Quincy Center Plaza
1385 Hancock Street
Quincy 02169, (617) 770-7517

Michigan
Department of Education
Teachers/Preparation and
 Certification Services
P.O. Box 30008
Lansing 48909, (517) 373-3310

Minnesota
State Department of Education
Capitol Square Building
550 Cedar Street
St. Paul 55101, (612) 296-2046

Mississippi
Department of Education
Office of Teacher Certification
P.O. Box 771
Jackson 39205, (601) 359-3483

Missouri
Teacher Education
Missouri Teacher Certification
    Office
Department of Elementary &
    Secondary Education
P.O. Box 480
Jefferson City 65102,
    (314) 751-3486

Montana
Certification Services
Office of Public Instruction
State Capitol
Helena 59620, (406) 444-3150

Nebraska
Department of Education
Teacher Certification/Education
310 Centennial Mall South
Box 94987
Lincoln 68509, (402) 471-2496

Nevada
State Department of Education
1850 Sahara, Suite 200
State Mail Room
Las Vegas 89158, (702) 486-6457

New Hampshire
State Department of Education
Bureau of Teacher Education and
    Professional Standards
State Office Park South
101 Pleasant Street
Concord 03301-3860,
    (603) 271-2407

New Jersey
State Department of Education
Teacher Certification and Academic
    Credentials
3535 Quakerbridge Road, CN 503
Trenton 08625-0503,
    (609) 588-3100

New Mexico
New Mexico State Department of
    Education
Educator Preparation & Licensure
Education Building
Santa Fe 87503,
    (505) 827-6587

New York
Office of Teachers Certification
Cultural Education Center
    Room 5A 11
Nelson A. Rockefeller Empire State
    Plaza
Albany 12230, (518) 474-3901

North Carolina
State Department of Public
    Instruction
Division of Certification
114 West Edenton Street
Raleigh 27603-1712,
    (919) 733-4125

North Dakota
State Department of Public
    Instruction
Teacher Certification
State Capitol, 9th Floor
Bismarck 58505, (701) 224-2264

Ohio
Department of Education
Teacher Certification
65 S. Front Street, Room 1012
Columbus 43266-0308,
    (614) 466-3593

Oklahoma
Department of Education
Hodge Education Building
2500 North Lincoln Boulevard,
    Room 211
Oklahoma City 73105-4599,
    (405) 521-3337

Oregon
Teacher Standards and Practices
    Commission
630 Center St. N.E., Suite 200
Salem 97310, (503) 378-3586

Pennsylvania
Department of Education
Bureau of Teacher Preparation and
    Certification
333 Market Street, 3rd Floor
Harrisburg 17126-0333,
    (717) 787-2967

Puerto Rico
Teacher Certification Division
Department of Education
Box 759
Hato Rey 00919, (809) 758-4949

Rhode Island
Department of Education
School and Teacher Accreditation,
    Certification and Placement
Roger Williams Building
22 Hayes Street
Providence 02908, (401) 277-2675

South Carolina
State Department of Education
Teacher Education and Certification
1015 Rutledge
1429 Senate Street
Columbia 29201, (803) 734-8466

South Dakota
Division of Education & Cultural
    Affairs
Office of Certification
Kneip Office Building
700 Governor's Drive
Pierre 57501, (605) 773-3553

Tennessee
Department of Education
Office of Teacher Licensing
6th Floor, North Wing
Cordell Hull Building
Nashville 37243-0377,
    (615) 741-1644

Texas
Division of Teacher Certification
William B. Travis State Office
    Building
1701 North Congress Avenue
Austin 78701, (512) 463-8976

Utah
State Office of Education
Certification and Personnel
    Development
250 East 500 South
Salt Lake City 84111,
    (801) 533-5965

Vermont
State Department of Education
Certification Division
Montpelier 05602, (802) 828-3124

Virginia
Department of Education
Division of Teacher Education and
  Certification
Box 6Q, James Monroe Building
Richmond 23216, (804) 225-2094

Washington
Office of the Superintendent of
  Public Instruction
Director of Professional Certification
Old Capitol Building, Mail Stop
  FG-11
Olympia 98504-3211,
  (206) 753-6775

West Virginia
Department of Education
Office of Professional Education
Capitol Complex, Room B-337,
  Bldg 6
Charleston 25305, (304) 348-2703

Wisconsin
Bureau of Teacher Education,
  Licensing and Placement
Teacher Certification
State Department of Public
  Instruction
125 S. Webster Street, P.O. Box
  7841
Madison 53707-7841,
  (608) 266-1027

Wyoming
State Department of Education
Certification and Licensing Unit
Hathaway Building
Cheyenne 82002-0050,
  (307) 777-6261

St. Croix District
Department of Education
Educational Personnel Services
#21, 22 & 23 Hospital Street
St. Croix, Virgin Islands 00820,
  (809) 773-1095

St. Thomas/St. John District
Department of Education
Educational Personnel Services
44-46 Kongens Gad
St. Thomas, Virgin Islands 00802,
  (809) 774-0100

**United States Department of
Defense Overseas Dependent
Section**
Recruitment and Assignment Section
2461 Eisenhower Avenue
Alexandria, Virginia 22331-1100,
  (202) 325-0885

Source: 1991 ASCUS Annual: A Job Search Handbook for Educators (Evanston, Ill.: Association for
School, College and University Staffing, Inc.), pp. 33–34. Used with permission.

Note: Adult education programs, while not separately delineated above, may provide instruction
at the elementary, secondary, or higher education level. Chart reflects typical patterns of progres-
sion rather than all possible variations.

Source: U.S. Department of Education, National Center for Education Statistics, *Digest of Education Statistics 1989,* Twenty-fifth Edition (Washington, D.C.: National Center for Education Statistics): 5.

ORGANIZATIONAL CHARTS

The Institutional Structure of Education in the United States

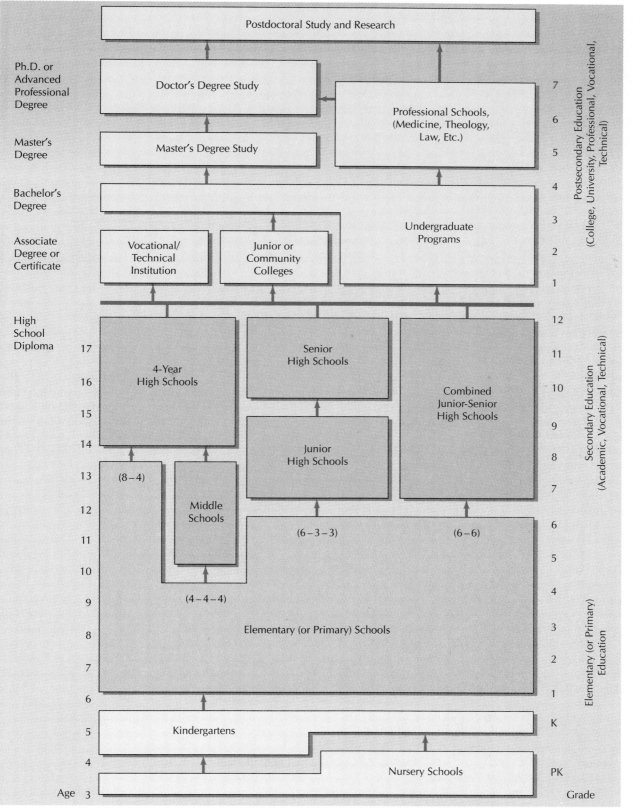

Organizational Structure of a Typical State School System

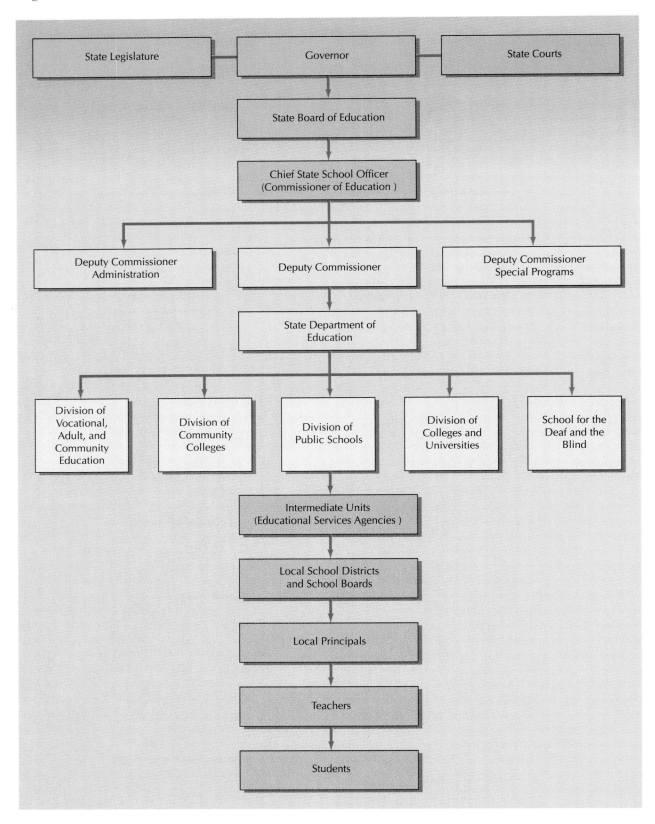

Organizational Chart for a Large Metropolitan School District

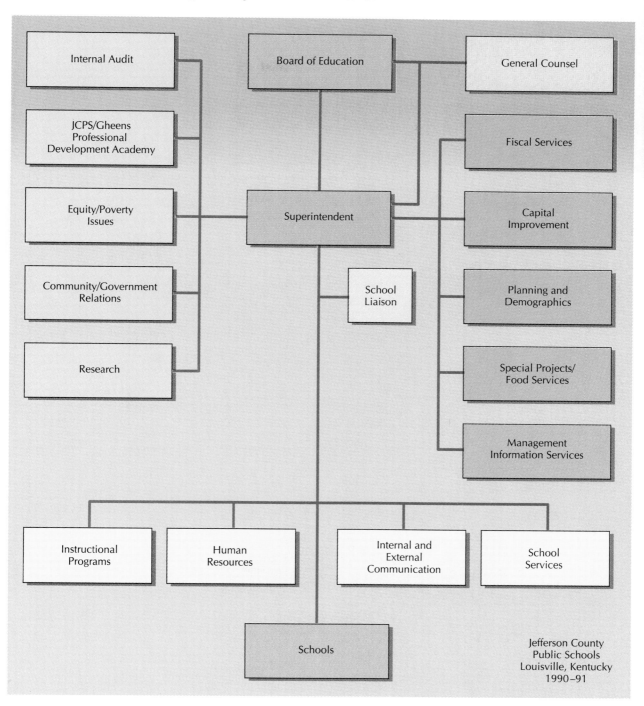

Internal Audit

Board of Education

General Counsel

JCPS/Gheens Professional Development Academy

Fiscal Services

Equity/Poverty Issues

Superintendent

Capital Improvement

Community/Government Relations

School Liaison

Planning and Demographics

Research

Special Projects/ Food Services

Management Information Services

Instructional Programs

Human Resources

Internal and External Communication

School Services

Schools

Jefferson County Public Schools Louisville, Kentucky 1990–91

Source: Jefferson County Public School System, Louisville, Kentucky, 1990–91. Used with permission.

Typical Organizational Structure for a Medium-Sized School District (20,000 pupils)

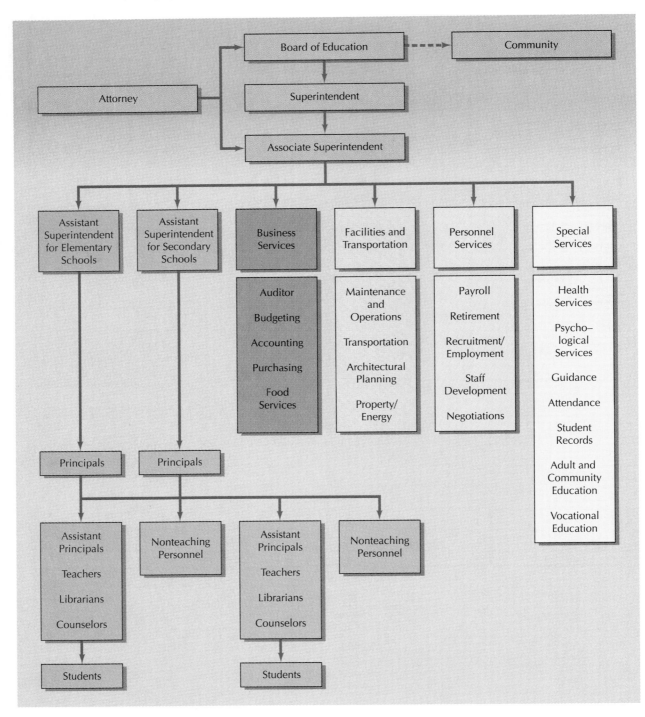

RESOURCES FOR MEETING THE CHALLENGE OF TEACHING AT-RISK AND EXCEPTIONAL STUDENTS

Organizations

American Red Cross
1730 D St. N.W.
Washington, DC 20006
*Has produced several publications
on AIDS. For sample copies,
contact your local office or write
AIDS Education Office*
*Ask for "AIDS and Children:
Information for Parents of School
Age Children" and "AIDS and
Children: Information for
Teachers and School Officials."
Single copy free, bulk orders
available.*

Center for Early Adolescence
University of North Carolina at
Chapel Hill
Carr Mill Mall
Carboro, NC 27510
(919) 966-1148
Middle school achievement issues

**Center for Successful Child
Development**
Robert Taylor Homes
4848 South State St.
Chicago, IL 60609
(312) 373-8680

Child and Family Policy Center
100 Court Avenue, Suite 312
Des Moines, IA 50309
(515) 243-2000
*Especially state policy on
collaborating to meet children's
needs*

Children's Agenda
155 Cottage St., NE
Salem OR 97310
(503) 373-7036

Children's Defense Fund
122 C Street, NW
Washington, DC 20001
(202) 628-8787
*Improving the quality of schools and
building parent and community
support for achievement*

The Family Resource Coalition
230 North Michigan Avenue
Suite 1625
Chicago, IL 60601
(312) 726-4750
*Particularly good on ways to build
support and resources that
empower families and enhance
the capacities of parents*

Foundation for Child Development
345 E. 46th St.
Suite 700
New York, NY 10017
(212) 697-3150

**Institute for Educational Leadership,
et al.**
1001 Connecticut Avenue, NW
Suite 310
Washington, D.C. 20036-5541
(202) 822-8405

Joining Forces
379 Hall of the States
400 North Capitol Street, NW
Washington, DC 20001
(202) 393-8159
*For ideas on specific programs that
link education and human service
systems to help children and
families at risk, contact this
clearinghouse.*

**National Coalition for an Urban
Children's Agenda**
c/o National Assoc. of State Boards
of Education
1012 Cameron Street
Alexandria, VA 22314
(703) 684-4000
*Collaborative interagency models of
service delivery*

**National Coalition of Hispanic
Health and Human Services
Organizations**
1030 15th St. N.W.
Suite 1053
Washington, DC 10005
*Assists those needing AIDS
information in Spanish.*

National Collaboration for Youth
1319 F St., NW
Suite 301
Washington, DC 20004
(202) 347-2080

**National Community Education
Assoc.**
801 North Fairfax, Suite 209
Alexandria, VA 22314
(703) 683-0161
*Good resource on ways to get
broad-based community
involvement to increase academic
achievement and improve school
climate*

National Education Association
NEA Communications
1201 16th St. N.W.
Washington, DC 20036
*Published guide for members, titled
"The Facts About AIDS."
Write for NEA AIDS Booklet*

**National Forum on the Future of
Children and Their Families**
National Research Council
2101 Constitution Ave., NW
Washington, DC 20418
(202) 334-3033

**National Network of Runaway and
Youth Services**
905 6th St., SW #411B
Washington, DC 20024
(202) 682-4114

**Networking Project for Disabled
Women and Girls**
YWCA of New York
610 Lexington Ave.
New York, NY 10022
(212) 755-4500

Outward Bound USA
384 Field Point Road
Greenwich, CT 06830
(800) 243-8520

Parent Aide Support Service
Nebraska Dept. of Social Services
1001 O St.
Lincoln, NE 68508
(402) 471-7000

Parents as Teachers
Marillac Hall
University of Missouri—St. Louis
8001 Natural Bridge Road
St. Louis, MO
(314) 553-5738

Teen Alternative Parenting Program
Child Support Division
143 E. Market St.
Indianapolis, IN 46204
(317) 263-6100

U.S. Department of Education
Disseminates a 28-page set of
guidelines, "AIDS and the
Education of Our Children: A
Guide for Parents and Teachers."
For free copies write to Consumer
Information Center, Dept. ED,
Pueblo, CO 81009.

Publications

- Copies of these three **Information Papers** are available for $5.00 each postpaid from: **William T. Grant Foundation Commission on Youth and America's Future,** Suite 301, 1001 Connecticut Avenue, NW, Washington, DC 20036-5541.

American Youth: A Statistical Snapshot by James Wetzel

Drawing on the latest statistically reliable government surveys, this demographic review captures much of the diversity inherent in a collective portrait of American 15–24 year-olds. Includes data on marriage, childbearing, living arrangements, income, education, employment, health, and juvenile justice. Historical trends as well as future projections are presented along with 12 charts, 18 tables.

Current Federal Policies and Programs for Youth by J.R. Reingold and Associates

Who is doing what for youth in the federal government? This concise survey of current federal policies and programs for youth in Education, Health and Human Services, Labor, Justice, and Defense provides a one-of-a-kind resource for researchers, practitioners, analysts, and policymakers who want quick access to accurate information about federal youth policy. Includes state-level allocation tables.

Facts and Faith: A Status Report on Youth Service by Anne C. Lewis. **Commentary** by Jane Kendall

Clarifies the underlying assumptions and reviews the current state of knowledge about youth service programs, including barriers and supports for such programs. The overriding challenge of youth service is to combine the dual needs that youth have: to work and to serve. Citing dozens of local, state, and national youth service programs, this analysis is a vital resource for policymakers and community leaders. Commentary stresses the value of service-learning.

- The following **Working Papers** are available for $10.00 each postpaid from: **William T. Grant Foundation Commission on Youth and America's Future,** Suite 301, 1001 Connecticut Avenue, NW, Washington, DC, 20036-5541.

Barriers to Developing Comprehensive and Effective Youth Services by William Treanor. **Commentaries** by David Richart and Dorothy Stoneman

A provocative discussion of the youth service world: prevailing attitudes toward youth, history, funding dilemmas, and leadership and staffing scenarios. Recommends a prototype for youth service systems.

The Bridge: Cooperative Education for All High School Students by Cynthia Parsons. **Commentaries** by Dennis Gray and David Lynn, Morgan V. lewis, Roy L. Wooldridge

Calling for a fundamental change in American high schools, the founder of a successful Vermont community service program presents a rationale and methodology for experiential and cooperative education models. Underscores the benefits of combining learning and doing in a school-based, supervised setting.

Communities and Adolescents: An Exploration of Reciprocal Supports by Joan Wynn, Harold Richman, Robert A. Rubenstein, and Julia Littell, with Brian Britt and Carol Yoken. **Commentaries** by Diane P. Hedin and Judith B. Erickson

What can communities do to be more responsive to youth and what can communities expect from youth? Explores the rich variety of community supports that can be made available to adolescents if individual communities decide to make youth a priority. Appendix includes 22 selected studies describing the differing impacts of community supports on adolescents.

Determinants of Youth's Successful Entry into Adulthood by Sarah Gideonse. **Commentaries** by Elijah Anderson and David F. Ricks

What prevents youth from successful entry into adulthood: individual defects or environment flaws? Addresses the factors which account for the difficulties youth have in assuming adult roles. Examines characteristics and circumstances that promote positive changes in young people and explains why it is never too late for interventions—even for youth with multiple problems.

The Difference that Differences Make: Adolescent Diversity and Its Deregulation by Melvin D. Levine, M.D. **Commentaries** by Michael S. Wald and John H. Martin

Discusses how teaching methods and expectations can constrict the ways in which young people learn, denying many access to education and employment opportunities. Contends that predetermined memory, verbal, and written criteria—to which a large number of students cannot and do not respond well—are often the only vehicles for showing knowledge. Argues for a wider lens through which to view young people and their abilities.

Family Influences on Transitions to the Adult Job Market by Robert I. Lerman and Theodora Ooms. **Commentaries** by Frank F. Furstenberg, Jr. and Margaret Simms

Analyzes the often ignored interrelationship of family influences and youth employment decisions. Emphasizes the critical connections among youth's living arrangements, the responsibilities of young people, and their choices about work.

The Interaction of Family, Community, and Work in the Socialization of Youth by Stephen F. Hamilton. **Commentaries** by John Ogbu and Paul Riesman

Explores the critical connections among family, community, and the workplace as they interact with young people. Calls for establishing intentional policy among these three spheres of influence to bolster their separate, but interconnected roles in socializing youth.

Mutuality in Parent-Adolescent Relationships by James Youniss. **Commentaries** by Ann C. Crouter and John H. Lewko

Through a comprehensive review of recent research, counters popular mythology that adolescent relationships with parents and peers are negative. Provides a context for adolescent-parent and adolescent-peer relationships to guide program development and policy considerations.

The Transition to Adulthood of Youth with Disabilities by David Vandergoot, Amy Gottlieb, and Edwin W. Martin. **Commentaries** by Sharon Stewart Johnson and Diane Lipton and Mary Lou Breslin

Cites youth with disabilities as an economically disadvantaged subgroup and explores family support, education, and employment issues as well as the barriers to community participation and self-sufficiency particular to these youth. Includes extensive research findings and policy recommendations.

Transitional Difficulties of Out-of-Home Youth by Joy Duva and Gordon Raley. **Commentaries** by Eileen M. Pasztor and Peter R. Correia III and Anita Fream

A targeted look at a vulnerable part of the youth population—foster care youth and runaways—who they are, how many they are, what programs serve them, what special problems they encounter in their transition to adulthood, what more needs to be done. Examines independent living programs that assist older out-of-home youth in preparing for life and work.

Youth Transition from Adolescence to the World of Work by Garth L. Mangum. **Commentaries** by Marvin Lazerson and Stephen F. Hamilton

Summarizes labor market realities, employer expectations, parental influences, and the difficulties youth experience as they move into the world of work. Highlights vocational education, apprenticeship, and on-the-job training opportunities available for youth. Makes recommendations for how families, schools, and workplaces can aid youth in the transition to work.

Youth and the Workplace: Second-Chance Programs and the Hard-to-Serve by Thomas J. Smith, Gary C. Walker, Rachel A. Baker, (Public/Private Ventures). **Commentaries** by Gary Burtless, Jacqueline P. Danzberger, Morton H. Sklar, Richard F. Elmore

Second-chance education, training, and employment programs of the last decade are detailed. Includes tables and an appendix of model programs for at-risk youth. Four commentaries expand the research and policy recommendations.

Vanishing Dreams: The Growing Economic Plight of America's Young Families by Clifford M. Johnson, Andrew M. Sum, and James D. Weill. (Published by Children's Defense Fund with partial assistance from Youth and America's Future.)

- **"Teens & AIDS: Playing It Safe"**
  A free brochure published by the American Council of Life Insurance and the Health Insurance Association of America. Packages of 100 are available for $10 from 1001 Pennsylvania Ave. N.W., Washington, DC 20004.

- The following three publications are available from: **Realizing America's Hope,** South Carolina ETV, P.O. Drawer L, Columbia, SC 29250, 1-800-277-0829.

Changing Delivery Systems: Addressing the Fragmentation of Children and Youth Services, by the Education Commission of the States and the National Conference of State Legislatures.

This work describes collaborative strategies state agencies can use to improve youth services and stretch limited fiscal resources.

Guiding Youth to Success: What Schools and Communities Can Do?, by MDC, Inc.

This book provides a vision of comprehensive guidance that involves parents and the community as well as the schools.

Let's Do It Our Way: Working Together for Educational Excellence, by MDC, Inc.

This handbook for everyone explains why it is important that all members of the community work with schools to educate young people and outlines step by step how to set up a collaborative.

Video Productions

- The following six video productions are available from: **Realizing America's Hope,** South Carolina ETV, P.O. Drawer L, Columbia, SC 29250, 1-800-277-0829.

All Our Children with Bill Moyers, produced by Public Affairs Television, *90 minutes.* Moyers and his colleagues examine the efforts of several programs and schools across the country which are achieving small victories in the lives of those young people who have known defeat.

Investing in Our Youth, produced by South Carolina ETV, *30 minutes.* Half-hour documentary edited from case studies produced for the legislators' teleconference, **Investing in Our Youth: A Nationwide Committee of the Whole.**

Investing in Our Youth: A Nationwide Committee of the Whole, produced by South Carolina ETV, *120 minutes.* This two-hour teleconference aimed at state legislators demonstrated how collaborative strategies are proving to be highly cost-effective by cutting through bureaucratic red tape while serving clients more effectively.

Making the American Dream Work for Our Children, produced by South Carolina ETV, *30 minutes.* Half-hour documentary edited from the case studies produced for the guidance teleconference, **Making the American Dream Work for Our Children: A New Vision of School Guidance.**

Making the American Dream Work for Our Children: A New Vision of School Guidance, produced by South Carolina ETV, *60 minutes.* This teleconference demonstrates how schools and businesses are being drawn into the school guidance process in order to better serve the nation's young people.

Responding to 'All Our Children'—Bill Moyers Live from Longstreet Theatre, produced by South Carolina ETV, *60 minutes.* Representatives from education, business, government, and the family engage in lively discussion with journalist Bill Moyers in response to the challenges facing the nation's youth described in the Moyers' documentary, **All Our Children with Bill Moyers.**

- **"AIDS Prevention Program for Youth"**
A new program for high school students from the American Red Cross. Materials include: "Letter from Brian," a video free on loan or available for purchase for $95; Teacher's Manual, $8.75 for five copies; Student Workbooks, $25 for 25 copies; Parents' Brochure, $4.50 for 100 copies. Order from American Red Cross, AIDS Education Office, 1730 D St. N.W., Washington, D.C. 20006.

Telephone Hotlines

DRUG RESISTANCE EDUCATION
Alcohol and Drug Helpline (Offers referral to local treatment centers and support groups.)
1-800-821-4357
Cocaine Abuse Hotline (Provides crisis intervention and information about treatment for abuse of all substances, not just cocaine.)
1-800-992-9239

Dare America (Arranges for specially trained police officers to present drug resistance education programs in the schools.)
1-800-223-3273

Drug Abuse Information & Referral Line, National Institute on Drug Abuse
1-800-662-4357
Drug Prevention and Education Inc.
1-800-342-3691

AIDS HOTLINE
Most states and local communities now have hotlines with up-to-date information on AIDS. The following is a national hotline.
- The U.S. Public Health Service has a 24-hour, toll-free number. Call 1-800-342-AIDS for a recorded message.

MISSING CHILDREN
Child Find
1-800-426-5678
Kid Net
1-800-543-6381
National Child Safety Council Missing Children International
1-800-872-7875
National Runaway Switchboard
1-800-621-4000

SUICIDE HOTLINE
Humanistic Foundations
1-800-333-4444

CURRICULUM RESOURCES

Curriculum Materials Evaluation Criteria

Publication and Cost

1. *Authors:* Are the authors known and respected professionally?
2. *Cost:* Is the cost of the materials reasonable relative to other, comparable materials?
3. *Development History:* Were the materials adequately field tested and revised prior to publication?
4. *Edition:* Is this edition to be in publication for several years, or is a new edition to be released shortly?
5. *Publication Date:* Were these materials published within the last two years?
6. *Publisher:* Does the publisher of these materials have a good reputation among educators?
7. *Purchase Procedures:* Are the purchase procedures clear and easy to use?
8. *Quantity:* Are there likely to be difficulties in obtaining sufficient quantities of the materials for each student who will be using them?
9. *Special Requirements:* Do our schools have the special resources required for use of the materials?
10. *Teacher Training:* Does use of the materials require skills that our district teachers are not likely to possess?

Physical Properties

11. *Aesthetic Appeal:* Are the materials likely to appeal to the user's aesthetic sense?
12. *Components:* Do the materials contain so many components that teachers will have difficulty in keeping track of them and using them?
13. *Consumables:* Does the product make unnecessary use of consumable materials?
14. *Durability:* Do the materials have components that are especially vulnerable to wear?
15. *Media:* Does the developer make appropriate use of the media included among the materials?
16. *Quality:* Did the publisher use high quality materials in the production process?
17. *Safety:* Are there possible hazards to students or teachers in using the materials?

Content

18. *Approach:* Does the developer use an approach consistent with the district's curriculum?
19. *Instructional Objectives:* Are the materials' objectives compatible with the district's curriculum and acceptable to teachers?
20. *Instructional Objectives—Types:* Do the materials contain affective objectives in addition to cognitive objectives?

21. *Issues Orientation:* Are the materials free of biases that are misleading or that are likely to be unacceptable to teachers, students, and the community?
22. *Multiculturalism:* Do the materials reflect the contributions and perspectives of various ethnic and cultural groups?
23. *Scope and Sequence:* Are the scope and sequence of the materials compatible with the district's curriculum?
24. *Sex Roles:* Is the content of the materials free of sex stereotypes?
25. *Time-Boundedness:* Does the content of the materials reflect current knowledge and culture?

Instructional Properties

26. *Assessment Devices:* Do the materials contain tests and other assessment devices that will be helpful to the teacher and his or her students?
27. *Comprehensibility:* Will the materials be clearly understood by the students who will be using them?
28. *Coordination with the Curriculum:* Are the materials compatible with other materials currently being used in the school?
29. *Individualization:* Does the design of the materials allow teachers to use them differently according to student needs?
30. *Instructional Effectiveness:* Does the publisher provide any data on the effectiveness of the materials in actual use?
31. *Instructional Patterns:* Is the primary instructional pattern likely to help the learner achieve the materials' objectives?
32. *Learner Characteristics:* Are the materials appropriate for the students who will be using them?
33. *Length:* Are the materials an appropriate length so that they can fit conveniently into the teacher's instructional schedule?
34. *Management System:* Is the use of the materials easily managed by the teacher?
35. *Motivational Properties:* Are the materials likely to excite the interest of students and teachers?
36. *Prerequisites:* Are the students likely to have the prerequisite knowledge or skills necessary for learning the content of the materials?
37. *Readability:* Are the materials written at an appropriate reading level for students who will be using them?
38. *Role of the Student:* Do the materials include activities that students are capable of doing and that they will enjoy doing?
39. *Role of the Teacher:* Do the materials include activities that teachers will find interesting and rewarding?

Source: Meredith Damien Gall, *Handbook for Evaluating and Selecting Curriculum Materials* (Boston: Allyn and Bacon, 1981), pp. 118–120. © Meredith Damien Gall, University of Oregon.

For articles on current techniques and materials in the various subject areas, consult the following periodicals.

The Arts
Art Education
Music Educators' Journal
School Arts

Foreign Languages
Modern Language Journal

Language Arts
English Education
English Journal
Language Arts
The Reading Teacher

Mathematics
Arithmetic Teacher
Mathematics Teacher
School Science and Mathematics

Physical Education
Journal of Health, Physical Education and Recreation
Physical Educator

Science
American Biology Teacher
Physics Teacher

School Science and Mathematics
Science and Children
Science Education
Science Teacher
Studies in Science Education

Social Studies
History Teacher
Social Education
Social Studies Journal
The Social Studies

Free Curriculum Materials

For free curriculum materials, consult the *Educators' Index of Free Materials,* an index published annually by

Educators Progress Service, Inc.
214 Center Street
Randolph, Wisconsin 53956
(414) 326-3126

As there is a rapid turnover in the availability of free materials, consult the most recent edition of the *Index;* (most college libraries subscribe to the *Index*). To give you an idea of the range of free materials available to teachers, the 381-page *Index* for the 1990–91 school year included the following analysis of 2,631 free materials available from 549 sources ("New" materials are those listed for the first time in the *Index*).

Analysis of Educators' Index of Free Materials, 1990

	New	*Old*	*Total*
Administration			
Board of Education	1	4	5
Superintendents and Principals	28	14	42
Fine Arts			
Music Education	0	1	1
Health and Physical Education			
Health Education	187	282	469
Nutrition Instruction	28	34	62
Physical Education and Recreation	28	79	107
Safety and First Aid	5	16	21
Language Arts			
Reading, Writing, Spelling, and Literature	2	23	25
Television and Radio	0	6	6

	New	*Old*	*Total*
Science and Mathematics			
Earth-Space Science	17	14	31
Environmental Education			
Conservation	1	11	12
Forestry	4	8	12
General	40	39	79
General Science	32	27	59
Life Sciences	0	4	4
Mathematics	0	17	17
Physical Science	3	84	87
Social Studies			
Citizenship	10	31	41
Economics	34	99	133
Geography			
United States and Territories	16	53	69
Various Other Countries	82	131	213
History	12	26	38
Sociology	4	12	16
World Affairs	19	82	101
Special Areas			
Cocurricular Activities	4	30	34
Consumer Education	63	110	173
Driver Education	12	1	13
Guidance	93	179	272
Special Education	26	11	37
Transportation	1	2	3
Vocational Education			
Agriculture			
Animal Husbandry	1	8	9
Crops and Soils	3	8	11
Farm Management	0	33	33
Business Education			
Distributive Education	0	20	20
Office Practices	0	1	1
Home Economics Education			
Clothing Instruction	0	15	15
Cooking Instruction	28	93	121
Family Life Education	11	52	63
Home Management	6	19	25
Industrial Education	27	31	58
Visual and Audiovisual Aids			
Charts, Pictures, and Posters	5	22	27
Exhibits	1	6	7
Magazines and Newsletters	15	32	47
Maps	0	12	12
Total	**849**	**1782**	**2631**

Source: Mary P. Parent (ed.), *Educators Index of Free Materials,* 99th ed. (Randolph, Wis.: Educators Progress Service, Inc., 1990), p. X.

Conventional Unit Plan Form

Grade: _____ Course/Subject: _____ Teacher: _____

Unit Topic: _____ Duration: _____

1. *Introduction:* State briefly the nature and scope of the unit; include the significance or justification of the problems, concepts, issues, skills, or activities that will be specified in the unit.

2. *Instructional Objectives:* (anticipated outcomes stated in behavioral or performance terms—cognitive, psychomotor and affective):
   a. What do I, the teacher, expect the students to accomplish?
   b. What changes in the students' behavior do I intend to bring about?
   c. What would each student be doing which would demonstrate that he has achieved the objective?

3. *Unit Content—Problem/Concept/Skills:*
   a. When and what am I going to teach or do? (Dates and topics)
   b. List the topics, subtopics, problems, concepts, issues, information, or skills involved.
   c. The activities should be identified and an approximate time indicated for each (e.g. 1 week, 2 sessions).

4. *Procedures/Activities/Approaches/Methods:*
   a. How am I going to teach?
   b. Instructional procedures to be used should be identified; informal lecture, discussion (large or small groups), oral or written reports, panel or committee work, audiovisual activities, educational games, guest speaker, field trip, and so on.

5. *Instructional Aids or Resources:*
   a. List the materials or equipment that you will need.
   b. List all materials that the students will need except conventional teaching aids such as chalk, chalkboard, and pencil and paper.
   c. Identify the textbook or reference materials in a standard bibliographical form (author, title, publisher, and year published).

6. *Evaluation:*
   a. In what ways am I going to measure and evaluate the students' progress or achievement?
   b. How am I going to find out whether or not I have achieved the stated objectives?
   c. How am I going to find out whether I have successfully communicated with the students?
   d. What evaluation devices could I use besides quizzes, tests and classroom participation?

Source: Reprinted with permission of Macmillan Publishing Company from *A Resource Guide for Secondary School Teaching: Planning for Competence,* 3d ed, by Eugene C. Kim and Richard D. Kellough (New York: Macmillan, 1983), p. 45. Copyright © 1983 by Eugene C. Kim and Richard D. Kellough.

American Alliance for Health, Physical Education, Recreation and Dance (AAHPERD)

1900 Association Drive   Phone: (703) 476-3400
Reston, VA 22091   Dr. Charles H. Hartman,
     Exec.V.Pres.
Founded: 1885. **Members:** 42,000. **Staff:** 54. **Budget:** $5,200,000. **Regional Groups:** 6. **State Groups:** 54. Students and educators in physical education, dance, health, athletics, safety education, recreation, and outdoor education. Purpose is to improve its fields of education at all levels through such services as consultation, periodicals and special publications, leadership development, determination of standards, and research. Operates Information and Resource Utilization Center devoted to physical education and recreation for the handicapped and programs for senior citizens. Maintains biographical archives; sponsors placement service; bestows awards. Cooperates with the President's Council on Physical Fitness and Sports in administering the Presidential Physical Fitness Awards. **Publications:** *AAHPERD Update,* 9/year. Newsletter. • *Fitting In,* monthly. Newsletter for 5th and 6th graders about health, nutrition, fitness, and exercise. Includes games and a guide for teachers who wish to utilize the information in the classroom. • *Health Education,* bimonthly. Professional journal for health educators. Includes advertisers' index and book reviews. • *Journal of Physical Education Recreation and Dance,* 9/year. • *Leisure Today,* semiannual. • *News Kit on Programs for the Aging,* semiannual. • *Research Quarterly.*

American Association of Teachers of French (AATF)

57 E. Armory Avenue   Phone: (217) 333-2842
University of Illinois   Fred M. Jenkins, Exec.Dir.
Champaign, IL 61820
Founded: 1927. **Members:** 11,000. **Budget:** $513,000. **Local Groups:** 76. Teachers of French in public and private elementary and secondary schools, colleges, and universities. Maintains Pedagogical Aids Bureau, offering French maps, postcards, and medals, at cost; conducts annual French contest in elementary and secondary schools and awards trips to the winners; awards annual summer scholarships to teachers for study in France or Quebec, Canada; maintains a placement bureau and a high school honor society. Furnishes traveling exhibits and provides a pen pal agency for exchange of letters between French and American boys and girls. **Publications:** *AATF National Bulletin,* quarterly. Newsletter reporting on the French language and culture and the problems of teaching French in the United States. • *Directory,* annual. • *French Review,* bimonthly. Journal.

American Association of Teachers of German (AATG)

112 Haddontowne Ct., #104   Phone: (609) 795-5553
Cherry Hill, NJ 08034   Helene Zimmer-Loew,
     Exec.Dir.
Founded: 1926. **Members:** 6500. **Staff:** 6. **Budget:** $850,000. **Local Groups:** 62. Teachers of German at all levels; individuals interested in German language and culture. Offers in-service teacher-training workshops; presents awards and scholarships to outstanding high school students of German. **Publications:** *American Association of Teachers of German—Newsletter,* quarterly. • *Die Unterrichtspraxis: For the Teaching of German,* semiannual. Journal; includes pedagogical articles, reports, teaching tips, news, and discussions. Also contains some articles in German, book reviews, obituaries, software reviews, and index. • *German Quarterly.* Scholarly journal on German literature and language. Includes some articles in German, volume index, book reviews, chapter news, review essays, and announcements of professional activities.

American Association of Teachers of Spanish and Portuguese (Hispanic) (AATSP)

P.O. Box 6349   Phone: (601) 325-2041
Mississippi State, MS 39762   James R. Chatham,
     Exec.Dir.
Founded: 1917. **Members:** 12,000. **Local Groups:** 74. Teachers of Spanish and Portuguese languages and literatures and others interested in Hispanic culture. Operates placement bureau and maintains pen pal registry. Sponsors honor society, Sociedad Honoraria Hispanica and National Spanish Examinations for secondary school students. **Publications:** *Directory,* annual. • *Hispania,* quarterly. Scholarly journal containing critical studies and annotated bibliographies on the literatures and languages of Spain, Portugal, and Latin America as well as papers concerned with the teaching of Spanish and Portuguese. Includes articles written in English, Spanish, or Portuguese, book reviews, and chapter news.

American Classical League (Language) (ACL)

Miami University   Phone: (513) 529-4116
Oxford, OH 45056   Ed Phinney, Pres.
Founded: 1919. **Members:** 3500. Teachers of classical languages in high schools and colleges. To promote the teaching of Latin and other classical languages. Presents scholarship. Maintains placement service, teaching materials, and resource center at Miami University in Oxford, OH to sell teaching aids to Latin and Greek teachers. **Publications:** *Classical Outlook,* 4/year. Journal. • *Newsletter,* periodic. • Also publishes books, mimeographs, pamphlets, and booklets, and produces posters.

American Council on the Teaching of Foreign Languages (ACTFL)

Six Executive Plaza   Phone: (914) 963-8830
Yonkers, NY 10701   C. Edward Scebold, Exec.Dir.
Founded: 1967. **Members:** 8000. **Budget:** $1,200,000. **Regional Groups:** 32. **State Groups:** 53. Individuals interested in the teaching of classical and modern foreign

languages in schools and colleges throughout America. Included in the ACTFL structure are state, regional, and national organizations of foreign language teachers and supervisors from all levels of education. Operates materials center which produces inexpensive classroom and professional materials. Conducts seminars and workshops. Offers group insurance plans. Presents Florence Steiner Awards for Leadership in Foreign Language Education; Paul Pimsleur Award for Research in Foreign Language Education; Nelson Brooks Award for Excellence in the Teaching of Culture; Emma Birkmaier Award for Doctoral Dissertation Research in Foreign Language Education; National Textbook Company Award for Building Community Interest in Foreign Language Education. Founded by the Modern Language Association of America, council is now incorporated and exists as a corporate entity. **Publications:** *Foreign Language Annals,* 6/year. Professional journal covering teaching methods, educational research and experimentation, and professional concerns. Includes book reviews, calendar of events, information on employment opportunities, research reports, advertisers' index, and annual directory. • *Public Awareness Newsletter,* quarterly. • *Series on Foreign Language Education,* annual.

American Federation of Teachers (Education) (AFT)
555 New Jersey Avenue, N.W.   Phone: (202) 879-4400
Washington, DC 20001   Albert Shanker, Pres.
Founded: 1916. **Members:** 715,000. **Budget:** $40,000,000. **Locals:** 2200. AFL-CIO. Works with teachers and other educational employees at the state and local level in organizing, collective bargaining, research, educational issues, and public relations. Conducts research in areas such as educational reform, bilingual education, teacher certification, and evaluation. Represents members' concerns through legislative action; offers technical assistance. Seeks to serve professionals with concerns similar to those of teachers, including civil service employees, through the Federation of State Employees, and healthcare workers through the Federation of Nurses and Health Professionals (see separate entry) division. Operates Education for Democracy Project. Bestows awards; compiles statistics. **Publications:** *AFT Action: A Newsletter for AFT Leaders,* weekly. • *American Educator,* quarterly. Magazine. • *American Teacher,* 8/year. Tabloid covering union news; includes conference report. • *Healthwire,* 10/year. Association and industry newsletter for AFT members involved in health care. • *On Campus,* 9/year. • *Public Service Reporter,* 9/year.

Association for Childhood Education International (ACEI)
11141 Georgia Avenue,   Phone: (301) 942-2443
Suite 200   A. Gilson Brown, Exec.Dir.
Wheaton, MD 20902

Founded: 1931. **Members:** 15,000. **Staff:** 13. **State Groups:** 31. **Local Groups:** 175. Teachers, parents, and others interested in promoting good educational practices for children from infancy through early adolescence. Seeks: to promote the inherent rights, education, and well-being of all children in home, school and community; to promote desirable conditions, programs, and practices for children from infancy through early adolescence; to raise the standard of preparation for teachers and others who are involved with the care and development of children; to encourage continuous professional growth of educators; to bring into active cooperation all individuals and groups concerned with children; to inform the public of the needs of children and the ways in which various programs must be adjusted to fit those needs and rights. Conducts workshops and travel/study tours abroad. Bestows awards. Maintains liaison with government agencies, cooperating organizations, teaching institutions, and manufacturers and designers of materials and equipment for children. **Publications:** *ACEI Exchange,* monthly. • *Childhood Education,* 5/year. • *Journal of Research in Childhood Education,* biennial. • Also publishes books and booklets.

Association for Supervision and Curriculum Development (ASCD)
1250 N. Pitt Street   Phone: (703) 549-9110
Alexandria, VA 22314   Gordon Cawelti, Exec.Dir.
Founded: 1943. **Members:** 120,000. **Staff:** 92. **Budget:** $12,000,000. **Affiliated Units:** 57. Professional organization of supervisors, curriculum coordinators and directors, consultants, professors of education, classroom teachers, principals, superintendents, parents, and others interested in school improvement at all levels of education. Provides professional development experiences in curriculum and supervision; disseminates information; encourages research, evaluation, and theory development. Conducts the National Training Center and National Curriculum Study Institutes; provides Research Information Service (free to members). **Publications:** *ASCD Update,* 8/year. Newsletter discussing the improvement of curriculum, instruction, and supervision in elementary and secondary education. • *Association for Supervision and Curriculum Development—Yearbook.* • *Curriculum Update,* quarterly. Newsletter. • *Educational Leadership,* 8/year. Magazine. • *Journal of Curriculum and Supervision,* quarterly. Includes abstracts of selected doctoral dissertations. • Also publishes books and booklets.

Council for Exceptional Children (Special Education) (CEC)
1920 Association Drive   Phone: (703) 620-3660
Reston, VA 22091   Jeptha V. Greer, Exec.Dir.
Founded: 1922. **Members:** 54,000. **Staff:** 80. **Student Associations:** 47. **State and Provincial Groups:** 57. **Local Groups:** 970. Teachers, school administrators, teacher ed-

ucators, and others with a direct or indirect concern for the education of the handicapped and gifted, defined as those children and youth whose instructional needs differ sufficiently from the average to require special services and teachers with specialized qualifications. Council is concerned with children who are mentally gifted, mentally retarded, visually handicapped, hearing impaired, physically handicapped, and those with behavioral disorders, learning disabilities, and speech defects. Champions the right of exceptional individuals to full educational opportunities, career development, and equal employment opportunities. Provides information to teachers, parents, and others concerning the education of exceptional children. Sponsors workshops, academies, and symposia on special education topics; provides technical assistance to legislators, state departments of education, and other agencies; disseminates information. Coordinates political action network to support the rights of exceptional people. Conducts special projects in areas such as special education technology and software and training teacher educators. Maintains 63,000 volume library. Operates the ERIC Clearinghouse on Handicapped and Gifted Children. **Publications:** *Exceptional Child Education Resources,* quarterly. • *Exceptional Children,* 6/year. Research journal covering all facets of special education. • *Teaching Exceptional Children,* quarterly. Magazine; includes classroom-oriented information about instructional methods, materials, and techniques for students of all ages with special needs. • Also publishes search reprints, books, and other materials relevant to teaching exceptional children; produces audio- and videocassettes, films, and microfilms.

Division for Early Childhood (Special Education) (DEC)

Council for Exceptional Children
1920 Association Drive   Phone: (703) 620-3660
Reston, VA 22091   Dr. George Jesien, Pres.
Founded: 1973. **Members:** 6000. **Staff:** 1. **State Groups:** 45. A division of the Council for Exceptional Children (see separate entry). Teachers, program administrators, students, parents, persons involved in health-related fields, and individuals interested in the development and education of handicapped infants and preschool children. Objectives are: to promote education for young children and infants with special needs; to initiate programs that cooperatively involve parents in their children's education; to stimulate communication and joint activity among early childhood organizations; to encourage professional development; to disseminate research findings and information addressing issues of early childhood. Believes that the provision of services to handicapped children from birth through the age of five must be made a priority in today's society. Encourages a national initiative to establish plans for systematic coordination between the social, educational, and health agencies currently serving hand-

icapped children through the age of five. Conducts workshops and professional meetings; bestows awards. **Publications:** *Division for Early Childhood—Communicator,* quarterly. Newsletter providing information on working with handicapped children; covers current trends and practices as well as recently published materials and resources. Includes book reviews; calendar of events; reviews of assessment instruments. • *Journal of Early Intervention,* quarterly. Provides information on current research and practice for individuals who work with disabled children. Includes book review.

Foundation for Exceptional Children (Special Education) (FEC)

1920 Association Drive   Phone: (703) 620-1054
Reston, VA 22091   Robert L. Silber, Exec.Dir.
Founded: 1971. **Members:** 1000. **Staff:** 7. Institutions, agencies, educators, parents, and persons concerned with the education and personal welfare of gifted or disabled children. Established to further the educational, vocational, social, and personal needs of the handicapped child or youth and the neglected educational needs of the gifted. Seeks funding from public memberships, foundations, and corporate and government grants. Conducts special programs and awards scholarships and grants for innovative educational projects. Bestows awards; operates charitable program and children's services. **Publications:** *Foundation for Exceptional Children—Focus,* 3/year. Newsletter providing information on the foundation's programs, committees, financial support, and board of directors. Carries profiles of scholarship recipients and of active members. Features award winners and grant recipients.

Home Economics Education Association (HEEA)

1201 16th Street, N.W.   Phone: (202) 822-7844
Washington, DC 20036   Catherine A. Leisher,
          Exec.Dir.
Founded: 1927. **Members:** 3700. **Budget:** $54,000. Teachers and supervisors of home economics education. Promotes effective programs of home economics education; supplements existing services available to home economics educators; cooperates with other associations in related fields. **Publications:** *Home Economics Educator,* quarterly. Newsletter. • Also publishes booklets, reports, monographs, and other materials.

International Reading Association (IRA)

800 Barksdale Road
P.O. Box 8139   Phone: (302) 731-1600
Newark, DE 19714-8139   Dr. Ronald R. Mitchell,
          Exec.Dir.
Founded: 1956. **Members:** 90,000. **Staff:** 75. **Budget:** $5,624,000. **Local Groups:** 1200. Teachers, reading specialists, consultants, administrators, supervisors, researchers, psychologists, librarians, and parents interested in

reading at any school level. To improve the quality of reading instruction at all educational levels; to stimulate and promote the lifetime reading habit and an awareness of the impact of reading; to encourage the development of every reader's proficiency to the highest possible level. Disseminates information pertaining to research on reading, including information on adult literacy, computer technology and reading, early childhood and literacy development, international education, literature for adolescents, and teacher education and effectiveness. Presents citations and awards; maintains placement service, library, and more than 60 committees. **Publications:** *International Reading Association—Desktop Reference,* annual. Directory listing association committee chairpersons and members, officers of various councils of the association, and editors of affiliated publications. Includes calendar of events. • *Journal of Reading,* 8/year. Journal on the theory and practice of teaching reading skills to adolescents and adults. Includes index, cumulated annually. Features book reviews and research reports. • *Lectura y Vida,* quarterly. Spanish language journal on reading skills. Includes index, cumulated annually. • *Placement Newsletter,* monthly. • *Reading Research Quarterly.* Journal on the theory and practice of teaching reading skills. Includes research reports. • *Reading Teacher,* 8/year. Journal on the theory and practice of teaching reading skills to elementary school children. Includes index, cumulated annually. Features book reviews and research reports. • *Reading Today,* bimonthly. Tabloid providing news on reading education; includes legislative updates and news for parents. • Also publishes catalog, books, and monographs (8–10/year).

Kappa Delta Pi (Education)

Box A   Phone: (317) 743-1705
West Lafayette, IN 47906   J. Jay Hostetler, Exec.Sec.
Founded: 1911. **Members:** 50,000. **Budget:** $1,100,000.
Active Chapters: 407. **Alumni Chapters:** 40. Honor society—men and women, education. Bestows annual Distinguished Dissertation Awards and Book-of-The-Year Award; offers scholarships. Conducts research projects.
Publications: *Educational Forum,* quarterly. • *Handbook,* biennial. • *Record,* quarterly. • *Scroll and Stylus,* quarterly. Newsletter. • Also publishes monograph and booklets.

Music Teachers National Association (MTNA)

617 Vine Street, Suite 1432   Phone: (513) 421-1420
Cincinnati, OH 45202   Robert J. Elias, Exec. Dir.
Founded: 1876. **Members:** 23,500. **Staff:** 9. **Regional Groups:** 7. **State Groups:** 51. **Local Groups:** 500. Professional society of music teachers in studios, conservatories, music schools, and public and private schools, colleges, and universities; undergraduate and graduate music students. Seeks to raise the level of musical performance, understanding, and instruction. Sponsors competitions;

bestows awards. **Publications:** *American Music Teacher Magazine,* bimonthly. Topics include American music, chamber music, aesthetics, composition, criticism, musicology, and performance. Also contains biographies and original research. Includes book and music reviews, local and state association news, and member news. • *Con Brio,* semiannual. Newsletter. **Price:** Available to members only. • *Music Teachers National Association—Directory of Nationally Certified Teachers,* annual. • Also publishes national courses of study and books.

National Art Education Association (Arts) (NAEA)

1916 Association Drive   Phone: (703) 860-8000
Reston, VA 22091   Thomas A. Hatfield, Exec.Dir.
Founded: 1947. **Members:** 13,000. **Staff:** 12. **Regional Groups:** 4. Teachers of art at elementary, secondary, and college levels; colleges, libraries, museums, and other educational institutions. Studies problems of teaching art; encourages research and experimentation. Serves as clearinghouse for information on art education programs, materials, and methods of instruction. Presents awards; sponsors special institutes and workshops. Cooperates with other national organizations for the furtherance of creative art experiences for youth. Maintains placement services. **Publications:** *Art Education,* bimonthly. Educational journal reporting on current issues, problems, and approaches in visual art education, including curriculum, teaching strategies, and innovative and exemplary programs. • *NAEA Newsletter,* bimonthly. Reports on national and state activities, events, and policies of the association. • *Studies in Art Education,* quarterly. Scholarly journal providing empirical, historical, and philosophical research in art education. Includes book reviews. • Also publishes bibliographies, books, pamphlets, and monographs.

National Association for Bilingual Education (Bilingualism) (NABE)

Union Center Plaza
810 First Street, N.E., 3rd Floor   Phone: (202) 898-1829
Washington, DC 20002   James J. Lyons, Exec.Dir.
Founded: 1975. **Members:** 3000. **State Groups:** 32. Educators, administrators, paraprofessionals, community and laypeople, and students. Purposes are to recognize, promote, and publicize bilingual education. Seeks to increase public understanding of the importance of language and culture. Utilizes and develops student proficiency and ensures equal opportunities in bilingual education for language-minority students. Works to preserve and expand the nation's linguistic resources. Educates language-minority parents in public policy decisions. Promotes research in language education, linguistics, and multicultural education. Coordinates development of professional standards; organizes conferences and workshops; supports state and local affiliates; and establishes contact with

national organizations. **Publications:** *Journal,* 3/year.• *Newsletter,* 8/year.

National Association of Biology Teachers (NABT)

11250 Roger Bacon Drive, #19   Phone: (703) 471-1134
Reston, VA 22090   Patricia J. McWethy, Exec.Dir.
Founded: 1938. **Members:** 7000. **Staff:** 9. **Budget:** $600,000. Professional society of biology teachers and others interested in the teaching of biology at all educational levels. Works to achieve scientific literacy among citizens. Promotes professional growth and development; fosters regional activities for biology teachers; confronts issues involving biology, society, and the future; provides a national voice for the profession. Sponsors summer biology updates. Bestows Outstanding Biology Teachers and Student Science Fair awards. **Publications:** *American Biology Teacher,* 8/year. Journal informing biology teachers of new research and teaching strategies. Contains audiovisual, book, and software reviews. • *National Association of Biology Teachers—News and Views,* 5/year. Association professional newsletter. Contains information on available grants, calendar of events, member news, research updates, and teacher workshops.

National Association for the Education of Young Children (Childhood Education) (NAEYC)

1834 Connecticut Avenue,   Phone: (202) 232-8777
N.W.   Dr. Marilyn M. Smith,
Washington, DC 20009   Exec.Dir.
Founded: 1926. **Members:** 70,000. **Staff:** 35. **Budget:** $2,000,000. **Local Groups:** 380. Teachers and directors of preschool and primary schools, kindergartens, child care centers, cooperatives, church schools, play groups, and groups having similar programs for young children; early childhood education and child development professors, trainers, and researchers. Open to all individuals interested in serving and acting on behalf of the needs and rights of young children, with primary focus on the provision of educational services and resources. Sponsors a public education campaign entitled "Week of the Young Child." Offers voluntary accreditation for early childhood schools and centers through the National Academy of Early Childhood Programs. **Publications:** *Early Childhood Research Quarterly.* • *Young Children,* bimonthly. Journal covering developments in the practice, research, and theory of early childhood education. Includes book reviews, calendar of events, research reports, and Washington update. • Also publishes books, brochures, and posters.

National Association for Gifted Children (NAGC)

4175 Lovell Road, Suite 140   Phone: (612) 784-3475
Circle Pines, MN 55014   Peter Rosenstein, Exec.Dir.
Founded: 1954. **Members:** 7000. **Staff:** 3. **Budget:** $600,000. **State Groups:** 22. Librarians, teachers, university personnel, administrators, and parents. To advance interest in programs for the gifted. Seeks to further education of the gifted and to enhance their potential creativity. Distributes information to teachers and parents on the development of the gifted child; sponsors annual midwinter institute to provide training in curriculum planning, program evaluation, and parenting and guidance relevant to gifted children. **Publications:** *Gifted Child Quarterly.* • *National Association for Gifted Children—Communique,* quarterly. Newsletter on the educational and familial needs of gifted children. Reports on federal legislative actions that affect gifted children and describes new educational materials for the gifted. Includes news of association activities.

National Association for Trade and Industrial Education (NATIE)

P.O. Box 1665   Phone: (703) 777-3421
Leesburg, VA 22075   Dr. Ethel M. Smith,
                Acting Exec.Dir.
Founded: 1974. **Members:** 1400. **State Groups:** 24. Educators in trade and industrial education. Works for the promotion, development, and improvement of trade and industrial education. Provides leadership in developing support for greater identity in federal legislation. Supports instructional programs for members to prepare for job entry level and supplementary instruction, apprentice training, adult retraining, and special training for industry. **Publications:** *NATIE News Notes,* quarterly. Association and industry newsletter; includes book reviews, calendar of events, research updates, and statistics. • *State Supervisors/Consultants of Trade and Industrial Education,* semiannual. Directory. • Has co-published *National Standards for Program Administration, Philosophy and Standards of Excellence, Supervision and Implementations,* and *Trade and Industrial Education.*

National Business Education Association (NBEA)

1914 Association Drive   Phone: (703) 860-8300
Reston, VA 22091   Dr. Janet M. Treichel, Exec.Dir.
Founded: 1892. **Members:** 18,000. **Staff:** 8. **Budget:** $1,000,000. **State Groups:** 54. Teachers of business subjects in secondary and postsecondary schools and colleges; administrators and research workers in business education; businesspersons interested in business education; teachers in educational institutions training business teachers. Administers keyboarding proficiency tests for high school and college students preparing for careers in business. Bestows awards. **Publications:** *Business Education Forum,* 8/year. Educational journal on accounting, basic business and economics, communication, information processing, keyboarding/typewriting, marketing and distribution, office procedures, business classroom and laboratory equipment, research, business ownership and management, administration and supervision. Includes annual index. • *NBEA Yearbook.*

National Council for the Social Studies (NCSS)

3501 Newark Street, N.W.   Phone: (202) 966-7840
Washington, DC 20016   Frances Haley, Exec.Dir.
Founded: 1921. **Members:** 25,000. **Staff:** 17. **Budget:** $1,600,000. **State Groups:** 49. **Local Groups:** 60. Teachers of elementary and secondary social studies, including instructors of civics, geography, history, economics, political science, psychology, sociology, and anthropology; interested others. Promotes the teaching of social studies to the best advantage of the students. Bestows awards. **Publications:** *Bulletin,* semiannual. • *Social Education,* 7/year. Journal containing articles by scholars, curriculum designers, and teachers on all aspects of teaching and learning the social studies. Features book reviews; instructional media; new resources; research reports. • *The Social Studies Professional,* 5/year. Tabloid covering council activities and news of the profession. • *Social Studies and the Young Learner,* 4/year. Journal providing new and creative classroom activities, content, research, and theory for social studies teaching in grades K–6. • *Theory and Research in Social Education,* quarterly. Journal providing scholarly articles and research findings about purposes, conditions, and effects of schooling and education about society and social relations. Includes book reviews.

National Council of Teachers of English (NCTE)

1111 Kenyon Road   Phone: (217) 328-3870
Urbana, IL 61801   John C. Maxwell, Exec.Dir.
Founded: 1911. **Members:** 102,000. **Staff:** 80. **State Groups:** 50. **Local Groups:** 89. Teachers of English at all school levels. Works to increase the effectiveness of instruction in English language and literature. Sponsors Conference on College Composition and Communication, Conference on English Education, and Conference for Secondary School English Department Chairpersons (see separate entries). Presents achievement awards for writing to high school juniors. Provides information and aids for teachers involved in formulating objectives, writing and evaluating curriculum guides, and planning in-service programs for teacher education. **Publications:** • *CSSEDC Quarterly.* Newsletter for secondary school English department chairpersons. Includes book reviews. • *English Education,* quarterly. Journal on preservice training and inservice education for teachers of English and language arts. • *English Journal,* 8/year. Magazine on the teaching of literature, language, and composition to middle and high school students. Covers classroom techniques, theory, and issues affecting English teachers. Includes book reviews, poetry, and reviews of teaching materials. • *Language Arts,* 8/year. Journal providing practical, classroom-tested ideas for helping children learn to read, write, and speak more effectively. Covers language development, ethnic studies, creativity, and uses of media. • *NOTES Plus,* quarterly. Newsletter providing secondary English and language arts teaching ideas. • *Research in the Teaching of English,* quarterly. Journal covering research into the teaching and learning of the English language. • *SLATE Newsletter: Support for the Learning and Teaching of English,* 4/year. Newsletter discussing social and political issues affecting the teaching of English. Provides bibliography. • Also publishes books and pamphlets; issues cassettes and literary maps.

National Council of Teachers of Mathematics (NCTM)

1906 Association Drive   Phone: (703) 620-9840
Reston, VA 22091   Dr. James D. Gates, Exec.Dir.
Founded: 1920. **Members:** 76,000. **Staff:** 50. **Budget:** $5,033,000. **State and Local Groups:** 222. Teachers of mathematics in grades K–12, two-year colleges, and teacher education personnel on college campuses. **Publications:** *Arithmetic Teacher,* monthly (during school year). Journal featuring articles on innovative and practical methods of teaching arithmetic and information on metrics, problem solving, basic fundamentals, and new technologies. Contains book, course, and product reviews, and cumulative index. • *Journal for Research in Mathematics Education,* 5/year. Reports on research, philosophical and historical studies, and theoretical analysis. Contains volume index and annual monographs. • *Mathematics Teacher,* monthly (during school year). Journal providing information for secondary and two-year college teachers on algebra and calculus. Includes information on new concepts and theorems, innovative approaches to teaching, interpretation and application of mathematical formulas. Contains: book, course, product, and software reviews; calendar of events; cumulative index. • *National Council of Teachers of Mathematics—Yearbook.* Monograph series presenting scholarly papers on a selected topic. • *NCTM News Bulletin,* 5/year. Newsletter reporting on association activities, legislation affecting education, new learning and teaching techniques, and new programs. • Also publishes booklets, pamphlets, reprints, and teaching aids.

National Education Association (NEA)

1201 16th Street, N.W.   Phone: (202) 833-4000
Washington, DC 20036   Don Cameron, Exec.Dir.
Founded: 1857. **Members:** 1,600,800. **Staff:** 600. **Budget:** $75,000,000. **State Groups:** 53. **Local Groups:** 10,000. Professional organization and union of elementary and secondary school teachers, college and university professors, administrators, principals, counselors, and others concerned with education. **Publications:** *Handbook,* annual. • *Issues,* annual. Magazine. • *NEA Today,* 8/year. Tabloid covering news and events affecting public education (kindergarten to twelfth grade). • *Today's Education,* annual. Magazine for nonteacher members.

Phi Delta Kappa (Education)

8th Street and Union Avenue   Phone: (812) 339-1156
P.O. Box 789   Dr. Lowell C. Rose,
Bloomington, IN 47402   Exec.Dir.

Founded: 1906. **Members:** 130,000. **Staff:** 60. **Budget:** $3,000,000. **Chapters:** 650. Professional, honorary, and recognition fraternity—education. To enhance quality education through research and leadership activities. Conducts seminars and workshops. **Publications:** *News, Notes, and Quotes,* quarterly. • *Phi Delta Kappan,* 10/year. Magazine; includes book reviews and Washington report. • Also publishes *PAR (Practical Applications of Research)* and monographs.

Reading Is Fundamental (RIF)

600 Maryland Avenue,   Phone: (202) 287-3220
S.W., Suite 500   Ruth P. Graves, Pres.
Washington, DC 20560

Founded: 1966. **Members:** 3227. **Staff:** 43. Volunteer groups composed of community leaders, educators, librarians, parents, and service club members who sponsor local grass roots reading motivation programs serving 2,100,000 children nationwide. Purpose is to involve youngsters, preschool to high school age, in reading activities aimed at showing that reading is fun. Provides services to parents to help them encourage reading in the home. Sponsors book distribution which emphasizes each child's freedom of choice and personal ownership of selected books. Is supported by corporations, foundations, and private citizens and through a federal contract. Presents awards. **Publications:** *RIF Newsletter,* quarterly.

Teachers of English to Speakers of Other Languages (TESOL)

1600 Cameron Street,   Phone: (703) 836-0774
Suite 300   Richard Orem, Exec.Dir.
Alexandria, VA 22314

Founded: 1966. **Members:** 11,500. **Staff:** 12. **Budget:** $1,500,000. **Regional Groups:** 28. **State Groups:** 41. School, college, and adult education teachers who teach English as a foreign language; students and professional people in the field; colleges and schools are institutional members, and publishers are commercial members. Aims to improve the teaching of English as a foreign language by promoting research, disseminating information, developing guidelines and promoting certification, and serving as a clearinghouse for the field. Offers placement service; bestows awards; maintains library; operates speakers' bureau. Sponsors annual summer institute. **Publications:** *Directory of Professional Preparation,* periodic. • *TESOL Membership Directory,* biennial. • *TESOL Newsletter,* bimonthly. Covers organizational news, refereed articles, book reviews, conference news, and employment opportunities. Lists TESOL awards and grants.

Source: From *Encyclopedia of Associations,* 1991, 25th Edition, Volume 1, edited by Deborah M. Burek. Copyright © 1990 by Gale Research, Inc. Reprinted by permission of the publisher.

PREAMBLE

The educator, believing in the worth and dignity of each human being, recognizes the supreme importance of the pursuit of truth, devotion to excellence, and the nurture of democratic principles. Essential to these goals is the protection of freedom to learn and to teach and the guarantee of equal educational opportunity for all. The educator accepts the responsibility to adhere to the highest ethical standards.

The educator recognizes the magnitude of the responsibility inherent in the teaching process. The desire for the respect and confidence of one's colleagues, of students, of parents, and of the members of the community provides the incentive to attain and maintain the highest possible degree of ethical conduct. The *Code of Ethics of the Education Profession* indicates the aspiration of all educators and provides standards by which to judge conduct.

The remedies specified by the NEA and/or its affiliates for the violation of any provision of this *Code* shall be exclusive and no such provision shall be enforceable in any form other than one specifically designated by the NEA or its affiliates.

PRINCIPLE I

Commitment of the Student

The educator strives to help each student realize his or her potential as a worthy and effective member of society. The educator therefore works to stimulate the spirit of inquiry, the acquisition of knowledge and understanding, and the thoughtful formulation of worthy goals.

In fulfillment of the obligation to the student, the educator:

1. Shall not unreasonably restrain the student from independent action in the pursuit of learning.
2. Shall not unreasonably deny the student access to varying points of view.
3. Shall not deliberately suppress or distort subject matter relevant to the student's progress.
4. Shall make reasonable effort to protect the students from conditions harmful to learning or to health and safety.
5. Shall not intentionally expose the student to embarrassment or disparagement.
6. Shall not on the basis of race, color, creed, sex, national origin, marital status, political or religious beliefs, family, social or cultural background, or sexual orientation unfairly:
    a) Exclude any student from participation in any program
    b) Deny benefits to any student
    c) Grant any advantage to any student
7. Shall not use professional relationships with students for private advantage.
8. Shall not disclose information about students obtained in the course of professional service, unless disclosure serves a compelling professional purpose or is required by law.

PRINCIPLE II

Commitment to the Profession

The education profession is vested by the public with a trust and responsibility requiring the highest ideals of professional service.

In the belief that the quality of the services of the education profession directly influences the nation and its citizens, the educator shall exert every effort to raise professional standards, to promote a climate that encourages the exercise of professional judgment, to achieve conditions which attract persons worthy of the trust to careers in education, and to assist in preventing the practice of the profession by unqualified persons.

In fulfillment of the obligation to the profession, the educator:

1. Shall not in an application for a professional position deliberately make a false statement or fail to disclose a material fact related to competency and qualifications.
2. Shall not misrepresent his/her professional qualifications.
3. Shall not assist any entry into the profession of a person known to be unqualified in respect to character, education, or other relevant attribute.
4. Shall not knowingly make a false statement concerning the qualifications of a candidate for a professional position.
5. Shall not assist a noneducator in the unauthorized practice of teaching.
6. Shall not disclose information about colleagues obtained in the course of professional service unless disclosure serves a compelling professional purpose or is required by law.
7. Shall not knowingly make false or malicious statements about a colleague.
8. Shall not accept any gratuity, gift, or favor that might impair or appear to influence professional decisions or actions.

Source: Code of Ethics of the Education Profession, adopted by the NEA Representative Assembly, 1975. The National Education Association, Washington, D.C. Used with permission.

As a citizen, a student, and a future member of the teaching profession, the individual student teacher has the right:

1. To freedom from unfair discrimination in admission to student teaching and in all aspects of the field experience. Student teachers shall not be denied or removed from an assignment because of race, color, creed, sex, age, national origin, marital status, political or religious beliefs, social or cultural background, or sexual orientation. Nor shall their application be denied because of physical handicap unless it is clear that such handicap will prevent or seriously inhibit their carrying out the duties of the assignment.

2. To be informed in advance of the standards of eligibility for student teaching and of the criteria and procedures for evaluation of his or her classroom performance.

3. To be consulted in advance and have effective voice in decisions regarding assignment, with respect to subject, grade level, school and cooperating teacher.

4. To be assigned to a cooperating teacher who volunteers to work with the student teaching program, who is fully qualified to do so, and is appropriately remunerated for the work, and given sufficient time to carry out its responsibilities.

5. To be reimbursed by the college or university for any financial hardship caused by the student teaching assignment; e.g., for the costs of traveling excessive distances to the cooperating school district, or for the expenses incurred when the student teacher is assigned to a location so remote from his or her college/university that it is necessary to establish residence there, in addition to the college or university residence.

6. To be informed, prior to the student teaching period, of all relevant policies and practices of the cooperating school district, including those regarding personnel, curriculum, student requirements, and student teaching program.

7. To confidentiality of records. Except with the express permission of the student teacher, the college or university shall transmit to the cooperating school district only those student records that are clearly necessary to protect the health and welfare of the student teacher, the cooperating teacher, the students, and others in the cooperating school. All persons having access to the records of student teachers shall respect the confidentiality of those records, as required by law.

8. To be admitted to student teaching and to remain in the student teaching assignment in the absence of a showing of just cause for termination or transfer through fair and impartial proceedings.

9. To a student teaching environment that encourages creativity and initiative. The student teacher should have the opportunity, under the perceptive supervision of the cooperating teacher, to develop his or her own techniques of teaching.

10. To a student teaching environment that encourages the free exploration of ideas and issues as appropriate to the maturity of the students and the topics being studied.

11. To carry out the student teaching assignment in an atmosphere conducive to learning and to have authority under supervision of the cooperating teacher, to use reasonable means to preserve the learning environment and protect the health and safety of students, the student teacher, and others.

12. To participate, with the cooperating teacher and college/university supervisor, in planning the student teaching schedule to include, in addition to work with the assigned cooperating teacher, observation of other classes, attendance at professional meetings, and involvement, as appropriate, in extracurricular activities that will enrich and broaden the range of the field experience.

13. To be assigned to duties that are relevant to the student teacher's learning experience. Student teachers shall not be required to act as substitute teacher or teacher aide, nor to handle any nonteaching duties that are not part of the cooperating teacher's duties.

14. To request transfer in the event of prolonged illness of, or serious personality conflict with the cooperating teacher and to have that request given favorable consideration without damage to any party's personal or professional status.

15. To a cessation of student teaching responsibilities in the event and for the duration of a teacher strike at the cooperating school or school district to which the student teacher is assigned. If the strike is a prolonged one, the college or university has the responsibility to reassign the student teacher to another school district.

16. To the same liability protections as are provided by the school district for regularly employed certified teachers.

17. To influence the development and continuing evaluation and improvement of the student teacher program, including the formulation and systematic review of standards of student teacher eligibility, and criteria and procedures of student teacher evaluation. Such influence shall be maintained through representation of student teachers and recent graduates of the student teacher program on committees established to accomplish these purposes.

18. To frequent planning and evaluative discussions with the cooperating teacher.

19. To systematic, effective supervision by the college/university supervisor. Such supervision shall include (1) regularly scheduled classroom observations of sufficient frequency and length to permit thorough insight into the strengths and weaknesses of the student teacher's performance; (2) conferences with college/university supervisor immediately following observation, or as soon thereafter as possible, to discuss results of observation; and (3) regularly scheduled three-way evaluation conferences among student teacher, college supervisor, and cooperating teacher, to ensure that the student teacher is fully apprised of his or her progress and is given substantive assistance in assessing and remedying the weaknesses and reinforcing the strengths of his or her performance.

20. To see, sign, and affix written responses to evaluations of his or her classroom performance.

21. To an equitable and orderly means of resolving grievances relating to the student-teaching assignment. The college/university grievance procedure shall incorporate due process guarantees, including the right to be informed in writing of the reasons for any adverse action regarding his or her assignment, and to appeal any such action, with the right to have both student and teacher representation on committees formulated to hear and adjudicate student teacher grievances.

22. To be free to join, or not to join, on or off-campus organizations, and to enjoy privacy and freedom of life-style and conscience in out-of-school activities, unless it is clearly evident that those activities have a harmful effect on the student teacher's classroom performance.

Source: National Education Association, 1201–16th Street N.W., Washington, D.C., 1977.

SELECTED RESOURCES FOR MULTICULTURAL EDUCATION

Banks, James A. and Cherry A. McGee Banks, eds. *Multicultural Education: Issues and Perspectives.* Boston: Allyn and Bacon, 1989. *(Issues and strategies for multicultural education in race, gender, social class, religion, and exceptionality)*

Butler, Johnnella E. and John C. Walter, eds. *Transforming the Curriculum: Ethnic Studies and Women Studies.* Albany: State University of New York Press, 1990. *(Integrating content about ethnic groups and women into the mainstream curriculum, applicable to K–12)*

Derman-Sparks, Louise and the A.B.C. Task Force. *Anti-Bias Curriculum: Tools for Empowering Young Children.* Washington, D.C.: National Association for the Education of Young Children, 1989. *(Resources and activities for engendering positive intergroup attitudes)*

Grant, Carl A. and Christine E. Sleeter. *Turning on Learning: Five Approaches for Multicultural Teaching Plans for Race, Class, and Disability.* Columbus, Ohio: Merrill, 1989.

King, Edith W. *Teaching Ethnic and Gender Awareness: Methods and Materials for the Elementary School,* 2d ed. Dubuque, Iowa: Kendall/Hunt Publishing Company, 1990. *(Rationale, activities, and teaching strategies for integrating ethnic and gender awareness into the elementary school curriculum)*

Lee, Enid, *Letters to Marcia: A Teacher's Guide to Anti-Racist Education.* Toronto: Cross Cultural Communications

Centre, 1985. *(Guide for reducing racism in the classroom and school)*

Lynch, James. *Multicultural Education in a Global Society.* New York: Falmer Press, 1989.

Multicultural Leader. Quarterly newsletter published by the Educational Materials and Services Center, 144 Railroad Avenue, Suite 107, Edmonds, Wa. 98020. *(News on current theory, research, and teaching materials on race and ethnicity, gender, social class, and exceptionality)*

Pedersen, Paul. *A Handbook for Developing Multicultural Awareness.* Alexandria, Va.: American Association for Counseling and Development, 1988.

Sleeter, Christine E., ed. *Empowerment through Multicultural Education.* Albany: State University of New York Press, 1991. *(Issues and problems of teaching in multicultural classrooms)*

Sleeter, Christine E. and Carl A. Grant. *Making Choices for Multicultural Education: Five Approaches to Race, Class, and Gender.* Columbus, Ohio: Merrill, 1988. *(Multicultural teaching strategies)*

Wasserman, Paul and Alice E. Kennington. *Ethnic Information Sources of the United States,* 2d ed. Vols. 1 and 2. Detroit: Gale Research Company, 1983. *(Lists of organizations, agencies, foundations, institutions, and media that focus on ethnic groups in the United States)*

Whether you're a high-tech expert or just a beginner, the following organizations and associations, on-line networks, and free teaching tools may help you make technology come alive in your classroom.

Additional information may be available from your state department of education's instructional technology department. Most provide technology-related inservice training sessions, as well as lists of local and regional resources and consulting services. *Teacher Magazine*'s "Extra Credit"

section and "Software Directory" regularly list grants, resources, and workshops related to technology.

If you're a member of an educational association or union, check to see if they offer technology-related grants, awards, newsletters, or conferences. Many hardware and software manufacturers offer workshops, 800-number help lines, free supplementary materials, and the opportunity to field-test products in the classroom.

Associations and Organizations

Association for Educational Communications and Technology
1025 Vermont Ave., N.W. Suite 820
Washington, DC 20005
(202) 347-7834

For $50, teachers can join this nonprofit organization and receive a subscription to the bimonthly magazine *Tech Trends* and membership in one of nine special interest groups. A more "comprehensive" membership, available for $80, includes a subscription to the quarterly journal *Educational Technology Research and Development.* Both publications profile leaders in the field of technology and provide information on copyright laws, new products, and conferences.

Challenger Center for Space Science Education
1101 King St., Suite 190
Alexandria, VA 22314
(703) 683-9740

This nonprofit educational organization invites teachers to join the Challenger Center education network for $40 a year. As a member, teachers receive *The Challenge,* a quarterly educational newsletter that includes lists of multidisciplinary resources. Members also qualify for fellowships and workshops. Anyone can purchase the videotape and teacher's guide for the satellite teleconference, *Suited for Space,* which aired January 28, 1991.

Computer Equity Program of the Women's Action Alliance
370 Lexington Ave., Suite 603
New York, NY 10017
(212) 532-8330

This nonprofit educational institution conducts projects and publishes and distributes books, brochures, and reports designed to encourage girls to use technology in school and at home.

Computer Learning Foundation
P.O. Box 60007
Palo Alto, CA 94306-0007

This nonprofit organization promotes October as "Computer Learning Month" and sponsors a number of contests

and programs. The group offers 12 resource guides for $6 to $10 each, plus shipping and handling. The guides list 1987-1989 winners of various CLF contests and describe the winning strategies for using computers in the classroom. *Computer Learning Month,* CLF's free annual publication, provides information on other resources, programs, and contests. A computer bulletin board containing *Computer Learning Month* can be accessed, via modem, by calling (415) 856-6719.

Institute for the Transfer of Technology to Education
1680 Duke St.
Alexandria, VA 22314
(703) 838-6722

This nonprofit organization, a division of the National School Boards Association, provides a technology leadership consortium for school board members. For $75, teachers can subscribe to *Insider's Letter,* a newsletter published nine times a year that provides news on technology in education. The group also offers conferences, publications, and site visits to "schools of the future."

International Society for Technology in Education
1787 Agate St.
University of Oregon
Eugene, OR 97403-1923
(503) 346-4414

This nonprofit educational association is dedicated to the improvement of education through the use of computer-based technology. For $36 a year, teachers receive eight issues of *The Computing Teacher Journal, Update Newsletter,* and a 10 percent discount on the price of books and software.

Learning Initiatives International
1201 W. Peachtree St., N.E., Suite 2900
Atlanta, GA 30367-1200
(800) 233-9233

An independent membership organization for educators who use IBM equipment and compatible software. The group publishes newsletters, sponsors conferences, and provides electronic mail services for members. Individual memberships are available for $45 a year, and institutional memberships cost $500 a year.

Public Broadcasting Service

1320 Braddock Place
Alexandria, VA 22314-1698
(703) 739-5038

Public television's National Instructional Television Satellite Schedule offers more than 1,300 hours annually of noncommercial programming for classroom use in all subjects and grade levels. The majority of local PBS television stations provide inservice training, curricular materials for instructional programming, on-line services, and more. For more information and a catalog of programming, contact the Learning Services Division of your local PBS television station or call the number above.

Satellite Educational Resources Consortium

P.O. Box 50008
Columbia, SC 29250
(800) 476-5001

This organization, an alliance of state departments of education and educational networks, provides for-credit high school courses in math, science, and language arts via satellite. By using telephone, computer, and keypad technologies, students can interact directly with their teachers on television. The group also offers inservice and graduate courses for teachers.

On-Line Networks

America Online

8619 Westwood Center Drive
Vienna, VA 22182
(800) 227-6364.

The network provides electronic mail, conferencing, news, technical help, games, and shopping services for Apple II and Macintosh users. Monthly fee: $5.95, plus surcharges.

CompuServe

Customer Service Ordering Department
Box L-477
Columbus, Ohio 43260
(800) 848-8199

CompuServe offers an information network with more than 1,400 databases, including extensive research databases. It also provides financial reports, news, weather, sports, electronic mail, shopping, games, an encyclopedia, and more. There is a one-time membership fee of $39.95, plus varying fees for different databases.

GEnie

General Electric
Box 02B-C
401 N. Washington St.
Rockville, MD 20850
(800) 638-9636

G.E. provides more than 100 on-line services, including news, weather, sports, travel information, stock market quotes, an encyclopedia, electronic mail, bulletin boards, games, shopping services, and a magazine. Monthly fee: $4.95, plus surcharges.

GTE Education Services

8505 Freeport Parkway
Suite 600
Irving, TX 75063
(800) 634-5644

Subscribers receive communication and information-gathering services, including electronic mail, databases, and more than 50 bulletin boards, one for special educators. "World Classroom"—a new project—links students around the world in science, social studies, and language-arts activities. Prices vary.

LinkNet Inc.

CEN
1400 E. Touhy Ave., Suite 260
Des Plaines, IL 60018-3305
(708) 390-8700

This service links teachers with other teachers locally and nationally through two networks, Learning Link and IntroLink. The networks offer computer bulletin boards, electronic mail, and conferencing. Information files contain research articles, notes, and teacher guides. Databases also contain scheduling information for instructional programming on public television. Individual subscriptions range from no charge to $189.

Long Distance Learning Network

AT&T
P.O. Box 716
Basking Ridge, NJ 07920-0716
(800) 367-7225

This on-line network links elementary and secondary school teachers and students around the world by matching up schools with similar curricular interests. The network offers *Computer Chronicles*, an on-line newspaper, as well as course work for students on such subjects as creative writing, energy systems, geography, and social issues. Subscription rates vary from $315 to $375 per semester.

NGS Kids Network

National Geographic Society
17th and M streets
Washington DC 20036
(800) 368-2728
in Maryland, call (301) 921-1330

The on-line network offers structured science and geography projects for grades 4–6. Teachers subscribe for eight-week study units. Students across the world work as scientists, collecting data, developing hypotheses, and drawing conclusions. Prices vary from $325 to $375.

Free Teaching Tools

Computer Posters

IBM offers free posters for teachers of grades K–3, 4–8, and 9–12. They show students how to use computers to achieve their goals. Each one contains a lesson plan on the back. Contact: IBM Corp., P.O. Box 3900, Peoria, IL 61614; (800) IBM-7257.

Educational Photography

Through the Polaroid Education Program, teachers can receive a Polaroid camera and ideas on how to use it to enhance learning in the classroom. To get the camera and join the program, send 10 proof-of-purchase seals from Polaroid 600 Plus film boxes. The program also provides inservice training for teachers around the country. Contact: PEP, Polaroid Corp., P.O. Box 227092, Dallas, TX 75222-7092; (800) 343-5000.

Space Network

NASA Spacelink is an on-line information network that provides lesson plans and activities, NASA news, and historical information. Teachers can also post their own questions on a computer bulletin board. The service is free, although there may be phone costs. To log onto the network directly via modem, dial (205) 895-0028. To get a brochure or more information, contact: NASA Education Affairs, Code XE, NASA Headquarters, Washington, DC 20546; (202) 453-8388.

Special Education

The Council for Exceptional Children's Center for Special Education Technology offers free "tech use guides," which summarize important ways technology can be used in special education, and "resource inventories," which list state and national technology resources. Teachers with questions about special education technology or wanting to request materials can call (800) 873-8255 between 8:30 a.m. and 4:30 p.m. (EST).

The organization also provides access to a bulletin board called TECH LINE, on SpecialNet, and international special education computer network. Contact: CSET, 1920 Association Drive, Reston, VA 22091; (800) 873-8255.

Whole Language

Using Whole Language Software is a free quarterly newsletter and catalog for K–8 teachers. The newsletter gives specific advice for using commercial software with a whole-language approach. Contact: Willy Billy's Workshop, P.O. Box 6104, Cleveland, OH 44101; (800) 628-4623.

Source: Mary Koepke and Sharon K. Williams, "Resources," *Teacher Magazine* (January 1991): 54, 56–57.

1. *Educational content and value:* Is the content accurate? Clearly presented? Appropriate for the intended audience? Free of stereotypes? Important? Does the program seem to achieve its objectives? Is it easily integrated with classwork?

2. *Mode of instruction:* What is the program intended to teach: concepts, principles, skills, visualization, and/or problem solving? Is the appropriate form of instruction or are the appropriate classroom aids (such as simulation, tutorial, drill and practice, visualization materials, problem-solving materials) being used?

3. *Technical features:* Did you have any technical problems with the program? Is the layout visually attractive? Are graphics, color, and sound used effectively to enhance instruction? Could you modify the program?

4. *Ease of use:* Are the instructions clear? Can students operate the program easily? Control the pace? Review the instructions? End the program? How is inappropriate input handled?

5. *Motivation:* Does the program hold students' interest? Do students want to use it again? Does the program vary when repeated?

6. *Feedback:* Is the feedback positive and constructive? Appropriate for the grade level? Immediate? Varied? Does it provide help or an explanation?

7. *Record keeping:* Are students' records stored on disk for later retrieval? What information is stored? For how many students? Is the record-keeping system easy to use? Is it reasonably secure?

8. *Documentation:* Are the written instructions clear? Well organized? Comprehensive? Are the objectives, prerequisites, and intended audience specified?

9. *Summary and recommendations:* What are the program's strengths? What are its weaknesses? Does it take advantage of the computer's capabilities? Does it involve the learner in the learning process? How does it compare to others with similar objectives? Would you buy and use it?

Source: Janice L. Flake, C. Edwin McClintock, and Sandra Turner. *Fundamentals of Computer Education* (Belmont, Calif.: Wadsworth, 1990): 286–288.

Name Index

Subject Index

Photo and Cartoon Credits

Photo Credits

Chapter One—Opener, Tom Stack / Tom Stack & Associates; p. 2, F. Siteman / The Picture Cube; p. 8, B. Daemmrich / Stock, Boston; p. 17, courtesy of Joyce R. Miller.

Chapter Two—Opener, Susan Fish; p. 33, B. Daemmrich / Stock, Boston; p. 36, P. Menzel / Stock, Boston; p. 41, S. Resnick / Stock, Boston; p. 52, Studtman Photo Service.

Chapter Three—Opener, MacDonald / The Picture Cube; p. 77, A. Brilliant / The Picture Cube; p. 84, F. Siteman; p. 85, courtesy of Bruce Johnson.

Chapter Four—Opener, Laima Druskis / Stock, Boston; p. 103, Susan Fish; p. 115, Pam Benham; p. 117, J. Chenet / Woodfin Camp & Associates.

Chapter Five—Opener, Bob Daemmrich; p. 138, B. Daemmrich; p. 150, Wide World Photos; p. 151, Sudhir Group / The Picture Group.

Chapter Six—Opener, Courtesy of the Abby Aldrich Rockefeller Folk Art Collection / Colonial Williamsburg; p. 183, Culver Pictures; p. 185, The Bettmann Archive.

Chapter Seven—Opener, Bohdan Hrynewych / Stock, Boston; p. 211, R. Pasley / Stock, Boston; p. 215, J. Anderson / Woodfin Camp & Associates; p. 223, North Wind Picture Archives.

Chapter Eight—Opener, Bill Gallery / Stock, Boston; p. 238, Sepp Seitz, Woodfin Camp & Associates; p. 252, M. Sullivan / TexaStock; p. 257, The Bettmann Archive.

Chapter Nine—Opener, Michael Going / The Image Bank; p. 276, The Bettmann Archive; p. 279, B. Daemmrich / Stock, Boston; p. 287, D. Dietz / Stock, Boston.

Chapter Ten—Opener, Frank Siteman / The Picture Cube; p. 310, F. Siteman; p. 318, F. Siteman; p. 321, courtesy of Gloria Marino; p. 323, B. Daemmrich.

Chapter Eleven—Opener, Mary Kate Denny / PhotoEdit; p. 339, J. Chenet / Woodfin Camp & Associates; p. 350, K. Vandivier / TexaStock; p. 355, courtesy of Shirley Hopkinson.

Chapter Twelve—Opener, Willie Hill / Stock, Boston; p. 381, F. Siteman; p. 392, courtesy of Eric McKamey; p. 397, B. Daemmrich / Stock, Boston; p. 399, B. Daemmrich / Stock, Boston.

Chapter Thirteen—Opener, Michael Salas / The Image Bank; p. 420, J. Ficara / Woodfin Camp & Associates; p. 424, B. Daemmrich; p. 426, R. Pasley / Stock, Boston; p. 432, courtesy of Thelma Holmes.

Chapter Fourteen—Opener, Murrae Haynes / The Picture Group; p. 449, M. Winter / The Picture Group; p. 455, M. Lunenberg / The Picture Group; p. 459, J. Chenet / Woodfin Camp & Associates; p. 463, F. Siteman.

Chapter Fifteen—Opener, Vandivier / TexaStock; p. 485, S. Lapides / Woodfin Camp & Associates; p. 494, J. Wilson / Woodfin Camp & Associates; p. 500, courtesy of Karin Marchant.

Cartoon Credits

Chapter One—p. 10, David Sipress; **Chapter Two**—p. 47, Ford Button; **Chapter Three**—p. 71, David Sipress; **Chapter Four**—p. 110, David Sipress; **Chapter Five**—p. 135, Randy Hall; **Chapter Six**—p. 188, David Sipress; **Chapter Seven**—p. 212, David Sipress; **Chapter Eight**—p. 256, Harley Schwadron in *Phi Delta Kappan*; *Chapter Nine*—p. 275, Edwin Lepper; **Chapter Ten**—p. 313, David Sipress; **Chapter Eleven**–p. 341, Glen Dines; **Chapter Twelve**—p. 393, David Sipress; **Chapter Thirteen**—p. 416, David Sipress; **Chapter Fourteen,** p. 449, David Sipress; **Chapter Fifteen**—p. 493, David Sipress.